# LIFE THROUGH MY EYES

# LIFE
# THROUGH
# MY EYES

**STEVEN M. RIPPIN**

Matador
9 Priory Business Park,
Wistow Road, Kibworth Beauchamp,
Leicestershire. LE8 0RX
Tel: 0116 279 2299
Email: books@troubador.co.uk
Web: www.troubador.co.uk/matador
Twitter: @matadorbooks

ISBN 978 1838595 418

British Library Cataloguing in Publication Data.
A catalogue record for this book is available from the British Library.

Printed and bound in the UK by TJ Books Limited, Padstow, Cornwall
Typeset in 11pt Sabon by Troubador Publishing Ltd, Leicester, UK

Matador is an imprint of Troubador Publishing Ltd

# FOR MY MUM AND DAD. THANK YOU

Thank you, Mum and Dad, for helping me through my eye operations, and for being there when I was bullied as a child and assaulted twice later on in my life. Thank you for those special memories we have shared, for all the days out and holidays you both took me on when I was a child and for helping me with my homework to showing me the error of my ways. And thank you, Dad, for bringing me home the latest *Star Wars* figures after you had a busy day at work. Mum and Dad, you're more than parents to me; you're my best friends, who I can talk to about anything. If I have a problem, I know that you're there to listen and help me through it. Although, I know one day you won't be there, and until that day arrives I will treasure every moment we get to spend together. And, after all is said and done, I will remember the good times we shared and the life lessons you both taught me, always.

Mum and Dad, I will cherish you both with the fondest of memories and make you proud of me. I will not dwell that you're no longer here because I will always keep you both close, in my heart, mind and soul. And I will live, laugh and continue to improve my life, and spread happiness and positivity to everybody I meet, because I know that's what you would want me to do. And, wherever I may be, I will always remember that you're both there by my side continuing to guide me on my journey through life. With your guidance and positive attitudes, you have helped get me through so many difficult times I have faced. You have also taught me many valuable lessons along the way as well, which have always been to have a positive outlook on life, to believe in myself and always to be courteous, respectful and honest to others. We have been through so much together, and I can't thank you enough for being there for me. Mum and Dad, you were and will always be my rock and where I draw my strength and positive attitude and zest for life. I love you both very, very much; you're my most prominent inspirations in life, and I'm so proud to call you my parents. Thank you for bringing me into this world and raising me how you have. With all my love, I dedicate my book to both of you.

Steven M. Rippin

# CONTENTS

It matters not how strait the gate,
How charged with punishments the scroll,
I am the master of my fate:
I am the captain of my soul

William Ernest Henley 1849–1903

The greatest discovery of my generation is that human beings can alter their lives by altering their attitudes of mind

William James 1842–1910

If there's any message to my work, it is ultimately that it's OK to be different, that it's good to be different, that we should question ourselves before we pass judgement on someone who looks different, behaves different, talks different, is a different colour. I am doing things that are true to me. The only thing I have a problem with is being labelled

Johnny Depp 1963–

Superman feeds off the power of the sun,
where I feed off the power of hardstyle music,
and the more I listen to hardstyle,
the more energised and focused I become
on chasing after my dreams
The powerful baselines, and the euphoric
melodies and lyrics in hardstyle, happy hardcore and
trance music have helped me stay
positive and optimistic through the challenging
times I have been faced with in my life.
And this is why, hardstyle, happy hardcore and
trance will be my style forever
Music is the one thing in life that helps to connect us all
Make things happen by living in the moment
Believe in the magic of positivity
and spread love and happiness to everyone

Steven M. Rippin

# ACKNOWLEDGEMENTS

My book is also a dedication to Sophie Lancaster, who was brutally murdered on 24 August 2007 for being an alternative individual, which is something very close to my heart. I also dedicate my book to Sophie's mum, Sylvia Lancaster, who campaigns against hate crimes against alternative subcultures. Sylvia Lancaster is also the chief executive of the Sophie Lancaster Foundation, which she set up in honour of her daughter: sophielancasterfoundation.com

My heart goes out to Sylvia and to her family with what they have had to live with all of these years because of the uneducated and small-mindedness of discriminating people in today's society who have issues with people, such as myself, who live an alternative lifestyle.

All my love goes out to Sophie Lancaster, Sylvia Lancaster and to all of Sophie and Sylvia's family and friends, who have been affected by Sophie's senseless killing. I write more about Sophie Lancaster and all the exceptional work her mum, Sylvia, does at the beginning of the chapter 'Be Unique, Be Yourself, Be Positive, Be Individual'. My book is also dedicated to my family, mates and online friends and followers who have supported, believed in me and contributed to my book. Furthermore, I would like to dedicate my book to all of the victims of the coronavirus who sadly lost their lives. We are now living in a new world; we have learnt many valuable lessons. Together we can move forward. Let's honour those who lost their lives by creating a more civilised society they would be proud of by showing more reverence and compassion towards our fellow humans. One world, one love, peace to all.

And finally, I guess you could say I'm not your average man, because on first appearances you might think, 'Why on earth is this guy dressed as a pirate? What could he possibly be able to teach me?' Looks can be deceiving, though, and, as they say, you should never judge a book by its cover because you don't know what lies within the pages before you. Now let's make the world a happier place for you and me to live in together and remind each other that we are never alone.

Steven M. Rippin

Thou shall not judge or have distain,
Thou shall never look down on anybody,
Thou shall not bully or intimidate others,
Thou shall believe in thyself,
Thou shall love thy family and friends,
Thou shall stay away from negative people,
Thou shall not do wrong upon those
who have done wrong upon thee,
Thou shall move on and rise above
the hatred of others,
Thou shall stay strong, positive and determined
throughout thy life,
And thou shall always do thy best to
Smile and be happy every day

Steven M. Rippin

# FOREWORDS

There is a deep, underlying, meaning why you choose to identify with a pirate. Now I know pirates are tough, pirates are ruthless, and people are afraid of them and what they may do. Due to your life experience, you created an alter-ego to combat against the pain that others have inflicted upon you. Somehow, in your mind, if people thought of you as a pirate, then perhaps they will stop their actions. While you are not a pirate in the traditional sense, it's what you have had to do in your life to help you confront and face your fears. It's not the long-term solution, but a defence mechanism to help you to arrive at a long-term solution. That is, discovering who you are, defining your purpose, and then living it without fear.

Ron Cichy II, California, USA, lifezynth.com

Steve is a truly unique and wondrous individual who leaves joy and laughter in his wake. Despite more than his share of heartaches and personal challenges, he strives to make the world a happier place. My life has been enriched in knowing him, and his story is one well worth telling.

Jim Scott, USA, instagram.com/jimscottauthor

I think you are a kind, charismatic, charming guy and Jules is flattered by your videos. You're one in a million. Most people wouldn't go out of their way to do something so kind, and if you believe in karma – what goes around, comes around. Thank you, much appreciated and good luck with everything Steve.

Amanda and Jules O'Riordan, London, England

You're an inspiration to so many, including me, kind people like you inspire me, that tomorrow will be a better day. You are very intelligent and compassionate, a wonderful combination. You're a sweetheart, much love to you and appreciation. You're the best xx.

Stacey Hayes, California, USA, instagram.com/hoststaceyhayes

I know this is an important journey for you, and your stories will be an inspiration and give hope to others who face the same trials and tribulations in life. It is you, my friend, that has been an inspiration to me as you have shown how you take life's challenges and turn them into such positive actions. Seeing your journey with your father his illness, his recovery, you thanking all of your donors to the charity, your daily inspirational quotes, your simple yet powerful messages on how to lead a good proper and purposeful life is a true inspiration to me.

Jeff Shumate, Atlanta, USA, instagram.com/jeffshumate13

I think Steve, you are a very amazing person. You love to use your uniqueness to inspire others to do what makes them happy. You help people to find themselves and to grow. You sure make me laugh with the pirate voice you do. Hope your book is a huge hit and helps people who are going through hard times to know how to cope with the bad.

Kimberly Barnard and Debbie Barnard, Arkansas, USA

Dear Steve Rippin, you rock! By far, my favourite pirate. What you do for others is wonderful. How you love your dad and helped him through his sickness is awesome… How you make people laugh… How you make people feel good about themselves and inspire them to be unique. That IS unique, my friend! Be blessed and know God loves you. A big hug from your friend in Norway.

**Anita Nystrand, senior pastor at the Way Church, Norway, instagram.com/anitanystrand**

Hiya Steve, I think you're a great genuine down to earth person. You have a soul I think that's been around for many lifetimes. You gain my respect in expressing yourself in how you dress. You are a very friendly, bubbly character. Who, one I think is someone who I may add can learn a lot from, from your life experiences. You always have the time to speak and have left me with some lovely memories working at the top bar in Kings. You've done great charity work and a true inspiration xx.

**Dani Rust, Market Harborough, England**

# PREFACE

Here are two videos to say thank you for purchasing my book, and to give you a concise description of what my alternative self-help autobiography is about: bit.ly/ThankyouForBuyingMyBook

There are six main reasons why I decided to write my book. The number one intention stems back to when I was raising money for Cancer Research UK in June 2017, when my dad was diagnosed with mouth cancer. You see, after my month of fundraising was over, I felt like my own journey had only just begun. The response I received inspired me to create a positive lifestyle leaflet, which I wanted to hand out to people to spread more love and happiness in the world around you and me today. So I told my dad what I was going to do, and he said, 'Go on, then let's hear what you've written so far for your leaflet.'

So, I read a piece of it out, and after he had finished laughing and joking with me, my dad said, 'Seriously though that sounds really good, you could write a book.' And that's when my dad inspired me to write my alternative self-help autobiography.

Thank you, Dad; you were and still are my biggest inspiration in all that I do, and I'm forever grateful to you for that. You and Mum have supported me from the very start with my book, and I hope I make you both proud.

Steven M. Rippin

Intention number two is because of friends who I have sadly lost due to mental health problems.

Intention number three is because of the health conditions my dad's been through and how he's coped with them.

Intention number four is because of how I've been treated for living my life as an alternative individual. And to let people know who have faced similar situations to what I've been through that they are not alone and can overcome how others may have left them feeling about themselves.

Intention number five is because I wanted to write a self-help book which isn't all one-sided, with me telling you what you should and shouldn't be doing to help improve your life without you knowing a single thing about me and the difficulties I've faced and learnt to overcome. Plus, I thought by doing this it would give you a more real and raw in-depth view on how the sincere people in today's society master their fears and dilemmas in life.

And intention number six is because I wanted to help those who only know me as Pirate Steve understand who I genuinely am on the inside and not how I portray myself to the world as the pirate they see me as when I'm out in public.

So, is this alternative self-help autobiography for you? It is if you want to live a happy and positive lifestyle. I would say, though, that it depends on how open-minded you are, and if you have ever felt like: you have never fitted into society, just how I've felt sometimes and still do – You're an alternative individual and have had to contend with small-minded people treating you differently because you're not the stereotypical woman, man, girl or boy the world expects you to be – You've been bullied – You've been insulted – You've suffered from anxiety and depression – You've suffered from low self-esteem – You have mental health problems – You've had to deal with patronising and condescending people – You have health or disability problems – You've been assaulted and you know what it feels like to lose a loved one, or you would like to know how to feel inspired, how to turn your life around and how to become more positive. Then I would say you'll be able to benefit from my book and understand how I've felt over the years.

And, as this is an autobiography, you will also learn about who I am, from personal stories about my life to my health issues, the times when I was bullied and assaulted and why I chose to look the way I do today, along with much more I hope you will be intrigued to read. Through my book there will be stories of mine which will be hard for you to read, along with a few of my friends' own tragic life stories as well, which they have kindly shared. Their stories broke my heart when I read them.

My alternative self-help autobiography will make you think, make you laugh, and make you cry. It will also take you on a journey through the diverse life experiences we go through. And I believe it will help you learn more about who you are as a person as well.

I hope when you have read how I've coped with my struggles that it helps and inspires you to conquer any hardships you might have been through or are dealing with in your life right now.

Some parts of my book might not appeal to you, which I will understand. I've included what I believe feels right to me, though, so you get a good idea of the person I am and that I'm not just some guy claiming that he has all the answers to everything I write about, because I haven't and I would only be lying if I said I did.

I'm going to be as real and as down to earth with you as I would be talking to one of my best friends as you read through my book. And a great piece of advice I was given when I first started to write it was to keep it as raw and as real as I possibly can, which I believe I have.

The video links you will come across can be found on my YouTube channel – The Positive Pirate – or by following this link: bit.ly/ThePositivePirate

I've also added a playlist to my YouTube channel as well, called 'Life through my eyes: Videos to go along with my book'. And you can find this playlist here: bit.ly/LifeThroughMyEyesPlaylist

If you have a printed version of my book, to access the website links type out the web addresses precisely how you see them into your browser; also include any capital letters when necessary.

Here are my social media links if you would like to keep up to date with what I'm up to.

# SOCIAL MEDIA LINKS

YouTube: The Positive Pirate – youtube.com/xxxpiratestevexxx
Instagram: thepositivepirate – instagram.com/thepositivepirate
Twitter: positive_pirate – twitter.com/positive_pirate
Facebook: Steve Rippin – facebook.com/PIRATESTEVERIPPIN
LinkedIn: The Positive Pirate – linkedin.com/in/thepositivepirate
Snapchat: The Positive Pirate – snapchat.com/add/piratesteveshow
And if you type in 'The Positive Pirate' on Facebook, my Like/Fan page will appear. So, without further ado, much love and respect from me to you.

Steven M. Rippin

# THE ASSAULT

I didn't see it coming; I turned around and saw this fist come flying at me from out of nowhere! Then it connected with my left eye, and I fell to the floor. There I was clutching at my left eye as I felt blood pouring down my face where the guy's ring had split my eyelid right open. I was looking around for help, but nobody was there.

The guy who had assaulted me was standing only a few feet away laughing, then he turned around and walked away with his friend as I lay there with my hand to my face covering my left eye as I felt the wet sticky residue of blood oozing through my fingers from out of my split eyelid. All I could think was, 'My dad isn't going to be happy about this. Is my contact lens all right? Will I be able to see out of my left eye again?' I couldn't see out of my right eye very well either due to my cataract, but I did my best, and I managed to stumble to the entrance of the nightclub where I was, and they called for an ambulance and made sure I was all right.

I was only twenty-one years old, and I had already undergone six significant operations on my right eye. So, the last thing I needed back then was to have more surgery done on my eyes, which were already in an extremely bad way. My poor parents had gone through enough already with me during their lives, and this was something they could have done without. Welcome to my life. If only I'd known what else was in store for me in the years to come.

Steven M. Rippin

# PART ONE

PART ONE

# INTRODUCTION

Well, here I am in my forties writing an alternative self-help autobiography on my life and the dilemmas I've faced. Don't get me wrong: I know there are other people out there in the world who have been through far worse circumstances than I've had to contend with in my life, and my heart sincerely goes out to all of those people. I wish none of us had to suffer in life. Unfortunately, though, life isn't a bed of roses, is it? You and I do experience afflictions from time to time with the problems life throws at us.

> When you have gone through a traumatic event in your life, it's down to you how you move forward from it. If you don't it might affect the direction your life takes from that moment onwards.

And now I thought I would start my book off with a song my good friend Georgie Gorman kindly wrote for me, and, if you would like to sing along to it, here is a video link and the first chorus of it: bit.ly/ MyFriendPirateSteve

> I wanna tell you a story about my friend Steve,
> He's the kind of mate
> he's really great
> and would you believe,
>
> He always looks so happy I can see him right now,
> His life's a bit of a bubble

he keeps out of trouble.
And when Steve goes by all the people say, 'Wow'

Pirate Steve's got a trick up his sleeve and I always knew he would.
And if you're wearing a frown
and you're feeling down
Pirate Steve is going to make you feel good.

**Georgie Gorman Sligo, Ireland; to be continued…**

Well, I hope you enjoyed Georgie Gorman's song. It's a lot longer than that, and I explain more about Georgie and this excellent song he wrote for me later on through my book. For now, though, it's time to explain who I am, and the trials and tribulations I have endured throughout my life and how I have overcome them.

A lot of people think I'm trying to emulate Captain Jack Sparrow with how I've styled myself. I'll put my hand on my heart and tell you, though, that the honest truth is that resembling Captain Jack Sparrow was and has never been something I went out to do. I didn't even know who Captain Jack Sparrow was! I changed my appearance because of my eyesight, if I'm truly honest, plus the fact that I had always wanted to have long hair and grow two plaits into my beard because of my love for the television show *Worzel Gummidge*. Worzel, you see, had two long pieces of straw jutting from his chin, which I thought looked cool when I was younger! I honestly can't help the way I like to look, by resembling a certain pirate; that's really just a coincidence. I'll tell you something, though: it's been hard work explaining to people over the years that I'm just being myself and not copying the fictional character who is known as Captain Jack Sparrow.

I can understand, though, how people who don't know me will presume that I must be a big fan of pirates, with how I look and act with the videos I make on social media. If I saw some guy looking how I do, then I'd think exactly the same thing and that he wants to live his life as a pirate, which I don't, but they don't know that because they haven't sat down with me and gone through a psychological evaluation on the inner workings of my mind, have they? So, I don't mind explaining to respectable and polite people why I chose to look how I do; I just get annoyed when I have rude and disrespectful people talk down and laugh at me because of it!

Over the years a lot of people have been in touch with me on social media telling me what they have been through in life. And they've said I've helped to inspire them with my own quandaries I've posted on social media. I never thought in a million years I would receive messages from people I don't know online telling me how much I've helped to inspire them in their lives. I've even had people explaining to me that I have saved them from wanting to commit suicide! When I've received messages like those, it makes me feel incredibly humbled to know that I have been able to touch their lives in such a powerful way. My friends and followers have told me they always look forward to my new posts online because they always help to put a smile on their faces and lift their spirits whenever they are feeling down.

I hope, by the time you've read my book, you will understand my appearance is who I am and how I feel comfortable living my life, as there's a lot more about me than resembling a pirate.

We should always share how we are genuinely feeling on the inside with our family and friends, and never bottle our problems up. I have known too many people who have suffered in silence over the years, which has done them no good, and sadly some of those individuals I knew have taken their own lives because they didn't open up and talk about their difficulties. By sharing my afflictions throughout my book, I hope they help you disclose any dilemmas you might be going through in your life with your loved ones.

I believe the stories and advice you're about to read will help you, benefit you and make you realise that you're never alone in life, especially if you can relate to being singled out and made to feel like an outcast. I'm also going to ask you questions to answer and write down, through specific chapters, which will help get any thoughts you might have out of your head. It will be a bit like keeping your own personal diary. Please remember: I'm no self-help guru. I'm just me. I'm a carpet cleaner who's an everyday lad from Leicestershire here in England, who's been raised by very loving parents. Everything you're about to read is coming straight from my heart and is one hundred per cent true, and nothing is fabricated or exaggerated. And when I write about extra-terrestrials and what is out there in space, they are only my personal views and opinions from what I have read and believe is true. I completely understand if you disagree with me on this subject as it is a very controversial topic.

I sincerely hope my book inspires you and gives you the encouragement and determination to get out there into the world to become the best version of yourself. And finally, thank you once again for purchasing my book. I truly appreciate it.

An inspiration to everyone – I always show your posts on Facebook to my little girl as a shining example of how to live your life!

**Kris Taft, Valenciana, Spain**

# WHO IS STEVEN M. RIPPIN, AKA PIRATE STEVE?

Well, I was born on Friday, 12 December 1975, at one o'clock in the morning in the city of Leicester in England, and little did my parents know what I had in store for them over the next forty-plus years. My parents were raised in Nissen huts, which were used during the war, and they both, along with their families, had it tough while they were growing up, not like you and I have it nowadays with all our creature comforts, which we take for granted. My parents even had to share their bathwater with their brothers and sisters, you know! Can you imagine getting in the same bathwater your brother or sister has just been bathing in? No, neither can I. I have no idea what it must have been like for them!

I come from a working-class family, and we have never been given anything in our lives. My dad has grafted extremely hard over the years and has earned every penny he's made; he's one of the hardest-working men I know, and I admire him very much for that.

I should start by telling you this strange little story from when I was only six months old. Once upon a time on a cold winter's night – I have no idea if it was a cold winter's night or not; I'm just trying to set the scene and make it sound all nice and cosy. Anyway, there was my mum back in 1975, after a busy day looking after her new-born baby boy, standing in the bedroom taking a photograph of her husband, my dad, while he held me in his arms looking down into my eyes, which was going to make the perfect father and new-born baby son family photograph. Well, that's what my parents thought was going to happen!

So, after my mum had taken the photograph, she then sent it off to be developed, which meant a photograph company of your choosing would print out your pictures and then send them back to you two or three weeks later. How annoying would that have been, especially if half of them came back blurry, which quite often they did! Thankfully, technology has come a long way since then, hasn't it?

Once my parents got their photographs back from the developers, the picture of my dad holding me in his arms shocked my mum and dad when they saw it, because there was my dad, who was supposed to be holding me while he looked down into my eyes, but I wasn't there. I was nowhere to be seen! And still to this day we have no explanation of my whereabouts, or where I disappeared to! It was like I had been abducted by aliens for a split second and then returned without any of us being any of the wiser. Who knows how long I was gone! I have no recollection of being beamed up by extra-terrestrials, that's for sure! I guess it does answer a lot of questions as to how I've turned out as a human being though, doesn't it? So, if you know any professional photographers you think can solve this mystery, then please let me know, thank you so much.

When I was two and a half years old, my parents noticed I was struggling to walk, then two years later I was diagnosed with Still's disease, which is a form of rheumatoid arthritis.

When I was around the age of four, living with arthritis, my parents and I moved to Syston in Leicestershire, which was closer to Potters Carpets in Anstey, where my dad used to work. I always remember the girl next door coming round to play with me when we lived there. Hold on, hold on, don't get any funny ideas now, I can see you laughing away with that grin on your face. The girl next door was around six years old, and I guess you could say that I was her toy boy! Anyway, the girl next door and I would often play in the mud together, digging holes and making mud pies; good times. Unfortunately, though, my rheumatoid arthritis gradually got worse, so my parents decided to move back to Market Harborough when I was five and into a bungalow to help me. Thus, my mud pie-making days with the girl next door were sadly over. Thankfully, though, my rheumatoid arthritis seemed to clear up on its own when I was around six years old. Whether that was because my mum had started giving me Seven Seas cod liver oil, I will never know.

I then started Fairfield Road C of E Primary School, when we moved back to Market Harborough, where all my troubles started, and the bullying began, which continued into my adult life. When I had my first school medical examination done, they picked up that I wasn't able to see the letters on the screen, which you get told to read when you go for an eye test at your opticians. So, the school medical team referred me to go and see an eye specialist in Leicester. And, when my parents took me to see the eye specialist, he told them that the inflammation from my rheumatoid arthritis had damaged my eyesight and caused me to have cataracts, plus other eye conditions as well!

My rheumatoid arthritis and eyesight problems changed the course my life was going to take forever.

Can you believe what one teacher said to my parents when I first started primary school? She told them I wouldn't amount to much in life! Well, I guess she was right, wasn't she, because look at how I turned out and what her school turned me into: a blooming pirate! So, whatever you do, always check, when you enrol your kids into a school, that they haven't got a policy where if your kids aren't doing too well they turn them into pirates and send them on their way! I'm only joking. What a thing to say to my mum and dad, though: 'Oh, by the way, your kid might only be five years old, but I can guarantee you, he isn't going to amount to much in life.' 'Wow' is all I can say to that. I hope teachers no longer go around saying cynical and cruel things like this to parents about their children nowadays!

When people have pulled me down, they have always made me more determined to show them that I will amount to something in life!

I was timid as a child, quite hairy, and was one of only a handful of kids who wore glasses, so the children loved calling me hairy monster and four-eyed goggle box. The children at my school always made me feel like some freaky monster who must be avoided at all times; it was horrible. It was as if bullying, demoralising and insulting me was a reasonable thing to do!

Adults often used to tell me that being bullied and called names was a normal part of growing up and was something I would have to get used to!

Well, that's totally wrong if you ask me. It didn't do me any favours, and I'm sure that kind of advice hasn't helped a lot of other children either, especially the ones who have sadly taken their own lives because of being bullied, demoralised and insulted!

When I was at school, if a child looked different in any way, then they were a target for bullying, no questions asked. I wish there had been a lot more support back then for children, such as me, who were threatened. I would tell my parents about what was going on with the ridicule and bullying, and they would report it to the teachers, but nothing would ever change, and the bullying would continue! One teacher I did adore, though, when I attended Fairfield Road C of E Primary School was Miss Howe. She truly made going to school a pleasure for me. I loved her classes. Liz – Miss Howe – used to put my eyedrops in for me in the mornings and at dinner times, which I sincerely appreciated her doing. And she told me, even though my eyes were very sore, I never complained once.

Thank you, Liz, for being the best teacher I ever had.

Steven M. Rippin

The impression I used to get when I was at school was teachers would focus all their attention on the children they liked and knew would do well in life. The other children, like me, they didn't seem all that bothered about; well, that's how I saw things anyway. Mind you, there were some outstanding teachers I was taught by, so they weren't all bad.

As children, you and I are socially conditioned from an early age to become successful in our lives, and we're led to believe that to be prosperous you need to be very intelligent and if you don't pass your exams at school, college or university, then you're not going to amount to much. And the pressure that puts you under as a child or a teenager at exam time can make you feel extremely stressed and worried about the direction your life's going to take. It shouldn't be like that, should it? You can only do the best to your ability! I didn't do too well in my exams, if I'm honest. I got a lot of Es, Ds and Gs, which was terrible. Oh, I did get a C in photography, though, so I was pretty proud of that. And, even though I didn't do too well at school, I think I've done all right, because I've got my own carpet cleaning business that my dad helped me set up, which I've had for over twenty-five years. And, can you believe, my dad never took any exams while he was at school, and he's owned his carpet and flooring business for well over forty years now! So, it just goes to show you that it isn't all about how many exams you pass or how clever you are because having common sense and being a hard worker indicates just how far you can go in life.

When I became a teenager, I was very timid, and I would keep myself to myself and play on my computer most of the time, then one day I was introduced into a local Pathfinders group by my good friend Simon Wellard, who my dad introduced me to when I was around thirteen. At Pathfinders, lots of events and activities were organised for us to do, and I had a great time there and made a lot of good friends, plus Pathfinders helped my confidence and shyness a lot as well.

> Thank you, Simon, for taking me under your wing. I never knew back then just how much yourself and your friends were going to help change my life around. I appreciate all you have done for me.

> Steven M. Rippin

I got to know a lot of Simon's friends by playing football with them down at Great Bowden park. I wasn't very good at football, so my friends always put me in defence. I didn't mind, though, because it felt fantastic to finally feel accepted and have real mates who were there for me. When I was fifteen or sixteen, I had a couple of different jobs while I was growing up at school, from picking mushrooms at the local mushroom factory to working in a photography shop, and, can you believe, I even used to handle thousands of tampons every day when I packed them in a distribution factory! And one day, while I was packing those menstrual devices into their packages ready to be sent off as free samples for women around England, the factory manager asked if any of us would like to earn a bit of extra money by taking a few boxes of them home with us. So I volunteered. What I didn't realise, though, was that there were thousands of these little blighters to be packed away, and I had eight enormous boxes of them to get through! So that night, there I was in the lounge with all my new-found friends – Tommy, Tammy, Thomas and Tarah Tampon, plus so many others I was getting acquainted with, which were spread all over the lounge carpet, making it look a right mess. My mum, though, bless her, offered to help me pack my little buddies away into their new dwellings to be delivered across England. And I gladly accepted her help that night.

When my dad arrived home from work that evening, he walked into the lounge and couldn't believe his eyes, as he stood there in disbelief with his mouth wide open as he looked at thousands of little tampons everywhere! The first thing my dad said to me was, 'I'm not happy about this, Steven. I don't want this happening every night, look at all this mess. I don't want to see this lot here tomorrow.' So, I had to get all those menstrual devices packed away that evening, which was going to take forever, but my mum and I got it done. I'm so grateful to my mum for helping me out that night, and I'll tell you something else as well: I've never touched another tampon in my life. Well, I guess it would have sounded pretty strange if I had, wouldn't it? Luckily, though, I've had no need.

Anyway, moving on, when I left school at sixteen, I went and worked at MRM, which incidentally was the place where I used to pack the tampons! This time, though, I was working in the offices.

Unfortunately, I only lasted one day because I couldn't stand it, if I'm honest. You see, I had to move computers from the attic to the offices downstairs, which got my white shirt all messed up, which I wasn't happy about, and the work I was doing was dull. So straight away, I knew that job wasn't for me. I gave it a go, though, and lasted one whole day!

Then I went and worked for my dad's carpet business. Unfortunately, though, tucking the carpets down with the knee kicker didn't do my arthritis any good and it came back with a vengeance, leaving me having to take a month off work! I then had to have an injection done on my left knee to drain the fluid away which had built up in it. And I was also put on tablets to help the inflammation go down. So that made me realise I would never make it as a carpet fitter.

Once I was fit again, I turned into a labourer for my dad instead, where I prepared the carpet jobs and then my dad would fit them, which is still what I do today, and we work well together, if I do say so myself.

Now at the age of seventeen, I started having driving lessons, and once I was confident enough I went for my driving test. Still, to this day, I have no idea how I managed to pass it, if I'm honest, because it took me three attempts until I did pass. And I think I only just scraped by at that! When I took my driving test for the first time, while I was driving around a roundabout, my driving instructor said, 'Keep on following the road around.' But for some reason, when I saw the sign to Market Harborough, I went to take it and started cutting across the lanes! My driving instructor went crazy when I did that, as you can imagine, and screamed, 'What are you doing? It's that way.' I think I scared him half to death after I nearly caused a major pile-up! So my driving instructor quickly took over the controls and drove us back to the test centre. I didn't have to ask him if I had failed or not; it was pretty apparent I had!

My first driving test shook me up after nearly causing a major pile-up, and I was put off driving straight away, but my parents gave me the encouragement to carry on even though I didn't want to at the time! The second time when I took my test, I drove well and got on great with my driving instructor, then, when the driving exam was over, I forgot to turn into the test centre car park and I ended up driving up a one-way street! What an idiot I was, and another fail! I was gutted. Then I thought, 'Oh no: I'm going to have to go through this all over again now!' So, I booked myself in for a third test a few weeks later!

Eventually, the day of my third driving exam finally arrived, and, while I was waiting to be called out by my driving instructor, I thought, 'I've got nothing to lose, I might as well go for it and stop acting like a pathetic idiot.' Then, before I knew it, I was being beckoned to my fate.

The first thing my driving instructor said to me when we were on the street outside was, 'Can you read the number plate for me please Mr Rippin?'

'Sorry, I can't read that,' I replied. So, he told me to step closer and try again, which I did, but still I couldn't read the number plate! At this point I'm thinking, 'I'm going to fail my test before I've got into the car at this rate,' which made me wonder what my family and friends would think of me blundering my driving test for a third time! I thought my driving instructor was going to turn around and say, 'Sorry Mr Rippin, but you've failed your driving test because you can't see further than your nose,' which luckily he didn't, and instead he asked me once again to move a bit closer to read the number plate, which I finally managed to read, much to my relief. My driving instructor then said, 'Right let's continue with the test,' which I was glad to hear. And I'm happy to say that the rest of the driving exam went well, and, yes, I finally passed at long last. I couldn't believe I'd succeeded, if I'm honest. It was all down to my parents, though, who had encouraged me to continue with my driving lessons, which I'm so grateful for them for doing.

I've had problems with arthritis all my life, and my doctor told me I'm in the worst job imaginable with the condition I have. So, when I was nineteen, my dad helped me set up a carpet cleaning business with the primary purpose of it helping to get me off my knees. My dad's helped me out a lot with my cleaning business over the years, mainly because I struggle to drive due to my eyesight, which I have sincerely appreciated him doing so much. I can still drive, but when I drove the work van I drove into fences, bushes and trees, and also took a few metal railings down with me as well. Oh, and I struggle driving in the dark so don't worry: there's no reason to feel concerned if you're in a car with me behind the wheel! If you were able to see what I saw through my eyes when I used to drive at night, you would see something like Catherine wheels at a fireworks display shooting off in all directions when you look at the street lights and car headlamps when they're coming towards you, which can be pretty disorientating; my cataract in my left eye causes the firework effect. I think I'm best kept off the roads really, aren't I?

My dad has helped me to carry on working throughout my life, and I'm forever grateful to him for his support and encouragement.

When I was working with my dad, we would fit carpets for customers I remembered from my school days, who were now settling down with their partners having babies. And I used to think to myself back then, 'Oh, should I be settling down and having babies as well? I'm still single and living at home with my parents while everybody else around me seems to be living their lives and growing up!'

My dad, though, always said to me, 'You do what you want; the main thing is, are you happy, Steve?'

And I would always tell him, 'Yeah, I am happy.'

Then he would say to me, 'Well, as long as you're happy, then I'm happy; you do what you want in life.' Society sadly puts too much pressure on people from an early age to meet a partner, settle down, get a house, have a baby and grow old together, doesn't it? I believe you and I should be allowed to live our lives how we choose to and not how we're told to by society, don't you?

Now in my twenties, I enjoyed going out partying and over to Ibiza, which I still do. Then I was assaulted when I was twenty-one, which affected my confidence and caused me to suffer from social anxiety, but I continued to be myself and live my life how I wanted. And so the years went by, I went to work, went out partying at the weekends and had a few lads' holidays, which were fantastic. Then, when I was around twenty-five, I decided to change my image and grow my hair long, which turned a few heads! So now, in my late twenties, I had long hair, and it was the beginning of a whole new chapter in my life because that was when I was to become known as Pirate Steve to everybody. Then, when I was thirty-two, I was assaulted again! And that's when my life took on a new direction all together because being attacked for a second time caused me to suffer from more mental health issues, which was a real low point in my life.

What helped me through those times, though, was when I created The Pirate Steve Show on YouTube, auditioned for *Big Brother* and appeared on *The Weakest Link* television game show. All those things helped me to overcome my mental health problems and also helped me rebuild my confidence and low self-esteem, which had been taken away from me.

Well, I hope that has given you a bit of an insight into my past. Now let's move on to who I have become today.

# MY EYESIGHT ISSUES MADE ME WHO I AM TODAY

Well, believe it or not, the look I have today started with my eyesight issues; they were the foremost reason I changed my image. If I'd been born with no problems with my eyes, then there's a good chance I wouldn't have written my book. So luckily I was born with eyesight problems, and I say lucky because I wouldn't have met all the fantastic people I have had the privilege of getting to know or had any of the incredible experiences I have had over the years, which have contributed towards helping me become who I am today.

I grew my hair long because I didn't like how my eyes looked due to the operations I have had done on them. And having people say how red, strange and sore they appear only made me more conscious about them when I was in public. It didn't help either when random strangers said, 'Oh you look weird; you're a stoner or a druggy, aren't you?' in a condescending way. Then they would laugh in my face and say, 'Whatever, mate,' when I told them I wasn't. So, as you can imagine, being told those things took my confidence away. Also, my confidence to chat women up has been affected as well, because when I see women I like nowadays I go all quiet and won't say a word to them, all because I don't want them to see what my eyes look like. So, no wonder I have been single for so many years! When I was younger, my friends were full of confidence and chatting women up all the time, while I would be the timid, quiet one in the background.

I guess the people who made me feel insecure and took my confidence away have helped to create Pirate Steve and put me on the path I'm on today! I've got a lot to thank those disrespectful people for thinking about it.

People have astonished me with how discourteous they have been and still are about my eyes! How would they like it if I turned around to them and said something impolite about their appearance? I still get people mentioning how red my eyes look today, which does upset me. I know my eyes look red from time to time, but there's nothing I can do about it; my eyes are who I am. Why can't some people learn to keep their thoughts to themselves instead of picking fault with others?

Because I was still receiving negative comments about my eyes after the surgeries I'd had done to make them look more normal, I said to myself, 'Enough is enough, I don't want to keep being insulted anymore when I'm out in public. I'm going to take the attention away from my eyes and grow my hair.' So that's what I did. Then, when I was growing it, everybody kept telling me to get it cut because I looked a mess. I didn't listen to anybody, though, and I carried on growing it. To this day, growing my hair was the best thing I ever did. It boosted my confidence and changed my life more than I could have ever imagined! So, if you want to change your image, do it and don't let anybody stop you.

Q: Hi, Steve, my question would be for you. What inspired you to portray Captain Jack, aka Johnny Depp? Did you do other personalities or was Johnny Depp your sole inspiration? You really do deserve to go on to great things; you have a great talent there. Hopefully, someone will see it and make things happen for you lol xx.

Jean Bushell, Kettering, England

A: Hey, Jean, excellent questions. I never intentionally went out to become a pirate or resemble Captain Jack Sparrow, believe it or not. And in this chapter I explain how it all came about. And to answer your question, Jean, no, Johnny Depp didn't inspire me, but he is one of my favourite actors. And that's very kind of you to say; thank you so much.

Steven M. Rippin

After a couple of years, I finally had the long hair I had always wanted. Then I needed something to tie it back with because it was getting in my face at work. And when I was watching Wimbledon one year, I noticed Rafael Nadal was wearing a red bandana to tie his hair back with and I thought, 'Rafael Nadal looks really cool with his red bandana. I'd love one of those,' so I looked on eBay, found one and ordered it for myself. Who would have ever thought by me watching Wimbledon all those years ago that Rafael Nadal was going to inspire me in such a big way, and not to become a famous tennis player but to become known as Pirate Steve! I should also point out that I had never heard of Captain Jack Sparrow or any of the *Pirates of the Caribbean* movies. I was just happy to have long hair, which I was hoping would take the attention away from my eyes.

The first time I was told I resembled Captain Jack Sparrow was on 23 June 2007, when my dad and I were on a *Buffy the Vampire Slayer* cruise around Alaska. Ashley Motes, who we became friends with on that cruise – the daughter of the organiser of the convention, Joe Motes – said, 'You look like Jack Sparrow.'

'I have no idea who that is,' I told Ashley. And she was shocked when I said that, and then Ashley told me I was going to have to watch *Pirates of the Caribbean* when I got back home, and I would understand what she meant. So, as you can see, even back then I had no idea who Jack Sparrow was. So, when my dad and I got back home to England, we watched *Pirates of the Caribbean*. Only then did we understand why Ashley had mentioned that I looked like this pirate called Jack Sparrow!

The first time I wore my bandana was when I was at home in May 2007. Then I wore it again for the second time when I was in Alaska in June 2007. And the third time I wore it was when I was in Milton Keynes, England, in July 2007 for my friend Tom Cooper's birthday. While we were celebrating Tom's birthday in a nightclub called Oceana, I hadn't been wearing my bandana, which I had safely tucked away in my pocket, so I thought for a bit of fun I would go and put it on. So off I went to the men's room, did my hair and put it on. I then joined my mates on the dancefloor, and within a few minutes the DJ announced that Jack Sparrow was in the building! I thought for a minute there was a Jack Sparrow lookalike in the nightclub, so I turned around to look for one, but couldn't see one anywhere. Then I saw the DJ pointing over at me! I couldn't believe it. So, I put my hand up to the DJ, gave him a nod and thanked him for the shout-out.

I had never experienced anything like that in a nightclub in my life. Then as I was going to the bar to get the drinks in a woman came over to me and said, 'Oh you do look just like Captain Jack; can I get a photo with you, please?'

'Yeah, of course, that's really good of you to say. I can't believe the DJ thinks I look like Jack Sparrow as well. I don't think I look anything like him, if I'm honest,' I replied. I don't think my mates could believe what was going on because they were used to seeing me shying away and blending into the background while they chatted the women up. So, for a woman to come over to me was unbelievable! Oh yeah, and that was the very first time somebody had ever asked me for a photo, you know. It was such a surreal night and one I will never forget. It still amazes me how a piece of red material wrapped around my head can cause such a commotion when I'm out in public from time to time. If it puts a smile on somebody's face, though, then that's awesome; after all, life's about having fun and making those around you happy.

So now, at the age of thirty-two, I've got a whole new image going on, and people have started calling me Pirate Steve. My dad, bless him, worried to death every time I would go out at the weekends when he saw how I was dressed, though, even more so when he saw me wearing eyeliner! He would often say to me and still does, 'Be careful and stay out of trouble. You know what people are like when they've had a drink.' And he was right, wasn't he, because I ended up getting put into hospital a couple of times.

From around 2008 a lot of people got to know who I was in my hometown. I think that was because I had appeared in my town's local newspaper twice within the space of a few months for being assaulted and auditioning for *Big Brother*. So, with those news stories, plus my social media activity, people soon got to know the name Pirate Steve. Gradually, over the years, more and more people were intrigued to find out who I was. I just didn't understand what the interest was if, I'm honest, as most of my life I had shied away. And now all of a sudden people were messaging me left, right and centre. It was pretty surreal.

I believe the majority of people in my hometown are OK with how I look, although there's always going to be a small minority of people who think I'm some crazy attention-seeking idiot. If they genuinely knew who I was, then they would understand I'm nothing like that. I just live my life out of the box and do what I want to do. I don't mind if people do think I'm strange, weird or eccentric; that's fine because I know I am; everybody's entitled to their opinions, aren't they? People should never judge others in a negative way without getting to know them first, though.

In 2009 I asked my dad if he fancied going to Warwick Castle in England with me, which he did. You should have seen the look on his face, though, while he was eating his bowl of cornflakes when I walked into the kitchen dressed in my full-on Captain Jack Sparrow outfit before we headed over there. My dad burst out with 'You're not going dressed like that are you?' as cornflakes and milk came flying out his mouth and across the kitchen table.

'Yeah, it will be awesome. We'll be able to get some really good photos as well,' I replied.

After my dad had calmed down and had got over the initial shock of how I was dressed, he went and got ready while I cleaned up. Then off we went. Soon as we arrived at Warwick Castle groups of schoolchildren and their teachers came up to my dad and me, and the teachers asked us if it was all right for their students to have a photo with me, which of course it was. We also had parents with their children coming up to us all day long asking for photos as well. My dad and I had never experienced anything quite like it; it was so good to see how happy we were making everybody that day. Even the people in period costumes who worked at Warwick Castle said how impressed they were with how I looked, which I appreciated them saying very much because I was feeling so nervous and timid. I have no idea where I got the confidence from to dress up and walk around Warwick Castle that day; I guess I wanted to prove to myself that I could do it.

It did get a bit tiring halfway through the day wearing my costume, so around three o'clock in the afternoon my dad and I took a break. And that's when the day went downhill for me. We visited the owl sanctuary they have there, you see, which is excellent, apart from the guy who was in charge of the owls back then. Because, while my dad was chatting to the owl guy, the owl guy started asking my dad why I was dressed up. I would have answered him myself if I'd heard him, but I was busy admiring the owls. I was also shattered and just wanted to have a few minutes of peace.

The owl guy also said to my dad, 'What's up with him? Can't he talk? Why's he just standing over there?'

'That's my son, and he's looking at your owls. He's taking a break because he's been busy all day having photos taken with everybody since ten o'clock this morning and now he's worn out and hungry. Does it matter what he's doing?' my dad replied, and the owl guy said, 'Uh, right.' Then I looked around, and I could just hear what this owl guy had been saying to my dad, so I walked over to where they were and said hi. And all this owl guy did was give me one of those condescending sneers and said, 'All right,' like it was too much trouble to talk to me. I knew straight away he didn't like me one bit. You just know when somebody takes an instant dislike to you, don't you? It was a horrible atmosphere, and I couldn't wait to get away from that bloke's negative attitude towards me. He was starting to take away all my confidence and self-esteem. People know how to put a dampener on your day, don't they? I didn't let that owl guy get me down for long, though. My dad knew straight away what I was thinking after the owl guy had spoken to me like that, so we quickly ended our very awkward conversation with him and had a go at archery, which isn't the best idea when you've got eyesight like mine! We had a good laugh, though, while we shot a few arrows. And if you would like to see my archery skills, here is a video link for your entertainment: bit.ly/PirateStevesArcherySkillsWarwickCastle

I've found over the years some people I've met act how the owl guy acted towards me because they can't wait to pick fault with me for whatever reason they have against me, a bit like how some individuals have picked fault with my eyes. Whether it's because I come across as being too shy and quiet sometimes when I'm out in public or if I make them feel intimidated in some way, I will never know. The main thing is that my dad and I had a fantastic day out together at Warwick Castle, and to finish the day off we watched a spectacular firework display and swordfight. I'm so pleased I dressed up as Captain Jack Sparrow that day, even though I was timid and nervous about walking around in my costume. Once I had stepped foot into the grounds of Warwick Castle, though, I felt a lot more comfortable, confident and relaxed. The whole experience unquestionably helped me to step out of my comfort zone a lot more as well.

Q: When did you start cosplaying, and what inspired you?

Yok Tsin, London, England

A: Hey, Yok, thanks for your question. I didn't get into cosplaying until I was around thirty-three. That's when I bought my Captain Jack Sparrow wig and started YouTubing. I gradually got introduced to the cosplay community by my friends, although I don't go to many conventions. There wasn't one central thing that inspired me, to be honest, Yok. I just grew into cosplaying a pirate over the years. When I was younger, though, I did love dressing up as a cyber kid with spikey-coloured hair when I went out clubbing, which I guess could have influenced my love for dressing up in costumes. Thank you so much for your question, Yok.

Steven M. Rippin

From 2009 to the present day I have continued to change my style. I have also carried on with the Pirate Steve Show on social media, now known as the Positive Pirate, and learnt a lot about myself along the way. It has been an incredible journey so far being Pirate Steve. Unfortunately, though, I have seen how shallow and fake some people can be towards you when you stand out in a crowd; certain individuals, you see, will only want to be your friend because of how you look, while others will enjoy insulting you. Onwards and upwards, though, as they say.

Q: What are the best/worst parts about being a pirate mate?

Sven Blackheart, Austin, Texas, USA

A: Hey, Sven. I like this question. When I'm dressed as Captain Jack Sparrow, I would say the worst parts about it are how jealous men can be towards you, which surprised me, if I'm honest, and something I never expected. Also, when I've been out in public, some men can take an instant dislike to me, especially in bars and nightclubs. When I'm not in my Captain Jack Sparrow costume, I don't feel like a pirate at all; I feel like my normal self, Steven Rippin. Not everybody sees this, though, and people will still presume I'm a pirate, even though I'm wearing my jeans and a T-shirt. Also, the insults I've received are something I never anticipated; they used to upset me a lot, over time, though, I have learnt how to ignore them as best as I can. And I would say the best part about looking like a pirate, Sven, is the number of people I make smile when they see me out in public. Furthermore, matey, looking like a pirate has given me confidence and helped me overcome my mental health issues. It's also made me feel accepted by a lot of people for the first time in my life as well. Thank you so much for your question, Sven, and all the best with your career.

**Steven M. Rippin**

I have got a lot to be thankful for, even though it has been a bumpy ride for me so far because I never thought I would have gone through half the negative experiences I have encountered for looking how I do.

Well, there you have it: the story on why and how I became known as Pirate Steve to a lot of people, which I hope you found interesting. Also, as you continue to read through my book, you will see I have taken on a lot of challenges and experiences in my life that I wouldn't have done if I hadn't changed my image all those years ago. So please remember to dress how you want to dress, look how you want to look and be who you want to be.

# FROM CHILDHOOD TO MANHOOD THIS IS WHO I AM NOW; MY VIEWS ON LIFE

I was timid and lonely when I was younger, and frequently in hospital for eye operations. So, I guess, with the time I had to take off school, it distanced me from the other children; they must have seen me as being this weird kid who wore a patch on his eye, who was away a lot. So, I ended up becoming an easy target for them to bully and insult because they didn't know any better, unfortunately.

Now, in my adult life, whenever I hear from my friends online who tell me how much I inspire them, make them laugh and cheer them up, I feel very honoured and humbled that the timid and lonely child I was can make them feel this way. Hearing them say that touches my heart because, when I was growing up, I used to hide away as much as I could from teachers and children, all because of how they treated me. These days, though, I feel good about myself once again thanks to my online friends and followers.

I've always been open and honest about my feelings, and I'll admit I can be an emotional and sentimental person who gets upset and takes things to heart quickly. And, when you look how I do, that can be very difficult in today's society, especially when you receive insults from strangers for no reason. Again, my friends online always help me through those times. So, I'll always do my best to keep on fighting the good fight for everyone who's suffered at the hands of the small-mindedness of bullies who think they're better than you and I are!

I don't know about you, but I'm done with negative-minded individuals treating people such as me like garbage, I won't stand for it anymore because I don't want anybody to have to go through what I've been through in my life. I have always been myself and wore my heart on my sleeve.

Remember, it's all right to be whoever you want to be in life. If you want to be a Disney cast member and dress up every day as your favourite character, then do it, and if you want to grow up and be a pirate, then make it happen. You can be anybody you desire.

From thirty-two until the age I am today, my life has improved slowly, and I'm now a much happier and positive person once again, just like I used to be before I started school. I'm still working with my dad, who helps me carpet cleaning, and my friends I grew up with have mostly settled down, so I don't get to see them very often. I've got a lot of new friends, though, and I still get to go out at the weekends from time to time partying with them, so life's good. Well, it still has its ups and downs, just like most people's; that's what makes life interesting, though, isn't it? I have loving parents and incredible friends who are always there for me, a roof over my head and food on the table; what more could I ask for?

I now live my life by spreading as much positivity to those around me as I can. Well, I hope that has given you a glimpse into the kind of person I am. And please remember: it's all right to be different and unique, so love who you are. And everything that has happened to you in your life so far has made you the person you are today.

Face your fears and believe in yourself because you can be whoever you want to be in life, so chase after your dreams and don't let anybody stop you from doing so. All I want to see is people getting along with one another and being happy. Is that too much to ask?

# HOW I FEEL ABOUT THE WORLD YOU AND I LIVE IN

Don't be socially conditioned by the world around you. Accept people for who they are and love the life you have been given – Be creative, be individual, be yourself.

When you see people with health problems, disabilities or deformities, remember they are no different to you or me; they have feelings and emotions as well. And, hey, we both have difficulties in life to deal with; nobody's perfect. Imperfections are what make us human, so embrace your flaws and turn them into beautiful things that will help you love yourself for who you are – Live your life how you want to live it.

You and I are both born with our own unique qualities. Some people are born leaders, while some are born followers. Whatever you do, though, don't become a sheep. Use your mind and follow your heart with what you want to accomplish in life – chase after your dreams.

We turn the news on every day, and all we hear about is either war, terror attacks, shootings, stabbings, the rich getting richer, people suffering from starvation, the prices of food, electrical goods and services going up, or we're being told this is good for you, and that's bad for you, eat more of this and eat less of that, which only leaves our heads spinning! Then they will try and brainwash us with advert upon advert between our favourite television shows to get us to buy the latest must-have items, which we don't need – don't be socially conditioned.

Why can't all the different countries of the world join forces as one for the sake of our civilization and find PEACE? Because, if you ask me, we should be thinking of our children and their children's children instead of fighting against one another. And, even as you're reading this right now, children are dying in their thousands all over the world because some countries are fighting for reasons I will never understand – let us unite and move forward to create a better world for the new generations of our planet tomorrow.

What's going wrong with our civilisation? I don't have all the answers to these dilemmas; I'm a carpet cleaner. I just want to bring peace, love and happiness into everybody's lives, and show them that there is hope for a brighter future tomorrow. I can't make that happen on my own, though, so you and I must fight for this world we love so much together if we want to see it thrive into the future so much more than it is doing right now – fight for what you believe in.

It's a corrupt society you and I are living in, where the rich get richer, and the poor get poorer, especially with some of those bankers and politicians who pay themselves ludicrous bonuses every year, which we eventually get to find out about once their despicable shenanigans are splashed all over the media. Then a week later we will find out they have resigned or stepped down from their high-powered positions with a ludicrous payoff! And, over time, those despicable individuals are never heard of ever again, while they live the rest of their lives out in their stately homes off the money they have taken from us! What I would like to know is: when will these criminals of today pay back the money they have taken from under our noses? And why do they get away with paying themselves so much money with their bonuses time and time again? Isn't it time it was put a stop to – money is the root of all evil.

There's more good happening in the world than wrong, though, so not all is lost for humankind. For a start, communities all over the world are stronger than ever, and countries come together when tragedies occur. If only people came together and helped each other out more on a daily basis, though, and not just when significant disasters occurred, then it would definitely make the world a much safer place to live in – always be there for somebody when they need help.

Our children get bullied at school, which can affect them for the rest of their lives, and their health, confidence and self-esteem can get taken away from them because of it. Then, as they grow up, some of those kids can start feeling isolated from society because of the small-mindedness of other children's parents who have made their offspring not understand how vital it is to be open-minded and accepting of others for who they are and not what society expects them to be or how they are required to look – never judge, always accept people.

Alternative individuals like myself are made to feel like outcasts and that it's all right for the general public to point and laugh at us because we're classed as the rejects of society who don't follow the rules. It's the alternative individuals in today's culture who make the world a more exciting and loving place to be a part of, if you ask me. And alternative-innovative individuals such as Elon Musk, Jeff Bezos, Richard Branson, Mark Zuckerberg, Bill Gates, Larry Page and Sergey Brin to name just a few of the entrepreneurs of our society today are the people who come up with creative ideas, new start-up businesses and moonshot ideas for the human race to progress forward in AI and technology bringing us closer to the singularity – be an alternative individual who has a creative mind.

Our lives can be corrupted the day we start school. Can you remember back to your childhood, when you would have been around four or five years old? If you can, there's a good chance you would have been full of confidence and loved learning and asking questions about everything around you. You would have talked to anybody, you would have sung your heart out and danced like there was no tomorrow, and nothing would have stopped you from doing anything you wanted to do. You and I would have felt this way because, when we were younger, we wouldn't have been influenced by anybody or anything around us. And our thoughts and emotions as the children we once were would have been untouched. Unfortunately, though, as we get older, our minds and belief systems can get corrupted by the various types of people we come into contact with.

People can have a notable influence on the course our lives take from the day we attend school to the day we leave, either positively or negatively, for example. Somebody might have been bullied or not encouraged throughout their childhood years, which has now affected the rest of their lives. And maybe the confidence and self-esteem we used to have bundles of as children were taken away from us when we were younger and growing up at school, which could have caused you and me to become more insecure, anxious and depressed about ourselves without us even realising it due to how we were treated as we were growing up. That might also be the reason why some people suffer from mental health issues and have negative thoughts about themselves today, which I can relate to all too well.

It isn't until we have grown up and turned into adults that we realise that life isn't a bed of roses as we once thought it was when we were children. Hopefully, though, you weren't made to feel insecure, anxious and depressed like I was made to feel when I was at school. So, as you can see, some people who come into our lives as we're growing up can change who we are from a young age. So, STOP believing in any negative comments those individuals might have said to you through the course of your life because they are NOT TRUE!

When I was at primary and secondary school, my confidence and self-esteem were taken away from me, and all I believed in was destroyed. I used to believe I was worthless because certain children and teachers said cruel things about me, and, when you're a child, you take what people say to you to heart, especially teachers because you believe what they say, don't you? Well, I did, and it wasn't until I left school when I slowly started to pick myself up and realise that the things I was told about myself were all lies. Certain youngsters and teachers at my schools were the ones who corrupted my belief systems.

Some kids, adults and schoolteachers can destroy our hopes and dreams we have while we're growing up, which can leave us feeling empty on the inside. Then, once you and I leave school, maybe not the happy children we once had been when we first started, we might need to rebuild our self-esteem, confidence and belief systems back up to what they once were again. You might have been one of the lucky ones, though, and enjoyed every day while you were at school. And, in that case, please take a moment to think of the children who suffered while they were growing up because of how they were treated. Thank you.

If you feel like you were left behind, like I feel I was, and you want to get your life back on track again to how it once used to be when you had your hopes and dreams to look forward to, then don't give up hope, because that happy, confident little child you once were is still inside you. You just have to believe in yourself and focus on your strengths and the activities you love the most, and that will help you back on your way to finding true happiness and contentment once again – Stay strong, stay positive, and stay true to yourself.

While at primary school, teachers should learn us how to deal with bullies, how to cope with mental health problems and how to accept people who look different in today's society, whether it's out of choice or because they have a medical health condition or deformity. And they should also teach us, when we're at secondary school, necessary life skills, such as the basics of DIY repairs around the home, how to cook, how to survive in the wild, first aid skills, communicating and connecting with others and understanding the basics of finance and banking. Along with how to negotiate with people like your banker or your boss at work. What do you wish you had been taught when you were at school, I wonder?

Social media, mobile phones, do you like me, don't you like me, oh no, boo-hoo-hoo, what am I going to do? We have our heads down looking at our phones 24/7, oblivious to the real world around us while we check to see how many people have followed us on Facebook, Instagram, Twitter and Snapchat. This is the society we live in, where the majority of people crave for fame and fortune. Does this apply to you? Am I famous yet? Instagram famous? Oh, wait a minute, no, because people have been unfollowing me, which means I'm even less well known now than I was this morning; what am I going to do? I need more friends, more likes, more followers! I need to feel accepted! How many likes did I receive today? Do people approve of what I'm wearing, the way I look and what I have to say? Do they accept me for who I am, or do I need to keep on proving myself to strangers on social media more and more every day? I just want to feel accepted!

You and I need to stick together and be there for one another in these dangerous times we're living in today, and move on past the social differences other people don't agree with on how we choose to live our lives – people should show more compassion towards one another.

Why do we have to moan, fight, create wars, attack each other's countries and kill innocent people along the way? Well, three words spring to mind: money, power and religion. The human civilisation should all come together as one and unite across the world so we can help our children and the world today, so they don't make the same mistakes tomorrow we have made. I envision a future where I see a united world, where everybody is connected via implants and artificial intelligence is making the world a much better and safer place for us to live in. Elon Musk, Jeff Bezos, Aubrey de Grey, Peter Diamandis, Facebook, Google, Boston Dynamics, SENS and Hanson Robotics, to name a few individuals and companies, I believe will take us there to this brighter and safer future I foresee of tomorrow.

# HOW I VIEW THE WORLD AND THE UNIVERSE AROUND US

We live on a beautiful planet where there is so much we could achieve together; if only we could put our differences aside and learn to love one another more instead of judging, insulting, being small-minded and attacking innocent people when they are out in public because we don't like how they look, along with putting a stop to all the senseless wars from happening, then we could move forward as a race and create an exceptional world to live in and accomplish so much.

If another civilisation were looking down on our planet today, they would be appalled at what they saw. My guess is they would think we are a pretty primitive species with how some of us act and behave towards our own kind! We should also be building bridges and putting a stop to all the destruction and devastation we are inflicting on our planet as well, if you ask me. The problem our world is always facing, though, is RELIGION, MONEY AND POWER! Which is such a shame because you and I should be allowed to have our own religious beliefs, shouldn't we? You might laugh when I say this, but I pray to the Universe, the Anunnaki, to Anu and his consort; the earth goddess Ki, and also to the creator who devised this civilisation we are a part of. To help explain who the Anunnaki were, here are three Wikipedia links which give a full description about who Anu, Ki and the Anunnaki were:

en.wikipedia.org/wiki/Anu, en.wikipedia.org/wiki/Ki_(goddess)
en.wikipedia.org/wiki/Anunnaki

The Anunnaki were believed to be the offspring of An and his consort, the earth Goddess Ki. Samuel Noah Kramer identifies Ki with the Sumerian mother Goddess Ninhursag, stating that they were originally the same figure. The oldest of the Anunnaki was Enlil, the God of air and chief God of the Sumerian pantheon.

### Taken from en.wikipedia.org/wiki/Anunnaki

For a more in-depth look into the Anunnaki, a fantastic book to read is by the late great author Zecharia Sitchin, which is titled *The Anunnaki Chronicles: A Zecharia Sitchin Reader*, and here is a link to Wikipedia explaining who Zecharia Sitchin was, who sadly passed away back in 2010, along with a link to his website – en.wikipedia.org/wiki/Zecharia_Sitchin – www.sitchin.com. So, I believe an extra-terrestrial civilisation created us, and every so often they come along to see how we are developing as a species. Unfortunately, though, I don't think they are very impressed with our progress and are looking down on us as a failure of a species at the moment. Also, it is thought the Moon might have been an ancient space station where the extra-terrestrials resided and may still do so, which would make sense after the number of structures I have seen on there. If you would like to see some of those images for yourself, here is a fantastic YouTube channel to check out, called 'MARS ANOMALIES and BEYOND' and a Wikipedia link on how some people think the Moon is hollow on the inside:

bit.ly/MARSANOMALIESandBEYOND

en.wikipedia.org/wiki/Hollow_Moon

Also, if you are interested in researching more about extra-terrestrials here is a list of some fantastic websites to take a look through – www.4biddenknowledge.com – bit.ly/PaulWallis – divinecosmos.com – bit.ly/OfSoundMindAndBody – bit.ly/MatrixWisdom – bit.ly/The5thKind – www.mufon.com – bit.ly/ThirdPhaseOfMoon – www.boblazar.com – SilvaRecord.com – dwilcock.com – bit.ly/ArtAlienTv – siriusdisclosure.com

Sorry I'm getting a bit sidetracked now, aren't I? So, I pray to the sky gods Anu and Ki, who I believe created you and me, and to the creator of our Universe and civilisation, who I can only imagine is a being of consciousness beyond anything you and I can envision. And, hey, for all I know, we could be a simulation created by a civilisation which exceeds our very own many times over, just how we have created the video game *The Sims*. And who is to say when the characters in *The Sims* will become self-aware, like you and I are today, and wonder who created them. Because then that would mean we are their creator, or as some would say their God! I don't understand why religion causes so much pain, affliction and death in our world today; there's no need for it, is there? And I realise not many people will believe in who and what I do. That's all right; I can understand why they wouldn't. I would like to hope, though, that those individuals don't criticise me on my beliefs just as I don't scrutinise them on theirs.

> The Anunnaki are the most powerful deities in the pantheon, descendants of An and Ki, the God of the heavens and the Goddess of earth, and their primary function is to decree the fates of humanity.

**Taken from en.wikipedia.org/wiki/Anunnaki**

I know religion brings a lot of happiness and comfort into many people's lives, including mine, unfortunately, though, it also brings so much sadness, because of all the wars it creates as well. I thought religion was all about peace, love, unity and respect for one another. Money and power have corrupted so many people over the years, yet you and I need it to survive, don't we? What if, though, we didn't need it? You see some people envision a world that's run without money, politicians or leaders. How cool would that be, although something would surely have to be set up to contain law and order, wouldn't it? And if you look up the Venus Project online, it will help explain how those people envision an alternative future for humanity where there's no longer a need for money and where poverty and war no longer exist either.

Also, did you know that free energy exists and the technology we have today is hundreds and hundreds of years out of date. Secret organisations are holding so much back from us, preventing humankind from moving forward. And there is a significant possibility there's an extra-terrestrial base deep underground in the Antarctic. They have even found the tops of pyramids starting to emerge from beneath the ice sheets there as well.

Oh, hold on a minute, I can hear my dad saying to me. 'Come back down to reality, Steve. You're away with the fairies again, aren't you? Come on, clean those carpets; we've got another job to get to after dinner!' Can you imagine it, though? A world where money and power no longer exist, and there's free energy for all. I wonder what kind of world that would be like to live in. Unfortunately, I doubt very much that will ever happen with how the planet is run today.

What kind of world are you and I living in today? For me, the world is inspiring and magnificent. Sadly, the world can also be hateful, depressing and a very lonely place as well. Most importantly, though, the world is what YOU and I make it. So make the world a beautiful place for everybody to live in and then, together as one, you and I will be able to unite and work towards a more civilised and peaceful planet where we can hopefully one day in the future put a stop to war, famine and senseless killings every day – Peace, love, unity and respect.

I'm more curious about the world around me today than I have ever been before in my life, plus I don't worry about what other people think of me anymore. Let them judge and criticise me; it's my life and I will live it how I want, just how you should be living your life as well. So, do what makes you feel happy and live your life the way YOU want to live it. Be unique, be yourself, be positive, face your fears, and become the best version of you.

However you and I view the planet, there's one thing we should always remember, and that it's a wonderful world we are both a part of. I would now like to end this chapter on one of my all-time favourite songs, which was sung by the late, great and all-time legend Louis Armstrong. Unfortunately for you, though, if you follow the link to this video I've made, you will find me, Steven M. Rippin, and my alter ego, Pirate Steve, singing a duet together of 'What a Wonderful World': bit.ly/WhatAWonderfulWorldPirateSteve

# PART TWO

PART TWO

# BULLYING

I want to do all I can to help you if you have ever been bullied or are going through a form of bullying right now through this chapter with the help of my friends on social media, who have also contributed by sharing their own advice and experiences of bullying. So, let's begin.

I was very unpopular when I was at school. I was classed as a geek, and got bullied and made fun of a lot, just like so many other children do in today's society. Whoever said your school days are the best days of your life must have been from another planet, if you ask me. Anyway, as you already know, the children at my primary school used to love calling me the four-eyed goggle box and hairy monster; jeez, what would they think if they saw me now? I think they would have a fit! I was also continuously teased and threatened by kids in other years as well, which left me feeling scared going to school every day because I didn't know what insults I was going to receive or if I was going to be beaten up, spat on or have my lunch money taken off me. No child should have to go through bullying when they're at school and made to feel this way, should they?

I know some children have it a lot worse than I did when I was at school. I just want them to remember that they are not alone when it comes to being bullied because so many people of all ages go through some form of it through their lives. My bullying days, unfortunately, have continued into my adult life because of my appearance. So, for me, the threats and insults have never stopped. And, as you can imagine, being bullied and ridiculed all my life has changed who I am as a person while I have been growing up over the years.

I never fitted in when I was at school, so the cool kids never let me join in with them no matter how much I wanted to be part of their inner circle, plus I wasn't very bright either. And it was only when I left school that I started to feel better about myself and who I was as a person, if I am truly honest with you.

So, let's start at the beginning. My school days were the worst days of my life. I attended Fairfield Road C of E Primary School, Welland Park Academy and the Robert Smyth Academy. And, truth be told, I hated going to all three of those schools, because of how I was treated!

Some of the older children at Fairfield Road C of E Primary School used to tell me to hand my dinner money over to them because they said my parents told them I should, and if I didn't they would beat me up after school, which scared the bejesus out of me! And I always remember this one huge girl, who was about eleven, doing that to me when I was around seven years old; she made me cry a lot when I was at school.

So-called friends always taunted and took the mickey out of me, which made me feel very isolated from the other kids, plus I felt very alone and didn't know who my genuine friends were. Sometimes things would be great, and then it was like someone had turned a switch on in particular kids, and they would go full-on into hate mode for the four-eyed goggle box, then they would switch it up a gear to see if they could make me cry as well. I was such a weakling and never stood up for myself. Well, apart from one time when I was around ten years old, that is. You see, while I was waiting along the corridor with the rest of my class for the next lesson to start, one kid kept teasing and threatening to hit me while all the other kids just stood there and watched. And, while this kid was doing that, I could feel my hatred towards him building up and up inside. What I was doing, without knowing it at the time, was pulling on my inner strength. Then all of a sudden I couldn't control myself anymore, and I just started shouting and screaming at the top of my voice at this kid! Then I threw my hands in the air and charged at him while I screamed, 'PACK IT IN RAWRRRRR.' I then picked these chairs up, which were stacked along the side of the corridor, and I started chucking them at him, then I chased him down the hallway while I carried on screaming, throwing chairs, and roaring at him! You should have seen his face! I'm sure he peed himself. Serves him right, the little t**t!

I think I scared all the other kids that day as well because they had never seen me react like that before, and the kid teasing me never hassled me again, you know. Steve Rippin does not endorse going around chucking chairs or any objects of any kind at people who you don't like.

When bullies know what your weaknesses are, they will only continue to do what they see upsets you all the more because they get enjoyment out of your suffering. You see, most bullies have problems going on in their lives, which cause them to act the way they do towards you. Kids can be evil, can't they? I was so happy to leave Fairfield Road C of E Primary School.

When I moved up to Welland Park Academy, I thought things would improve and that my bullying days would be over. Unfortunately, that wasn't the case, and the bullying just continued as it did before. I always remember one lad at Welland Park Academy, who used to stand next to me when I was talking to my friends in the courtyard, who would continuously punch me in the arm no matter how many times I told him to stop! I might as well have been talking to a brick wall! This bully knew I was weak because I never retaliated, which fuelled him to do it all the more. Luckily, though, my good friend Neil Page stuck up for me back then and got this bully to stop punching me when he was around. Neil helped me out a lot with bullies at school, and I'm forever grateful to him for that.

Thank you, Neil. You helped me get through so much back then at Welland Park Academy.

Steven M. Rippin

One time when Neil and I were walking down Church Street in our hometown, this lad who I recognised from Welland Park Academy came walking towards us. And I could hear him mumbling away to himself while he was looking at me, then out of nowhere when he was within a couple of feet he head-butted me! I was in shock and couldn't believe what he had just done! And still, to this day, I have no idea why he did it. So, I told my dad when I got home what had happened, and he informed the school, who I believe spoke to this lad about his actions. And my dad, bless him, even went round to this lad's house and talked to his dad about what his son had done to me, and all this lad's dad said was, 'Well, boys will be boys.' With that kind of mentality and attitude, no wonder there's still so much bullying going on in schools today if this is how some parents bring their children up!

I also used to have kids hurl abuse at me, throw stones at me, threaten me and call me a loser. Some teachers even treated me like I was a waste of space. Oh, I just loved school, as you can imagine! Gradually how I was treated at school took a toll on my self-esteem and confidence, which then caused me to get upset regularly. I also became more sensitive, withdrawn, anxious, nervous and timid around other teenagers and adults. I told my parents how I was feeling because they would often see me coming home from school crying, so they did all they could to help me by talking to my teachers, but, as usual, nothing would get done; my bullying problems just got brushed under the carpet. On the upside, though, I only got head-butted once by a kid from Welland Park Academy, and I didn't get beaten up after school either, like I thought I was going to. One of my friends, who went to Welland Park Academy, also got bullied severely by a lad who used to pull a knife on him! Then there was a teenager who was only a few years older than me who committed suicide by jumping off a building! Like, what the hell was going on when I was at school in the '90s? So many children and teenagers were suffering back then and weren't getting the help they desperately needed!

> Some parents are not telling their children what's right, and what's wrong anymore! But, hey, what do I know? I'm not a parent; I'm just another victim of bullying.

I hope things have improved nowadays in schools. Unfortunately, though, I don't believe they have, because I still hear on social media about children being tormented, bullied and taking their own lives because they can't stand what they are being put through anymore by other children and teenagers. What does and will it take to get things to change, before somebody you know decides to take their own life because of bullying? All I ever wanted while I was growing up was to be accepted by the so-called cool kids who unfortunately always looked down and never approved of me. The so-called cool kids really used to get on my nerves and p**sed me off.

It's weird because, even today, I still get those same feelings when I go into particular bars in my hometown, where I get that feeling of not being accepted by the so-called mature wannabe cool adults. You have to laugh about it, though, don't you, really? And, luckily, I've learnt to ignore those kinds of people nowadays because I know I don't need their acceptance.

I've never fitted in, and I've always been made to feel like an outcast by certain individuals.

The reason I didn't like retaliating back to the bullies at school was because of my eyesight, and back when I was at Welland Park Academy I had just been through some significant operations on my right eye to fit it with a Molteno tube, so the last thing I needed was my eye being knocked about by a bully. Because I didn't stand up for myself back then, the bullying continued with the threats, insults, and me being used as a human punch bag.

When I went to school, I was bullied a lot, my advice is, always keep your head high and make sure you get help and don't keep it inside yourself. Bullying sucks, my kids get it all the time. It will never stop Steve Rippin; just need prayers!

**Jodie L. Chapman, Henderson, Nevada, USA**

So, I got through Welland Park Academy, and then I had one more school to contend with, the Robert Smyth Academy, where I had more cruel and negative-minded teenagers to put up with, which was where I had stones thrown at me. I was also insulted and threatened there a lot as well. Furthermore, as an added bonus, I got spat on!

I always thought, 'Why is it always me being bullied?' And it wasn't until I left the Robert Smyth Academy that I realised that it wasn't just me being tormented, because millions of other children and adults were also being bullied every day of their lives as well sadly.

My Grand Daughter was bullied in 2016 and had to put up with physical abuse as well as verbal. And threats to gang up and beat the c**p out of her as well as her teacher bullying her had appointed her bullies, his watchdogs. And they were to watch her and keep her facing the wall at recess, etc. We finally had to get the police involved and a local Anti-Bullying group I finally found. And they got with the superintendent of our school district and had a long talk with the principal, teacher and kids. It's horrible.

Jackie Taylor, USA

I was bullied at school for the way I looked. I have weak muscles, and it made my eyes look a bit different. I spent about six years in and out of hospital having tests to find out what was wrong. Then I had an operation on my eyelids. I didn't think anyone would ever want me. Then one day I met someone, and he accepted me for me, seventeen years we have been together. He gave me my confidence back. He loves me for who I am. I have been through a lot, and it made me stronger. If someone looks at me or says something about my looks, I brush it off, smile and walk on. I don't know them, and they don't know me or what my problem is. I am now happy with my life. Be true to yourself, I didn't believe I would ever be where I am today, but things get better as time goes on x.

Paulette Jones, Somerset, England

Luckily, I had some fantastic friends who stuck up for me while I was at Welland Park Academy and the Robert Smyth Academy, who I'm forever grateful to. Also, I would like to say that all those schools I have mentioned are great schools to attend; I just didn't have the best experiences at them, because of specific individuals.

All the negative situations I had to go through at school have definitely made me want to show all those people who found it funny to give me abuse, spit, throw stones, punch, head-butt and assault me along with everything else they put me through mentally and emotionally, that they didn't destroy me because I am an even stronger person on the inside today than I ever was before. Now I would like to thank the following people who were always there for me through those dark school days of mine.

Thank you so much, Jason Price, for always sticking up for me and having my back at the C of E Primary School, you have always shown me a lot of respect, and for that, I am forever grateful to you. All the best to you and your family, mate.

Steven M. Rippin

Big thanks to Neil Page, who was my best friend through Welland Park Academy and the Robert Smyth Academy. Neil was an excellent mate while I was at school; he was always there for me and diffused a lot of situations I was in with bullies who wanted to beat me up or insult me.

Thank you so much for always being there for me, Neil. Much love and respect to you and your family, mate.

Steven M. Rippin

Now moving on to the legend Chris Gregory, who I have had the privilege of calling a fantastic friend of mine for many years. Chris is a charming guy who's been through so much in his life but still he always has the time to help his friends out when they need him just like how he has always been there for me, especially when he helped my parents and me out after I had been assaulted when I had a lot of threats and abuse from specific individuals where we live! What I love about Chris the most is that he is always thinking of others; for example, he donates money for children's cancer each month and is always looking out for his family and friends, so, as you can see, Chris has a big heart and bucket loads of love to give.

Thank you, Chris; you have helped me out so many times over the years which I have sincerely appreciated you doing, you were always there for me through my school days and later on in my life as well, especially after I was attacked. Much love and respect to you and your family, mate. And please remember, Chris, I'm always here for you whenever you need me. Oh yeah, and thanks for teaching me how to throw some shapes down on the dancefloor at the Broadway nightclub.

Steven M. Rippin

Also, I would like to thank Sally Scurrell, Zoe Hodgkin and Renée Street, because they always had time to talk to me and treated me with respect and kindness, which not many people did. They also helped me feel more accepted and got me through some challenging times I faced at the Robert Smyth Academy.

Zoe, Sally and Renée, all three of you will always have a special place in my heart because you treated me as an equal and as any other normal human being while I was at school; I will always remember that. Thank you for being there for me, and much love to you all and your families.

Steven M. Rippin

When you were bullied it made me sick, I could never understand why you were a target, one of the loveliest lad's in my year, I could never understand how they could be so cruel to you, but their opinions never mattered to me, I have my own mind and no one could have made me dislike or bully you xxxx.

**Zoe Hodgkin, Market Harborough, England**

You are such an inspiration to other people out there. You are such a kind-hearted person and didn't deserve to get hurt in your younger years. Look how far you have come and you have achieved so, so much. You are an amazing person, and I thank you with all my heart of knowing you for so long x x x.

**Sally Scurrell, Market Harborough, England**

Growing up is tough, yet it makes you and I who we are today and I'm proud of who I've become just as you should be proud of who you've become. Always stay strong and don't let anybody pull you down. And remember to stand up for yourself or people will treat you like a doormat and walk all over you, and nobody wants to be treated like that, do they!

I was for far too many years believe me. Also, always talk to your family or friends or somebody who's in authority if you're being bullied, because they should be able to do something about it. And, if they don't, keep on telling them the bullying hasn't stopped and that something needs to be done to put an end to it RIGHT NOW. Please don't suffer in silence.

What would your advice be to somebody who's being bullied, and what would you advise them to do about it?

If the bully's in a group, I would confront the main culprit, but not in a violent way and ask them why they're doing it. And I would also, when they're on their own, confront them and say, how come you don't bully me when you're on your own, is it because you're afraid without your friends to back you up?

**George W. Rippin, Market Harborough, England**

I went through this for five years at school, then saw it as a teacher.

1. Don't keep it between you and the bully. It's often done covertly because the bully knows it is unacceptable. Go to the right people for help and be persistent if nothing is done.
2. You don't deserve it, and you're NOT to blame – if you boil it down to its bare components, bullies have no right to victimise anyone, and I often tell pupils if that's done in the world, they could be taken to court and sued for harassment.
3. Bullies are cowards – they behave the way they do because they're deeply inadequate in some way and trying to have power over someone else makes them feel better. They tend to be very unhappy people inside.
4. There's nothing wrong with YOU. You're not fat/ugly/stupid etc. It's a tactic they use to hurt your feelings, no matter how inaccurate.
5. It won't last – especially at school. I go back to my hometown in East Durham now, after travelling the world and getting all sorts of wonderful experiences, and the people who bullied me

are still there. They look a hell of a lot older than they should, and they usually have no job and loads of kids.

Kathryn Pope, Buckinghamshire, England

I would tell them they are not alone and that I am there for them if they ever need me. Telling them to stand up for themselves or that the bully is jealous does not help. Knowing there is one person that loves you for who you are and is beside you gives you the strength to get up in the morning. Tell them it is ok to feel upset/angry etc. And say I'm here for you and ask if there is anything, they want to do about it? Tell them we are all perfect individuals and to be proud of who they are because you are proud of them.

Maria L. Mills, Market Harborough, England

# HOW BEING BULLIED MADE ME INTO THE MAN I AM TODAY

Bullying affects people in many different ways. And being bullied, assaulted and criticised has made me want to dress and look how I want! So looking how I do today doesn't bother me in the slightest. If I'm honest, I don't think I look all that different to anybody else in society anyway, plus I know a lot of very cool alternative people who stand out way more than I do, and they look incredible.

I have learnt a lot from being threatened over the years. And today I can see how much being bullied affected the outcome of my life – in the right way, I'm happy to say, because when I look at my personality traits I now have I can see I'm a kind and caring person and somebody who wants to inspire others to be who they want to be in life.

People show me a lot of respect because I'm not afraid of being who I want to be. I've even had members of the public say they wish they had the courage to dress how I choose to, which to me is a massive compliment. I always tell those people to be themselves and don't worry about what other people think; it's your life and you should live it the way you want. Today, I feel how I look and dress has boosted my self-esteem and confidence no end. It has also helped me to develop as an individual and get me through the anxiety, shyness, mild depression and emotional state of mind I was left in because of being bullied and assaulted.

This is what I would say to those who have bullied me through my life: 'Yeah, look at how you affected me and changed my life for the better, with all your insults, hurt, pain and beatings you gave me. I'm now the biggest geeky nerd out there who people look up to. I help to inspire others against individuals like you who went around bullying innocent people like me, just because you were so unhappy with your own life!'

> I have been bullied many times being a quiet person. I would show the bully that whatever they do, you will keep going and prove you are a higher being, sensitive and caring. NEVER let them get you down.

> **Gordon Harrison, Leicestershire, England**

Now you have got a good idea of how my school days went and how popular and loved I was by everybody. NOT! Anyway, let's leave my school days behind and move on into my adulthood, where I have continued to be ridiculed and insulted with rude comments and insults, such as: Grow up and act your age – Get a life – Stop being a pirate – Are you gay – You're too old to go to nightclubs – What are you, are you real? – You're not being true to yourself – You don't know who you are – You're hiding behind your look and persona; learn to be yourself – You're an idiot, along with other numerous comments and insults I've received as well; the list goes on and on.

Those small-minded people who criticise me need to understand in their own minds why I'm different to them, and because they can't accept I'm happy with who I am as a person. It winds them up, I believe, and I get the impression they want me to be just like they are and conform. The problem is, though, I love living my life outside the confines of modern-day society! So why can't they accept that? Oh, I forgot: it's because they're shallow-minded! Well, let me tell you something. I'm never going to conform to how society and feeble-minded people have told me to; that's never going to happen, not in their lifetime, not in my lifetime and not in anybody's lifetime. The sooner those negative-minded people can understand and get it through their heads that I'm happy with who I am, the better!

Those individuals need to stop worrying about how I'm living my life; they need to start thinking and concentrating on what direction their own lives are taking, and also, while they're at it, they should take a look in the mirror and ask themselves, 'Why don't I accept other people who don't conform to society? They've never hurt, harmed or insulted me! I should learn to leave them be and let them carry on with their own lives just as I should be doing with mine.' Some people don't realise when they're stepping over the line and being insulting with their remarks in today's society towards you or me, do they? What I would like to know is: what gives them the right to throw insults and accusations our way?

I know so many people who are living their lives just how they want to, by being the remarkable and inspiring individuals they are in the world today. Take my good friend from New York, Mari Ashley, for example. She dresses how she wants. Some people might think Mari dresses a bit over the top, but that's how she chooses to dress, and I think she looks outstanding. Why can't people just be happy and accept others for who they are?

> Just wanted to say that I admire you for just being you. It was tough times at school for me. It was pretty much all through primary and secondary school. When I left Robert Smyth, I chose to be different. My hair was different, my makeup and my clothes. I wanted to be different, as that is how I was always made to feel. It takes long journeys to discover who we truly are. They are never easy. The way you are doing yours is brave and wonderful and is sticking a big V sign up to those that hurt you. I chose to confront all those that bullied me, and I got an apology off all of them, mainly because they have turned into nothing more than silly adults with as much vision as a mole! Keep strong and show everyone the wonderful kind-hearted person you have always been. Remember that before the light, there is always dark. People are very narrow-minded and seem to think being normal is what makes the world tick. In fact, in my experience, it's those that don't follow the norms that lead the fuller life. Ok, so you dress like a pirate and have a poorly eye, but you are not afraid to stand out and be different, AND that is what makes YOU, a very unique and special human being. Let people judge, but don't allow them to affect your heart. Violence shows what total imbeciles these people are, and I'm so sorry you were a human punch bag. Unfortunately, that is the only way these people can behave due to lack of brain cells! (that's my conclusion anyway). YOU are a voice for all the victims, past, present and future. An inspiration

for generations who somewhere lost themselves through no fault of their own, who made life choices. Some better than others, some with a positive impact on their lives. And some a negative impact. But all in all, struggling to find reasons for what happened, to come to terms with how it felt, to accept and finally to move on. Be that voice so people know there is an end and it was never the victim's fault and that sometimes in this world, people can be s\*\*t, rude, ignorant and bullies. These people will not die with a clear conscience. Somewhere in their darkened souls, it will come back to haunt them. Live your life the way you choose with your head held high, for you have a pure heart xx.

### Claire Farrar, Market Harborough, England

Being bullied really affected me – as you can see; I turned into a pirate. Seriously, though, children and adults don't realise how much damage they can cause when they say and do the things they inflict on us; their actions can affect the rest of our lives. And, ever since children poked fun at how my eyes looked, I have always had a complex about them. My eyes are who I am, and they go red because of the operations I have had done and a condition I have called band-shaped keratopathy, which people don't always believe when I tell them!

# HOW TO DEAL WITH BULLYING

All bullies want is attention, because most bullies are unhappy with themselves through emotional events that have taken place in their lives, which could be causing them to take their frustration out on others. As soon as a bully gets a reaction out of you, and sees you're emotionally hurt and feeling uncomfortable with what they're doing or saying, they will continue to do what they're doing even more, because it will make the bully feel happy to have finally found an outlet for their pent-up frustration, which they now know they can take out on you. They will class you as an easy target. Remember, there's nothing wrong with you; it's the bully who's suffering deep down inside. So, remember, you're an amazing and beautiful human being.

As a former victim of bullying, I'd advise anybody who is being bullied to put focus on their own self-esteem. It is important never to forget that you are not in any way less of a person than anybody else. People will try to make you feel otherwise, but you have to remember to stay true to yourself. Remind yourself of who you are and who you want to be. Focus on that. And don't give a damn what others say. They are not in charge of your life. You are. It took me a long time to get there in the end, but I did. And I hope every victim of bullying will be able to do the same

Sina Sparrow, Germany instagram.com/sinasparrow

I got bullied as a kid A Lot in school, and I've been in a place lately where I'm now dealing with it as an adult. I started to really let it get to me, and a dear friend of mine gave me this advice: When people bully you, it's not about you, it's about them. They feel so small and so weak inside that their only way to build themselves up is to go after others. Regardless, it is so wrong, but if you can realise this, you can bring yourself to the point where you know with all of you're being that they are jealous, they want to take your joy because they have none, and they wouldn't be busting on you in the first place if you weren't wonderful!

Jessica J. Peterson, Tennessee, USA

Bullies will follow you around school hitting you, calling you names, tripping you up… and their friends join in. Do not ignore them. See a teacher. Tell your mum or dad.

Lee Easterlow, Market Harborough, England

Q: What are your views on school bullies. And what are the best ways to deal with them? Did you have such issues in school? And if so, was taking on a comedy style persona a part in that to deflect their attention. (I'll let you guess why I ask)

Lez Briddon, Yorkshire, England

A: Hey, Lez, thanks for your questions. Yeah, I was bullied all through my school days which affected me pretty badly, and it's taken me years to feel good about myself again. The best way I believe in dealing with bullies is to inform somebody in authority, and also let your family and friends no what's going on as well.
Also, if it's cyberbullying somebody's going through, my best advice would be to print out all the comments and profiles of the culprits who have been harassing you. And inform the police

about what they have been doing and saying, which is what I did. The harassment soon stopped when the bullies found out my parents and I had printouts of their names, comments and private messages which they had sent me on Facebook, which we had shown the police! Oh, and to answer the last part of your question, Lez. No, the persona I took on didn't have anything to do with the bullying while I was at school; that was more to do with my eyesight, which is a whole different story. Thank you so much for your questions, Lez.

Steven M. Rippin

Bullying can happen at any age and anywhere, at school, the workplace, online, in elderly care homes, at your own home, in bars, nightclubs, and out in public, to name a few places.

Ignoring bullies can be difficult, but when you do, by showing them no interest at all, it can sometimes help, as most bullies will get bored and walk away and find another victim to upset. Unfortunately, though, that doesn't work all the time, it all depends on what sort of bully you're dealing with. So, remember a bully might turn aggressive towards you for ignoring them! If they do tell somebody in authority, such as a teacher, the boss at work, or the police.

Always do your best to avoid bullies and don't go where you know they will be. If that's not possible for you to do, though, keep with your friends if you can because bullies don't like getting into trouble, and if they see other people around you there's a less likely chance they're going to torment you. Unfortunately, this doesn't always work because bullies from when I was at school would continue to bully me even if my friends were around.

Taking up self-defence classes and joining a gym can help give you more self-confidence if you're being physically bullied, and never slouch or shuffle your feet when you're out in public; instead, hold your head high and walk with confidence, then if a bully is lurking about, they will see you are full of courage, and nothing worries you. Furthermore, when you're on your own, always know your surroundings and where you are. And be on your guard. Always believe in yourself and say, 'Nobody will ever treat me like trash again! I'm going to stand up for myself from this day on. And I will always tell somebody in authority if things do start getting out of control because nobody is going to ruin my life! I'm a strong, confident and positive person with a lot to offer the world. And I'm going to make my parents and my friends proud of me.'

Walking into bars after I was attacked was and still can be very intimidating and difficult for me to do, which must sound crazy. So nowadays I like to be surrounded by my mates when I go into social environments, even more so around my hometown, where I was assaulted. My confidence has come back over time; I'm just a lot more cautious when I'm out at the weekends these days. I'll admit, I still get nervous but not as much as I used to because I have now learnt how to become more confident with who I am as a person. I stand up for myself a lot more as well, especially if I come across anybody I think is about to kick off with me. I'll tell them I don't want any trouble because I've been here before and I can see where this is leading!

Don't try getting along with bullies to defuse any situations you find yourself in by agreeing with everything they say about you; this will lower your value of who you are as a person, and you will also be lowering yourself to the bully's level. Although, if a bully makes a joke about you, you could try laughing along with them because this isn't the kind of reaction they would be expecting. All the bully wants to do is hurt your feelings, so seeing you laughing will hopefully throw the bully off guard. This might not work in every situation, though; it all depends yet again on what type of bully you are dealing with.

Now here are the various types of bullies you might come across in life.

The physical bully: Who hits, slaps or punches you – Causes you harm – Damages your property – Hides your belongings – And who puts stickers on your back like, 'Kick Me'.

The verbal bully: Who insults you – Teases you – Makes racist or homophobic comments about you – Intimidates you – Who does their best to pull you down – And who makes you feel worthless.

The social/cyberbully: Who spreads rumours about you behind your back, online and out in public to other people – Who will give you nasty looks when they see you out in public – Who will give you physical and negative gestures when nobody is looking – Who will get other people to exclude and ignore you – Who will use social media sites to harass you –

Who will create social media groups to blacken your name – And who will try and destroy your reputation.

The sexual bully: Who will bully and intimidate you – Who will touch you inappropriately – Who will make advances on you – Who will make rumours up about you – Who will victimise you, because of your appearance – Who will threaten you with gestures of violence – And who will put pressure on you, and make you feel uncomfortable if you don't want to do something. All these various types of bullies can damage you emotionally and physically if you let them, so please be careful and be on your guard if you come across any of them. Well, there you have it, they are the different types of bullies most people come across at some point in their lives. If you know someone who's going through bullying right now, please do your best to help them. I had my parents and friends there for me.

Q: I was going to ask if you think bullying's worse today with the internet or back in our day? I was affected by bullying, also. And yes, they've all tried to add me on Facebook over and over again! Crazy huh? All I can say is that karma does happen, even if you don't see it, because you're too busy living your life x.

Sam Bingham, Waikiki, Western Australia

A: Hey, Sam, thanks for your question. I think bullying is worse today because bullies can now harass you 24/7. Also, I get messages from parents telling me how their children are being affected by bullies who ask for my advice on how to deal with it which I sincerely hope helps them. I'm sorry to hear you were bullied as well, Sam. I hope the bullying didn't affect your life too badly, as it did mine. All my very best to you and your family.

Steven M. Rippin

Have you ever suffered from cyberbullying where people send you nasty emails and spread rumours online about you? I have, and it's not pleasant. It can be extremely intimidating, especially when people are threatening to beat you up and are telling you you should leave the country for your own safety! I was cyberbullied and had hate groups made up about me online because specific individuals didn't approve when I pressed charges against one of their friends who had assaulted me. It's unbelievable how some people act, isn't it? I have also had just about every insult you could imagine thrown at me, which used to upset me a lot; nowadays, I laugh when I receive them. I just haven't got the time to waste worrying about what other people think of me. I've got more important things to do and people to devote my life and time to. You have to learn to rise above the haters.

I love and support individuality, creativity and humour. The ones who step out of the box are the leaders. People, unfortunately, are afraid and ridicule what they don't understand. Enlightened people don't. We are free in ways they cannot be. All love all day. Love you, Pirate Steve. The sea separates us, but navigate by the stars, my friend. I love you because you are being you, that's huge.

**Audra West, Texas, USA**

Q: How did you deal with the bullying at school?

**Kimberly Barnard, Arkansas, USA**

A: Hey, Kimberly, to be honest, I didn't deal with the bullying at school very well. I just put up with it and went home crying most nights. It was a horrible time of my life and like a living hell. My family and friends definitely helped me through it, though. Thank you for your question.

**Steven M. Rippin**

I have seen much evidence of cyberbullying, and it can be very disturbing and worrying. I have turned around to some on groups who do this and said, 'I don't care what you think or say about me because your opinions mean nothing to me.' Letting someone get to you is only effective by the amount of power you give to them. Having said that, if you are vulnerable, it's easier said than done. I will not allow these bullies to have any power over me. Face to face is a different matter altogether and needs a different tack. Many bullies are cowards themselves and have issues which they need to address. They think by picking on you it will make them feel better, but I don't think it's a solution for them. They need to be able to admit they're shortcomings and face their fears instead of deflecting those fears onto others. Some awful bullies are very narcissistic and manipulative with massive egos. They don't or won't admit they are at fault. The Narcissistic personalities also manipulate the vulnerable bullies amongst them to attack others.

### Vittoria Franchino, London, England

A quick word of warning: in the next few paragraphs I'm going to write about sexual bullying, which you might find hard to read.

One thing that shocked me while I was writing my book and asking my friends on social media questions were the number of women who private messaged me and told me they had experienced sexual bullying and forms of rape! Who the hell do those men who do those heinous acts on women think they are? They need castrating and locking away from civilisation forever to rot away in a cell. I can't even begin to imagine the traumatic effects of being raped can have on a person. My heart sincerely goes out to all the women and men who have been affected by these malicious acts scumbags have done on them. Men should always respect a woman's decision if there's something she doesn't want to do, just as women should respect a man's decision if there's something he doesn't want to do!

I get timid and embarrassed when it comes to talking about sex because I haven't had much experience of it, if I'm honest. I'm very reserved, you see, and find it a challenging subject to write about. So, when I hear how women in our society have been mistreated, it sickens me to my stomach. I just don't understand how a man can do something so low, vile, disgusting and evil like that to a woman! It is a sad, sick and twisted world you and I live in, isn't it? Now here is my good friend Karen's advice on this subject which she has so sadly been put through herself.

Anybody whether an adult, child, male, female or disabled, speak out and report the person abusing you mentally or physically, both are a crime. Nowadays, there is more recognition of abuse and many more laws to help the victims. Don't believe your abuser when they say, 'Tell anyone, and no one will believe you' or 'Tell, and you will be taken away from the parent that isn't abusing you.' The abuser will always say things to drag you down, make you depressed and make you feel like you cannot get free or live a better life without them. Report it, you will be amazed at life's new possibilities, new friendships and much, much more which life has to offer.

Karen, England

Many thanks to Karen for sharing her advice and what to do if you or someone you know is going through a traumatic experience like this today. Seek help from your family, friends, your local GP or a counsellor who you can open up and talk to, to get the best possible support and advice you need. Above all else, think what you're most passionate about in life, and chase after your dreams just like Karen has done. Karen is now doing well and has a diploma in child daycare and works as a nanny. I sincerely hope Karen's advice helps you or somebody you know.

As many others have said, 'You are an inspiration.' You can't get closer to the truth than that. You have helped me through a lot of things, even though you're across the pond. I have Indy, Sparrow, and Ironman as heroes, but you are a real-life inspiration, my friend. You are a hero.

Matt Werner, Washington, USA

Learn what your inner strengths are, and learn your weaknesses and how you can improve on them, then every time you're faced with a bully who is giving you insults and has been spreading vicious rumours about you, you should hopefully feel more confident from within yourself when they try to pull you down.

Always ignore the negative comments bullies give you; you're so much better than they will ever be; bullies are the ones who are weak and insecure.

Do your best not to answer bullies back as well because sometimes, when you answer a bully back, you will end up provoking them and giving them an excuse to either insult or hurt you even more.

Never be ashamed of coming forward and telling somebody what's going on if you're being bullied, because the more you talk about your problems, the better you will feel, believe me.

Now here are some questions I would like you to answer to help you get any negative and upsetting thoughts out of your head if you're going through any form of bullying right now. And please, be as truthful, open and as honest as you can. Even better, talk about what's on your mind to your family and friends.

Do your best to tackle your dilemmas as soon as you can.

So on with the questions, along with my own answers as well.

Q: Have you ever been bullied; if so, has it affected your life?
A: Yes, being bullied took my confidence away and made me feel insecure, anxious and nervous around people.
Q: If you were faced with the person or persons, who bullied you right now, what would you like to say to them?
A: 'Why did you bully me? What was it you had against me? Have you grown up now and stopped threatening others? Can I get an apology from you?'
Q: Do you think you could ever forgive the bully or bullies, for what they put you through? And why?
A: Yes, because, if I didn't, I wouldn't be able to move on with my life.
Q: What have you learnt and gained from being bullied?
A: I have become a more confident and positive person, and I love to help others who are going through difficulties in their own lives.

These are just a few questions you can ask yourself if you have ever been bullied. I sincerely hope they help you so you feel more comfortable talking to somebody about how you might be feeling.

Are you a former bully who's changed your ways and are now a reformed character? If so, how did you change your ways, and do you have any advice for other people who might still be bullies today?

Going to hold my hands up. Always shocks people when I say it, I'm not sure if it's because I'm female or because people just don't have me down as someone who could do it. I was bullied badly at school, so I picked on a girl, and it made me feel great at the time because for once I was the bully, not the other way around. It gave me a sense of empowerment after all the times I had felt like I was worth nothing more than just something you stepped on in the street. What I didn't realise at the time was that I would look back upon this and cringe. Bullying is a really cowardly thing, and it's something I deeply regret. I went on as an adult to gain some qualifications in counselling studies, and I hope in the future to work with people who have been bullied to empower them to realise that it isn't them that has the problem.

**Lisa Parratt, Market Harborough, England**

I admit and hold my hands up to it. I'm ashamed to say that, yes, I did pick on people at school. I've since seen people I was nasty to and apologised to them. In fact, I was just a little s*#t at school in general, but I was also picked on. The thing that changed me was getting kicked out of Robert Smyth and going to the Blaby pupil referral unit. Once there, I was never in trouble, I kept my head down at school and just got on with school in general, maybe it was knowing that I had hurt them emotionally enough to be kicked out of school that stopped me. The worse thing about being a bully is the bully doesn't know they are until its too late. My advice to any bullies would be, Don't, it's an awful thing on both parties, and for the victim to go through and later on in life the guilt, you will live with. It's not clever, it doesn't make you hard or funny, and if you were to continue in life after school in the workplace, you would be out of work, just love in life, it's much easier and happier to love than hate. I've tried to change my life for the better, I used to hold a lot of anger and hate, I just can't be bothered with it now and I think that was a key trigger to my depression, I just want a happy simple life and to make my little boy's life the best I can. Positives always outweigh the negatives in life, the guys that bullied you will forever live with it at the back of their minds and till the day they offer to apologise, no forgiveness is needed.

### Simon Harrald, Market Harborough, England

I have personally found hearing what my friends on social media had to say on bullying very informative because it's made me realise why bullies may act the way they do, especially when they're younger. Adult bullies should know better, though, shouldn't they? If you don't like somebody, just disassociate yourself from that person.

You and I both suffer from problems in life, and we don't always know how to deal with them. Unfortunately, though, some individuals release their frustration and negative attitudes on to others they see as easy targets because it makes them feel good. Instead of threatening people, bullies should focus on their own lives by joining a club, taking up a sport, or doing something they enjoy doing. On that note, I would like to thank, Lisa Parrott and Simon Harrald, who opened up about their past bullying days and how they have now turned their lives around.

# HELP AND ADVICE ON BULLYING

What do you think is the best advice to give to somebody who is being bullied either at school, at home or in the workplace?

In most circumstances, the bully/bullies are doing it to prove they are cool to mates. My advice is to get the bully or bullies on their own and talk to them and tell them how they are making you feel. If this doesn't work talk to someone you trust, can be anybody, and try to come up with a way of avoiding or putting a stop to it. Also, don't ever think it's your fault because in the world we live in, we certainly cannot please everybody or make everyone like us. Love yourself and carry on knowing you'll be the best person you can be!

Samuel J. T. Conway, Leicestershire, England

It's not your fault. There is nothing wrong with you and you did nothing to deserve this. It is a reflection upon their character, not yours. You are so much more than the opinion of others. Do not take to heart what they do or say, it ultimately shows that they are insecure and are jealous of something you reflect that they want but will not admit to wanting. You, unfortunately, cannot make everyone like you or understand you. And that's perfectly fine. You were not born to please others. Love yourself

Sabrina Gomes, Portugal

Join a martial arts class and learn to stand up to bullies. This is from my own rather extensive experiences with being bullied as a child. All that changed when I started training karate and I was able to defend myself against bullies, and I got a reputation as someone not to be messed with.

Victor 'V2DHeart' Vargus, St Vincent, Caribbean

As someone who has been, physically, mentally, emotionally and sexually bullied… I would tell them. Keep going. You're stronger than you think. Be proud. You are strong enough to get out of bed and face the day, even knowing it's going to be bad. And Talk, talk to your doctor and get referred to therapy. Do it even if you're a teen. I wish to god my Mum would have and as I got older my GP didn't take me seriously, now I'm 35 and I'm a severe depressive with bad suicidal tendencies because nobody listened. If you're in school nobody will help you, and that's the truth, sounds drastic to recommend therapy but they are neutral and will actually listen, get it ALL out or like me and so many others you will end up with a pit of poison inside eating away and it will affect aspects of your life. Don't be ashamed to get help. It could save your life in more ways than one. I've been hurt so much, so I try to be as kind and understanding to people, there's to much hurt and suffering in the world, a little kindness goes a long way. I wish I'd of had a neutral person to talk to, its hard to talk to family and friends, they have distractions and emotional ties which makes it hard, if the parents get upset or angry the child can sometimes feel it's their fault for adding stress and strain, in a bullied child's state of mind they feel everything is their fault, I know I did and in my family life I still get made to feel that way even now. Being bullied/abused in any form is the worst thing, but I know it can be overcome with the right help and if that help is given soon enough, then they won't end up broken like myself and many others.

Natasha Smith, Buckinghamshire, England

Speak to whoever is in charge of the institution etc. And document everything when it happens, it's unfortunately rare that things get sorted right away, but at least if someone knows about it and things escalate further, it helps your case. Sadly I had this experience in college recently, and unfortunately there was little they could do, due to lack of evidence and he said/she said stuff, but it has at least all gone on record, so it's there if it occurs again which makes it a less stressful environment to be in then.

Shannon Purcell, Ireland

I would say a bully usually doesn't like you because they see something in you, they can't possess. If you have love in your heart, they want it. If you have hope or talent in something, they don't. It's usually based out of jealousy and insecurity on their part. Never change those amazing parts of you that make others feel uncomfortable. Those things are what make you special. You can always get away from them, but they can never get away from themselves, and that is their punishment and their weakness.

April Dalaman, California, USA, instagram.com/aprildalaman

Forget the haters and just be true to yourself. Nobody likes a bully!

Ben Wood, Leicestershire, England

So, as you can see from all these replies from my friends on social media, there is an unmistakable message that starts to emerge, which is that you should always tell somebody what's going on when you're being bullied because it's not you who's at fault; it's the bully who has the issues. Remember, if you're being bullied seek help from somebody you trust whether that's a member of your family, a close friend, your local GP, a counsellor, or a person in authority, such as a teacher or a policeman. Now, here is a very touching poem by Sarah-Louise Morris.

I'm stronger now I realise I don't need to fit in, It doesn't matter what I do, they will say I sin, I'm not ashamed of the scars I carry anymore, If they don't like me this way, there is the door, I stand tall allowing myself to feel the courage I have found, Gaining confidence I'm starting to feel more proud, That all the things they say and do to hurt me, Will never keep me down, I did it so I can be free, Born to be different no two are the same, Expressing is a choice we shouldn't feel shame, The fire burns inside, I start to drop all that apply, I'm learning now when it's time to say goodbye, I'm off on my journey, trying my best to keep focus, I can't control their actions, that's on them if it broke us, As I start to find colour, I see that not everything is grey, I want to enjoy my life for me, and that's all I have to say

Sarah-Louise Morris, Nottingham, England

# MY EXPERIENCES OF BEING BULLIED

If you remember at the beginning of my book, I opened with 'I didn't see it coming; I turned around and saw this fist come flying at me from out of nowhere!' Well, I think it's now appropriate to tell you the full story of what happened that fateful night when I was twenty-one years old.

It all started when I was in my local nightclub one Saturday night with my mates partying. While I was standing on the edge of the dancefloor admiring all the women, I happened to look to my right as I could feel somebody's eyes on me, and that's when I spotted this guy looking straight at me in a menacing way. I just ignored him and thought nothing more of it. Luckily, I knew the bouncers at the nightclub, so I mentioned it to one of them, and he said, 'It's probably best if you leave, Steve. Not worth the hassle, mate,' so I left through the entrance to the club. Little did I know, though, when I left, this other guy who had been staring at me left through the fire exit with his friend. And the fire exit was on the same side as the entrance to the nightclub.

So, as I was leaving the club car park, all of a sudden, I saw this fist come flying at me from out of nowhere that connected with my face, well, with my left eye, which split my eyelid right open! Then I could hear this guy and his friend laughing away as they both walked off while I was lying there on the ground clutching at my eye. So there I was unable to see due to the blood oozing out of my split eyelid and down my face all disorientated and not knowing if I'd be able to see again out of my left eye, which has glaucoma and a cataract forming on it; I was also wearing my contact lens that night as well, which I wasn't sure was still in my eye or not. And the first thing that went through my mind was, 'What's my dad going to think?' which was the least of my problems right then! So, I managed to clear my head and stagger to the nightclub entrance, where I alerted Jannine Haines, who was working there that night about what had happened to me. Jannine helped to clean me up and called an ambulance for me; she was fantastic. Jannine saved me that night, and I'm forever grateful to her for all she did for me back then.

> Thank you so much Jannine. I will never forget you looking after me and calling for an ambulance. Much love to you and your family.

> Steven M. Rippin

When the ambulance turned up at my parents' house, my dad popped his head out of his bedroom window and said, 'What's happened?' And I told him not to worry, then he came down the stairs, answered the door, and he must have gone into shock when he saw me holding my eye and covered in blood, bless him. That night I spent at the Leicester Royal Infirmary, and luckily an eye surgeon was on duty, who came along and stitched my eyelid back together for me, who I'm forever grateful to. It wasn't that painful when the eye surgeon was stitching my eyelid back together, to be honest; I think it was because I was still in shock!

Can you believe my contact lens survived and didn't break while it was in my eye when I got punched in the face? Woohoo! At the time, you see, I was wearing hard gas permeable contact lenses, which cost around £120 each. I was so relieved they survived! My left eyelid, which was split open, now has a scar on the inside and outside of it, which causes me a lot of problems and pain, which I suffer from every day of my life. I believe that pain is the leading cause of my left eye going red a lot, which my eye specialist, Dr Kumar, has called band-shaped keratopathy. If it gets any worse and starts to obscure my vision, then one day I might need an operation to help me see more clearly and also to help me deal with the discomfort it causes. Band-shaped keratopathy is caused by a traumatic injury to the eye and is a corneal disease derived from the appearance of calcium on the central cornea.

> I'll always remember the look on my attackers face when he turned and walked away as I lay there covered in blood clutching at my eye; not a nice feeling or place to be in, I can tell you.

One of the reasons why I wear eyeliner is to cover the gap between my eyelid. You see, I had to have a procedure done to remove some ingrowing eyelashes, which now grow at the wrong angles due to being punched in the face. The operation I had done wasn't successful; when they burnt my ingrowing eyelashes away, they must have cooked some of the others away as well because they never grew back again, which has caused the gap to appear in the centre of my left eyelid. I now have to go to my opticians regularly to have my ingrowing eyelashes removed. And, when I call my opticians, Lisa, at the other end of the phone, always says, 'Are you ready for another plucking,' which always makes me laugh.

Another time when I was in my local nightclub, I narrowly missed a pint glass smashing into my head. This guy, you see, thought I was chatting his girlfriend up when all we were doing was having an innocent conversation together. Luckily, I had just moved out the way in time when this guy threw his pint glass at my head. Unfortunately, though, the contents of his drink drenched my friend instead! And it wasn't until my mate informed me that some guy went to throw his pint glass at me that I even realised what had happened! I believe it's mostly down to people being insecure why they act this way.

Now moving onto another one of my unfortunate incidents, which happened when I was around twenty-three years old. While I was in a pub talking to my friend early one Saturday evening, these two old blokes in their late sixties or early seventies came up talking to my friend who I was with. Then one of the old men started talking to me, and out of nowhere he slapped me around the face hard for no reason at all. I couldn't believe it. I stood there in shock thinking, 'What have I done wrong!' Then my friend and the old man who he was talking to turned around and were as surprised as me at what had just happened. They made sure I was all right, and the old man told his friend who had slapped me to calm down, then they both apologised. I still to this day have no idea why that old man slapped me round the face. All I can think he was jealous of me for some reason and was trying to impress his friend. I was so young and naive back then; looking back, I wish I had stood up for myself more. I did ask him why he slapped me, but he just stood there in front of me and said nothing. I guess I have one of those faces men don't like!

I could sit here and think to myself, 'Why is it always me who gets assaulted?' So many people sadly do, though, for no reason.

Well, back to my series of unfortunate events, and onto the time when I was assaulted for a second time. In this attack, I thought I was going to lose the sight in my right eye where I have got a cataract, glaucoma, a Molteno tube, plus many more eye conditions to contend with. This assaulted happened on the August bank holiday weekend in 2008, after I had come back home with my parents from a lovely couple of days down in Bournemouth. I had a fantastic time that weekend away with my parents, and I always remember walking around the hotel gardens with my mum and dad taking photos of the flower displays on the Sunday morning before we left; they looked spectacular. And, when I looked over at my mum, she looked so happy that day. We arrived back home from Bournemouth early Sunday afternoon, then in the evening my mates called me up to see if I wanted to meet up with them. So, I decided because it was a bank holiday I'd go out. If only I knew what that night had in store for me, though! If only, eh? How many people have said that over the years, I wonder.

I had a great night out with my friends that bank holiday Sunday night in the Enigma nightclub in Market Harborough. While I was in the club, I got chatting to a guy I knew while the rest of my friends headed downstairs to the dancefloor. Then after I had finished talking away to this guy I knew upstairs in the club, I turned around to go and join my mates, but this guy, who must have been at least six foot four and built like a brick s**thouse, who I had never seen before in my life, was standing right there in front of me blocking my way looking extremely aggressive, then out of nowhere he head-butted me for no reason! I stood there in disbelief and said, 'What did you do that for?' He didn't answer me, he just stared at me, then head-butted me a second time! I'll say this, though: he didn't put me on the floor.

So, one positive that came out of that negative situation for me was I found out that I can take a couple of damn hard head-butts to my face, and still not get put on my backside, and that guy was a damn big unit! After that guy had head-butted me a couple of times, he then walked off and disappeared into the nightclub, leaving me there with my head cut open just above my right eye. Then the lad I had previously been talking to came up to me and said, 'Hey, mate, I can't believe what just happened to you; your head's bleeding. You'd better get it looked at.' I then thanked him and quickly headed downstairs towards the restroom to get some tissue to clean my wound up. By now my shirt had blood all over it from the blood coming down my face, and I was still in shock wondering what the hell had just happened to me!

My first thought was, 'Oh no, not again, what's my dad going to think this time?' Then I started worrying if my right eye was going to be all right, or if I was going to lose the sight out of it because it had just taken two serious knocks where my Molteno tube was! I then started having déjà vu from years before when I had been through something very similar to this situation I was in right now. Anyway, as I was on my way downstairs towards the restroom one of the bouncers saw me and got some tissue for my head, and he said, 'Would you be able to recognise the person who did this to you?'

'Yes, I would,' I told him. The bouncer then took me back upstairs into the nightclub, and standing right there, in front of us both, was the guy who had head-butted me! I was then asked if I would like to press charges against this man, which I did. My attacker was then escorted away by the police, who were already outside the nightclub. I want to say a big thank you to the bouncer who looked after me that night, because, if it hadn't been for him, that guy who head-butted me might have gotten away with it!

I always remember, when I was getting into the ambulance outside the club that night, a lad was stood there smirking at me as I was holding a big wad of tissue to my head just above my right eye, which surprised me as he was an alternative guy with a great punk look going on. I used to see this guy around town quite often, and I had always thought he was pretty cool for expressing himself how he did; how wrong I was. So I learnt another valuable lesson that night, which was: just because somebody else is alternative, doesn't mean they are going to like you because you're an individual as well. You would be surprised at the number of alternative people who have looked at me like I'm a freak, you know. What's that all about?

When the ambulance took me home in the early hours of that bank holiday Monday morning, I had to wake my dad up, and that was something I dreaded having to do because I didn't want to put him through seeing me after I had been assaulted for a second time! That was one tough night. I had to be strong and hold it together, though, especially when I saw my parents crying.

When my dad answered the door to me that Monday morning, I remember him saying, 'Oh no, Steve, what's happened this time?' then he passed out and fell on the hallway floor. The ambulance crew then quickly helped my dad and brought him back around and told him he had just gone into shock. What an excellent job those ambulance guys do. I felt sick to my stomach when I saw my dad passed out, and it was me who had caused him to feel this way even though I knew it wasn't my fault! Still, though, I felt guilty seeing my dad hurting so much. It's moments like these in my life that I will never forget, and which always make me feel very emotional when I think back to how people have not only affected me but how they have also affected my whole family as well. I can't even begin to explain to you how upsetting it is when you see your mum and dad crying. Once my dad was feeling better, he then followed the ambulance in his car to Kettering General Hospital, where I had my head stitched back together just above my right eye. The nurse at Kettering General hospital was fantastic.

> I'm sure men don't like the way my eyes look, because both assaults
> I have been through, have been on my eyes, or very close to them.

After I had been assaulted and reported my attacker to the police, I then went back out into public a week later. And the guy who had head-butted me came up to me in the King's Head pub to apologise for his actions the weekend before. I appreciated him doing that, but the damage had already been done to me mentally and physically. I felt very vulnerable back then, but my friends around Market Harborough said, 'We've got your back mate; if you need us just let us know,' which I appreciated them saying. And the number of people who said that was unbelievable! Being a victim of an assault made me want to get a message out to everyone that this kind of behaviour had to stop because I didn't want it happening to anybody else, which, unfortunately, it still does. So, I created a Facebook group called 'What's happening to Harborough with all the violence?' where I had around 147 people join and support me. Now here is the *Harborough Mail*'s news article they did on me after I had been assaulted and the message, I wanted to get out there to everybody.

# HEAD BUTT VICTIM USES WEB TO CALL FOR PEACE

A MAN nearly blinded in one eye after he was head-butted while on a night out has called for an end to violence in Harborough. Steve Rippin, known to friends as Pirate Steve or Jack Sparrow, was enjoying a night out in the Enigma nightclub with friends when he was hit twice in the face. The attack, on Sunday, August 24, has left Mr Rippin with five stitches in a wound above his right eye and feeling nervous about going out in the town again. But the 32-year-old is determined to raise awareness of what he feels are increasing levels of violence in Harborough and has set up a group on the social networking website Facebook calling for it to stop. Speaking about the incident, he said: 'This big bloke came out of nowhere and head-butted me for no reason. I'd never seen him before in my life. I said, "what did you do that for?" He didn't answer me then did it again. Then he walked off,' An ambulance was called and Mr Rippin was taken to Kettering General Hospital, where he spent the night receiving treatment. Mr Rippin suffers from glaucoma and as part of his treatment has a tube in his right eye, which drains fluid away and releases pressure. He said he was initially worried the attack might cause him to lose the sight in that eye. 'The pressure of the swelling is pushing down on my eye, and as I have weak sensitive eyes, it's really hurting,' he said. 'I've had enough eye problems with glaucoma, so this is the worst thing to happen.'

The Facebook group set up by Mr Rippin in response to the attack has so far attracted 147 members. 'I set up the group because I was furious at what had happened to me and wanted to vent some of my frustration,' he said. 'I didn't realise I'd have such a big response from people supporting me on it. I feel sick to the stomach with all the stories I keep hearing from people whose sons have been in fights or been head-butted and didn't deserve it. I think it's about time someone stood up and brought it all out in the open. If that's got to be me, then I'll do it. I've had enough of seeing fights in Harborough because people have had a drink and can't control themselves.' Mr Rippin thanked bouncers at the club and ambulance staff for helping him during the ordeal as well as friends and family who have supported him since.

*The Harborough Mail*. **Published on Tuesday, 22 September 2008**

I didn't feel embarrassed sharing my story in this way. Yeah, I got stares from certain people in my hometown whose friend I had reported to the police, but I had done nothing wrong. It was the guy who had attacked me who was at fault. One guy who came up to me a few weeks after the incident said to me, 'You should think about moving out of Harborough, you're not safe here.' I stood my ground, though, and said, 'I'm not going anywhere, this is my hometown, and no one is going to threaten me.' Then my good friend Carl Andrews stuck up for me that night, which I really appreciated him doing, and he told that guy to leave me alone and go away, which he did. So don't be afraid, or feel intimidated of coming forward if you're faced with a situation like I have been in because if you don't say anything about any form of bullying you might be going through, it will only continue. So, the more you talk and let people know about what you have, or are going through, the better. And remember, talking to family, friends and to counsellors can help.

The two incidents where I was assaulted were both unprovoked, and I was set upon when I was least expecting it, so I had no chance of defending myself. So, please, be aware of your surroundings when you're out, because you just don't know who's lurking about. And, if you or somebody you know has been through anything like what I have, you will know how emotionally upsetting it can be for you, as well as for your family and friends as well.

Bullies don't realise the knock-on consequences their actions have. It's like a domino effect: once you knock one down, then the rest will follow, but, just like dominoes, you and your family can get back up again. Bullies should stop and think how they would feel if somebody attacked a member of their family or one of their friends.

I had to dig deep to get through all I was put through, but I came out of it the other side an even better version of myself than I was before! And then four months after I was assaulted, I created The Pirate Steve Show on social media, because of all you have just read. Nowadays, though, I'm known as the Positive Pirate online. To finish, here are some lovely words on how we should treat one another as humans from my good friend Harry Diver.

We've only met a few times; however, you are probably one of the most genuine, honest, memorable and calming individuals I've ever met. I genuinely love meeting people like you who are individual, warm, and a unique representation of themselves – such a rare quality in 2019, where everyone wants to be someone other than their true self. I always say and I quote, 'Me being born, shouldn't offend your visual view of me. I'm like a fingerprint. I shouldn't have to fit into your selected version or what you think I should be.' We all can have an opinion, which we are entitled to. However, when it's hurtful, derogatory or isn't constructive, then it's not worth saying. I wish we all lived in a world, where a hug was mandatory, and hate was eradicated, where help was offered, and segregation was eliminated. We are only tenants in this world. We don't own it. The only thing we all have in common should be race. It's called the human race. So, live today, with the hope of tomorrow, and if we are lucky enough to awake tomorrow, then make a difference to someone who isn't as fortunate in this life. There isn't one person on this planet who is better than us. We are no different to a tin of beans or a carton of milk in a supermarket, everything and everyone has an expiration date. So, keep being you, Steve.

**Harry Diver, London, England**

# IT'S TAKEN ME SOME TIME TO GET OVER THOSE ASSAULTS

I would say it wasn't until around 2016 that I started to feel more like my old self again and safer when I was out in public! After the second assault, I went to see a counsellor, and she said I had a good positive outlook and attitude towards life. So, thankfully, I only had to see her once. If you're struggling after any ordeals you might have been through, and you don't feel comfortable talking to any members of your family or close friends, remember, there are counsellors and support groups out there you can turn to for help if you need them. The people who have helped me the most through my ordeals have been my family, mates and online friends. And they are the ones who can help you get through any tough times you might be facing right now as well.

When I go out at weekends, there is one thing my mum and dad always say to me nowadays, which is, 'Well, look after yourself and stay out of trouble.' And they are words I will never forget because they show me just how much my parents love, care for and worry about me. One of my mum and dad's favourite sayings, when they know somebody has said something to upset me, is, 'Well, you need to learn to expect it where you go and with how you look, because people will say things, especially when they've had a drink,' which is so true, isn't it?

Do, and be who you like to be, if everyone were the same, it would be a s**t world. You look on Facebook, YouTube and wherever you look some are different, so what if you don't like what you see, don't look and who cares, I'm not going to stop talking to someone for looking different. People should not listen to what other people say. You should make your own mind up.

**Lee Easterlow, Market Harborough, England**

Pray, Trust in God to help you through whatever you're anxious about. Join an active church with people who can be there for you. Meditate. It's also how I live my life! It's worked and helped me through MANY situations that were almost unbearable in hindsight. So sad what you went through Steve Rippin, and I'm glad you've recovered. You can still use all this advice because you'll probably have flashbacks, something will trigger its memory, etc. What also helps is forgiving whoever it is that attacked you. This doesn't mean your approving or even liking the person. But forgiving someone who has wronged you is allowing you to let go of what happened. Forgiving someone helps you to cope and move on. Just think, if that hadn't happened, you wouldn't be reaching out to all of us now and getting all this great advice!

**Carla Nelson, Ohio, USA**

I was at a very low point in my life after the second time I was attacked. And, to make matters worse, a lot of nasty rumours were made up about me in a hate group on Facebook. Coming from a small-town community, rumours soon get spread around. What annoyed me the most, though, was seeing how much those rumours were upsetting my parents, especially my mum, who I often saw crying because of specific lowlife individuals from my town who had made those untrue accusations up about me. One rumour why the guy head-butted me was because of my appearance; another was that I was a local drug dealer, which was just ludicrous! And this next rumour made me laugh because, apparently, I had slept with this guy's girlfriend! Which I think I would remember if I had, wouldn't I? It was made even more ridiculous because I had not slept with a girl or had sex for over ten years back then! And I would never in my life do anything like that when someone is in a relationship with somebody else! When I found out who this bloke's girlfriend was, I knew of her because her mum and dad and my parents had been good friends for many years. I couldn't even remember the last time I had seen their daughter! I was told the primary reason why he head-butted me, though, was because of my appearance; how much truth is in that, though, I don't know.

The hate group I mentioned earlier was made up about me on Facebook to blacken my name and a place where certain people could insult me. On top of that, I also received a lot of evil private messages from individuals about how much they hated me and what they wanted to do to me! Oh, and get this: I even had one guy come around my house asking me to drop the charges against this guy who had head-butted me twice in the face! I was an innocent victim, and when that hate group was set up on Facebook, it was very distressing for my family and friends.

When the police came around my house, I showed them the messages, comments and Facebook profiles of individuals who had been harassing and threatening me, which my mum had printed out. The police just laughed and said, 'Don't worry Steve, it will all settle down, just ignore it.' The torment kept happening, though! My dad wasn't happy at all with what was going on and didn't want to stand by doing nothing watching his son's name being blackened. So, he went down to his solicitors to see what we could do to bring charges up against those people who were threatening, harassing and spreading malicious rumours about me, for defamation of character. The solicitors told us to wait and see what happens. So, we did, and thankfully the Facebook group was taken down. I think that was because the culprits behind the hate group found out my parents and I had gone to the police and showed them their Facebook profiles and all their defamatory comments and messages they had sent me. Because of that hate group, though, the damage to my name had already been done, because particular people who we thought we knew around our town said to my dad they believed the rumours being said about me were genuine! You always find out who your real friends are when things like this happen, don't you? Also, a lot of people thought because of what had happened to me I was going to stop being Pirate Steve and cut my hair short so nobody would recognise me. That had never crossed my mind and was something I would never have even considered doing. If anything, everything that had happened to me made me want to be Pirate Steve more than ever before!

I, too, have experienced the cyberbullying, and that was also very traumatic. I don't understand why people wanna be mean for, for no reason, but this is the downside to social media. Cruel people love to hide behind the computer to put other people down. The only consolation, I suppose is, maybe we are in good company. If you look at any of the Kardashians social media, people post nothing, but terrible evil things, I believe, that it comes down to, envy and jealousy on their part.

Stacey Hayes, California, USA, instagram.com/hoststaceyhayes

All the evil messages I received online from those cyberbullies, empowered me all the more, to become who I am today.

Always think, when you're going through a difficult time, how you can turn that situation around to your advantage, just like I did when I created the Pirate Steve Show in 2008; now known as the Positive Pirate. Back then, I turned all my negative emotions I was having into positive ones to show people how strong I was through the videos I uploaded to YouTube. And that has enabled me today to inspire so many people. As they say, good always conquers evil. And everybody who genuinely knew me when I was attacked in 2008 knew those rumours were untrue.

If you're a victim to online harassment, like I was, my best advice to you would be to take screenshots of that person's social media profile along with their picture. And print out all the comments and messages they have been tormenting you with, then you can use those as evidence which you can hand over to the police or your solicitors if things end up going to court. And remember, you can also report those cyberbullies to whatever social media platform the harassment is happening to you on and block their accounts. If the cyberbullies make another fake account up and the intimidation continues, you will hopefully have a good idea which individuals it's coming from.

There are a lot of things you can do when you're being slandered on social media. I looked up online when you can contact the police about these matters. And if what's being said about you is indecent, very offensive, obscene, threatening or menacing the police call this an offence of malicious communications. And the police will then investigate the matter further for you. If what is being said about or to you, doesn't fall into being indecent, very offensive, obscene, threatening or menacing, then this is called defamation of character because it is a false statement that is being made up about you, which could be causing personal damage to your reputation just like it was doing to mine with the false statements that were being made up that I was a local drug dealer! If it's defamation of character you're a victim of, you can go to the civil courts because it's more of a civil matter, and the police won't be able to help you with this. Also, you can go to your local Citizens Advice Bureau and a solicitor to learn more about what the best steps are to take before taking any further action. Cyberbullying should not be tolerated in any way, shape or form in today's society!

Stronger laws need to be introduced to help protect people of all ages from cyberbullying if it's happening to them. And the people who are committing these acts of cyberbullying need to be brought to justice and made to pay for their crimes against the innocent people they are hurting and upsetting! Maybe the perpetrators should do community service, or for the more severe acts of cyberbullying, where people's lives are threatened, they should be given short-term prison sentences for emotionally damaging innocent lives. In some cases, people can be left feeling traumatised and too scared to leave the safety of their own homes when they have suffered cyberbullying, while others won't be able to cope and will resort to committing suicide to put an end to their emotional stress, anxiety and depression they have been left to live with. If community service and prison sentences sound too harsh, though, then maybe what my good friend Gordon Harrison has to say is a good idea. All I know is that something has to be done to make more awareness of this online harassment so many people are living with today.

> I think cyberbullying is horrible. Having been bullied emotionally up to my late teens, I know that it can cause severe damage. Like most things, legislation is a way to deal with serious matters. However, taking people to court, or, sending them to prison, is difficult to enforce, costly to administer, and puts the offender with other like-minded people. Often, bullying behaviours are learnt from parents, or, peer groups. Recently, things like the NHS – tax credits and minority groups have been promoted by TV adverts

or in Soaps. I would think the Government should put a series of information films out trying to educate the uneducated. This should be a long and primetime campaign. And also, advertisers and tv programmes should be encouraged. A name and shame campaign could be introduced. I would recommend, anyone, being cyberbullied, to try to explain to the perpetrators, why they are wrong. And to protect their mental health, they withdraw from social media, and the premise, that they need to protect themselves from abuse.

**Gordon Harrison, Leicestershire, England**

Don't be a victim and don't suffer in silence, speak up and let's put a stop to cyber bullying once and for all.

If you're going through cyberbullying in your life, please don't bottle up how you're feeling by keeping your problems to yourself. Always report those bullies/cyberbullies to an authority figure, such as your parents, the police, your boss or your schoolteacher. And this will show that you're not scared of coming forward and facing your fears. Your family and friends will also look up to you for being so brave. And don't be worried about what the bullies might do after you have reported them. You might think they will want to take their revenge out on you. Remember, they are already harassing and upsetting you, so you have nothing to lose and everything to gain. And by reporting them, everything will be out in the open, plus you will start getting the help you need and also love and support from your family and friends. Don't feel scared when you resort to reporting people; it's your life and you deserve to be happy.

A far better man you are Steve, those who use violence to win their wars, bring darkness to their world only to one day end up alone needing help from the very ones they hurt. Time age and body will catch up on us all. You, my friend, have brought nothing but light, as long as I know you, Shine, Shine, Shine on Steve Rippin.

**Georgie Gorman, Sligo, Ireland**

I hope what I have written about here helps you or somebody you know, because nobody deserves to live in fear, do they? One of the hardest things about being an alternative individual is when other people take an instant dislike to you for no reason. I love to get on with everybody; some people, though, are very small-minded and get jealous of others. So, you can look like an alternative individual, like I do today, or like I used to look when I first got assaulted, with short hair and no pirate look going on, and still get trouble.

A few days after I was assaulted, I dressed in my Captain Jack Sparrow outfit to show my online friends that nobody was going to stop me from being who I wanted to be. And would you believe, before I got assaulted for a second time, I was thinking of cutting my hair short and getting rid of my beard. Instead, though, I decided to do the opposite and go full throttle into pirate mode! The night I was attacked is the foremost reason I created the Pirate Steve Show, now known as the Positive Pirate on YouTube. So, out of that negative experience, a positive outcome came of it. Also, in March 2013, I uploaded a video to my YouTube channel, where I dressed as Captain Jack Sparrow and made a video where I talked about bullying. If you would like to watch that video, here is a link to it: bit.ly/BeAStarNotABullyVideo

Writing down all I have been through, with my accounts of being bullied and assaulted, has helped to clear my head of all the negative thoughts and feelings I used to have. I'm also now able to see things a lot clearer, even though those memories of being attacked, are still there with me. Remember, you're stronger than the bully, and the bully will always do their best to take away your confidence, self-esteem, positive attitude and inner strength. You see, the bully wants to make you feel weak and worthless, and that they are way more powerful and superior than you are, which isn't true at all; they are the weak ones. So always look deep down within yourself and focus on that inner strength you have, and by doing that it will help to empower you.

When you have been through a traumatic experience, you can quite easily feel sorry for yourself and hide away from everybody. Please, though, never let your self-pity get the better of you because you will only drown in that. What you need to do is pick yourself back up and get out into the world as soon as you can, so you can show your family, friends and those who have hurt you the best damn version of who YOU were always born to be! Focus on the positives and never the negatives. Facing your fears and pushing yourself to carry on after you have been through a distressing ordeal can be extremely difficult; you have to take it stage by stage, and then, over time, everything you feared and were worried about will gradually lessen, just as I have found its done for me. Now here are a few kind words from my friends on social media when they heard I had been assaulted.

Yes, same here, since I have been bullied, it made me into the strong person who I am today! You know what, I have a strong feeling that they didn't just attack you just for your differences but ALSO because of your good looks! There is this quote I once heard that goes something like – If you are too brave, too beautiful, or too clever, the world will try to kill you! – I believe this to be totally true! I see nice-looking people get hated on all the time, and for no reason even, just because they are attractive. This sort of thing happens to me a lot.

Rose Colbert, California, USA, instagram.com/rose_red_rum

I'm sorry you went through that Steve but proud you were able to turn it around into something positive. You are strength, warmth and hope in one, you give so many people hope. In the same situations, never, never give up is what you shout through all of your postings, it's a message that is helping lots of people, whom are or have gone through so much but giving them hope that things can and will change if we can turn our bad experiences in to good, we then are able to stand tall and smile once again. Bless you, Steve, for all you have done and still do, what a beautiful person you are inside and out. I'm sure your parents are proud of you as we whom know you are also. Keep up the good work.

Maxine Sirs, Hartlepool, England

It's just so disgusting that someone would attack somebody else just because they look different. It would be a boring world if everyone looked the same. It's so good you didn't let it stop you from being who you want to be. I have been bullied in the past but now see it as almost a compliment, the bullies recognise I'm not the same as them, I'm not narrow-minded, judgemental or unkind, I would feel worse if they thought I was like them! I never judge others by their appearance. I prefer to find out what someone thinks, feels and says, know them by their actions and how they treat others, how they present themselves in their appearance makes no difference. You are the best of both, you look individual and interesting, but most importantly, you have a kind heart, a positive attitude and put yourself out to help others. Let no-one tell you otherwise, you're perfect the way you are.

**Lisa Twinkle, Rochester, England**

Jealousy is terrible, and you shouldn't have been attacked for being you. You're an awesome person, and a great friend to have. You always cheer me up when I'm down, I can always count on you to be there.

**Harley Schram, USA, instagram.com/countrygirl7959**

Steve, I am so sorry this happened. Thank you so much for sharing. And for taking this moment in your life to change the life of others. It is definitely easier to love than to hate, takes less muscles to smile than to frown. One day we'll all get it right, and the world will surely be a much better place. You're Amazing

**Ty Swint, Nashville, Tennessee, USA**

Steve, you're a lovely fella. The f***wit that did that to you is one sad, sad person. The fact that he did that to such a nice guy says more about him than it ever does about you. I only ever see you once in a blue moon, but when I do, you are always having a

great time, and have a big old smile on your face. Keep on Rockin'
Brother Rippin, Keep on Rockin

**Mark Timson, Market Harborough, England**

Thank you so much, Rose, Maxine, Lisa, Harley, Ty and Mark, for
your kind words; they truly mean so much to me.

Steven M. Rippin

# CAN I FORGIVE THOSE WHO HAVE HURT ME?

Anyone would think I'm a troublemaker after reading about those assaults I have been involved in, wouldn't they? And some people might say, 'There are always two sides to a story, and he must have provoked those people in some way.' All I can say is: people who know me know I never go out to cause trouble; all I ever wish is for everybody to get along, be happy and enjoy their lives. If I had done something wrong, then, yes, I would have deserved getting attacked. When you know you haven't done anything immoral in the first place, though, that's what hurts. What also annoys me is how some human beings think it's OK to go around making untrue accusations up about other people and assaulting them for no reason! It's been a long road for me, but I'm finally happy where I am now.

Q: If you could tell anyone that's getting bullied one thing, what would it be? And I just can't understand why people would assault you. You are so kind-hearted, I just don't get why, just pure scum that's all they are, nothing else. You're someone who a lot of people know. You mention Pirate Steve in Harborough, and most of the people go oh yeah I know him!

Susan Dilks, Market Harborough, England

A: Thank you for what you said, Susan. The foremost thing I would tell somebody who is being bullied is to talk to their family and friends about what's going on. Thanks for your question.

Steven M. Rippin

Can I forgive the people who have made my life hell? That's a question I have asked myself many times over the years. It wasn't until 2018 when I was able to answer that question with a YES or a NO. What helped was when I watched a video on Facebook about a lovely old lady called Eva Moses Kor, a Holocaust survivor. Eva and her twin sister Miriam were both born in the small village of Portz in Romania on 30 January 1934, where Eva, Miriam and her family had many good years together. That was until 1944 when a Hungarian Nazi armed guard told Eva's family to gather their belongings together because they were being relocated to the Auschwitz–Birkenau death camp, where Eva and Miriam were to be separated from their parents forever. Eva's parents and two older sisters were sadly killed. Eva and her twin sister Miriam, though, were selected, along with other sets of twins, to be used in horrific experiments at the Auschwitz–Birkenau death camp, at the hands of Josef Mengele.

Approximately 1,500 sets of twins were experimented on at the Auschwitz–Birkenau death camp, which is extremely hard to imagine, isn't it? What poor Eva and Miriam must have gone through I will never know. It must have been like hell on earth back then for all of those unfortunate innocent victims of the Holocaust. Sadly, most of the twins who were experimented on died. Eva became very ill, but thankfully she survived and helped her sister Miriam to survive as well – Eva's now forgiven Josef Mengele. If you would like to know more on Eva Mozes Kor's story of what she went through during the Holocaust, here is a Wikipedia link: en.wikipedia.org/wiki/Eva_Mozes_Kor. I found the video of Eva explaining what she and her sister had been through truly unbelievable. I still can't believe this kind of thing went on all those years ago. And it's what Eva explained that struck a chord with me when she said, 'We cannot change what happened, that is the tragic part, but we can change how we relate to it,' which is so true, isn't it? After watching Eva's video, I believe I can now forgive those who inflicted pain and hurt on me. And now I say to myself, 'Once you learn to forgive somebody for hurting you, you can then begin to move forward with your life once again, and know you're healing yourself from within.' At first, living with a mindset like this didn't come easily for me, but over time, I have started to feel liberated and free. So, YES, I can forgive those who have tormented and assaulted me in the past. I have learnt those who hurt me, are the weak ones, and that I am the powerful one. I feel a lot better within myself since realising that. So please remember, no matter what has happened to you in life, you can't change your past but you can choose how you move forward from this moment on.

> I have achieved a lot since I was bullied at school and assaulted later on in my life, and I'm proud to say, I battled my demons and WON!

Since being bullied at school, assaulted and through anxiety and mild depression, instead of feeling sorry for myself, I picked myself up and now I own my own carpet cleaning business, I've appeared on national television, auditioned for *Big Brother*, had encounters with bears in the Great Smoky Mountains of Tennessee, created my own brand called the Positive Pirate and made a lot of fantastic new friends as well, plus so much more. And I mention a few of those things I've accomplished because I want you to know, if you're going through a hard time right now, you can achieve anything you put your mind to as well. And, when you focus on what you want to accomplish in your life, it will help motivate you, so you don't let anything or anybody destroy your hopes and dreams. Over time, you will learn to cope and get over what you have been through. It will be tough, but things will gradually improve. It might take years, as it did for me, but stay focused and you will get there. And remember to always concentrate on what you're passionate about in life, which will help you have a more positive outlook so you can move forward once again.

Well, I would like to end on a good note, and let you know that the two guys who assaulted me both went to court and got fined for what they had done. If I hadn't prosecuted them, then there might have been other innocent victims who would have had to have gone through the same as I did, and I couldn't let that happen. Hopefully, the two people who assaulted me have learnt from their past mistakes and are now living much happier and positive lives. Coming forward and pressing charges against individuals who harm you in any way is very important, so always stand up for what you believe in, because good always conquers over evil, and believe in the justice system, because it does work. And the power of social media will help you get the truth out there, just as I found it did for me. It's your life, so make it the best damn one you can, because you deserve all the happiness in the world. Also, believe in yourself and never let anybody hold you back or intimidate you.

# BEING ASSAULTED CHANGED MY LIFE

On 25 August 2008, my life took on a whole new direction after I was assaulted and head-butted twice in the face.

I was supposed to have gone to Myrtle Beach in America with my friends a week after I had been attacked; that was the last thing I wanted to do, though. I didn't want my mates or anybody seeing me looking like an emotional wreck with a big gash on my head full of stitches, plus my confidence and self-esteem were at an all-time low. Then I decided that I didn't want to wallow in my self-pity anymore, so I spoke to my parents and Auntie Janet, and after talking to them I decided I was going to go to America because I knew I would have only regretted it if I hadn't gone.

I always remember breaking down in tears once my friends and I arrived at Orlando International Airport because I felt so alone; it was a horrible feeling. The friends I was with, though, really helped me through those emotions I was having, which I appreciated so much, plus I met some awesome people over at Myrtle Beach: one charming young woman was Rebecca Roundtree, who worked in a restaurant. And I also met a great guy called Chris Davis, who my friends and I partied with.

Hell yea! I'll never forget the night I met you and your friends in South Carolina was the greatest night.

**Chris Davis, Myrtle Beach, South Carolina, USA**

The rest of my time over at Myrtle Beach was awesome, and it helped me to forget about what had happened to me only weeks before. And I'm happy to say, when I arrived back home in England, around 14 September 2008, I felt a lot more comfortable and confident within myself. When I was catching up with my posts on Facebook after my holiday, I received a message from a girl called Alice Cave, whose message read as follows.

> If you ever fancy coming out, you're welcome, mate drives us there, and we know people who live in Leicester. If you don't mind hanging out with a strange group of chavs, skaters and goths lol.

> **Alice Cave, Northampton, England**

I appreciated Alice asking me this very much, and still do, to this day. Alice Cave opened my world up to a whole new culture back then in 2008, along with many new friends who she introduced me to as well, all because of how kind and thoughtful she was. Alice has a heart of gold and is an adorable human being who couldn't believe what had happened to me. So, I started going over to Leicester a lot more and hanging out with Alice and her friends. I loved those nights out we had, and still do, when I get a chance to go over to the rock and goth clubs over there. Alice helped me through an extremely low point in my life when I was feeling lost on the inside, so going over to Leicester on nights out helped me no end. And, truth be told, I was scared to death about going out in my hometown, which I had grown up in, ever again. The more I went over to Leicester to meet up with Alice and her friends, the more my confidence and self-esteem gradually improved, and over time I began to feel less anxious as well, although the anxiety and mild depression I had, did take quite a few years to get over fully.

> Thank you so much, Alice, for getting in touch with me in 2008. I will never forget what you did for me back then by introducing me into your world and to all your awesome friends. All my very best to you and your family.

> **Steven M. Rippin**

In October 2008, my good friend Lynda Hill got in touch with me and said, 'Steve, you should think about auditioning for *Big Brother*,' so I listened to her, and did just that. After taking Lynda's advice, I started piecing together an audition video for *Big Brother*. By focusing on that, it helped take my mind off the assault I had gone through only a couple of months before, plus it gave me a purpose and a new challenge to take on. When I had finished making my *Big Brother* audition video, I made a YouTube channel, where I posted it. And it was from that point on that I created the Pirate Steve Show, which is now known as the Positive Pirate. I gained a lot of support from everybody in my hometown when they heard I was auditioning for *Big Brother*, which also helped with my emotional recovery process.

Thank you to everyone who supported me back then on my journey to enter the *Big Brother* house.

**Steven M. Rippin**

Then, on Tuesday, 16 December 2008, I was invited to my cousin Sandie Hart's school, where she worked as a teacher in Melton Mowbray, to dress up as Captain Jack Sparrow and say hello to her class. I felt nervous when my cousin first asked me to do that because I didn't know if I would have the bottle to dress as Captain Jack and parade myself around her classroom. I told myself I was going to do it, though. So, my dad drove me to Melton Mowbray to Sandie's school, where I had photos taken with all the children, as well as a few of the teachers who appeared in my cousin's classroom while I was there, who I think were intrigued to see a pirate. I also gave out chocolate button sweets to the children as Christmas presents, and can you believe even the teachers, after they had a photo taken with me, held their hands out waiting to be given some chocolate button sweets as well, bless them. See, it just goes to show you we're all big kids at heart, aren't we? Then, after I had finished giving out sweets to the teachers, we finished the day off singing Christmas carols.

I knew the children and teachers had appreciated me going over and dressing up as Captain Jack Sparrow that day because a few weeks later my cousin Sandie handed me a folder where all the children had made drawings and written out thank-you messages for me. That really touched my heart, you know, so I made them a short thank-you video message for taking the time to do that. And, for the first time in years, I felt proud of myself because I had made other people happy and had brought smiles to their faces. What a great experience it was going over to my cousin's school back in 2008, especially after the year I had gone through.

Everything that happens to us makes and changes us every step of the way on our journey through life. So, no matter what you have been through, focus on improving your life by taking challenges and stepping out of your comfort zone just how my friends and cousin helped me to do. Always look at harmful events you go through in a positive way, because those experiences help toughen you up in life. I finished 2008 on a good note and accomplished so much in the four months after I had been assaulted. My life has been quite the adventure so far, and I have loved every moment of it, even though I have been bashed about along the way.

After you have been through a terrible ordeal, it comes down to how you move on from it, with how your life is going to turn out. I could have quite easily fallen into a deep depression, but instead I surrounded myself with my family and friends. Auditioning for *Big Brother* and going to my cousin's school dressed as Captain Jack helped progress me forward through the emotional hurt, pain and misery I was going through in 2008. So, by getting yourself out there into the world, it will help you conquer any worries you have. So, stay active and always talk to somebody if you're suffering. Please remember, you can achieve your goals no matter what anybody has said or done to you; don't hide away. Be proud of who you are and don't be intimidated by people who have caused you misery. Live your life with the confidence and determination that will show everybody who has ever hurt you that they can never destroy who you are. Being assaulted changed my life and I faced my fears. So, if I can do it; so can YOU; believe in YOURSELF and never let the bad guys win.

# KEEP SELF-CONTROL IN NEGATIVE SITUATIONS

Come on, admit it, you have had negative thoughts, just like I have at some point in your life, and thought things you would love to say to somebody who's annoyed you, haven't you? There are things I would love to say to certain people, but instead of going off at them and saying something like, 'What's your problem, why are you acting like that, I know you don't like me, so why don't you just leave me alone?' I will let them have their say, nod politely, then walk away from them because that person insulting me isn't worth my time of day. Saying that, I did once turn round and say to a guy who had urinated down the back of my leg while I was at a festival, 'What do you think you're doing, you're peeing all over me,' which he completely denied because he was drunk! I had to control my temper that day, I can tell you! Anyway, I managed to keep my cool, and I walked away from that situation before it got out of hand. What I'm trying to get across here is that you should always, instead of lashing out at somebody for something they have said or done to you, do the opposite instead, and either walk away or ignore the person who's irritating you. And, please, never try reasoning with someone who is drunk, because they won't listen to a word you say. Those encounters could lead you getting involved in a fight, which is the last thing you want.

Or, if it's a different kind of circumstance you find yourself in, say, for example, a member of your family has upset you, you could try, in a non-patronising way, asking them if you could have a quiet talk about what they have said to upset you, to try and resolve things. Or, if it's gone past speaking with them, do what I do and be as courteous as you can when you're around them. Why families can't all get along together I'll never know. I understand it's hard to bite your tongue sometimes when somebody has wound you up, especially a family member; please, though, DON'T let them get to you; be mature, and you will gain a lot of respect from all the other members of your family. When you act negative towards someone, you will always attract negativity into your life.

You and I are unable to control every situation we find ourselves in; we can, though, control the overall outcome of those encounters we have, just as I did when I was attacked in 2008 in the way I conducted myself towards my assailant after he head-butted me. And, because I responded by not retaliating back, I showed that guy I was the more civilised man. I kept that situation under control by talking to him politely. Unfortunately, doing that didn't help my situation though because, as you know, he then head-butted me for a second time after I said 'What did you do that for?' Anyway, the point is, the incident didn't escalate further, which it quite easily could have if I had fought back. It might have even turned into a very nasty fight in the nightclub, which could have left me more worse off than I already was. People might say I attracted that situation into my life, because of how I look and choose to dress. As individuals we should be allowed to wear and look however we want when we're out in public, though, and not be singled out because of it, shouldn't we?

After that incident happened in the nightclub, I started to attract a lot of fantastic people into my life. And those individuals were always there for my parents and me once they had heard about what had happened. And their support was amazing.

# HOW I BEAT MY LOW SELF-ESTEEM

If you have suffered from having low self-esteem, just like me, then I want to help you as best as I can to improve it. Let's say goodbye to low self-esteem forever. I used to be very self-conscious and anxious about what other people thought of me, I had no ambitions in life, I let people walk all over me, my relationships never worked out, I was always trying to please everyone around me, and I was very timid and found it hard to communicate with others; basically, I was unhappy with my life. I'm much more confident and content in my life now than I used to be, and when I look back at myself from twenty years ago I cringe and think, 'Who was that person? That wasn't me, was it?' I was so pathetic. It wasn't until I was at least thirty-three that I started to rebuild my life, confidence and self-esteem.

The best thing to do to find out what your self-esteem is is to write down any negative thoughts you might be having about yourself, or your life in general. For me, it was how I looked – What people thought of me – What my eyes looked like to people – Being afraid and intimidated – Having no direction in life and feeling like a failure and reject. If you're having any negative thoughts, like I was, that can be a sure sign you have low self-esteem, but if you're having positive thoughts and feel happy with your life, then that's an excellent sign you have high self-esteem. If you're suffering from low self-esteem, though: Did something happen to you as a child? – Has anything traumatic ever happened to you in your life? And what thoughts and feelings do you try and suppress and put into the back of your mind?

Now here are the kind of thoughts you might have. 'Oh, another day at work. Let's get on with it; the quicker I get started, the quicker it will be over with' – 'I feel so demoralised; where's my life going?' – 'Oh, I look terrible today, I feel so fat and ugly' – 'Why can't I have the job I've always wanted' – 'Nobody cares about me' – 'There isn't any point in my existence' – 'People don't appreciate me' – 'I always fail at everything I do' – People are always laughing at me'. Also, have a think back throughout your life and try and remember when you didn't have low self-esteem problems. To improve your low self-esteem, try writing down all the things that have been upsetting you into a diary; doing that can be very therapeutic. Also, you could write down a list of challenges you want to take – What aspects of your life you want to enhance – What your positive personality traits are – What your goals are, and what achievements you have accomplished. I hope this helps you if you do this.

When you have high self-esteem, you're full of confidence, and you love and accept who you are as a person.

If you suffer from low self-esteem, try talking to your family and friends. Ask them what they think your best qualities are, and what aspects of your life they think you need to improve on. Furthermore, it's also a good idea to book an appointment to see your local GP, who can give you professional medical advice on how you're feeling. Whenever I'm feeling down, I'll think, 'I have very loving parents, a roof over my head, a great job, and lovely friends who are always telling me how much I inspire them,' which lifts my spirits and makes me feel happy. Also, when I get myself in the gym and blast some hardstyle music out, that puts me in a positive mood and makes me feel fantastic as well.

To help lift your spirits if you're feeling down, think of the incredible experiences you've had in life, or play your favourite music, go shopping with your friends, plan a weekend away, or join a club. Another great thing to do is laugh – yes, it's as simple as that: start laughing to yourself wherever you are. Well, maybe not if you're in a lift full of strangers all around you, like I was when I was with my dad once when he decided to let one go! Blimey, those situations can be so embarrassing, but, hey, my dad always gets me laughing when he lets one go in public! Anyway, where was I? Oh, yeah: if you're on your own at home, have a go at laughing out loud to yourself, and see how good it makes you feel; laughing releases endorphins around your body, which will make you feel great just like that feeling you get from exercising. Honestly, by laughing and smiling, it can help lift your spirits and how you're feeling on the inside.

I was a perfectly fine and happy child before I started school. By the time I left at the age of seventeen, though, I was a broken mess.

Low self-esteem is usually caused by something that has happened to you in your life. My low self-esteem issues started with how schoolchildren treated me. Schoolchildren also caused my lack of confidence and anxiety issues. So, I always looked at myself as being unimportant, worthless and insignificant to everybody else around me while I was growing up. Then, as I gradually got older, I became more and more self-conscious about myself because of how I was treated. My eyesight problems made me feel vulnerable at school, especially when I had to wear an eye patch. I've felt I've been pointed and stared at for one reason or another throughout my life!

The next time you have a negative thought like 'Nobody likes me. I'm just a waste of space'. Turn that feeling into a positive impression instead, and into an affirmation: you can say to yourself every day, for example, something like this if you're being bullied: 'I'm going to show my bullies they can't push me around and bully me anymore. And I'm going to be a strong, confident person from this day on.' Saying affirmations to ourselves are a great way to improve the thoughts that go on inside our heads. Now I would like you to write down a list of affirmations you can read out loud to yourself into a mirror. It's even better to hear yourself speaking the words you believe in because it will make those words sound so much more real. And to help you think of some affirmations, here are a few I say to myself.

'I'm going to have a great day today carpet cleaning' – 'I'm so grateful for my eyesight and health' – 'I feel fantastic; I can't wait to see what today brings' – 'I love my life, my family and all my friends who are there for me' – 'I feel so lucky to be alive to enjoy everything life has to offer me' – 'I'm extremely grateful for the money I have in my bank account' – 'I'm going to help and inspire as many people as I can today' – 'I'm so privileged to have the job I have' – 'I'll bring positivity and happiness into the world'.

Those affirmations I say to myself show me that I have high self-esteem, and are the kind of affirmations you should be saying to yourself every day. If you can get into the habit of saying a statement to yourself when you wake up either out loud or in your head, it will make you feel good and set you up for the rest of the day. Now here are a few more affirmations.

'I'm going to start living my life the way I want to live it' – 'I'm going to start being more positive from now on and push those negative thoughts out of my head I've been having' – 'The past's the past, and it's now time I moved forward with my life' – 'Nobody can stop me from accomplishing the ambitions I have' – 'Nobody will treat me like a doormat ever again' – 'I will always surround myself with honest, happy, positive people' – 'I have learnt to accept myself for who I am'.

Read your affirmations daily and gradually you will rebuild your low self-esteem and push those negative thoughts out of your mind, and you will replace them with all those positive and happy affirmations you have been saying to yourself. It won't happen overnight, so please be patient; it took me a long time to rebuild my low self-esteem, well, years, if I'm honest. I got to where I am today by focusing on my goals and what I'm most passionate about in life. I love making videos for my social media sites, spending time with family, working hard cleaning carpets, keeping myself fit, listening to music, and also hanging out with my friends at the weekends. And those things have helped my low self-esteem and lack of confidence tremendously.

Never feel sorry for yourself, always pick yourself up, and remember, you're a confident individual who knows what they want out of life.

Another way to help improve your low self-esteem is to do something that makes you feel good about yourself, such as raising money for charity. When I raised money for Cancer Research UK in June 2017, I gained so much confidence and self-esteem. So, if there's a charity close to your heart, I would highly recommend organising a fundraising campaign. Doing so will help you become more confident and happier within yourself, plus you will learn a lot about the type of person you are as well.

Finding time for yourself is vital. I know a lot of people who want to do things they love doing, but by the time they have got home from work and settled down there's never enough time for them to do anything. It happens to me as well. Once I get caught up in my work, I find the things I want to do, I haven't got time for. So, I have to be strict with myself and make time for my family and friends, to get myself in the gym, or to relax and watch my favourite television shows. Always remember to delegate your time to all aspects of your life, or before you know it your life could spiral out of control.

Simple things like watching what you eat, exercising daily, looking after your appearance and hygiene can all make you feel good about yourself. It can also boost your low self-esteem and confidence. So, if you're feeling sluggish and run down, take a look at what foods you're eating and if you're getting enough exercise. Always focus on your health and fitness, your social life, your family and friends, and any interests you have. If you're struggling to fit everything into your daily life, then write down what you want to do and delegate a certain amount of time each day for that activity. Doing what you love doing will help boost your low self-esteem no end, and make you feel a lot happier as well.

> I've always told my parents and my close friends what's on my mind. And I have always asked for their advice when I've had a problem. Don't keep your quandaries bottled up inside.

Since I started making videos and posting them on social media, my low self-esteem has soared. I have now regained my confidence as well, thanks to my friends online, who I appreciate so much. Always surround yourself with people who have similar interests to you and start living your life the way you want to live it today.

When somebody compliments you, or when you have accomplished something extraordinary in your life, write those decisive moments down into a diary to look back on so you can read them to yourself whenever you're feeling down. And remembering when somebody has complimented you or when you have accomplished something exceptional in your life will help remind you of that fantastic feeling it gave you and how good you felt about yourself. Can you imagine if we complimented, motivated and helped each other every day? We would feel so much better about ourselves, wouldn't we? So always do your best to praise, encourage and assist others.

Nobody is perfect in life; for a start, I have wonky eyes. It has taken me years to accept how I look, especially when I have had to put up with people saying to me, 'You look weird, what's up with your eyes?' We have to learn to accept our flaws we have, though, don't we, because they make us who we are? People will always find fault with you, no matter how you look or how you act in life; some human beings, unfortunately, love to criticise others because deep down they're not happy with themselves in one aspect or another. And those people like to pull others down because, for a short while, it makes them feel better about themselves for a few minutes.

With plenty of determination, confidence and integrity,
you'll go far in life.

I still need to be more confident within myself. I want to be able to approach people more easily and talk to them without becoming shy, which, I admit, I still do get from time to time. I do push myself, though, and speak to people when I'm out in public. I get so nervous when I do, though, especially when it comes to talking to women!

Keep positive people in your life and get rid of those negative individuals, because they will only bring you down. If, on the other hand, those negative types are family or friends of yours, then do your best to help them through any difficulties they might be experiencing. They will appreciate you being there for them if you do.

Never worry about not being perfect in life because nobody is; we all make mistakes and upset those we love and care about without meaning to. We are only human, after all! The lessons we learn from the mistakes we make, help to make us better people.

If you want to become happier and have high self-esteem, you can achieve it. You just have to love yourself for who you are, and, whatever interests you have, get yourself out there and learn as much as you possibly can about them, and, hey, you never know, if you become really good at what you love doing, you might even be able to make a career out of it: how cool would that be? So, don't let your low self-esteem get the better of you. Remember, you can accomplish anything you put your mind to; never let anybody tell you otherwise. I was able to turn my life around, and I know you can too. Learn to love yourself and do what makes YOU happy.

Again, please remember, if things get too much for you, talk to your family and friends, or to your local GP, who can give you their best professional medical advice on how they can help you improve your low self-esteem issues. Please don't suffer in silence.

# ASK QUESTIONS THROUGHOUT YOUR LIFE

You should never be afraid to ask for what you want in life. I was always too scared to put my hand up in class and ask questions or tell the teacher that I didn't understand what he or she was talking about. I was afraid of getting laughed at by the teachers and children, you see, so I kept quiet and didn't say a word! On the odd occasion when I did pluck up the courage to ask questions in class, some teachers would just roll their eyes up in the air and say something like, 'Steven, haven't you been listening to a word I've been saying? Extra homework for you. Yes, have you got a better question to ask, Sarah?' Can you imagine how that made me feel? Not good at all!

Have you ever wanted to do something, but were too afraid? Well, why not write down all the things you have wanted to do, and a list of the reasons why you haven't done them yet. And then think to yourself, 'What's stopping me from doing them now?' Just let go of your fears and do what you have always wanted to do in life, and remember: time's short, so act now before it's too late. And, on another subject, don't be like me and let every opportunity of asking somebody who you fancy out on a date pass you by because you're too afraid of being rejected and making a fool of yourself. Can you believe: one girl I liked when I was seventeen, who I never asked out on a date even though we used to make out with each other in the nightclub most weekends, told me since we've been back in contact that she was waiting for me to ask her out all those years ago! And when she told me that my heart sank, because I now wish I had asked her out. I feel like I missed out on so much by not asking her those simple words, 'Would you like to go out on a date with me?' So, if you can relate to this, and there's somebody you really like who you want to ask out on a date, just ask them out and don't be a big wet blanket like I was.

Now here are a few of the principal reasons for feeling afraid, and not asking people questions and telling them how you feel. You might lack in confidence – You might think you're not good enough, and that there's somebody else who will do a much better job than you will – You might have a fear of rejection – You might have a lot of painful childhood memories from your past you still haven't fully moved on from yet – You might have negative thoughts running riot through your head – You might be visualising what the worst-case scenario will be to something you have to do, or you might have low self-esteem and insecurity issues caused by how other people have treated you.

Now let's find out if you're a confident person or somebody who puts up with what life throws at them, with the following question. What do you do if you're in a restaurant and your soup has been served to you cold? Do you carry on eating it because you don't want to cause a fuss, or do you tell the waiter politely to go and heat it back up for you? Remember, it's you who's paying for the soup. I hope your answer was that you would tell the waiter to go and heat it back up for you, because that would show the confident person you are and that you're not afraid of asking for what you want. When you're asking somebody a question, visualise you get what you're inquiring for; be persistent and full of confidence.

Raising money for charity every day for a month in 2017 helped my confidence and changed my outlook on life. It also pushed me out of my comfort zone, because I knew I was going to have to talk to a lot of people and ask them questions to help me with my fundraising campaign, which I was petrified about doing at first, but I pushed myself, and I did what I was always afraid of doing. And I can tell you it felt good to break out of my shell I had been cocooned in for far too long. So, take that step forward, let go of your fears, and stand up for yourself and ask all the questions you have been wanting to ask but were always too scared to, and, when you do, you will change your life forever. And remember, you only live once so make the most of every opportunity that comes your way. The more you put into practice asking people what you want, the more you will get out of life.

# HARMFUL MEMORIES; DON'T LET THEM BRING YOU DOWN

A great way to deal with those hurtful memories is to close your eyes and think of a memory that upsets you the most. And if you can, turn that vision into something you can rise above, because, at the end of the day, you're still here and getting on with your life and showing yourself as well as your family and friends that the perpetrators who hurt you didn't win or destroy you. Or you could try saying to yourself, 'Why on earth did I let that lowlife make me feel this way! I have so much going for me! From this day forward, I'm not going to waste my time and energy thinking about what they did to me and how they made me feel because I'm so much better than they are. So, from now on, I'm going to focus on things I love doing and make my family and friends proud of me.'

Don't let your damaging memories hold you back. If it's a traumatic memory, though, you should turn to your family and friends or somebody you know you can trust to talk to about how you're feeling. If, on the other hand, you don't feel comfortable talking to your family and friends, you can always talk, like I have mentioned before, to your local GP or a counsellor, who can help and advise you on the best possible course of action to take.

You have the power to move on and live the life you deserve.

Don't create harmful thoughts out of past experiences you have had. If you're afraid of something happening to you – say, for example, somebody wants to harm you, just how I used to feel after I was assaulted when

I thought the friends of the bloke who had head-butted me wanted to beat me up – it's you who's imagining and creating those fears you're having. And the more you think about them, the more you will attract negative situations into your life. So do your best to stop thinking about those fears, which will most likely never happen anyway, and visualise the positive outcomes you want to happen instead. Talk to people who have been through similar circumstances to yourself and learn how they have overcome their problems.

Posting fun and inspiring videos on social media, which I started creating in 2008, helped me conquer eighty per cent of my harmful memories.

Focus on what makes you feel happy and the things you love doing in life to help you move forward from any past harmful experiences you have been through. Open up and tell the world how you feel through the power of social media, and those who truly care about you will shine through.

# PART THREE

# MENTAL HEALTH

In the chapters to follow, you will find the best advice I can personally give on mental health issues. And I share with you stories on how I have tackled generalised anxiety disorder, social anxiety, panic attacks and depression. I'm not going to sit here and tell you I know all about mental health because I don't. I know my problems will have been nowhere near as severe as most other people's; the more this subject is written and spoken about, though, the better it will be for everybody. Remember, it's OK to not be OK. I hope the help and advice to follow will benefit you as you learn how I have overcome my anxiety and mild depression, plus there will be helpful information from my friends on social media as well.

I would also like to say, please take my advice I share with you lightly, because I'm no health care professional. At the end of the day, I'm a carpet cleaning tradesman, so I'm unable to give you expert advice on what the best thing to do is when and if you do suffer from having mental health issues. For more in-depth and professional advice, you should make an appointment to discuss any problems you might be going through, with your local GP, or counsellor.

You should never let your health or disabilities stop you from doing anything you want in life. It's surprised me just how many people do though. And please remember, you're never alone suffering from mental health; there are millions of people all over the world suffering, so the more you and I talk about our problems, the better.

It's said there are around one in four people who will experience a mental health issue in England each year. These figures are changing all the time, but it's said every week around one in six adults – it might be more, or it might be less, experience symptoms that are associated with having a mental health problem, such as anxiety or depression. And around one in five adults have considered committing suicide at some point in their lives. Just like one of my friends sadly thought of doing in the past; thankfully, he sought professional advice and is now continuing to battle through his depression with a more positive attitude. Now here is a website to the charity organisation MIND, with statistics on mental health: bit.ly/MindMentalHealthStatistics

In 2013 there were around 8.2 million cases of anxiety disorders diagnosed in the UK, and there are roughly 40 million cases of anxiety disorders diagnosed in America every year. In 2016, there were 5,668 suicides recorded in the United Kingdom, seventy-five per cent of which were men and the other twenty-five per cent women. I took those statistics from the websites www.mentalhealth.org.uk and adaa.org. With statistics like these, it shows you how severe and devastating mental health problems have become today, doesn't it?

Looking back to when I was at school, there wasn't any help or advice with the mental health issues I was going through. I remember the first aid courses they taught us, which were excellent. That's all I remember being taught, though, when it came to our health and well-being. If only teachers had been trained to look out for signs of mental health years ago, such as generalised anxiety disorder, depression, phobias, OCD, panic disorders and PTSD, then I know they would have helped me out no end, especially when I was being bullied; I felt scared going to school because I was feeling anxious, mildly depressed, and lonely. There I was, thinking there must have been something wrong with me when all along it was because I was suffering from anxiety and mild depression. I would just get told to buck my ideas up and get on with it like everybody else was. I also remember people saying, 'What's up with you? Are you a man or a mouse? Stop acting like a wimp,' which didn't help or make me feel any better about myself either!

When I finally thought my life was going well and I had beaten my mental health issues from my childhood school days, I then went and got assaulted twice, which resurfaced all my problems, this time though into my adult life!

In 2016 the National Association of Headteachers in the United Kingdom did a survey and found that three-quarters of schoolteachers said they lacked the resources they needed to help schoolchildren who might be suffering from mental health problems. In 2017 schoolteachers still hadn't been trained to learn about mental health or what signs to look out for. If only the National Association of Headteachers had addressed this issue years ago and understood how devastating mental health problems were for children and teenagers. It would also have been fantastic if they had come up with a mental health awareness class for the school curriculum because then they might have been able to save many schoolchildren's lives, who have regrettably committed suicide over the years. All because those schoolchildren didn't know which way to turn to seek the help and advice they so desperately needed. It hasn't helped either with government cutbacks on funds which schools need to help tackle mental health problems. Although the British government did invest three hundred million pounds into mental health programs, along with training hundreds of mental health workers to work in schools back in 2017, sadly though, that money will only reach around a quarter of schools in England, leaving hundreds of thousands of schoolchildren still without the help they seriously need today! So, when will the government wake up, listen, learn and invest more in this ever-growing problem?

So, let's hope that what the British government have done by investing three hundred million pounds into mental health for schools is just the beginning. And I hope the British government decide to spend millions more into this severe problem schools are facing all over England in the coming years. By doing so, they would help the future generations of schoolchildren and teenagers of tomorrow.

I unquestionably turned out unconventional, because of not being taught about mental health from a young age. I know I'm one of the lucky ones, though. I managed to overcome my issues, and survive.

I do understand teachers have to be careful when giving advice on these issues as it has to be as accurate as possible. I have also read there are courses for teachers to go on so they can learn how to have in-depth conversations with their students on mental health issues and know when to refer them to see their local GP or a counsellor.

In 2017, the Duchess of Cambridge, Kate Middleton, launched a website to help teachers talk about mental health problems with the charity Heads Together for Schools, which can help students who might be suffering from depression, anxiety, PTSD or the loss of a loved one, which I think is an excellent step in the right direction to helping children and teenagers while they are at school and college.

In today's society, some people are afraid of letting others know how they feel on the inside, which I believe is because they don't want to get laughed at or classed as being that kid or that adult who has a mental health issue. Sadly, in today's society, we all suffer ridicule from people's small mindedness about topics they don't understand. Some individuals' attitudes need to change and fast. Never feel embarrassed speaking about your mental health problems to your family, friends or local GP or counsellor.

There isn't enough being done to tackle mental health in our society today. And, from time to time, I will hear of somebody I either know or someone online losing their battle with it. They will sadly take their own life because, unfortunately, they never spoke about how they were genuinely feeling on the inside to anybody. This is why I want to let as many people know as I can that they are not alone and there is help out there. With the right help, they will begin to understand why they are feeling the way they do. Then hopefully, over time, they can learn how to get their issues under control so they can lead a healthy life. Together, you and I can help one another.

# WHAT DEPRESSION AND ANXIETY MEAN TO ME

Even though I have never suffered severely with anxiety and depression, I wanted to share with you how they have made me feel. So here we go.

Anxiety and depression made me feel all alone, and like a BIG DARK BOTTOMLESS HOLE had opened up beneath my feet everywhere I would go. With each step I would take, the anxiety and depression would drag me further and further down into its depths and continue to suffocate and consume me. I wanted to climb out of that hole. The longer I focused on the negative thoughts and emotions I was having, though, the more they kept pushing me further and further down until that hole swallowed me up and made me its prisoner.

On the inside, I felt like a blackened-out empty shell of a man, while to the world around me I put a smile on my face and pretended everything was all right. That was very hard for me to do when I was bombarded by society rubbing my face in what I could never have. Everywhere I looked I would see people living their lives full of love and laughter, falling in love and living happily ever after, with not a care in the world. And I would look at my own life and think, 'What have I got to offer the world? I'm just a joke to everybody who nobody takes seriously. Who would ever love me? In their eyes I'm just that weird pirate guy who got beaten up.'

One of the lowest points of my anxiety and mild depression was caused after I had been assaulted and put into hospital. At that point, I felt a lot of people hated me and were happy to see that I had been attacked, especially that one guy who was sniggering at me when he saw me getting into the ambulance covered in blood, I will never forget that. I also feared for my own life because I thought specific individuals wanted to kill me! You see, I kept thinking a group of men were going to beat me up or murder me when they would see me on my own! All those thoughts of anxiety I was having, kept spinning around inside my head. They made me feel sick to my stomach and empty on the inside. I didn't want to see anybody or do anything. I just wanted to be left all alone. I was in a bad place; I was an emotional mess and petrified every time I went out in public. And I could have quite easily slipped into a deep depression if I wasn't careful. When I went to work with my dad after I had been assaulted, I would go to the work van to get some kit for the job we were doing, and I would always feel nervous and anxious being out on the street on my own; I would continuously look over my shoulder just in case somebody was coming towards me with a knife or looking out of their windows pointing a gun at me! I feared for my life, and everything was getting too much for me; I was at the lowest I had ever been.

My dad feared for my safety as well, and always told me to get a taxi home after I had been on a night out in Market Harborough at the weekends because he said, 'You just don't know who's lurking about in the streets or alleyways when you're walking home on your own, so always get a taxi back.' So, I always did, purely out of fear of somebody attacking me from out of nowhere and beating me to death! Then my mind switched off because everything was too much for me to handle, and my attitude turned decidedly negative; I didn't know what to do anymore. The best way to describe how I was feeling is that feeling you have when you have just lost somebody close to you. And that emotion coursed through my mind, body and soul every minute and every hour of the day.

After being assaulted and receiving hate messages on social media from people threatening me, my depression and anxiety really kicked in, and that's when that BIG DARK BOTTOMLESS HOLE appeared at the bottom of my feet everywhere I would go. Anxiety made me feel like my head was a mass of jumbled up thoughts and emotions I couldn't control and that nobody liked me. When I was out in public and I heard somebody laughing with their friends, I presumed they were laughing at me; I felt I was being ridiculed because of my appearance. And that only added to my anxiety and how I felt on the inside. I just wanted to scream from the top of my lungs, 'WHY ARE YOU LAUGHING AT ME, DOES MY APPEARANCE AMUSE YOU? YOU DON'T KNOW WHAT I'VE

BEEN THROUGH IN MY LIFE!' And I thought people were going to start on me when I was out with my friends at the weekends. My mates would always tell me to calm down and tell me that nothing is going to happen, nobody is looking at me and that I was getting paranoid because of what I had been through. My body language back then was terrible; even my friends noticed how I was acting, and the negative attitude I was portraying to those around me.

What I have learnt when you feel your anxiety coming on when you're out in public is to concentrate on your friends and the people you're with – To listen to what they're talking about – To give them your full and undivided attention – To contribute to the conversations you're in with them, and most of all, to laugh, smile, have fun, and be happy that you're alive and out enjoying your life with your mates.

I would always push the negative thoughts I was having about people wanting to beat me up and murder me when I was out with my friends, to the back of my mind, where, unknowingly to me, they would fester away. And I would start thinking to myself, 'I'm worthless, I'm pathetic, I live at home with my parents, and I'm a grown man who should have a wife and family by now. There must be something wrong with me because nobody likes me.' What had society done to make me feel this way? Oh, of course, it was the small-minded idiots who liked to treat me like dirt, walk all over me and assault me for no reason! Escapism was going to be my saviour, and that's where I went, so I hid away in my own little world where nobody could bully, hurt, laugh or ridicule me anymore. I just wanted to be all by myself, and not have any communication or connections with anybody. Being on my own in my room, felt like the safest place for me. In the end, it was my sanctuary.

If I had carried on isolating myself away, I would have driven myself into a mental breakdown. Eventually, I would learn who I was as a person on the inside, and over time I would realise the world around me didn't have it in for me, and nobody wanted to kill me; I came to the understanding that I was stuck inside my head with the negative thoughts I was having.

I knew, with enough determination, I could change my negative attitude and that I could pull myself out of that BIG DARK BOTTOMLESS HOLE of anxiety and depression I was in! So, I looked for guidance to my dad, who has always been my inspiration and the most positive man I know. And that's when I threw my hands in the air and grabbed hold of that rope which had appeared at the bottom of that HOLE OF DESPAIR. Then I mustered up all my courage and resolution and, bit by bit, I pulled myself out of that PIT OF DOOM I had been in. It didn't matter how many scrapes, insults, bruises, bullies, cuts and assaults I received on my way back to the top because the small-minded people who didn't like me weren't going to stop me from climbing out of that BIG DARK BOTTOMLESS HOLE. I knew I was worthy and that I deserved to live a happy and positive life full of love, happiness and support from my family and friends, who I knew I could count on to be there for me! Now I was back I had a purpose and a mission to spread my message of love, hope and encouragement to everybody who had ever felt like I used to feel.

After I had reached the top and climbed out of that BIG DARK BOTTOMLESS HOLE of anxiety and depression, that's when I focused on doing something I was passionate about, which was making videos on social media. The videos I have made have helped me no end to conquer my fears.

I went to speak to a counsellor after I was assaulted, and the counsellor asked me how I was feeling, as well as a series of questions about my mental state of mind and the world around me. I'm happy to say the counsellor said I had an excellent attitude and I was doing well after everything I had been through. Although I think I went to see the counsellor too soon, if I'm honest, because my emotions were still all over the place. Looking back, I think I was hiding how I genuinely felt on the inside. By going to that one guidance session, though, it did give my morale a real boost.

You and I are here to help one another through the low times we face. And also to make sure there is somebody there who is going to throw that lifeline down that BIG DARK BOTTOMLESS HOLE we may regrettably find ourselves in when we least expect it.

Music, family and friends were all key factors that kept me strong while I was going through my mental health problems.

One thing I'm happy to say is I never once had any thoughts of committing suicide; life's so precious to me, and I love being alive. I always knew when I was in that BIG DARK BOTTOMLESS HOLE that I wanted to live a happy life. Being surrounded by my loving family and friends is extremely important to me. And I'm pleased to say I'm in a fantastic place in my life right now.

Always be there for your family and friends if they are having suicidal thoughts.

Hope for the Day's website has loads of excellent information and resources for individuals suffering from mental health issues, which you can find at www.HFTD.org. Now here are Hope for the Day's six ways you can be supportive to somebody you know who might be suffering right now.

LISTEN: Let someone really express their experiences. Being someone they can talk to is essential when giving support

BE NON-JUDGEMENTAL: Don't criticise or minimise the way they feel. You may not be able to understand exactly what they are going through, and that's OK

ASK WHAT, NOT WHY: When you ask questions, avoid asking 'Why' questions, and instead ask 'What questions.' Asking why can have a judgemental tone, even if you don't mean it that way

GIVE INFORMATION – DON'T DIAGNOSE: Don't assume they have an illness or condition. Provide direction to resources that can identify and treat mental health issues

ACT AS A BRIDGE: You can connect someone to mental health resources. Resources include family, school guidance, mental health professionals and organisations like HFTD

TEAMMATE IN SUPPORT: Being supportive doesn't mean your duty is to 'fix' someone. Mental health is complicated, and solutions aren't overnight. As a teammate, the best support you can give is by being a trusting ear, helping to navigate resources, and acting as a source of encouragement

# HOW DOES ANXIETY AND DEPRESSION MAKE YOU FEEL?

Everybody experiences anxiety and depression in their own way, so to get a clearer picture of how these mental health issues affect other people, I asked my friends on social media the following question.

How would you best describe depression and anxiety make you feel? And have you learnt any tips and tricks to help you cope with them?

Depression makes me feel numb. Like I couldn't care less if I died. And if I did, it would do the world a favour. Makes me want to hide from the world, that I have nothing to offer. Anxiety makes me feel like I'm annoying everyone. I care too much. I overthink EVERYTHING. I think everything I say or do is annoying and that I'm in the way. It destroys my confidence. Makes me feel lost and uncertain. Having both of these things makes me feel like I'm trying to breathe underwater, that I'm being suffocated. Sometimes it was too much, and I turned to self-harm to turn my brain off from the nasty thoughts inside my head. I know now that's unhealthy, and I'm still battling not doing that. But luckily, I have some supportive people in my life. And I am grateful for that.

Delina, Australia, instagram.com/delinadamage

Worthless… Even if I anchor feeling depressed, I will always carry depression with me. It will so easily raise its ugly head. I have learnt to cope with it. Practising the 'Art of NOW' and learning to show, COMPASSION, to myself, as well as to other people.

Maria, Finland

Depression for me is, I find myself unable to be happy. I don't feel like getting out of bed. And I hate myself for not getting out of bed. I either don't eat at all, or I eat everything. I don't feel like being creative, because what's the point when I'm not good enough. I feel like I'm a burden on everyone I know. But I need to talk to them because they make me happier.

Morgan Rockanne, Michigan, USA
instagram.com/morganrockanneofficial

First, depression feels like an overload of sadness. Eventually, you feel so sad that it grows into numbness, and you start to feel like you have no energy. Then, most of the days go by without you noticing it, and it becomes more and more crap. After a huge amount of time, all you will want to do is to get to bed, which could result in oversleeping as well. Anxiety, on the other hand, causes irritability, and it easily makes me sad within a couple of seconds. Anxiety is always there, and it can really easily trigger a panic attack, which makes everything worse. I also think that depression and anxiety never really goes away, it's always there, but with time, people will be able to control it. It's hard, but life is hard. I turned my depression and anxiety into workouts, and I was able to lose 20+kgs.

Zsófia Nagy, England, originally from Hungary,
instagram.com/punk_rock_prom_queen

You have been one of the few people who have boosted me up when I was down Steve. Well, in my life, I've never had anyone. Well, yes, I did, but for a short time, but mostly never had anyone I could turn to, but I'd help others with their depression! Anxiety is a whole other beast! Because there are social, intimate, and lonely anxieties! So, with that, I try to tell people to take it easy and make steps towards getting used to it. I used to have severe anxiety over being photographed, so I made IG, and posted a pic a day, and six months later, I got over it! But with depression, when it overtakes me, I try reaching out but I also, don't wanna be a burden. So, I try to find stuff that makes me laugh or find something that consumes me, so my minds occupied! It's always about taking little steps because the whole picture is way too much for anyone, but bit by bit, it's not so bad. There will be struggles but keep at it, and you can beat the anxiety!

Raziel Necronomicon, USA,
instagram.com/raziel.necronomicon

Powerless and weak, deep breathing, yoga, eating healthier, positive affirmations, and trying to let go of negative self-talk have helped me feel a little better.

Joshua Pipes, Ohio, USA, instagram.com/jpipes32

Like I can't do anything, and I have no energy to try. I have no motivation to make art or see my friends. I never want to go anywhere or do anything. I hate myself for not trying to make myself feel better when I feel hopeless. And anxiety just makes it worse by always feeling like something is wrong or going to happen. Waking up in fight or flight mode every morning trying to calm myself down and remembering that I'm ok. But it's gotten a lot better.

Bri Heartbreak, North Carolina, USA,
instagram.com/hintofsadness

Very scared, alone, guilty and drained. It didn't matter who I was with, or where I was. There was always a barrier in front of me, stopping me from being happy or letting anyone close. Just in case I was hurt again. I felt like people were judging me because I didn't smile or laugh with them, they didn't understand that I couldn't, so people started to leave me alone, nothing was funny to me. I was too tired to laugh or smile. I just wanted to sleep, but I couldn't with all the thoughts spinning around my head. I felt guilty because my children needed me and I had to give my all just to go to them, one thing that I always did during my illness was to make sure they were looked after by me and were happy and still giggling every day. This was my illness, not their's. Yes, I occasionally cried in front of them, but it's a natural emotion. They didn't know why as much as me, but they kept me going with cuddles and seeing them be them, made me a proud, strong mom no matter what else was going on. One thing the illness didn't take away from me, was me being the best mom I could be. I refused the medication and therapy offered as I wanted to get myself through it, which I did, and now I feel stronger than ever.

CJ, United Kingdom,
instagram.com/cjrocks35

Thank you so much to everybody who answered my questions on how anxiety and depression make them feel. I hope you have found my friends' advice and the problems they go through insightful and helpful.

# ANXIETY AND PANIC ATTACKS: MY EXPERIENCES AND ADVICE

Now, here are a few times when I have suffered terribly with my anxiety problems: When I was at school – While I was taking my exams – When I went for my driving lessons and tests – When I've had to stand up in front of a crowd of people and talk – When I've had to use the phone to speak to people, which might make you laugh, but it's the truth – When I've been out in public, especially when I've been in bars, pubs and nightclubs – When my dad had a cardiac arrest, and also when he had cancer; my anxiety levels were off the scale on both of those occasions – When I've thought people were laughing at me, and also, when I thought people wanted to kill me after I had been assaulted.

Q: How would you advise dealing with depression and anxiety? And generally, getting through the troubles life throws at us?

**Claire B. Hughes, Leicestershire, England**

A: Hey, Claire, excellent question, thank you. For me personally, the way I've dealt with my anxiety and depression is to make sure I don't isolate myself away from the world anymore like I used to. I also like to speak to my parents and friends about how I'm feeling and what I'm going through which I find helps me a lot. Facebook and Instagram have also been supportive as well, Claire. You and I have to stay as positive as we can when we're feeling at our lowest, and it's always best to avoid drinking alcohol, because alcohol is a depressant and will only make us feel worse, and we also need to focus on the things we love doing in our lives. I've always dealt with my problems head on, so I suggest facing your fears, writing down everything that goes on inside your head and dealing with each of those problems one at a time. You and I need to look after ourselves when times are hard, and we should surround ourselves with positive people who make us feel good and encourage us to achieve our full potential in life. By taking a walk in the countryside, being creative, doing yoga, meditating, listening to our favourite music, exercising regularly and having a well-balanced diet can also help us in a small way when we're suffering from anxiety and depression as well. Thank you so much for your question, Claire. I hope my answer helps you.

Steven M. Rippin

I feel fortunate I have only had a few panic attacks in my life; some people can suffer from them regularly. If you have ever experienced having a panic attack, you will know only too well what they are like. Panic attacks are brought on by all sorts of stressful or traumatic circumstances; for example, you could be worried about test results from your doctor – The bully at school – Your teacher – Exams – Your boss at work, or you might have a family member who is ill in hospital; on the other hand, you might have been involved in a car accident – You might have witnessed a robbery or a murder – You might have been assaulted, or you might have been threatened or intimidated by somebody. Any number of reasons can trigger panic attacks. They can also be brought on if you have a medical condition, such as having hyperthyroidism, an overactive thyroid gland – Medication withdrawal – Hypoglycaemia, low blood sugar – When you suffer a mitral valve prolapse; a minor cardiac problem that occurs when one of the heart's valves doesn't close correctly, or overuse of stimulants, such as amphetamines, cocaine and caffeine.

Now here are a few signs to look out for if you think you're going to have a panic attack. You start to worry uncontrollably – Your head starts to spin, and you feel dizzy – You start having heart palpitations – You break out in a cold sweat – You feel like you're going to pass out – You find it difficult to breathe and have shortness of breath – Your legs turn to jelly – You start going hot and cold – You feel detached from reality – You have a knotted and sick feeling in the pit of your stomach, and you feel like you're not in control.

The worst panic attack I had was when I saw my dad die on the doctor's examination bed when he had a cardiac arrest in 2014, which, thankfully, my dad survived, and this is how it made me feel: the world around me just melted away and didn't exist to me anymore. I felt dizzy, nauseous; my legs turned to jelly. I couldn't think straight or focus. I broke out in a hot and cold sweat. I was having heart palpitations; my head was spinning, and then I collapsed on the floor. I will never forget how I felt back then. Panic attacks are horrible, aren't they?

The following self-help tips on panic attacks are very similar to the ones I have written about in more detail on social anxiety throughout this chapter. I hope you find them helpful.

- Avoid alcohol, caffeine, smoking, and some cold and flu remedies, because they might have stimulants in them, which are best avoided.
- Controlling your breathing helps because when you have a panic attack, you can become short of breath and find it difficult to breathe. So, learning to control your breathing will help you a lot. It will also help you stay calmer and lessen the intensity of the attack you're having. Also, learning to relax is very important and practising yoga and meditation techniques are a great way to help you as well.
- Connect with your family and friends and don't isolate yourself away from them. It is always good to have somebody to talk to about your problems. Join groups you're interested in, in your local area if you don't have anybody to connect with online.
- Exercising at least thirty minutes every day can help you relieve anxiety, just like dancing, swimming, walking or running can as well.
- Keep your mind active and, if there are any hobbies you have, focus on them.
- And always do your best to get a good night's sleep. Try and

get at least a maximum of eight to nine hours of sleep in a night. Lack of sleep can raise your anxiety and how you think and perform during your day. If you're still struggling to get your panic attacks under control, you should seek medical advice from your local GP, who can recommend the best treatment options available to help you.

One type of treatment your doctor might suggest is called CBT: cognitive behavioural therapy. CBT focuses on the way you think and will help work out what might be triggering your panic attacks. This kind of therapy can help you and your doctor look at what you're afraid of in a more realistic way.

I used to get really anxious when I had an appointment to see my doctor, and one time I got so nervous I ended up breaking out in a hot sweat, and felt all dizzy and nauseous; I thought I was going to have a panic attack and black out right there in the surgery! Luckily one of the receptionists gave me a glass of water, which sorted me out. Then, a minute later, my doctor called me in, and that caused my heart rate to skyrocket, and I went all dizzy and passed out! Sorry, I didn't really; I'm only joking. Luckily, I was able to control myself and I managed to get through my appointment without collapsing; some pirate I make!

Ever since that experience, I have now changed my mindset when I go to see my GP. And, if I'm waiting for some blood test results or to ask my doctor something serious, I'll say to myself, 'My test results are going to come back positive, and even if they don't, my doctor will inform me what needs to be done to get me healthy again.' Or, if something is wrong with me, I'll think to myself after seeing my doctor, 'I'm so happy I came to see my GP today. Now he can get me on the road to recovery to sort my issue out and make me feel better.' Saying these statements to myself has helped me and, after a while of repeating them, I'll stop worrying as much. My heart still beats fast when I'm waiting to see my doctor, though. Whose doesn't; that's just a normal reaction when you visit your GP, isn't it?

So, when you next visit your doctor. Remember, just as soon as you step foot into your GP's examination room, he or she will already be examining you on your body language, how you look, your mannerisms, the expressions on your face, and how you speak to them. So what you want to do is make sure you walk into your doctor's surgery room full of confidence with a big smile on your face, which is precisely what I do now, although I most probably scare my GP as I walk into his surgery room like this, because he's probably thinking I'm ready to burst into a song and dance routine and audition for *The X Factor*!

It's crazy, isn't it? When I was only twelve years old and told I was going to have a tube fitted into my right eye, I wasn't worried one bit; waiting to see my doctor to ask him a question about my manhood, though, I end up nearly having a panic attack and collapsing on the floor in front of everybody in the waiting room. Like, what's that all about? Anyway, before I had surgery done on my eyes, I would think to myself. 'They'll get me right, I'm in good hands here, I can't wait for the anaesthetic; come on, let's get on and do this operation so I can wake up and have some hospital food.' Now that's the kind of attitude you want to have. Unfortunately, I lost that mindset as I grew up. Luckily, though, I have now thankfully regained it. These days I have my anxiety, which contributed to my panic attacks, under control.

# ADVICE ON ANXIETY AND DEPRESSION

There isn't really much you CAN say, but being there for them, encouragement, now that's what really matters, to me any ways. Let them know, that each day they make it through is an achievement and should be rewarded with a smile, hug, food (ha-ha) and even if you can't physically be with them just the fact that you are there talking to them; it means the world to them. I suffer daily with depression AND anxiety, and I have such amazing online friends, who have dropped their entire day just to talk to me about random things, to make sure I'm okay. And I can't forget my girlfriends (all 3 of them) who have done absolutely everything to see me smile. Surround yourself with positive energy, and the output will be something amazing!

**Ginny Cash, Georgia, USA, instagram.com/xtoxic.venomx**

Talk! I've suffered badly recently and wasn't talking enough to those that care about me. As soon as I did open up about how I was feeling, they can then work from that to help. It got to the point that it was affecting my home life, and wasn't fair on my parents, so I went back to the doctor's. The new meds seem to be working. The past few days, I've felt like a new person. I've been enjoying getting up in the mornings now. It's a horrible disease that's brushed under the carpet by too many people and missed, which causes it to be one of the world's biggest killers.

Simon Harrald, Market Harborough, England


This is a message I give myself, as I suffer from both anxiety and depression. If my 90-year-old Grandad, who is severely poorly and doesn't have long left. Can make the effort to stand up and show me to the door when I visit him in hospital, let alone get out of bed. Then so can I. It took him all his might to pull himself up and see me to the door. He is attached to a catheter and a few other things, but he did it. His strength has made me think, never give up and always try.

Lisa Parratt, Market Harborough, England

# GENERALISED ANXIETY DISORDER

Generalised anxiety disorder, GAD, affects millions of people all over the world. And I'll admit I still get anxious from time to time, although I now know how to control it. It isn't always easy for me to do, though, just like anybody who suffers from anxiety problems knows. So, to control my general anxiety disorder, what I do is think positively, calm my breathing and think about the dilemmas that are causing it. Then I'll break the problem down and focus my thoughts on things that are important to me and what make me happy, such as my family and friends. Doing that helps to relax my mind, so I don't lose control and end up having an anxiety attack.

Staying in control is vital when you feel an attack coming on, especially if you find yourself in a situation like I was in when I saw my dad having a cardiac arrest. Unfortunately, though, I didn't stay in control and I ended up passing out on the floor!

If you suffer from generalised anxiety disorder, the widespread symptoms are feeling on edge and worried – Having low energy levels and feeling tired – Struggling to concentrate on work and everyday things around the home – Feeling tense in your back, neck and shoulders, and thinking negative thoughts. If you have any of those symptoms and they're not going away, there's a good chance that you might be suffering from generalised anxiety disorder.

Connecting with people with similar issues to our own through support groups online could help us through some of our mental health issues with the advice they share with us. Now, here is some advice and questions to ask yourself, on the best ways to cope with generalised anxiety disorder. Always connect with your family and friends who you know will be there for you. Make sure, though, whoever you do talk to, that they don't have a negative attitude. A person with a negative manner will only make you feel worse about yourself. So, make sure you talk to somebody who has a positive attitude towards life, which will rub off on you. When you feel an anxiety moment coming on, and your family and friends aren't around, don't worry: try listening to some of your favourite music instead or go for a walk in the country, have a workout, meditate, or do some deep breathing exercises. Those activities should hopefully help you relax and lessen that anxiety moment you felt coming on. One minute I might be feeling anxious about something that's on my mind, and I won't want to do anything or go anywhere. Then I'll say to myself, 'Get yourself in the gym, Steve, don't just lie around here feeling sorry for yourself. Get some hardstyle podcasts on; they always make you feel good and put you in a positive state of mind, COME ON, DO IT.' And, sure enough, once I'm exercising to some hardstyle I feel fantastic in no time. Hardstyle, cinematic, progressive house and trance music all help to clear my mind.

And finally, to help any anxiety moments you feel coming on, take a time out and treat yourself. Just remember my three favourite words: 'Everything in moderation'. Also, pets can be relaxing and may help your anxiety as well.

# DON'T LET YOUR ANXIETY WORRIES GET THE BEST OF YOU

Anxiety and how it makes you and me feel on the inside isn't taken seriously enough. Just because people are unable to see the condition physically, they think you're all right, and you're just having a bad day; how wrong they are, though! Thankfully, so many people nowadays are talking about mental health on social media and in the news, which is helping to make it a more recognisable illness in today's society. So, please, don't bottle your feelings up, if you or somebody you know is suffering right now talk about your problems, because it's OK to not be OK.

So how do you cope when you're worrying about things on your mind that are making you anxious or upset, I wonder?

When you're worrying about something, you might think that you're working out a way to solve the dilemma you're facing, when in reality you're getting nowhere at all. So, when you next start feeling concerned over something, ask yourself: is this a problem I can sort out, and is there a solvable solution to it? – Is the problem I'm facing something that's happening in my life right now? – Is the problem something I think might happen, or am I imagining and overthinking about it? – Is there something I can do to prepare myself for the problem I'm facing, or is it out of my control? – How true do I believe my thought or dilemma to be? Or how untrue do I think my thought or dilemma to be? – Is there a more positive and realistic way of looking at the situation I'm facing? – How likely is it that what I'm afraid or scared of is going to happen? Or how unlikely is it that it will never happen, and what could be some of the possible outcomes? – Is what I'm thinking about helpful? And how will worrying about the problem I'm facing help me, and how will it hurt me? And what would I say to a friend who's worrying about this problem?

It's also a good idea to write down the emotions you might be going through during your week into a diary or a journal so you can get a good look at the kind of thoughts and feelings you have been experiencing. Then you can begin to work out what's been triggering those emotions off in the first place. So, just as soon as you start feeling anxious, panicky or worried, write down what brought that worry on, who you were with and what you were doing at the time. Look at the people you surround yourself with as well, so you can see how they make you feel. If they bring the worst out in you, then maybe it's best to stay away from them and introduce more happy, positive and uplifting individuals into your life instead. Don't let your anxieties take control of you.

# HOW I FELT BEFORE MY DAD WENT INTO HOSPITAL

Before my dad went into hospital for his operation, we both carried on working every day as normal, which helped us both tremendously, and, by keeping ourselves busy, the build-up to the day of my dad's operation came around a lot sooner than it would have done if we had been moping around the house all day long. Every day was a struggle for me personally; I couldn't help but think about what my dad was facing. To help me through those days, though, I would wake up every morning and turn my podcasts on, on my phone, which helped me focus on the day ahead. The atmosphere at home was very tense as well, but we had to stay as positive as we could for each other. Getting to sleep at night was difficult, because that was when I had so many emotions running riot in my head. So, I would listen to audiobooks to help me focus on something else for a few hours as I drifted off to sleep. Listening to those audiobooks at night definitely helped to clear my mind from all the worrying I was doing.

# HOW I FELT WHEN MY DAD WAS IN HOSPITAL

When my dad was in hospital, all I did was worry and get anxious all the time; I kept thinking I was going to lose him. In my mind, I was worrying about the possible outcomes of what could happen and what the future held. Those were thoughts I generated in my head, which hadn't even happened yet, and thankfully never did. When you let your feelings run wild just like I was doing, they will drain you mentally and emotionally. Your energy levels will drop, and you will start to struggle and concentrate on your everyday life. All those things happened to me when my dad was in hospital. After a while I ended up breaking down. I couldn't cope, you see, because I felt emotionally drained, physically and mentally, and my anxiety levels must have been off the scale. Luckily, though, my mum was there for me and helped to calm me down when she saw me in tears one night. My mum was my rock, and I love her so much for helping me through those extremely tough times we both went through when my dad was in hospital. So my best advice yet again is to open up and talk about how you're feeling to your loved ones and close friends when you're going through a turbulent time.

# LEARN TO CONTROL YOUR WORRIES AND ANXIETIES

Getting your homework in on time, paying your credit card bills off and preparing for a job interview are all worries and anxieties you can sort out and solve right away, whereas worrying about the outcome of how you did in an exam, what your blood test results will be, how the operation will go you're having done, or if you're going to get a severe illness one day are all worries out of your control. For the worries you can solve, though, you can start by making a plan of action on how you're going to work through them, then you will start seeing things much clearer and feel less concerned about the difficulties you're facing. When my dad had his two major health scares, those situations were out of my control. I had to put my trust and faith into the medical staff who were operating on him; I couldn't concentrate on anything. I kept myself as busy as I could, though, which was hard to do but by doing so it did help me.

I knew that while my dad was in hospital I had to be there for my mum and stay strong for her, so I embraced all the negative and anxious emotions I was feeling, and I turned them around and focused on being as supportive and as positive as I could for her. And, when times like those arise in your life, all you can do is your very best to face those problems head on and be as positive as you can. And never feel ashamed if you do need to ask your family and friends for their help and support when you need them.

When circumstances are out of our control, they show us what we're made of. I won't lie to you, it's tough, but your real character of who you are as an individual will shine through. Also, you will find out what your strongest personality traits are you might not have known you had and what personality traits you need to improve on as well.

# SOCIAL ANXIETY: TRIGGERS, SIGNS AND ADVICE

Here are the common types of social anxieties that can be triggered when we're out in public, which include: When we think people are staring and judging us on how we look – When we walk into bars and think everybody is looking at us – When and if we have to stand up and give a speech in public – When we meet new people, go out on a date or take exams – When we make small talk with our family, friends or strangers – When we think we're going to embarrass ourselves in front of everyone – When we find ourselves in the spotlight – When we're summoned to the office or the headmaster/headmistress's room – Or when we're going to chat up a girl or a guy we fancy.

And here are some physical signs other people might notice about you and me if we're suffering from social anxiety, which include: Finding it challenging to speak to other people, and having shortness of breath – Blushing and going red in the face – Feeling sick and having that horrible knotted feeling in our stomachs – Having heart palpitations and tightness in our chests – Shaking and breaking out into a cold sweat, or we might start feeling dizzy and need to sit down.

And, finally, here are some signs on how we might start acting, because of our social anxieties, which include: Staying at home and avoiding going out to meet our friends during the day – Acting invisible when we're out with our mates, by hunching our shoulders and blending ourselves into the background so nobody notices us – Always wanting to be with somebody, no matter where we go, because we don't like doing things by ourselves anymore, or we might start becoming dependent on alcohol before we go out to steady our nerves. Never become dependent on alcohol; stop and break that habit straight away. The last thing you want to do is turn yourself into an alcoholic; also, don't turn to substance abuse to escape your problems either!

Again, it's an excellent idea to go and see your local GP if social anxiety is having a significant impact on your daily life. What your local GP will do is ask you how you're feeling, what kind of things you like doing, what interests you have, and how you act in social environments. If your local GP thinks your social anxiety is severe, then he or she will refer you to go and see a mental health specialist, who will do an assessment on you and go through all the various treatment options that are available to help you with your condition. Hopefully, though, things won't get that bad.

Always stay in the NOW, instead of thinking, 'What if I make a fool of myself and people laugh at me when I'm out in public? What if people judge me? What if I don't know what to talk to my friends about? What if people stare at me? What if people don't like me?'

As you can see, all the above questions contain the words 'What if' and things which haven't happened to you yet. So, change those 'What if' outcomes into more positive 'What if' outcomes instead, just like my good friend Morgan Rockanne practises.

I suffer from Social Anxiety. I'm going to say what works for me. I tend to think in what-ifs, 'What if I f**k up? What if I say something stupid?' My best friend always says, 'What if you don't f**k up, what if you do something great?' You need to try and think this way. It's a lot less harmful.

Morgan Rockanne, Michigan, USA

Fantastic advice there, I think you'll agree. Thanks, Morgan. Also, train your mind to start thinking in the following ways with these statements I have written out below when you're out in social situations which will help you have a positive attitude towards life.

I don't mind making a fool of myself, because that's what life's all about, having fun and joking around. And if I do spill a drink down myself when I'm out in public, so what, it's not worth worrying about, is it. And if I trip up and land on my backside as I walk into a bar, I'll stand up, bow and say, 'Thank you, my next performance will be in an hour's time,' then I'll walk away with my head held high hopefully having made a few people laugh, but not at me, with me. And if I chat a man or woman up and they reject me, who cares, it will be their loss, plus I'll have my friends with me to enjoy the rest of my night.

If people judge me on what I'm wearing, I won't care because I know I look awesome, and they're probably just jealous anyway. People judge people all the time, and it won't just be me who they're judging, they're probably judging everybody else around them as well.

I'll have loads to talk to my friends about, such as that new television show, that band I want to go and watch, what happened to me at work this week, the holiday I'm going on next year, that rave I'd love to go to, and that man or woman who I really fancy, also I'll ask how my mates and their families are. I'll never run out of things to say.

So, as you can see, these statements will hopefully help you feel more relaxed when you're out in public, plus it's easy to come up with conversational pieces, isn't it? If you're someone who finds it difficult to start up a conversation with somebody, though, start by asking them about themselves, and what their interests are; it's as easy as that. And if you're out in public and you feel yourself becoming anxious, remember to find somewhere nice and quiet so you can take a few deep breaths to relax your mind.

When you focus too much on how your thoughts are making you feel, you will start becoming anxious, so do something to take your mind off how you're thinking, such as going for a walk, painting, reading a book, calling a friend up or anything at all; occupying your mind will help you snap out of that anxious train of thought you were in. Don't let your anxious thoughts take control of you.

Body posture: if you feel your body posture isn't what it used to be because of your anxieties and you have found yourself slouching, hunching your shoulders and withdrawing into yourself more, that's going to make you feel worse about yourself and won't help your social anxiety. So, start practising better body posture and better body language. Keep your shoulders back, stick your chest out, stand tall, and be proud of who you are every time you look at yourself in the mirror.

When you're walking around, either at home or when you're out in public, imagine you're wearing a gown, the kind of gown that drapes over kings' and queens' shoulders. And imagine that gown you're wearing is pulling your shoulders back and making you stand a foot taller. I've tried this, and it does work. It might sound silly to some people, but you have to have an open mind and believe in yourself. I always feel a lot more confident within myself when I imagine wearing a king's gown. Straight away, my whole body posture will straighten and improve my body language to those around me. And it also makes me feel great on the inside as well as on the outside.

So, go on, give it a go. What have you got to lose? Just imagine that king or queen's gown pulling your shoulders back and making you feel more confident within yourself. And, by practising wearing an imaginary gown over your shoulders, it will hopefully help your social anxiety when you're out in public and give you the self-assurance you deserve. It might feel strange at first when you practise this technique, but the more you do, the more natural it will become. Trust me. I'm a pirate. I'll have you standing up straighter and more upright in no time. Some people even balance books on their heads don't they to help their body posture, so you could try that as well if you like; be careful not to smash anything, though, or your parents, girlfriend, boyfriend, husband or wife will have your guts for garters.

Because I stand out a bit more than most people when I'm out in public, I tend to get a few people staring at me. So, for somebody who suffers from social anxiety, it's imperative for me to feel confident within myself as a person. If I don't, I'll start getting nervous and anxious wherever I am and with whoever I am talking to.

Studies have shown that laughter is beneficial for your mental health and well-being, plus one study mentioned that laughter could even help lower your anxiety more than exercise! Although exercising can relieve your anxieties in the following ways. Exercising can: Distract you from what's on your mind – Reduce and burn away stress hormones, excess energy and tension – Exercising releases endorphins, which help improve your mood, and exercising, walking and running without question benefit you a tremendous amount as well.

Affirmations are also a great way to change your mindset and help improve your mood when practised every day. So, here are a few I say which you can try out too.

'I feel great today, and nothing is going to get me down' – 'I don't worry about what other people think of me' – 'I have so much to be thankful for in my life' – 'I live for today' – 'I will never let negative people into my life' – 'I have loving family and friends who are always there for me' – 'I will only think positive thoughts' – 'I will not let people intimidate, patronise or belittle me' – 'I'm in control of my life' – 'I will always stand up for myself and my family and friends' – 'I love who I am and what I have achieved' – 'I'm just as good as anybody else'.

If you let your social anxiety fears take over your life, they will never go away. What you need to do is address your fears. Like I did when I found myself coming face to face with the guy who had assaulted me. I think I coped with that situation well when my attacker apologised to me, which I didn't know he was going to do at the time. It was very much appreciated on my part. When my attacker approached me, I stood my ground and had no fear, which surprised me, if I'm honest, even though my hands were all sweaty and clammy, and my heart was beating faster than a locomotive steam train! I was also very polite to him, although I did feel nervous the whole time this guy was talking to me. I didn't know if he was going to assault me again! So, as you can imagine, I wanted to get out of that situation as fast as I could. And, even though I wasn't afraid, I could feel my social anxiety levels starting to rise! So that was the first real test my social anxiety was put through after I had been assaulted and I thought, if I could get through a situation like that, then I could gain back control over my fears, and become somebody who other people who had or who were going through similar situations could look up to, which they did, because I started receiving a lot of private messages from people online telling me how much I had inspired them because I had stood up for myself and not backed down or felt intimidated by the perpetrator who had assaulted me!

So always do your best never to avoid situations you know you need to face because you're worried or nervous about what the outcomes might be, such as if you have ever been victimised or assaulted and are afraid of going out into public again. And, if you're scared of taking on a new challenge, push yourself and face those fears that have been holding you back and let go of them. Don't lose out on opportunities through your life because of your social anxiety worries; perseverance, determination and having a positive attitude helped me through mine.

To help improve your overall social anxiety, here are a few simple steps you can take.

- Cut out caffeine. Caffeine acts as a stimulant that can cause anxiety symptoms. I like my coffee, though, but I will only have a few cups of it in a week.
- Exercise at least thirty minutes every day.
- Add more Omega-3 fats into your diet, such as salmon, herring, mackerel, sardines, anchovies, seaweed, flaxseeds and walnuts. They all help support a healthy brain, improve your mood, your outlook on life, and your ability to cope with anxiety.
- Reduce your alcohol intake. Drinking increases your risk of having an anxiety attack and it can make you feel depressed; alcohol is a depressant and can disrupt our thoughts and feelings; alcohol can also have a long-term effect on our mental health.
- Quit smoking. Smoking can lead to having higher levels of anxiety; nicotine is a potent stimulant.
- Get a good night's sleep. You should try and get at least eight hours of sleep in a night. Getting a good night sleep will help you stay more focused and relaxed in social situations, and you will function much better throughout your day as well. If you do struggle getting to sleep though, make sure you keep mobile phones, tablets and game consoles switched off, or out of your bedroom completely. Or you could try listening to an audiobook; they always help me fall asleep much faster.

Say NO to social anxiety; let yourself go and feel free and feel happy: Letting yourself go crazy for a few minutes can be an exhilarating experience for your mind, body and soul. Just like it was for me when I was letting all my frustration out by dancing to DJ Mad Dog and Noize Suppressor vs Rob Gee with their track 'MFFYF' while my dad was having his cancer surgery done. Or you could scream from the top of your lungs, and throw your arms in the air, which is a liberating experience as well. Serotonin, dopamine and endorphins get released from your brain to various parts of your body when you let yourself go crazy for a few minutes. Those chemicals help you feel happier on the inside. It always feels like a weight's been lifted off my shoulders when I've had a mad moment and just let myself go. So, go on and give it a go, just go crazy and enjoy letting all your social anxiety fears out. SHOUT, KICK, PUNCH the AIR with your FISTS and rid yourself from all that negative energy that has been dragging you down for far too long!

# HOW I DEAL WITH MY ANXIETY WHEN I'M WITH MY FRIENDS

Coping with my social anxiety after I had been assaulted used to be very hard for me to do. I would often break down and cry in front of my friends. What they must have thought of me I will never know; I was one big emotional wreck. My mates stuck by me, though, and I will always remember that. Going out at the weekends over the years with my mates has unquestionably helped improve my social anxiety. Nowadays, I like to get out nice and early at the weekends so I can watch the night gradually build up. I also like to get a good view of the room or bar I'm in so I can see what's going on and everybody who's around me, just in case somebody decides to cause trouble. I have developed having this mindset because of being assaulted.

I should point out that it's normal to feel a bit nervous and anxious in certain situations in our everyday lives. So, don't think you're suffering from social anxiety when you feel yourself getting anxious when you're out in public; they are ordinary feelings to have from time to time. It's when and if those anxious feelings start to interfere with your everyday life that you should take action to control them. Also, to help improve your social anxiety, it's a good idea to take up new activities and do things you usually wouldn't do. Doing this, you see, will help your social interactions with people when you're out in public. So, by joining, for example, a fitness class, a gym, a book club, a walking group or anything at all that will help improve your social skills with other people will benefit your social anxiety no end.

Over the years, while I have been going out in public during the daytime and out at night with my friends, I often used to think, 'Oh no, I really stick out here. I feel like everybody's looking at me.' And just as soon as I would start thinking that way, my whole body language would change and I would become extremely nervous. Then my shoulders would hunch over, my head would go down, and I would want to leave the place where I was because I was feeling so self-conscious and anxious the longer I stayed there. And by being in that negative mindset I attracted more people to stare at me, because there I was resembling a pirate, who's supposed to be full of confidence and not give a damn what people think of him, but instead I was coming across as a very timid man, which must have been very confusing to everybody around me.

When you're out with your friends, concentrate on them and don't keep focusing on yourself. Ask them general everyday questions to take your mind off how you're feeling if you feel your social anxiety coming on. These days I have learnt the best thing to do when I know people are staring at me and I start feeling anxious is to relax, take a few deep breaths, put a smile on my face, acknowledge the people who are looking over in my direction and either give them a polite smile or a wave, then focus my attention back on my friends who I'm out with. When you're an alternative individual, people are going to be intrigued by how you look and wonder why you dress the way you do; you have to learn to accept the positive and the negative attention you'll receive. If you're somebody who dresses unconventionally, over time you will get used to people looking at you; they may even ask you for a photo. If that happens, take it as a compliment and enjoy the moment. Don't let your social anxieties hold you back.

Well, that's all the advice I can give you on how I have coped with my social anxiety issues when I have been out with friends in public. If none of my advice has helped you, it might be time for you to seek out professional help from your local GP. Your GP might recommend cognitive behavioural therapy that works best for people who suffer from social anxiety. Cognitive behavioural therapy works on what you think, how you feel and how your feelings affect your behaviour. So, by changing the way you think, when you're in social situations that cause your social anxiety to flare up, CBT will help you feel and function much better in your everyday life.

I hope what I have written has helped you in a small way. These techniques I have mentioned have helped me and they might or might not help you. If they haven't, you will have to find out what does by focusing on your strengths and by talking to your family and friends. And hopefully, they will be able to help you through your issues.

What I have written here have been some of the most anxious times I have been through in my life which have changed me as a person. I still suffer from a bit of social anxiety today, just like everybody does. It all comes down though to how you control it, so it doesn't take over your life. By incorporating the correct methods, your anxiety will lessen when you find out what works best for you. Then all those anxious feelings you might have been having about yourself will hopefully start to disappear gradually. Even if they don't go completely, don't worry, just as long as you feel you're beginning to take back control of your thoughts, then that will be a good sign you have started to learn how to improve your anxieties you might have been having. You have the power from within yourself to face your most anxious fears and conquer them, just like I have.

I'm now in a great place and feel a lot better within myself with my social anxiety, and I hope over time you are able to get yours under control as well. I'm no expert on mental health, as you know, and I can't emphasise enough that, if social anxiety is affecting your life severely, then you should seek out professional medical advice from your local GP, or a counsellor if you think that's the path you need to take to get your life back on track again.

# ADVICE FROM MY FRIENDS ON ANXIETY AND DEPRESSION

Before we get to the advice on anxiety and depression, here are a few tips if you have a friend or a family member suffering from mental health and what they can do to help themselves.

Talk about your anxiety and depression to your family and friends, or your local GP or counsellor – Do something you enjoy doing and what makes you happy – Keep fit and eat healthily – Avoid smoking, alcohol and drugs – Do things to help other people, such as charity work, which will help boost your social skills, self-esteem and confidence – Never be afraid to ask people for help – Treat yourself with kindness and respect – Surround yourself with positive people – Take up meditation to relax your mind – Write down realistic goals you want to achieve – Listen to music – Take a walk in the countryside or along the beach – Have fun – Make sure you don't isolate yourself away from people – Hang out with your mates – Appreciate and be grateful for everything and everybody in your life, and spend time with your family.

Well, I hope those tips help. Above all else embrace life and appreciate every morning when you wake up to the wonders of the world around you. Now here is the question I asked my friends on social media to find out what advice they would give.

Do you know anybody who suffers from anxiety or depression? If so, what advice would you give to help them through it?

I would say, go and talk to your doctor and they will find a counselling group for you to join, which can help you.

George W. Rippin, Market Harborough, England

Don't go through it alone. I hid it from people for years as at the time I felt embarrassed and ashamed. The longer I held it in, the worse it got. As did I. Once I finally spoke to some friends who have/had anxiety issues, I finally felt a sense of relief and the more people I opened up to, the more apparent it was that I wasn't alone. In fact, there were a hell of a lot of people who were in a similar position. Going to the doctors was the next step where I was put on a few different types of medications and various strengths until we found what was right for me. I refused counselling because I just don't like counsellors, friends and family are a much better option for me personally. Don't be afraid to talk about it, don't be scared to go to the doctors (I was incredibly surprised at how helpful and supportive mine was, and still is) make sure you discuss it with friends, so they understand if you can't make it to certain social occasions, having their understanding and support eases your mind if you can't go. Also, (as hard as it is) try not to be hard on yourself, don't blame yourself, or hate yourself.

Ashlee Gardner, Market Harborough, England

Just keep moving forward, the view at the top of the mountain is amazing!

Eddie Davis, Townsend, Tennessee, USA

Remain positive, create a support network of people who you can talk to, and always ask for help as hard as it may be. And remember that the only person that can save you is yourself. I have learnt a lot this past year with my PTSD. And without my change in perspective and being more positive towards life, I wouldn't be where I am today, plus, I have an amazing support network in place, and with them, I know that I can keep on improving.

Clare King, Market Harborough, England

I suffer from anxiety, and while I'm managing it a lot better now, the best advice I can give to people with loved ones who have anxiety is: Be patient. We know you'll have to handle us getting anxious over small things at times. And sometimes the same things, over and over again. Please don't stop telling us it's okay, even if you have to say it over and over. That reassurance can help. Having consistent support can be so, so important to an anxious person, and especially with someone who is patient and won't get angry at us, or tell us we're stupid, or silly, or we shouldn't feel like we do.

LaiLai Berry-Wilson, Leicester, England

I moved to Ibiza 8 years ago. Best thing I've ever done. I've never been in one club. I just do my own thing, and I'm happy as I could be. Paddle-boarding – walks in the hills – beautiful food. I Just stay away from what the general population are doing. If they go left, I go right. I don't have Facebook, don't do Tinder or any of that sheep stuff. Make a plan and go for it. I moved here and had 300 euro to my name. Now I train celebrities, and I'm just off to L.A for a week to get my boxing coach certificate. I use a quote by the Wu-Tang clan to help me, P. E. A. C. E. Positive Energy Activates Constant Elevation. You can do it. Just stick to the plan and don't listen to anybody but yourself. Newspapers – news – soaps – X-Factor, reality tv. All those things have to go. They are all extremely toxic and should be forgotten about if you go to start a new life. Create your own life; don't let the media create it for you. And don't try to please anybody. Be yourself. It's your world; you create your own happiness. Surround yourself with only positive people who want to change and evolve. Also, do daily exercise and watch what you eat. Take control and live a happy, healthy life.

Adam Hart, Ibiza

Talk to your friends or go for counselling. Give yourself a treat every day, preferably in the evening so that you have something to look forward to. It can be a treat as simple as a bubble bath or watching your favourite DVD. If you wake up feeling low, have a note pad by your bed and write down whatever comes into your head, and write for 20 mins non-stop, even if you repeat what you've written. Don't read it back; just put it away. Read self-help books. Louise Hay – You can heal yourself, and Eckhardt Tolle – The power of now is very good. Go to Iyengar Yoga classes. Lastly, when you feel better, you can read those notes and see how far you've come.

Sylvia Slingo, London, England

Yes, I can help with that. Anxiety and depression come from internal learnt behaviours and a lack of belief in one's own thoughts. This makes life complicated and will lead to subconscious beliefs resulting in internal pressure – this fuels negative self-image. Hence anxiety creeps in and leads the mind to believe all is bad. Only the individual has the power to rewire the anxious brain and turn negatives into positives so that a complete life can be enjoyed. Depression is horrible as it descends on you like a dark cloud. You have to realise you're going into a depression and then work hard to steer yourself out of it. Look at it like a car going into a dead-end road; you can either sit and do nothing or reverse the car out. My tip is to write down your negative thought then turn it into a positive thought. It's hard work and draining but works for me. Also, breath and focus on your breath rather than on the negative thought. I hope this helps.

Gordon Harrison, Leicestershire, England

One of the most common misconceptions over depression is not understanding the reasons behind it… yes, there are causes that trigger it: bullying, abuse, mental, physical, verbal, post-traumatic disorder, postnatal depression, grief. There are so many, but depression is an illness, and also the brain produces too much serotonin which YOU CANNOT CONTROL. Taking the HAPPY PILLS, as people call it, all it does is level you out to try and live a functioning life. It doesn't take the issues away. You need help from counselling, loved ones and also others that are going through something similar xxx and talk to people who you trust xx People with depression and anxiety CAN live with it, it's learning the tools to make you do so. I have and still do live with it. My way may not work for all, but I have helped many others along this path. The most common thing over anxiety or depression is that people are too scared to talk about it. People say, oh get over it; it's nothing really, get a grip etc. That's rubbish. You can't do that until you understand it, which a lot of people don't. The first thing to do is REALISE you actually have an issue that YOU CANNOT CONTROL. It's out of your hands. It's your brain reacting to situations that you cannot control. You don't want this to happen. You don't want to wake up and feel this way. It's sh*t, but somedays you do. You cannot control it at all. Life can be amazing and joyous and full of love and laughter. The next it can be a quiet room with the walls coming in.

Heather Smith, Leicester, England

Work out what the trigger is and when it's starting, and what calms it. I used to have it badly. I worked out when the onset was starting and tried many things until tapping my feet was my answer. Nip it in the bud before it goes full tilt. Ten years on, I have it seriously under control.

Warren Lee, Wellingborough, England

A massive thank you to everybody who contributed their answers and excellent advice on how to cope with anxiety and depression. I think you'll agree there has been a lot of fantastic help and guidance here from all of my good friends on social media, which I sincerely hope has helped you in some way, just as it has done for me. With enough determination, perseverance and by keeping a positive mindset, you and I can gain control over our anxiety and depression issues to live a good life. We have to stay strong, never give up, and remember to always believe in ourselves and be there for one another.

# MENTAL HEALTH: DO YOU SUFFER FROM DEPRESSION?

Depression is said to be one of the most common mental health problems people face in England today. You might know someone who is always the life and soul of the party, but behind closed doors it's a completely different story for them because that person might feel like the loneliest and most isolated person in the world; you just don't know how people are feeling on the inside, no matter how well you think you know them.

Mild depression, which I have suffered from and still do from time to time, can be caused by being bullied – Being beaten – Work – Worrying about money – People insulting you, and general everyday concerns, while severe depression can make you feel worthless and suicidal. Depression can be brought on by many things that happen to us throughout our lives, such as – Bullying – Losing loved ones – Living on the streets – Being put into foster care – Being in an abusive relationship – Going through a divorce – Going through a traumatic event – Losing your job, and also, being dependent on alcohol and drugs, feeling uncomfortable in social situations, and giving birth. Furthermore, you might have a higher risk of depression if you suffer from an illness, such as having heart disease, cancer or an underactive thyroid or if somebody in your family has suffered from mental health all their lives.

When, say, you lose your job, or you break up with your partner, if you're not careful depression can grab hold of you, then, before you know it, your life can take a downward spiral; you may even end up turning to alcohol to forget about your problems. Doing that will only make things worse and leave you feeling even more depressed than you were in the first place. So, please, don't become dependent on alcohol, whatever you do! Depression can affect you and me at any age. And if you're like me and have suffered from having low self-esteem and worried about how you come across to other people, this could be another cause of your depression. If it wasn't for this book I'm writing, I would have never understood why I used to feel so upset and down all the time when I was younger. Everything makes so much more sense to me now, though.

Everybody deals with depression in their own way. I dealt with mine by putting myself out there on social media and expressing my feelings in a number of videos I made. It's an exhilarating feeling when I share a video online of how I'm truly feeling to the outside world. Social media has been incredible and has got me through so much in life. I know if the internet wasn't around, though, my family and friends would be there for me. Now, here is a video I made from January 2013, when I was feeling depressed about my eyesight; it's extremely tough for me to watch this video. These thoughts you're about to hear me say to myself still go on in my head today: bit.ly/InsideSteveRippinsMind

Nowadays, I only have depressing thoughts from time to time. They range from what my life will be like when my parents are no longer here to what the outcome will be for my eyesight in the future, and when I see people out in public who bullied and insulted me after I was attacked. Those depressing thoughts will only last a few days, though, then I'll be back to my usual self again, thankfully. If you're having depressing thoughts that last longer than a couple of weeks, though, and however much you try to block them from your mind, you can't because they're always there nagging away at you and interfering with your daily life, then you might have a form of depression you need to address, which could mean it's time for you to make an appointment to see your local GP, who you can talk with to discuss how you've been feeling and what the best course of action is for you to take. That course of action might either be therapy, going to see a counsellor, or prescribing you with medication to help you for a short period, until you have a better handle on your depression. If you think you're suffering from depression, remember depression is rated from mild to severe, and it affects us in many various ways.

Now, here are the symptoms people might be suffering from who have mild depression. They might: Feel irritable or angry – Feel a sense of hopelessness – Have feelings of guilt and despair – Have an attitude of self-loathing – Experience a loss of interest in the activities they once used to love doing – Find it difficult to concentrate at work – Lack motivation – Have a sudden disinterest in socialising with their friends – Start to have aches and pains for no reason at all – Feel sleepy in the daytime – Suffer from insomnia – Have changes in their appetite – See changes in their weight, and they might start acting differently to how they usually behave, for example by drinking more alcohol, taking drugs, and hanging around with the wrong kind of people. So, if you or somebody you know is showing these symptoms, talk to your family and friends about how you're feeling and maybe see your GP if those signs don't improve. It's a bit like my good friend Warren Lee says, 'Nip it in the bud before it goes full tilt.'

If mild depression is the issue, a few lifestyle changes might help, such as exercising, keeping to a regular sleep pattern, eating a balanced diet full of fruit and vegetables, and taking up yoga and meditation. And incorporating these lifestyle changes could help boost your serotonin levels in your brain, which can help contribute to battling your mild depression. Also, doing things you enjoy doing, such as going out with your friends, dancing, reading, taking a short break, playing sport, or listening to your favourite music, can help you as well.

Even though I mentioned a few lifestyle changes that might help, that doesn't mean the mild depression will clear up all on its own. If your symptoms are left untreated, they could gradually get worse over time. So, it's essential to visit your local GP to discuss the signs you or somebody you know might be portraying. Mild depression is said to be challenging to diagnose. And if you went along to your local GP to find out if you're suffering from it, they would do a physical examination and ask you in-depth questions about your health to find out what's causing it. Sometimes it might be an underlying physical health problem you have that's causing or contributing to your mild depression. Your local GP might also do some lab tests on you as well to rule out any other medical health conditions, such as a thyroid function test to see if your thyroid is underactive: hypothyroidism. Or your GP might suggest a psychological evaluation, which is better known as talking therapy or psychotherapy. If you are referred to go and talk to a psychotherapist, they would ask you about your thoughts, feelings and the kind of behaviour you have been portraying. By taking these steps, it can help your local GP work out if you have what they call, persistent depressive disorder, or another condition that can affect your mood, such as severe depression, bipolar or seasonal affective disorder.

GPs can sometimes prescribe SSRIs, which stands for selective serotonin reuptake inhibitors: medication in the form of an antidepressant, which can take up to six weeks to take effect. SSRIs block the reabsorption (reuptake) of serotonin to the brain that makes more serotonin available, but they are more effective in people who have moderate and severe depression. SSRIs might also be used to treat anxiety problems as well. Although taking medication for depression might make you feel better, please remember it isn't curing the root of the problem. That's why it is recommended you go and talk to a counsellor, who can help you find out why you're feeling depressed in the first place.

Now, here are the symptoms people might be suffering from with moderate depression. They might: Have problems with their self-esteem – Unable to be as productive as they usually are – Feel worthlessness and unimportant to the world around them – Feel more sensitive to what other people say to them – Worry a lot more about things.

Moderate depression is pretty similar to mild depression, although it can cause more problems in your daily life, more than mild depression, such as how you function at home, school or work. Moderate depression is more straightforward to diagnose because of how the symptoms have more of an impact on your daily life. When you visit your local GP with moderate depression, you have to make sure you explain ALL the symptoms you have been having so they can accurately diagnose you.

Now, here are the symptoms people might be suffering from with severe depression. They might – Feel down and want to cry – Feel empty on the inside or numb – Have low self-esteem – Have no motivation to do anything – Find it difficult making decisions – Find no pleasure or enjoyment in the things they used to love doing – Feel guilty and worthless – Feel isolated from other people, or become easily irritated – Feel hopeless, helpless or in despair – Start self-harming themselves, or start having suicidal thoughts.

The physical symptoms people might show who are suffering from severe depression can include: Finding it difficult to sleep – Observing differences in their appetite, such as eating less, or comfort eating – Finding it hard to speak, or think clearly – Finding it a challenge to concentrate or to remember things – Having unexplained aches and pains – Having no interest in sex – Having no energy – Moving slowly – Feeling restless or agitated, and they might also feel constipated.

Having severe depression is classed as having mild to moderate depression. The symptoms are a lot more critical and noticeable, especially to those around you, such as family, friends, classmates and colleagues at work. Bad episodes of severe depression can last up to six months or longer.

Depression can sometimes clear up after a while, but it can also come back for some people as well. If you know anybody who has been acting differently lately to how you're used to seeing them act, make sure they know you're there for them whenever they need you. Also recommend that they book an appointment with their GP, who will be able to suggest various medical treatment options that are available to help them, such as SSRIs, CBT, psychotherapy, lifestyle changes, visiting a counsellor or herbal remedies. I realise I don't understand how someone who suffers from severe depression feels on the inside. So, I have only been able to write about so much on this subject as I don't want to put the wrong information out there. Talking to your family and friends and doing things you enjoy doing is vital when you suffer from mental health issues.

More people are starting to talk about their mental health. And that will help medical health professionals understand the conditions many are sadly suffering from in today's society; the more information that's out there on these issues, the easier it's going to be to diagnose. Please remember, somebody you know who might look full of confidence to the outside world and everybody around them might be suffering from depression and full of sadness and misery on the inside, which they don't want to feel; they just don't know how to put a stop to those thoughts and feelings they're having. Also, they might not know how to explain how they're emotionally feeling to their family and friends. They don't want to be a burden to them and be looked down on for not being the strong and confident individual their family and friends thought they were. It's these misconceptions about mental health problems that need to change, so you and I can show people who sadly suffer that it's acceptable to talk about how you're feeling on the inside to the outside world; it's OK to not be OK.

YOU and I will only find out how somebody we know is genuinely feeling on the inside when we talk to them. Remember, always look out for any slight changes in your family and friends' personalities or behavioural patterns that you're not used to seeing them portray. I sincerely hope with the small amount of knowledge I know and have shared with you here through my stories and advice on mental health that I have been able to help you or somebody you might know, if only in a small way.

# ADVICE ON COPING WITH MENTAL HEALTH

To help you and me understand how other people cope with their mental health problems, I asked my online friends what advice they have on these matters and here is what they had to say.

For me, suffering from depression is like being trapped in a lift on your own. The walls are slowly closing in, and you hear the echo of your own voice. In the end, you have to press that button to get help, though. Mine started back in 2015 from a tough break up, I channelled it with all the wrong things from cocaine to alcohol and being involved with football violence, my main problem was becoming addicted to strong painkillers such as codeine and tramadol to block the thoughts out. I was taking 30 codeine at once and ten tramadol's, sniffing up to 4 grams of coke at once plus other substances and drinking from early in the morning till late at night. Until one day, I saw the effect it was having on my family, friends and all my loved ones. I knew it had to stop after my mum found me trying to kill myself, so I sought the help I needed from a doctor, spoke to a counsellor and therapist, and I also opened up to all my friends. Since that day I have had relapses and my downtimes, the thing to remember is depression and anxiety never truly goes, it's like a monkey sitting on your back calling at you, but you need to ignore it and talk.

Thankfully, now I'm a father to a beautiful little boy, and he is my reason for wanting to wake up every morning as I want to give him a better life, so he doesn't make the mistakes I have. I have a strong support network around me of friends and family. Three people in my life truly helped me. They sat with me when I cried or didn't want to be here anymore; they are my three best friends, Benny Corr, Jonny Marabella and Anna Puffett. From just taking me out when I have nothing to cheer me up to sitting there listening to me unleash my pain and aches on them, or even just talking to me to take my mind off everything. So, next time you feel low, stop what you're doing, pick your phone up and phone that one friend or family member you know you can count on, because trust me, it helps, and it's worth seeing your friends and family every day a lot more than it is ending it and knowing the pain and anguish they will be going through. Positively look at life, always try to outweigh the negatives first. If I have helped one person in life from you reading this, I have achieved one more thing in my life. Love, Light, and Peace to you all. Stay Positive and Stay True.

### Simon Harrald, Market Harborough, England

I've battled with eating disorders, OCD and depression since being at school. I think they all go hand in hand for me, as it's all about control. I feel if I had more support from the NHS earlier on, it might have nipped it in the bud. I also don't think there's that much support out there for families who are supporting their loved ones through mental health issues, those in the NHS do their best, but they're just isn't enough resources, and charities like BEAT and MIND are picking up the slack.

### Sophie Webster, Oadby, England

I think the best advice is that everyone is different and has different ways to cope with stuff… there isn't a one thing solves all. I got through mine by running. It gives me head space-time and being out in the fresh air with my dogs helped me, but I know that wouldn't be everyone's answer. Also reading a lot, trying out different things and knowing there isn't an instant fix, so not to be disheartened if you revert and have a sh*t day/week/month/longer. And 'Humans' by Matt Haig, brilliant book, helped me no end, I think you'd like it. And as above, talking definitely helps, you don't always need a professional, a decent mate/colleague that will just listen and not judge or advise but only gives you the time to get to your own answers is just as good xx.

Kelly Eldridge-Smith, Loughborough, England

My son and I suffered depression and anxiety very heavily until we changed to a plant-based lifestyle. It's mind-blowing how changing what we are, changed so much in our physical and mental health. I am a firm believer that food plays a huge part in mental and physical health. One would never think to change their daily diet. If we are raised on a typically processed food lifestyle, we would never link it to our problems, until we reboot the body with healthy foods.

Elicia A. Baca, Colorado, USA

I was diagnosed with depression after the birth of my 2nd son (1995). I was raped, 7-8 yrs ago by an old work friend. My depression took a massive nosedive. I started suffering from anxiety and panic attacks. I sometimes don't want to leave my house. Anyway, I was diagnosed with bipolar after the rape. My mental health team referred me to the necessary people to help me with the tools, to help me through the anxiety, panic attacks and also, counselling, which I needed. Mental health should no longer be a taboo subject, and society needs to learn to accept it and help if they see someone in crisis. I'm a support contact for someone with mental health (as you know Steve Rippin, as you put the person in contact with me) I apparently make my buddy laugh regularly too, laughter can also be a healer. Sometimes, even someone that suffered from a mental health condition, to be a buddy for another mental health sufferer can help, due to the fact they know exactly how it feels to feel alone, etc.

## Karen, England

I would like to add in here the story regarding the young woman I put in touch with my friend Karen. You see, I have a lot of private messages from people on social media explaining their problems to me, and I do my very best to help them with the limited knowledge I know with what I have been through myself. And the young woman I put in touch with Karen told me she was thinking of ending her life, which shocked the hell out of me, as you can imagine! At first, I wasn't sure how to reply to her, because I knew I had to be very careful with what I said, so I opened my heart and told her about the difficulties I have faced throughout my life, which she really appreciated. Then, after we had chatted online for a while, I put her in touch with Karen, who had also been through some very traumatic experiences in her life as well. The young woman is now doing a lot better, I'm happy to say, and she has sought the help she so desperately needed from her doctor. I'm not going to mention the lady's name out of confidentiality; here, though, are a few words of gratitude from her, which meant a lot to me. I'm just so happy I was able to help her when she was going through such a tough time in her life.

Thanks, Steve, your words speak volumes! They hit home. I'm going to try because I can't live like this! I really feel for you. I don't know how you got through it! You are a genuine inspiration, and I respect you for that. I'm going to give it one last chance. You gave life a chance and look where you are! Steve, you should be proud of yourself and what you have overcome! You really may be a beacon of light for me. Thank you for your kind words. But words of reality. Words of reason. You talk so much sense! You really are an amazing person and deserves better. You've come along way now, Steve, you got this. I believe in you. Wow, you are a dude. Thank you for listening to me. But also sharing yourself, which I found really interesting. Steve, I can see that you're a brave bloke; who cares a hell of a lot. You don't let em in. I don't know how you do that. You are a blessing and an honourable man. Forget the haters, live for YOU because it's YOU what counts xxx.

**Anonymous, England**

I feel very humbled when people share their problems with me, and when they do I like to share mine with them, which I think helps those individuals because it makes it less one-sided when somebody does have the courage to open up. And one more story I would like to share with you is when another good friend of mine got in touch on Facebook one year, who couldn't thank me enough because his friend, who he had written to me about, spoke to him about how he was feeling suicidal on the inside, that was until he read my post on Facebook regarding depression. And my buddy who messaged me told me he believes my post saved his friend's life. And now with his permission here is the message my friend sent me about his mate who was feeling suicidal.

Hi mate, I really hope you don't mind me messaging you on here – I just wanted to say an enormous thank you to you for doing what you do. As I'm sure you'll remember, you posted a status a while ago about depression/mental illness and how it helps to talk to people, etc. A friend of mine came to me earlier in the week and admitted to me he'd really struggled with depression and anxiety, to the point he'd planned taking his life, and he said to me he'd read your status and felt it might help to tell me how he's been feeling. He's now under close medical supervision and receiving help for his problems as I was able to make arrangements after speaking to him (he'd like to remain anonymous in everything, so I shall not name him). But he didn't feel ashamed to speak to me after reading your post. He was mentioning about your status, when he first told me, how he was feeling as he said it was so genuine and from the heart, which made him realise that talking, really would help, so I am just so glad he did, and grateful to you for posting! I spoke to my friend about how he was feeling before he opened up to me, and he said before speaking, he felt very isolated, and as if nobody knew how it felt. He also said, he thought people would consider him 'weak' if he was to talk, although, after taking time to read your status he realised this was not the case, and he described opening up to me about things as, 'a weight off his shoulders.' So, I just wanted to say an enormous thank you – without your posts, he may not be here to this day, due to his severe problems, so in my eyes, you have genuinely saved his life. I really do owe you one! Thanks again! You're doing a great job of raising awareness mate, and good on you for that!

Anonymous

Thank you so much, Anonymous, for your message on Facebook regarding your friend. I hope with all my heart that your friend is getting on much better now since he's spoken to you about how he was feeling. He has a fantastic mate in you for being there for him in his time of need. He is an inspiration to all sufferers of depression and mental health problems all over the world for opening up about how he was feeling. He should be proud of himself. If only more people like your friend spoke about their issues, then so many more lives could be saved in the world today. All my very best to your friend for the future, and to yourself. I'm just so happy I was able to help your mate with the post I made on Facebook.

Steven M. Rippin

And here is the post which helped to save my friend's mate's life.

# MY FACEBOOK POST ON CYBER BULLYING

Cyber Bullying: Cyber Bullying is a very serious problem and one I have personally been through where I had my own life threatened. I think tougher laws should be brought in to put a STOP to the very serious acts of Cyber Bullying, where people's lives are threatened, and they are traumatised to the extent of suffering from mental health problems because of it, and also scared to leave their homes. Prison sentences should be introduced or some kind of penalty as well. Some people very sadly, take their own lives because of Cyber Bullying, so something definitely needs to be put into place to ERADICATE this evil problem in our society which we face today! I went to the police with printouts and names of all the harassment I was receiving, which was coming from people in my hometown. So, Don't Ever Be A Victim and Don't Ever Suffer in Silence, Speak Up and Let's Put A Stop to Cyber Bullying Once and For All.'

Steve Rippin, 9 August 2018

I have been diagnosed with chronic PTSD (after birth trauma with my first child). The community midwife was so unsupportive and patronising towards me, we begged for help at the local GP. I eventually saw a counsellor, but she just told me to not think about it as it was unhelpful thinking (I was a total mess). Some people would think I was making a fuss, and that it wasn't a big deal, but I felt like I was dying on the inside and no-one could see it. It was only a helpful Health Visitor, that put me in touch with Home-Start. I could go to a group there and not be judged; it was a great support and the people there understood. A voluntary counsellor at Home-Start helped me, and without her, I wouldn't be here now – she was amazing. Sadly, there aren't enough people to support us; everyone can see a broken leg; no-one can see that your mind is broken. I always take the time to listen to people. And tell people my story – talking helps me. And it raises awareness and might help other people to become more understanding. And also, for other people in need to seek help. I find that doing puzzles, crafting and pottery are a real help to calm the craziness in my head. Just focusing on something creative really helps and gives a sense of satisfaction and achievement, especially if I feel I'm failing elsewhere. I know I'm not failing, it's just the feeling you can't help obsess over. I often don't even want to leave the house, as the thought is too stressful. My emotional brain takes over my logical brain – need to get the logical back in charge again. You're doing an amazing job raising awareness, Steve.

### Kim Oldfield, Market Harborough, England

I suffer from GAD and depression on and off, both of which I have had diagnosed by doctors. I'm fine at the minute. Having researched into it and have been to counselling, I also think I have a category C personality disorder. All of this stems from developmental trauma from my childhood. The earliest memory I have of this manifesting itself was when I was at primary school – I would have been about 5 or 6. I had a school dinner lady who used to force me to eat things, even if they made me gag, and as a result, I developed depression and didn't want to go to school. At the time, it was never acknowledged, or diagnosed as being a mental health issue, and I didn't get help until I was 19, by which point, I had had several bouts of (some pretty serious) depression.

Since then, I have had counselling and been on antidepressants on three separate occasions. Both of which I found very helpful at the time. And I am glad to say; I'm a lot better now. When I suffered worst of all (through my teen years, age 12-17) I just thought I was actually insane, and just an over sensitive pain in the arse, so I didn't think to get help – to me, it was a fault with who I was as a person and something I just needed to stop doing, and not an illness that I needed help with.

I think things that helped me most were – CBT – Art therapy (example: writing postcards to the people upsetting me, telling them what I really thought, of course with no intention of posting them)! – A website called 'No more panic' (a good way to talk to others and gain support anonymously, if you aren't comfortable talking to people you know) – Samaritans (I think people think they are just there if you're suicidal, but that isn't the case) – Antidepressants (although, these are just a splint to help you get by, while you treat the core problem. On their own, they will make you feel better, but they won't fix the actual problem – that's what counselling is for) – The doctors – Counselling (I think there's a common misconception that counselling is costly, but there are a lot of organisation's that will do it on a donation basis if you look for them) – Mind is also very good for sources and for information. I also think it is good to take solace in not feeling alone – whether that means talking to likeminded people in groups or online. Or even relating to a character from a book or a film. I found Ronald Dahl's, Matilda, and Elizabeth Bennett, from Pride and Prejudice, were my inspiration when I was trying to recover. I am a firm believer in this quote, 'You are not responsible for the programming you picked up in childhood. However, as an adult, you are 100% responsible for fixing it. When you blame others, you give up your power to change.' I think to consider yourself a victim all your life and not try to help yourself, is basically giving in to the bullies or your demons, or whatever you want to call them. You should fight them and come out stronger. I may have/have had anxiety and depression, and whatever else, but my god, they don't have me.

By Anonymous

Well, I would like to say a HUGE THANK YOU to everybody who contributed their advice and the struggles they go through with their mental health; it sincerely means a lot. Keep fighting and never give up.

Thank you so much if YOU reading my book right now were one of the lovely people who shared your mental health issues and advice on how to cope with them.

Steven M. Rippin

I have learnt some very valuable information from the advice people have shared with you and me here throughout these chapters on mental health. It has been heartbreaking hearing what other people have been through and are still going through in their lives today. If you or anybody you know is struggling from mental health issues, here are a few helpful links to check out.

The first link is for anybody who has had suicidal thoughts. At the HFTD (Hope for the Day) website, you can find resources and information on suicide prevention. HFTD achieves proactive suicide prevention through outreach and mental health education. Have hope; It's OK to NOT be OK – www.HFTD.org

The Bemindfulonline website is a course you can take that can help you understand your thoughts and feelings better. Bemindfulonline can also help you when things get too much in life – www.BeMindfulOnline.com

And for more in-depth information on mental health, there's the mental health website that will give you a lot more professional advice and guidance than I can – www.MentalHealth.org.uk

Here is a link to a very useful and helpful booklet that is all about mental health, from the various types there are, to preventing it, to treatment and care: – bit.ly/FactsAboutMentalHealth

This next link can help people who suffer from anxiety, panic disorders, phobias and OCD. The nomorepanic.co.uk website offers great support and advice, plus you can make new friends who might be going through something similar to what you're going through right now – NoMorePanic.co.uk

Home-Start is one of the family support charities in the UK, which offers help to families with young children to deal with whatever life throws at them – www.Home-Start.org.uk

And, finally, here is a link to the Mind website, which provides advice and support to anybody who's experiencing mental health problems. Mind's campaign is to improve mental health services, raise awareness and promote understanding of mental health issues. They won't give up until everybody experiencing a mental health problem gets the support and respect they deserve – www.Mind.org.uk

I hope you find these website links helpful. And now here are my closing thoughts on what needs to be done about mental health in our society today in my own opinion. From an early age, you and I are continuously learning and experiencing about the world around us, which is one of the most significant times of our lives. Once in a while, though, we need a little guidance to comprehend what those thoughts are whirling around inside our heads which we don't fully understand yet. So, I believe there should be at least one counsellor in every school to help children from an early age understand what mental health means.

So just as long as the school curriculum gives children the correct coping skills and resources to help them through any problems they have while they are growing up, as well as assisting them not to feel embarrassed or ashamed when speaking about how they are genuinely feeling, then enough children will stand up and question without fear why they might be upset, scared and confused. And then they will hopefully be more open to talking about their issues, instead of bottling up their emotions on the inside. Then, as they turn into adults, they will have a better understanding of what those thoughts were which disconcerted them when they were younger.

You and I need to start building on the communities around us where we live today and, on the relationships, we have with our families and friends who we can confide in. We should also find out what our best attributes and life skills are so we can help either a family member or a friend who is suffering from mental health problems as well; by doing so, we will then make a better future for ourselves and our children. And, at the same time, we will start to get a better understanding of how we can tackle and eliminate mental health for the generations of the future to come tomorrow.

# PART FOUR

PART FOUR

# COPING WITH THE LOSS OF A LOVED ONE

This chapter is very close to my heart, as I can imagine it will be for you. I had to think long and hard on whether I should write about the loss of a loved one, then I thought: you and I should be able to open up and talk about how we are feeling when we lose somebody who meant so much to us, shouldn't we? So, this chapter is dedicated to all those I have sadly lost...

I have lost all my grandparents; my uncle; my cousin, who was only sixteen; and a lot of friends, who I miss very, very much. I would do anything to be able to see them again. It's knowing you're never going to see those who you have lost and the not being able to talk to them or hold them in your arms ever again that hurts the most, isn't it? You can't even begin to explain to somebody who hasn't lost anyone what that pain feels like. Never feel embarrassed to show your feelings to those you love and cherish every moment you get to spend with them. Let them know how much you love them every day.

Also in this chapter I write about my grandparents, who I have sadly lost, who meant so much to me throughout my life; how my online friends cope with the loss of a loved one; my good friend Arron Micklewright, who very sadly took his own life in 2017; and help and advice on grieving.

Live your life and chase after your dreams. You don't know what's waiting for you around the corner.

# MY GRANDPARENTS, WHO I MISS EVERY DAY OF MY LIFE

What a lot of people don't know about me is that I am part Italian, Iranian and English. My mum's mum, Theresa Kirkucki, my grandma, was Italian, you see. And my mum's dad, Marek Kirkucki, was born in Iran.

My grandma, Theresa Kirkucki, was born in the village of Chialina. Chialina belongs to the municipality of the town Ovaro in the province of Udine. Chialina village is on the slopes of Mount Zoncolan, which stands at a height of 1,750 m. In Chialina village you will find the church of San Nicolò, which was built in 1944, and the private oratory of Santa Teresa, of the eighteenth century. Udine, which is close by to Chialina village, is in the north-eastern part of Italy, where there are several art museums which feature works by Tiepolo and Caravaggio. You can also see the impressive views of Udine and the surrounding mountain ranges there; I would love to visit one day.

My grandma was a lovely woman; she was one in a million. When I was younger, I used to try and get my grandma to say certain words. She pronounced specific words in an amusing way because of her Italian accent, which would make the whole family laugh, bless her. And one word, in particular, I used to ask her to say, was Ethiopia. She would always pronounce Ethiopia, as 'Ifinokio'. And just hearing my grandma's voice in my head right now brings a tear to my eye. When I used to visit my grandparents, I would often hear my grandma say to my grandad from time to time, 'What are you do it, man,' in her fantastic Italian accent, while my uncle Nino would say, 'Ah, leave it, mam, he's done nothing wrong, let him relax.' It's funny the things you remember, isn't it? My grandparents were always there for each other and loved one another very much. They were together for over sixty years, you know! How many people nowadays can say that, I wonder! My gran was always so happy to see me when I went around to visit her. And I can picture her face right now lighting up with that beautiful smile of hers. While my gran and I would sit there in her lounge together, she would tell me stories from her past, of when she used to live in Italy; I always loved hearing those stories. I think she used to get up to some tricks, bless her. My gran also told me her family's distantly related to Madonna somehow. My gran's maiden name was Deprato, you see. And one of my gran's relatives had the surname Ciccone, which is the same surname Madonna has. So somewhere along the family tree is the Madonna connection. Although none of my family or I have ever met Madonna. And I doubt, very much, Madonna knows we even exist.

My gran never wanted for anything in life and was happy with what she had; she also had a strict upbringing when she was younger, but never moaned or complained about anything. Even when she fell ill in her later years, she kept a smile on her face and got on with it. She appreciated all she had, especially her loving family. When I was young, I remember my gran and grandad taking me into Leicester to a jumble sale; they both loved jumble sales and looking for a good bargain, bless them. Then, later on in their lives, they enjoyed doing car boot sales on Sunday mornings as well.

When my grandma came over to England, she spent most of her life working at Weddel Swift, which is a distribution company for the frozen meat industry; she worked extremely hard there. My gran was unquestionably one of the hardest working women I've known, and there wasn't a day went by that she didn't go into work.

I love you so much gran. You're never forgotten, and you're always in my thoughts. My parents and I talk about you and the great times we all shared often, especially that time in Italy at Hotel Frank, when my dad pushed you into the swimming pool! Until we meet again. I love you.

Steven M. Rippin

My mum's dad, my grandad, Marek Kirkucki, came from Kirkuk, which is a city in Iraq. He was a real gentleman and was always so laid back, with a big smile on his face. My grandad's father was a policeman, who was sadly shot in the line of duty. And when my grandad was ten years old his mother strapped a money belt around his waist and sent him away on a bus! He then had to live and fend for himself on the streets, where he had an extremely tough time. My grandad eventually ended up in a Polish camp in Kirkuk, where a Polish family took him in and raised him as their own. My mum's family and I have so much to thank that Polish family for; unfortunately, though, we have no idea who they were. Because my grandad couldn't remember what his surname was, the Polish family who took him in gave him the surname Kirkucki, because they found him in Kirkuk. My grandad arrived in England on 12 December, which is the same date as my birthday. Unfortunately, this is all we know as my grandad's past is very sketchy.

My grandma and grandad were amazing together, and they would always put a smile on your face when you saw them.

My grandad had a fascinating life and was never educated, but he learnt to speak three different languages: Italian, Polish and English. And there I was at school trying my best to learn the French language, and I only got graded a G after five years of studying it! My grandad also worked as a lorry driver most of his life, and when he retired he worked for the local council, where everybody loved him. People used to love being around my grandad because he was one of those individuals who would always make you feel relaxed when you were in his company. I loved my grandad very much; he was so kind, happy, caring, generous and loving. My grandad was without a doubt one of the nicest men I have ever met; nothing was ever too much trouble for him, and he would always love to feed you.

My grandad never knew his real age, and sadly none of my mum's family know anything about my grandad's parents, so there has never been a way of finding his true age out.

I used to give my grandad lots of shoulder massages when I went around to see him, which he loved. And he would often say to me, 'Hey, Steven, can you come here and rub my shoulder for a minute, please.' Although those shoulder massages never lasted for just a minute because when I'd stop my grandad would say, 'Aw just a few more minutes please, Steven,' then half an hour later he'd be happy, bless him. Giving my grandad those shoulder massages and listening to his stories from his past are the times I miss the most, and of course hearing his fantastic laugh.

> I love you with all my heart, Grandad. I always think of you, and how kind-natured and loving you were to your family and me. I hope to be half the man you were, with your happy and loving attitude towards life. I'm so proud to call you my grandad. See you again soon. I love you.
>
> **Steven M. Rippin**

On a side note, it does upset me when I hear how some people I know talk about foreign people who live in England. What they don't realise is that my mum and I are both part Italian and Iranian. So, are those individuals saying that my mum and I should leave the country we were born in just because we have foreign blood flowing through our veins? I have found people from other countries are very hard-working and do our country an excellent service. Just look at all the Polish delivery drivers; they work all hours of the day, so you and I receive our parcels we order online. My grandparents, who were both from abroad, were very hard-working citizens of the United Kingdom when they were alive and, between them, they created a lovely family. So, I believe just as long as people who do come to England from other countries respect our laws, respect the way we live our lives, respect our culture and, most importantly, show respect to our citizens there shouldn't be a problem.

My dad's parents were both English; my dad's mum, my grandma, Catherine Zeta Nash, was born in 1926, in Pune, which is the second-largest city in India, and was once the centre of power of the Maratha Empire, which was established by Shivaji in 1659 from the victory at the Battle of Pratapgad. My dad's mum was born in India because her dad served in the King's Royal Rifles during WWI, where he was wounded by shrapnel in his shoulder and arm, and also where he was gassed before being transferred to the Shropshire Light Infantry after the war. My grandma sadly passed away the day before my second birthday, when she was only fifty-one years old. My dad told me my grandma was a lovely lady; I just wish I'd had the chance to have got to know her.

> I love you so much, Grandma. I just wish we could have had more time to have got to know each other and created many special memories together. I hope we are reunited again one day so I can hear all about your life in India. I love you.

Steven M. Rippin

My dad's dad, Gordon William Rippin, was born in Melton Mowbray in 1925, at Mapperly Terrace. He was an ex-Coldstream Guardsman, who served in the Oxford and Buckinghamshire Light infantry, which existed from 1881 until 1958. And my grandad's brother, George Herbert Rippin, sadly died in action in Italy in 1943, at the age of only twenty-two. He was a lance corporal in the Coldstream Guards and was buried in Monte Casino, Italy. My dad told me my grandad was wounded by mortar shrapnel while he was in the Reichswald forest towards the end of the Second World War in 1944, and when a couple of soldiers came across my grandad lying on the ground they thought he was dead. So, they put him in a shed with all the other fallen soldiers, then a few minutes later my grandad woke up wondering where he was! Luckily, one of the soldiers on guard saw my grandad moving around in the shed and said, 'We've got a live one here!' I can't even begin to imagine what that experience must have been like for my grandad when he came around to find himself in a shed full of dead soldiers all around him! Thankfully that soldier on guard saw my grandad moving around that day!

When my grandad returned home from the war, he found himself a job working on a building site, and when he wrapped himself up to keep warm in the winter months, he got nicknamed Nobby, because his nose would always turn bright red. That nickname stuck with my grandad for the rest of his life! He then went onto work for Pet Foods in Melton Mowbray, as a production service operator.

My grandad was a bit of a character bless him, and he would always be smiling, watching cartoons, messing about, laughing and cracking jokes when I went around to visit him; he had a fantastic sense of humour. My dad told me he would often hear his dad saying things like, 'Did you hear about Doris down the road boy, she died last week didn't she, and guess what: she never did return that tin of yellow paint!' That's just the kind of sense of humour my dad's dad had. My grandad was a very happy, upbeat and positive guy, and I miss him very much.

I love you with all my heart, Grandad, and I will never forget that fantastic sense of humour you had. Whenever I think of you, I always picture you laughing away pulling funny faces and watching cartoons. Oh yeah, that reminds me: do you still have that country and western record I lent you when I was twelve years old? I never did see it again! Only joking; I hope you enjoyed listening to it though. Grandad, I love you.

Steven M. Rippin

It's funny to imagine that, if certain events hadn't happened, such as if it hadn't been for my mum's mum and dad coming over to England, and my dad's dad being found alive in that shed, my parents would have never met, and I wouldn't be here today. It has been incredibly difficult writing about my grandparents and looking back on their lives. At the same time, though, it has been lovely thinking about them and remembering the good times we shared together, as well as remembering what they accomplished and went through.

I also very sadly lost one of my cousins, Ian, when he was only sixteen years old; I would have been fifteen at the time. Ian was in a car accident, you see, and sadly he didn't make it. It was and still is very difficult for me to get my head around why Ian was taken away from us at such a young age. Sadly, I didn't get to know my cousin very well. I did get to know his dad, David, though, who was also sadly taken away from us at the age of only sixty-one. David was my uncle, my dad's stepbrother. David was a real down-to-earth guy and easy to get along with. I miss Uncle David a lot.

Cousin Ian and Uncle David, wherever you are, I'm still thinking of you both and love you very, very much.

Steven M. Rippin

Life can be so cruel; it gives, then it takes away those who we hold close to our hearts and leaves us heartbroken and feeling empty on the inside. As they say, though, the passing of a loved one gets easier over time, and, although you never entirely get over the loss of somebody close to you, you have to learn how to cope as best as you can. It's the little things during your everyday life that can sometimes remind you of your loved ones, isn't it, such as hearing a piece of music, or when a memory of them pops into your mind unexpectedly? My dad told me once, while he was lying down on his bed one afternoon, a butterfly flew in through the window and landed on his hand, and straight away he thought of his mum. That butterfly visited my dad three more times that day, and my dad believes that butterfly was his mum coming by to say hello to comfort him. I know many people might not understand that, but only when you have lost somebody close to you will you genuinely comprehend how you can see your loved ones in many various shapes and forms all around you.

# HOW PEOPLE COPE WITH THE LOSS OF A LOVED ONE

Here follows advice from my friends on social media with guidance on coping with the loss of a loved one. The stories you are about to read are very emotional and heart-warming; they brought a lump to my throat, and, I don't mind admitting, they also brought a few tears to my eyes.

> Having lost loved ones, it's hard, very hard, but as time passes, it does get easier, you have to think of the happy times you had together and talk about them. I miss saying, 'Mom.' When I'm on my own, I will say, 'I love you mom', or I will wish her a happy birthday. It may sound funny but saying it out loud feels good.
>
> George W. Rippin, Market Harborough, England

> I would tell them to do EFT (emotional freedom technique). It quickly heals the pain of loss. After tapping (another name for EFT), the grief is gone, and the love remains. It's like a miracle, and it's literally at your fingertips.
>
> Heather Ambler, USA, instagram.com/the30daytappingchallenge

> Always remember that the person who you've lost lives on in you and your children. Look out for little things such as robins, butterfly's, feathers, or, even a type of music they used to listen too,

always means that they are close by. That always makes me smile. Eventually, things do get easier, and it's always ok to have a cry xx.

Kathryn R. Dickenson, Leicestershire, England

Hi Steve, lost dad years ago, he was 47, he took his own life. It's been hard to cope with this all these years, as my dad was a beautiful, caring man. He would talk to people and would help anyone. Years have gone by supporting mam through things. Mam was not just my mam. She was my best friend. We went and done lots of things together. She became poorly four years ago, she started having tests, and found out she had lung cancer, this then went to the brain over the next couple of years, I lost her early February. This was the biggest pain I have ever felt; part of me has gone with her. I feel I'm not the same person anymore even though I try to do the things I like or did with mam. Part of me isn't there anymore. I remember mam in everything, the days out and her laughter. I saw her in pain, and when she was confused. It's hard to say how do we cope with losing a loved one. I don't think we ever do cope. I am always looking for ways to connect with her in a sign of a feather, or a robin. Or a gust of wind when I'm standing at the beach. It's a longing I long for, and a pain I cannot get rid of. I know she wouldn't want me like this, so I do try every day to find the me I was when mam was with me.

Maxine Sirs, Hartlepool, England

I think the main thing is that there is no blueprint on how to deal with loss. Everyone will react differently, and there is no right or wrong way to grieve. Some people go to grief counselling, some to therapy, some may throw themselves in work or even exercise to clear the head of sad thoughts. Of course, there will be good days and not-so-good ones. It is important to have friends and/or family to support you, so you don't go into a 'dark place' (drugs/alcohol/depression) and people who you can talk to. Even if they just listen, that is fine too.

Shaggy, USA, instagram.com/shaggywaggys

I know it's probably wrong, but I try to use the visual of my relatives out enjoying a grand vacation or working out of town. It makes things feel not quite so permanent. It's probably denial, but it works for me. I also try to do things that they enjoyed or share stories about them with my son.

Melissa, USA, instagram.com/mshoneybee73

I think everyone grieves in their own way when they lose people that they love. I have lost my parents and my three brothers. Even though it's been years ago now, I'm still very sad at times. I'm not sure if you ever really get over that kind of loss. I just try to get through each day and remember the wonderful times I had with them. I know they wouldn't want me to be sad, but I can't help missing them every day.

Debbie Barnard, Booneville, Arkansas, USA

My Grandad passed away on the 1st of Feb 2017, he was practically my best friend as well as family, to this day I still feel the pain of losing him, I will say my best advice is to let your emotions out, Cry, shout, get angry at the world and feel however you do feel at the time deeply, hold close the memories and thoughts of the good times, let go of the bad. Talk to others close to you, share good or happy stories with others who knew them (It may make you cry like it does myself, but it's a good kind of cry) Always keep in mind they live on through the family and friends, and they will forever be in our hearts! R.I.P Granddad Tommy, rest easy, p.s, it was quite emotional writing and thinking about this, but I am happy I get to share my experience and feel those emotions again, as it reminds me of him.

Samuel J.T. Conway, Leicester, England

Firstly, remember that there is no rule book dealing with grief... everyone deals with it differently, losing a child, parent, or friend, there is no right or wrong, but YOU MUST let it out somehow, in whatever way or comes to you, and as much as you miss their voice, their touch, know that one day, you will meet again in any way shape or form. My husband lost his daughter 6 years ago to cancer, aged 17 xxxx they are around you, they just can't be seen in a physical form, white feathers, robins, butterflies, music that comes on when you're thinking of someone etc., a feeling that you're seeing something out the corner of your eye, certain smells you can't explain etc.

Heather Smith, Leicester, England

There is no rule for grief. You may constantly cry or not at all. You may be angry or laugh at the memories. My wonderful father died unexpectedly in February (2017). I know I am in denial. I cannot bare to think I will never see that wonderful man again. He is on holiday to me. You don't get over mourning your loved one; you just adjust to living with the pain.

Heidi Kirkland, Leicestershire, England

I lost my dad 21 years ago. And when he first passed, I couldn't grieve fully xx Took me about 10 years after to completely breakdown xx Now I talk to him daily, usually when I'm on my own xx I think of him daily, and always see things that are significant xx Sunday morning, I saw a robin xx I said hello dad, and it came nearer xx I was just chatting away to a robin xx He came back three times in all, but I always see that robin xx And that gives me both, hope and strength xx We all deal in different ways, but my only regret, is that I didn't grieve earlier xx.

Lynda Shepherd, Leicestershire, England

It's ok to grieve. Let it out. Cry, get angry, go through the phases of grief. It is ok, and it is going to be ok. Once the grieving process is over, remember them and celebrate them, always celebrate them. The sadness never goes away, but it does get easier. Love them and celebrate them, and never forget. I first lost my mom over ten years ago to health, and this is how I handle her loss. When I lost my stepbrother and his wife, in the Brussel's Airport bombing, I continue that tradition. I also go out and do a random act of kindness to celebrate their memory too.

Erin A. Shell, Florida, USA

My simple advice comes down to something I have learned from many deaths in my life, 'Let their legacy live on through you.'

Matt Werner, Silverdale, Washington, USA

When I lost my brother out of the blue on Christmas morning – he went to bed Christmas Eve and never woke again! I wasn't prepared at all – but I went about dealing with things by trying in my head to make him proud of me every day from that day on. I try my best to enjoy the things he loved so much. And try never to forget to keep looking around and taking notice of the little things that reminded me of him each day. And I try hard to let each and every one of those little things that I see bring a smile to the back of my mind, even if it's not possible to necessarily show it in my face. Love to all those that have loved and lost.

Kris Taft, Valenciana, Spain

Thank you so much to everybody who shared their very compelling and emotional stories of the loss of their loved ones. And also for their advice on how they have coped in the years that have gone by since. I don't know about you, but I got very emotional while I was reading through my friends' replies on this very delicate subject. I sincerely hope my friends' advice on grieving has helped you in some way and let you know that you are never alone when coming to terms with the loss of a loved one in your life. Always remember your loved ones are never truly gone, especially when you and I share those special memories we have of them with our families and friends to look back on.

The more we open up and share our feelings when we have sadly lost somebody close to us, the easier it will become over time to gradually take our first steps forward in the healing process of our grieving, even though we will always miss our loved ones so very, very much. My dad has learnt over the years how to cope with grieving for his parents through his positive attitude and sense of humour. And, to give you a great example of this, my dad used to tell me his mum died before my second birthday, so she didn't have to buy me a birthday card! That's just the kind of sense of humour my dad has and is the way he copes and remembers his parents.

I have spoken to a lot of people who have bottled their feelings up after they have lost loved ones and they told me they wished they had spoken to their family and friends a lot sooner about how they were feeling because, just as soon as they did, they said it helped them on the inside to gradually move on with their lives again, plus it was something they knew deep down their loved ones would have wanted them to do. If you or somebody you know has recently lost somebody, here are a couple of website links to help through the grieving process:

bit.ly/NHSDealingWithGriefAndLoss
bit.ly/MarieCurieCopingWithGrief

Those you have loved and lost will be guiding you onwards through your journey in life. They will always be with you and around you wherever you go. So, remember to look out for them because they will take on all shapes and forms and reach out to you when you least expect. And you know that bright star up there in the sky, well, that's your loved ones shining a light letting you know they will always be there for you whenever you need them.

# A SPECIAL TRIBUTE TO MY GOOD FRIEND ARRON MICKLEWRIGHT

In loving memory of Arron Micklewright 23/1/1990–20/6/2017

We will never forget you,
You will always be in our hearts and thoughts,
Now and forever.

One of the saddest days of my life and one I will never forget along with so many other people was the day when I heard about the tragic loss of my good friend Arron Micklewright. I still can't believe he's gone. I always expect to bump into Arron when I'm out in Market Harborough. I used to see him all the time down the King's Head pub with his brothers Casey and Adam Robertson, where we would always have a good laugh together and take a few selfies. One thing I will remember about Arron was that he was always surrounded by gorgeous-looking women wherever he went. The women loved Arron, there was no mistaking that. Well, who wouldn't? He was a handsome lad. Arron had a fantastic personality and was full of confidence and charisma by the bucketloads, which all added up to make the perfect combination of a truly remarkable individual who Arron's friends and I fell in love with just as soon as he came into our lives.

It was on Tuesday, 20 June 2017, when I first heard about the tragic news of an incident that had taken place at Little Bowden Park in Market Harborough. At the time, my dad and I were out on one of our walks raising money for Cancer Research UK, and while we were walking down

Leicester Road we bumped into a friend of ours who asked us if we had heard about a body that had been found in Little Bowden Park in the early hours of the morning! My dad and I hadn't heard anything, and this news shocked the hell out of us, as you can imagine!

It wasn't until a few days later when I came across my good friend Casey Robertson's Facebook status when I realised the body that had been found in Little Bowden Park was Casey's brother, Arron. For a moment, I couldn't believe what I was reading; it just didn't make any sense to me. Arron taking his own life! The funny, cheeky, lovable guy who I knew, who was always full of life and bringing happiness to everybody wherever he went. I was in total shock and disbelief; my heart sank. Then my head started spinning; I felt sick to my stomach and extremely nauseous. I felt as if I was having an out-of-body experience, and that this was all just a bad dream – well, nightmare! I was mortified, eventually, though it started to sink in that this was real. I then messaged Casey and told him how shocked and upset I was after hearing this devastating news about his brother. I told Casey, if he needed anything, to just let me know and that I would be there for him and his family. I became friends with Arron through his brother Casey, who I've known since he was fifteen.

> Thank you, Steve, means a hell of a lot! And thank you for the donation on that page! The funeral has been put up, and you're more than welcome to join us, but if not, then the wake is at the royalist on the 10th, July. You're more than welcome to join us x.

### Casey Robertson, Market Harborough, England

It's very emotional writing about Arron and remembering the good times we shared. Even as I'm writing this right now, I'm getting the same emotions of his loss coming back to me all over again. So, I can't even begin to imagine what it must be like for all of Arron's family and close friends.

Arron's mum, Joanne Pursglove, always loves it when she sees stories and photographs on her son's Facebook page appear. It reminds her that Arron's family and friends are still thinking of him and that he will never be forgotten and will always be remembered.

I wish you knew how many people's lives you touched, but most of all, you touched mine from the day you came into this world. I loved you, and I will never stop until we meet again, my baby. I so miss you xxxxxx.

## Joanne Pursglove, Market Harborough, England

Joanne and Steve Pursglove, Joanne's partner, live on a narrowboat called *Floating Dolly Lady*, where they sell Russian dolls, along with other cool bits and pieces. You can find Joanne's Floating Dolly Lady Facebook page, by visiting bit.ly/FloatingDollyLadyFB. What I love about Joanne and her family is that they are thoughtful and down-to-earth people who always treat you with the utmost respect. I love people who portray those qualities. Steve Pursglove was always there for Arron and was a fantastic stepdad and father figure to him. Steve misses Arron very, very much, and was so touched by all the heart-warming messages Arron's family and friends posted on social media when they heard about his tragic loss.

I knew Arron for around ten years, and we always had a good laugh together when we saw each other out in our hometown. I will admit, I didn't know Arron as well as his close friends knew him, because of our age differences. I'm quite a bit older than Arron, you see, and we both had different social circles of mates, but regardless of this we still became good mates and had so much time for one another when we did see each other out.

I had always wanted to do a shout-out for Arron to show my love and respect to him for being such a good friend, so on Monday, 23 February 2015, I uploaded one of my Facebook Entertainment News episodes where I gave him a shout-out. Arron loved it and here's the comment he left on Facebook for me: 'Ha, this made me laugh Steve Rippin.' I know it doesn't seem like much; I'm just so pleased I made that shout-out video for Arron. And if you would like to watch it, here is a video link to it: bit.ly/SpecialShoutoutForArronMicklewright2015

I only knew Arron from hanging about with his brothers, he always had a big smile on his face and always looked on top of the moon! We always spoke to each other if we saw each other out. Such a shame that he's gone, and he's missed by so many people. Life is life, we can't change anything, if only we could though. Arron was a top lad, and I will always remember him as one.

### Brad Woolnough, Market Harborough, England

I will always remember one night when I was out, because when my friends I was out with disappeared and left me on my own, I went into the Square Bar in Market Harborough, wondering what to do for the rest of the night. Then I heard somebody calling my name out, so I turned around and saw it was Arron. So I went over and joined him and his mates, and we all had a great night out. Arron and his friends made me feel really welcome back then and made my night one to remember. Arron was, and his mates are, all very friendly, genuine, kind, caring and good down-to-earth honest lads, who I have been lucky and privileged enough to get to know. A few of them include Ashley Topham, Stevie Newbold, Dan Large, Dan Overton, Sam Hendo, Scott Wright, Jarrod Burke, Ash Pears, Lee Smithhurst, Arron Lee Brace, Brad Woolnough and Rory Rattray.

Another memorable night I will never forget was when I met Arron and Casey along with the ladies; they were out with in the King's Head; we owned the dancefloor all night long that Saturday night. Those Robertsons and Micklewrights certainly know how to attract the women. Every time I used to see Arron out, there were always a lovely group of ladies around him. I definitely need some of that Robertson and Micklewright magic, I know that! I will always remember and cherish those nights and memories I made with Arron. It's just not the same anymore when I go out in Market Harborough at the weekends, because that magic spark Arron used to bring with him everywhere he went is something I genuinely miss. I'm so pleased I had the opportunity of getting to know such an incredible guy and be a small part of his life.

Not a second goes by without you in my mind! You and Adam brought George and me up into men. You were not only our brother but our father for many years. You stepped up for us when no man could. And we will always cherish that! No one can take away the memories. Then Steve came along with his sons, and we created a bond that can never be broken. We finally found a family who understood us, who loves us, and who wanted to be with us, regardless of how chaotic we were! I'll never forget you! You'll always be the first thought of my day! And you will always be my ginger brother that the women loved! Michelle Keegan's secret admirer! Only if she knew! Let's be honest, though! She wouldn't have a chance;) You and Adam never let us down, and I will never forget that. I will never be the man you were! You were already a father without knowing because you raised two little brothers into men! And I'll make sure everyone knows that. You will never be forgotten! I love you always big bro.

**Casey Robertson, Market Harborough, England**


Well, where do we even start? You were like the annoying baggage that came as part of me being with Ash, something I quickly had to learn to accept, and eventually, learn to love. Some of my funniest stories involve you. You were the light and soul of any party, and your laugh was infectious! I can't believe it was only two days ago you were sat in our living room thinking you were a professional racing commentator! If only you could see how loved you were, and how missed you would be. RIP Giglet, our world is a quieter place without you.

**Ellie Booler, Market Harborough, England**

Arron's close family friend Ellie Booler set up a JustGiving page where Arron's family and friends donated money to help raise £4,000, to enable Arron's family to give him the best possible funeral and send-off he so rightly deserved. The donations soon started pouring in, and within just over a week Ellie Booler had raised an astonishing £4,413.

Arron's funeral was one of the saddest days of my life. It was, as you can imagine, extremely emotional. At the same time, though, it was a beautiful service as well. Arron would have been so proud of everybody who turned out to show their love, support and respect for him that day. Arron would have especially loved the speeches his brother Adam Robertson and his best friend, Ashley Topham, made and read out for him as well, which were very emotional and heart-warming; there wasn't a dry eye in the building. Over four hundred people attended Arron's funeral service, which shows you how well loved and how much Arron will be missed by so many people. Arron will never be forgotten, and he will be with each and every one of us, in our hearts, always and forever.

What a roller coaster of emotions today, going to sleep with an extremely heavy heart! It just doesn't seem right that you are gone! There will never be a day that goes by where you are not in people's thoughts, memories and laughs! See you on the other side, Jiglet x.

Ellie Booler, Market Harborough, England

Arron had a big heart and was always so kind and caring to everybody he knew, whether they were old friends or new. I learnt a lot about Arron during the funeral service. From all the love he had for his family and friends. To finding out Arron wanted to become a policeman. He would have made a mighty fine one as well, if you ask me, and soon whipped this town, Market Harborough, back into shape. Another thing I never knew was Arron's love of the sport Enduro, which is a form of motocross Arron loved taking part in every year at the Red Bull Romaniacs events with his best mate, Ashley Topham. Arron was damn good on his motorbike as well, from the videos I've seen of him. The Red Bull Romaniacs events are the brainchild of Martin Freinademetz, who created the event back in 2004.

Never thought I could miss a pain in the arse as much as I miss you. Not an hours passed that you're not in my thoughts. Love you, brother x.

Ashley Topham, Market Harborough, England

Arron hated Anyone to be mardy, down or upset. There are not many people who have the ability to change a person's mood by just being in the same room as them. Or with one look, or infectious laugh – But he couldn't fail.

Jasmin Thorne, Market Harborough, England

After the funeral, we all went back to the Royalist pub in Market Harborough, where the wake was taking place, and while I was at the wake I got to catch up with Arron's mum, Joanne, who really appreciated me being there but was disappointed I wasn't wearing my bandana because she had told her family who were travelling to Market Harborough from out of town that a pirate was coming! I didn't wear my bandana out of respect for Arron, you see, and to be honest I didn't think it would be appropriate to wear it. Around 6 pm, I did put my bandana on, though, after speaking to Joanne, which she was pleased about. Arron's mum, Joanne, is a genuinely lovely and down-to-earth woman, and you always know where you stand with her, which are personality traits I love in people. My dad and I admire people who are down to earth and take you as they find you because we have both come across so many people in our lives who are so full of themselves and look down on you; I can't stand those kinds of people. You should always be yourself, and if somebody doesn't like you, then that's their problem. Being down to earth, open and honest goes a long way in life, doesn't it?

One of the funniest moments of the day while I was at the wake was when Dan Large and Dan Overton came out in their mankinis! They turned a few heads when they were dancing around the beer garden with their bits 'n' bobs bobbing and weaving all over the place! Plenty of photos were being taken, as you can imagine. The two Dans certainly got everybody laughing that afternoon, which was great under the circumstances. Arron would have loved it.

> Sometimes, you will never know the true value of moments until they become memories, and we had too many moments Arron Micklewright, but now they will be memories I will cherish forever! Today is going to be a rollercoaster of emotions for everyone involved, but all said and done, the celebration of your life is going to be f**king BIBLICAL! Love ya mate, forever and a day.
>
> **Dan Large, Market Harborough, England**

I also got to meet up with my good lifelong friend from my school days, Kerry Robertson, who is Arron's auntie. Kerry loved Arron so much, and she was always there for him whenever he needed her, just as Arron and his brother Adam, were always there for their Auntie Kerry whenever she needed them. Family is so important, isn't it?

Arron and Adam were always protective over me when I was out in town, they looked after me, even when it wasn't needed, they were like my bodyguards. It has been really hard on us all, but knowing Arron was loved by so many, help's in a way if you know what I mean. I miss him so much and don't want to say goodbye to him, my nephew, love him so much xx.

### Kerry Robertson, Market Harborough, England

I spent all day at the wake with Kerry, her family, and her relatives who had travelled to Market Harborough from various parts of England to be there for Arron; it was great meeting them. One of Kerry's relatives who I was talking to was telling me all about Benidorm and that I should take a trip over there because they have some excellent entertainment on, including a great Tom Jones tribute act! 'I'm not really into Tom Jones,' I told Kerry's relative. 'I'm more into hardstyle.' Still, though, we both had a lovely conversation together that afternoon while we talked about Tom Jones, hardstyle and Benidorm.

When I was in London, with my good friend Troy Goodman, in July 2017, while I was dancing in a nightclub, I suddenly thought, 'I'll never get to see Arron enjoying himself like everybody here is doing ever again,' then I broke down and cried. Another time when it hit me was when I was in the King's Head in Market Harborough with my good friend Dan Hewitt. I started thinking of all the good times Arron and I had shared in there. And I kept imagining I was going to see him come walking up to me with his trademark white shirt or T-shirt on, along with that loveable cheeky smile of his on his face; then I couldn't help myself and I started crying again. I still find it difficult when I go in the King's Head today, knowing I'll never see Arron in there where I first met him ever again.

A lot of people who knew Arron must feel the same way as me and have had moments like these themselves; it just doesn't seem right, does it, that here, Arron's friends and I am, carrying on with our lives, knowing we will never get to see Arron who we all loved so much again?

Well, yesterday was a very sad day for the boys and me, but we got through it with the strength of family and friends. Saying goodbye to you was the hardest thing ever, and seeing the devastation on everyone's face, hurt like crazy! The amount of people that turned up to show love for you Arron was amazing! Fly high now angel, Me and the boys, love and miss you millions.

### Lauren Overton, Market Harborough, England

Arron was an amazing person and had a heart of gold. The sun always shone when Arron was around. One thing he would do was turn people's frown upside down. Anyone Arron touched in his life would never be forgotten. I still can't believe he's gone...

### Sheryl Fernley, Market Harborough, England

I still miss Arron so much, Arron, Adam, Casey, and George, have been like brothers to me, and I have known them since I was born, and I still remember being with everyone when little George came home from the hospital! I will also never forget us all playing in the apple tree together when we lived next to them on Walcot Road.

### Sam Hendo, Bristol, England

I always love it when I see either, Joanne, Steve, Kerry, Adam, Casey or George out, because as well as being awesome people, who I'm privileged to call my friends, they remind me that Arron will never be forgotten with the love they all have for him. I have no idea how Arron's family must feel, or what they have all gone through and do so every day of their lives. My heart sincerely goes out to them.

I don't ever not want people to talk about him. I miss him so badly, some days are hard to get out of bed, but seeing memories and pics pop up on Facebook and timelines, helps. Means he's still in people's thoughts, same as me x.

### Joanne Pursglove, Market Harborough, England

Love and light to you, mate; you truly made a significant impact on my life, because you never judged or had a bad word to say about me; you made me feel accepted when some of my friends never did. You always brightened my nights up when I saw you out at the weekends as well. And I will always remember how you welcomed me to hang out with you and your mates when mine had left me on my own. Arron, you were a big inspiration to so many people's lives who you touched, mine included. I always looked up and admired you because you lived your life to the fullest, and although I only knew you from going out in Market Harborough and the times we shared around town and on the dancefloor together, I still classed you as a very good friend of mine; I honestly wish I had half the confidence and charisma you had. Arron, everybody loved you and will do eternally. I hope you're having a blast wherever you are right now, mate, and no doubt you have an army of women after you. Love you always and forever.

Steven M. Rippin

Arron has sadly left behind his mum, Joanne Pursglove; his stepdad, Steve Pursglove; his dad, Darren Micklewright; his brothers, Adam Robertson, Casey Robertson and George Vellam; his sister, Tamzin Micklewright Kershaw; his auntie, Kerry Robertson; his girlfriend, Amy Thomas; and his best friends, Ashley Topham, Ellie Booler, Dan Large, Dan Overton, Lauren Overton, Stevie Newbold, Ash Pears, Rory Rattray, Scott Wright, Aaron Lee Brace, Sam Hendo, Jarrod Burke and Brad Woolnough; there are so many more people I wish I could mention; you know who you are, though.

Never shall we forget those who have influenced and inspired us. We should always celebrate their lives and the times we were lucky enough to spend with them.

In loving memory of Arron Micklewright
23/1/1990–20/6/2017

# HELP AND ADVICE ON GRIEVING

Here are a few ways people grieve. Some people like being left alone while others find comfort in talking to their family and friends, which I think is good because we should always remember those special memories they have left us with – Some people find it helps getting involved in charity work – Some people like to keep as busy as they can, which I don't believe is the best way to cope, because it can prolong the grieving process, and I think you should always talk to other people about how you're feeling – Some people will learn to appreciate all the small things life has to offer them, and they will see the world in a different way from how they used to see it before. Furthermore, you and I should honour our loved ones by letting them know we will grow stronger every day in their memory and carry on with our lives after they have passed on because that is what they would have wanted us to do; they would want to see us happy and fulfilling our goals in life.

When you and I lose somebody close to us, there's no guidebook on how we're supposed to feel and cope in the coming days, months and years that lie ahead for us is there. We will find the comfort we're looking for from our family and friends when we remember the good times we shared with them. Then, over time, the burden of grief we are carrying on our shoulders which is weighing us down will hopefully lessen. Social media has helped me in the past when it comes to grieving. I was able to talk to my friends online, you see, who had been through the grieving process themselves. And, by doing so, we were able to be there for one another. Never isolate yourself away from your family and friends, and make your loved one, who you have sadly lost, proud of who you have become today. Let their memory live on through you.

Now, here are the five stages of grief you can expect to go through, although they might not happen in the order I have listed them in here, and some people may not go through any of these stages at all.

Denial – This can't be happening to me.
Anger – Why is this happening? – Who's to blame?
Bargaining – Make this not happen and in return I will…
Depression – I'm too sad to do anything.
Acceptance – I'm at peace with what's happened.

Now I'm going to share with you what I believe we can do to help ourselves through the grieving process.

Turn to your family and friends and let them know how you're feeling. Maybe they can be a shoulder to cry on and help with funeral arrangements. Never be alone.

Draw comfort from what or who you believe in. If you're a religious person, you can turn to your religion to help and comfort you, just as my auntie did when she lost her parents, or, if you find you're questioning your faith, try talking to your local vicar or to somebody else in your religious community. For me, I find it hard to turn to religion, although I do believe in a higher power, so it's the Universe I turn to. And I put all my faith into the Universe because it created everything you and I know that's around us. So, I believe our loved ones who you and I have sadly lost are never truly gone; I think they transcend into a higher state of consciousness, which we don't yet fully understand. You and I might even come from the skies above. We may even be descendants of extra-terrestrials and have their DNA within us, for all we know. That's a whole other subject though, isn't it?

One lady I spoke to who had recently lost her husband told me that it helped her having her dogs because it gave her a purpose to venture out every day. Pets can help you so much when you're grieving.

Joining a group or a class will help take your mind off grieving as well. So, if you felt up to it, you could join a gym, a salsa dancing class, a walking group, an art class, learn a new language or anything at all. By joining a group or a class, you will also be making new friends and increasing your social circle at the same time, plus it will help take your mind off everything you have been going through and thinking about lately.

Sharing your losses with other people who have gone through the same emotions as you have can help. So, if you're struggling with your grief, you could join a local bereavement support group in the area where you live. To find out where they are, you can search online or contact your local hospitals and counselling centres.

If you don't feel comfortable talking to your family and friends about the loss of your loved one, you could find online forums where others are also grieving and connect with them. Or you could talk to a therapist or a grief counsellor if your grief is becoming too much for you; they will be able to help you work through the painful emotions you're experiencing.

My next-door neighbour's husband sadly passed away over twenty years ago; unfortunately, his widow never moved on with her life. So, she gradually declined and ended up turning to alcohol. She also didn't listen to anybody's advice they would offer her. It was so sad to see. Then one day her taxi driver wasn't getting a reply when he knocked on her front door, so he called my dad, who went around her house to find out what was going on. And my dad and the taxi driver ended up having to break the front door down to her home because they weren't getting a response from her. And when they entered her house they found her passed out on the settee. My dad then called for an ambulance, and our neighbour was rushed into hospital, where she sadly passed away a few weeks later. Our neighbour's grief consumed her over the years because she didn't get the help she needed to move on with her life. If she had spoken about how she was feeling to somebody, she might still be alive today; please, don't let your grief consume you.

Q: How do you rush the grieving process? I've had this feeling for nearly six months; it's driving me insane. I miss my friend so much. I've never felt this pain before, and I'll never wish it on my worst enemy. I just hope she knows how much I love her and what an inspiration she has been in my life.

**Hayley Peachey, Barry, Vale of Glamorgan, Wales**

A: Hi, Hayley, I'm so sorry to hear about the loss of your friend. Unfortunately, you can't rush the grieving process; it's something you have to learn to cope and live with over time. Yes, it's difficult, and it changes you and me as people when we do go through these tough emotional times in our lives, but we must carry on and honour the memory of those who we have so sadly lost because that's what they would want us to do. It helps as well, Hayley, to talk to your family and friends about how you're feeling. So never isolate yourself away from them and know that your friend is always with you in your thoughts, and everywhere you go. Think of all the good times you spent together with them, and how they would want to see you carrying on living your life. There are going to be times when you feel emotional, which is normal, but those feelings should gradually lessen. And, Hayley, remember to stay as strong as you can and look after yourself. Love and light to your friend, who will forever be with you always.

Steven M. Rippin

Sadly, there's no quick fix to get over the grieving process, so please remember to stay strong, carry on, and make your loved ones proud of you. Moving forward with your life is essential when you have lost a loved one.

# HOW TO HELP SOMEBODY WHO HAS SUICIDAL THOUGHTS

I once had a friend of mine say they had suicidal thoughts, which shocked me! So, I had a good talk with my friend about what was on their mind, which helped them. I knew they had suffered from depression in the past. I just never realised it was this severe for them to contemplate suicide! You don't know what's going on inside someone else's head, no matter how well you think you know them. I told my friend to go and book an appointment with their doctor just as soon as they could, which thankfully they told me they had already done. And their GP diagnosed them with having depression and put them on antidepressants. The doctor also told my friend to go and see a counsellor. There's still a long way for them to go, but I believe they will pull through.

If you think a friend of yours or a family member might be having suicidal thoughts, here are some of the symptoms to look out for.

- Is your friend acting differently to how they usually behave?
- Are they coming across as being negative about things in their life they never used to be negative about?
- Does your friend get agitated or act anxious, or do they get angry for no reason at all?
- Do you feel your friend is withdrawing into themselves, and not joining in as much as they used to with you, such as meeting up with you for a coffee or going out at the weekends? Are they becoming more secluded?
- Are they taking care of their personal appearance and

hygiene? Or have you noticed a steady decline in the way they look and appear to you these days?

- Has your friend or a family member been looking more tired lately? Are they getting enough sleep? Because when you have got a lot on your mind emotionally and find it hard to switch off all the thoughts and feelings going on inside your head, you can start to get stressed and have broken sleep. And if you notice your friend or family member getting sleepier and more worn out during the day, that could be due to the emotional anxiety they are going through.

- Have you noticed any of your family or friends gaining or losing weight recently, or have you seen a change in their eating habits? It's said that a lack of appetite can sometimes be a sign of depression, while an increase in appetite could be a sign of emotional distress.

- Have any of your family or friends started to drink more alcohol or abuse drugs, which are things they never used to do? This could be a hard one to notice straight away, so watch how they are acting and how they look. And, if you do suspect something, here is a website to help you spot any changes when people have started to take drugs and drink more alcohol: sobercollege.com/telltale-signs-of-drug-use

- Hopelessness: do any members of your family or friends come across as if everything in their life is getting too much for them to cope with? And do you remember a time when they were positive, full of confidence and somebody who you would look up to? You might have even heard them say things like, 'The world would be better off without me' or 'Who would miss me if I wasn't here?' Just as I have heard one of my friends say to me. And if you have heard them say anything like that at all, that's when you need to have a serious talk with them about what's going on inside their heads and tell them that they have got everything to live for and that you're there for them whenever they need you. Furthermore, ask them to book themselves an appointment straight away to see their local GP for professional help and advice.

- Also, is there a family history of problems associated with mental health?

I wonder if you have noticed any of those changes in your family or friends. If you have, please try your best to speak with them about how they might be feeling. They might secretly be battling their demons right now and crying out for help without you even realising it.

Remember, if you do talk to your family member or friend about how they are feeling, don't come across as being patronising. Show them you're concerned because you love and care about them. And also, because you have noticed they are not acting like themselves lately. You could even try asking them something like this, 'Hey, you know how much I care about you, and that you're one of my best friends, well, I just wanted to have a chat with you, just the two of us, if that's all right? I've noticed you haven't been acting yourself lately. And I just wondered if there's been anything on your mind you want to talk to me about? And remember, you can talk to me about anything. I will never judge you because I love you; you're my best friend.' And, by showing compassion to your family member or friend, they will hopefully want to open up and confide in you about what's on their mind. I was just so glad my friend opened up and talked to me about how they were genuinely feeling on the inside.

Remember to look out for the signs of suicidal thoughts in someone close to you, which are: Getting agitated and anxious – Withdrawing into themselves – Not taking care of their appearance – Gaining or losing weight – Drinking more alcohol and taking drugs, and continuously moaning about everything and everybody. For further help and advice, here is a link to Hope for the Day's suicide prevention website: www. HFTD.org

Always open up and talk about what's on your mind to those you trust and those you know will listen to you.

You will always and forever have your grandad, grandma, mum, dad, child, partner or best friend by your side who you might have sadly loved and lost everywhere you go through life. And you will also have those special memories and happy times you shared with them to look back on as well. So, look up into the stars at night, because that's where your loved ones now reside, they are those stars you see shining down on you which are helping to guide you through your journey in life; you're never going to be alone.

Honour your loved ones by keeping their memory alive. Your loved ones are now with you and forever in your heart until the day you're reunited with them once again. Until that day arrives, get out there into the world and make them proud of you by living a happy and beautiful life. When you're feeling at your lowest and you don't think life's worth living, STOP and THINK how you will affect your family and friend's lives. Always appreciate the ones you love today.

When somebody's alive, we can quite easily put off going to see them and think, 'Aw, I'll go next week,' then before we know it, months have gone by, and we lose contact with those who we love so much. So always make that extra bit of effort and visit your family and friends who you haven't seen for a long time and show them how much you love and care about them.

Life is so precious, and we only have one chance at it to achieve great things, so let's make our loved ones who we have sadly lost proud of who we are today and embrace the wonder of LIFE we have been given.

# PART FIVE

PART FIVE

# HEALTH AND FITNESS: MY EYESIGHT AND ARTHRITIS AND MY DAD'S HEALTH ISSUES

Over the years, I have spent a lot of time in hospitals and had numerous eye operations done. On top of that, I have also had to cope with arthritis since I was two years old. I have had an underactive thyroid for many years as well, which caused me to sleep a lot when I was younger. I know other people are a lot worse off than I am, and when I see what they have to go through my heart goes out to them. I'm always inspired by people who have health and disability problems who take challenges, go on adventure holidays and play sport. I think those individuals are amazing. And they show you and me that our health and disability issues don't have to stop us from living fulfilled, active and incredible lives.

When people can't see a physical health or disability problem somebody has, it's hard for them to understand what that person is going through in their everyday life, isn't it? For example, a lot of my family and friends don't realise the pain I'm in every day. You see, most days, I suffer from pain in my eyes and also with my arthritis, which flares up from time to time. I always do my best to hide the pain I'm in. And I will put a smile on my face and get on with life as best as I can. It isn't easy, especially when I'm out in public and somebody turns around and mentions how sore and red my eyes look. I have tried explaining to my friends over and over again about the medical conditions I have. Unfortunately, though, I don't think they fully understand how severe they are. The problem is they can't physically see anything wrong with me on the outside. I guess it's a bit like a car; the problems lie underneath the bonnet, which you can't see.

People who suffer from health and disabilities are the real super-heroes of today, along with all the medically trained staff all over the world.

You will find people with disabilities make the most of what they have. They will get on with their lives as best as they can, and you won't hear them complaining either because they are so happy to be alive.

# PIRATE STEVE'S EYE PROBLEMS: EYE, EYE, CAPTAIN

I have suffered from eyesight problems since I was five years old. They first detected them when I was at primary school, when I wasn't seeing as well as I should have been in the school eye examination. So, they sent me to an optician in Leicester, who then referred me to see an eye specialist at the Leicester Royal Infirmary. There I was examined by the eye specialist, Dr John Cappin. And Dr Cappin found I had a cataract on my right eye, which needed to be operated on and removed, which he did in 1982.

> Steven's arthritis started when he was about two years old. It affected his knee joints. When they discovered he had arthritis in his knees, they put him on six tablets a day. They called the arthritis stills disease. It then went on to affect his eyesight. When he was five years old, he had his eyes checked at school, and they noticed he could not see out of his right eye. We went to see a specialist, and they told us there was a cataract. So, they had to operate on the right eye to remove the cataract when he was seven years old. The left eye also had a cataract forming, but they will not operate on that eye until the cataract is fully ripened. Steven has also had six operations done so far on his right eye. He developed glaucoma after that because the pressure in his eye was high. Also, in the end, they had to fit a Molteno tube into his right eye to drain the fluid to keep the pressure low. He has been on eye drops since the age of five and is still on them. He has to wear contact lenses because he is long-sighted in one

eye and short-sighted in the other. At the moment he is on two drops a day for his right eye, which is betnesol N. He has had no operations on his knees. The arthritis cleared up for a few years but came back in October 1992.

**Sheila Rippin, Leicestershire, England**

My mum always kept a record of my medical history. And I'm so grateful to her for doing that for me.

You might not find this interesting, so please don't worry if you want to skip by it. If you are interested, though, here is a list of the operations, eye conditions, and a few other things that have affected me throughout my life. I don't mention everything, or you would be here all day reading through my medical history! I hope this will give you a better understanding of the kind of childhood I had while I was growing up as well. You will also see why I had to take a lot of time off from school.

1977 – When I was two years old, I was diagnosed with rheumatoid arthritis; Still's disease.

1982 – My cataract was removed from my right eye.

1987 – A capsulectomy operation was done to remove the lens in my right eye.

February 1988 – I had my first trabeculectomy vitreous operation done, which lowers the intraocular pressure inside your eye.

29 June 1988 – I had my second trabeculectomy vitreous operation done due to complications when they first attempted the procedure.

4 November 1988 – My goniotomy operation was done, which is a surgical procedure where the surgeon uses a lens called a goniolens to see the structures of the front part of your eye.

1989 – I had my Molteno tube implanted into my right eye.

5 May 1989 – My contact lens was fitted.

October 1989 – Corneal degeneration was happening in my eyes, which meant my vision became blurred because the cells in my eyes were dying.

October 1989 – I was told I had band-shaped keratopathy, which is a corneal disease where you see the appearance of calcium on the central cornea. It can also be caused by trauma, such as having eye surgery.

October 1989 – I had an operation on my right eye done where they removed part of it. They removed what they call the vitreous body, which is the clear gel that fills the space between your lens and the retina part of your eyeball.

27 March 1993 – I had an injection into my left knee for arthritis.

1994 – I developed acute iritis, which is recurrent and is caused by trauma.

1996 – I had an operation done at the Leicester Royal Infirmary to stitch my left upper eyelid back together from the first assault I went through.

September 1997 – They found I had juvenile epithelial corneal dystrophy, a group of genetic, often progressive, eye disorders, where abnormal material often accumulates in the transparent outer layer of your eye, the cornea.

1 November 2004 – I was told I had, patellofemoral maltracking, which is another cause for my knee pain.

1 May 2004 – My doctor found I had an underactive thyroid, so I started having thyroid function tests, and they found I had hypothyroidism.

26 May 2005 – I had electrolysis done on my left upper eyelid, due to when my eyelid was split open from the first assault I went through, which left me with ingrowing eyelashes, and also with permanent pain in my left upper eyelid.

29 October 2005 – I was told I have thyroid eye disease.

1 April 2006 – I had my right upper eyelid lowered. My eyelid had always been high up due to the operations I had done on it. And my left upper eyelid had trichiasis done on it. Trichiasis is an eyelid abnormality, where your eyelashes grow in the wrong directions and grow in towards your eye. So, I had trichiasis done to remove my ingrowing eyelashes again. Unfortunately, the operation wasn't a success, and I still have painful ingrowing eyelashes today.

25 August 2008 – I was assaulted for a second time and had my head

stitched together just above my right eye where my Molteno tube is fitted. That was done at Kettering General Hospital, and they did a fantastic job fixing me up.

Well, there you have it, a brief recollection of my medical history that you might or might not have found very interesting to read. As you can see though, I was in and out of hospital quite a lot up until 2008.

Aw sweetie, so sorry to hear that you have had to endure so much from such a young age. You're a shining light, and you're doing good things with your life, and you will only be rewarded for that. Miracles happen every day to good people, and improvement can sometimes come out of nowhere, bless xx.

Stacey Hayes, California, USA, instagram.com/hoststaceyhayes

My eye specialist, who performed all my eye operations up until the late eighties, was Dr Cappin. The doctors and nurses at the Leicester Royal Infirmary used to call him God because he was renowned for his incredible eye surgical skills. I was so happy to have Dr Cappin as my eye consultant back then.

When I was thirteen, I had three trabeculectomy eye operations done; I only thought I had had two done, but I have been informed it was three. And all three of those operations happened in the same year because it was a race against time to save the sight in my right eye. A trabeculectomy means, when Dr Cappin operated on me, he inserted a needle into my right eye to release the fluid build-up, which was causing me to have very high eye pressure. My right eye pressure was in the region of between 70 and 80, you see, which was terrible and extremely high. An average person's eye pressure is anywhere between 12 and 22. Unfortunately, all three trabeculectomy eye operations I had done were unsuccessful, which meant it wasn't looking good for my eyesight.

My parents, I remember, were worrying no end, bless them, and didn't know what to do when those procedures kept failing. The surgeons thought I was going to lose my eyesight! At the time, I had no idea that might have been the case! But I let the medical staff and Dr Cappin do what they thought was best for me; I trusted them with my life. I actually enjoyed going into hospital, as strange as that might sound, although it was a bit scary going into theatre. I did enjoy the anaesthetic they would give me, though, that made me feel great for the ten seconds I remember of it. And still, to this day, I remember telling the anaesthetist, and his crew, my name and counting down from 100. When I was recovering on the ward, a lovely nurse called Louise who looked after me would always comment on my long eyelashes. And I always remember her saying all I would have to do when I was older would be to flutter my eyelashes at the ladies and they would fall at my feet! She must have needed her eyes checking! Who would want to fall at my feet? That was really lovely of Louise to say though, wasn't it?

And I was right: no women have ever fallen at my feet, unless they have tripped up by mistake, plus I have never been able to flutter my eyelashes at the ladies because half of them on my left eye have been burnt away! So back to my eyesight, which needed saving. Because the trabeculectomy eye operations never worked, there was one more eye procedure Dr Cappin suggested he could do to save the sight in my right eye. It was a very complicated and risky operation to do, plus there was also a chance it might not work as well, he told my parents! What other options did I have left, though?

And so, the final showdown for my right eye began. A bit like in a western when the movie is about to end, and you see the cowboy going to rescue the damsel in distress. All you want to know is: will the cowboy and damsel live happily ever after? In my case, though, it was whether my right eye was going to live happily ever after, after Dr Cappin had sliced and diced it and implanted the Molteno tube into it! So, would my right eye and the Molteno tube be a match made in heaven, or would the Molteno tube be awkward, throw a tantrum and not want things to work out? Well, I am happy to say it was a match made in heaven between my right eye and the Molteno tube because they have now been together for over thirty years and bonded beautifully. My Molteno tube is now part of who I am, and I could never live without her.

Well, I had that major eye operation done when I was fourteen and today my Molteno tube is still working perfectly and draining away the fluid that helps to keep my right eye pressure low. Whenever my eye specialists of today see the Molteno tube Dr Cappin fitted for me, they are always extremely impressed by his work from all those years ago. I was told I was the youngest patient to have a Molteno tube implanted at the time, although I'm not sure how true that is; they might have meant in England; I honestly don't know. I am just so grateful to everybody who was involved in helping to save my eyesight back then. And especially to Dr Cappin, because without him, I could have lost the sight in my right eye.

Thank you so much, Dr Cappin, for everything you did for me, and for saving my eyesight all those years ago. I can never thank you and your team enough. I am forever grateful to you all.

Steven M. Rippin

One day, my mum drove me over to see Dr Cappin at his home for a private consultation. Unfortunately, Dr Cappin had a pretty awkward driveway to drive up. So, I got out of my mum's car to help guide her into his driveway easier. At the time I was holding a thank-you card in my hand I had brought along with me to say thank you to Dr Cappin for all he had done for me over the years. Well, the thank-you card fell out my hand while I was helping to guide my mum into Dr Cappin's driveway. So I put my hand up to tell my mum to stop reversing, then once she had stopped I bent down to pick it up then, all of a sudden, my mum started reversing again and ran over my hand and the thank-you card! Luckily the driveway was made out of pebbles, so my hand sunk into them a bit, so it didn't hurt me that much. I did have to shout to my mum to stop and drive forward, though, so I could pull my hand free, which luckily she did when she heard me!

Then I went to the passenger window to tell my mum what had happened, and she felt so bad when I told her she had just run over my hand. I told her not to worry about it, then she must have tapped the car into reverse because she then drove over my foot! Luckily it didn't hurt too bad. By now, though, my mum, bless her, was really upset, and again I told her not to worry about it because I was OK and no harm had been done. Eventually, my mum managed to reverse the car into Dr Cappin's driveway without running over me for a third time! By now, though, I was running late for my appointment, and Dr Cappin must have been wondering where I was. Then a moment later I saw Dr Cappin's wife come out of her house looking for me, where she saw my mum in tears while I was telling her not to worry and that everything was all right.

So, while Dr Cappin was examining my eyes, Dr Cappin's wife was looking after my mum and telling her not to worry about running over my hand and my foot. My mum, bless her, was so upset that day, as you can imagine. My mum only ever drove me over to see Dr Cappin one other time for my eye appointments. On that occasion, my mum drove straight into Dr Cappin's fence, which left a big white scratch mark down the side of my parents' car! So, when my mum and I got home, my mum got a tin of red paint to cover the scratch mark up with so my dad wouldn't see it. Then, as my mum was painting the car, my dad pulled into the driveway and saw what she was doing. He thought she was polishing the car so when he realised she was painting it he wasn't very impressed at all!

Mum, you're one in a million. I love you very, very much.

Steven M. Rippin

Although the pressure in my right eye now reads an average of four, which concerns my optician. I'm assured by my eye specialist, Dr Kumar, that it's at a normal level after all my right eye has been through.

Every day I wake up, I thank the Universe for the eyesight I do have so I can see and experience the natural wonders of the world around me today. It wasn't until I was in my twenties that I realised how serious that Molteno tube operation was that I had done when I was fourteen. It has made me appreciate my health and my eyesight so much.

The planet you and I live on is an incredible place, isn't it? And I love how there's so much to explore and study. Every living object and everything that has been made by Mother Nature, I find truly incredible. And I unquestionably see the world you and I live in from an entirely diverse perspective today, because of my eyesight.

When I was younger, I never worried about having eye operations done. I guess it was because I was so used to going in and out of hospital. It's like with anything in life: the more you do it, the more natural it becomes, just like brushing your teeth or riding a bike, I guess. So the next time I have to have a procedure done on my eyes, I'll think, 'Ah right cool, I'm off to have my eyeballs sliced and diced again, which can only mean one thing: I get to have a week or two off work. Woohoo.'

Always make sure you go for your regular eye check-ups and any other important medical appointments that come through for you because they all help to keep you and me fit and healthy throughout our lives for longer.

After my Molteno tube operation had healed, I had to have eight stitches removed from my right eye, and, let me tell you, that was one of the strangest sensations I have ever felt. So, imagine, if you can, feeling the white part of your eyeball being tugged about and then pinging back and forth into place half a dozen times. Well, that's what it felt like to me when I had eight stitches removed from my right eye! Now here is a video from 2014, when I had an appointment to see my eye specialist at the time, Miss Bibby, who was a charming woman, and also when I had another eye appointment to see my opticians in Leicester, While Opticians, who are fantastic: bit.ly/StevesEyeAppointments

I have been going to While Opticians since I was eight years old and they have always gone above and beyond with the professional service they have provided for me over the years. While Opticians used to be run by Simon Gavzey and his family; they then sold the business to Swati Modi. Swati and her team of optometrists are incredible, to put it one way, especially when it comes to my glasses prescription, which can be very complicated, and not forgetting when I call them up for my annual pluck, as Lisa, who works there, likes to call it. Swati, who runs and owns While Opticians, removes a lot of my unwanted ingrowing eyelashes every five to six weeks, you see.

My dad and I always have a good laugh with Swati and her team of optometrists when we go to visit them for our eye appointments. Those girls in While Opticians are wild and have a fantastic sense of humour. For example, one time when my dad was in While Opticians he said, 'Have you seen Edward?' I wondered who on earth my dad was going on about, then all of a sudden the optometrists started laughing hysterically behind the reception desk, and this was while the shop was full of customers. Swati's team of optometrists thought Edward was a man's private parts! Naughty optometrists! So, every time my dad and I go to While Opticians now, there's an ongoing joke about where Edward is, and my dad will often say, 'So, have you seen Edward lately?' I don't know!

Swati Modi and her team have given my parents and me so much excellent advice over the years, which has helped me no end to cope with my eyesight conditions, which I am forever grateful for. So, I highly recommend if you or anybody you know requires an optician, to check out While Opticians, that is, if you live in the Leicestershire area here in England.

> Having my eyesight problems has made me feel a lot more vulnerable in my everyday life because a lot of the time when I'm only wearing my glasses I can only see out of my right eye.

My attitude has mostly been positive when it comes to my eyesight, even though I still worry from time to time about what the future holds for me, because at some stage in my life I will have to have my cataract removed from my left eye that's forming on it right now. The primary thing that worries me about having my cataract removed is if there are any complications, like there was when they removed the cataract from my right eye, which was the reason why I needed to have a Molteno tube fitted. So, for the time being, I just hope my eyesight lasts as long as it can, so I can continue on with my carpet cleaning job. Even now, though, I'm having trouble seeing the stains on carpets that customers point out to me!

I believe it's always best to keep a sense of humour when you have health issues. Having a sense of humour has definitely helped me with my eye conditions.

I'll admit, my illnesses have held me back in the past and changed how my life has turned out, but I'm happy and I wouldn't change a thing because, without my health problems, I wouldn't be who I am today. And finally, can you believe, I actually got a can of Coke stuck in my eye once! Don't worry, though: it was only for Halloween purposes. And now here is a short video of me wishing everybody a happy Halloween with a can of Coke stuck in my eye: bit.ly/CanOfCokeInEye

> Never let anything hold you back if you suffer from health or disability problems; you can do anything you put your mind to.

At school, I wasn't always able to join in playing sport because of the eye operations I had done, so that made me feel like an outcast back then. I always thought I was being looked down on by other kids and some of the gym teachers as well; well, that's the impression they gave me with the way they used to speak and look at me. They always made me feel like I was the lad who was trying to get out of playing sport when I wasn't at all!

When I've been at work, from time to time, I'll suffer badly with my arthritis and have to shuffle along on my backside while I nail the gripper rods down because I can't stand the pain I'm in when I'm kneeling. And sometimes if I have shooting pains I'll jump up in the air in pure agony and scare the customer half to death, bless them, then I'll have to tell them what's wrong with me! I've also had to explain to carpet fitters that I don't fit carpet because of my arthritis. I can do a bit of prep work, but if I used the knee kicker, which all carpet fitters use to stretch carpets in, I would be in a wheelchair by now without a doubt!

My eyesight, arthritis and underactive thyroid have affected and changed the direction my life has taken over the years. I'm happy with how things have turned out, though, because, as I have said before, I wouldn't be who I am today if it wasn't for my health conditions. I'm now relying on the advancements of medical science and technology to help me in the future, which I hope will prolong my eyesight and improve my arthritis and underactive thyroid.

I cope with the medical health disorders I have with the love and support I receive from my parents and my online friends who have helped get me through a lot of the difficult times I've faced. Never give up, and never feel down or depressed when you're suffering from a medical health problem. And remember, you're never alone because there are always people you can talk to, whether that's a member of your family, a close friend, your local GP or a counsellor.

Your true inner self will shine through when you live with a medical health condition because that's when your best personality traits will reveal themselves to your family and friends, and show them that you're positive, strong and determined to carry on with your life as best as you can.

# LIVING WITH DISABILITIES

I have had to live with two different forms of disabilities throughout my life, those being my eyesight and arthritis. Although my limitations are nothing compared to what some have to live with. I feel blessed to be able to wake up every morning knowing I'm able to use my legs and see out of one of my eyes with my glasses on. I'm also grateful to be able to go to work, go out with my friends at the weekends, and enjoy life. Unfortunately, not everybody who suffers from disabilities has these opportunities that I am blessed and lucky to have, and I really do feel for those people; never take your health for granted.

I'm always inspired by people who are disabled because I see how much passion, love and determination they have within themselves to live their lives to the fullest. And they never let anything stop them from doing what they want to do in life. A good friend of mine, Sylvia Slingo, has a disabled son, Matt, who is a really lovely guy. Matt was in an accident many years ago, sadly, and has gone through so much in his life when it comes to his health. So, to help cheer Matt up a bit, Matt's mum, Sylvia, kindly shows her son videos I make on social media. And Sylvia has told me my videos always put a smile on Matt's face and make him laugh, which I am so happy to hear. Sylvia works with learning disabled people, and she has witnessed how the general public react to people with learning disabilities. So now, here is a short story from Sylvia, who witnessed a learning-disabled young man trying to make awareness of bullying.

One evening, I popped into the shop connected to the petrol garage. I was choosing some flowers when a young adult man came up to me wearing a t-shirt that said: FREE HUGS TO ALL WOMEN. He came up to me and said, 'Do you like my T-Shirt? I am trying to raise awareness for being bullied at school and thought this was a nice gesture. My friends are away at the moment, and I'm feeling very lonely.' I said I liked the shirt and he said it was lovely to meet me. I said likewise (It was obvious that he had a learning disability). The reactions of people were very interesting: One lady was obviously embarrassed, so refused to answer when he approached her. A young girl in her late teens was embarrassed too and said: 'Why would I want to hug you.' He then said, 'When you have children, I hope you don't say that to them.' A man then became aggressive shouting at him and telling him, 'The lady said she doesn't want to hug you, leave her alone.' The young man then became distressed and was asking the assistants if they would hug him if they weren't behind their tills. I found it quite sad the way that people reacted, but I guess its fear.

I had another incident at London Waterloo, where one of the autistic clients I support, was afraid to go on the down escalator. I was coaxing her and said I would go down backwards and face her, which would allow her to look at me, and I told her not to look down and hold my hands. A guy in a hoodie then got on and pushed her out of the way, which made her nervous. And it ended up with her losing her grip on my hands, and me going off without her. I then had to run up the down escalator, and I shouted at the guy saying, she's learning disabled, I was so worried she was going to run off. On a plus note though, I recently took my disabled adult son away on holiday – he's in a wheelchair, and he is brain injured. We went out to a disco, and a lovely lady asked him to dance in his wheelchair. I think it's made his life. He became disabled from an accident many years ago, and he was so happy to be chatted up bless him. I would like to campaign for more activities to be carried out in care homes. As I know only too well where my son is, they're happy to take megabucks for the clients, but not provide a good service. I have even got my MP involved with the funding cuts to disabled people. My slogan is – There's ability in disability, and they should be treated like the rest of us.

**Sylvia Slingo, London, England**

I'm so sorry to hear about your son being involved in an accident and becoming disabled, Sylvia. I sincerely hope one day there is a cure to help Matt. All my very best to you both and thank you once again for sharing your stories of how you have personally witnessed learning-disabled people being treated in today's society. I would have hugged the learning-disabled young man in the petrol station. Some people can be so cruel, can't they? Others get afraid of what they don't understand, and this is how they react, sadly!

Steven M. Rippin

It sickens me when I see somebody either pointing, pulling a face of disgust, or insulting somebody who is learning disabled. It's such a disrespectful thing to do, isn't it, just like how that poor learning-disabled young man was treated in that petrol station? Small-minded people should stop and think how they would feel if somebody turned around to them and started pointing and throwing insults their way, or to one of their family or friends.

It's a very sad society you and I live in when we see this kind of behaviour happening. I really feel for the young man who tried his best to make more awareness of bullying. It sounds like he was a victim of bullying himself! Society needs to learn to accept people no matter what disability they have or how they look. What I think needs to be done is that schools make more awareness of people who have learning disabilities in our society; they should teach children from an early age how to accept others who are disabled no matter how different they are. By doing this it will hopefully help those schoolchildren understand how learning-disabled people are no different to you and me. Then, once those schoolchildren have grown up, they will hopefully no longer judge or react in negative ways to learning disabled people.

I believe that being taught to accept people who are disabled while you're at school would help so much in today's society. For a start, it would help young children from feeling insecure about themselves if they're unhappy because of a disability they are suffering from. When children grow up feeling insecure about themselves, as I well know, it can lead to developing mental health issues if you're not careful. Those children need to know they're accepted by others, no matter what health conditions they have. Always treat other people who have learning disabilities how you would treat your own family and friends: with the love and respect they deserve.

If you suffer from a health or disability, have your illnesses ever held you back from doing something you have always wanted to do in life? If so, why? And think to yourself, 'Why are these problems holding me back?' Also, do your very best to think of ways you can overcome those dilemmas if they're holding you back. If you do see somebody who's learning disabled when you're out in public, always be courteous and don't go looking around every five seconds at them. If you're intrigued and want to know more about them, similar to how some people have been curious to find out more about me, then why don't you go up and ask them politely if they don't mind explaining to you their health problems they have. They will either be happy to tell you, or they will politely say they would rather not talk about them. And that's when you should respect their wishes and end your conversation. People who are disabled are no different from anybody else. They have emotions and can get upset by the cold-hearted words small-minded people say to them just as much as you and I can. So, please remember, we're all the same on the inside.

I have always appreciated it when somebody has taken the time to come up and ask me politely what happened to my eyes and how I got the scar on my forehead, or what inspired me to dress how I do, because then I will quite happily explain my story to them, which they are happy to listen to. If you find people stare at you when you're out in public, what I have learnt to do when they do that to me is to stand tall, be confident within myself and show everybody around me that I'm not ashamed of how I look. Own any imperfections you might have and turn them into defects you're proud of. I'll admit, I have found this hard to do over the years when I've had people say negative things about my eyes. Nowadays, though, I love how my eyes look and I will do my best to keep a smile on my face and rise above any hurtful comments thrown my way. There are too many people in this world who will quite easily pull you down and make you feel like a piece of dirt, insult you and tell you you're worthless. And, by letting those small-minded people treat you that way, you're only going to let them destroy you slowly on the inside. So, stand tall and love who you are.

Other people don't know how to react, because they don't understand. My eldest has Williams Syndrome, and I know by looking at her, it's not always visible unless she's having a meltdown. It's hard to accept you're different from the rest, and society is full of judgemental a**e holes. It's just a good job; we don't care about their opinions.

Kylie, Norwich, England, instagram.com/kystar87

Deformities and abnormalities are f**king beautiful, and disabilities are a challenge that makes you smart and strong. Why be normal and boring and have an easy life? It makes you stupid and ungrateful and stagnant. I may sound harsh, but my constructive and bitter way of thinking has brought me joy and peace. Literally, everyone suffers once in a while, some more and some less, that's life. And as long as you are living it to the max, then there is no time to focus on the pain. Instead, be proud of how far you have come, regardless of obstacles.

Alice, Sweden/Germany

Embrace your health problems and turn them into what I like to call PHP: positive health power, because your health conditions you think are holding you back right now, might give you the power within yourself to climb that mountain you never thought you could climb. My eyesight, arthritis and mental health problems have helped me elevate my life to levels I never thought I could. And, if you want to reach new heights in your life, all you might need is that extra push of encouragement from your family and friends to help you along the way to finding your true potential. Your health makes you who you are. Having health issues is not a drawback. I see it as an advantage because it helps you see your life from a whole new perspective to everybody else. So, remember those three magic words: PHP, positive health power. It doesn't matter what kind of disability you suffer from. You can always achieve greatness like anybody else; never hide away.

# SCARMAN USA AND SCARGIRL

Two people I have had the pleasure of getting to know through Instagram suffer from health and disability problems every day of their lives. And those two awe-inspiring individuals are Ward Foley and his good friend Mónica Ovalle León, who were both born with arthrogryposis. Ward Foley created ScarmanUSA.com many years ago to help empower children and adults of all ages who have been born with arthrogryposis. And Mónica Ovalle León runs the South American branch of scarmanusa.com called ScarGirl.

What is arthrogryposis, though, I hear you ask. Well, arthrogryposis is where the joints of your body take on a curve; they also call this joint contracture, which can cause shortening and weakening of the muscle tissue; arthrogryposis can be found throughout the body at birth. Medical professionals think genetic and environmental factors could cause it, yet the actual causes of arthrogryposis are still unknown.

Scarman was created from some of my scars but represents all of us. We all have scars. Some we can see and some we can't. Every scar on Scarman is real, and each scar has a story behind it. We can grow from our scars, from our struggles, and from our failures. Scarman celebrates that growth while helping us accept and love everything about ourselves.

**Ward Foley, Norton, Kansas, USA, scarmanusa.com**

When babies are born with arthrogryposis, the muscles around their joints can become thin, stiff, weak or missing. And, after having a lot of surgeries, babies can be left with scars which, sadly, Ward Foley and Mónica Ovalle Leon have both been left with. Ward has undergone decades of surgery and intense rehabilitation, has been laughed at, beaten up, faced terrible humiliation, badly burned in a deep fryer and nearly killed by a drunk driver. So, this caring and inspirational man has been through a lot in his life, as you can see. Ward's never let his health and disability problems ever get him down, though, and instead of feeling sorry for himself he's embraced his arthrogryposis and it's empowered and inspired him to show sufferers of the condition that you can still live a beautiful and meaningful life, and achieve greatness just like Ward himself has done.

> You can be in the wrong place at the wrong time… a lot. In fact, your whole life can seem like one big wrong turn. But that's exactly what it takes to get you to the one place you want most.

### Ward Foley, Norton, Kansas, USA, scarmanusa.com

Ward's organisation, scarmanusa.com, holds Scarfests all over the world where families who have been affected by arthrogryposis all come together, make new friends, share stories and give hope to others who are living with this condition today. Ward also shares his own life story of living with arthrogryposis to the families at his Scarfests. And he explains to them how we should all love ourselves for who we are.

> Everybody has Scars, including me. We have to accept them and life with them, but it's not easy. Nobody should judge people on their looks. Character is more important! Everybody is Beautiful with scars or without them.

### Rommel Bommel, Germany, instagram.com/rommel_bommel_g

Mónica Ovalle León also goes around bringing positive vibes, smiles and happiness to all the families and children who suffer from arthrogryposis in South America, along with helping to organise Scarman USA events. What a lovelier world it would be to live in if there were more people like Ward, Mónica and all the individuals who work at Scarman USA and ScarGirl.

Ward Foley has inspired me to accept my own scars I have been given by cruel negative-minded people in today's society. Whether they are the real scars on my body or the hurtful scars, those cold-hearted individuals have left me with on the inside. Those scars represent my stories of where I have been, what I have been through, where I am going, and how I have overcome them.

Scarman USA is about:

> Helping others to feel so-called normal just the way they are. Being proud of themselves, their struggles and every single scar. Spreading a message of hope, courage and self-acceptance while providing support, friendship and unconditional love. We are not given a good life or a bad life. We are given life, and it's up to us to make it good or bad.

**Ward Foley, Norton, Kansas, USA, scarmanusa.com**

When I first got to know Ward, he kindly sent over from America a Scarman shirt and colouring book for me, which was exceptionally generous of him to do; those gifts meant so much. I wanted you to know about Ward Foley and Mónica Ovalle León because, no matter what kind of disability you have, remember you're accepted for who you are, you're loved for who you are, and you will grow more every day into the person you're truly meant to become because of your disability. I highly recommend checking out the fantastic work that Ward Foley and Mónica Ovalle León are both doing right now by visiting ScarmanUSA.com. You can also follow Ward Foley by visiting instagram.com/inscargram and Mónica Ovalle León at instagram.com/monica.ovalle.l

Thank you so much for your friendships over the years Ward and Mónica. Also, thank you for the shirt and colouring book, Ward. All my very best to you both and your families.

Steven M. Rippin

# FOUR INSPIRATIONAL PEOPLE WHO SUFFER FROM DISABILITIES

Your life is what you make it, and these following four inspirational individuals, who have all suffered from health and disability conditions, have certainly proved that. The first guy I would like to tell you about is Morris E. Goodman, who the doctors named 'The Miracle Man'. Morris E. Goodman was left fully paralysed from a plane crash he was involved in, which left him unable to breathe, talk or swallow on his own, plus he could only communicate by blinking his eyelids! Because of Morris E. Goodman's will and determination to live, though, he survived and rebuilt his body along with his mind and outlook on life; he truly is a remarkable individual. Morris E. Goodman is now a motivational speaker and goes around the world inspiring other people with his life story of survival and the extraordinary amount of will and determination he has to live. If you would like to learn more about Morris E. Goodman's story and the journey he has been on, here is a link to his website: www. TheMiracleMan.org

The second guy I would like to mention is Nick Vujicic from Australia, who was born without any arms or legs. Nick Vujicic now swims, surfs and plays golf. To learn more about how Nick Vujicic lives his life and what he has accomplished, here is a link to his website:www.LifeWithoutLimbs. org. The third inspirational individual I would like to mention is Michael J. Fox, who was the star of the *Back to the Future* movies in the mid-eighties. Michael J. Fox was diagnosed with Parkinson's at the age of twenty-nine. Since being diagnosed, Michael has now become an advocate for finding a cure for the disease. Michael's not let Parkinson's stop him from continuing to do what he loves doing best either, which is working in the entertainment industry. Michael has continued to star in many TV shows and has done a lot of voiceover work in movies as well. So, as you can see, Michael J. Fox is a very inspiring man who is living his life to the fullest.

And, finally, the fourth inspiring individual I would like to mention is Stephen Hawking, who was one of the world's greatest minds of our time. Stephen Hawking was diagnosed with amyotrophic lateral sclerosis (ALS) at the age of twenty-one. Stephen Hawking was only given a few years to live after being diagnosed with the disease but lived until he was seventy-six years old! And, although he couldn't speak and was wheelchair-bound, he became one of the most famous physicists the world had known since Albert Einstein. Stephen Hawking was a theoretical physicist, cosmologist, author and the director of research at the Centre for Theoretical Cosmology at Cambridge University. So, without a doubt, I think you will agree Stephen Hawking was a remarkable man who didn't let his disabilities stop him from achieving greatness in his life. These four extraordinary gentlemen are a few of the inspirational individuals who have and did not let their disabilities hold them back from living their lives to the fullest and accomplishing great things. They show you and me that anything is possible. So, if you have a disability, do you want to mope around feeling sorry for yourself all day long? Or do you want to be remembered for being that person who inspired other people who have disabilities to become the best versions of themselves? The choice is yours, all depending on what kind of medical health issue you have, of course. Remember, having a positive attitude and plenty of perseverance and determination can help you accomplish great things. So, it comes down to you how you want to live your life.

# HELP AND ADVICE WHEN LIVING WITH A HEALTH OR DISABILITY ISSUE

To get a better understanding of how other people cope daily with their health and disability conditions, I asked my friends on social media the following question.

If you have a medical health condition, visible deformity, or disability. How does society treat you, and what advice would you give to somebody who suffers humiliation from the public because of this?

Hi Steve, I have many thoughts on this one. Disability in anyway is horrid. I do not feel that many people are aware or understand mental disability. Disability is much the same – I.E, it's not the norm, so many do not understand. I have empathy for those that have this disability, but it is not visual and so can't be understood. I feel some people hide their disability, but others ride on the back of it by declaring their status. Often in my opinion and experience, those with nonphysical disability lose out on sympathy and compassion that is so important to us all. I myself have a disability that is not visible. I do not broadcast it. If you are physically disabled, I feel for you and would pass the word around, but you should also realise there are a great majority of disabled people who do not bang a drum for empathy. We have a deep divide between physical and mental disability that requires much thought by the NHS. I very much doubt in today's society that a physically disabled person could be treated badly, unless they used their disability for unfair advantage. Oh, I do like stirring the cauldron lol.

Gordon Harrison, Leicestershire, England

People love to judge what they can't see or experience for themselves. The Truth is to never expect others to understand, but always give them the chance to think a little!

Fior Avona, London, England,
instagram.com/stormgirl_370z.official

Being in a wheelchair and in pain 24 hours a day sometimes makes me cranky. Everyone offers you the best ways to deal and cope with it, although most people have never gone through what you're going through. The advice is helpful, but when living with chronic pain, you have tried everything. So please, if we are not the life and soul of the party all the time, don't take it personally. Also, many people who have a disability, either physical or mental, don't mind talking or answering questions about it, because it helps with ignorance. So, don't stare or whisper and point. ASK, and we would tell. We are all human; people with disabilities are not aliens; we are humans with special gifts xx.

Wendy Rudge, Basildon, Essex, England

Usually, people will never be able to understand your disability, especially if it isn't obvious to them. The best thing to do is educate and distance yourself from toxic people. As a person with Asperger's Syndrome, I may struggle with social skills, but I do the best I can. If other people don't see the effort you make just to seem normal; they're not worth your time. There may be plenty of instances where people think you're normal because you don't 'Look <insert disability here>,' and put too high of expectations on you, because of that. I've realised that all people are strange, but in various ways. For anyone that also has mental health issues, remember, you're NEVER alone.

Bethany, Nashville, Tennessee, USA,
instagram.com/broken_mindsette

I too live with some form of mental illness. I have Diverticulitis, Asthma, Arthritis and a knackered back. My answer would be to never give in. There is always inspiration knocking on the door.

Tim Wykes, Brixworth, England

I live with mental illness, and I am also a mother of an autistic child. The stigma is awful, but you can always educate, answer questions, politely smile at their unwarranted advice (deep breaths help too) and most importantly be true to yourself. You are not the disability; you're a human who lives with certain medical issues (it just could be your superpower, who knows) One small thing; I have a daughter that points out one thing not many may know about autism; that girls are affected too. Sometimes it's not picked up on and diagnosed until they are older. Some think autism is a disease, but it's a neurological disorder affecting various areas of development and function. It can't be cured but can be well managed. Kate's sensory issues are her superpower. Kinda like Spiderman's spider senses.

Rebecca Tompkins, Adelaide, Australia

Having an invisible disability makes it hard. Unfortunately, people can't grasp it, which is frustrating. Some people are limited in their ability to understand. I'll continue pushing through helping others who truly want to know. Honestly, it's sad to see how people don't understand a medical condition which someone has no control over. It can damage a person on an emotional level. It breaks my heart that people can be cruel with no empathy…

**Tammee Clark, Brown City, Michigan, USA**

Thank you to all my friends who contributed their advice on how they cope with health and disability problems. I sincerely hope they are coping as best as they can with their conditions. And I wish them, and you if you are struggling, all my very best for the future.

Health and disability problems come in all various forms. In some instances, they can lead to further conditions once you have had them treated. If I hadn't had arthritis, I would never have developed the eye conditions I have had to live with since I was five years old, which are only getting worse.

If I had been born today with the arthritis I was born with back in 1975, there is a good chance they would have been able to treat my arthritis a lot better and I might not have developed the eye conditions I have because of how far health care and medical procedures have advanced over the years. Like they say, though, you should be thankful for the health you do have, which I truly am.

So, if you come across anybody who insults you because they don't understand the medical problems you have, please don't let them upset you. If anything, those individuals are the ones who have a problem that seriously needs addressing. They obviously are unable to live in a civilised society and don't know how to interact with other human beings appropriately. Furthermore, they are the ones who need to seek out help from either a psychiatrist or a life coach, if you ask me. Oh, and learn some people skills as well while they're at it!

Living with a health or a disability will change your life and might make you stand out to those around you. So, remember, OWN your condition, or it will OWN YOU and take over your life, which you don't want to happen! Let your ailment help you become the best version of who you were always born to be.

No matter what people say or what dilemmas you face throughout your life, always be ready to take on the world and make your family and friends proud of who you are because your health or disability make you special and unique. And, just like Rebecca Tompkins says, her daughter's sensory issues are her superpower, kinda like Spider-man's spider senses. To me, that makes Rebecca's daughter Kate all the more awesome. I love that way of viewing health and disability problems, don't you? Now let's get out there and change the world for the better and bring hope and justice to those who need our help who are suffering today.

# WHEN MY DAD HAD A CARDIAC ARREST AT WORK

Through the following chapters, I'm going to tell you how my dad survived having a cardiac arrest and battled cancer. So, let's begin. My dad's troubles all began on one brisk cold winter's morning. On Tuesday, 11 November 2014, my dad and I had a job to do in East Farndon, Northamptonshire, fitting carpets in the local village church. Everything was going well, and the church carpet we had laid was looking great. Then when I had a few spare minutes while my dad and I were waiting for the glue to go off – we full stuck the carpet, you see – I went outside and made some video vlogs on my phone, then after I had finished making my vlogs I went back in the church, and my dad said he needed to lie down because he wasn't feeling too well. We both thought he must be coming down with the flu, so my dad had a lie down, then he said his shoulder was hurting him as well, which we thought must have been down to all the carpet fitting he'd done over the previous fifty years. My dad also told me he was feeling drained and worn out that day as well, which wasn't like him at all. Then after he had lay down and rested for a while, he seemed a bit better in himself. So, after we had finished the job we were doing, we continued with the rest of our work day.

That evening, when my dad called round to a customer's house, the customer said, 'Are you all right, George? You don't look too well.' And my dad said he was fine and just felt a little bit under the weather. That night, because my dad was still feeling drained and not his usual self, he took a hot bath to see if that would help him to feel any better, which he said it did. So, we just put why he was feeling the way he did down to the flu. Then on Wednesday, 12 November 2014, which started like any other regular day, we got ourselves ready and went off to work. That day my dad had a dining room carpet to fit, and I had a lounge carpet to clean in the same house over in the village of Rothwell.

As we were driving over to Rothwell, I asked my dad how he was feeling, and he said, 'Yeah, I'm feeling much better.' So, we carried on as usual and helped each other to set up the jobs we were doing that day. Then when I had nearly finished cleaning the lounge carpet, my dad came into see me, and he didn't look well at all! He said, 'Steve, I'm not feeling too good, I think I'm going to have to call the doctor.' And when I heard my dad say that I started to worry.

'What's up?' I said, sounding concerned.

'I've been having a pain across my shoulder, and I'm having chest pains,' my dad replied. So, with no messing about, we left our work equipment in the house, locked up and got in the van, where my dad then called our local doctors' surgery up in Market Harborough, who recommended him to go over to Kettering General Hospital.

I said to my dad, 'I'll drive,' but he was having none of it because he knew I had just got a new pair of glasses, which I was having trouble focusing out of properly because my lenses in my frames had been changed. I would have scared my dad half to death, anyway – pardon the pun – if I had driven us both over to the hospital that day! I felt terrible, although I guess it was safer I didn't drive, or I could have caused an accident, knowing me! So, my dad drove himself over to Kettering General Hospital while in the early stages of having a cardiac arrest. As we were driving to the hospital, I could see how much my dad was struggling, and he said to me, 'I'm not feeling good, Steve… but I'll be all right, don't worry.' And that's when I really did start to panic!

I kept saying, 'Let me drive, I'll be all right.' My dad still wouldn't have any of it, though; he's one stubborn motherf***er; I know that!

The critical moment of that journey occurred when my dad and I drove off the A14, where you take the exit for the A43, because when we pulled up at the traffic lights where the massive roundabout is I looked over at my dad to make sure he was all right and that's when I saw he had passed out across the steering wheel! 'DAD, DAD WAKE UP ARE YOU ALL RIGHT?' I started shouting, then after a few seconds, thankfully, he did wake up, and he was covered in sweat. My dad then said to me, 'I passed out, didn't I? It's all right; we're nearly there.'

I can honestly say I don't know anybody who is more strong-willed, resilient and determined than my dad. His will to survive and continue astounded me that day! So, there my dad was, covered in sweat and having a cardiac arrest at the traffic lights, which had just turned green, with cars parping their horns as they drove by. It was all so surreal; it was like we were both living in a horrible nightmare we couldn't wake up from! Luckily, we arrived safely at Kettering General Hospital, but then we had to queue up to park the van! After ten minutes of waiting, which seemed like a lifetime, we managed to park up only to find out it was the wrong car park! Eventually we managed to park the van up thankfully! Hospital car parks, eh!

Then my dad and I ran as fast as we could to the A&E department, which we were so pleased to get to at last. Once we were in what we thought was the A&E department, I remember looking at my dad and he was literally dripping with sweat, out of breath and could hardly stand up by himself; it looked as if he was about to drop dead any second! Then the receptionist told us we were in the wrong area! And that the A&E department we needed to be in was further down from where we had just come from! I couldn't believe it and wasn't sure if my dad was going to make it or not! All I can think was his adrenaline must have kept him going that day.

So we both hurried back the way we had come to the A&E department, which seemed to take forever to get to, then once we finally arrived my dad told the receptionist he was having chest pains and finding it hard to breathe. Unfortunately, while my dad was having a cardiac arrest, the receptionist had to ask him for his full name, where he lived, his occupation etc. Then that was it: my dad turned to me and said, 'Steve... carry on you'll have to do the rest.' Eventually when the receptionist realised how bad my dad was, she called for a doctor to examine him in a triage room while I finished giving her my dad's details. After signing my dad in, I went straight into the triage room, where I saw my dad lying on an examination bed while the doctor did an ICG on him to find out what was happening inside his body.

While the medic was doing a scan on my dad, my dad said to me, 'I'm going,' then I saw my dad's eyes roll up into the back of his head, and that was it: my dad had died right there in front of me! I shouted at the medic in hysterics, 'WHAT'S HAPPENING TO MY DAD?' The doctor then turned around, looked at my dad and pressed the emergency panic button. Then, within seconds, a whole team of surgeons and nurses came bursting into the triage room, which I was quickly taken out of a few seconds later by one of the nurses, who said to me, 'You don't want to see this; come outside and wait here a minute, dear.' Then she went off and left me all alone. While I was standing there on my own, the walls of reality melted away in front of my eyes. Nothing was making sense to me, and I felt as if I was in a dream. I started feeling sick all over. I couldn't focus, my vision went blurry, I broke out in a cold sweat, my legs turned to jelly, my head was spinning, I was having heart palpitations and shaking, and, basically, I was going into shock. I then slid down the wall I was leaning against and fell to the floor.

I remember everybody in the waiting room area of the A&E department looking and wondering what was up with me while I was there on the floor in shock, thinking I would never see my dad alive again. Luckily, the nurse who had taken me out of the triage room where my dad was came and helped me back onto my feet again, and said, 'Come with me, dear; I'll make you a cup of tea.' She then took me into a small room and brought me a cup of tea with sugar in it, which helped to increase my blood sugar levels, which had dropped considerably after seeing my dad die. Even writing this right now, I'm starting to shake and feel slightly nauseous all over. I'm actually breaking out into a cold sweat, if I'm honest with you!

After I had gained a bit of self-control over myself, the first thing the nurse told me to do was to call my mum and explain to her what had happened to my dad, which was really hard for me to do, as you can imagine. When I phoned my mum, I told her not to worry, but to come over to Kettering General Hospital as soon as she could. I then went on Facebook, because I felt so alone sitting there in that small room all by myself, not knowing if my dad was going to survive, and I posted a status saying 'I'm scared', if I remember correctly. And my online friends were fantastic that day. They showed my dad and me so much love and support, which I will never forget. Then I called Paul Tompkins up, who was cleaning some upholstery for us that day – we give all our upholstery cleaning jobs to Paul, you see, and he has been a good friend of ours for over twenty years. It was so good to hear Paul's voice when he answered the phone; he was fantastic and told me not to worry and that everything was going to be all right. Paul said, 'I'm here if you need anything at all, Steven.'

Thank you so much for being there for me that day, Paul; I've got a lot of respect for you, mate.

Steven M. Rippin

While I was being looked after by the nurse, you'll be happy to know that, thankfully, my dad was resuscitated! Then, after my dad was revived, he was then transferred to the cardiac department, where he was still in a lot of pain, so they gave him some aspirin and a Ticagrelor. My dad was also able to provide the surgeons with verbal consent to operate. Furthermore, he told the surgeons to make sure they gave his mobile phone to me to look after. Isn't it funny what you think of when you're going through something as traumatic as a cardiac arrest! It just shows you how important our phones are to us. It's so surreal thinking back what my dad went through.

Later that day, my mum arrived at the hospital, and she was so strong, bless her; she without a doubt helped me to keep it together, I know that.

Thank you, Mum; you helped me more than you will ever know, I love you so much.

Steven M. Rippin

Around six-thirty in the evening, my good friends Matthew Squibbs and Mark Perry came over to Kettering General Hospital because my mum and I needed to get my dad's work van back home and I wasn't in any fit state at all to drive it.

Thank you, Matt and Mark, so much for being there for my family and me in November 2014. It meant a lot knowing how much you both cared.

Steven M. Rippin

After six hours, my mum and I were informed by a surgeon that, while my dad had been in surgery, he died twice, but they had managed to resuscitate him on both of those occasions thankfully, which was the best news we had heard all day! The doctor also suggested that we should go home and try to get some rest because there wasn't much more we could do. We both felt so bad leaving him in hospital that night. All I wanted more than anything was to see my dad. Once my mum and I arrived home, we had a lot of messages and phone calls to reply to from our family and friends who had heard about what had happened to my dad. It was lovely reading their messages of support on Facebook.

After I had replied to my messages, I then got on the phone to my dad's brother, my uncle Andrew, and he said, 'I'll come over, Steven, and we can go over and see how your dad's doing in hospital if you like?' Which I wanted to do more than anything in the world. So, I called Kettering General Hospital to see how my dad was doing, and they told me he was back on the ward, but it would be best not to disturb him tonight. Still, though, my Uncle Andrew and I drove to the hospital, and we did get to see my dad, although it was heart-breaking because he had wires and tubes poking out of his body and machines all around him. My dad was in the land of the living, though, which was what I had wished for all day long, and he was being monitored by a lovely nurse twenty-four hours a day as well. The first thing my dad said when he saw his brother Andrew and me was, 'I'm back.' As you can see, my dad never lost his sense of humour, and he was so pleased to see us both that night. I then called my mum, and she spoke to my dad; she was so happy to hear his voice, and of course over the moon that he had survived. My mum felt so guilty for not being there at the hospital that night, though, but my dad understood she must have been feeling emotionally drained after the day she had been through.

What a day we had and to think, only hours earlier, my dad and I were both at work fitting and cleaning carpets.

That day, when my dad had his cardiac arrest, he died three times.

I felt so relieved when I saw my dad alive; it was like a weight had been lifted from my shoulders. It was also one of the most exhilarating and happy emotionally charged feelings I have ever experienced in my life.

It will undoubtedly be a day none of my family or I will ever forget. I can't thank the surgeons, nurses and rest of the medical staff at Kettering General Hospital enough for saving my dad's life that day. Now here is a short video message my dad wanted to make that night when my uncle Andrew and I went over to visit him after his surgery on 12 November 2014: bit.ly/GeorgeInHospitalNovember2014

None of the medical staff could believe my dad had driven himself to the hospital while he was having a cardiac arrest! You should have seen the look on their faces when they found out.

The day after my dad had his cardiac arrest, I remember seeing my mum crying, which I presumed was because of what had happened the previous day. The reason my mum was crying, though, was because she had come off the phone to a customer, who had said to her, 'Where's George? He's supposed to be here fitting my lounge carpet today.' And my mum's reply to that customer was, 'My husband had a cardiac arrest yesterday and is in the hospital recovering from it, I'm sorry, but there's nothing I can do about your carpet that needs fitting.' The customer then said to my mum, 'Well, I'm not happy about that, when's my carpet going to be fitted?' And that was when my mum started to cry and had to put the phone down. When I heard what this woman had said to my mum, I was fuming. I couldn't believe how inconsiderate she was being; she obviously had no feelings whatsoever for my dad. To this day, I still get annoyed when I think about how that customer spoke to my mum and made her cry! So, there my family and I were, who had just gone through one of the worst experiences of our lives. And there was that customer worrying about her carpet! What a sad world she lives in!

A few weeks later, once things had settled down and my dad had rearranged his fitting jobs while he was in hospital, I had to go and work at that customer's house with another fitter to fit her lounge carpet! All I can say is it took a lot for me to not say anything to her about how she had upset my mum. My dad told me to leave it, you see, because it just wasn't worth the hassle of getting into an argument with her, plus we had enough going on in our lives already. So, I respected my dad's wishes, and I didn't say anything, I wish I had, though, believe me! Some people are so self-absorbed in their little materialistic worlds, they forget about the real world around them, and focus solely on themselves without any consideration whatsoever for anybody else!

On the positive side of everything that happened to my dad, it did bring our families closer together. And the outpouring of lovely messages of support we received from everybody sincerely touched our hearts. My dad also couldn't believe the number of get-well cards he received either. He had never been one for buying and receiving cards; he used to see them as a waste of money, and would say to me, 'What a waste of money, don't bother getting me one.' He has since changed his tune and now sees how powerful words can be when you receive a meaningful and beautiful gesture, such as a get-well card.

A week after my dad had his cardiac arrest, the surgeons and medical staff were happy to let him go home. It amazed my mum and me how well he looked when we picked him up. And here is a video of my dad on the day he left the hospital: bit.ly/GeorgeLeavingHospitalNovember2014

My dad now has three stents in his arteries. The surgeons said his left main artery is normal. And that his left anterior descending artery has mild proximal stenosis, with long moderate stenosis in the mid vessel, while my dad's circumflex artery occluded proximally. And his right coronary artery is dominant with mild–moderate plaque disease only. As you can tell, these are notes from my dad's medical records, which I have tried my best to make into easy reading for you! Don't worry if they have baffled you because they have completely confused me!

My dad died for around two minutes on the operating table.

To think my dad led a pretty healthy and fit lifestyle before he had his cardiac arrest shows you that anybody can be at risk from having heart problems. So please look after your health as best as you can. My dad never drank and never smoked, and he always ate healthily. He did like a treat now and then, but who doesn't?

My dad told me when he knew he was going to die as he was lying there on the examination bed in the triage room that everything around him was white. He also told me he was in a long, white corridor that had white ceilings, white walls and white floors. What got me was when my dad said, 'Whoever fitted the flooring did a great job on it!' So, even on his death bed, my dad was still thinking about carpets and flooring; now, that's what you call dedication to your job, isn't it? And it doesn't end there, because right at the end of the white corridor, after my dad had finished admiring the craftsmanship of the white flooring, my dad told me he saw one of the ceiling lights go out, and then, one by one, he said he saw the rest of the lights go out individually, starting from the far end of the white corridor. And it wasn't until the very last ceiling light went out, which was above my dad's head, when he said to me, 'I'm going,' and that's when he knew his time was up and he died. My dad also said it wasn't painful when he died, and he didn't remember anything while he was on the other side; he just remembers waking up in the ICU ward. Now here is what my dad had to say after surviving his cardiac arrest.

I was glad I survived it; it's funny, when you have a cardiac arrest, in my case I wasn't in any pain you just drift off and die very peacefully, but it was good to wake up again.

**George W. Rippin, Market Harborough, England**

And to end my dad's cardiac arrest episode, here is my dad's thank-you video message we both put together to thank everybody for all their love and support throughout this tough journey he had been through. Well, that's what we thought, and all was well for a couple of years: bit.ly/ASpecialMessageFromMyDad

# WELLNOW EXERCISE FOR HEALTH

My dad now eats even healthier than he did before and he's cut out takeaways, which we all used to love eating at least once a week, plus he also goes to the WellNow Exercise for Health class, which is run by Liz Adams at our local leisure centre. My dad's always making the other members of the class laugh with his crazy fun and motivating attitude and shenanigans he gets up to while he's there. For example, one time, my dad downloaded a farting app on his phone and when he was on his way to his exercise class he walked through our local leisure centre with his farting app set to making a trumping sound with every step he made! My dad told me the young girl behind the reception desk was loving it and laughing away when she heard his fake gusty wind shenanigans coming from his phone. Also, while he was at his exercise class, every so often when somebody bent down while they were warming up and stretching, he would press a farting sound effect on his app, and everybody around him would burst out laughing. I think he makes those classes a lot of fun.

> Everybody who suffers a heart condition is referred to a rehabilitation exercise class.

Liz Adams, who runs the WellNow Exercise for Health classes, also organises walks for her members to go on. I went on one of those walks with Liz and my dad while we were raising money for Cancer Research UK in June 2017, and everybody who participated on that walk donated £1 each to help my dad and me with our fundraising campaign, which we appreciated very much. One lovely lady, who's ninety-eight years old and attends Liz Adams's exercise class, has stayed a lot more mobile, fitter and healthier than she could have ever imagined. So, you have no excuses for not exercising, and it proves it doesn't matter how old you are: you are never too old to start keeping fit.

Exercising will help invigorate your mind, body and soul. Just ask anybody who keeps fit, and they will tell you how good it makes them feel. If you have any medical health conditions, though, always consult your local GP first. And they will let you know if it's safe for you to take part in any physical activity you want to take up. Now here is a video I made of my dad in action at his WellNow Exercise for Heath class, which I put my own little spin on. So, are you ready to do some disco walking? If you are, please follow the following link: bit.ly/DiscoWalking. Keeping fit will make you feel fantastic on the inside and on the outside.

# I BELIEVE STRESS WAS THE CAUSE OF MY DAD'S CARDIAC ARREST

The medical staff told my mum and me that a cardiac arrest can be brought on by stress, or it can be in your genes. I believe my dad was under a lot of stress because of the number of hours he used to do at work; he used to do fourteen-hour days. My mum and I always used to tell him to slow down and take it easier, but his phone would continuously be ringing with customers putting pressure on him to get their jobs done straight away, which he felt obliged to do for them, plus he wasn't sleeping well at night either, because of the jobs he had on his mind. It was crazy.

You see, my dad would fit as many carpets as he could in a day, and if he got caught up he would pull another job in on top of his day's work! And not only that: he also had his night calls to do after he had finished fitting carpets as well, which kept him out until at least ten-thirty most nights! Some of my dad's customers didn't realise how much stress and pressure they were putting him under; it really was all too much for him, which he didn't like to admit, because he loved his job so much. And some customers who wanted their carpets fitting were an absolute nightmare when they were doing their houses up! Some clients, you see, will push you along to get their jobs done when it's obvious they're not ready for you. And, get this, I've been on jobs with my dad when the customer's house is still being built, and there are no floors down in the bedrooms we're expected to fit carpet in! Like, what's that all about? And the customer will turn around to us and say, 'Well we're project managing the build ourselves, and things haven't gone according to plan!'

We would love to say to the customer, 'Yeah, that's obvious isn't it; we can see that with the disorganisation you're in.' I'm just so pleased my dad no longer has to put up with that kind of nonsense from customers anymore!

Numerous workers in all kinds of industries are put under stress, and it isn't fair on them, is it? You and I should think about our health first, and how taking too much work on can take its toll on us, just like it has done on my dad and so many other tradespeople. If you haven't got the time to take a job on, tell the customer you don't have the time to do it unless they are willing to wait because it isn't worth the stress it can cause you.

To destress your life, you have to take a look at the kind of lifestyle you might be leading right now. For example: Do you get home late from work? – Do you have quality time to spend with your partner and family? – Do you go to sleep at night worrying about jobs that are on your mind? – Are you happy with your life? – Are there things you wish you could do, but you never seem to have the time to do them? – Do you feel down and depressed? Or do you feel like escaping the life you have right now? If you can relate to any of those questions, then there's a good chance you're living a pretty stressful lifestyle, which unfortunately a lot of people are doing nowadays without even realising it. So, please, do your best to make any essential lifestyle changes you believe you should be making right now to help improve your life before it's too late and you end up harming your health, just like my dad did!

Look after your health and happiness – Pace yourself – Spend time with your family and friends – Don't block the people you care about the most out of your life because you're working too hard, and if you're overworking yourself, take a step back, relax and delegate your work to other people if you can. Don't worry, be happy and live a stress-free life. And, before I end, please, always remember, if you ever feel weak, start having chest pains, or a pain across your shoulders and difficulty in breathing, get yourself to your nearest hospital straight away to get checked out.

# MY DAD'S BATTLE WITH CANCER

When I first heard my dad's GP had referred him to go and see a cancer specialist, it turned my mum's life and my life upside down. The last thing we expected my dad to say when he came home from the doctors in January 2017 was that he might have cancer! You just can't prepare yourself for news like that, can you? And when my mum and I went to see the consultant with my dad, it broke our hearts when he confirmed that he did have cancer.

By sharing my own experiences throughout this chapter, I hope I am able to help you or somebody you know who might sadly be suffering right now with this devastating illness. Before I told any of my friends on social media that my dad had cancer, I discussed with him first if he wanted to share his journey with them. He did because he thought it would help make more awareness of this deadly disease and also assist others who might be going through a similar ordeal in their own lives. Cancer is something you and I should always be talking about, so we can help one another through any hardships we might be facing alone. Now here is the video message my dad made to let everybody know he had been diagnosed with having squamous cell carcinoma mouth cancer: bit. ly/WhenMyDadWasToldHeHadCancer

The support my dad received after everybody had seen his video was unbelievable. I soon started receiving loads of private messages on Facebook from people who had been through cancer, people who had just been diagnosed with it and people who knew somebody who was going through it. There were so many upsetting stories I was told about, along with the stories of individuals who had thankfully recovered from cancer as well, which was so good to hear because it gave me hope and lifted my spirits a bit. Every day, my family and friends were asking me for news and updates on how my dad was doing, which was lovely of them and what also reminded me that I wasn't alone on this journey my dad was going through. So, I started posting regular updates on Facebook and Instagram to help keep everybody informed on my dad's progress, which they really appreciated.

One nurse at a pre-op appointment my parents and I attended a couple of weeks before my dad's major mouth cancer operation said to my dad while my mum and I were in the room with him, 'This is a very serious operation you're going through, Mr Rippin; it will be a long, hard recovery process, and you may not talk again. The worst-case scenario is that you could die.' My parents and I thought she put that very bluntly with no feeling at all! So, as you can imagine, it didn't go down to well with us and made us worry all the more. Some nurses need to show more compassion when talking to patients and their families.

One car journey I will always remember was when my Auntie Lella drove my mum, dad and me over to Northampton General Hospital on Monday, 3 April 2017, which was the day before my dad's operation. My parents and I really appreciated Auntie Lella driving us over that day and being there for us so much. As we drove through our hometown on our way to Northampton General Hospital, I was looking around at everybody on the streets of Market Harborough, who were busily getting along with their everyday lives, holding hands with their loved ones, and chatting on the streets to their friends with smiles on their faces. And I thought to myself, 'Will I ever be part of this world again? I feel so cut off from everything and everybody who I know and love so much.' I felt like I had been torn away from the reality I once used to know, and now I was looking in on the world from an entirely different perspective. I can only best describe the feeling I was having, if you have watched the movie *The Matrix*, when Neo got pulled out of the world he once knew and into the reality he was woken up in, where Morpheus told him that the world he used to know didn't exist how he believed it did. So that's the feeling I had and still do, to this day.

So, there I was, deep in thought about life as you and I know it and then I was snapped out of my daydream when Auntie Lella said, 'Who wants to do a bit of car karaoke?' Which was the last thing I thought my parents and I would be doing that day! So, there we all were, on our way to the hospital the day before my dad's major mouth cancer operation, karaoke-ing to Lady Gaga's 'Poker Face'! If you do watch this next video, you will see my dad dancing away with his funky dance moves in the back seat of my Auntie Lella's car. And this video really does bring a lump to my throat when I watch it back: bit.ly/DrivingToHospitalDoingCarPoolKaraoke

> Thank you so much, Auntie Lella, for driving my dad over to the hospital in April 2017. You helped my family out so much back then, and I will never forget that, especially the car karaoke, that was great fun and helped to lighten the mood that day. Much love to you.

Steven M. Rippin

The day before my dad's operation was all quite surreal! My emotions were all over the place, and I wanted to burst into tears one minute and then laugh and smile the next. Deep down, though, I wanted to show my dad I was all right and that I was staying strong for him and my mum while he was going to be in hospital. I can only imagine how my dad must have been feeling back then. Now here is another very emotional video where I broke down in tears, along with my mum and Auntie Lella, when we left my dad in the hospital: bit.ly/LeavingMyDadInHospital

Leaving my dad that day was one of the toughest moments of my life, and I still remember so vividly the doors to the ward closing as I stood there waving goodbye to him, not knowing if I would ever see him again. I can't even begin to explain to you how that felt.

The night before any serious operation, a doctor talks you through the worst-case scenarios that could happen to you during your procedure. And dying was one of the scenarios my dad was told could happen to him! I asked my dad what he said when he was told by one of the surgeons, that the operation he was about to go through could end his life, and this is what he said.

> F**king hell, well, what's got to be done has got to be done. I just hope I wake up. I'm glad Sheila and Steven weren't here to hear you say that.

George W. Rippin, Market Harborough, England

My dad was able to cope with being told he could die because of his positive attitude, even though he was scared on the inside, which is just a normal reaction anybody would have, isn't it? That evening, once my mum and I had arrived home, my dad Facetimed us from the hospital after being told by his surgeon that there was a chance he could die. And he said to us, 'I love you both,' which made my mum and me feel very emotional, as you can imagine, and is making me feel upset right now as I write this. These were the last words my mum and I heard my dad say before his operation. The next thirty hours or more were going to be the toughest my mum and I had ever been through in our lives, well, apart from when my dad had his cardiac arrest!

The medical staff recommended that my mum and I stay at home while my dad was being operated on. There wouldn't have been much we could have done by going to the hospital due to the procedure lasting over ten hours! So on Tuesday, 4 April 2017, the day of my dad's operation, my mum and I were finding it an extremely tough day to get through. What helped us, though, was when my mum's sisters, Lella and Janet, my aunties, came round to see us both at home. They supported my mum and me so much that day, as did all my dad's family as well. During my dad's operation, one team of specially trained surgeons worked on my dad's tongue and neck, while another group worked on his arm to remove a piece of skin, vein and artery which were going to be inserted and joined together onto his tongue, where the cancerous growth had been removed.

When my dad was having his operation done, to help me through the day, don't ask me why, but I decided to vent my frustration and how I was feeling on the inside by dressing as a devil and dancing my heart out, which for a few minutes made me feel so good! And the song I danced to was by DJ Mad Dog and Noize Suppressor vs Rob Gee, 'MFFYF'. Please be warned though, because if you watch this next video, I do swear, but singing the lyrics in this song really helped me to vent out how I was feeling that day: bit.ly/DancingLikeADevil4thApril2017

Around 6 pm we were told to call the hospital to find out how my dad was doing because that was when he should have been back on the ward. Unfortunately, though, when I spoke to the nurse, my dad still wasn't back, which worried my mum and me no end! So, I continued to call the hospital every hour to find out what was going on. It wasn't until 10.30 pm that my mum, Auntie Lella and I were finally told my dad was back on the ward, which was such a relief to finally hear! That was one stressful day! The reason my dad was late arriving back on the ward was because they had to rush him back into surgery to stop a minor bleed on his neck, which was bleeding from where they had made an incision to remove one of his lymph glands. My mum, Auntie Lella and I were just so happy to hear my dad had made it through the operation, though, and was ALIVE! My dad was kept asleep, with the anesthetic they gave him, until 3 pm the following day to let his body recover; he was out of it for around thirty hours!

I didn't get to see my dad again until Wednesday, 5 April 2017, when my dad's brother, my uncle Andrew, came over from Melton Mowbray and drove us both over to the hospital to see him, although the nurse did have to make sure it was all right with my dad first, though, because he had only just started to wake up from the anaesthetic. I thought the first time when I saw my dad after he had his cardiac arrest was tough. This time, though, it was even tougher because there were more wires and tubes going into him, and machines all around monitoring him, plus he couldn't talk because the surgeons had cut part of his tongue away! Luckily, Uncle Andrew and I had brought over a notepad for my dad to write on. And that's how we communicated with each other that day. I really had to hold the tears back when I saw my dad. It was so heart-breaking seeing this prominent and powerful human being, who was my dad, lying there not able to talk back to me. He also looked very emotional and ready to cry when he saw his brother and me appear in the ITU ward.

I just had to take a moment to compose myself, because I am actually crying right now as I write this. The feelings going through my head right now are unbelievable as I recall the events of that day.

When Uncle Andrew and I were standing around my dad's bed in the ITU ward, my dad reached out as best as he could to hold my hand as he looked into my eyes. And that's when I saw his tears trickling down his face as he began to cry. When I was looking into my dad's eyes as he was looking back into mine, I had to quickly turn away and make out I needed to blow my nose because I was going to burst into tears if I didn't. I knew I couldn't let my dad see me getting upset, because, if he did, then that would have made him feel even more emotional. Fortunately, I managed to pull myself back together.

When Uncle Andrew saw how I was feeling, he came to my rescue by producing two big bolts from the inside his jacket pocket, which completely threw me! I had no idea what he was going to do with these two huge bolts of his! So, I asked my Uncle Andrew what they were for, and he said, 'I thought your dad would make a great Frankenstein.' Then Uncle Andrew turned to my dad and said, 'All we have to do, George, is get some strong super glue and stick these two bolts to either side of your neck. It would make a great photo. What do you reckon, eh?' I was shocked and had no idea what to say! All I can say, is that my dad didn't look too impressed, and I noticed Uncle Andrew soon put his two large bolts away! Because the surgeons had removed one of my dad's lymph glands, there was a Frankenstein-like scar full of stitches around his neck. So, I could see where my Uncle Andrew was coming from that day with his Frankenstein exploits. Uncle Andrew has quite the sense of humour. It's always good to have a sense of humour, though, when you're visiting relatives and friends in hospital, isn't it? As they say, laughter is the best medicine after all.

The rest of our visit went really well, and we only spent a few more minutes with my dad because we could see he was feeling tired and needed to rest. So, we said our goodbyes and left my dad to have a sleep and recover. It was so good to see my dad that day, and considering all he had been through I thought he looked pretty good. Looking back to when I first saw my dad in the intensive therapy unit, it was like another world. There was a computer station that reminded me of something you would see on a *Star Trek* television show and an army of medical staff working around the clock looking after their patients, who were all hooked up to life-saving support systems. It's incredible to think what goes on in hospitals every day while we are at work or at home, enjoying life with our families and friends isn't it?

One thing my dad never lost while he was in hospital was his sense of humour because he wrote down on his notepad how the nurses would fight over who was going to give him a bed bath, which I secretly think he enjoyed. I also asked my dad a few months after his operation how it made him feel being told he might not wake up again, and this is what he said.

It's really scary. What choice do you have: you either don't have the operation and your cancer spreads… and will probably kill you.

You're in the hands of the experts, and you got to let them get on with what they got to get on with. You have to trust them.

**George W. Rippin, Market Harborough, England**

The procedure my dad underwent, explained: the operation was treated by the Maxillo-Facial team at Northampton General Hospital, and he underwent major surgery after being diagnosed with having squamous cell carcinoma on the left-hand side of his tongue at Kettering General Hospital. Before my dad's operation, the nurses at Kettering General hospital made an incision into my dad's stomach, where they inserted a feeding tube down his neck; they then pulled that feeding tube through the incision in his abdomen they had made. My dad was fitted with a feeding tube because he wasn't going to be able to eat any solid foods for a while and would be on a liquid diet for some time after his procedure.

Then the surgeons at Northampton General Hospital inserted a tracheostomy into my dad's neck, so he could breathe while the operation was taking place. Also, just in case he had difficulty breathing after his surgery. On the left-hand side of my dad's tongue, the surgeons performed a partial glossectomy, which means they removed the infected cancerous part of his tongue. They then reconstructed my dad's tongue with a radial forearm free flap from his left forearm, which means they took a skin graft from his left arm and inserted that piece of skin onto his tongue to fill in the gap where they had cut part of it away. Then the surgeons joined the artery and vein of my dad's tongue together with the artery and vein from the skin graft. Unbelievable, eh? And that's not all; the surgeons also dissected the left side of my dad's neck, where they removed one of his lymph glands as well! The operation went according to plan, although an hour after surgery the surgeons had to take my dad back down to the theatre again because he had a minor bleed on his neck.

It's fantastic what they can do nowadays, isn't it? My dad's surgeon, Dr Harrop, said before his operation that it's one of the most significant procedures they perform at Northampton General Hospital. And I can see why. After the operation, my dad spent a small amount of time in ITU. Then he was moved to the head and neck ward, where he spent the rest of his time in hospital recovering and being monitored by the fantastic team of doctors, nurses and staff who work there. My family, friends and I are forever grateful for all the hard work the surgeons, nurses and members of staff at Northampton General Hospital and Kettering General Hospital provided my dad with. Everybody who works at the NHS do such an excellent job and are a massive credit to our nation here in England, and I will never be able to thank them enough for saving my dad's life. I admire my dad so much for being the super strong and super positive man he is and forever will be in my eyes.

How my dad's mouth cancer started: my dad's mouth cancer started when an ulcer appeared on his tongue; he thought it would go away on its own. When after a month it didn't, that's when my dad decided to go to his local pharmacy, who told him to crush a paracetamol tablet and put it on the ulcer, which he did but that only made it worse and made the ulcer come up like a mushroom! When that happened, my dad booked an appointment to see his GP. The reason why my dad didn't go to see his GP any sooner was because there had been a campaign on the news about not wasting your GP's time with petty little problems. My dad told me he will never listen to that kind of advice ever again! When my dad saw his GP, he asked him why the ulcer had mushroomed as it had. And he said the paracetamol tablet must have brought the ulcer/cancerous growth to the surface quicker. My dad's GP then referred him to go and see a cancer specialist over at Kettering General Hospital, where he was diagnosed with squamous cell carcinoma cancer on the left-hand side of his tongue, which was the size of a golf ball! If you have had a mouth ulcer for more than two weeks just like my dad did, it is advised that you go to see your local GP and get it looked at as soon as possible. Now here are a few tips to help prevent you from getting mouth cancer.

Always keep a clean and fresh mouth, and remember to brush and floss your teeth regularly – Don't smoke or chew tobacco of any kind – If you have got an ulcer in your mouth, it is a good idea to swill your mouth out with salt water, which you should boil first and then let cool down for a few minutes before gargling. Gargling saltwater is a great natural disinfectant. And if the ulcer doesn't disappear after two weeks, then you should book an appointment to see your local GP to get it looked at – Always maintain regular dental check-ups at least once every six months. You can also ask your dentist for an oral cancer screening – Avoid alcohol; if you do like a drink though, drink in moderation – Exercise regularly, because it will help boost your immune system, which wards off cancer – Be careful how much exposure to the sun you have, and always protect your face and your lips. UV-A-B-blocking sun protection lip balms are good to use – Eat healthy, and include cancer-fighting foods and drinks in your diet, such as sweet potatoes, green leafy vegetables, garlic, pumpkin seeds, flaxseeds, tomatoes, cabbage, broccoli, berries, fruit, grapes, oranges, blueberries, water, and ginger and green teas. And finally, check your mouth at least once a month. You could buy yourself one of those dental mouth mirrors to help you check those hard-to-see areas. And remember, check the back and roof of your mouth, underneath your tongue, and the inside of your cheeks. And if you do feel anything unusual, such as any lumps, bumps, tender areas, red, white or grey patches, then you should book an appointment to see your dentist to have them checked out as soon as possible.

Q: How did you deal with getting through your father having cancer?

Kimberly Barnard, Arkansas, USA

A: Thank you for your question, Kimberly, I got through my dad having cancer with the help of my mum, family, friends and everybody who was there for me on social media. And also by staying as positive, strong and determined as I could, which I know is what my dad would have wanted me to have done. Music helped me a lot as well, but it was tough, Kimberly. Thank you so much for your question.

Steven M. Rippin

My dad told me, it helped him a tremendous amount by sharing his mouth cancer journey with everybody on social media.

One thing I did when I called the hospital to find out how my dad was doing after his operation, which I don't think he agreed with me doing, was when I went live on Facebook. My dad said to me, you see, 'I don't think you should have gone live like you did. What if you'd have rung the hospital up and they said your dad's dead?' I could totally understand where he was coming from when he said that to me. I just felt it was the right thing for me to do at the time, plus I did ask my mum if she minded me going live on Facebook, and she was happy for me to do so; I just followed my heart with how I was feeling. I think it also helped my mum as well, if I'm honest, because it gave us both comfort knowing we weren't facing this alone. And here, if you would like to watch it, is the Facebook live video telephone conversation I had, when I found out how my dad was doing after his mouth cancer operation: bit.ly/RingingUpTheHospital

My dad doesn't usually get emotional, although when he read messages from his family and friends on Facebook and Instagram those messages would make him choke up and cry. Seeing your dad, who's this big strong man you have always looked up to, break down and cry shows that you and I are only human, and we both have emotions we can't continually control. So please remember it's good to cry and let out how you're truly feeling on the inside. It's such an emotional journey your loved ones go on when they're facing a serious medical health condition. You can't begin to explain to anybody how it makes you feel on the inside when you see somebody you love so much suffering unless you have been there and gone through it yourself. Nothing else matters when our loved ones, or ourselves, are facing a severe medical problem, and it's at times like those when trivial conversations and people's stupidity really wind me up. And here are a few examples of what I mean.

People talking about their relationship problems – People speaking about you behind your back – Somebody pinching your parking space or cutting you up – Spilling a cup of coffee or glass of wine on your carpet – Waiting in a queue, and somebody pushing in front of you – When a job you're having done around your house doesn't work out, because a tradesperson hasn't turned up for one reason or another – Somebody commenting on the way you look – Finding a scratch on your car – When someone is ill with the flu and won't stop moaning about it, or when you find out somebody doesn't like you; so what? Let them waste their time and energy talking and thinking about you if that's all they have to worry about in their pathetic little lives. I realise these are everyday problems we face from time to time, I just think, why should we be worrying ourselves so much about them when there are more serious real-life issues going on!

When my dad was in hospital having his operation, all that mattered to me was that my dad was going to survive, so that made me see things in a totally different light, and now when I hear people whinging about their mundane problems it makes me laugh! A good example of this was when my dad and I met a friend of ours a few days before he was due to go into hospital. You see, when we asked our friend how he had been, he said he had been off work for a few weeks with a terrible cold. I knew what my dad was thinking, but we didn't say anything about him going in for major surgery to save his life in a few days; we just said to our friend we were glad to see he was feeling better. It makes you smile to yourself, though, doesn't it, when you hear about your friend's trivial life problems, such as having a cold, while you're going through a critical medical health condition in your life.

Again, my dad has never smoked or drunk alcohol, plus he has always kept himself fit and healthy throughout his life, but he still got this evil disease! So, no matter how fit and healthy you think you are, nobody's safe from cancer! If my dad had been a smoker or a drinker, his chances of survival would have been a lot slimmer, just as they would have been when he had his cardiac arrest in 2014 as well. The doctors and nurses said, because my dad was fit and healthy, it helped with his fast recovery, which amazed them. To help you stay healthier, have a well-balanced diet, do a minimum of thirty minutes' exercise daily, don't smoke and, if you do like a drink, drink in moderation, or, even better, don't drink alcohol at all.

One thing my dad thinks might have caused his cancer is glues, sprays and adhesives he's used over the years at work. Whether they have contributed in any way at all we will never know. All I know is that you have to be very careful using glues, sprays and adhesives. So, I always wear a mask at work now, and I even wear a mask when I use hairspray on my hair at home.

Q: My question is, where do you draw your strength from to keep going? Your dad appears to be your rock, and when he was ill, you still managed to keep us all informed and entertained us. Where did that stoicism come from?

Kazzie Lemmon, Queensland, Australia

A: Hey, Kazzie, thank you for your question; that's lovely of you to say. I think, no matter what life throws your way, you have to knuckle down and get on with it as best as you can. If you don't, you can quite easily fall into depression and end up isolating yourself away from everybody around you if you're not careful. You also have to keep moving forward with whatever you're facing in life. I know there will be more challenging times ahead for me. I can only just like the rest of us, though, face those times with a positive attitude. None of us know what the future holds, so we have to live for today and make the best of our time here. I believe I've learnt to cope with my life problems much better because of what I've been through. I mainly though, draw my strength to carry on, through my family and friends and from my dad, who, like you say, Kazzie, is my rock. Thank you so much for your excellent question.

Steven M. Rippin

First off, I just wanted to say how amazing it was following your journey to raise cancer awareness. My mother passed away from cancer nine years ago. It was terrible and probably the most heartbreaking thing I've ever had to go through. If there's anything I can help with to bring awareness to your cause, please let me know, and secondly, I just wanted to thank you for being one of my first followers, and one that has liked almost every single post. It means the world to me. My page is small and my following smaller, but I'm trying every day, to bring a little light to an alternative Community.

Kat M. Gavin, Florida, USA

Thank you so much, Kat, for all your love and support while my dad was going through cancer. I am sincerely sorry to learn about the passing of your mother. I cannot even begin to imagine what that was and is still like for you. Love and light to your mum, who will forever be with you everywhere you go.

Steven M. Rippin

When I was doing my best to be there for my dad in hospital and my family and friends, it eventually caught up with me and I ended up feeling emotionally and physically exhausted. I thought at the time I was holding it together pretty well. That was until I got home and broke down in tears. My mum, though, was there for me, and she helped no end. So, if you ever find yourself in this position, you really must look after yourself by asking your family and friends for help when you need them. And also get plenty of sleep and eat properly as well.

The world you and I think we know is all just a mask on the outside, a bit like how we get ourselves ready in the bathroom every morning for the day that lays ahead of us. We make ourselves look and feel great on the outside, with the masks we wear once we have had a shave or put our make-up on. Then when we're ready, we'll face the world and portray to everybody who we meet that day that everything in our lives is wonderful. Is that how you and I are genuinely feeling on the inside, though? Nobody knows how somebody is truly feeling or what they are going through in their lives, do they? And behind the scenes of the world you and I live in while we're busy at work, or meeting up with friends, so much is going on that's hidden away from us. For example, just think somebody somewhere is being wheeled into surgery right now to have a life-saving operation done. And their family and friends are all there at the hospital, or at home worrying and praying for their loved ones to survive the medical health condition they are sadly going through. So, please, always be thankful for your health and the medical staff who look after us when we need them. Life is amazing and being able to spend it with the ones we love makes it even more magical. And simple things like meeting up with our family and friends for a coffee, going for a walk, feeling the grass beneath our feet, hearing the wildlife in the countryside and experiencing the beauty of the world around us are just some of the pleasures in life that you and I should be so grateful for.

Thank you to all the hard-working medical professionals, surgeons, doctors, nurses, cleaners and maintenance staff, who make the NHS possible for all of us to benefit from here in England. In today's society, they are the real celebrities and superheroes, if you ask me.

Steven M. Rippin

Q: I have a question. Not sure if anybody else has asked, but it's kind of relevant to me right now. You have been through and are going through an awful lot yourself. So, where do you find the strength to keep on going? What you have done for your old man and cancer research is phenomenal, and most probably myself included, would have broken by now, but you just keep going, so yeah, where the hell do you find the strength and do you have some I could maybe borrow?

Chris Chambers, Leicestershire, England

A: Hey, Chris, thank you so much for what you said, that truly means a lot to me. I find the strength to carry on with everything my parents and I have been through over the years, through my family and friends on social media; they have genuinely helped me to carry on. Music and exercising help me a lot as well. Also, I always stay as positive as I can, and I'll say to myself, 'This isn't going to beat me; I'm going to beat it and be there for my family.' Thank you for your question, Chris, and all the best to you and your family.

Steven M. Rippin

Sharing my dad's journey through mouth cancer helped a lot of people. And that showed me we should always share our problems with our family and friends because it can help lessen the burden of worry off our shoulders. And the people who sincerely care about us will shine through. I have unquestionably learnt who my real family and friends are since my dad was diagnosed with cancer. And finally, since my dad has had his cardiac arrest and been through cancer, this is how those traumatic experiences have changed me. My senses and emotions feel like they have been switched up a few levels, and I can honestly say, today I feel more alive and in tune with myself than I have ever felt before!

Together, I believe you and I can beat cancer; we just need to keep on raising as much money and awareness of it as we possibly can to help the medical professionals who are trying their very best to come up with the cures to eliminate this evil disease on the planet today. Knowing my dad had pulled through his twelve-hour mouth cancer operation and was on his road to recovery made me realise I wanted to raise money for Cancer Research UK as my way of saying thank you to everybody who had been there for him and my mum and me. I also wanted to help other people who were going through some form of cancer in their lives as well, and fundraising was my way of doing this. So back in June 2017 I did just that and walked 10,000 steps every day for Cancer Research UK. To finish this chapter here is what my dad had to say about the health problems he's been faced with.

I'm in no pain, so I'm quite happy, and I'm so pleased we have the NHS; it makes you feel safe living here in England. I've been lucky that I have had no pain, whether it's been my cardiac arrest or cancer I've never suffered. I think going through cancer, and my cardiac arrest stops you worrying about the trivial things in life, and it makes you live for today, but I have always been a positive person throughout my life, it's just how I am, and my dad had a fantastic sense of humour, and I think that rubbed off on me as I grew up.

George W. Rippin, Market Harborough, England

# FUNDRAISING FOR CANCER RESEARCH UK WITH MY DAD

Throughout the whole month of June 2017, my dad and I walked well over 10,000 steps every day for Cancer Research UK. The response we had from the general public and local businesses from Market Harborough was fantastic. There was a raffle competition organised by Wesses Bakery, where many local companies donated prizes, plus Wesses Bakery, the Roebuck and Bowden Stores had collection jars on their counters where people gave to our fundraising campaign as well. Now here is a video I made to help promote and explain what my fundraising campaign was all about: bit.ly/WalkingAllOverCancer2017

Throughout June 2017, my dad and I walked three hundred miles.

The community of Market Harborough is incredible, if you ask me, and I feel so proud to live here and be a part of it. The town has shown me how kind, generous and supportive the residents of Market Harborough genuinely are. Our local radio station, 102.3 Hfm, covered my dad's journey with having squamous cell carcinoma mouth cancer along with my fundraising campaign. Also, the *Harborough Mail*, the *Leicester Mercury*, BBC Radio Leicester, the *Northampton Telegraph*, BBC Radio Northampton, and the *Melton Times* covered our stories as well. I couldn't believe the amount of support we had from the media. And with all this free publicity my dad was able to help make more awareness of mouth cancer to the general public, along with what symptoms to look out for. I am forever grateful to the newspapers and radio stations who covered my dad's mouth cancer journey and my fundraising campaign.

A couple of weeks before I started raising money, my arthritis flared up in my knees, making it a struggle for me to walk. Typical, eh? But I wasn't going to let a bit of arthritis stop me from walking 10,000 steps, and it didn't. So, I got training and made these two videos to get me ready to Walk All Over Cancer:

bit.ly/GettingReadyToWalkAllOverCancer2017
bit.ly/TrainingForMyCharityWalk

At the beginning of June, I received a message on Facebook from a guy who worked at BBC Radio Leicester, and he asked me if I would like to go on Ben Jackson's morning show and talk about my fundraising campaign, which I thought was a fantastic idea. Although I will admit, I felt pretty nervous when I was first asked to go on! So, the day arrived when my dad and I went live on air to thousands of BBC Radio Leicester listeners to tell them what our fundraising campaign was all about. First, though, we had to get ourselves there, and that was quite a fiasco. Firstly, we got caught in traffic on our way to Leicester, which made us late. Then, secondly, once we had arrived in the city, we had no idea where the BBC Radio Leicester studios were! And there was me thinking I had everything planned out on Google Maps!

So, my dad and I kept our cool as best as we could and walked to the Clock Tower in the city centre of Leicester, where one of my dad's customers saw him and started chatting away to him. I had to be as polite as I could and tell my dad that we didn't have time to stop and talk, so my dad said his goodbyes to his customer and off we went. Then we spotted a police officer, and we asked him if he knew where the BBC Radio Leicester studios were, which he did thankfully. Then a minute later I had a phone call from BBC Radio Leicester asking me where my dad and I were; we were supposed to be going on air in two minutes' time! So just as soon as I got off the phone, I told my dad we only had two minutes to get to the studios! You should have seen us; we ran through the streets of Leicester and past an HMV music store faster than Superman chasing after a pair of speeding bullets! We must have looked like a right pair in our bright pink fundraising T-shirts! Anyway, once we had finally arrived at BBC Radio Leicester, we were then rushed straight into the studio, where Ben Jackson was waiting for us. We then had a quick chat with Ben before we went live on air, while he played the *Pirates of the Caribbean* theme music. And I'll tell you something: I felt much more relaxed and confident than I thought I would. When the *Pirates of the Caribbean* theme music ended, Ben Jackson introduced my dad and me. And I explained what we were going to be doing throughout June, while my dad spoke about his journey with having a cancerous growth on his tongue. The whole interview went really well, and Ben Jackson was a lovely guy. It felt like my dad and I had known Ben for ages, and that we had just popped round his house for a cup of tea and a slice of toast. If you would like to watch the interview my dad and I had with Ben Jackson, here is a video link to it, followed by the interview Nick Shaw from our local radio station, 102.3 Hfm, did, which also went great:

bit.ly/RadioLeicesterInterview
bit.ly/HFMRadioInterview

Here is the kind of incredible generosity my friends on social media did to help support my dad and I while we were fundraising. First off, Ruth Gamble of Wesses Bakery in Market Harborough organised a raffle competition with her husband and work colleagues.

> Thank you, Ruth Gamble and all your lovely staff at Wesses Bakery for organising the raffle competition, and also for all your support throughout June 2017. My dad and I love you guys.
>
> Steven M. Rippin

A lovely woman, who I have had the privilege of getting to know through Instagram, Nicole Morcos, from California, was kind enough to make some beautiful handmade bracelets for my fundraising campaign, which people loved; they sold out pretty fast, I can tell you.

> Thank you so much for the bracelets you made, Nicole. That was so kind of you to do, All my very best to you and your family.
>
> Steven M. Rippin

Jez West of Market Harborough donated a signed Leicester Tigers Rugby shirt that went up for bidding and raised an astonishing £1,000! And a MASSIVE thank you to Ruth Moore, who won the signed Leicester Tigers rugby shirt. Here is a video of Jez handing over his signed Leicester Tigers rugby shirt for our fundraising cause: bit.ly/LeicesterTigersSignedTshirt

> Thank you so much, Jez, for donating your Leicester Tigers rugby shirt; that was extremely good of you to do. And many thanks to you, Ruth, for bidding and winning, well done. All my very best to you both and your families.

> Steven M. Rippin

And a good friend of mine from London, Lorna Spike Watson, baked a load of cupcakes and raised over £100, which was fantastic. I couldn't believe how much time and effort Lorna had put into all the baking she must have done to help my fundraising campaign!

> Thank you so much, Lorna, for baking those cupcakes you made. I was very overwhelmed by your support and kindness. All my very best to you and Chris.

> Steven M. Rippin

The true spirit of people's generosity really shines through when you're raising money for such a good cause, doesn't it? Now without this next lovely young woman, LeeAnne Murrell from America, the pink fundraising T-shirts people around Market Harborough wore, including my dad and me, would never have been made. LeeAnne, you see, wanted to donate a few hundred pounds so I could get some fundraising T-shirts printed to help raise money and make more awareness of cancer. At first, I didn't want to take LeeAnne's money because it just didn't feel right as I only knew her through Instagram. Then she said to me, 'We're both fighting for the same cause Steve, and all the money is going to Cancer Research UK,' which did help change my mind. I'm so glad I decided to accept LeeAnne's generous offer because those pink fundraising T-shirts helped spread the word of our fundraising campaign no end, especially when a group of us got into our local newspaper wearing them. I never thought in my life that somebody who I have never met would spend $300 on fundraising T-shirts for me. LeeAnne Murrell is, without a doubt, one of the kindest individuals I have ever had the honour and privilege of connecting with online. I cannot thank LeeAnne and her family enough for their overwhelming generosity and support while my dad and I were raising money.

> Thank you, LeeAnne, from the bottom of my heart for your donation. Those fundraising T-shirts helped so much. You truly are an amazing woman with a heart of gold. Much love to you and your family.

> Steven M. Rippin

To help our fundraising campaign, I decided to dress up as Captain Jack Sparrow and walk around my hometown and the city of Leicester in my full-on pirate regalia, which I was a bit worried and nervous about doing at first. After thinking what my dad had been through though, I soon changed my weak-minded mindset and realised how pathetic and stupid I was being.

Now here is the *Harborough Mail*'s news article, which was published on Thursday, 11 May 2017, to help raise awareness of what my dad and I were up to for Cancer Research UK.

# BETTER HAND OVER YOUR MONEY TO PIRATE STEVE!

If you're out and about in the Harborough area next month, don't be too surprised if you see a pirate. He'll be looking like Captain Jack Sparrow from the film series Pirates of the Caribbean and striding along purposefully. It's not Johnny Depp, obviously – it's Market Harborough's lookalike Steve Rippin. And he'll be walking every day in June to raise money for cancer research. Steve (41) was inspired by his dad George Rippin, who was diagnosed with mouth cancer this year and underwent a 12-hour operation to remove it. 'Basically, I'm walking 10,000 steps a day (about five miles) every day in June to help raise awareness of cancer.' Explained Steve, who runs a carpet cleaning firm in town. Steve, who'll be walking much of the time in full pirate kit, will be part of a national 'Walk All Over Cancer' campaign run by Cancer Research UK. Dad George (64), who runs a carpet supply and fitting firm in Market Harborough, was diagnosed with cancer of the tongue. He went into hospital in April and is now (touch wood and thinking positively) recovering amazingly well at home in Market Harborough. 'Don't make me out to be special though. I'm just another person who got cancer.' He told the Mail. 'I try to stay positive, and I think that's helped me through. And I tried to be strong for other people – without pretending it wasn't worrying me.' Much of the journey through the cancer wards and afterwards has been recorded in live blogs by Steve and George, on Steve's Facebook page. Many people say they have been helped by them. The live blog on April 3, as George stands in a hospital corridor before his operation, with son Steve trying to be supportive, is simply lovely; true, awkward, charming and tender. George had a piece cut off his tongue and replaced with a skin graft from his arm. He also needed a tracheotomy to keep him breathing. Steve said: 'It was a tough day saying goodbye to my dad at the hospital and not really knowing what the outcome would be.' The duo's openness has brought an outpouring of messages of support on social media. 'It's been overwhelming really,' said Steve. 'And it really helped me to get through the operation,' said George – 'Especially messages from people who I didn't know who'd seen a Facebook post or whatever and said how it had helped them.' More than anything, the whole cancer scare episode has reminded a close-knit Harborough father and son, what they've got in each other. As Cap'n Jack Sparrow himself once said: 'Not all treasure is silver and gold mate.' Steve has raised more than £500 so far.

Article by Alex Dawson, Thursday, 11 May 2017,
facebook.com/theharboroughmail

Here follow a few short stories of some of the days out my dad and I had while we were fundraising. On the first day of our campaign, my dad and I headed to Bowden Stores, which is run and owned by Dominie Cripps, in the lovely village of Great Bowden in England. My dad laid the flooring, coincidently, when Dominie first opened Bowden Stores in 2016. It was an entertaining morning because there I was dressed as Captain Jack Sparrow, pestering Dominie's customers for money while they were all innocently enjoying a nice quiet cup of coffee, and I'm happy to say they donated generously. Andrew Carpenter, a freelance professional photographer, also came along to take some photographs of my exploits that Saturday morning as well for our local newspaper, the *Harborough Mail*. My dad was really enjoying himself that day down at Bowden Stores. And it was so good to see him out and about on the first day of our fundraising campaign so soon after his surgery. I couldn't believe he was there with me, if I'm honest; he unquestionably gave me an extra boost of confidence that day.

Thank you, Dad, for being there for me, and thank you so much for all your support, Dominie. We couldn't have asked for a better start to our fundraiser.

Steven M. Rippin

Later that day my dad and I came across the television personality Timmy Mallett, who used to have a TV show called *Wacaday* here in England in the eighties and nineties. Timmy Mallett was famous for his enormous pink foam mallet and his word association game he used to play. You would often see Timmy on his television show, bopping people on the head with his huge pink foam mallet when they either hesitated or said an incorrect word; Timmy Mallett is a national treasure. I met Timmy in Croft Wingate's portrait gallery in Market Harborough, where he had an exhibition of his paintings on display. I never knew Timmy Mallett was an artist; he's a mighty fine one, as well you know. Timmy had quite a shock when he turned around in Croft Wingates and saw me standing behind him in my Captain Jack Sparrow outfit! Luckily, he didn't have his enormous pink foam mallet with him or I'm sure he would have bopped me on the head with it; instead, we had a lovely chat together. The following week, the *Leicester Mercury* got in touch with me and asked if I would like to be featured in their newspaper about the day Captain Jack Sparrow met Timmy Mallett, which of course I was. And now, here's that very news feature.

# JACK SPARROW RUFFLES A FEW FEATHERS AS HE MEETS TIMMY

Former Tv presenter Timmy Mallett was all at sea when he met a pirate at a Leicestershire art gallery. The celebrity known for his trademark giant pink foam mallet was lost for words when he bumped into Jack Sparrow lookalike Steve Rippin, at the Croft Wingates Gallery in Market Harborough. Timmy, who was promoting a collection of his artwork at the gallery in St Mary's Road, said: 'I was gob smacked. It's not often I am lost for words, but when I turned round to be faced by a very tall pirate, I was quite surprised.' Timmy who used to live in Leicester, and recently had work on show at the Oberon Gallery in the city centre, chatted to guests at the gallery about his art and posed for photographs. He said: 'I have real affinity for this county, I stayed the night at a hotel in Market Harborough and went out for a bike ride in the countryside. It was beautiful. I took some photographs and painted a watercolour which I put into the exhibition at Croft Wingates. I have been to the gallery a few times and love the people there. To meet Steve, the Pirate was a treat. I think what he is doing raising money for Cancer Research is great.' Steve had popped into the gallery to see Timmy after fundraising for Cancer Research UK in the nearby village of Great Bowden. The 41-year-old carpet cleaner is walking 10,000 steps every day in June to raise awareness and cash for Cancer Research UK. He has been inspired to do so by the care and treatment his father George received during his battle with mouth cancer. Steve, who has collected more than £900 on an online fundraising site, said: 'Timmy was cool. I kind of bumped into him and there he was looking up at me. We had a fun chat about things. His art is brilliant, and he's a little treasure.'

Article by Adrian Troughton, 10 June 2017, *Leicester Mercury*,
www.leicestermercury.co.uk

A couple of weeks into my fundraiser, my good friend Susan Dilks invited my dad and me to her annual dog show, called 'Suzy's Dog Show', which was held in the village of Lubenham in England. Susan said my dad and I could do some judging, and the proceeds would be allowed to go to our fundraising campaign, which was so kind of her. What Susan didn't know, though, was that I'm scared to death of dogs! So, this was my chance to overcome my fear of them!

My dad and I didn't realise we would be given a microphone each to talk to the audience with that day, so a lot of ad-libbing was going on, plus I had no clue what I was talking about when it came to the various breeds of dogs I was judging. I ended up saying things like, 'This dog looks nice,' or 'Oh jeez, I don't think this one likes me: he keeps barking. Help!' I don't think the owners liked me saying that, though, as they were trying to win a rosette for their dog! So, to give myself something else to say to the audience, I helped advertise one of my friend's hard house events he was putting on. I have no idea what everybody in the audience thought that Sunday morning, though, and even if they knew what a hard house event was! All in all, it was a great day, and my dad and I met loads of lovely people at Suzy's Dog Show, some of whom I'm still in contact with today. What an experience it was for me, though, being surrounded by so many dogs at one time that I'm scared to death of being around! I think I scared the dogs as much as they petrified me! So, I doubt I'll judge another dog show again.

Thank you so much, Susan, for helping my dad and I raise money for Cancer Research UK. It was certainly an experience I'll never forget.

Steven M. Rippin

I met you at a fun dog show in Market Harborough, while you faced your fear of dogs, whilst raising money for Cancer Research UK. We certainly were not aware that you had a fear of dogs. You are a true crusader battling on through life whilst battling your demons; truly an amazing person and I am happy to call you my friend xx.

Karen May, Kettering, England

While my dad and I were walking around Market Harborough raising money with our pink fundraising bucket, we had a lot of people pulling up in their cars on main roads handing cash over to us; it was unbelievable! We even had one guy pull up on his bike who donated £50! My dad and I couldn't believe how generous everybody was. We both felt very humbled to have touched so many people's hearts with my dad's mouth cancer journey. Cancer touches so many people's lives around the world, and there is a good chance you know either somebody who is, sadly, going through cancer right now or somebody who has had it. So, the more money and awareness we make to eliminate this evil disease the better. Now here is a video of one of the many walks my dad and I went on. I did my best to post a video diary daily so everybody could see our progress and know we were doing our 10,000 steps: bit.ly/MyDadAndIWalkingForCancer

When my parents passed away, it was hard as you can imagine, there's not a day goes by, that I don't think about them. I've tried to focus on the positive side of things and do my bit for charities, such as Cancer Research and LOROS, by doing sponsored walks, the race for life and not forgetting, joining Steve and George Rippin, on their 10,000 steps a day on one occasion. I want to help others in a similar situation to my parents, who both passed away with cancer. I found by doing all of this; I feel proud of myself for contributing to these charities.

Jeanette Lovell, Market Harborough, England

My dad and I were joined on a few of our daily walks by my good friends Troy Goodman, who's Market Harborough's very own lovable postman;

Bobby Gamble, who used to work at the Roebuck pub and restaurant as the quizmaster every Thursday night, and by, Arron Shelton, who has a heart of gold. Having friends join my dad and me on our walks was fantastic and showed me just how much they cared about what we were doing. Bobby Gamble has the gift of the gab and will go up to anybody and everybody, which are personality traits I admire about him. When we walked around our local Market Hall in Market Harborough while we were fundraising, Bobby went up to the stallholders asking them if they would like to have their photo taken with Captain Jack Sparrow for a small donation, which I thought was a fantastic idea.

Thank you, Bobby, I'm forever grateful to you for all the support you gave my dad and I while we were fundraising. You're a true inspiration to many, mate.

Steven M. Rippin

A day I will never forget is the day when Bobby Gamble, Troy Goodman, Arron Shelton and Vanessa McBride came over to Leicester with me when I had another interview with Ben Jackson on his morning show for BBC Radio Leicester. Troy Goodman, who loves to get in on the action filmed Bobby Gamble and me on his phone while Mr Jackson interviewed us both.

Thank you, Troy; you are a legend, sir.

Steven M. Rippin

If you were wondering where my dad was, he was doing an interview for Radio Northampton, which unfortunately fell on the same day as my interview was scheduled in for BBC Radio Leicester. Ben Jackson, appropriately named Bobby Gamble as Bob the Pirate, and it was Bobby's mum, Ruth Gamble, who came up with the idea to have a raffle competition at Wesses Bakery, where she works. While I was on the air, I mentioned to Ben Jackson that my motley crew and I would be going around the shopping mall in Leicester and, if anybody saw us, to please come and say hello. I also told Mr Jackson how my fundraising campaign had been going along with the fun adventures my dad and I had been on. If you would like to hear what Bob the Pirate and I had to say, here is a link to our radio interview with Ben Jackson: bit.ly/ BackOnRadioLeicesterWithBenJackson

Once my motley crew of pirates and I arrived at the shopping mall in Leicester, we headed to the John Lewis retail store, where we met Gary Roundtree, who is one of the MDs. I first thought Mr Roundtree was going to politely tell us all to leave and call for the security to escort us off the premises; luckily, he didn't. I think he was more intrigued to find out why on earth Captain Jack Sparrow was walking around the toy department playing with a big blow-up pink flamingo! My fellow pirates and I then had a great conversation with Mr Roundtree, and I explained to him what we were up to. Bobby Gamble then asked Mr Roundtree if he would like to donate a prize to the raffle competition his mum was organising at Wesses Bakery, which he was more than happy to do. And John Lewis, on behalf of Mr Roundtree, contributed an outdoor candle holder.

Thank you so much for your generosity, Mr Roundtree, and the John Lewis retail stores.

Steven M. Rippin

After our visit to John Lewis, we all proceeded to the shopping centre in Leicester, where we had lots of excellent interactions with the shoppers and some of the store managers as well. Then I was approached by a member of the security team who said, if I didn't have a permit to fundraise, my friends and I wouldn't be allowed to stay on the premises; I didn't realise I needed to have a licence. The security team told me though that I could make a phone call to the shopping centre's head office and ask them for permission. So off I went to do my best to get through to the shopping centre's head offices, which, unfortunately, I was unsuccessful at doing. So, we decided to head to the exit before we were kicked out by the team on patrol! On our way out of the shopping centre, though, we had more interactions with the shoppers, who asked us what we were up to, which delayed us from exiting the premises. And every time I looked around I saw members of the security team following my motley crew of pirates and me; they weren't looking very impressed that we were still there!

By the time we had finished talking to the shoppers, there must have been around four security guys after us, and one kept pointing towards the exit to me. I was doing my best to gather the crew, but Bobby kept trying to work his magic on one of the store managers, who wanted to meet me. Thankfully, though, I managed to gather my mischievous crew mates up in the end, much to my relief. And, as we were finally leaving, I took one last look in the direction of the security team, and there they were waving goodbye to us. Can you imagine if I had got arrested for fundraising, though? The news headlines that evening might have read something like 'The day Captain Jack Sparrow was nearly caught raising money for Cancer Research UK'. Now that would have been excellent publicity, wouldn't it?

Thank you so much, Troy Goodman, Bobby Gamble, Arron Shelton and Vanessa McBride, for coming over to Leicester and supporting me that day. I really appreciated it.

Steven M. Rippin

One day, when Andy 'Chappers' Chapman and 'Dizzy' Debs Chapman came on a walk with my dad and me, we went into the Pets at Home pet store in Market Harborough, and we asked them if they could help us out in any way with our fundraising campaign. And they did in a very unexpected way! You see, the store manager of Pets at Home said we could borrow their eight-foot pink mascot, which caught us all off guard! But it sounded like it would be hilarious to have one of us dressed up walking around town in an outfit like that. The only problem was: who would be able to fit into this giant pink mascot of theirs? Lo and behold, 'Dizzy' Debs Chapman was the perfect fit. So 'Dizzy' Debs went off to change, while my dad, Andy and I waited patiently outside the store for her return. So, we waited, and we waited, and we waited some more, still though there was no sign of 'Dizzy' Debs Chapman. We started to wonder where on earth 'Dizzy' Debs had disappeared to. Finally, though, 'Dizzy' Debs Chapman made her grand entrance, well, exit from the Pets at Home pet store, and it was well worth the wait! The first thing Andy my dad and I saw when 'Dizzy' Debs emerged was this eight-foot-tall bright pink tapeworm! We couldn't stop laughing. 'Dizzy' Debs Chapman looked spectacular! What a morning we all had; you should have seen the looks on people's faces when they saw Captain Jack Sparrow being chased by an eight-foot pink tapeworm through the streets of Market Harborough; it was priceless! We certainly turned a few heads and raised a lot of money that day. If you're interested in seeing Captain Jack Sparrow being chased around Market Harborough by an eight-foot pink tapeworm, here is a video link for you to check out: bit.ly/JackSparrowAndTheTapeWorm

Massive respect to you, 'Dizzy' Debs Chapman, and thank you for being such a good sport that day.

Steven M. Rippin

After our tapeworm adventures, my dad, 'Dizzy' Debs Chapman and I went for dinner at Emerson and Wests, which is a great little bakery and restaurant in our town. 'Dizzy' Debs's husband, Andy 'Chappers' Chapman, had to go unfortunately because he had an appointment to attend. While we were in Emerson and Wests, I met Tim Wykes and his wife, who I made jump when they entered the restaurant that afternoon for a quiet cup of tea and a slice of cake. After the initial shock of nearly being held up by Captain Jack Sparrow, Tim Wykes, his wife and I had a lovely conversation together. Tim genuinely inspired me with his life story he told me that day. What I learnt from Tim Wykes was that we should never let our lives pass us by and we should do our best in everything we do. I believe meeting Tim Wykes and his wife that day was meant to be.

All my very best to you and your wife Tim, it was a real pleasure meeting you both in Emerson and Wests. Oh, and sorry for making you both jump.

Steven M. Rippin

And one more unforgettable experience my dad and I will remember from our fundraising month was when my cousin Sandie Hart invited us both to the Sherard Primary School in Melton Mowbray where she worked, to talk about my dad's battle with cancer at her assembly in front of three hundred children. I was so apprehensive about getting up in front of those children when Sandie first asked me. I had never done anything like that before, you see. Again, I didn't let it faze me because it was nothing compared to what my dad had been through. So, on the day of my cousin's assembly, I dressed up in my Captain Jack Sparrow costume, and off my dad and I went to Melton Mowbray. Once we had arrived at my cousin's school, Sandie told us to hide behind some black curtains, while she spoke about what cancer was and what my dad had been through. Then, when we heard her call us out, my dad and I made our grand entrances from behind the black curtains, and the kids loved it when they saw us appear.

The funniest moment from that day was when Sandie asked the children, 'Now, have you all brought some pennies?' And the children all said together, 'Nooo.' Sandie, my dad and I stood there in surprise when we heard them say that because they had been told to bring in some loose change. So again, Sandie asked, 'Has anybody brought any pennies?' And yet again it was a big long 'Nooo' from all the children. Sandie did her best bless her to save the situation by saying, 'Well thank goodness Mrs Evans has; yours is the only one going in the bucket.' Then a sweet little girl's voice spoke up and said, 'I've brought pennies.' Quickly, Sandie turned around in the direction of her voice and said, 'Who's brought pennies? Put your hand up if you brought pennies.' Then the little girl replied to Sandie and said, 'I did. I brought some pennies.' Then my dad and I started clapping, and my dad said, 'Aw, good girl.' And another child called Oliver said he had brought some pennies in as well. So, it all turned out pretty well in the end, because we made a grand total of three pence for our fundraiser. Luckily, some of the parents and staff had brought pennies in that day as well. So, the pennies soon started rolling in. And, as they say, look after your pennies and the pounds will look after themselves. Now here is a video from that day when we were on stage at my cousin's school: bit.ly/HasAnybodyBroughtAnyPennies

After the assembly, the staff, parents, Sandie, my dad and I went outside with the children and walked around the school grounds with them class by class, so they were able to take part in our fundraising campaign. It was a great morning, and we managed to raise around £300, which was fantastic.

Thank you so much, Sandie and your staff, for helping my dad and me raise over £300 for Cancer Research UK, at the Sherard Primary School in Melton Mowbray.

Steven M. Rippin

I never imagined how rewarding fundraising was going to be. I learnt so much about myself as a person, plus it was great sharing those experiences with my dad. I honestly didn't think he would have been able to join me fundraising because it had only been around six weeks since he had undergone major surgery. Walking 10,000 steps every day helped my dad move on from his cancer experience in a positive way.

Thank you to everyone who invited my dad and me to their events in the summer of June 2017 and for supporting Cancer Research UK. My dad and I will never forget how generous you were. We love you all.

Steven M. Rippin

The good of society always comes through, doesn't it? And I hope my fundraising stories and what my dad has been through has helped you see that sometimes there is light at the end of the tunnel, especially if you or somebody you know is going through an illness right now. And please remember, your family and friends will always be there to help and support you through those challenging times.

Q: When I lost my parents in 2011, they died three weeks apart. My entire outlook on life took a huge shift. I appreciate the small things, memories. I am more grateful. How did your recent trial with your dad's health (Hi dad!) change you?

**Cindy McFarland, Orange County, California, USA**

A: Hey, Cindy, I am so sorry to hear about the loss of your parents. Love and light to the both of them. After my dad had survived his cancer ordeal, I had no idea it had changed me so much on the inside. And, for the first time in my life, I decided to stop giving a damn what people thought of me. I had always lied to myself before, you see, and it did use to bother me, which I know is pathetic. I also knew I wanted to inspire as many people as I could to live their lives with positive attitudes and to also help them appreciate and enjoy the beauty of the world around them. Thank you so much for your question, Cindy.

Steven M. Rippin

The health problems you and I are faced with through our lives make us appreciate the world around us a lot more than we would have done if we hadn't had them. Furthermore, they always remind me that we are not invincible and that we should treat our bodies with the utmost respect they deserve.

While my dad was in hospital, he told me to take his mind off things he would focus on everything he was looking forward to doing once he was home again, such as spending time with his family and friends, taking walks in the countryside, getting back to work, relaxing with the cat and listening to the birds chirping away as he would wake up to another lovely day feeling lucky to be alive to appreciate all life has to offer him. Once my dad was back home and fit enough, I went on a walk with him along the canal. And he said to me, 'I've been looking forward to this so much, Steve; it's the simple things in life you miss the most.' And hearing my dad say that really touched my heart, and is something I will never forget hearing him say.

> I'm so proud of how well my dad's done since his operation. He's now semi-retired, but still working, and loving life so much more than he did before.

My parents used to call me Steve Austin as a joke when I was younger. I had no idea who Steve Austin was though; then I found out, as I grew up, he was the Bionic Man in a television show. And, just like Steve Austin, the surgeons helped to rebuild and put me back together again when they saved my eyesight just as the surgeons have helped to rebuild my dad over the years, by placing three stents into his arteries after he had his cardiac arrest, and by rebuilding his tongue after he had been diagnosed with cancer. So always think to yourself when you're going into hospital, 'The surgeons are going to rebuild me, and make me feel much healthier and stronger than I have ever felt before.'

Also, if you or somebody you know is in hospital, do your best to focus on the things you're going to look forward to doing once you recover. For example, you could think of that holiday you have been planning on going on, that restaurant you have always wanted to take your family to, that night you're going to have out with your mates, or that walk you're going to go on in the countryside with your grandparents, wife, husband, father, mother, son or daughter. Having a positive attitude is vital when you're in hospital. And a great way to help you think more positively is to say out loud and into a mirror, the following affirmations:

> 'I am Focused, I am Positive, I am going to beat this' – 'I am Fit. I am Healthy. I can do anything I put my mind to' – 'I have all the love and support of my family and friends to help me through this turbulent time I am going through'.

There are people I have read about who have willed themselves back to full health even when the doctors have told them they will never recover, but those patients have proven the medical staff wrong because of their positive mindsets!

Also, while my dad was lying in his hospital bed, to keep his joints from stiffening up, he used to exercise his legs by raising them up and down regularly, which helped to keep him a lot more mobile, then, as soon as he was allowed to, he was walking around the hospital grounds in no time at all. The nurses even had to call his mobile phone one day to find out where he had disappeared because he had been gone so long!

After my dad had recovered, and our fundraising campaign was over, our local newspaper, the *Harborough Mail*, did one final write-up to conclude the month of fundraising we had done.

# WHEN HIS DAD GEORGE GOT CANCER OF THE TONGUE, MARKET HARBOROUGH'S STEVE RIPPIN KNEW HE WANTED TO DO SOMETHING TO HELP

'It was a tough day saying goodbye to my dad at the hospital and not really knowing what the outcome would be' Steve (41) said. 'I made up my mind soon after, that I'd start fundraising for Cancer Research UK.' Fortunately, George (64) who runs a carpet supply and fitting firm in Market Harborough, is recovering very well from his operation. During which he had a piece cut off his tongue and replaced with a skin graft from his arm. In fact, he recovered so quickly, that he joined Steve in a whole month of daily walks averaging 10 miles a day to raise an amazing £6,348 for the charity as part of their national Walk All Over Cancer Campaign.

The 300 plus miles they walked is the equivalent of travelling from Market Harborough to Edinburgh. Steve, who runs a carpet cleaning firm, did most of the walks dressed as his alter ego Pirate Steve, a pretty convincing Captain Jack Sparrow lookalike (from the Pirates of the Caribbean films). 'The month of walking was fantastic' said Steve. 'I've never done any charity work like this before, and it was an incredible journey. I'd like to thank everybody who donated, all the people and all the businesses.' Steve has special thanks for Wesses Bakery in the town, who raised £1,250 with a big raffle, and for the Roebuck pub, Bowden Stores and all the media who covered his story. And there were thanks for Jez West too, who donated a signed Tigers Rugby shirt that raised £1,000 for the charity.

Dad George said: 'Personally, I'd like to say thank you to the medical staff at Market Harborough, Kettering and Northampton. My doctor in Market Harborough spotted the problem, Kettering Hospital was fantastic and Northampton, wow, what a brilliant team they've got there.' He added: 'I'm quite proud of Steve raising all that money. I think the charity experience showed us both what a lot of great people there are out there. Next time we'd like to do something for local charities.'

Article by Alex Dawson, Thursday, 3 August 2017,
facebook.com/theharboroughmail

My dad and I are extremely grateful to everyone who supported us. And to show our thanks, here is a video we made: bit.ly/ThankyouForYourSupport

My dad and I raised an incredible £6,348! We initially thought we might raise, if we were lucky, £2,000, so to raise £6,348 just blew our minds, and it was all down to the general public who came out in force to support us because without them it wouldn't have been possible. I wish I could mention everybody who donated to our fundraiser; you know who you are, though. And in this next video I get quite emotional, because it's the day when my dad was given the all clear by his doctor, Dr Harrop, at Kettering General Hospital: bit.ly/MyDadGetsTheAllClear

Now here is a question I asked my dad on what advice he would give to somebody who's going through cancer right now.

Listen and trust your doctors; also, if it helps, change your lifestyle, and try and keep as fit as you can, eat healthy and have a good balanced diet, plenty of fibre, fruit and veg. And get out walking, or you can go to a gym; basically, keep active.

George W. Rippin, Market Harborough, England

My dad is one of the most inspiring human beings I know. He has shown me with everything he has been through just how much will and determination he has got built into his very soul, which has always helped him fight back every time he has had a severe illness. My dad has never let anything faze him, and he has always got on with life, 'Well, I've got it; let's deal with it,' he would say, which is an attitude we should all have. June 2017 was a month I will never forget, plus a year that changed my dad's life and my life forever.

# FUNDRAISING TIPS

A lot of people have asked me, since my dad and I raised money for Cancer Research UK, what the best ways are to go about fundraising. So, I thought I would share with you my fundraising tips if you're thinking about raising money for your favourite charity.

Think carefully about which charity you would like to raise money for – Think how much you would like to raise; remember to be realistic, though – Believe in yourself; be devoted to the cause you're raising money for, and have plenty of passion, commitment and determination – Write down when you will start your fundraising campaign – Work out how long you want your campaign to last. Mine was for one month, so I had thirty days to raise the £2,000 target I had set myself. And, remember, you can start promoting your fundraising campaign a month or two ahead of schedule.

Write down the reason why the charity you're raising money for has affected, you, your family or your friends – Get in touch with local media, such as your local newspapers and radio stations, who will be more than happy to help you with your fundraiser – Let people know what charity you're going to be raising money for and where they can donate by sharing your fundraising page on your social media sites – Get your family, friends and local businesses involved by organising a raffle competition they can donate prizes too. And sell raffle tickets for a pound each – Walk through your local community in fancy dress to grab people's attention – A good tip while fundraising is to never go up to people in the street shaking your collection box at them as they walk by you. My dad and I never did this. If somebody wanted to donate, we would let them come up to us on their own accord. I, for one, have never liked it when I have walked by someone in the street and they start shaking their charity box in my face! I think that's rude and impolite, plus that person puts me off donating to them.

Get in touch with local schools, and ask them if you can come along and talk about the charity you're raising money for – If there's a local pub you like drinking in, you could ask the landlord or landlady if they would like to help your fundraiser. Maybe you could get a local band to perform, and have a fancy dress night with a raffle competition going on while volunteers walk around with donation buckets – You could organise a sponsored walk with your family and friends, where they all donate £1 each to join in with you. And, finally, you could have a car boot sale, and sell all the unwanted items you have got stored away. Or, you could set up a gofundme or justgiving page online.

Well, I hope my fundraising tips have helped give you some ideas of what you could do if you're thinking of raising money for your local charity. Helping to raise money for charity can lift your spirits and make you feel so good on the inside, especially if you're feeling down and have a loved one who's poorly. Also, if you would like to help other people who are less fortunate than yourself, then I would definitely recommend fundraising. You will not only be helping yourself on the inside; you will also be helping to find a cure for medical health conditions so many people are sadly facing in the world today. I thought I was an outgoing person before I started fundraising. After a whole month of going out in public raising money, though, I became even more uninhibited and confident within myself as a person. Fundraising has also helped my confidence, self-esteem and shyness. So why not look up a charity you care passionately about, and organise a fundraising event around your local area? Go on, give it a go: you'll love it, and you'll be able to look back one day and say to yourself, 'I helped to make a difference in the world, and possibly helped to save somebody's life.' Now, how proud would you feel about yourself if you knew you had helped in contributing in saving somebody else's life?

# LOOK AFTER YOUR BODY AND KEEP YOURSELF FIT

My dad and I often get asked how we keep ourselves fit, so here in the chapter to follow I'm going to write how we stay as fit and as healthy as we possibly can with the medical health conditions we have.

By eating the wrong foods every day and not exercising our physical fitness and appearance will start to suffer, which is the last thing we want to happen! So, remember to keep active and have a well-balanced diet. If you've got an office job or you're sitting down for long periods, you most probably go to your local gym a few times a week or go on walks. If you're not doing anything physical at all, though, then I would advise you to start doing some form of exercise. The more activity you squeeze into your daily life, the better. Even if you only went on a forty-minute walk every day, that would be fantastic as well. I'm no health expert, that's for sure; I've just picked tips up over the years and learnt a lot since my dad had his cardiac arrest in 2014 on the best ways to live a healthier lifestyle.

At home, I do a lot of cardio and a few weights, but nothing over the top because of my rheumatoid arthritis. My rheumatologist has always told me, 'It's good to exercise, Steven, but it's best not to go over the top with your condition.' So, just as long as I stay lean and fit, I'll be happy. And if you suffer from an illness, remember to consult your local GP first before taking up any form of physical exercise, or making any changes in your diet.

A sport my dad loved was walking football, which he had to stop playing, unfortunately, due to a knee injury. Walking football is a slower-paced version of the game that's aimed at the over-fifties where no running's aloud. So, if you have reached a certain age, or you know somebody who has and is looking for another activity to take up, then why not let them know about walking football. To find out if there's a walking football team in your local area, you could try getting in touch with your leisure centre and asking them if there's a team where you live. If there isn't, you could ask your friends if they're interested in being in one you're putting together. Please, though, be very careful if you or somebody you suggest walking football to does decide to take this sport up because injuries can occur no matter how careful you are. And consult your local GP first to make sure walking football is an activity that's safe for you.

The team my dad was in was called 'The Hornets' and they would compete against other walking football teams around our local area, playing in friendly matches and competitions; my dad used to love taking part in those games. Walking football is a great way to keep fit, look after your heart and make new friends. Now here is a promotional video I put together for my dad's walking football team if you're interested in learning more about this sport: bit.ly/thehornets

I know you have heard it said a million times before, but it's vital to warm up and cool down properly when exercising. I remember going all dizzy and nearly passing out once because I hadn't cooled down properly; I hadn't drunk enough fluids either. Warming up helps you before exercising because it raises your body's core temperature – it increases blood flow to your muscles, and it also helps to reduce muscle soreness and lessens your chance of injury. Cooling down helps you after exercising because it helps to lower your heart rate back to normal. It gets your muscles ready for your next exercise routine, you won't go all faint and dizzy after you have finished exercising, and it will help you get rid of any lactic acid build-up. Cooling-down exercises help to stretch those muscles out you have been working so hard. Since I have been exercising more over the years, the arthritis in my knees no longer aches as much it used to and I don't have to take tablets to control the pain, which I am so grateful for.

My dad's played sport all his life, from boxing, basketball, running marathons, playing tennis, walking football, and going to his WellNow Exercise for Health Fitness classes each week. He also loves walking regularly, as well. At first, I was never too bothered about going on country walks with my dad, over time though I have thoroughly enjoyed them. I have also seen the benefits walking has.

Walking is just as good as running, because a brisk walk can help reduce the risk of diabetes, heart disease, high cholesterol and high blood pressure just as much as running can, plus walking is less damaging on your joints. To burn the same number of calories as you would by doing a fifteen-minute run, you will have to go on a brisk half-hour walk. Do your best to get into a regular habit of going on a thirty-minute walk every day if you want to become fitter; if you do, you will see your overall health and well-being improve no end, plus you will have a lot more energy as well. An excellent thing to do when you're out walking is to punch your fists in the air, which helps to get your heart rate up.

Charles Eugster, who was a ninety-seven-year-old retired dentist, was a bodybuilder and a track and field athlete who broke records. Charles was known as the fittest ninety-seven-year-old on the planet, who started his physical fitness at the age of sixty-three, which changed his life forever; he was an inspiration to everybody. Sadly, Charles Eugster is no longer with us and passed away at the age of ninety-seven.

Thank you so much for inspiring so many of us, Charles.

Steven M. Rippin

The next time you say to yourself 'Urgh I'm tired. I can't be bothered to do anything. I feel so worn out', remember, exercising always gives you more energy. When you feel exhausted, though, the last thing on your mind is to start exercising isn't it? Well, that's the first thing that should be on your mind, because when you start exercising that's when neurotransmitters are released from your brain and throughout your body, such as serotonin, dopamine and endorphins, which all help to make you feel great again. Serotonin is produced by long-term cardio exercise, and is said to regulate your anxiety and happiness. Dopamine can help to improve how you're feeling and your long-term memory, and is responsible for that euphoric feeling you get from exercising. Endorphins give your body that good positive feeling and make you feel happier as well. You know that euphoric feeling you get after you have been running or dancing, well, that's those endorphins at work your neurotransmitters have released into your body. Endorphins also help to reduce stress and boost your self-esteem. When you don't exercise, there's more chance of you falling ill and feeling sluggish.

It doesn't take much of your day up when you exercise. For example, a thirty-minute workout takes around five per cent of your day, a forty-five-minute workout takes about seven and a half per cent and an hour of physical activity takes almost ten per cent. So, you have no excuses not to exercise. And, hey, who wouldn't want to live a healthier and fitter lifestyle? If you don't have time to keep fit during the day, do your best to incorporate your exercise routine while you're at work. For example, if you live close to your employment, you could either walk or cycle there instead of taking the car. And if you work in an office, you could start using the stairs instead of the lifts, plus you could go on walks during your lunch breaks as well, just like my good friend Andy 'Chappers' Chapman does. There are always opportunities to stay fit and active in whatever job you do. It's down to you, though, how fit and healthy you want to be. Always look after your body and treat it like a temple. One more thing: if you're ill with a bad case of flu, then you should rest up and let your body recover before taking part in any form of physical activity.

# FOOD, DRINK AND LIVING A HEALTHY LIFESTYLE

As they say, you are what you eat, so I guess you could call me a melon! Which some people might agree with. Sorry: my bad attempt at a joke there! Now I'm going to write about the diet my dad and I have, and what foods we have incorporated into our daily lives since he had his cardiac arrest in 2014, plus I will tell you what foods you should avoid, along with lots of other helpful advice as well.

My dad's done really well after being told to change his eating habits. He didn't eat too badly before, although we did use to have a takeaway once a week from our local Chinese, which we have now put a stop to. Nowadays, we cook our own healthy Chinese stir-fries with lots of vegetables and chicken. We only use a pinch of salt and no harmful spices in our dinners.

Other than the Chinese takeaways, my dad's diet was pretty good, plus he has never been a drinker or smoker either. I, on the other hand, do like a drink now and then when I'm out with my friends, although I have cut down a lot over the years. I used to go out every weekend with my mates partying and have a few ciders, you see, which are bad for you, especially when you have arthritis! When I go out these days, I like to have half-pints and glasses of water, which my friends find very amusing. It's my body, though, and I want to do my best to look after it.

My dad and I have never smoked in our lives; we can't stand the smell of it. And whenever we are out in public, we will both hold our breath and wave our hands in front of our faces fanning people's second-hand smoke away as we walk by them. I can understand why the Japanese wear those face masks. It's an excellent idea, if you ask me; they're a great fashion accessory as well; then again, I guess my fashion sense has a lot to be desired for, doesn't it?

If you smoke and want to give up but always find it hard, think of the benefits quitting smoking will do for you. For a start, it will help to improve your health and your bank balance. Now, I'm no Derren Brown, with any unique hypnosis or mind-changing suggestions to bamboozle your mind with. I'm just your average everyday carpet-cleaning tradesman. So, what I would suggest when you want to quit a bad habit is say to yourself, 'I want to have more energy. I want to treat myself and my family more. And I want to live a long and healthy life.' It's also a great idea to write down all the POSITIVES that will come from you quitting smoking, such as the health benefits and the amount of money you will save. That is of course if you do smoke. If you don't, then that's fantastic. Now here are the benefits people would see if they did decide to quit smoking over a specified period.

Within the first twenty minutes, their blood pressure and pulse rate would return to normal – Within eight hours their oxygen levels in their blood would return to normal, and their levels of carbon monoxide would be reduced by more than half – Within twenty-four hours carbon monoxide would be eliminated from their bodies. And their lungs would start to clear out mucus and other smoking debris – Within forty-eight hours their ability to taste and smell would improve – Within seventy-two hours their breathing would become easier, their bronchial tubes would begin to relax, and their energy levels would increase – Within two to twelve weeks their circulation would improve throughout their bodies, making walking and running much easier for them – Within five years their risk of having heart attacks would fall to about half that of a smoker – Within ten years their risk of lung cancer would fall to about half that of a smoker – And within the first fifteen years their risk of heart disease would nearly be the same as somebody who has never smoked. Information taken from nicorette.co.uk. I hope that has encouraged you to stop smoking if you're a smoker.

To stop smoking, start by cutting down bit by bit each day, then, day by day, week by week and then month by month. By doing this, you will hopefully slowly start to retrain your brain to kick that bad habit you're in and know from within yourself that you can quit. Please, though, don't start vaping instead, because there are so many chemicals in those things that might lead onto other health problems for you in the future. Feel good and feel alive: quit smoking today.

When it comes to our diets, my dad and I eat very similarly, apart from I don't eat white bread, potatoes or anything with white flour in it. Those ingredients blow my belly up; well, not literally: I just have a reaction to white flour and potatoes, you see, plus it's all stodgy food that's no good for your body anyway. So, instead of potatoes and white bread, I will eat sweet potatoes and wholemeal bread, which taste great and are healthier alternatives. As a family, we eat a lot of fish, spinach, kale, brown rice, salad and fruit. My dad always starts his day off with a big bowl of porridge, and I start my day off with a bowl of bran flakes, with either rye flakes or bran sprinkled on top of them. Rye flakes are a great alternative to porridge and can be even healthier for you to eat. Then we will put pumpkin seeds, blueberries, apples, oranges and sometimes a banana in with our cereals as well.

What makes me laugh is when somebody asks me about my eating habits. And the first thing they will do when I tell them what food I eat is laugh or say something like, 'I'm not eating that rabbit food, give me a good old fry up any day.' Well, those kinds of people can laugh and say all they want to me. They have to remember one thing, though: all those bad saturated fats and processed foods they are eating daily are doing their overall health no good, and if they're not careful their arteries will build up with plaque; plaque can become loose and cause blockages in your arteries which can lead to having a stroke or a heart attack! So please be careful how much saturated and processed foods you eat: everything in moderation.

Pirate Steve's Cuisine will make you a lean, mean fighting machine. To give you an idea of what sort of food my dad and I enjoy eating at mealtimes, here is the kind of menu you would expect to see if we ever held a dinner party, which would never happen because we're not into dinner parties, if I'm honest; we would much prefer to go out and eat in a restaurant. Dinner parties are too much hassle and hard work, if you ask me.

# PIRATE STEVE'S CUISINE MENU

**Monday night main meal:**
Salmon, kale, spinach and basmati rice

**Tuesday night main meal:**
Fresh vegetables, chicken and sweet potato casserole

**Wednesday night main meal:**
Healthy homemade chilli con carne made with chicken

**Thursday night main meal:**
Healthy homemade chicken curry stir fry, which is fried in extra virgin
olive oil with either sweet potato wedges or basmati rice

**Friday night main meal:**
Haddock, garden peas and sweet potato wedges

**Saturday night main meal:**
Homemade pea and mint, or sweet potato and cauliflower soup,
followed by a green leafy chicken salad

**Sunday night main meal:**
We usually go and buy a chicken from Marks and Spencer down the road
and make a salad to go with it

We don't use sugar, and we only use a tiny pinch of salt in our meals and soups my mum makes.

And, for puddings, my dad and I eat a lot of fruit. One treat we love, though, is my mum's homemade tea loaf, which is made with oatmeal flour, eggs, raisins, almonds and pumpkin seeds, then soaked overnight in ginger tea. And it tastes fantastic.

Well, there you have it, Pirate Steve's Cuisine Menu. What do you think? Hope you liked the sound of those meals. And, hey, remember to tell all your family and friends because our meals are the healthy choice for anybody looking to get in shape.

Always be careful how many bananas and eggs you eat in a week; well, that's the advice food nutritionists have given my dad and me.

A tasty treat my dad and I enjoy is a smoothie. Of course, though, it has to be made of healthy ingredients. So, we put things like kale, spinach, ginger, almond nuts, bananas, oranges, lemons, apples and avocados in them. Oh, a word of warning, though, if you do make yourself a healthy smoothie, it will give you the runs, so make sure you're stocked up on plenty of toilet paper for the following morning. Also, please don't rely on healthy smoothies as part of your daily diet; they're great once in a while, though.

If you do change your diet, do it gradually, as I only know too well, because when I first increased my fibre intake I started having a bloated belly and a lot of wind. And I couldn't work out why I kept feeling so unwell and had uncontrollable gas when I was at work! It was so embarrassing, you know, especially one day when I was bending over to empty the waste tank on my carpet cleaning machine because all of a sudden from out of nowhere I let a noisy little trump out while the customer was standing right behind me!

I thought I was feeling unwell and breaking wind all the time because of either eating or drinking something that wasn't agreeing with me. So I read online about cauliflower, which I had introduced into my diet. And that's when I realised it was the cauliflower that was causing me to have an upset stomach and plenty of wind! And soon as I cut my cauliflower intake down, I felt so much better, and my belly went back to normal, along with my uncontrollable bowel movements! Every 100 grams of cauliflower contains two grams of fibre.

So always make sure you don't overdo it on your fibre intake, or you might end up giving yourself a bloated belly and finding yourself running for the loo every five minutes.

Drink at least eight glasses of water every day.

I drink a lot of water every day, along with ginger and green tea, especially ginger tea – that's one of my favourites: ginger tea is good for your digestive system. You know that feeling you sometimes get when you have had a big meal, and you feel all bloated afterwards, well, if you have a cup of ginger tea, that will help break the food down in your stomach, causing your belly to feel all bloated. Ginger tea has always come to my rescue, along with a couple of Deflatine tablets from my local pharmacy, especially if I'm going on a night out.

Always be careful how much red meat you eat.

Eating a lot of red and processed meat might cause bowel cancer, and it is recommended to eat 70 grams or less of it a day. To give you an idea if you're eating too much red and processed meat, think of the typical English breakfast, where you get two sausages and two rashers of bacon, well, that's equivalent to 130 grams! I only eat red meat once in a while, and not very often; in fact, I probably only eat it five times a year. So, on the odd occasion when I do, I love to treat myself to a steak and ale pie. And one of the best I have had was at a restaurant in Pigeon Forge in the state of Tennessee, called Paula Deen's Family Kitchen. And WOW what an incredible place that is; it was cheap to eat in there as well. Furthermore, the food at Paula Deen's Family Kitchen was some of the tastiest food I have ever eaten in my life. Luckily, I don't get to go there very often, which is a good thing because, if I did, instead of people calling me Pirate Steve they would be calling me Roly Poly Steve instead!

Always make sure you eat right, keep fit and cut out the wrong food from your diet.

Everybody likes a treat now and then, don't they, and I'm no exception. I love a piece of carrot cake or banoffee pie and a few drinks when I'm out with my friends. I never snack on biscuits, crisps or sweets, though. Also,

I don't eat cheese unless I'm in a restaurant and it comes with the meal I'm eating – I don't like fizzy drinks – I don't add salt or sugar to anything I consume – I don't eat pizzas, and I'm a chicken and fish man. Please remember, too much salt and cheese are no good for you so do your best to cut those out of your diet as much as you can, along with any other unhealthy sauces you might be adding to your meals as well. Once I cut cheese out of my diet, I lost weight.

All those diets you hear about in the media I think are a waste of time. They tell you you can't eat this and you can't eat that. I think you should be allowed to eat what you want in moderation. Have a treat now and then; just don't go making a regular habit of it, and stay away from fatty foods. Once you start a diet, you should stick to that way of eating for the rest of your life, I believe, and not just for the next six months or few years, because once you stop that diet you have been on you might slip into your old eating habits and put weight on again! So, include more fruit and vegetables in your diet – Exercise regularly – Don't drink excessively – Don't smoke – Cut cheese, salt, biscuits, sweets and sugary drinks out, and be careful how much red and processed meat you eat.

People often ask me my age, and they are always surprised when I tell them how old I am! They always say, 'What's your secret?' And I tell them I have never been married – I have never had children – I have never smoked – I make sure I have time for myself – I put time into activities I enjoy doing – I don't get stressed – I don't eat cheese – I eat sensibly – I drink at least eight glasses of water every day – I'm careful how much salt is in my diet – I drink ginger, turmeric and cleanse teas every day – I drink alcohol sensibly – I will have a coffee occasionally, maybe five in a week – I eat whole meal brown bread – I exercise regularly – I don't eat white potatoes; I eat sweet potatoes – And I moisturise every morning and night! By now, though, the people who asked me what my secret is have either fallen asleep or wished they had never asked me my age in the first place! Seriously, though, it's all about taking care of yourself and not letting life's problems get you down.

Well, I hope what I have written so far has helped to explain how my dad and I do our best to eat, drink and live healthy lifestyles. Honestly, it's surprisingly easy to cut out a lot of the wrong foods and drinks you might consume. And it's even easier to introduce healthier ways of eating, drinking and keeping fit instead. You have to learn to discipline yourself, and, instead of reaching for that slab of cake or those biscuits and chocolates you walk by in the supermarket every week, reach out for those delicious pieces of fruit and healthy vegetables instead. And ditch that glass of wine you have been looking forward to drinking all day and have a lovely refreshing glass of water or a cup of ginger tea instead. It really is up to you how healthy you want your life to be. As they say, your life's in your hands, and you are what you eat.

# PIRATE STEVE'S CHOLESTEROL TIPS AND ADVICE

I know I have been getting a bit serious through this chapter. It is important, though, to understand how to live a good clean, healthy lifestyle – well, within reason, of course, because life would be pretty dull if we didn't let our hair down once in a while, wouldn't it? So, if you can bear with me, I'm now going to write about lowering your cholesterol, which has a lot of benefits for our overall health, then afterwards there will be some entertaining health videos to watch.

When there's a history of heart problems in your family, such as my dad suffering a cardiac arrest, the doctor recommends any sons or daughters to go for a cholesterol test. So, when I went for my cholesterol test and was told it was too high, I knew I had to do something about it, which I did, and the following pages are dedicated on how I did that.

Right, then. I hope my following tips and advice on lowering cholesterol will help put you on the right track if you have been told your cholesterol is too high. To get us started, here is a brief explanation of the various types of cholesterol that are found in our bodies. We have got LDL cholesterol: low-density lipoprotein; HDL cholesterol: high-density lipoprotein; and triglycerides, which can affect our cholesterol as well. LDL is the bad cholesterol and is laid down in your blood vessel walls; it carries your cholesterol from your liver to your blood vessels. And if you have got high levels of LDL in your blood, it increases the risk of you having heart disease or having a stroke. HDL is the good cholesterol, and it helps to remove surplus cholesterol from your bloodstream. Having high levels of HDL helps to protect you against heart disease and having a stroke. Triglycerides are another type of blood fat; they produce high calorie intake and can come mainly from alcohol and sugar in your diet. High triglyceride levels increase your risk of heart disease and having a stroke. Keep your overall cholesterol levels down by eating the right foods, exercising regularly and not going over the top on alcohol, takeaways and sugary treats. Remember to discipline yourself.

Back in December 2017, being first told by my GP that I had high cholesterol shocked me because I'm always cautious with what I eat and drink, plus I exercise regularly. Apparently though it's down to your genes in your body, which can affect how high your cholesterol levels are and also if there have been any cardiovascular problems in your family. So, on 18 December 2017 I had my first cholesterol test done, and my overall cholesterol was 6.1 mg/dL – 5 mg/dL is the recommended level or lower. My GP then suggested that I should have another cholesterol test done in a few months to see how my levels were doing; that's when I was concerned my doctor was going to put me on statins if my cholesterol didn't drop.

Then three months later, on 26 March 2018, I went back and had another cholesterol test done. I didn't think my levels would have come down, if I'm honest, because I had had a few drinks here and there with my friends and treated myself to the odd dessert or two in restaurants, plus I hadn't exercised much after Christmas. So, I was pleasantly surprised that my overall cholesterol levels were now down to 5.4 mg/dL. Still, though, I wanted to see if I could get my levels down even further. So, to really test how my cholesterol was reacting to how I lived my daily life with what I ate and drank and how much I exercised, I had yet another test done on 15 May 2018. I decided not to drink any alcohol and have no meals out or desserts whatsoever in those two months to follow; I just couldn't have eaten and drunk any healthier. And guess what my cholesterol was after those two months? It was 4.5 mg/dL! I was so happy I had managed to lower it even further by changing a few things in my daily diet and by exercising more.

The main things I did to help lower my cholesterol levels were to drink more ginger tea along with my eight glasses of water every day and I increased my bran/fibre intake; not too excessively though! I ate more fruit and vegetables, and I exercised daily as well, which I still do today. So, it proves, the healthier you live your life by eating and drinking sensibly and exercising regularly, you can lower your cholesterol levels. You just have to discipline yourself to change any bad lifestyle habits you might have. Although I do realise that some people, no matter how healthy and fit they are, still have problems with their cholesterol levels and need help to keep them under control by taking statins. Now here is a video I made on health tips for cholesterol: bit.ly/HealthTipsOnCholesterol

Our cholesterol levels do go up and down over time; if you're concerned about your overall health, though, you should go and have some blood tests done or ask your local GP to organise a health check for you where they will check for diabetes, heart disease, kidney disease, stroke and dementia. For more information, here is a link to the NHS Health Check webpage, which is available for everybody who lives in England: bit.ly/NHSHealthCheckEngland

Having a health check done by the NHS is a bit like how you have your car MOT'd every year to make sure it's still running smoothly and safe to drive on the roads. And what's more important than giving yourself a full MOT check to make sure you're still working and at your full potential?

If you're over twenty, you should have a cholesterol test done once every five years.

I don't believe one hundred per cent that the diseases and illnesses you and I can get throughout our lives are all down to our genetic make-up or that they are hereditary conditions passed down to us from our families; they might contribute in a small way, but we can always help ourselves and prevent the outcome of either having a stroke or a heart attack or developing diabetes.

From what I have learnt, having too much cholesterol in your body can cause a build-up of plaque on the walls of your arteries. Then, after a while, if nothing is done about that plaque, the build-up of it will eventually narrow and harden your arteries' walls. And if some of that plaque/cholesterol breaks away it can cause blood clots that can lead you to either having a heart attack or a stroke.

If you have a history of heart disease of any kind in your family, I would advise you to make an appointment with your local GP to have a cholesterol test done because it could help save your life. How you look after yourself today will help you live longer and healthier when you're older.

As you know, the recommended level for cholesterol is 5 mm/dL or lower. People say, though, your levels can go up and down from day to day and that it's hard to get an accurate reading. So, to help you understand the recommended borderline high and low cholesterol and triglyceride measurements for adults as of 2020, here is a cholesterol table I have made. All the values are in mg/dL – milligrams per decilitre and are taken from the National Heart, Lung and Blood Institute website. Also here is a website link where you can find out more information and advice on cholesterol: bit.ly/YourGuideToLoweringCholesterol

|  | Total cholesterol mg/dl | HDL mg/dl | LDL mg/dl | TC mg/dl |
|---|---|---|---|---|
| Good | Less than 200 | 40 or higher | Less than 100 | Less than 150 |
| Borderline | 200–239 | n/a | 130–159 | 150–199 |
| High | 240 or higher | n/a | 160–189 | 200 or higher |
| Low | n/a | less than 40 | n/a | n/a |

If your cholesterol levels are too high or you have a family history of heart and cholesterol problems, your GP might suggest you taking a statin tablet if you're struggling to lower them. From what I have read and been told by people, statins can help save your life; they help lower your risk from having a heart attack or a stroke. Then you will also hear the other side and that statins are dangerous to take, so it's up to you if you do decide to take them or not when advised by your GP.

The benefits of taking statins are that they help to lower your LDL – They help to reduce the risk of you having a heart attack, stroke or other vessel-related diseases – They work better than any other cholesterol treatment – They help lower the risk of narrowing of your arteries – They help fight inflammation off, which can reduce artery damage – They help stabilise your blood vessel lining, which benefits your whole body, and make it less likely that plaque will rupture your heart. Furthermore, statins help to relax blood vessels which lowers your blood pressure.

The possible side effects of taking statins are they can cause you to develop type two diabetes or higher blood sugar levels – They can mess with your immune system – They can cause confusion and memory loss as well as making you feel nauseous – They can give you cramps, and they can also cause liver damage – Muscle damage – Dizziness – Headaches – Kidney damage – Flushing of your skin, and drowsiness. Not everyone suffers these side effects while taking statins, though. The Mayo Clinic says you're more likely to experience side effects if you're female – Over sixty-five – Have type one or type two diabetes – Take multiple medications to lower your cholesterol – Have a smaller body frame – Have liver or kidney disease or consume too much alcohol. Statins block an enzyme called HMG CoA reductase, which the liver uses to make cholesterol. And, finally, there is a risk of liver damage and kidney failure when statins are mixed with grapefruit. Grapefruit contains a chemical that can interfere with your body's ability to break down or metabolise certain statin medications. People who take statins and eat a lot of grapefruit will increase the level of statins in their blood, which can cause possible side effects.

Statins help reduce your blood cholesterol, and health risks related to atherosclerosis and heart disease. If you or anybody you know suffers from having high cholesterol, here are some ways you can help to lower it.

When you're out shopping it's important to avoid saturated and trans fats; trans fats are very similar to saturated fats. Saturated and trans fats include foods that increase your LDL cholesterol levels. Now here are the sort of foods you should avoid. Full-fat cheese, milk, cream and yoghurt – Butter and lard – Fatty meats and sausages – Biscuits, cakes, puddings, sweets and pastries – Processed foods, burgers, chips, pizza, pies, etc. – Palm oil.

Buy foods that contain higher amounts of unsaturated fats. Unsaturated fats are the fats you should include in your diet because unsaturated fats help you keep a healthy cholesterol level, and by doing so you will stay fit, feel better on the inside and live a lot longer. There are two types of unsaturated fats; there's monounsaturated and polyunsaturated. You will find monounsaturated fats in: Olives – Sunflower oil – Peanut oil and butter – Avocados – Sesame oil – Nuts, and some vegetables, oils and spreads. Monounsaturated fats help to maintain healthy HDL cholesterol, and they help to lower the levels of the bad LDL cholesterol. You will find polyunsaturated fats in some vegetables, oils and spreads – Walnuts and pine nuts, and flaxseed, flaxseed oil, sesame seeds and sunflower seeds.

Polyunsaturated fats help lower LDL cholesterol and provide you with the correct fatty acids your body can't make, such as Omega-three and Omega-six. And you will find Omega-three in oily fish, such as: Mackerel – Salmon – Tuna – Herring – Sardines and trout.

I guess after reading all that you're thinking, 'Well, what can I eat, then, Pirate Steve?' Well, what you can eat is meats, such as chicken, fish, turkey and lean cuts of beef, lamb, pork and ham – All fruit and vegetables – Fish; eat fish at least three times a week, and make sure one of the fish is of the oily type – Eggs: boiled, poached and scrambled, along with omelettes; only eat eggs in moderation, though – Oils: olive oil, rapeseed oils, sunflower, corn and soya; spreads based on these oils are acceptable as well, and when it comes to pulses and soya; baked beans, peas, lentils, tofu, Quorn and textured vegetable protein/soya mince are good choices. So, remember, saturated and trans fats are bad for you and monounsaturated and polyunsaturated fats are good for you.

And last but not least good drink choices to add into your daily diet to help lower your cholesterol include green, ginger and peppermint teas. Regular teas might have cholesterol-lowering effects, but they don't work anywhere near as well as herbal teas do. Other good drink choices include water, proactive and Benecol drinks, and freshly squeezed orange juice because it contains folic acid that helps lower your levels of homocysteine which can cause heart attacks. Drinks to avoid include fizzy drinks, energy drinks and alcohol. If you do drink alcohol, though, drink responsibly and don't go over the top. Also, avoid spirits and limit how much coffee you drink.

If you would like to learn more about what foods are good for you and what foods are bad for you here are a couple of website links for you to take a look at that have excellent food charts explaining all about the saturated and polyunsaturated fats I have written about:

bit.ly/WikipediaFoodChart
bit.ly/FoodDataCharts

If you want to live a healthier, prolonged life, by introducing some of the foods and drinks I have recommended they will help you achieve this and give you a better fighting chance of pulling through any harmful medical health conditions you might face throughout your life, just like my dad was able to pull through his cardiac arrest and cancer scares, all because he looked after himself, ate the right foods, didn't drink alcohol, didn't smoke and exercised daily.

# HEALTH AND YOGA BENEFIT VIDEOS

As I promised, it is now time for a few fun videos on health, fitness and face yoga exercises featuring me dressed up as Captain Jack Sparrow. And to start, here are the benefits of bananas.

Bananas have many benefits and the first one I'm going to tell you about is how they can help nourish and make your hair lovely and shiny, although it can be a bit of a messy process accomplishing this because you have to rub banana in your hair, so it's best to wear protective gloves. Right, let's get started. What you will need is one banana, a bowl, a pair of gloves and some tin foil.

Now mush your banana in the bowl and rub it in your hair – Then get your tin foil and cut it into strips, depending on how long your hair is – Wrap the strips around your hair then leave them on for thirty minutes – After the thirty minutes are up, you can then go and give your hair a good old washing or you will have people saying you smell like a ripe banana! Now here is a video of the benefits of bananas: bit.ly/HealthTipsBananas

Bananas can also help reduce the puffiness around your eyes. All you have to do to accomplish this is, again, mush some banana up and dab it lightly around your eyes, starting from near your nose and working your way out to the sides, just as you would with any regular eye cream – Then leave the mushed-up banana on for fifteen to twenty minutes before washing it off. Whether this will help reduce the puffiness around your eyes, though, I don't know because it's not worked for me, I know that! And, finally, bananas can be a great face moisturiser as well; yet again, though, get your protective gloves ready, because you have got to get on down and do some serious banana mushing. Then rub your mushed-up banana all over your face and leave it on for thirty minutes before washing it off. Your skin should now be feeling all lovely, clean, smooth and soft. Just be careful if you leave any stray banana peelings lying around, though, because you don't want anybody to go slipping up on them, plus you never know when a cheeky little monkey will come along and cause havoc with you once they get a whiff of banana in the air; if you have watched my benefits of bananas video, you will know what I mean! And they are the benefits of bananas; who would have thought bananas could do so much for you? Now before reading and watching the following health benefit videos, please be careful if you have arthritis or any other medical health issues because I don't want you to go and cause yourself a mishap! Please consult your local GP first before taking part in any physical exercise programme or change in your diet.

# THE BENEFITS OF WALKING EVERY DAY

Walking helps your mood improve – Increases your creative juices – Slashes your risk of chronic disease – Helps you beat colds quicker because walking everyday mobilises your immune systems warriors that patrol your nose, throat and lungs. People who walk thirty minutes every day are forty-six per cent better off than somebody who works out at least once a week – If you have arthritis walking will help strengthen your joints and help you burn calories; a brisk walk can also help lower harmful cholesterol levels, and walking at least a minimum of thirty minutes every day will help you lose weight as well.

Here are two videos on the benefits of walking:

bit.ly/TheBenefitsOfWalking
bit.ly/BenefitsOfWalkingBonusVideo

I walk more than I drive nowadays; that's because my eyesight is getting worse, plus I don't want to go causing any mischief on the roads!

# THE BENEFITS OF DRINKING WATER DAILY

Drinking water increases your energy – Relieves fatigue – Promotes weight loss – Flushes out toxins – Improves your skin complexion – Helps relieve constipation – Boosts your immune system to help you beat those nasty colds – Helps your aching muscles and joints – Prevents cramps and sprains – Is a natural headache remedy, and might be a good brain booster too. Here is a video of the benefits of drinking water: bit.ly/ BenefitsOfDrinkingWaterDaily

# THE BENEFITS
# OF DRINKING GREEN TEA

Antioxidants in green tea might lower your risk of various types of cancer – Reduce free radicals in your body while protecting your cells and molecules from damage – Help improve your brain function – Lower your cholesterol – Increase how much fat you burn – Protect your brain in old age – Lower your risk of Alzheimer's, Parkinson's and type two diabetes, and green tea can also enhance your overall physical performance. Here is a video about the benefits of drinking green tea: bit.ly/TheBenefitsOfGreenTea. I love herbal teas, plus I love my little diffuser teapot I pour my green tea into. So why not give green, ginger and peppermint tea a try for yourself and see how refreshing and good it makes you feel?

# THE BENEFITS OF DRINKING
# A HEALTHY SMOOTHIE

When you drink a smoothie, you get your daily allowance of fruits and vegetables; just remember not to exceed the recommended daily allowance. A healthy smoothie can help you lose weight – Improves your digestive system – Detoxes your body – Gives you more energy – Helps you look and feel fantastic – Gives you a radiant complexion, and clearer skin – Nourishes your hair and helps it grow – Boosts your brain function – Is full of nutrients, vitamins and minerals, and a healthy smoothie can also help you build muscle and improve your physical fitness. Here is a video about the benefits of drinking a healthy smoothie: bit.ly/ DrinkingASmoothieBenefits. A healthy smoothie packed with fruits and vegetables will help get your children, that is if you have any, drinking healthier drinks from a younger age.

# THE BENEFITS OF EATING BLUEBERRIES

Blueberries help you maintain healthy skin and bones – Lower your blood pressure – Manage diabetes – Ward off heart disease and cancer – Reduce wrinkles – Improve mental health – Protect cholesterol in your blood – Give you healthy digestion – Are the king of antioxidants and help protect your body from free radicals that can damage your cells that contribute to ageing and diseases, and blueberries are also one of the healthiest fruits for your eyes because they are packed with nutritious vitamins and minerals. Here is a video about the benefits of eating blueberries: bit.ly/TheBenefitsOfBlueberries. I always put blueberries on my cereals in the mornings. I love them.

# THE BENEFITS OF USING TEN PER CENT SULPHUR SOAP

Sulphur soap is excellent for treating acne, blackheads and the oiliness of your skin – Decreasing those nasty little whiteheads – Dermatitis – Unblocking your pores – Relieving itching, burning, scaling, chafing, redness and skin rashes – Restoring and regenerating your skin – Helping heal wounds – Toning your skin along with making it tighter, while also improving the elasticity and firmness of it – Drying out any excess sebum production and also killing bacteria. Always use a moisturiser after using sulphur soap because it can dry your skin out. Furthermore, be careful not to get any of it in your eyes because it can make them sting. Here is a video about the benefits of using sulphur soap: bit.ly/TheBenefitsOfSulphurSoap. It has been said the Romans used to bathe in warm water filled with sulphur to cleanse their bodies of any acne problems they had. And the ancient Egyptians, it has been said, used sulphur to treat eczema and acne over 5,000 years ago. Also, sulphur has been reported to have been used in traditional Chinese medicine in skincare ointment over 2,000 years ago.

# DO YOU SUFFER FROM STRESS?

If you do, let your feelings out by writing down all the things that bother you, and break each problem down so you can see how you're going to solve them – Think of the things you enjoy doing – Go dancing – Try meditation; meditation can help lower your heart rate and help your breathing become slower and more profound, which then in turn can help your blood pressure drop and stabilise which will help your muscles relax giving your body a chance to heal – Exercise regularly – Listen to your favourite music – Go shopping and treat yourself – Have a night out with your friends or a few days away – Learn breathing exercises, and a walk in the countryside is always great to help relieve your stress levels as well. Here is a video I hope you find helpful if you suffer from stress: bit.ly/ SufferingFromStress. Why get stressed? It just isn't worth it. It will only make you ill, so say goodbye to stress and either get yourself down the gym or dance like crazy to your favourite tunes; that's what I do!

# THE BENEFITS OF CYCLING

Cycling will help you lose fat and burn calories – Your strength and endurance will increase, including the vital muscle groups in your legs: quadriceps, glutes, hamstrings and calves, and pedal power is low impact, so for people who can't put too much pressure on their joints cycling or swimming can be a great alternative. Here is a video demonstrating the health benefits of cycling: bit.ly/TheBenefitsOfCycling. Just make sure you wear all the protective gear, such as a helmet, knee pads, arm pads, a bright fluorescent visor and protective eyewear when you're cycling. And not a Captain Jack Sparrow costume because your breeches could get caught up in your bike chain, leaving you in a right pickle.

# THE BENEFITS OF WEIGHTLIFTING

Weightlifting helps lift depression – Gives you more flexibility – Increases your energy levels – Lowers your risk of diabetes – Gives you a healthier heart – Gives you better blood sugar control – Helps prevent back pain and improves your balance. Always remember to get a qualified instructor to help you with any new weightlifting programmes you take up, so you don't go and cause yourself a wrongdoing! Here is a video about the benefits of weightlifting: bit.ly/TheBenefitsOfWeightLifting

# THE BENEFITS OF WARMING UP

Warming up helps to increase movement of blood through your tissues, making the muscles more pliable – Increases the delivery of oxygen and nutrients to your muscles – Prepares your muscles for stretching – Gets your heart ready for an increase in activity; preventing a rapid rise in your blood pressure – Reduces your risk of injury and aches and pains – Assists your circuitry system in pumping oxygen-rich blood to all your working muscles to help increase the circulation throughout your body, and safely prepares your body for the increased demands of physical activity you will be doing. Always remember, never overdo it and know your body's capabilities while you're working out. Here is a video about the benefits of warming up: bit.ly/TheBenefitsOfWarmingUp. And please drink plenty of fluids to replenish your body or you might find yourself going all dizzy and faint, as I did once.

# THE BENEFITS OF
# EATING PUMPKIN SEEDS

Pumpkin seeds contain a lot of beneficial plant compounds known as sitosterols and free radical-scavenging antioxidants, which help give your health an added boost – Benefit your heart, liver and immune system – Help you fight off diabetes – Offer unique benefits for men's prostate health – Are packed with nutrients from magnesium, copper, protein and zinc, and also help women from the relief of menopause symptoms. Here is a video about the benefits of pumpkin seeds: bit.ly/TheBenefitsOfPumpkinSeeds. So, don't go sprinkling sugar all over your cereals in the morning; go and grab yourself a handful of pumpkin seeds and sprinkle them on your cereals instead, just as I do.

# THE BENEFITS OF STAYING HAPPY AND POSITIVE

Staying happy and positive helps to protect your heart – Gives you a healthy immune system – Combats stress – Wards off disease and disability – Lengthens your life and eliminates aches and pains. You will also have a lot more energy and self-control by staying happy and positive as well. Here is a video about the benefits of staying happy and positive: bit.ly/TheBenefitsOfStayingHappyAndPositive

# THE BENEFITS OF DANCING: FEATURING MY DAD

It doesn't matter how old you are; you're never too old to dance. Dancing helps to improve the condition of your heart and lungs – Increases your muscular tone, strength, endurance and aerobic fitness – Keeps you in shape – Reduces your risk of osteoporosis, and you will also have better coordination, agility and flexibility when you dance as well. Here is a video of my dad and me dancing, well, trying to, along with what the benefits of dancing are: bit.ly/TheBenefitsOfDancing. So, what are you waiting for? Put your groovy shoes on, get your favourite style of music playing and shake, rattle and roll like the legend Mick Jagger with ants in your pants.

And there you have it; they are my top tips and advice to help you live a healthy and fit lifestyle. Remember, always do at least thirty minutes of moderate to intense exercise five times a week to maintain good health. And, if you want to lose weight, you should increase this to at least thirty to ninety minutes of moderate to intense exercise, five times a week.

Always consult your doctor first before taking up any form of physical exercise if you have any health conditions. And talk to a professional personal trainer when taking up a new fitness regime.

# FACE YOGA TIPS AND ADVICE

Now it's time for a few face yoga exercises that can help you maintain a healthy young-looking beautiful face with smooth-looking skin, which are unfortunately demonstrated by me yet again dressed as Captain Jack Sparrow! Now what I would like you to do is invite your family and friends round to your house while you practise these face yoga exercises so they can have a good laugh at you while you entertain them pulling and stretching your face around in all sorts of various positions. I'm only joking. So, without further ado, here is the first face yoga exercise.

# ~ THE SMILE SMOOTHER ~

The Smile Smoother is excellent for helping improve your cheek lines and sagging skin. This technique is an alternative to a facelift and using fillers. And here is a video for you to follow along to with step by step instructions: bit.ly/TheSmileSmoother. Hide your teeth with your lips to make an O shape with your mouth – Then smile widely while keeping your teeth hidden – Repeat six times – Now hold the smile O shape while placing your index finger on your chin – Then move your jaw up and down while your head tilts gently back. And, finally, relax and repeat twice more.

# HOW TO INCREASE CIRCULATION IN YOUR FACE

This technique was used for many years in India as a form of medicine. And here is a video to help you follow along to with instructions below as I perform this face yoga exercise: bit.ly/IncreaseCirculationInYourFace. Take your finger and thumb in both hands and pull your earlobes down gently three times – Then do the same to your outer ears three times tenderly, and, to finish, pull the top of your ears upwards three times lightly. You should now feel a lovely glow across your face as your blood circulation is increased. Now here is a bonus video to improve skin tone: bit.ly/FaceYogaSkinTone. Place your index finger in-between your eyebrows while breathing deeply in and out through your nose. By pressing this point, you will increase the circulation around this area. Then circle in one direction for a count of fifteen seconds with your finger and then in the other direction for a further fifteen seconds. And then relax. This technique will also hopefully work in times of stress and is supposed to help you sleep better at night as well.

# THE FLIRTY EYES YOGA TECHNIQUE

This technique helps deep eye hollows and drooping eyebrows; it is an alternative to an eyebrow lift. And here for your enjoyment is a video of myself demonstrating this face yoga exercise to get those flirty eyes of mine ready for a Saturday night out on the town followed by step-by-step instructions on how to achieve this: bit.ly/FaceYogaFlirtyEyes. Place your index fingers under each eye, pointing inwards towards your nose – Then hide your teeth and tease your top lip and your bottom lip away from each other at the mouth – Finally, flutter your upper eyelids while you gaze towards the sky for thirty seconds. Please be careful when you're doing this, though, if you're wearing contact lenses because mine nearly fell out when I was demonstrating this technique! And, if you have had any luck on achieving those flirty eyes, please let me know because I haven't.

# HOW TO IMPROVE DROOPING EYELIDS, CROW'S FEET, EYE BAGS AND PUFFINESS AROUND YOUR EYES

This technique is an alternative solution to Botox and eye surgery. And here is a video where you catch me at work in my dad's garage dressed as Captain Jack Sparrow demonstrating how to improve your eye area using the step-by-step instructions below: bit.ly/FaceYogaEyeImprovements

Place both of your middle fingers on the inner corners of your eyebrows, then with your index fingers do the same to the outer corners – Now look to the ceiling and raise your lower eyelids upwards to make a strong squint. And then relax. Repeat six more times, then finish by squeezing your eyes tightly shut for ten seconds.

# THE GIRAFFE

The Giraffe technique is great for lines and loose skin on and around your neck; it is also an alternative to a neck and jowl lift. In this video, I got caught doing a bit of gardening dressed as Captain Jack. Anyway, without further ado, here is how to do the giraffe. Oh, blimey, that sounds like a 1970s disco dance I'm about to perform for you, doesn't it? bit. ly/FaceYogaThegiraffe. Slightly tilt your head backwards and place your fingertips just below your chin, then lightly stroke your skin downwards – Now jut your lower lip out to pull the corners of your mouth down and place your fingertips on your collar bones with your chin pointed upwards – Then hold for four deep breaths. And relax.

# HOW TO IMPROVE YOUR JAWLINE AND RELIEVE TENSION

And here is the final video where I come running out from behind a tree dressed as Captain Jack Sparrow to demonstrate how to improve your jawline and relieve tension with this face yoga exercise technique: bit.ly/ImproveYourJawlineAndRelieveTension. First, take two fingers and your thumb on either hand – Now pinch with your two fingers and thumb all the way along your jawline starting from your chin then working your way up – Then repeat another six times. And relax. If you get tension in your jaw area, this is a great technique to help relieve that tension apparently.

One final word before I finish. If you don't believe any of these face yoga exercise techniques have worked in the slightest after you have tried them out for a few months, please don't blame me. I'm just a pirate, and you know what they say about us pirates, don't you, that we're just a bunch of old scallywags up to mischief wherever we go: yo-ho-ho! Seriously, though, face yoga exercise techniques can take a long time until you start to see any improvements. If you stick at them, though, you will gradually begin to see a difference.

Well, I hope you found my advice helpful on how to lower your cholesterol and also enjoyed watching my videos. Please remember I'm no expert in this field of keeping fit and eating healthy, so only take my advice lightly. And, as you have heard me say before, it all comes down to common sense; for example, if you're going to eat all the wrong foods, drink a lot of alcohol, smoke every day and not exercise, then there's going to be a high risk of you having medical health problems later on in your life, so please do your best to look after yourself and, in return, your body will look after you.

The health advice I have written about has genuinely helped to improve my family's health and fitness over the years, and we're now a lot fitter and healthy because of it. And I believe, if you follow my advice, you will be too.

# PART SIX

# THE SOPHIE LANCASTER FOUNDATION

I would now like to dedicate Part Six of my book to Sophie Lancaster, who was brutally murdered on 24 August 2007. Sophie Lancaster and Rob Maltby – Sophie's boyfriend at the time – both dressed alternatively and had their own fantastic and individual unique looks. Tragically, though, one day, while they were walking through Stubbeylee Park in Bacup, Lancashire, one evening, they were set upon by a gang of teenagers. The gang of youths first assaulted Sophie's boyfriend, and then when Sophie pleaded for the gang of teenagers to stop what they were doing they turned on Sophie as well. The gang then proceeded to kick and stamp on Sophie and Rob, until they were lying on the ground unconscious and covered in blood. Rob survived the horrific assault. Sadly, though, Sophie died from her injuries.

Since Sophie Lancaster's senseless murder, the Sophie Lancaster Foundation has been set up by her mum, Sylvia Lancaster. On the Sophie Lancaster Foundation website, you can learn all about the fantastic work Sylvia and her staff are doing to help put a stop to hate crimes, plus there is also a merchandise store where you can buy Backstreetmerch products from in honour of Sophie Lancaster to help raise money for the foundation, which you can find on the following link: bit.ly/TheSophieLancasterFoundationWebsite

The founder of the foundation, Sophie's mum, Sylvia Lancaster, now goes all over the UK and into Europe, raising awareness of hate crimes; she is also a voice in government for alternative people who have been victims of hate crimes. In 2014, Sylvia was awarded an OBE, at the Queen's birthday honours, which was for 'Community cohesion in the reduction of hate crimes' for all the hard work she had done since Sophie's death in 2007. Sylvia was presented with the award in December 2014 by HRH Prince Charles.

I'm Sylvia, more often known as 'Sophie's Mum' these days, and I am the Chief Executive of the charity I established as a lasting legacy to Sophie. It's a busy role that sees me working all over the U.K and into Europe, delivering presentations and training to raise crucial awareness of the damage of hate crime and its impact on victims and communities. I'm a regular key-note speaker at conferences, but just as happy working on the S.O.P.H.I.E stall at Bloodstock, Rebellion or Download! Since 2010, I have been a member of the U.K Government Cross Party Hate Crime Independent Advisory Group, which allows me to be a voice for alternative people and victims of hate crime. Using my experience as a youth worker, I feel that reaching young people, and those who work with them is at the centre of all we do.

**Sylvia Lancaster, chief executive of the
Sophie Lancaster Foundation**

The S.O.P.H.I.E. wristband you can buy to show your support for Sophie Lancaster stands for Stamp Out Prejudice, Hatred and Intolerance Everywhere. After Sophie sadly died, her Myspace website was inundated with people sending in their deepest sympathies and condolences. They also shared their own personal stories of how they were attacked because of being alternative individuals.

I realised that prejudice and intolerance was the new racism, and my hope was what happened to Sophie, would lead to a greater understanding and acceptance of all people.

**Sylvia Lancaster, chief executive of the
Sophie Lancaster Foundation**

What tragically happened to Sophie Lancaster is one of the main reasons I decided to write my book because I have had enough of all the hate and abuse small-minded people in our society today have against people such as myself who choose to be alternative! All alternative individuals are doing are being who they want to be; they're causing no harm to anybody.

It's a sad world we live in, isn't it, when a small minority of people can't accept others and think it's fine to go around insulting and attacking them because they wear slightly different clothes and have tattoos and piercings!

> Following the horrific murder of Sophie Lancaster, her family wanted to ensure a lasting legacy to their beautiful, bright, creative daughter, and so, The Sophie Lancaster Foundation was established, and it became a registered charity in 2009. We do this through various means, including education, to create a lasting legacy to Sophie Lancaster. The charity aims to raise awareness of prejudice against subcultures through campaigning and educational work. We also work to have UK Hate Crime extended to include, Alternative Subcultures.
>
> The Sophie Lancaster foundation,
> bit.ly/thesophielancasterfoundation

All it takes is one person to see you getting attention when you're out in public for them to turn on you because of their jealousy and lack of understanding of what it's like to be creative and alternative. If you ask me, those people should learn to love and respect others who choose to look differently and grow up. I'm so grateful to Sylvia Lancaster for creating the Sophie Lancaster Foundation because it's making more awareness of hate crimes against individuals like me in today's society. Hopefully, it will help put an end to atrocious hate crimes so many alternative individuals suffer.

You and I now have a voice and are being heard like never before, thanks to Sylvia. There is still a long way to go and a lot of work to do with educating people on individuality in today's society, but we will get there, and we will never stop until hate crimes against alternative individuals have been eliminated forever! And, until that day arrives, all of us alternative individuals will stand together, side by side, hand in hand and walk tall and be proud of who we are.

Even though I didn't know Sophie Lancaster, I still feel, just like so many other alternative individuals, a powerful connection to her and what she must have gone through throughout her life. What I mean by that is when you don't know if somebody is going to throw an insult your way or want to assault you for looking different when you're out into public just like what happened to me when I was attacked. Luckily, though, I'm still here to get my message out there to the world that hate crimes against alternative individuals need to be put a STOP to!

All of my love and respect goes to Sophie Lancaster and to all of her family.

Thank you so much, Sylvia, for letting me include your daughter, Sophie, yourself and your foundation in my book.

**Steven M. Rippin**

For more information on the Sophie Lancaster Foundation, please visit the following links:

Website: sophielancasterfoundation.com
Facebook: bit.ly/TheSophieLancasterFoundation
instagram.com/Sophie_Lancaster_Foundation
twitter.com/Sophie_Charity

# BE UNIQUE, BE YOURSELF, BE POSITIVE, BE INDIVIDUAL

I always used to feel worried, anxious and afraid of going out in public after I had been assaulted. I was frequently thinking somebody was going to attack me again because of how I looked! I also ended up losing my confidence, and I was continually looking over my shoulder. I knew deep down, though, I had to face my fears and be the alternative individual I wanted to be and not let anybody stop me from doing so. So, over time, I did just that with the help of my family and friends. Also, what helped me was when I turned all the negative thoughts I was having into positive thoughts; I wasn't going to be beaten. Furthermore, I wanted other alternative individuals to know that they are not alone when they face ridicule and hate from cruel members of the public! We need to STAMP OUT HATE CRIMES in our society today, so we can move past this caveman-like Neanderthal behaviour small-minded people portray!

Another significant change in my life which helped me face my fears was when I created my alter-ego Pirate Steve and the Pirate Steve Show on social media, now known as the Positive Pirate. Creating the Positive Pirate helped me regain my confidence and self-esteem. It also gave me the perfect outlet to express how I had always wanted to express myself for the first time in my life as well. I used to be afraid of going out in public dressed in my Captain Jack Sparrow costume because of being cyberbullied by individuals in my hometown. Luckily, though, I had a lot of people say, 'Dress up in your costume. You look great in it.' For some reason, though, I would keep coming up with excuses not to wear it. If I'm honest, it was because I would worry what other people would think or do to me who didn't like me. I didn't want any more trouble from anybody anymore, you see. I have learnt now, though, to never worry about what other people think of you because they have the problem, not you.

I'm happy to say I no longer worry about going out in public dressed up in my costume. I find it great fun, and it's definitely done my confidence and self-esteem no end of good as well.

From an early age I have always felt like an outcast. I believe it's because of how people have treated and looked down on me over the years. I have never understood why particular people have had something against me. I have never gone out to cause trouble or upset anybody; that kind of behaviour isn't in my nature.

When you stand out in a crowd people will look at you, and they might think to themselves, 'What on earth possesses somebody to want to look and dress like that? They're only out for attention.' Some people presume alternative individuals want attention from others. That's far from the truth, just ask any punk, goth, emo or alternative individual why they dress how they do, and their answer will be because they want to. They do it for themselves; there's no reason. You and I dress diversely because we feel comfortable doing so. Alternative individuals don't choose to be different; it's who they are.

If you're an alternative individual or somebody who likes to dress distinctly and gets negative comments from people when you're out in public, remember you are unique – You are loved – You are a beautiful human being – You have so much to offer the world – Dress how you want to dress – Stand tall – Never have regrets and remember to stay true to who you are on the inside, as well as who you are on the outside. Show the world your magnificent self. I never judge anybody on how they choose to look, and I think to myself, when I see alternative individuals, 'If only more people were like you in the world and expressed themselves; respect.'

I have met loads of awesome alternative individuals over the years, and I'm always impressed with the amount of effort they put into their unique styles and looks they have. These guys and girls are awe-inspiring and are genuinely friendly, lovable people. When I hear how they get insulted by insensitive members of the public, it pi**es me right off!

In my hometown, the majority of people know who I am or have heard of me, so I feel pretty safe, although I still have to be careful because I don't know who's out and about and might take a dislike to me. Sometimes people come up to me and say, 'Ah, man, you're Pirate Steve. I've heard so much about you; it's great to meet you; you're amazing,' which is really lovely of them to say and makes me feel very humbled. I must admit, though, I always get incredibly embarrassed when somebody does say something like that because I'm nobody amazing, although I'm going to contradict myself now, because I do believe you and I are both extraordinary in our own individual ways. And there have been other times when strangers on the street will introduce themselves to me because they're intrigued by how I look. I love those interactions I'm privileged to have because deep down I'm timid; approaching people I don't know isn't something that comes naturally to me. So I feel fortunate in this respect that I get to know a lot of people who I wouldn't usually have the good fortune to meet if I didn't resemble a pirate. I never thought I would experience what it feels like to be accepted by the majority of people in my hometown; ninety-five per cent of them have accepted me for who I am. And I say thank you.

When you live your life as an alternative individual, you will get the odd idiot here and there who will get jealous of you and want to pull you down. That's life, sadly, and the way some human beings are. Some people sicken me with how they think it's OK to disrespect you because they don't like your appearance. I always get caught off guard when somebody disrespects me, but I will never insult them back as I don't want to lower myself to their level. I find it's best to be as polite as you can, walk away and be the more grown-up individual in those situations. People have tried telling me over the years how I should be living my life and that I should change how I look because I'm not getting any younger and I will only have regrets if I keep the look I have. Have you ever had somebody talk like this to you? I would never dream of speaking like that to anyone! I believe they talk this way because they have lived sheltered lives and are now caught up in the rat race and have become slaves to the system, so, when they see somebody like me not conforming, they instinctively feel the need to find out why I haven't followed the laws of society as they have. And, just like an error on your computer screen, some people think there must be something wrong with you when you dress unconventionally; therefore, they find it perfectly acceptable to throw offensive remarks your way! Never change for anybody.

I get looks quite often being goth and living in Newfoundland Canada as well as being 41 years old. I tried to be a normie (normal everyday citizen), but the pull of the goth lifestyle kept pulling me back. So, I finally said screw it and screw them. I'm a loner most of the time, but oh well, I'm strange and unusual, and I embrace it. Others should embrace it too. You can't be anyone else; they are all taken. So just be you and surround yourself with people that accept that.

Laura, Newfoundland, Canada

Have you ever been laughed at, singled out and made to feel like a freak for being alternative? If your answer is yes, you're not alone. People all over the world get ridiculed for being individual. Don't let those imbeciles win; stay strong and stay positive because you're awesome; everybody should be accepted for who they are. I have been told by my friends I'm one of the friendliest people you could meet, and still I get insulted and spoken to like I'm a piece of filth and that I don't belong in particular bars because of how I look! It sickens me to my stomach how people think it's OK to treat me this way! Well, let me tell those people something: they're the ones with the problem. They have the wrong attitude towards others, such as myself in today's society. They need to learn how to accept people for who they are. They should also stop judging them on their appearances, just as we don't judge them on theirs! Nobody is any better than anyone else in life. If I didn't feel comfortable wearing the clothes I wear, I would never have dreamt of going out in public looking the way I do, but this is who I am, and I am happy! How you style yourself shows those around you who you sincerely are. So never feel afraid or intimidated by small-minded people when you express your true inner self.

# HOW FRIENDS AND THE PUBLIC TREAT ME BECAUSE OF HOW I LOOK

Unfortunately, I lost friends when I changed my image, and so-called mates stopped inviting me out at the weekends and on holidays with them. I even found out through one of my buddies that this one guy I used to go out partying with most weekends said he was ashamed to be seen out with me in public because he didn't like how I dressed and thought I looked like a clown! That hurt when I heard what he had said about me; I never realised he felt that way. I wonder if any of your friends have stopped being mates with you because of how you look. There are so many men in today's society who have long hair and beards. It makes me wonder if they have had half as much grief about their appearances as I have! You unquestionably learn who your genuine friends are when you live your life as an alternative individual because they're the ones who accept you however you choose to look. So please remember, its what's on the inside that counts – well, obviously not to my ex-friends it wasn't, as I found out.

> I used to have some fantastic nights out with my mates who dropped me; there's now a bit of an atmosphere when I see them out.

I will speak to anybody. Unfortunately, though, when my friends have seen me talk to random strangers when we have been on nights out, they will say, 'What you doing speaking to them for, they're weird,' which really annoys me. I'll tell my mates who are being discourteous, 'These guys are cool. Please don't say things like that; you wouldn't like it if somebody said something like that about you, would you?' Again, people are always judging others, aren't they? If you judge people by their appearance, you will limit your social circle and become small-minded. I have had a lot of awe-inspiring conversations with people I don't know over the years, from homeless people to druids, an FBI agent, a politician, professors, millionaires, actors and magicians. Only once I got talking to those individuals did I learn what their occupations were, well, apart from the homeless people. You never know who you will come across in life, so always accept everybody, no matter how they look.

Homeless people and millionaires are the same as you and me and are made out of flesh and bone. The only difference is one has money and the other doesn't. The homeless person might have once had a highly respectable job and has just had an unfortunate run of bad luck, which is something that could happen to any one of us! So, that being said, nobody is any different to anybody else in life; we are all the same.

One year I was asked to go on holiday by a friend of mine so he invited me to Manchester where he lived to have a night out with his buddies who I would be going on holiday with. My friend's mates were lawyers, who were very polite and respectable people, and we had a great night out together in Manchester. So, I came away from my friend's house that weekend looking forward to going away with him and his buddies on holiday. Around a week later, though, my friend messaged me saying his mates didn't like me because of how I looked and didn't want me going on holiday with them! I couldn't believe it; I was shocked, annoyed and distraught by what they had said. My friend was embarrassed about the whole situation and apologised to me no end, which I appreciated. His friends were so false when they met me, which I didn't realise they were being towards me at the time. They clearly didn't like me from the moment they met me. Why do some people find it acceptable to judge others without getting to genuinely know them first? I thought lawyers would have more common decency.

Oh yeah, and there was a lad I was good friends with for years who got married and didn't even invite me on his stag do because of my appearance! I only heard about that through my mates. We have never spoken or had anything to do with each other ever again. It's disheartening to find out what somebody's real guises are when you have been friends with them for years, isn't it? I will never forget how those so-called buddies of mine and other people have made me feel by rejecting me how they have.

One Christmas Eve my friend and I were having a good laugh with a bunch of strangers who we met in a bar, then my mate left to go to the men's room while I carried on chatting with everyone, then all of a sudden a mother and daughter who were sat in a corner started insulting me for no reason! The daughter said I would be better off with my own sort in another bar, then her mother and herself kept sniggering and laughing at me, which killed the happy Christmassy atmosphere in the pub. Nobody could believe how the pair of them were acting; I then stood up, slammed my pint glass down on the table and walked off, leaving the room in total silence. I probably should have said something to the two of them, but I'm not like that. I know it sounds petty, but this is the typical kind of nonsense I have to put up with from specific people when I'm out in public, and still do, unfortunately!

I always like to be more mature and rise above idiots who find it funny to insult me. A bit like the time when this guy came up to me in a pub in my hometown and said, 'Are you Pirate Steve? I don't like you,' then just walked off, leaving me standing there feeling afraid because I thought he wanted to beat me up! Luckily, nothing happened. I had no idea who that guy was, but I did find out around two weeks later that he was a police officer! Unbelievable, isn't it: there's me thinking the police are there to protect us; instead, though, I get threatened and intimidated by one of them!

Just be you and the hell with the haters. You got a good inner soul that these stupid humans can't see.

Rhonda Whitlow, Las Vegas, Nevada, USA

This next incident happened in a bar in Nashville, Tennessee, after my dad and I had been to watch Dolly Parton perform live at the Grand Ole Opry. And while my dad was chatting to the owner of the bar we were in, in Nashville, I got speaking to a couple of the girls in there, then after a few minutes I ended up having trouble with a guy who kept butting into the conversation we were having; he kept questioning my appearance. I did my best to ignore him, but he wouldn't go away, and he continued saying behind my back, 'Why are you dressed like that?'

'This is how I always dress,' I told him.

'That's weird,' he replied.

'Ah right, well, I'm sorry about that,' I responded. I should point out here that you should never apologise to somebody who's being rude towards you, which is a lesson I have now learnt! Saying sorry to a stranger who's insulting you lowers your value and makes you look vulnerable and weak. Then I carried on talking to these two girls while this drunk guy stood behind us. I was pretty nervous if I'm honest because I didn't know if this guy was carrying a gun or a knife on him! The two girls then told the impolite guy to go away and leave us alone, which he didn't.

Luckily, my dad saw what was going on, so he came over to this irritating guy, which I hadn't seen him do, and he said to him, 'What's the problem?'

'He dresses weird, why's that?' the guy replied.

'He's my son. I want you to apologise to him,' my dad said.

'I'm not apologising,' came the response of the obnoxious guy.

'Well, we're going to have a problem then aren't we?' replied my dad.

'Are we? why's that?' the drunk said.

'Because you're not apologising to my son!' my dad returned, becoming angry. Then my dad and this drunk guy stood there in silence looking at each other for a good minute. The discourteous guy then offered to shake my dad's hand, which my dad squeezed tightly and said, 'You're going to apologise right now.' Then the staff saw what was going on and stepped in and kicked this annoying guy out the bar. The drunk guy never did apologise to me, and after he had gone the waiter said, 'I'm really sorry about that; he comes in here all the time causing trouble.' Things then calmed down, and my dad and I chatted with the two girls I had been talking to for a few more minutes before we left.

To this day, my dad and I look back on that situation and we count ourselves extremely lucky because for all we knew that irritating guy could have been waiting for us outside with a loaded gun and his friends ready to attack us. It's just not worth even thinking about what could have happened, especially when you hear about the amount of gun crime that goes on these days. Other than that circumstance, my dad and I had a great night out in that bar in Nashville. You have to be so careful when you're out in public no matter where you are these days, even more so when you're in another country. What a shame a small minority of people act like that guy did, though, and love to get drunk and intimidate others.

These situations I have found myself in with people have assuredly affected me over the years and made me warier how I dress when I go out in public. Don't get me wrong: I still wear alternative clothes when I'm out; nobody will ever stop me from doing that. I just pick and choose my outfits more carefully these days.

Now, here is another incident I had while I was at work with my dad when I was made to feel like a reject of society. One day, when we were cleaning carpets in a village, a customer of my dad's saw him outside the house we were working in, so she came over and had a chat. Then after I had finished carpet cleaning and had packed all the equipment away, I went and introduced myself to my dad's customer, who seemed like a pleasant woman. That was until she turned around to my dad and said, 'Your son will never get a girlfriend with how he looks, will he? Who would want to go out with him!' My dad and I stood there incredulously! She then started laughing her head off and wouldn't stop! My dad quickly ended his conversation with this woman as politely and as soon as he could because he knew I was fuming and wanted to say something to her, which I wish I had! Then once we were in the van I told my dad how I felt, and he told me not to take what she had said to heart and that she doesn't know any better because she's one of those small-minded people who doesn't get out into the real world much. Which was good advice my dad gave me that day because, instead of getting upset when somebody does say a negative thing to you, you have to turn that negative comment around and think what kind of person they are to say something like that in the first place; that woman was undoubtedly a very judgemental person! Some people speak before they think, don't they? Then before they know it they make complete fools of themselves because of their lack of people skills.

> Just be yourself, who cares what other people think. The people that are mean to you don't understand you. Find people who do understand you, because those people are your tribe. I have been made fun of in the past for being different, but I have found people that understand me. I know you will too.
>
> Hester Armstrong, Gainesville, Georgia, USA

You won't believe this story either, which happened to me while I was on holiday with my parents back in 2013. You see, when my parents and I visited Southwold on the east coast of England, while we were walking along the beachfront after having a fantastic meal out, we came across a guy who must have been in his mid-fifties renting beach huts out. And as I walked by him, I said, 'Hi, it's lovely around here isn't it, what a great part of England.' And as I was saying that he gave me a peculiar look and didn't bother answering me back! So off I went thinking what a strange bloke he was while I made a few video vlogs on the beach.

My mum and dad were a short distance behind me, and when they encountered the beach hut guy they said hi to him as well; I should point out that the beach hut guy didn't realise they were my parents. And he said to them, 'He's a strange one, isn't he,' as he pointed over in my direction.

'What do you mean?' replied my dad.

'Well, look at the state of him and how he's dressed!' answered the beach hut guy. At this point, I happened to turn around and saw where my parents were, so I went over to join them, and I heard the rest of the conversation, which went like this:

'Yeah, this is my son,' my dad said.

'Oh, right, I just don't get it, why?' replied the beach hut guy as he stood there examining me. My mum, dad and I then looked at each other and couldn't believe what he had just said!

It didn't seem to faze this guy that he was making a fool of himself by disrespecting me in front of my parents! My mum, dad and I just stood there staring at him in astonishment. After a few seconds, my dad said, 'Yeah, whatever, mate,' then we all walked off offended at how rude he had been! It just shows you that it doesn't matter how old somebody is; they will always have plenty to say to you if they don't like how you look. Those kinds of people don't stop and think about how they might be making that person feel on the inside with their hurtful words. Would you criticise or tell the Rolling Stones, Russell Brand, Rob Zombie, Lady Gaga, Miley Cyrus, Alan Carr, Johnny Depp, Alice Cooper, Marilyn Manson, Bjork, Madonna, Michael Jackson (RIP), Prince (RIP) or any extroverted and eccentric celebrities to start dressing more appropriately or to grow up and start acting their ages? Of course you wouldn't; well, I don't think you would anyway. Nobody is going to tell a celebrity they can't do something or look a certain way, are they? They will always wear what they want. Now imagine if one of those celebrities had been strolling down the beachfront in Southwold in England. They wouldn't have been questioned and criticised about their appearance by the beach hut guy, would they? Instead, beach hut guy would have asked them for a selfie, then offered them a free beach hut to hire for whenever they wanted!

Certain people can be very shallow-minded and give you no encouragement when you decide to change your image. Thankfully, though, there are not many people like that around; there are more positive people who will encourage you, and they are the individuals you should surround yourself with. And when you come across any offensive fools, don't give them your time of day; be polite, then walk away from them with your head held high, feeling proud of who you are.

Now and then when I have been out in public people have asked me particular questions with a snigger on their faces. A bit like how this one woman did who came up to me once and ask me why I look the way I do, which I honestly don't mind when I am asked in a courteous way. It was the way this woman came across, though, while also having the audacity to say I am hiding away from who I genuinely am! Here are a few of the questions she bombarded me with: 'Why are you a pirate?' – 'Why do you dress the way you do? Isn't it time you stopped?' – 'When will you grow up?' and 'Why are you hiding behind this persona you have made for yourself?' What does a stranger know about me, and what gave her the right to question me like that? I found her extremely rude, and I didn't like the way she was sniggering at me. After a few more minutes of her interrogating me in her condescending way, I said, 'Right, I'm bored. You're doing my head in! You're not listening to a word I'm saying in reply to your questions; goodbye.' Then I turned my back on her and walked away. I think she was quite shocked when I did that; I made sure, though, I did it graciously. Some people should learn to keep their thoughts to themselves if they have nothing constructive to say other than the offensive comments they find funny to throw your way. Then there was one guy who said in a patronising way to me that I'm not real, I'm fake and who do I think I am? I could go on and on like this.

Well, there you go; they are just a few of the situations I have found myself in when the general public have discourteously insulted me. Having gone through so many incidents like this over the years has taken its toll on me; at the same time, though, I have certainly learnt a lot about people and how they react when they see alternative individuals in today's society, which has opened up my eyes and shown me what some of the human race are genuinely like, which saddens me no end. A small minority of the public don't realise the damage they can cause with their words when they say the hurtful things they say to people such as myself. If somebody wants to sincerely get to know someone they are intrigued by, they should speak and treat that person how they would like to be treated and spoken to in return. The majority of citizens in public are very courteous and know how to ask questions about my life in a friendly and non-patronising way, thankfully.

> It's ok to be different, always remember that. Those who stand by you will love and support you. You carry on shining while the insulters are left in the shade. I have a friend, called Ted Parrotman, some may have seen him on Jeremy Kyle, and This Morning, he gets insulted and judged, he's heavily tattooed, has small horns on his head, had his ears removed to mimic a parrots head (he donated his ears to a friend who didn't have an ear), etc., but he's a gentle giant who loves his parrots (he even changed his surname).

> Hayley Peachey, Wales

> If someone is insulting another, that person is probably jealous or threatened by something different. Always be your unique self.

> Gliem, Canada, instagram.com/gliemmusic

Whether you're an alternative individual or not, when you see somebody who dresses slightly differently to you in society, and you decide to address them, think about what you're going to say to that person. If it's something negative about their appearance, consider how it would make you feel if someone approached you and criticised how you looked. Your words can have a devastating effect on some people, so why not pay them a compliment and make them feel happy and accepted just how they accept you for who you are? Don't be the cause of that person's depression because of your small-mindedness! Remember, they are no different to you; they express themselves because they feel comfortable with who they are just as you feel comfortable with who you are. If people have disrespected you, don't let them get to you. If they do, stay as positive as you can and remember there's nothing wrong with you; it's those feeble-minded ones who are at fault and have a problem.

When I have heard what my alternative friends have had to put up with, it really annoys me! One of my mates who dresses alternatively told me when she went out one night residents where she lived started throwing chips and taunts at her because of how she was dressed! How would those people like it if somebody threw chips and hurled abuse at them, I wonder! What a tragic society you and I are living in when people do things like that.

Be prepared to face criticism from people when you live your life as an alternative individual.

There are a lot of fantastic people of all ages where I live, and I am happy to say the majority of them always tell me how much respect they have for me because of how I choose to look and the positive messages I put out there on social media.

Thank you Market Harborough, I am so proud of where I live. I love everybody I know who lives here. Respect.

Steven M. Rippin

Young lads who are bodybuilders have opened up and explained to me how they used to feel on the inside. And it's been fascinating why they got into bodybuilding in the first place. They either had insecurities about themselves or used to get bullied a lot at school and decided to do something about it, so they got themselves down the gym, where their confidence grew and grew, and they felt good about themselves once again. I'll tell you something: I can sincerely relate to how they felt, even though I'm no bodybuilder.

If you can relate to anything I have written about, write down those experiences and emotions you had and explain to yourself – How they made you feel – How you can turn them around to your advantage, such as by creating your own blog or YouTube channel where you can help other people who have also suffered from similar experiences, and also think how those negative circumstances have helped or will help you grow as a person in the future just how my negative experiences have helped me. Writing down your experiences can be very therapeutic and help you move on with your life.

When somebody says a negative thing to me nowadays, I will walk away and won't give that person any more of my precious time, or I will say, 'You can read all about why I look the way I do in my book.' And that gets them every time because either they are intrigued and want to know more about me, or they can't wait to get away from me!

Always learn from your past negative experiences with somebody so you know how to deal with those encounters the next time a negative-minded individual says something disrespectful to you. Being an alternative individual doesn't mean you're put into a particular category, such as being labelled as a goth, emo, rocker, clubber, hipster or pirate; anybody can be an alternative individual. It doesn't all come down to how you look; it's how you feel and think on the inside.

I have found my inner strength and confidence by dressing how I feel comfortable.

The people who are genuinely at peace with themselves are the ones who live their lives outside the confines of modern-day society who you might call eccentric, weird, freaky and strange because of how they wish to live their lives. Those people, though, are the most down-to-earth individuals you will ever have the good fortune of meeting. They will never give you any nonsense, and they will always treat you with respect. Don't let anyone stop you from becoming who you want to be, so be unique, be individual and become the best version of you.

The next time you see somebody who dresses alternatively, don't laugh at them; treat them as if you would treat your own family and friends, with the LOVE and RESPECT they deserve.

With all the hurt and pain, I have endured because of my appearance, it has given me the STRENGTH, DETERMINATION and MOTIVATION to carry on being myself.

# HOW TO LIVE YOUR LIFE AS AN ALTERNATIVE INDIVIDUAL

There's one thing being an alternative individual isn't, and that's easy, principally because of how you get treated by particular members of the public. Believe it or not, even some of your friends as well. I never intentionally set out to become an alternative individual and resemble a pirate; it's just how my style has developed.

Have you ever thought, 'Where's my life going? I never have time for myself anymore? I used to have so much fun when I was younger. Now look at me, I'm old, and my life is flashing before my eyes. I wish I had had the confidence to dress more alternatively, gone to that nightclub my friends never wanted to go to with me, changed my image, dyed my hair bright pink and shaved it at the sides, been more adventurous and got those tattoos and piercings I had always wanted to get but never did because I didn't want to get laughed at by my mates. I just wanted to fit in and be accepted by them and not feel like an outcast. I was always too scared to be who I wanted to be when I was younger. It's too late for me now, though. If only.' IF ONLY! If only this; if only that! Jeez, if you and I lived our lives in a world of if onlys, we would never do anything and we would have so many regrets, wouldn't we?

So, STOP and LISTEN right now. It's NEVER too late to change who you are; it doesn't matter how old you are either to make changes in your life today. I was around twenty-five when I first decided to change my image, and I didn't start enjoying myself until I was thirty-three. I'm now living my life and enjoying every moment of it, and I have no plans on changing because I've found the person I'm happy being; nobody will ever take that away from me.

People used to tell me to cut my hair when I was growing it because they said I looked much better with it short. If I had listened to those people, Pirate Steve as I'm known today wouldn't exist. So, I stuck to my guns, and I grew my hair, then once it was pretty long I started feeling more confident within myself. Always follow your heart when you want to make a change in your life and don't be influenced by what other people say to you.

Dress and style as you want. The radiance that you have with it makes you feel so self-assured that all others are envious. Be yourself.

### Julia Spaniol, Germany, instagram.com/thebluedarklight

Over the years, a lot of people have said to me, 'I wish I had the guts to dress how you do.' And I always tell those people, 'Dress how you want to! What's stopping you? it's your life.' So, if you're in your late twenties, thirties, forties, fifties or even your late eighties and you have always wanted to dress alternatively and never have, then make that change happen today. It's a liberating feeling to wear what you want, and, when you do, the real you will emerge. Being an alternative individual isn't about how you dress; it's about your whole outlook on life and what you want to get out of it. Now here are some questions to ask yourself if you have thought of becoming an alternative individual.

Have you always wanted to dress differently but have held yourself back from doing so because you feel worried about what other people will think of you? – Are you changing your image or outlook on life for all the right reasons and not just to please other people around you, so you fit in with them? – Do you want to be somebody who makes a difference in the world? And do you have goals you want to achieve but you're not too sure if to take that final leap of faith and lean into what you truly want to get out of life?

Well, I hope those questions have helped you if you have been thinking of changing your appearance and outlook. Don't hold yourself back on the goals you have and never have regrets. Also, try asking your family and friends for their advice when it comes to making important life-changing decisions.

I took a look back at the things I have done since leaving school from notes I have written down to the hundreds of videos I have made on social media, and there was one clear message I kept noticing, which was this:

It's all right to be different. And whatever you do in life, people will scrutinise you, so embrace who you are and don't be afraid to show the world the real you. You only live once so love, laugh, cry, be true to yourself, and stay positive in everything you do.

After looking back on my life, this message made me realise who I genuinely am on the inside and that I have always subconsciously wanted to bring love and happiness into as many people's lives as I can, which might sound cheesy but it's the honest truth.

When you're an alternative individual, some people will be intrigued and ask you questions on what made you decide to be different, while others will admire, respect and want the confidence to be just like you in their own way. Unfortunately, there will also be people who won't want anything to do with you, and they will talk cruelly about you behind your back. Don't worry about those people; they don't understand what it's like to have an awe-inspiring creative mind like you. All those small-minded individuals have done is follow the herd and lived sheltered everyday lives.

I have had to put up with my fair share of negative comments, as you know. The one good thing that has done is that it has toughened me up on the inside and I have learnt to accept what people's negative opinions are of me. Luckily, most have been said positively, I am happy to say. You will never make everybody happy or understand where you're coming from with your alternative style and outlook on life because everyone has their views on what they like and what they don't like. My problem is I always go to bars and nightclubs where you wouldn't usually see a guy who looks like me. So, I often end up sticking out like a sore thumb in those places; people always expect to find somebody like me in a rock club. I will always go where I want, though, and I won't be made to feel intimidated by anybody!

In my hometown, most people have now accepted me for who I am, even though there is still a small percentage who will take the mickey out of me. So what? Let them mock me; I'm doing nobody any harm. I just want to be happy, enjoy my life and make others around me smile along the way. Is that too much to ask?

My Hubby and I dress how we want to. I don't care what people think. I'm a care worker for the Elderly, I have tattoos and piercings, and my clients love me. Never judge a book by its cover, be you xxx.

Vicky M. Allen, Lancashire, England

People rarely judge me on my appearance when I go to big cities and places I have never been to before, which I love. I do catch them on occasion staring in my direction, though.

Here are a few of the most common criticisms I receive from people when they see me in public, which are said in a very disrespectful and patronising way. 'It's Pirate Pete!' – 'Where's your boat?' – 'Are you in fancy dress?' – 'What's the special occasion?' – 'Is the circus in town?' – 'Is that a wig you're wearing?' – 'Why are you dressed like a pirate?' – 'Are you gay?' – 'Why do you look like this?' – 'Are you real?' – 'I don't understand what you're doing this for?' – 'You look like an idiot' – 'I don't like you' – 'You're scary' – 'Who do you think you are?' – 'You're not being true to yourself' – 'You don't belong here; you're weird' – 'I F***ING HATE YOU, FREAK!' Plus, I have received many more comments like these. And, like I said earlier, don't take to heart what these small-minded people say to you if you have ever been insulted for looking different in today's society. Always rise above their insensitive remarks.

If you're living an alternative lifestyle, some members of the public may want to embarrass you in front of your friends – Pull you down in front of their mates – Have a girlfriend or boyfriend they want to impress by making you look like a fool, or they could be jealous of you and wish they had the courage to be different themselves. On the brighter side, though, people will give you compliments and want their picture taken with you, plus you will inspire many as well. When I'm insulted, I take that negative feeling it gives me, and I let it empower my mind, so it enables me to get my message out there into the world that it's acceptable to be unconventional and individual.

Geeky kids, nerdy kids or whatever you like to call them are the new cool kids of today's generation because they are the creative ones; they are the individual free thinkers; they have the big ideas that help change the world, although they might not know it when they are being bullied and humiliated by other children and teenagers when they are at school. I know I didn't and look how I turned out! Hmmm, maybe that's not the best example!

My advice to anybody who's alternative when going out at the weekend is: To keep your friends around you when you're out in public, especially when you're in bars and nightclubs – To think about the type of places you're going to – To never leave pubs or clubs alone, and to always get a registered certified taxi home with your mates. Above all else, please stay safe out there because you don't know who's lurking about and ready to start on you for looking different.

My alternative friends have to put up with a lot of abuse when they go out at the weekends clubbing from insensitive people. Even when they go out in the daytime, they will get insulted because of how they look. And get this: the offensive comments come from people you would least expect them to come from, such as an old couple in the supermarket doing their weekly shopping or from an office worker who will say, 'Look at the state of you! You're a disgrace; what must your parents think of you?' So, yet again, it shows you that some of the so-called 'Normies' who fit into society and dress appropriately can be very impolite to those of us who dress alternatively in today's society.

To be individual shows a strong character, people who mock are normally the weak ones. I think most of us would like to stand out but haven't the courage. So, to those who dare, I have the utmost respect for, be true to yourself, it's not about appearance, it's what comes from within, and to be colourful is a bonus.

**Tracy Ingman, Market Harborough, England**

When you hear people spreading untrue rumours about you, envision how a celebrity would think when they receive hateful remarks from people online and also when they're out in public. They ignore them because they haven't got the time to waste on such trivial matters. So why should you worry about what somebody says about you who you don't know; let them carry on concerning themselves about you if that's all they have to fret about in their dull little lives.

Don't let the negative people hurt you, because if they get you down, they win. Don't let them win. Show them that you are strong and that you are the winner, not them.

Gavin Franz, Indiana, USA, instagram.com/__gavin_of_steel__

Every once in a while, a woman will approach me asking for a selfie and depending on where I am this can wind men up; I get the impression they think, 'Look at him getting all the attention, the self-centred idiot.' So, I do my best to get those men involved in the photos being taken to make it clear that it's not all about me and that it's just as much about them as well. I want to see everybody having fun and being happy. Also, if a woman wants a picture taken with me who's with her boyfriend, I will introduce myself to him as soon as possible, so he knows I am no threat to him, and I do that because of the looks I have been given by some girlfriends' boyfriends in the past. I can honestly say I get shy and embarrassed when somebody approaches me for a photograph.

The benefits of being an alternative individual for me have been meeting all the genuine members of public I have had the privilege of speaking to who I wouldn't have met if I didn't look the way I do. And I always feel humbled when they ask if I'm the pirate guy they have heard about and seen on social media. When I tell them that's me, they can't believe it and are so happy. I always tell them, though, I'm nobody special, and I'm just as excited to meet them as well. I always appreciate members of the public introducing themselves to me; I have never been very good at approaching people. So, as you can see, the positives do outweigh the negatives when you're an alternative individual.

# SHOW YOUR CREATIVE INDIVIDUAL SIDE TO THE WORLD

Alternative individuals are very creative people, although I never thought I was a creative person myself until people started saying, 'You're creative, aren't you? It's clever how you make those videos you post online. Some are pretty crazy, but you do talk a lot of sense.' I have never thought much of the videos I have made, if I am honest, because they are very amateurish. As they say, you can't always see what's right there in front of you until somebody points it out. So now I realise the videos I make show the creative side of my personality with how I like to express myself to the world.

You can be whoever you want to be in life and if somebody like me can choose to be different, then so can you. To find out how creative you are, make a list of the things you love doing. You could include your interests and anything that makes you happy.

You might like travelling: if you love travelling, you could work for an airline company, be a tour guide or make documentary videos of the area where you live to help promote your community. You might like sewing: if you like sewing, you could start your own online business by selling your creations online and seeing where it leads for you. You never know: you might end up selling your pieces to major outlet stores. You might like music: so for that budding musician in you, all you have to do to be that next badass rock star guitar player is put a lot of practice in and ask your friends if they want to be in a band with you and go from there. You might want to write a book: everybody has a story to tell, so sit down and write about the most meaningful moments of your life, like my good friend

Ron Cichy II of the website lifezynth.com would say. Or come up with an original idea for your very own detective series or magical fantasy fairy tale. Just think: you might have a book inside that mind of yours waiting to pop out onto paper, just like J.K Rowling did, or you might like gaming and movies because these interests can all lead onto so much more for you as well. So, if you're into gaming and movies, you might be interested in going to conventions and cosplaying, or you might want to become an app developer for games you have had ideas for, then again you might like to become an extra for a movie or a TV show.

How creative are you, I wonder. Whatever interests you have, they will show your creative side and the kind of person you are. So, get out there and put your artistic skills to the test and see where they take you. Everybody has creativity built into them; it's just a question of finding out what that creative flair is which you have.

Dress differently, make an impression on the world, embrace your passions and let your creativeness flow, so you become the alternative individual you were always born to be. And by doing so you will open up new windows of opportunity for yourself. At the same time, you will feel alive to the world around you as well, just like how being an alternative individual has made me feel.

# DON'T LISTEN TO PEOPLE WHO TELL YOU TO ACT YOUR AGE

I will always dress and look how I want no matter what insults people give me. When somebody does tell me to cut my hair and to dress more appropriately, that always makes me want to do the opposite, so I will grow my hair longer, paint my nails black, wear crazier clothes and wear even more eyeliner around my eyes! Don't let your age or anybody stop you from being the alternative individual you want to be. Age should never defy who we are and how we live our lives.

I often have people say to me, 'When are you going to grow up and act your age?' Which doesn't make any sense to me because I am already grown up and acting my age; age is just a number, after all, isn't it? And can you believe this: when a customer asked my dad if he liked reading and my dad told them that he was reading the *Harry Potter* books, they said he was too old to read them because they are very childish; how narrow-minded! Luckily, my dad told that customer they were fantastic to read. Good on you, Dad, for putting that customer right. I also remember going into a shop called Woolworths when I was thirteen, and while I was looking at the toys deciding on whether or not to buy a Batman figure a kid from my school saw me and said, 'What are you doing? You're not buying that, are you? You're too old for kids' toys.'

'What's it got to do with you what I buy?' I replied to him. Then the kid from my school turned around and walked off, shaking his head, laughing at me. The next thing I knew an old couple came over to me and the old man said, 'Well done for sticking up for yourself and telling that boy what you thought of his remark.' He made me feel a lot better. Jeez,

I have got friends in their forties who love buying toys for themselves. One of them even goes over to Japan buying himself movie action figures, while another friend of mine buys *Transformers* and *Star Wars* figures. I think, if that's what they're into, then fair play. They're not hurting or harming anyone, are they?

My point with these stories is that it shouldn't matter how old you are; if you like something, you should buy it if you can afford to. And if you love reading children's books, read them. Don't let people dictate how you should be living your life because of your age.

I'm also a big fan of Disney and love going to Disneyworld when I can. I feel sincerely sorry, though, for people who think Disneyworld is just for children because it isn't; it's for people of all ages to enjoy. And for adults who have forgotten what it's like to have fun and be that child they once were again, they should get themselves over to Disneyworld and stop moaning at people like myself who love enjoying life. I feel very sorry for people who have this closed-off mindset thinking because you reach a certain age you have to stop acting a particular way. It's a bit like someone telling me to stop clubbing and listening to electro and hardstyle music because that music is only for the younger generation to enjoy and somebody my age should be listening to Radio Two instead! Well, let me tell those people something: that's never going to happen. I have been listening to electro and hardstyle music most of my life. So why on earth would I suddenly stop listening to it because somebody tells me to! And, on that note, all that leaves me to say is: don't let your age confine you and don't think you have to dress a certain way because society tells you to!

# BECOME A CONFIDENT ALTERNATIVE INDIVIDUAL

Now I am going to give you tips and advice on how to become a confident alternative individual.

Tip 1: if you suffer from confidence and have terrible body language, people will see you as weak and won't give you the respect you deserve, which is what I found when I acted that way. So what you should be doing is feeling comfortable with who you are and portraying a value of self-confidence to everyone around you. You also want people to know you're a self-assured and approachable person who they feel relaxed being around and not somebody who comes across as being pathetic, condescending and intimidating. Also, surround yourself with people who appreciate you and don't pull you down. Remember: stand tall, keep your shoulders back, keep your eyes off the ground and give people eye contact.

Tip 2: alternative individuals like to express themselves, so why would you want to follow everybody else and do what they do, wear what they wear and have the same haircuts they have? Well, that way of life might be for some people, but it's certainly not for me, although I will admit that's how I used to be because I used to copy what clothes and hairstyles my friends had as I wanted to feel accepted and fit in with them. I used to be exceptionally unoriginal with my appearance and I had no individuality whatsoever. So, if you would like to change your look and style, don't be afraid of buying clothes you wouldn't usually buy. Let your creative side out and mix and match various styles together, then over time you will see what looks good on you and what doesn't.

I have only this to say, no matter how we dress, we all bleed red.

**Eddie Davis, Townsend, Tennessee, USA**

Being alternative has meant I have always had my own opinions and views on things, especially when it comes to extra-terrestrials, science, space, technology, health, what the future holds for humanity and the Universe. And even though some people laugh at what I believe in it doesn't bother me one bit, firstly because they are fundamental issues I am very passionate about and secondly because I am an alternative individual with my own mind. When you live your life as an alternative individual, stick to what you believe. And never let anybody change your opinions on anything you hold close to your heart.

> Your individuality comes from within you and will develop over time as you grow as a person and have new life experiences.

If you have an opinion on something, let your family, friends and work colleagues know how you feel about the topic of conversation you're having with them, and if you're in the workplace don't be one of those 'yes, sir, no, sir, three bags full, sir' kinds of people who come across all creepy just so everybody likes them; you will end up being known as a sheep who follows the herd if you do that.

Tip 3: always take challenges and step out of your comfort zone. Stepping out of my comfort zone gave me the confidence to appear on *The Weakest Link* and audition for *Big Brother*. I will admit I felt nervous and timid when I took those challenges on; those experiences, though, were incredible. So never feel afraid to take on a new task. Think outside the box and do something spectacular.

Tip 4: you might lose so-called friends by choosing to be an alternative individual. Don't let that worry you, though, because you will learn who your genuine mates are, and, hey, would you want friends in your life who don't understand you and criticise you for how you look? I know I wouldn't! Those kinds of mates will only stop you from reaching your full potential in life. I have made some awesome mates online and in my hometown through the years, and they have all helped me feel more confident within myself as a person because they accept

**Top left:** Baby me aged four, 1979.

**Top right:** This is when I disappeared in my dad's arms, 1975.

**Bottom left:** Here is Worzel Gummidge and me after I had my cataract removed, 1982.

**Bottom right:** Here I am aged twelve when I attended Welland Park Academy, where I was bullied daily.

Here are a few photos after I was head-butted twice in the face when I was thirty-two, 2008.

'Jack Sparrow' lookalike attacked in town nightclub

Full story on p3.

Headbutt victim uses web to call for peace

A few months after I was head-butted, I went to the Sherard Primary School in Melton Mowbray, and this is one of the teachers who loved her chocolate button sweets which I was giving out as Christmas presents. Also, below are the thank-you messages the schoolchildren did for me for going over to visit them, which I sincerely appreciated them doing for me.

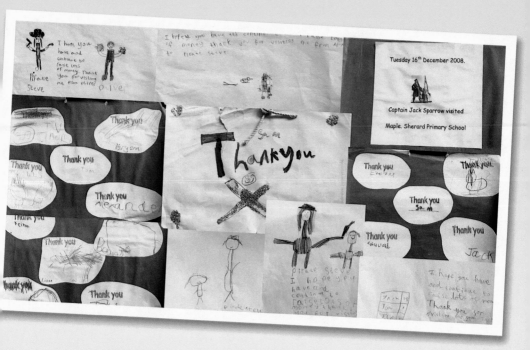

**Left:** My mum's parents: my grandparents Marek and Theresa Kirkucki.

**Right:** My dad's parents: my grandparents Gordon William Rippin and Catherine Zeta Rippin.
**Below:** My good friend Arron Micklewright and me.

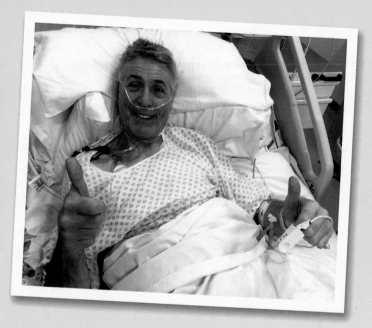

**Above:** My dad recovering in hospital from his cardiac arrest, November 2014.
**Right:** My dad recovering after his mouth cancer operation, 5 April 2017.

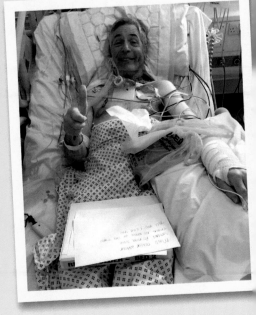

**Left:** Here is my dad's skin graft healing up.

**Top left:** Timmy Mallett and me at Croft Wingates in Market Harborough, June 2017.

**Top right:** Fundraising for Cancer Research UK at Bowden Stores in Great Bowden, June 2017.

**Middle left:** Here is Andy and his wife, Debbie Chapman, who is dressed as a tapeworm, and me fundraising for Cancer Research UK.

**Right:** And here we all are at Wesses Bakery fundraising in Market Harborough.

**Left:** The Pirate Steve Show.
**Below:** The Positive Pirate, as I am now known on social media.

**Left:** Here I am on The Weakest Link on Thursday, 14 October 2010.

**Right:** Here, my dad and I are on top of Mount Harrison overlooking the Great Smoky Mountains.

**Top left:** Fun and entertaining times at the Sweet Fanny Adams Theatre, 2009.
**Top right:** My dad and Bill Owens at Dollywood, 2009.
**Middle right:** Stacey Annette Morgan and me at the Tennessee Shindig, 2009.
**Bottom left:** Here I am on stage at the Tennessee Shindig trying to be a Blues Brother, September 2009.
**Bottom right:** Here is my dad being sung to by the late, great Stacey Annette Morgan, at the Tennessee Shindig, September 2009.

**Top left:** My dad and me at Dollywood with a bunch of lovely old ladies in 2009.

**Top right:** Here is the awesome ventriloquist Stephen Knowles and me at the Comedy Barn, 2016.

**Middle left:** The singing Santa, who my dad and I had the privilege of meeting in 2009.

**Bottom left:** Horse riding in the Smokies was an unforgettable experience with my dad.

**Bottom right:** The Great Smoky Mountains: my dad and I love you.

**Above:** Peter Cunnah from
D:Ream and me, 1988.

**Above:** Here is Amanda
O'Riordan and Judge
Jules; this is the photo
where Amanda stole my
photo opportunity with
her husband.

**Above:** Judge Jules, Amanda O'Riordan and me, 2017.
**Right:** Me with blonde hair back in the day.

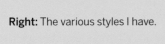

**Right:** The various styles I have.

**Left:** My alternative look.

**Right:** This photograph of
Michelle Foster and me in
Camden Town, London, was
taken on November 2017 by
David Griso; davidgriso.com

Here are the cybergoth goggles and respirators I made along with my Cyberlox wigs I bought and started wearing in my forties, as you do.

The T-shirt I am wearing in the middle picture portrays how I felt when I was head-butted in 2008.

**Top left:** Here is a photograph my good friend Philip Eldridge-Smith took of me on May 2019 — www.esphoto.co.uk — instagram.com/esphotoinsta

**Top right and below:** These two professional photographs were taken by John Robertson — www.jr-photos.com

**Top left:** My dad aged 10/11 years old.
**Top right:** My dad and me, 1978.
**Middle left:** My dad and me having fun when I was twelve years old.
**Bottom left:** I love you very, very much, Dad. Thank you for being the best dad a son could ask for.
**Bottom right:** Here is my dad and me after he had been given the all clear by his cancer specialist, Dr Harrop, 2017, a year my family will never forget.

My dad and I had a magical time at
Disneyworld and on our road trip over in
America, September 2012.
Dad, I love you with all my heart. Thank you
for these unforgettable memories we shared
together.

During the covid-19 lockdown in 2020 my dad and me did fifty shows each weekday evening over ten weeks to help lift people's spirits; as you can see, we were not afraid of making fools of ourselves and we helped a lot of people through some very emotional and tough times.

**Above:** Here my dad and me are doing our country music party show during the covid-19 lockdown June 4 2020.

Never forget who your true self is in life and always keep a smile on your face along with a positive attitude; have fun. Be unique, be yourself and be positive through all the turbulent times life throws your way.

me for who I am and never judge me. When you have got good friends in your life, they will always be there for you when you need them the most, especially when you're feeling down and need somebody to talk to. Genuine friends are the ones who accept you no matter how you look.

Tip 5: don't let people walk all over you and take advantage of your kind nature. Remember you're an alternative individual with your own mind. So, if somebody asks you to do something you haven't got time to do, tell them in a clear, confident voice, 'I'm going to have to give it a miss this time, I've got too much on. Thanks for thinking of me, though.' Some people find it difficult to say no to people, especially family and friends. Don't feel guilty if you have to turn them down, though, because it's not worth putting yourself under any pressure, is it? Think of your own well-being first before committing to anything. Be honest if you can't do something or be somewhere for somebody.

In the past, I have gone along to events with my mates just to please them when I haven't wanted to, and I always ended up not enjoying myself. It annoyed me as well because I wasted my hard-earned money when I could have been doing something a lot more productive and enjoyable with my time instead! My friends always expected me to do everything they did, no questions asked. What annoyed me as well were when my buddies let me down when I asked them to do things, such as going to Ibiza on holiday or nights out clubbing in England! I no longer do what they want to do, and I now focus on things I have my heart set on doing instead. The last thing you and I want is to have regrets in our lives. So, don't just sit there and be told what you're going to be doing and where you're going to be going by your friends; get out there and do what YOU want to do. Don't be held back by anybody!

Tip 6: having your own mind makes you who you are. Society, though, tries its best to mould your personality and the way you think to their manipulative ways so they can sell you their products to get hold of your hard-earned money. Don't let them. Don't be manipulated by the media. Don't follow the crowd!

Tip 7: only wear clothes you feel comfortable wearing. People will know if you're trying to get attention, which some people think I do. I have only worn clothes I feel suit my style and personality. I never try to be somebody I'm not, and I unquestionably don't dress how I do to get attention; trying to get that through to small-minded people who question me on my appearance, though, can be hard work!

The majority of customers I work for are OK with my appearance. I do get the odd funny look here and there though, and I have a lot of people ask me, 'Do you go to work dressed like that?' Then I have to think to myself, 'What do they mean? I'm wearing a pair of jeans, a shirt and a smart pair of shoes, just like they are.' Then it clicks: they're referring to my bandana and my beard plaits. So, when I tell them, 'Yeah, I do go to work dressed like this,' that's when they look down their noses and start sniggering at me. Those rude individuals can't believe I get away going to work looking how I do, which baffles me because, come on, I don't look that different, do I? I have two eyes, a nose and a mouth, for crying out loud! When I go to work, I wear my bandana along with my work clothes, and still some customers think I'm dressed as a pirate!

> Do and be who you like to be. If everyone were the same, it would be a sh*t world. You look on Facebook, YouTube, wherever you look, there is someone different. So what if you don't like what you see, don't look and who cares. I'm not going to stop talking to someone for looking different.

### Lee Easterlow, Market Harborough, England

Well, I hope you have found my tips on becoming a confident and alternative individual helpful. I would now like to tell you how my friends have been discriminated against because of how they look. One of my alternative mates, Anne, has tattoos on her fingers and piercings on her face, which look fantastic, if you ask me. Unfortunately, though, one year when Anne worked in a coffee shop an old lady complained about her tattoos to her manager and said she didn't want Anne serving her looking the way she did! Which then led Anne being given the sack and having to find another job, which luckily she did, and she now works as a tattooist.

> Back in my full-on goth days on nights out in Leicester, I'd get people like chavs, throw their food at me, spit at me, yell all kinds of idiotic things like, 'Oi, goth weirdo', along with too much other more abusive stuff that I won't go into. It doesn't make me angry

anymore if anything, I feel pity for small-minded individuals like them xx.

Louise Parker, England

I also had another friend of mine who had to cut his long hair short because of a new job he got working at a bank! I was shocked when he told me why he had to cut it! Why do people get discriminated against for having tattoos or long hair? I just don't get it. Small-mindedness is all I can put it down to. This kind of attitude really winds me up, and I find it disgusting how alternative people are discriminated against in today's society! I wish I could bring a law in where people aren't discriminated against because of how they chose to look. Why should you and I have to conform with what we wear to please other people? What a sad world we live in when we're told to do just that!

If somebody wants to have long hair, then let them have long hair; why should it matter what kind of job they have? It can be tied back into a ponytail, can't it? And if somebody wants to have tattoos or piercings on their body, then let them have as many tattoos and piercings as they wish. They're not causing any harm or any trouble to anyone. Oh, hang on a minute, though: bosses and managers can't go upsetting the customers, can they, with how creative and original alternative individuals who they employ want to look? Bosses and managers need alternative individuals to look all bland and boring, so they can keep those crazy kids under control or who knows what evil demonic spells they will cast upon their customers!

People should be encouraged to show their creative and unique sides more and not told to get rid of their uniqueness so they blend into society just like everybody else does. Why do certain citizens in society want to keep on controlling how you and I live our lives so much? At least we alternative individuals show the world the type of people we genuinely are on the inside. We have no secrets to hide.

The more you and I are allowed to express ourselves in the workplace, the better it will be for everybody, if you ask me, because your work colleagues, bosses and managers will get to see who you genuinely are as an individual. You might or might not agree with me, but this is my own opinion.

I love and support individuality, creativity and humour. The ones who step out of the box are the leaders. People, unfortunately, are afraid and ridicule what they don't understand. Enlightened people don't. We are free in ways they cannot be. All love, all day.

Audra West, USA

I love giving compliments to people I see have made an effort with their appearance because I know it will make them feel good about themselves and give them more confidence to be the alternative individuals they want to be. And just like my good friend Claire Smith says,

Be a flamingo in a flock of pigeons xx.

Claire Smith, Market Harborough, England, instagram.com/bradleyknockers

When you give people like me a compliment, it means so much to us because life's hard enough when we get judged and frowned upon everywhere we go, not knowing if we're going to get insulted or attacked when we're out in public because of how we look.

If you're still trying to find your true self and become an alternative individual, but you feel as if you're too shy, lack confidence and are worried about what people will think of you, please don't because by becoming that individual you want to be, it will help you overcome some of your shyness and confidence issues just as it has done for me. Furthermore, you will also learn to love and accept all the flaws you don't like about yourself, just like I'm doing today. My weaknesses are my lack of confidence, shyness and not always standing up for myself when somebody laughs or insults me.

If there's something you don't like about yourself, learn to love those imperfections because your flaws are what make you who you are.

Learn to own your flaws, and, once you do, people won't be able to hurt you anymore because they will see your imperfections don't bother you with what they say. All those small-minded people want to do is get a reaction out of you and bring you down when they see you out having fun with your friends and loving life. So, don't give those feeble-minded ones the satisfaction that they have got to you and made you feel down. Own your imperfections and turn them around to your advantage. For example, if you're shy, be that dark and mysterious man or woman who everybody is intrigued by and wants to get to know. And if you don't like how your body looks, then start exercising and change your diet, which will help you think more positively about the person you want to become. I think it's attractive having your own flaws because they make you all the more intriguing. So, embrace your imperfections and love everything about yourself.

# HOW I LIKE TO TREAT OTHER PEOPLE

Have you ever been given a negative comment by somebody about your appearance, such as, 'Oh you do look tired. Are you all right? You look ill,' or, 'Look, just don't bother. You're pretty useless at everything you do; just give up because you're never going to achieve your dreams.' I don't think some people realise how upsetting their comments can be when they say things like that to you, do they? For a start, say you're with friends, feeling happy and loving life, then you see somebody you know and they say, 'Hi, aw, you look pale and look at how red your eyes are. Are you all right?' Straight away those comments are going to make you feel low about yourself and take away how happy and confident you were feeling, then because of what that person has said to you; you will start thinking everybody around you must be thinking how pale you look and how red your eyes are as well. You might even want to go home and hide away from the world. As you can see, I was writing about the comments people say to me. I realise the person saying those things is only saying them because they are concerned and care about me, but their comments can take all my confidence away and make me feel insecure on the inside.

I always give positive compliments that will make someone I know feel good and put a smile on their face for the rest of the day.

I do my best to keep negative people out of my life nowadays and rise above any derogative comments they say to me and I'll always give that person a positive compliment back after they have made me feel terrible, such as 'Oh, thanks for pointing that out about my red eyes. By the way, you look fantastic tonight I love what you're wearing, have a great night,' which always catches them off guard. Hopefully, though, doing that will make them stop and think the next time they say something negative to somebody they know.

People should be more courteous when they talk to you and instead of saying 'You look ill' or 'You look tired; are you OK?' they should say something like, 'Hey, it's lovely to see you. You're looking really well. How are your eyes feeling these days? And how is your business going?' Now, wouldn't that be a much more gracious thing for them to say, which at the same time would make you feel good and boost your confidence?

They say eyes are the gateway to the soul, yours maybe red sometimes, but they are bright, open and honest, which tells me you have a beautiful soul. It's hard to ignore those who judge, don't want to listen to you and want to make fun of you, but stay strong and keep positive; you are an amazing person.

Lisa Twinkle, Rochester, England,
instagram.com/lisadeathrattleuk

One of our neighbours is known for his negative attitude towards life, which is a real shame because I think he is a great guy. Nobody else seems to see this, though, sadly. And one day when I saw him while I was out walking with my dad, we stopped and chatted to him for a bit, and he was pretty down and talking very negatively as usual. So, I said to him, 'You're looking really well today.' And just as soon as I said that his whole body language changed and a big smile appeared on his face; he also seemed to grow a foot taller, his shoulders went back and he held his head high, then he said to me, 'Thanks, Steve; that's the nicest thing anybody has said to me in a long time.' He looked like a different man once I had said that compared to the guy my dad and I had been talking to only moments before. Unfortunately, though, a few minutes later as we carried on our conversation his shoulders slumped, and he started speaking very negatively again. It just goes to show you, when you pay somebody a compliment it can have a significant impact on them, just like it did for my neighbour that day.

I have always adored your mum and dad, and it's down to them you have turned out as amazing as you have. You are an inspirational young man, and so positive and caring, and always thinking of others xxxx.

### Stacey Williams, Market Harborough, England

Some people don't realise how negative they come across to others because they might have been like it for years and don't understand they are coming across so negatively. Those people might also find it hard to break out of any negative habits they are in because they don't know any better. So, if you know anybody like that, try your best to be positive around them and make them feel good about themselves. It's up to them, though, if they want to change how they are coming across to others, because there is only so much family and friends can do to help them. Sometimes it's a good idea to advise your friend or family member to visit their local GP about their negative state of mind if you can see it is affecting their daily life.

Giving someone a small compliment while you're in a conversation with them will help brighten their mood and make them feel much better about themselves. So, the next time you're out and you come across a friend or family member who's known for being negative and grumpy, tell them how well they look and praise them on something they're wearing or on their new hairstyle they have just had done. And, by doing so, they will always remember you for making them feel good about themselves, plus they will associate you with being an uplifting and happy, positive person they will love being around.

Dare to be different, if not you'll just blend into the crowd and go unnoticed. Never be scared to be yourself, no matter how you decide to portray that. Being strange and unusual can be hard, but it's harder to be a stranger to yourself, so be true to you and to hell with anyone else.

### Paul Davies, England

# REMARKS FRIENDS AND PEOPLE SAY TO ME IN PUBLIC

Now I am going to share with you how some members of the public view me, along with a few short stories and interactions I have had with them. There will also be advice on how to cope and deal with any conversations you find yourself in with strangers who are intrigued by your appearance if you're an alternative individual.

Resembling a pirate has been very entertaining, especially when I see people's reactions as they walk by me on the street. I will often catch them looking out the corners of their eyes at me, then when they realise I have detected them looking in my direction they will quickly avert their eyes away, which always makes me laugh, so I will give them a wave or a smile, which embarrasses them even further! I have even caught a few people taking sneaky photographs of me while they are pretending to take a picture of their friends, but it's so obvious they are taking a photo of me instead. Then, after they have captured me on camera, I have often overheard them say to their mates, 'Yeah, we got him in the picture,' as they are giggling away.

I also find it funny when somebody is walking by me, and they whisper to their friends, 'It's Captain Jack,' 'It's Blackbeard,' or 'Ooh arr, where's the *Black Pearl*?' thinking I haven't heard them. What they don't know is that I have got pretty good hearing so when I turn around and acknowledge the people who have said something, I'll say, 'Hey there' or 'Yo-ho-ho,' which always surprises them and I'll hear them comment to their mates, 'Oh no: he heard us!'

Be you because you're the best person you can be! We weirdos have to stick together!

Bethany, USA, instagram.com/broken_mindsette

Certain buddies of mine don't like it when people call out to me on the streets. It's all just a bit of fun, isn't it? And, hey, wouldn't you be intrigued if you saw somebody resembling a pirate walking down your road? I know I would. What really annoys me is when I have been out with particular friends and they have turned around and said to those innocent people who have called out to me or asked me for a photo, 'Oh, here we go again; he hasn't been called that before, do you want a picture?' in a really patronising way! And that attitude really winds me up! I do try talking to those mates of mine and tell them it's all just a bit of fun and to get involved if photos are being taken, but they never do.

Those that matter don't mind, and those that mind don't matter. People shouldn't care what other people think about them, as long as they are happy.

Ash Pears, Leicestershire, England

I have even asked people I know if it bothers them how I dress. For some of them, it does! Real friends should accept you for who you are and however you want to look when you're out in public, shouldn't they? If they don't, they're not real mates, and maybe you should think of cutting ties with those individuals because they're not letting you be who you want to be. Those so-called friends of yours became buddies with you for a reason, and that reason was because they liked you for who you are. An article of clothing or how you wear your make-up shouldn't change that, should it? If strangers who have called out to me in public get on my friends' nerves, then I would rather them talk to me about how it makes them feel rather than them speaking negatively towards those innocent people who have done nothing wrong.

So, when friends of mine have shown their true colours and made me feel ashamed to be out with them, I will go over to those strangers who have called out to me in public, and I will have a chat and a picture taken with them, which, you can imagine, winds my mates up, but I'm not going to ignore anyone because I know only too well what it feels like to be unacknowledged by people. So, these are just a few of the positive and negative encounters I have had because of certain friends of mine in public.

Now onto some other negative experiences I have had. One night when I was on a night out with my friend he introduced me to his mum and her mates in a pub in Market Harborough and one of her friends said when he saw me, 'Why the look? I just don't get it; are you gay? Why do you do this?' Like who on earth in their right mind would have the audacity to talk like that to somebody they don't know? My general response when I get asked questions like those from shallow-minded individuals is to say to them 'I'm just being myself, there's no reason why I'm dressing this way. And no, I'm not gay because I'm wearing eyeliner. I'm no different from anybody else. Why do you dress the way you do?' Which they will often reply with, 'I dress this way because this is who I am and you're not being true to yourself. I still don't get it.' By this point, I get bored and politely end the conversation I'm in with them and walk away because I'm not being listened to by the other person insulting me. In the situation I was in with my friend's mum's mate, I kept my cool, finished my drink, then left the pub. I just can't be doing with small-mindedness like that anymore!

Being courteous in those circumstances is essential because if you're not careful arguments can quickly start up if you let them, which is the last thing you want to happen. So always choose your words carefully when talking to rude people.

Live and let live, be unique, be individual and become the best version of you.

One time when I was out in Northampton with my friends, I was at the bar ordering drinks when a woman came up and started talking to me, then a couple of minutes later her husband came along and put his arm around his wife as if to say, 'Stay away from my woman; this one's mine, all mine.' His body language was terrible, and how he spoke to me was very patronising. Basically, he was being a typical alpha male and making quite a fool of himself in front of his wife, while trying to make me look like an idiot. I could see in his wife's face how embarrassed she was at how her husband was acting. I felt quite sorry for her, if I am honest. Then the next minute, the alpha male dragged his wife away from the conversation we were innocently having together while she was trying to apologise to me, then they were gone. That encounter reminded me of how cave dwellers might have acted, with how they would supposedly drag their women back to their caves showing the other cavemen around them that this was their woman and nobody else's! What a horrible mentality to have. Unfortunately, though, some people still have this mindset today when it comes to their partners, which I believe is down to a lack of insecurity.

My kids told me, their dad and friends said I look ugly with my hair and ink. I've told my kids, I'm a non-conformist, and it doesn't matter what anyone else thinks or says. I'm happy in my own decorated skin. I want my children to be and dress who they want to be. It's worked, because my 7 and 9-year-old said I look beautiful, my world is complete.

Heidi, Florida, instagram.com/heidihappy1

Another strange interaction I had was when I was in Yorkshire, visiting Whitby for the Whitby Goth Weekend, which they hold twice a year. So there my dad and I were in one of the bars, which is a rare occurrence because my dad doesn't drink. Anyway, I had gone up to the bar to get a couple of drinks and a woman who must have been around 4'8" started talking to me while I was waiting to be served. Mentioning the woman's height will make more sense later on. Again, a lovely woman and then within a few minutes her husband came along and stood next to her, and his body language and the way he looked at me was very intimidating. I said, 'Hi, I'm Steve. Hope you're having a good night. Your wife's really cool,' which was the wrong thing to say because he got the completely wrong end of the stick and he said to me, 'What did you just say? My wife's really small?'

'No, I didn't say that. I said she's really cool,' I replied, taken aback. I had no idea what he was going on about; he obviously had a complex about his wife's height and didn't like me talking to her, so I quickly said, 'It was nice meeting you both. I've got to go now and take these drinks back over to my dad,' while the woman's husband kept giving me evil eyes!

My dad knew straight away something was going on, and said, 'Do you want me to go over there and have a word with him?'

'No, leave it; it's not worth it. I'm used to people acting like this; it's best to ignore him,' I replied to my dad. Then, when we had finished our drinks, we left the bar and had a much better night after that. It did put a bit of a dampener on our evening, though.

Unbelievable, isn't it? There I was at a Whitby Goth Weekend where I thought everybody would be friendly because they are alternative individuals and I still got hassle! That weekend showed me that it doesn't matter where you are and who you surround yourself with because trouble can start anywhere, even among people you think you would get along with. Those situations I have been in could quite easily have got out of hand if I hadn't been careful. Luckily, I don't like trouble, and I always defuse those circumstances I find myself in as best as I can and walk away. I have always been myself, and only ever wanted to go out and have a good time and dance. It's just some men, as you can see, who usually have a problem with me because of how I look, sadly! I don't mean to attract attention from people when I'm out, and even though there is a lot of positive attention the negative still finds me.

Always surround yourself with people who accept you for who you are.

One final situation I found myself in was when I was in a bar in my hometown with my friends, when this guy I only knew briefly questioned me about my appearance. I got into a right fluster talking to him. Anyway, here is how the conversation started that evening. 'Why is it that you look like Jack Sparrow?' asked the guy in the bar I knew briefly.

'I don't think I do look like him,' I said.

The guy replied with, 'You are, you're acting like him, you look like him, you are him.'

Then I told him I'm just being myself and I'm writing a book about my life and what I have been through with being assaulted and bullied because of how I look, which I wish I never told him about because he then said to me, 'I don't wanna hear about your problems. I've lived on the streets, been a heroin addict and had a tough life.' By this point, I started feeling intimidated and uncomfortable talking to this guy. I felt like it was a pretty awkward conversation, to be honest, which I was losing control of.

I don't know why I told him I was writing a book; I think, if I'm honest, I was feeling intimidated by him and said the first thing that came into my head. Anyway, he was genuinely intrigued why I was basing my appearance on Captain Jack Sparrow, which I have never meant to do, by the way, and he couldn't understand why I wasn't making any money out of the way I look. He then said to me, 'Why have you copied his character?'

'I haven't. It's just how my looks developed over the years and how I feel comfortable today. I never intentionally went out to resemble Jack Sparrow,' I replied.

He then asked me, 'Do you want to make money?'

'Yeah,' I said. He then wanted to help me make money by becoming a Captain Jack Sparrow lookalike, which was kind of him but it's something I have never been interested in doing. I then started to feel a lot more in control of the conversation by this point and not so nervous and intimidated as I was when we first started chatting. He turned out to be a genuinely friendly guy. How I came across within the first few minutes of that conversation showed me how much I lacked in confidence when members of the public questioned me on my appearance. I knew from that moment on I had to do something about that.

So here are a few valuable lessons I took away with me from that conversation to help not only me but also you with any future interactions you have with members of the general public if they question you about how you look if you're an alternative individual.

Always believe in yourself – Don't let what people say to you make you feel intimidated in any way – Calm yourself from within by taking a few deep breaths to gain back control – Steer the conversation in the direction you want it to go in – Listen to what the person has to say – Know who you are and what you want to do with your life – Always be courteous to the person you're in a conversation with – Let the person have their say – Never interrupt them while they are telling you how they feel about how you look – Stand up for yourself and think before you say anything in reply to their questions they ask you – Never defend yourself to members of the public because of how you style yourself; it has got nothing to do with them how you look. And if members of the public don't like how you dress, then that is their problem and not yours – Always be respectful to whoever you're talking to and never raise your voice to them – Talk to people in a polite manner even if they are making you feel uncomfortable or are intimidating you; they might not know they are coming across that way, you see, especially if they have had a drink – Always keep your cool and have lots of patience with members of the public; in most situations I have found myself in over the years, no matter how much you defend yourself and try your best to explain to somebody why you choose to look how you do, they will have already made their minds up that they either love how you look or hate how you look, plus nine times out of ten they won't listen to a word you have to say and will continue to question and berate you even more. And, finally, if somebody is making you feel uncomfortable with the questions they ask you, politely end your conversation with them and say your goodbyes.

Well, I hope that advice helps any conversations you find yourself in if you ever get questioned because of how you look if you're an alternative individual. And remember, always take control of the discussions you're in with the public from the start when they ask you about your appearance. Never let the other person lead the topic of conversation in the direction they want it to go in. I still have a lot to learn when it comes to certain situations I find myself in, but I am a lot more confident and know how to answer people much better nowadays when they do ask me why I resemble Captain Jack Sparrow, plus I have a bit of fun with those questions I get asked as well if I can.

When you're an alternative individual, always be prepared what to say when somebody asks you questions about your look.

Once I changed my image and became known as Pirate Steve, everything changed for me and for the first time in my life I felt happy. And, even though I had never gone out looking for attention, I will admit it was and still is fantastic getting recognition from people after all the horrible years I faced from being bullied, beaten up and ignored by so many people. I thought for once in my life I deserve a bit of happiness and to know what it feels like to be accepted. Furthermore, it was also time for me to move away from being the quiet little boy I had been all my life and to finally become the man I was destined to be. It's an overwhelming feeling to finally feel accepted and respected by the majority of people who know me; it's something I never thought I would experience. Nowadays, I feel comfortable in my own skin, and I love dressing how I do. I guess it's just the style I have chosen that turns a few heads for some reason, especially when you live in a small-town community like mine because you don't often see many pirates walking around your local Savers or Boots stores, do you?

It doesn't matter how you choose to look; you can still get singled out and beaten up or bullied for no reason.

One of my friends, Matt, told me once that his friend Sarah – that isn't her real name – asked if he wanted to go on a night out one weekend. And Matt said, 'Oh, I'm already going out with Steve – you know, who everyone calls Pirate Steve?'

And Sarah's reply to Matt was, 'Urgh, no, not him.'

'Steve's great; you'll love him,' was Matt's response, which I really appreciated him saying. And I mention this because I never knew Sarah, who's now a friend of mine, thought that way about me before she knew me. Isn't it a shame she judged me on my appearance without getting to know who I was as a person back then? How many other people must think this way about me I have no idea. Oh well. I can only be who I am and nobody else. If people want to judge on appearance alone that's up to them, isn't it. I feel sorry for those people, though, because their small-mindedness is stopping them from getting to know so many lovely, kind and creative alternative individuals out there in the world today.

When I receive an insult from somebody, I will think to myself, 'Rise above this small-minded idiot, Steve; you're better than they are; they're not worth your time of day.' So be as polite as you can to the insensitive offender, agree with what they say by nodding your head, and then reply with, 'Thanks, well it was nice meeting you, enjoy the rest of your day, take care.' Which will leave them flummoxed, because that's the last thing they would expect you to say.

Q: Do you feel having the extra persona which you have, gives you the chance to detach yourself from things that have touched your life or has it given you that extra boost of confidence knowing how much Pirate Steve has been taken into so many different people's lives?

Kaie Parker, Yorkshire, England

A: Hey, Kaie, great question, thank you, and yeah at first I was able to detach myself from events I've gone through because of becoming Pirate Steve. Over time, though, I've also learnt to accept everything that's happened to me as well. And having the extra persona of Pirate Steve has definitely given my confidence and low self-esteem a big boost. I've taken challenges and stepped well out of my comfort zone, which I would never have done if I'd stayed as the timid little boy I used to be. And everybody I've met in public and on social media has helped me along the way to become who I am today. It was the public, you know, Kaie, who first labelled me as Pirate Steve even though I'm not a real pirate! Thank you so much for your question.

Steven M. Rippin

Just because somebody dresses differently and has piercings and tattoos doesn't mean they are any different from anybody else. It shouldn't matter what clothes, jewellery, colour, country, shape, size, hairstyle, education or job you have, either, so why do some people find it difficult to get along with others, such as me? Which leads me nicely onto customers I have worked for.

Can you believe when I have been out at the weekends that some male customers I know turn their backs on me when they see me out, and others will ignore me as I'm standing right there in front of them while they're busy talking to my friends I'm out with! Then there has been the female customers who have seen me out in public who have come straight up to me and given me hugs and asked me how I'm doing, while their partners are standing right next to them with that if-looks-could-kill expression plastered all over their face because they are obviously thinking to themselves, 'I really don't want to be here right now; I can't stand this t\*\*t who thinks he's a pirate that my partner's talking to!' Those scenarios have happened to me quite a few times, you know. It's all good fun, isn't it? Surely, I can't be the only person this has happened to. Situations like this always make me laugh though because they are so trivial and pathetic, aren't they? Why do some men get so uptight?

I remember one time when I was in a bar a group of men said as they were walking by me, 'Hey, Jack Sparrow.' So, I turned around and said hi to them, and they all blanked me apart from one of them, who gave me a dirty look! People have a lot of confidence when they are out with their friends, don't they? If they were out on their own, though, it would be a completely different story, wouldn't it? I usually find rude and obnoxious people approach me when they see me on my own, especially when I'm in bars and nightclubs when my friends have disappeared off somewhere or when I'm walking home alone.

On a number of occasions when I have either been walking home by myself after a night out or when I have been walking with my dad during the daytime I have had people in their cars drive by me and shout obscenities at me through their car windows, such as 'prick', 'w***er', 'Arrrr' and 'f***ing idiot'! Which is very intimidating, as you can imagine! Those lowlife idiots don't realise how damaging their actions can be to somebody's well-being and mental state of mind when they do that. Now here are some wise words of wisdom from my online friends on this subject.

There are horrible people everywhere, but fortunately there are a lot more good people around. Focus on the good ones, don't waste any more energy on those that don't deserve it.

Faye Moore, Lincolnshire, England

Many people these days don't seem to have time for each other. They have small minds, no manners, very little education and no empathy with their fellow human beings. I see this every day, and it saddens me, to be honest. They feel safe from the cocoon of their car, or armchair when using the internet. Safe to shout out their horrible bile. Ignore them. In fact, forgive them inside yourself. You should feel very sorry for them, mate. Because something is definitely missing in their sad lives, which makes them so insecure that they have to behave the way they do!

John Robertson, Northamptonshire, England

I get it all the time mate, not just in Market Harborough, but everywhere, it seems that there are a lot of narrow-minded people around who just don't like anything that doesn't fit their criteria. I have to say; it's usually blokes that give me hassle, whereas women will say things like 'I like your style.' The only place I never get any grief is London; maybe I should move there lol.

Alan 'Yebut' Davies, Leicester, England


The more that people hate themselves, the more they want others to suffer. See them as the victim because they are failing at life. Negative humans waste energy, so don't waste energy thinking about them. Let the negativity fall away, like rain running down a windowpane. Take a breath, relax and appreciate the love you are surrounded with. Always remember that people who are secure and love themselves don't hurt others.

David Butler, London, England


It happens to myself and my partner also. On the positive side, we've also had positive comments and even had people inspired to be that little bit more confident in their individuality. Some people will always fear anything that isn't grey or beige.

Jason Haynes, Northamptonshire, England


I've had abuse also hurled at me through someone's car window as they've driven by me before. I've even had someone throw an apple at me. Thankfully it didn't hit my head too hard; otherwise, I could have collapsed. Didn't see the reg in time to report it as it happened so quickly. They were coming from behind. Take no notice of them. Probably just bored of their pathetic lives so needed to spice theirs up by trying to put others down. Morons that are a waste of space. Never change for anyone. I am vigilant every now and then when it comes to walking by the roadside for any passing cars or vans nowadays.

Scott Dickens, Leicestershire, England

Thank you to my online friends for their advice and how to deal with those types of negative individuals who they have also sadly encountered who hurl abuse at the general public as they drive by them. And that reminds me: one bar I enjoy going into in my hometown is where I have unfortunately had a lot of offensive remarks from people who look down on me and treat me like a joke when they have seen me on my own in there. I put up with it for years until one day when I had just had enough of it because the disrespectful comments kept coming from the same crowd of people every time, so I posted a status on Facebook, which caused quite a reaction in Market Harborough, along with a few apologies from the owners of the bar, who were disgusted at how some of their clients were behaving towards me. I received 282 likes in total, plus over 430 comments on that status I posted on 25 June 2018, which might not sound like many likes and comments to some people, but they were a lot for me. And now here is that post I made, minus the bar's name.

# TREAT PEOPLE WITH RESPECT

I didn't want to have to say this. First off, I love [pub name here] in Market Harborough, but why do I always get disrespected by A SMALL immature MINORITY of the women who drink in there? It always happens when I'm on my own as well. They have the balls to make fun of me as I walk by them, which I don't mind if it's done in the right way, but when it's done in a SARCASTIC way, there's just no need for it! I NEVER go around disrespecting anybody, because I love to get along with everyone who I meet, unfortunately, though I always get looked down on by this SMALL MINORITY of WOMEN in this pub, what the HELL have I done! AM I THAT HIDEOUS TO LOOK AT? It's like they don't think I belong where they drink! I write all about this kind of DISGUSTING ATTITUDE IN MY BOOK! SOME WOMEN IN THIS TOWN need to learn to RESPECT OTHERS on how they choose to dress, and if they have a problem with me, DON'T LOOK AT ME, SIMPLE! These immature, rude women need to learn a valuable life lesson if they're to get anywhere in life. Plus, there's been other incidents. One was when a guy was pestering me for a photo as I was trying to pee who continued to hound me and took a picture of me when I told him not to, then he showed all his friends who all burst out laughing at me when I left the men's room! Always Treat people HOW YOU wish to be treated in return, with RESPECT and POLITENESS, which I'm always saying and trying to get across to people!'

Steven M. Rippin, 25 June 2018

It's those situations that annoy me because it's obvious those people have no respect and are trying to make a fool out of me! Now here is what some of my friends had to say about that incident when I posted it on Facebook.

Well said, Steve. These people are ignorant and childish, and they have no idea what a lovely person you are. I think you have to feel sorry for them because they will probably never understand the true meaning of life. Try not to waste your energy on this Steve.

Sylvia Slingo, London, England

Interesting how they are in a group, and you are on your own when this happens. On a one to one basis or if you were surrounded by your friends, I doubt they would be so brave. Small-minded people and alcohol don't mix, and they are only jealous of a man that is being himself. Continue to be you. You have half the world on your side; they have nothing except their words.

Kazzie Lemmon, Queensland, Australia

God, this has made me angry. Your awesome and people should take a leaf out your book and be more true to themselves. Fake ass f\*\*\*ers. Keep being you. Stay awesome

Tanya Garner, Desborough, England

Shallow bitches! I bet they have badly drawn on eyebrows, look like cheap hookers and regularly act like them as well! Rise above them mate! It is your life to live as you want to, so be your wonderful self and love life to the full! Your Pirate Steve, so make them walk the plank!

Amj Wilford, Leicestershire, England

Hi, Steve – usually haters who band together and pick on someone who is self-assured enough to 'be themselves', are threatened by that level of confidence. It makes them seem mediocre – which they are, obviously of low intellect too. Is that all they have got in life – sitting in a pub picking on someone just because that individual chooses to walk along a more interesting path and display that confidence enough to do so? Tell you what – you are a crackin looking bloke and there's a pub at the end of our road here in Blackpool where I reckon the ladies around this neck of the wood would be absolutely thrilled to have someone like yourself in there ordering a pint! Sending hugs.

Sheila Dibnah, Preston, England

Well, they are just a handful of supportive comments I received out of over 400 on how I was treated in that pub by those women. I appreciated my friends sending me those messages so much. Now I'm going to tell you when I went on holiday to the beautiful White Isle of Ibiza in 2000, before I looked how I do today, then I'm going to tell you how I was treated when I went back to Ibiza again in 2007 as Pirate Steve. So, let's begin. After holidaying in Ibiza with my friends for the first time in 1996 I fell in love with the White Isle, so I decided to go back to visit my mates Adam Epsly and Steven Robinson, who both lived over there and still do.

So, in 2000, I booked myself a trip to the White Isle, where I stayed with my good friend Adam Epsly. Adam worked most nights on the Slingshot, so I didn't get to hang out with him all that much, unfortunately. Most nights while I was there, I would go out on my own for a meal, then I would head up to the West End in San Antonio and around the bay area to party, and during the days I would relax and soak up the Ibiza sunshine and atmosphere. I loved it; well, what's not to love about Ibiza? One night when I was in a bar around seven o'clock in the evening, which was empty apart from two women who were sitting down having a drink together, I thought to myself, 'I know, I'll go over and introduce myself and see if they're happy for me to join them for a drink.' You have to remember, I was really shy back then and I had no clue about how to chat women up, which I still don't, if I'm honest!

So, I went over to those two women and said, 'Hi, how's your evening going? Is it OK if I join you for a drink?' Yeah, I know, a very cringeworthy Steve Rippin moment, I think you will agree, and one I will never forget! Anyway, so there I was standing in front of those women waiting for a reply, and one of them said without any hesitation, 'No,' and carried on talking to her friend and acted as if I wasn't there!

They left me standing there feeling like a right plonker, and I replied to them with, 'Oh OK. Sorry to have troubled you.' Then I walked back over to where I was sitting, feeling pathetic and like a right pilchard. I then quickly finished the rest of my drink and made my escape out of that embarrassing situation I had caused myself to be in.

On another night, when I was walking to Cafe Mambo's to watch Pete Tong DJ and see the famous Ibiza sunset, a bunch of lads started mouthing off at me about the T-shirt I was wearing and said how stupid I looked, so that didn't do my confidence any good either and put me on edge for the rest of the night. I thought to myself, 'Oh, great, what a holiday this is turning out to be. Everywhere I go I either get rejected or insulted.'

Thinking back to when I was at Cafe Mambo's while I was watching the Ibiza sunset reminds me of how I felt inside because, truth be told, I felt incredibly lonely, insecure and nervous back then. The rest of that holiday I spent on my own a lot, apart from when I meet up with Adam when he wasn't working at the Slingshot. I did have some good nights out while I was over there, but it was nothing compared to when I had been there with my mates in 1996, though. All in all, looking back, it wasn't the best experience and holiday I had expected it to be, sadly.

Now let's fast forward to the year 2007, when I went back to Ibiza with my long hair, red bandana and the whole Pirate Steve look going on. And just as soon as I stepped out the taxi when I arrived in San Antonio, a few metres from where the Slingshot is, a couple of Italian guys started waving and shouted over at me in a friendly manner, 'Hey, Jack Sparrow,' and straight away they helped to relax the social anxiety I was feeling and I felt a lot more comfortable and confident within myself more than I ever had done when I had been in Ibiza in 2000; I just knew I was going to have a much better experience this time around.

When I walked along the harbour front from San Antonio bay, where I was staying, to San Antonio's West End in the evenings, I had no end of people staring at me and I could hear some of them saying to each other as

I walked by them, 'It's Jack Sparrow' or 'It's Johnny Depp.' Unfortunately, I was pretty shy back then, so I kept my head down and focused on where I was going. I did start to acknowledge people more as my confidence grew day by day while I was over there, though, so I knew that holiday was doing me a world of good. The difference in how people treated me because of how I looked was unbelievable, especially compared to the last time I had visited Ibiza in 2000. I was still the same person I was before; I just had long hair and I was wearing a bandana now.

While I was walking around San Antonio at night by myself, I had people offering to buy me drinks and groups of men and women asking if it was all right to have their photo taken with me, which was an excellent experience. I honestly lost count of how many group photos I must have been in back then. And when I was out having a meal in the evenings along the harbour front, I could feel the eyes of the people passing by staring at me, which again was quite a surreal experience because I had never encountered anything quite like that before in my life. I was always so used to being ignored, you see, so knowing people were staring and whispering to each other about me was pretty overwhelming. It just made me realise how different people will treat you when you change your appearance.

When I was in Ibiza in 2000 nobody wanted to know me and when I went back in 2007 everybody wanted to know me and was staring, approaching and buying me drinks.

I can understand why people were treating me differently, though, because I now resembled a pirate in Ibiza, and for all they knew I could have been related to corsair Antonio Riquer Arabí, who had been a resident of Ibiza in the 1800s. Antonio Riquer Arabí formed a vigilante group of pirates on the island to protect everybody who was living there from other pirates who were trying to invade it. To help protect themselves, the residents of Ibiza built watchtowers around the island to ward off any incoming threats and signalled each other from their lookouts by fire, allowing the locals to take refuge in churches.

Antonio Riquer Arabí was a phenomenal corsair captain and conquered over one hundred pirate ships.

The residents placed a memorial statue of Antonio Riquer Arabí to honour him for protecting the island of Ibiza, which is also said to be the only pirate statue in the world. Well, there's your little bit of pirate history for today.

I loved all the interactions I had when I was in Ibiza in 2007, and it did my confidence and self-esteem no end of good as well. After seeing how I was treated on those two separate occasions, I felt like I had been on an undercover social experiment to see how members of the public treat you based on how you look. It was quite an eye-opener, and I can honestly say it was sad to see and experience because Steven Rippin was insulted and ignored, while Pirate Steve was welcomed with open arms.

The majority of people I met in Ibiza were very friendly and lovely. And if you get the chance, visit the Slingshot and Foot-Darts, which are both next door to each other in San Antonio, right behind Es Paradis, where you can say hi if they are there to Steven Robinson and Adam Epsly, who are two awesome friends of mine.

I have learnt it doesn't matter how you look because you can be somebody who blends into a crowd and you can still get insulted or attacked. And if you do choose to be an alternative individual you are going to stand out and create attention for yourself, just like I have when I've been to Ibiza in the past, which drew to me the good, the bad and the most excellent experiences you can imagine.

I have also realised over the years I have to be careful who I become friends with since becoming Pirate Steve, and you should be too if you're an alternative individual because you want someone to get to know you for all the right reasons and not because of how you look or if, let's say, you're a well-known celebrity. You want somebody to get to know you and become a good friend of yours because they genuinely like you for who YOU are on the inside and not what they see you as on the outside. Well, I hope you have found what I have written on how people have treated me when I have been out in public interesting, insightful and helpful. And, as you continue to read through my book, you will see, I have had more positive interactions than I have had negative ones. And I sincerely hope you don't have to go through any of those negative interactions I have been through if you're living your life as an alternative individual today.

Why fit in when you were born to stand out. To be remembered after death, you must be unique and different.

Kate Ford, London, England

# ADVICE ON BEING AN
# ALTERNATIVE INDIVIDUAL

I thought to get a more general opinion other than my own on what it's like being an alternative individual, I would ask my alternative friends on social media what advice and encounters they might have had. There will also be help and advice from my non-alternative friends as well. And here is the question I asked them.

> What advice would you give to an alternative individual who loves to dress differently but gets insulted because of how they choose to look? It could be because they have tattoos, piercings, their clothes and hairstyles are different from what most people are used to or anything at all that sets them apart from everybody else.

> I admire and quite like seeing people who are individual and dress differently, whether that's clothes, hairstyles and tattoos. I think these people are more imaginative and have their own mind. And I think it would be boring if you didn't have these people around. I think people who are individual are quite brave who stand out, and it would be a funny world if we all dressed and acted the same.

> George W. Rippin, Market Harborough, England

We are educated by parents, our initial interactions with others and our own thought processes. Society, in general, expects us to conform to the 'norm', and if you are non-compliant with this then most likely you will be judged on your looks, for example, most people expect an accountant to be a maths expert who never laughs in a grey suit or a criminal to look like a thug. This is not the case. I have been brought up in a judgmental way, which I have now questioned. I was told to avoid 'different' people. Now I have changed as a result of personal turmoil that affected me badly, and I do not judge. Given my age, my employment and my insecurity, I chose to comply with society's rules. I admire and am interested to know more about reasons people dress as they do, Steve, your question has me thinking, which is unusual these days. Carry on with what makes you happy as long as you are a kind human being that's what is important.

Gordon Harrison, Leicestershire, England


Eh up Steve, everyone is an individual and dresses how they wish, no matter what they choose to wear, I've had plenty of comments in the past through my hobby. Most people just haven't got the confidence to be different and to be themselves. When I was younger, we had mods, skins, rockers, punks and northern souler's. BE You.

Andy 'Chappers' Chapman, Market Harborough, England


Be yourself. You don't have to follow the crowd. Individuals inspire creativity. Turn your backs on the doubters and take-in Ghostpoet's latest release, the aptly titled 'Freak show' – For further reading, why not seek out, 'Dark Days and Canapés' – a prose worthy of this new chapter (I am sorry if some find the director's interpretation of the song alarming – remember, it's only fiction).

Nick Williams, Market Harborough, England


I look at it this way. We are like the stars in the Universe of life. If we cannot shine our light as brightly as we can, there would only be darkness. Shine your light, be seen and be heard. The greatest gift in life is being an individual filled with love and uniqueness. That is what makes the world a better place. Never give in to fear, hatred or trying to be what others want you to be. Shine your light.

Becky Harris, Frackville, Pennsylvania, USA

My best advice is it to hold your head high, as just the other day, I had some neighbourhood teenagers single me out while I was walking one of my dogs. I had gone out with some friends for a birthday and was a bit dressed up and edgier than usual. Skeleton leggings, strappy, drop shoulder top and boots. They decided to start screaming about the devil worshiper, the goth bitch, Satan's whore, etc. Now, I have the mouth of a sailor and could have gone off on them. But honestly, with the way the world is these days, there's more than enough hate going around already without me contributing to it. I held my head high and kept walking. It's hard to do, and the s**t they said hurt, but reacting negatively and retaliating would have just spurned them on and created more drama. Sometimes being the bigger person and just walking away is the most peaceful option. Don't be afraid to stand your ground if the situation calls for it but being able to walk away isn't a sign of weakness. It's a sign of strength. As corny as it sounds, you're the only one who writes the story that is your life. This is just a chapter in that story. Be the good you want to see in the world.

Never judge someone by how they look, just like you never judge a book by its cover. You can never tell what's on the inside by what you see on the outside. Honestly, most of the time, the things people say, or do, regarding my appearance doesn't bother me. At the end of the day, they don't know me, my life, my struggles or anything that I've been through. They don't know that I could one day be the nurse saving their life, they just see the goth chick with her socially unacceptable makeup, and her too long hair and out of season combat boots. They don't see the 28-year-old woman. They don't see the artist, the animal advocate, the nursing student, the person. So, in all honesty, the way the world sees me doesn't matter to me. It's how I see myself that does. Because self-worth is a million times more important than proving yourself to a world that doesn't even know you.

Kat M. Bell, Florida, USA

It's all about fear me old son. People are afraid of anything different. It's the same reason there are racism and homophobia. Take an uneducated monkey out of their comfort zone, and they cannot compute how to react, so they will react in the only way they know-how, with Neanderthal results. Unfortunately, this is the majority of the population. However, since we were kids, this percentage has declined, and I expect it to be next to nothing by the time we are on our last legs mate! I would say to anyone who is vilified by the way they choose to look, to be strong and ignore the f**kwits who have no idea other than to conform. Easier said than done I know, but every time criticism comes your way, look at them with pity, rather than reciprocate the fear they are showing you x.

Adam Epsly, owner/operator, Foot-Darts, Ibiza, Spain

Society today has a lot to answer to. It is drilled into the heads of everyone that, 'This is in and this is last season,' or 'You're too overweight to wear that.' They say we all have to be ripped with a six pack or a size 10 to be perfect to wear the clothes millions of others do. But in reality, that only sells magazines. We are all beautiful in our own way. Tattooing, in many cultures, is a sign of strength and accomplishment. Be proud of who you are. If you have scars, show them to the world, be as unique as God intended. Hold your head high knowing that we all have something different about ourselves; some just prefer to hide it and live in the dream of media and social perfection. Maybe they say things to those who show who they are to hide their own fears or doubt, or maybe they are jealous of the strength it takes to be that person who is open and proud. We will never really know. Violence and distaste towards uniqueness isn't a way to make people change to the norm. It's a way to stereotype people. We are individuals, we feel, we bleed, we breathe the same, but inside and out we are beautiful. I mean, I'm ginger with too many freckles and tattoos, but I know I'm awesome. Diversity gives strength, courage and a beautiful array of visual enlightenment.

Maria L. Mills, Market Harborough, England

Why should we follow what society tells us to wear? Why should we be robots/clones? We were all born into a world where each one of us is unique. We shouldn't have to follow a stereotype. We are beautiful and unique in our own ways. We have flaws and make mistakes. We're only human. What you wear doesn't define the type of person you are! Each of us is as beautiful and unique as the next. Dare to be different, dare to be the change you wish to see in the world! Be crazy and live your life, for we only get one! Don't listen to people if they wish to be clones. LET THEM! I'd rather live in a world where I'm different and proud than a clone of someone who does the same thing every day.

Danielle Tredgett, Leicestershire, England

What a great question! I feel that some beings are most afraid of what they don't understand. Or that they are envious of one who can express themselves so radically and artistically without any reconciliation for conformity. It's an unfortunate truth, but if humans do not feed their mind someone else will do it for them, whether it be the media or mass marketing, we are being sold false ideologies/trends every day. Even on social media as we speak! So, to be yourself and original is the ultimate 'Gandhi.' Be the change you want to see and keep expressing yourself! No matter how hard it seems, you will thank yourself later and stand as an example and inspiration for others who wish to do the same.

Alix Hex, USA

I dress how I want in different looks every day or week sometimes. I really like eighties-style as well as rock chick, glamour puss, etc. I don't follow fashion I make my own trends and wear what I want when I want. I had a lady down the road where I live laugh and say, 'Look at her, what does she think she looks like,' when I was wearing an eighties style pink ruffled dress and accessories and makeup. It did upset me a bit, but I just ignored it as it was just petty of her, and my dad said it says more about her than me that she felt the need to laugh and be nasty. It takes courage to follow your heart and be different, unique and yourself. And the best thing to do is to be proud of yourself and ignore the nasty people; maybe they are even jealous that they don't have the guts to be different in a society that wants us all to be the same xx.

Vicki Vaughan, London, England

Say to yourself, 'I love myself unconditionally, and I do not need other people's approval, for who I am, what I do, or how I dress, in order to love myself fully.' Use this as your daily mantra, say daily into the mirror or as part of a daily meditation. If you do so regularly, you will soon notice the positive changes in your life.

Vicky Day, South Devon, England, instagram.com/telvicky.uk

Thank you to everybody who contributed their fantastic help and advice on how to live your life as an alternative individual. I hope my friends' advice has helped to give you a broader outlook of what it's like to be an alternative individual in today's society. I also hope it's given you some insight on how alternative individuals, such as myself, feel when small-minded people do comment or say negative things to us. Alternative individuals are no different from anybody else. Be unique, be individual and always be yourself.

# REMEMBER YOUR TRUE SELF AS AN ALTERNATIVE INDIVIDUAL

Do you know who you genuinely are or are you swamped down by the various identities you have been given throughout your life? I know precisely who I am; I am Steven Mark Rippin, a positive person who loves life. I am not hiding behind a mask or persona, as some think. I am who I am because I chose to be. I see a future where I am helping other like-minded individuals become who they wholeheartedly want to be and where small-minded people no longer intimidate or judge alternative individuals like myself because of our appearances, nationalities, beliefs, health issues or disabilities we may have.

I know who I am from the core of my being. I am at one with my true inner self, and I am willing to change as time goes by if and only if I choose to and not because some discourteous individual wants me to because they don't like how I look! I wonder if those ill-mannered people who have insulted and questioned me are genuinely happy with themselves? If they are, then great; they shouldn't go around judging others, though; they should learn to focus on their own lives. Impolite people who think they know me should never judge a book by its cover. They should get to know who I am first before being ill-mannered towards me. Well, I don't know about you, but I certainly feel a lot better after saying that.

Now, please stick with me here because you might laugh when I say this next part, but for a moment envision yourself as a tree. And all those branches of your tree are the identities that make you you. You see your true inner self comes from the roots of your tree, which is continuously growing year by year. Now here are a few types of identities we are given throughout our lives – grandparent – parent – brother – sister – nurse – postman – teacher – tradesperson – office worker – barista – shop assistant etc. For me, I'm a son – a tradesperson – an author – a video editor – a creator – a terrible dancer – a reader – an explorer – somebody who wants to help inspire others – an alternative individual, and someone who loves life. So, as you can see, there are quite a few branches on my tree other than being known as just a pirate and a guy who cleans carpets. Now, what I would like you to do is draw yourself a tree and see how many diverse identities you have. See, there's a lot more to you than you thought there was, isn't there? Never forget who you are.

Alternative individuals who have discovered who they are have nothing to prove to anybody, which leaves them able to live their lives in peace and contentment; criticisms and insults mean nothing to them. They see the bigger picture, and instead of worrying about petty comments and triviality they keep on improving themselves physically and mentally every day.

Throughout our lives, you and I are given labels that show people who we are and the responsibilities we have. What those labels don't show people, though, are the INDIVIDUALS we were born to be. So you might get called a doctor, a wife, a husband or in my case a pirate, but we are so much more than those labels people have given us.

If you feel like you have got more to offer the world, don't let the labels people have given you stop you from fulfilling your true potential in life.

Here are some excellent questions to ask yourself when you're alone and have time to think about your thoughts and feelings. These questions can help you think about the person you want to become deep down.

Who am I? – What am I most passionate about? – What are my goals, and where do I see myself in five years? – What do I want to accomplish in my life? – Am I happy with who I am? – Where can I make improvements in my life? – What are my most significant achievements? – What am I most thankful for? – Am I living the life I have always wanted to and following my dreams? – Do I love who I am today? – How would I best describe myself? – What would I do today if there was no tomorrow? – What are the biggest life lessons I have learnt so far? – What advice would

I give to my five-year-younger self? – What am I holding onto right now that I need to let go of? – If I was to die tomorrow what would be my biggest regret and how can I change it, so it doesn't happen? – What bad habits do I need to break? – What good habits do I need to introduce into my life? – When am I most inspired and motivated? – Who inspires me in my life, and how can I be more like them? – Who are the five most influential people in my life, and when did I last tell them how much I love and care about them? And, finally, what am I going to do right now to fulfil my dreams and ambitions I have?

When you're asking yourself those questions, it's a good idea to write your answers down as you go along so you can read them back to yourself and see a clearer picture in your mind of the person you are and who you want to become. This will be the first step you will have taken in learning who your genuine inner self is and what types of characteristics you have.

Our lives are constantly changing, and we are learning new lessons along the way that make us who we are today.

If you take a look back throughout your life, you will see how much you have changed and how far you have come. When I look back at how much I have changed, it makes me proud of how far I have come. I used to be timid; I had anxiety and mild depression issues; and I also lacked confidence and self-esteem. Now, though, I'm positive, confident and full of life and energy. I have also developed into somebody who loves spreading positivity to as many people as I can. I wonder how much you have changed throughout your life. Finding your true inner self isn't quick, and it's like learning anything in life: it takes time, maybe years.

To find your true inner self, remember the proudest moments of your life and all you have accomplished. Then write those times down and explain to yourself what motivated you the most to do them and how they made you feel; this will help you see what you genuinely value in life.

If you didn't have to work and had all the time in the world to do what you wanted to do from this moment onwards, I wonder what you would be doing instead. You might want to travel the world, write a novel, raise money for your local charity, build the house of your dreams or help the less fortunate children in the world today to have a better life tomorrow.

Whatever it is you would love to be doing right now, that's when you will realise who your true inner self really is.

Until you push yourself out of your comfort zone and take challenges in your life, you will never know what you're capable of achieving, just like myself right now writing this book. I am well out of my comfort zone, and I have no idea if anybody will even want to read what I have written. If I don't follow my heart and finish this journey I'm on, though, I will never know, so, just like me, if there's something you have always wanted to do, face your fears and go for it. Take that new challenge on and see where your journey leads you. Who knows what's waiting around the corner and what you could achieve; you will never know until you try. If you need help finding who your true inner self is, you can always ask a family member or one of your best friends who you know you can open up to and trust: What do they think of you? – What annoys them about you? – What your faults and flaws are you might have which you can't see yourself – What areas of your life they think you need to improve on, and what your best qualities are. Tell them to be as honest with you as they can.

My friend Matt has pointed out a few of my own flaws to me, which I need to develop. One of them is that I need to speak louder and project my voice when I'm in public. Another one is that I need to believe in myself more; he also thinks I need to have more confidence when it comes to talking to women. So, as you can see, having a good friend you can confide in can help you find the areas of your life you might need to improve on.

Please don't get labelled as one particular person for the rest of your life. Always acknowledge your identities which make you you, other than being known as a good son, daughter, mother, father or grandparent, because you have so much more to offer. If you don't know who your authentic self consists of yet, you might already be showing signs of it by what you're doing in your daily life. Maybe you like taking treats in for your work colleagues, which shows how kind and considerate you are, or perhaps you're always there for your family and friends when they need you, which shows how loving, compassionate and caring you are; when you know what your true self consists of, you become your best self. The values I hold within me are being caring, thoughtful, kind, courteous, respectful, hard-working, honest, happy, enthusiastic and positive. And I have also been told I am somebody who makes those around me feel inspired.

Well, I hope I have helped explain the various characteristics we have through what I have been writing about. I know it can get a bit confusing, so remember: the branches of the tree signify your identities, the tree is your body and the roots of the tree show your true inner self. So, learn all about your origins, which make you the person you are today.

I have always known who my authentic self has been since I was a child; I just lost my way because of the cruel things that happened to me. What helped me remember, though, was when I started making my amateurish Happy News videos on YouTube after I had been assaulted, which then led me on to posting positive and inspiring messages on social media. Ever since I have been doing that, I have felt like I used to feel when I was a five-year-old child before my mind got corrupted: happy and carefree once again.

Finding your genuine self is something you and I are doing every day of our lives; it can be a lifelong quest for some people. So, look inwards at the person you are today and keep learning about yourself and the world around you. If it helps, you could try taking up meditation, which can help you understand who you are as an individual on the inside as well. What helped me was being bullied as a child, being attacked in public on three separate occasions and witnessing my dad have a cardiac arrest and then go through cancer. So, remember you're more than just a wife, a husband, a girlfriend or somebody's boyfriend. You are a unique and fascinating human being with an incredible life full of all sorts of opportunities waiting for you. So, will you let your life pass you by or will you get out there and make it the best adventure ever? It's up to you.

Thank you, Mum and Dad, for raising me how you have and for giving me my one true identity, which is being your son.

Steven M. Rippin

You really inspire me to be my own version of myself. I have followed you for a long time now on Instagram; you are so amazing. I am mixed; I am white and Native American. I have always been torn with my own identity but seeing how you just throw everyone else's expectations of you in the trash and treasure your OWN expectations of YOURSELF and how you are so happy and carefree, it has encouraged me to do the same. So, here is to being US!

Kase, Tennessee/Alabama, USA

# SELF-CENTRED PEOPLE EXPLAINED

I would just like to say, as I have been writing my book, I have felt uncomfortable writing about myself all the time. It's like it's all about me, me, me, which is one thing I don't like writing or talking about, if I'm honest. I guess that sounds strange because here I am writing an alternative self-help autobiography; I guess it's like going on a date and all your date does is talk about themselves all the time. I would hate that, wouldn't you? I would come away from that date thinking, 'It was all about them; they didn't show any interest in me whatsoever. What was the point in me even being there if all my date was going to do was brag about themselves?' So, I do apologise if it gets annoying when I write about myself through my book. Anyway, let's move on.

When I'm out in public, and people ask me questions about my appearance, I always ask them about themselves as well, and that isn't to be polite; it's because I am genuinely interested in getting to know that person and show them that it isn't all about me. You always know if somebody is sincerely interested in getting to know you or not don't you because if they don't let you get a word in sideways there's a good chance they're self-centred, isn't there? Although I will contradict myself now because that individual might feel nervous in public places, which causes them to talk about themselves all the time. So, if you meet someone you like and they come across as being conceited, do your best to get to know that individual first before presuming they are. You don't know what underlying issues they might have about themselves.

Those first impressions when we meet somebody might not be the accurate representation of who they genuinely are on the inside; you have got to delve underneath the car bonnet to get a real feel of the person you're talking to before judging them as being someone who is self-centred. I can't believe a girl I dated once was warned by other people to not talk to me because they told her I was self-centred and loved myself! Again, another form of how people will judge and spread untrue rumours about you when they don't know you as a person! The girl I was dating said the people who called me conceited thought that way about me because when they saw me out at the weekends looking how I do they presumed I was seeking attention from everyone and that I must be somebody who thinks he's better than everybody else!

I found this out a long time ago, when I was around thirty years old. Back then I was very timid in public, although I was never afraid to dress how I wanted to because it never crossed my mind that what I would wear would grab people's attention so much for them to judge me how they did. I was shocked and upset that this was how I came across. I have always been myself and never in my life have I ever been self-centred! The girl I was dating said, after she had got to know me, she knew straight away I wasn't a conceited person looking for attention; she couldn't believe how some people had spoken about me to her in this way behind my back! All I can put it down to is when you're an alternative individual living in a small town you're going to get noticed by other people and attract good and bad attention from them.

I understand everybody is entitled to their own opinions, but people should never go judging others when they don't know them. If somebody is curious about someone they see when they are out in public, they should go up to that person and get to know them first before slandering their name behind their back to other people! Sadly, some people think all you want to be is the centre of attention when you're an alternative individual. So, if you come across someone unconventional who stands out in society who you have never spoken to before, please don't presume they are self-centred and seeking attention from everybody. All they are doing is being themselves, just as you're being yourself. People are always so quick to judge and spread rumours about others, aren't they, which can be very damaging to that person in question's reputation and also to their mental state of mind as well. So please always show love and respect to one another.

# HELP YOUR FAMILY AND FRIENDS IF THEY ARE SELF-CENTRED

When you come across a member of your family or a friend who talks about themselves all the time and never considers anybody else, try finding out if anything is on their mind that they need to speak to somebody about. If there is, let them know you're there to help and listen to them if they need someone to talk to. If things are too difficult for them to open up and speak to you, though, you could suggest they try talking to their local GP or a counsellor if they have serious problems.

Also, if your family member or friend is making you feel unimportant in the friendship you have with them, you could ask them politely, 'Why is it you never ask how I'm doing?' You could then explain how you have been feeling in the friendship you have with them. If they don't take this the right way or understand where you're coming from, then maybe this isn't the best friendship for you to be in with this person because now you can see the bond you have with them is very one-sided and that you're just a shoulder for them to cry on.

A real friendship works both ways and most times your family member or friend will understand where you're coming from when you say that you would like to have a chat about how they have been treating you, because they will be willing to listen to what you have to say so they don't lose your friendship. And that's when you know you have got a genuine friend you can build a better relationship with now you have sat down and talked things through together. Always do your best to stick by your family and friends who might be coming across as conceited. And please be extremely careful if you do decide to talk to them because you don't want to upset them or cause any arguments. So be as subtle as you can.

> Some people, not all, who talk a lot, might lack confidence, be hiding behind their insecurities, have personal problems or be generally nervous people.

I know one man who's very self-centred and talks solely about himself all the time, so when I have seen him out I have tried explaining to him how lucky he is to have everything he's got in his life because he's got a lovely family, a beautiful home and money to spend. Still, though, he's always talking about himself and how bad his life is, plus he's always negative about everything and looks so miserable! I wish I could help him see the more positive side of life. Unfortunately, though, some people no matter how much you try and help them won't listen to a word you say, will they? If you know somebody like this, you could try suggesting that they read *The Secret* by Rhonda Byrne, *Think and Grow Rich* by Napoleon Hill, *How to Win Friends and Influence People* by Dale Carnegie, and *The Seven Habits of Highly Effective People* by Stephen Covey. Those self-help books are fantastic and definitely worth reading.

Reasons why a person might be coming across as self-centred: Feeling insecure – Subconsciously worried about their appearance with how they look to other people – Feeling worthless and unimportant to those around them – Feeling scared or afraid they are unable to live up to other people's expectations of themselves – Feeling vulnerable in different surroundings they find themselves in, or suffering from mental health problems, such as anxiety or depression. It's also said people who use the words me, myself and I a lot suffer from more mental health issues in their lives because they are focusing on themselves, which might be because of a traumatic event they have gone through. So, to you and me, those people we know who might come across as being conceited could genuinely be unhappy, insecure or suffering from mental health problems. Furthermore, they will unlikely know they are coming across this way, just as I didn't realise I was, when I was out at the weekends years ago when I kept thinking about my safety all the time because of how anxious I was left feeling after I had been assaulted. I would continuously focus on myself, you see, and not my mates I was with, so to those around me I would have come across as very self-centred. So that's why it's vital you and I should never bottle up how we're feeling on the inside; we should always talk to our family and friends and make sure we get the help we need.

# MY PERSONALITIES EXPLAINED

Welcome to the strange reality which is the world I live in. This might sound peculiar, but over the years I have created another personality of myself, who is, as you know, Pirate Steve. And from around 2006 up until 2014 I had two personalities: there was Steven M. Rippin and then there was Pirate Steve. Steven M. Rippin would be very shy and quiet, whereas Pirate Steve was this overly confident and crazy pirate guy on social media. Since 2014, though, I have been merging my personalities together.

It must sound bizarre reading this, so I will do my best to explain it to you. My primary personality and who I am at the centre of my core is Steven M. Rippin, who has always been a timid and unconfident man, whereas my alter ego, Pirate Steve, has always been full of confidence, doesn't care what people think of him, lives his life doing what he wants to do and has never let anything faze him. Basically, Pirate Steve is the opposite of who I, Steven M. Rippin, am.

I was always held back with how I genuinely wanted to express myself when I was younger. That was, until I created Pirate Steve, then the Pirate Steve Show on YouTube in 2008, where I made crazy light-hearted videos about being happy and positive, which felt so good to make because I had finally found an outlet where I could be who I wanted to be. I am now known as the Positive Pirate on YouTube. Every time I made a video in the persona of my alter ego, it was like this other person emerged and manifested themselves into my mind, which must sound absurd, but I love being unconventional; it certainly makes life more interesting – well, it has done for me.

By letting myself act crazy and eccentric in my videos was where my Pirate Steve persona/alter ego first started to emerge, then the more

I acted like this zany pirate, the more my confidence grew. My low self-esteem, anxiety and mild depression, which I was suffering from in 2008, slowly began to recede as Pirate Steve starting to become part of me.

As soon as I put myself in front of a camera and hold a microphone, I feel at peace, well, to be honest, I feel on top of the world, more confident than you could imagine and so happy; my microphone is my comfort blanket.

The confidence, the not giving a damn what people thought of him along with Pirate Steve's overall positive attitude and body language were all personality traits I knew I wanted to incorporate into my own everyday life, yet, at the same time, I didn't want to forget who I was. Pirate Steve has always been their deep down inside my subconscious mind; it just took a few head-butts to my head for him to manifest himself. So, since 2014, I have finally become whole again and my authentic self with the combined bonus of incorporating Pirate Steve's personality traits into my everyday life.

Q: Hi, do you think you will always be Pirate Steve, or is a change about to happen?

Heidi Kirkland, Leicestershire, England

A: Good question, Heidi. I have thought about that myself over the years. There has been a couple of occasions where I considered reverting back to how I used to look. Then things have happened to me which have made me more determined than ever to continue being Pirate Steve. So, in answer to your question, yes, I will always be Pirate Steve, but Steven M. Rippin is who I genuinely am and is who I will always be. Pirate Steve is my alter ego, and he's helped me to become the man I am today. Thank you so much for your question, Heidi.

Steven M. Rippin

Little did I know when I first decided to grow my hair that it was going to change my life in so many ways for the better. You never know what's around the corner and will set you on a new path in life, do you? You and I cope with tragic events through our lives in many ways, and my alter ego was my way of dealing with mine. I guess being scared, anxious, upset, insulted, attacked, bullied and made fun of has made me a lot more determined in my personal life to make something of myself and to show all my haters that they can't beat me. Going through those conflicts has helped me create Pirate Steve, who, yes, I did use to hide behind!

So, in conclusion, because I loved being Pirate Steve so much, I merged him with my own personality. And now my two temperaments have become one. So now I am shy, crazy, quiet, odd, sensitive, eccentric and the kind of person people either love or hate. My confidence today has come from my alter ego. Unfortunately, though, some people still think I am hiding behind my Pirate Steve persona and not being true to myself; well, that might have been accurate years ago. It isn't anymore.

I think you will agree; being happy is essential in life, isn't it? And for the first time in mine I finally feel content with who I am. It has been a long journey to get to the stage I'm at in my life right now and, looking back on how I have arrived here, it has been a pretty bumpy and unbelievable voyage of self-discovery.

I am both Steven M. Rippin and Pirate Steve in mind, body and soul.

# HOW TO CHANGE YOUR PERSONALITY TRAITS

Personality traits. What are they? Well, our personality traits reflect the characteristics which make us who we are through our thoughts, feelings and how we behave. I would like to think I have good temperaments, and after asking my family and friends what they think of me, the most common responses I received was that they see me as an inspiring, fun, calming, loving, caring and approachable person. Also, though, they think I am too sensitive, too nice, somebody who can get taken advantage of easily and someone who needs to be more confident within themselves. A fifth personality trait I recognise I need to improve on is my shyness, because when I'm in public even if it doesn't look as if I am; I can be very timid! So, already, I have five traits I know I need to sharpen.

If you feel like you need to change any of your characteristics, ask your family, friends and online buddies the following questions or ones similar to them: 'Please be honest and tell me what you think of me – What annoys you about me – What negative personality traits I have you think I need to change, and any new ones you believe I need to incorporate in my life?' And don't let what they say hurt your feelings because they are only trying to help.

Then, once you have a list of traits people have told you they think you're lacking in or need to elaborate on, think why they suggested you need to improve on them. It might be you need to be more positive, compassionate or considerate. Then consider how much better your life would be if you did work on those traits. For example, if you're out with friends at a party, and you can feel that negative personality trait of yours coming through – let's say it's the self-centred one – then you should take a time out, relax your mind and take a few deep breaths and remember that isn't how you want to come across to people anymore because you're NOT someone who talks about themselves all the time. You're now a kind and thoughtful individual who listens to what others have to say. So, THINK, WRITE DOWN and VISUALISE the person YOU want to come across as to those around you.

To improve again, let's say your self-centred trait, try practising having conversations with your family and friends. And tell them to let you know when you're making them feel uncomfortable or saying the wrong thing. I know it probably sounds silly to do this, but it's the best way to learn how you come across to others.

Once you know the personality traits you want to incorporate in your life, practise them every day.

Think of the people who inspire you. It might be your mum, your dad, a work colleague, a friend or a celebrity. Also, read autobiographies on individuals you admire. I have read a lot of biographies on people I value, such as Napoleon Hill, Jack Canfield, Louise L. Hay, Andrew Carnegie, Rhonda Byrne, Stephen Hawking, Elon Musk and Martine Rothblatt. By doing this, it will help you find the characteristics you want to incorporate in your life. My dad has always inspired me, and ever since I was a young boy I have wanted to be just like him and have a lot of the temperaments he has. You see, my dad's a very positive, caring, compassionate, thoughtful, considerate, honourable and trustworthy man who has always been there for others.

Always treat people you don't know how you would treat your own family and friends: as if you have known them for years.

Now, if you have any negative traits, transform them to benefit you. For example, I have been a timid person throughout my life. Shy people though can be excellent listeners, which I think I am, and by being a good listener you could be an invaluable friend to someone who has got problems they need to speak to somebody about. And, if someone has got a fiery temper and loves to boss people around all day long at work, they could make a great leader. Personality trait tip: if you have a lot of diverse characteristics you want to change, focus on the most critical ones first. For example, if you have a hectic work life and don't spend enough time with your family, then you should focus on spending more time with them, or if you love spending loads of money but never make enough of it, then you should concentrate on sorting your money problems out.

Now, here is a great example of a bouncer who needs to change a few of his negative characteristics who I came across outside a nightclub in London one year.

One weekend I went to a club in London with a few friends, and, while we were queuing up waiting to get in, the women I was with started chatting to the bouncer about ages, then the bouncer looked over at me and said in a very condescending way, 'He must be 50, just look at him.' Which, clearly, I wasn't, then he gave me a dirty look and started sniggering. One of the girls I was with said to the bouncer, 'Of course he isn't; he could pass for early '30s; that's really rude what you said about our friend.' I just shrugged off what he said and told the women not to worry about it because that bouncer wasn't worth getting into an argument with. So, I stood there with a smile on my face and decided to rise above his negative remark. Silence is golden, isn't it?

So within the space of a few seconds that bouncer had firstly made an idiot out of himself with what he had said about me; secondly, because he wanted to ruin any chances he thought I might have had with those women I was out with; and, thirdly, because he was trying to impress my mates, who all happened to be women. What was funny was this bouncer also had a goatee beard and long hair, which only made it even more apparent why he had taken an instant dislike to me when he spotted me in the queue! He was unmistakably feeling very intimidated by my presence and had to prove his dominance to my friends. I bet he would have loved it if I had risen to his bait and started an argument with him so he could have said, 'I'm not letting you in tonight, mate, but I'll let your mates in.'

That bouncer needs to change some of his personality traits on how he conducts himself to other people, especially if all he does is go around being patronising towards the patrons of that nightclub who he doesn't like the look of. If he doesn't change his attitude, he will only continue to attract more negative situations into his life. The negative traits that bouncer portrayed were being obnoxious, disdainful and rude.

Changing your temperaments won't happen overnight. Once you know the traits you want to change, though, practise improving them one at a time and at every given opportunity you get. Always stay determined, committed and positive when you want to change any of your characteristics. And, if you do, over time you will gradually see a difference with how you come across to those around you, just like I have by developing my timid personality trait, which I am still working on today!

A few things that helped me improve my shyness have been making videos on social media, interacting with customers at work, fundraising, stepping out of my comfort zone and walking around in public dressed as Captain Jack Sparrow. By doing those things, it has helped me come out of my shell a lot more.

Always be yourself, don't put a front on and don't be somebody you're not because people will see straight through you.

I hope what I have written has helped you understand more about the personality traits you portray to your family and friends along with any you might need to improve on. If you feel you need to change any of your attributes, start working on them today.

# CONDESCENDING PERSONALITY TRAITS

The types of people I want to write about now are the ones who come across to you and me as being patronising, mock you and me as if to say, 'Ha-ha. You're pathetic: look at the state of you. I'm so much better than you will ever be,' and who belittle and treat us like a piece of dirt on the bottom of their shoes. Yeah you know the ones; they are the people you meet when you're at work, at somebody's wedding, or out with your friends partying. So, when you find yourself in contact with condescending people in public, and you feel uncomfortable in their company, either talk to them about how they are making you feel so you can resolve your differences or get yourself away from them as soon as you can. Surround yourself with people who love and respect you.

Now here are a few signs to look out for if you come across somebody who's condescending. Condescending people: Can act over the top and loud, so they know everybody can hear them – Are obnoxious, annoying, rude, insulting towards other people and disrespectful to the society around them – Like to show off – Will talk about themselves all the time – Like to be the centre of attention – Will come across to others as being lovely and friendly until you get to know them – Will take your confidence away – Won't let you get a word in because they always dominate the conversation – Will make cocky comments and remarks about you to impress their friends – Can be very arrogant and think they are better than everybody else, and finally condescending people can come across as being conceited, which means they have a very high opinion of themselves.

Have you ever come across somebody who has got those personality traits? Maybe one of your friends has, but you haven't had the stomach to tell them, or then again you might be able to relate personally to coming across this way. Well, if you do, don't worry because people can change their ways. Now here are some great affirmations patronising people should learn.

'I will be a more thoughtful person' – 'I will listen to others and ask them about themselves' – 'I will stop patronising people' – 'I will not pat people on the back and belittle them' – 'I will stop bragging about how awesome my life is' – 'I will stop being condescending towards others' – 'I will stop being arrogant, and I will start helping people out more' – 'I will stop making people feel uncomfortable in my company' – 'I am just like everybody else. I am no better than them' – 'I will accept people from all classes no matter what their backgrounds or religious beliefs are because we are all equals'.

The other types of people I find really annoying are the ones you sometimes find in shops who ignore you, just like the time when I was in a coffee shop in Leicester when the server didn't give me any eye contact while she was serving me because she was too busy on her phone! I hate that, don't you? I expect to be acknowledged, or is that too much to ask for these days? Well, unfortunately, it is! I have come across quite a few shop assistants in England, you see, who have been too busy to serve me because they are texting away on their phones or busy chatting up the other members of staff while I'm at the counter waiting to be served by them! So, when that happens, I throw the stuff I was going to buy down on the counter and walk off. It's unbelievable how some shop assistants treat you, isn't it? Thankfully we have the internet nowadays. I will say, though, that not all shop assistants are like that, thank goodness, because I have had some fantastic interactions with them in England.

Eye contact, being courteous and having time to talk to your customers are the three essential factors to have if you work in the service industry.

My dad and I have made some great friends in stores we go to England, and one of them is Bowden Stores in Great Bowden. Every time my dad and I walk into Bowden Stores, which Dominie Cripps runs and owns, she will always greet my dad and me with a lovely smile on her face and give us both a big hug, plus the servers and chefs go out of their way to say hello and ask us how we are doing as well, which means a lot. Now that's the kind of reception you want to receive when you go into a shop, isn't it? You don't want to be ignored and see somebody engrossed on their phone or too busy to serve you because they want to make out with the other shop assistant they are working with, do you?

> Big friendly smiles and lovely warm greetings from shop assistants
> go a long way.

Normal people scare me: this is so true from my own perspective because I never know what's going to come out of somebody's mouth when they see me, plus being bullied and assaulted by some of the so-called normal people who conform and live in today's society has made me a lot more wary when I do come across them. Somebody like myself, though, has always got to be careful when out in public, which is such a shame. Be who you want to be and never change for anybody. And one final thing that annoys me is when people take the mickey out of other individuals who don't realise they are being taken the mickey out of; I hate that, don't you? Well, they are just some of the types of people I find condescending. Remember, distance yourself as far away from those irritating individuals as you can.

# HOW TO COPE WITH
# CONDESCENDING PEOPLE

Here is a question I asked my friends on social media on what they think of patronising people along with how best to deal with them.

Have you encountered people you find condescending – Conceited – Loud – Obnoxious – Belittles you to impress their friends – Takes your confidence away – Thinks they're better than you? If so, how do you deal with those types?

I try to keep away from these people and avoid them, but if I come across them, I like to be very positive and happy.

George W. Rippin, Market Harborough, England

Yes, in my work, I have come across many like these, and until recently I was very intimidated by these types. Firstly, they are like this usually to hide insecurity and keep people away, as they probably feel inferior. They may also be testing people to see how weak they are. Money also can affect these types. I have earned respect from this sort as follows: Don't let them get the better of you. Share common interests. Be extra nice to them. Stand up if they bully – tell them you need respect, as they expect respect. Treat them as equals – in an indirect way, try and question them – crack jokes. If they overstep the mark, tell them this is unacceptable. Often, they have historical issues and overcompensate by patronising, and those weak enough fall for it, strong, well-rounded people question them, and they hate it. Question where they come from and what they have done in life, step into their shoes. Make your challenge to become their friend's – see it as a personal challenge. Above all, don't let them drag you down.

Gordon Harrison, Leicestershire, England

Toxic people like that are not needed in your life. It can be hard to expel them from your life because they need to be like that to make themselves feel better about themselves. After they have put you down for so long, you can start to believe what they tell you. You have to get into the mindset that you are a bigger person, and they are like that because they have issues and jealousy that they are not ready to deal with. If you can get into that mindset, you will get stronger each and every day until you realise you don't need that in your life. They need you more than you need them. Toxic energy is a waste of your time. Good positive energy is so much better, so surround yourself with that type of person xx.

Wendy Rudge, Basildon, Essex, England

Unfortunately, I went out with one of these people for five years. But love is blind, which made me blind to this too. When I look back, I realise how much of it I assumed was banter, wasn't.

Susan Dilks, Market Harborough, England, instagram.com/suzy0826

You need to remove them from your life, not slowly or with any compassion, immediately. Think of it like a band-aid on your arm. You can remove it slowly and have it tug each hair painfully, or you can rip it off in one go. After that stand back, light your pipe and admire your handiwork.

Jules Marshall, Manchester, England

There are always people like this. I deal with it by having my little bubble. Very few people are allowed in my bubble, and those that aren't in it, don't affect it. I just think how rude these people are, and it drives me away from them. Life has been way simpler since my bubble existed.

Claire Farrar, Market Harborough, England

I just keep on being nice and hope that my actions of patience will rub off on them, and they will do some self-reflection. There is usually something else going on in their lives, and you cannot judge them by that. What you can only do is what I formerly said.

Matt Werner, Washington, USA

You can either ignore them and stop being around them, or you can give them a big dose of truth or their own medicine if they persist and you have had enough. You don't have to be rude, but just point out their misinformation, that works well because it puts them on the back foot. They will then think twice before doing that to you again, and people will respect you for it. Be a doormat to no one. Sometimes, we also may dislike someone because we see something in them, we dislike about ourselves or how we once were, and perhaps coming to understand them, we understand ourselves better. And we might be able to help them.

Vittoria Franchino, London, England

Yes, and avoid them at any cost! They will really bring you down, btw, confronting them is pretty much pointless, just walk away!

Lydia, Belgium, instagram.com/lydialithos

Never ever lower yourself to their pathetic petty level. I have always found the best way to deal with people like this, is to be super sickly nice to them. I always make a point of rubbing in my happiness by only asking them how their day is when I know it's been a really bad one, it always really riles them that you are so much happier than they are. You have to make it clear that there's absolutely nothing they can do to drag you down. Being a pirate helps too, it makes me feel attractive, empowered and invincible. If they really pi** you off, just imagine giving them a good keelhauling. Works for me.

Captain Elizabeth Vane, England,<br>instagram.com/captainelizabethvane

Thank you so much to everybody who contributed their views and helpful advice on how to deal with condescending people. A pretty clear message reveals itself here, doesn't it, which is always to walk away from those types of individuals, laugh off what they say, and show them that, no matter how they come across, they will never upset us because we are confident people who are civilised and courteous.

# HOW TO LIVE YOUR LIFE WITH A POSITIVE ATTITUDE

When you have the wrong mindset, you will attract negativity into your life, so now I am going to write about how having the correct attitude can help draw positivity into your life again.

On occasion, we don't always have time for our family and friends. Sometimes we can be negative, portray a terrible attitude and be judgemental, which doesn't mean we're bad people; nobody's perfect; we are only human, after all, so don't worry: we all have our off days once in a while. The good thing is they don't have to last because it's up to us to overcome those negative days we have by doing things we enjoy so we regain our positive mindsets once again. So, let's keep on motivating each other, believing in ourselves, growing as individuals and learning from our past mistakes, and move on so we can develop and turn our errors into lessons we won't make again. So do great things, be magnificent and live your life with a positive attitude!

Why live your life with a negative mindset when you can live your life with the power of positivity? If you haven't always had the best attitude, it can affect various aspects of your life, just like it did with mine when I was attacked and cyberbullied, which caused me to think very negatively about myself; it also created my anxiety and mild depression. What I did to transform my mindset was to take all those hurtful memories I had and convert them into more positive thoughts instead, which I could help people with. So, I started posting positive and helpful advice on my social media sites, which I am happy to say have helped countless people over the years and have even saved some individuals' lives. One thing I love doing is giving hope and encouragement to people who have lost their way, so they believe in themselves once again. Now here are a few examples of the thoughts I used to have when I had a negative attitude and how I changed them, which I hope help you if you're suffering in any way today.

Negative thought: 'I wonder if they like me or not?' Positive thought: 'I really don't care if somebody likes me or not. I'm too busy to worry about what others think of me. I've got a life to live.'

Negative thought: 'Look at me lying on my bed, feeling sorry for myself. Come on, Steve, snap out of it.' Positive thought: so, I did, and I started writing ideas down for videos I wanted to create that would inspire people; by doing that it helped to take my mind off how I was feeling on the inside.

Negative thought: 'It's always me bad things happen to.' Positive thought: 'Things happen in life to everybody. There's always somebody who's far worse off than I am. I should be grateful for everything and everybody I have in my life.'

Negative thought: 'Why can't I get a girlfriend, but all my friends can?' Positive thought: 'Do I genuinely want a girlfriend? I should be focusing on what I love doing in life. If I'm meant to have a partner, it will happen when it's supposed to happen. Don't go looking for it, Steve; it doesn't work that way and in the meantime follow your heart and the passions and goals you have.'

As you can see, I turned those negative thoughts I used to have into more positive and productive resolutions instead, which have helped to make a significant difference in my life today. Start living your life in the moment instead of dwelling on the past. I also focused on my creative side a lot more, which is one of my strong personality traits. And, when you find out what your best qualities are, focus on them, and hopefully they will help you overcome your negative mindset.

When you're faced with difficulties in life, having a positive attitude will help you through them. Music has helped me a lot, especially when I have been feeling down. Well, apart from those songs that sound depressing and are to do with breaking up with someone! Why listen to those sorts of songs when you're already feeling upset? You want cheering up not made to feel even worse than you already do. So that's why I have always loved listening to hardstyle music; it's so uplifting. A lot of the lyrics in those songs are about the Universe, being at one with yourself, being with your friends, enjoying life and making the most of your time while you're here, as well as giving you that feeling of acceptance. Hardstyle has always boosted the way I feel about myself, especially if I'm in a negative mood. Hardstyle music is all about positivity and loving life. So, if you feel down in the dumps and need your spirits lifting, go and listen to some hardstyle music. I recommend Isaac's *Hard Style Sessions*. And here is a link to DJ Isaac's podcast if you are interested in checking his phenomenal podcast out: bit.ly/ IsaccsHardstyleSessions.

Now, here is a video link where I talk about my love for hardstyle music and don't worry it's only over one minute long: bit.ly/MyLoveForHardStyle.

Don't let your negative attitude destroy your life. Seek help from your family, friends or your local GP, who can help advise you on what you should be doing to get your life back on track again.

Stevieboy, you're such a lovely and friendly guy! It's always so cool to write with you, and you motivate me every day to live my dreams and fight for them because you always stay positive.

### Julia Spaniol, Germany, instagram.com/thebluedarklight

What kind of attitude towards life do you have? I used to be very negative, and I would always be moaning and groaning about everyday things. My dad, on the other hand, has always been a very positive person. When he used to hear me being negative, he would always say to me, 'Can you hear yourself, Steven? You're always moaning. Be more positive; you've got the wrong attitude, you have,' or he would say, 'Steven, you're very negative today. Come on, be more positive like you always tell me to be.' If only I had listened to my dad years ago and taken his advice. So please remember to listen to your family and friends when they tell you to buck your ideas up because they always speak the truth and only want what's best for you. Now here is a question from the late great public speaker Earl Nightingale; if you haven't heard of Earl Nightingale, then I highly recommend reading his book *The Essence of Success*, which is an excellent read.

What's your attitude? Just answer this question with a yes or a no. Do you feel the world is treating you well? If your answer is a quick, 'Yes' your attitude is good. If your answer is, 'No' your attitude is bad, and if you have trouble deciding your attitude is probably average.

Earl Nightingale, 12/03/1921–25/03/1989

Well, my answer to that question back in 2008/2009 would have been no. Today though, it's a quick and decisive YES. On a few occasions in 2008/2009, when men who were friends with the guy who had assaulted me walked by me in the street, I would get really nervous, and my whole body language would change. I would also look very stone-faced as well because I didn't know if they were going to start on me, plus it didn't help when they said, 'Hello, how are you doing?' And, because of my negative attitude back then, I always ignored them and looked away when they spoke to me. And to this day I still remember hearing one of them say something like, 'What's up with him? No wonder he got beaten up,' as he walked by me.

Because my head was all over the place back then, I remember thinking to myself, 'Those guys will only start on me once they get me into a conversation.' So, I thought the best thing to do would be to ignore them and they would leave me alone, which they did. Still, though, by disregarding them I drew more negativity into my life by acting that way. And they said what they said to me because of my attitude. I realised a few years later, once I was feeling more like myself again, that all those men were doing were being friendly and didn't have any bad intentions towards me at all. I had just jumped the gun, put two and two together and got five instead of four because I wasn't thinking straight and kept focusing my thoughts in a negative way towards anybody who was associated with the guy who had head-butted me. Unfortunately, over the years, I have continued to get nasty looks and the odd insult here and there from specific individuals who know the guy who attacked me. Because I had a negative attitude after I had been assaulted, I attracted negativity into my life.

I knew the sooner I changed my mindset back then, the better things would be for me, so that's what I did. I now live my life with a positive attitude every day, and it's helped enhance my life no end. So I urge you or anybody you know who might be struggling with their negative mindset to change that attitude around and show love and respect to everybody, or you will only end up attracting negative situations into your life and give the wrong impressions to people, just how I did.

How you think becomes your reality. When I used to go out at the weekends with my friends I would often think, 'I bet tonight's going to be a rubbish night,' and because I put myself in that mindset that's how my night turned out. So, I ended up making my thoughts become my reality. Has this ever happened to you, I wonder? If it has, please change how you're thinking straight away. Nowadays, before I go out at the weekends, I will go in the gym, do a workout, turn my speakers up and blast some hardstyle out, which always puts me in the right frame of mind for a fantastic night out with my mates. So that might be something you could try doing if you ever feel down before you go on a night out with your friends.

Affirmations, I have found, are a great way to change your attitude. To give you an example, here are a few I say to myself. 'I'm going to have a FANTASTIC night tonight, and I can't wait to get out with my mates and party'– 'Yeah, it's Saturday night, I've been working hard all week so now it's time to have a good laugh with my friends'. Or I will say, 'Tonight's going to be awesome; I'm going to be with my mates, have a good laugh, make a fool of myself dancing and meet the girl of my dreams,' which unfortunately still hasn't happened yet. Saying affirmations to yourself similar to mine will help change your whole attitude and the way you might be feeling on the inside about yourself.

Q: How do you keep so positive?

Stacey Williams, Market Harborough, England


A: Hey, Stacey, thanks for your question. I believe I keep positive because of the love my parents and friends give me and also by living my life in the present moment and appreciating everybody and everything around me today. Don't get me wrong: I still get down from time to time; I just make sure, when that happens, I pick myself up and carry on with more conviction than I had before, especially when somebody says something negative to me about how I look! Nobody will ever keep me down for long. I also believe in the power of the Law of Attraction, which has helped me become more positive in my everyday life as well. I hope this helps to answer your question, Stacey.

Steven M. Rippin

Here are a few key points to improve a negative attitude. Learn to manage rejection – Surround yourself with positive people – Don't be resentful of what others have – Always believe in yourself and focus on your goals and ambitions – Give at least one compliment to somebody a day – Keep a smile on your face – Read self-help books – Be enthusiastic about everything you do – Use positive words to describe your life and who you are – Never judge yourself against other people – Turn your failures into lessons – Keep a diary and write down each day all the positive things that have happened to you and what you are grateful for, and live in the moment; don't dwell on the past. Remember, believe in yourself no matter what anybody says to you! Everybody is good at something; it's just a matter of finding what that unique talent of yours is, such as if you're a good singer admit to yourself that you are a spectacular singer and don't let anybody tell you otherwise. I'm good at editing videos in my amateurish way, and I know how to inspire and make other people feel happy – well, I hope I do, anyway! So, remember, always focus on your inner strengths and build on them.

You have inspired me with your life and your positive attitude. You are the kind of person who is always trying to help others, make them smile, and make their day a bit brighter. You are true to yourself and who you really are in life. That is a great inspiration to others.

Debbie Barnard, Arkansas, USA

If you go around thinking in a negative way, 'Why does that person always look so happy, why do they know so many people, and why do good things keep happening to them?' you will become very bitter. Those individuals have good experiences because of their positive attitudes. Also, good things are most likely not happening to those people as often as you might think they are because everybody faces dilemmas throughout their lives, don't they?

> Surround yourself with people who make you feel happy. Take every opportunity that comes your way and learn something new about yourself today.

I only became well known in the town where I live because I took chances and did things a lot of people wouldn't normally do, such as by having the courage to walk around in public resembling a pirate, auditioning for television game shows and by putting myself out there on social media for the world and my hometown to see me for who I genuinely was. So, the people who sit around complaining because they see others doing well for themselves are the ones who need to get out there and do something different with their lives if they are unhappy with their own. They should also stop criticising others, change the way they think, and learn to have a better attitude towards life. When you smile and laugh, you give out positive energy into the universe and to everybody around you, which people love. Furthermore, they will be attracted to you all the more because of it.

Here is a quick and easy way to change how you're feeling if you find yourself having negative thoughts which might contribute to you having a negative mindset. First, find somewhere quiet to relax, then lie down and when you're feeling comfortable close your eyes and think about somebody who annoys you; they might have insulted you or pulled you down in the past – Now take a minute to think about that person – Can you feel that hatred you have towards them? – Right, now stop and take a deep breath – And when you're ready, now think of somebody who makes you happy and who you love being around – Now think of the last time you spent with that person and how good they made you feel. And, finally, open your eyes, breathe out and relax. There you go: you have just turned a negative feeling you were having about someone you don't like into a positive emotion about somebody you do by releasing the chemical serotonin into your brain, which as you and I know is the chemical that makes us feel good. So, the next time you feel down, take a deep breath and focus on somebody who makes you happy.

When I'm feeling depressed about how somebody has made me feel, I will post a message on Facebook and Instagram because the love and support I receive from my friends on those sites is overwhelming. Their words of comfort mean the world to me and help lift my spirits so much. I can never thank my online mates enough for helping me feel better about myself after someone has upset me. So if you're comfortable opening up about how you feel on social media, I would recommend posting a status because your online friends love you for who you are and will help you through any bad experiences you might be going through with their supportive messages and comments. Opening up about my problems on social media has been my way of dealing with my mental health issues over the years, which I understand is nowhere near the same as getting professional help from a counsellor. Still, my social media friends have helped me no end.

Now here is one of many messages I received on Facebook, which helped to lift my spirits when I was feeling down in December 2018.

Hi Steve, thinking of you at this low point you have expressed openly from your heart. We feel your pain and understand a heavy heart when you've lost loved ones. And although the years pass the anniversaries can seem like it was yesterday. Always remember the love you shared and how much joy you would have brought into their lives. As you have in your own circle of friends and Steve, it is a large circle you have of trust and love. Most of us have a very small circle of our family and a few very special friends who we can absolutely count on no matter what. But with you, there are so many who genuinely love you for who you are and mostly your oversized honest heart. Keep it real as you do, let it be water off a ducks back with any hurtful remarks because you have an army of friends behind you and not many people ever have that. And most importantly, a father many only dream about, and I am sure your mum is a beautiful person. Keep smiling from the inside out, Steve. You are always there lifting our spirits, so I just hope as one small voice amongst all those who love you, that you can feel a sense of peace in the things that can cause a troubled or sad heart. Enjoy a Blessed Christmas with Mum, Dad & family. God Bless you, our friend. Much love Ruth & Lochlan.

**Ruth Moore, Northamptonshire, England**

Thank you for writing such a lovely message, Ruth. All my very best to you and Lochlan.

Steven M. Rippin

Lovely people like Ruth are the reason I like to write positive messages online for my friends which hopefully inspire them to live their lives to the fullest. My social media buddies have never judged, insulted or criticised me; they accept me for who I am.

Now, if you can relate to any of the following statements, these are the typical thoughts you and I have when we are feeling down and negative. Also, if we're not careful, these statements we think to ourselves can damage our confidence and self-esteem – 'I can't' – 'I will never' – 'I shouldn't' – 'This is the way things always happen to me' – 'This is just how I behave' – 'Yeah, that's just what I'm like' – 'I'm clumsy' – 'What an idiot I am' – 'Yeah, that's me the one who's always failing at life' – 'I'm such a terrible driver' – 'I'm useless at everything I do' – 'It's going to be another one of those days' – 'I never have enough money'.

So, if you can relate to any of those statements, you should eliminate them from your mind immediately and STOP saying them to YOURSELF FOREVER! I'll admit I have thought comments like those about myself, which haven't done my confidence and self-esteem any good. A great example of this is when I see a woman I fancy who I'd like to ask out; you see, I'll usually end up thinking, 'I'll only make a fool of myself, and she's bound to have a boyfriend. Why would she like me?' So, I have had to turn those negative thoughts around and learn to think more positively by saying to myself, 'I feel fantastic. I'm full of confidence tonight. I'm great on dates, even though I've not been on one since I can remember. Right, I'm going to go straight up and ask that woman out who I like. And even if she says she's not interested, I'm not going to let that bother me because there's plenty more fish in the sea,' which does help boost my confidence. Unfortunately, though, I still get nervous going up to women and asking them out on dates! Also, instead of believing in those negative thoughts you might have had about yourself, try changing them into more positive thoughts instead. And here are a few examples of what I mean.

Negative thought: 'I'm useless I can't do that.' Translates into: 'I can do that, I believe in myself, and if I get stuck at any point I'll ask for help and advice from somebody.'

Negative thought: 'Why do I act so stupid?' Translates into: 'I'm not stupid at all, I've accomplished so much in my life. I'm going to prove everybody wrong who has ever doubted and not believed in me and show them what a successful person I can be.'

Negative thought: 'I'll never amount to much; I'm too dumb.' Translates into: 'I'm clever, and whatever I'm faced with I'll learn how to deal with that problem one step at a time. I might not be good at some things, but I'm good at football, making money and helping others.'

And one final negative thought: 'Why do I act so foolish?' Translates into: 'I might be a fool, but, hey, I love being a fool. I make people laugh, and there's nothing wrong with that.' So always change negative thoughts into positive beliefs instead, or your subconscious mind will start to believe how you are thinking about yourself is true. Don't let negative comments people say hold you back from fulfilling your true potential.

Say you're going for a job interview. If you think to yourself, 'I'll be rubbish in the interview today. I'll end up getting all the questions wrong they ask me, and I'll probably make a right fool of myself. I'm so nervous,' then that's probably how the outcome of your interview will go. So, you're going to have to change that negative attitude straight away, aren't you, and think instead, 'I'm going to be incredible in my job interview today. I'll breeze through the questions they ask me, and I'll make sure I keep a smile on my face and feel confident and relaxed. Come on bring it on,' then by thinking with this all-new and improved attitude, there's going to be a much higher chance of you getting the job you're being interviewed for. Even if you don't get the post, you know you went to that interview with a positive mindset. And you never know, the person interviewing you might recommend you to another firm that has been looking for somebody just like you because of the fantastic personality and positive attitude you portrayed to them.

Now, here is a little trick that might or might not help you erase any negative thoughts and experiences you have had in your life. So, to start, please find somewhere quiet to lie down and relax for a few minutes. Then, when you're ready, close your eyes and imagine a whiteboard in front of you. Now imagine you're holding a black bold marker pen in your hand, and with that marker pen write down any negative thoughts and experiences you have had on the whiteboard, then once you're finished start rubbing those feelings and events away with that pink eraser which has magically appeared out of thin air in your hand. With each rub you make you are subconsciously erasing those negative emotions and occurrences from your mind and memory forever! That's it, keep rubbing away. And remember, the faster you rub, the quicker those negative thoughts and experiences will disappear. Then, when you're ready, open your eyes. You should now have begun to eliminated those negative feelings and circumstances you had.

I sincerely hope my mind trick lesson helps you in some way. It might not help at all; if it doesn't, don't worry because over time you will find what does. It might be talking to your family, friends or your local GP or taking up a new sport or activity help you. Whatever you do, never give up. Now I would like you to write down a list of inspiring and positive affirmations you can say to yourself at least once a day, which will help you think with a positive attitude towards life. And to help give you an idea of the kind of affirmations I mean, here are a few I say to myself.

'I will learn to do that' – 'I will always do my best' – 'I am better than that' – 'I will do great things with my life' – 'We all make mistakes, and I'm going to learn from mine' – 'I'm going to look forward to every day' – 'I will not let anybody talk down to me' – 'I'm going to save up, go on adventures and buy things I have always wanted to treat myself to' – 'I am so grateful for everybody and everything I have in my life' – 'I'm so lucky to be alive today'.

Remember to repeat any affirmations you come up with every day to yourself. By doing this, you will help embed them into your mind, which will help change the way you think and see yourself. Once you have got used to saying affirmations, you will start believing and seeing yourself as a more confident and outgoing person. And the negative attitude you might have once had will slowly be eradicated from your mind; you will develop a more positive attitude towards life instead. If you are already living your life with a positive mindset, fantastic; if you know somebody who isn't, though, maybe you could suggest that they try writing down some affirmations to say to themselves each day to help them with their negative state of mind. It's up to you how much you want to change your attitude, the way you think about yourself and how other people see you. So please remember its only YOU who can make those changes happen.

Now here are a few things to remember when you want to turn your negative outlook into a positive one. Write down all the positive things that have happened to you during your day – Smile and laugh as often as you can – Stop thinking negative thoughts and always think positive thoughts – Don't judge other people because nobody's perfect – Take challenges and learn something new and, if people are rude, patronising or pretentious towards you, rise above their remarks and ignore them, then once they have finished trying to belittle or insult you for whatever reason, pay them a compliment because that bewilders them every time and, if anybody has ever said anything negative to you and made you feel down, upset or depressed, say to yourself, 'I am AWESOME, I can do anything I put my mind to. Nobody will ever stop me from chasing after my DREAMS. I will always focus on what I want to ACHIEVE because I BELIEVE IN MYSELF, and I am going to make everybody around me feel LOVED and HAPPY from now on. So goodbye old negative attitude and hello to my NEW POSITIVE MINDSET instead, which is helping me reach new heights of LOVE, HAPPINESS and FREEDOM.'

Everybody in my life has helped me to rebuild my confidence, low self-esteem, anxiety and mild depression. And, because of my family and online friends, I now have a well-defined mindset. I am forever grateful to those people for always believing in me, supporting me and accepting me for who I am. Don't let people walk all over you. Stand up for yourself and show them that you are a confident individual who has a positive attitude. So, start living your life for today because who knows what's around the corner. Become the MASTER of your EMOTIONS.

# STEPPING OUT OF YOUR COMFORT ZONE

Don't let opportunities that come your way pass you by. Grab hold of them and make things happen by stepping out of your comfort zone. I used to let so many chances pass me by because I was scared of venturing away from my safe place, then after I was assaulted in 2008 I said to myself, 'I'm going to live my life how I want,' so that's what I did, and I took challenges and opportunities that came my way from that day forward. And, since I have had this attitude, my life has changed tremendously. I always get nervous when I do step out of my comfort zone, don't get me wrong, but I think it's the adrenaline rush of venturing into the unknown that I love the most because I have no idea what to expect, and that awareness makes me feel so alive!

Another thing that has helped my confidence and, in a way, has also pushed me out of my happy place is my job because it involves being in social situations talking to customers, which for me is very difficult because of how shy I am. So, that being said, I never thought I would have the confidence to do radio and newspaper interviews, audition *for Big Brother* and *Deal or No Deal* and appear on *The Weakest Link* television game show.

Stepping out of our comfort zones at any given opportunity is a vital thing you and I should always do in our lives. Don't just sit back and let your life pass you by. If there are things you have always wanted to do, get out there and do them.

A fantastic affirmation to say if you are struggling to believe in yourself when you want to step into the unknown is 'I have the confidence and determination to achieve anything I put my mind to'. This affirmation will help you focus on the challenge or opportunity you have set yourself to accomplish. And repeat this statement daily; that way it will help you train your brain and give you a much stronger and more positive mindset to succeed.

When it comes to taking those first steps out of your cosy little world, do some research on the subject you want to take part in. If you're afraid, though, you should look ahead at what the positive outcomes will be. And, if there is anything you are worried about, think about the various ways you can deal with those dilemmas and eliminate them. Also, learn all about what you are going to be doing, and, once you feel untroubled knowing what the worst-case scenarios will be, you might be pleasantly surprised that they don't turn out as intimidating as you first thought they would. You will never know, though, until you give that challenge or opportunity a try.

If you are still scared of taking on something new, talk to your family and friends about what you want to do and hopefully they will be able to offer their help and advice just how my parents and friends helped and supported me when I auditioned for *Big Brother* and *The Weakest Link*. I was extremely nervous going on *The Weakest Link*. After appearing on the show, though, I felt proud of myself and thought, 'This is awesome. I can't believe I'm here. What was I so nervous about?'

Today is the tomorrow you worried about yesterday.

**Richard Willis, Leicestershire, England**

# FEELING NERVOUS ON THE RADIO

When I was forty-one, I found it extremely nerve-racking when my dad and I were invited to go onto BBC Radio Leicester and our local community radio station, Hfm. I had to really push myself out of my comfort zone back then to do those interviews. By doing them, though, they helped my self-confidence issues no end. I was apprehensive because I was worried about what certain people around my hometown who didn't like me would think of me when they heard me on the radio! How stupid was I? So I pushed all those negative thoughts I was having out my head because I knew I was going on the radio for a worthy cause as I was raising money for Cancer Research UK. Back in 2017, when I did those interviews, I was still inside my head and letting my anxious thoughts trap me in there, which I believed I was over. Luckily, they didn't catch me for long though, and once I was at the BBC Radio Leicester studios I felt a lot more relaxed and confident than I thought I was going to be. Also, before I was interviewed, I prepared some notes on what I was going to say, which helped me considerably.

Doing radio interviews is a great way to push yourself out of your cosy surroundings, especially if you suffer from having self-confidence issues or social anxiety. So if you ever find yourself being interview on the radio, the foremost factors to remember are to stay focused on what you're going to be talking about – Don't go off topic – Write down all the critical points of what you would like to get across to the audience – Have passion – Don't go on too long with each question you're asked or which you ask – Keep your audience entertained and wanting to know more about what you're talking about – Keep a smile on your face – Stay relaxed and don't fidget around – Treat the presenter and the radio listeners you're addressing as if they're your best friends – Prepare and learn as much as you can about the subject you're mentioning, and above all else enjoy the whole experience.

When you take on a new challenge that presents itself to you, you might not know anything at all on how to go about it and find the whole process very daunting. Well, don't be defeated or put off the challenge you have set yourself. What you should do is surround yourself with people who have done what you want to achieve. In my case, it was writing a book. And I found Instagram was fantastic for this because by using hashtags associated with writing I attracted authors into my life who helped me out as much as they possibly could. Or you could join LinkedIn and connect with like-minded people in the same fields as you are in on there.

Why not take on a new quest today? What have you got to lose? It doesn't matter if you succeed or fail because it isn't about winning, losing or competing against other people; it's about YOU becoming the best version of yourself. And, when you are passionate and committed about something close to your heart, everything will come more naturally to you, and you will be able to take on anything, no matter how nervous or scared you feel on the inside. Only you know from within yourself that you can achieve what you have set out to accomplish. So never feel afraid if you are asked to do something you don't feel comfortable with doing but would still love to take part in. Just go for it and enjoy the experience. Remember, life's what YOU make it.

The more confidence you have, the better you can cope with stepping out of your familiar little world. I wish I had more confidence within myself years ago and hadn't let opportunities pass me by. You should never think of what could have been though. So, I don't regret missing out on anything because everything happens for a reason and new opportunities have always presented themselves to me, just as they will to you as well. And, if somebody as timid as me can step out of their comfort zone, then so can you.

If you want to make a change in your life, you're going to have to give up the things that are holding you back right now and start focusing on what you want to do. For example, if you're an alcoholic, the first thing you will want to do is stop drinking because that will help change the direction your life would have taken you in, and it will give you the opportunities to achieve the things you have always wanted to accomplish. You will also feel more in control of your life and healthier at the same time. If you can relate to this, make changes in your life today before it's too late.

It's down to YOU to find a job you enjoy doing – The home you have always wanted – The partner of your dreams – To increase your monthly income – To eat healthier food and exercise more – To go to a self-development class, or to take up a new sport and interest to improve your life. YOU are the master of your destiny.

# NEVER BE AFRAID TO MAKE
# A FOOL OF YOURSELF

A genuine alternative individual can laugh at themselves and not take themselves seriously. I'm always making a fool of myself and embarrassing myself when I'm out in public; I don't mean to, though; it's just who I am. So, my best advice to you whether you are young or old is always be yourself. And if you do something embarrassing, don't hide away; laugh along with everyone else who has seen you make a buffoon of yourself; embrace your clumsy foolishness, as I do. I made a clown of myself on a couple of occasions in front of millions of people when I appeared on national television here in England! I will explain more about those situations I got myself in further on in my book. For now, though, here are a few occasions when I have made a spectacle out of myself in my everyday life.

Because of my eyesight, I tend to bump into things a lot, trip up and misjudge distances. One time when this happened, I was in a retail store called Boots, and after I had done my shopping I walked towards the cashier, tripped up and crashed into the counter, where I nearly fell on top of the clerk! So, as you can imagine, all the staff turned around to see what was going on and started giving me funny looks. Then I looked over at them and said, 'I always like to make an entrance,' which luckily got the girl who was serving me laughing; still, though, I couldn't wait to get out of that Boots store! This next embarrassing predicament I found myself in happened when I was rollerblading along the promenade in Venice Beach, California. So, picture the scenario: the sun's blazing and there are loads of gorgeous girls and guys flying around on their roller blades looking cool. Then there was me who was trying to rollerblade and act cool as well, which I wasn't doing a very good job of at all.

Anyway, as I was rollerblading past a bunch of exceptionally hot American girls, I thought, 'Hey, I'm pretty good at this,' then the next minute I know my feet went from under me, my hands flew in the air and I hit the pavement head first while my arms and legs went flying all over the place. I felt like such a plonker, and I must have looked like one too! To make it even more embarrassing, two of the most beautiful Californian girls I had ever laid my eyes on, who I had just skated by, stopped and asked me if I was all right. I told them I was and thanked them for their concern before they skated off into the sunset. I just wish I'd asked them for their numbers! Chatting women up has never been one of my strong points, unfortunately. Anyway, I then brushed myself down and carried on rollerblading, pretending as if nothing had happened after nearly knocking myself out. Luckily, I was wearing a helmet that day.

Those two times when I made a fool of myself are nothing compared to when I was on holiday with my mum and dad when I was five years old. One evening while I was on holiday with my parents sitting around a table having drinks well, I wasn't drinking; I was too young for rum back then – with another couple who my parents had got to know, my dad said to me, 'Come with me a minute, Steven.' So off my dad and I went to the men's restroom, which I always remember was down a flight of stairs. Anyway, my dad said, 'Promise me you'll not say anything about that man's big nose,'

'I won't say anything,' I promised my dad.

My dad and I then went and rejoined my mum and the other couple. After a few minutes, when the conversation went quiet, don't ask me why but you know what kids are like when they are told not to say something, well, I turned round to the man with the enormous nose and said, 'My dad told me not to say anything about your big nose.' You should have seen the looks on my parents' faces! My mum and dad went bright red with embarrassment. Then my dad took me by the arm and quickly escorted me back down the stairs to the men's restroom, where he gave me the telling-off of a lifetime! I had never seen my dad so angry at me and when you're only around four foot tall somebody like my dad, who's six foot, four inches can be a pretty intimidating presence! While I was getting the telling-off of a lifetime, my poor mum, bless her, was still upstairs with the couple I had just embarrassed her in front of. 'Sorry, Mum.'

After that incident, my parents and I kept bumping into the man with a large nose and his wife for the rest of our holiday; typical, eh? We saw them when we went for breakfast every morning, on the bus back to the airport, and on the plane home, where I took a photo of his whopper of a nose. Furthermore, we also saw this couple on the motorway in England as we drove by them! What are the chances of that? I have searched high and low for the photograph I took on the plane of this man and his ginormous nose. Unfortunately, I've not been able to find it, or you could have seen for yourself how gigantic it truly was! I think I can be forgiven for my actions back then because I was only five years old. I feel terrible now, though, because it must have been so embarrassing for that poor guy. I still wonder to this day if he ever got a nose job or needed counselling because of what I said to him all those years ago! Just think: my five-year-old self might have changed that man's life forever.

Now, I have one final story to tell you of when I made an exhibition of myself yet again, this time, though, with the help of my dad. I want to share this story because it shows you that you should always be yourself and never worry about what other people think. Firstly, though, never feel afraid to shed all your inhibitions away. Always show the world, your true inner self. So, if you want to make a spectacle of yourself on the karaoke down at your local bar, go for it. If you want to pull a moony at your best friend's birthday party, do it, or if you desire to walk around public with a pirate puppet on your hand then that's entirely up to you as well, which leads me nicely onto my final story at long last.

So, let me take you away to a land far, far away, well, to Las Vegas in the Nevada desert, to be precise, where my dad and I took a trip one year and stayed, yeah you guessed it, at the Treasure Island hotel. Now, to show you how much I don't care about making a laughing stock out of myself in front of loads of people, especially the ones who think they're cool, envision this scenario if you can. There you are, relaxing around a swimming pool in Las Vegas, the sun's beating down on you, beautiful people everywhere are drinking cocktails and making out with each other while the DJ's spinning some tunes. And then this perfect scene is interrupted when you see my dad filming me with a pirate puppet on my hand as I walk around the swimming pool area saying in a crazy pirate voice, 'Hello and welcome to the Pirate Steve Show. Here we are live in Las Vegas at the Treasure Island hotel; how cool is this, eh, Barnacle Bart?' I wonder what you would think if you encountered somebody doing that while you were relaxing on holiday! As you can guess, we got quite a few stares. I don't think anybody knew what was going on; I didn't either, if I'm honest! But this is the kind of mindset you should have when you're an alternative individual. So, don't be afraid of making an idiot out of yourself. Have the confidence to get out there and do things most people wouldn't even dream about doing but secretly wish they had the guts to do. And, when you can do that, that's when you know you're comfortable with who you are.

Most people are frightened they will end up being laughed at by everybody around them when they want to have a bit of fun, which, if you ask me, holds those people back from being their true selves. So what if somebody laughs at you? Let them laugh; you're the one being yourself and having fun. I bet deep down those people secretly wish they had the courage to be more like you. Yeah, I'll admit I must have looked like a right plonker that day with a puppet of a pirate on my hand, but, hey, I was having a good laugh and enjoying myself. So always do things that make you happy, just as inspiring others makes me happy. And, if you're interested, here is the video my dad filmed of me walking around the swimming pool area at the Treasure Island hotel in Las Vegas: bit.ly/TreasureIslandBarnacleBart.

So, get yourself out there and don't be worried about making a nincompoop of yourself. And if you do end up doing something embarrassing while you're out in public don't fret about it, embrace your foolishness and go along with it, such as if you tripped up on a banana skin in the street, and everybody turned around and started laughing at you; all you have got to do in that situation is take a bow and tell the onlookers you were practising your banana tripping skills for a scene in a movie you're going to be starring in. So, remember to turn your embarrassing moments around to your advantage and control them. Learn to laugh at yourself, have fun and don't take life too seriously. One thing I know for sure is that those foolish circumstances I have found myself in are moments in my life that I will never forget and ones I will treasure forever.

# CLOSING THOUGHTS ON BEING AN ALTERNATIVE INDIVIDUAL

For me, it's been quite a journey being an alternative individual. It's had its ups and downs but living an unorthodox lifestyle has unquestionably helped me learn so much about myself and how human beings treat one another based on their appearances. I have also grown a lot as a person, and I now understand myself more than I ever thought I would. People have always tried to change me through my life, and they will do the same to you if you let them.

Individuals who have questioned and insulted me no longer bother me because I know who I am. I have got nothing to prove to anybody, especially to strangers who don't know me. Those judgemental people should get out into the real world more. I'm not all that alternative, I know; I think I look rather average, if you ask me, especially when you compare me to other alternative individuals in the world who have extremely impressive piercings, tattoos and amazing styles they have created for themselves; me, I wear a red bandana, jeans and a T-shirt most days! If we lived our lives by following in everybody's footsteps and conformed to society, what a dull existence we would have, so I say thank you to the nonconformists out there who are unique and stand up for what they believe in. Those guys have taken risks and challenges in their lives, which a lot of people hold back from doing in today's society. I take my bandana off to anybody who lives an unorthodox life. Nonconformists should be welcomed into our society and not frowned upon like they are. The world needs more inspiring people who choose to live their lives outside the box and who are not afraid to make their mark on the world, if you ask me! And even if you don't dress alternatively, it doesn't matter because your heart, mind and soul make you an extraordinary human being.

Becoming an alternative individual isn't about becoming a goth, punk or pirate. It's about showing the world around you who you genuinely are on the inside. You might be a nonconformist who dresses and looks very respectable, who has big ideas and aspirations to change the world you live in but you're too afraid to speak up out of fear of getting laughed at by your peers. Well, don't be: voice your opinions to the world and tell everybody those significant plans you want to accomplish; make those notions of yours happen, so you help develop a better future for the generations to follow of tomorrow. Just like Steve Jobs, Bill Gates, Elon Musk, Stephen Hawking, Richard Branson, Albert Einstein, Wallace D. Wattles, Dale Carnegie, Earl Nightingale, Napoleon Hill and many others have done. It doesn't matter how you choose to dress; it's all about expressing yourself to the world in your own way with how you feel comfortable. So always express yourself as much as you can; embrace your individuality, and never let anybody tell you how to live your life. Being the unconventional man I am has made me a lot happier as a person more than I could have ever imagined. People have said many times they admire me for just being myself, which means a lot.

Never let the citizens of today pull you down or destroy your dreams. Believe in your heart that you can be that alternative individual you have always wanted to be. Furthermore, be proud of the person you are, and create a life for yourself that's full of excitement and adventure.

# PART SEVEN

# WHEN I AUDITIONED FOR *BIG BROTHER*

When my good friend Lynda Hill suggested I should consider going on the *Big Brother* reality TV show in 2008, at first I thought she was messing about, then after some consideration I thought it might not be a bad idea. It could also help me get my life back on track again because it had only been a few months before that I had been assaulted and put into hospital, which left me feeling down and depressed, as you know. So, on 20 December 2008, I uploaded my *Big Brother* audition video to YouTube, and to date it has had over sixteen thousand views, which might not sound like many to some people, but for me that's fantastic. I always remember the television presenter Davina McCall mentioning my audition video on *Big Brother's Little Brother*, and she said something along the lines of, 'Stay safe while making your audition videos and don't go hurting yourself by jumping out of any trees.' I believe she was referring to my audition video because I jumped out of a tree dressed up as Captain Jack Sparrow and hurt my manhood, you see! Then a few weeks later, after word got out that I was auditioning for the show, my local newspaper asked if they could do a story on me. If you're interested, here is the story the *Harborough Mail* published on 13 January 2009.

# CAP'N JACK LOOKALIKE IN BID TO ENTER THE BIG BROTHER HOUSE

A JACK Sparrow lookalike from Harborough has made a bid for TV stardom after producing an audition video for the hit reality show Big Brother. Steve Rippin, known to friends as Pirate Steve or Jack Sparrow, has submitted the two-and-a-half-minute clip to the video-sharing website YouTube explaining why he would make a good housemate for the popular Channel 4 programme. It has been uploaded to an official Big Brother auditions channel on the website which allows people to post videos for viewing by programme producers as well as fellow fans. Those who stand out from the crowd will get to meet the show's chiefs face to face and won't have to queue to see them. His entry has proven so popular it has been shown on the Big Brother's Little Brother programme recently, as well as in The Sun newspaper which ran an online story about it. Mr Rippin has also been supported by a campaign group on the social-networking site Facebook called 'We want Steve Rippin to make it into the Big Brother House.' Set up on Sunday the group already has more than 260 members. Some of the comments on the YouTube video compare Mr Rippin to comedian Russell Brand, while friends have left him numerous messages of support via Facebook. One comment says: 'He will bring laughter, calm and clumsiness to the house, and he is someone that could actually win it.' While another states: 'Hell yeah Steve! Saw your video and you should so be on Big Brother.' The video starts with

Mr Rippin introducing himself while a fake parrot sits on a perch beside him. He is then seen jumping down from a tree hurting his leg as he lands. Later in the video, the 32-year-old carpet fitter describes himself as a working-class lad who would make a good housemate because he is easy-going and charming.

*Harborough Mail*, 13 January 2009

A couple of months after my video had been on *Big Brother*'s auditions YouTube channel, I received a phone call from one of the production team, and they said they really enjoyed watching my video and would like me to attend a second audition down in London. I couldn't believe it and was so happy to have been given a chance to have made it through to the second stage. I had never been so nervous in all my life. I was way out of my comfort zone, that's for sure, and I loved it. So, I went down to London for the second stage of the auditioning process, and there were thousands of people dressed up in a variety of costumes. One costume which stood out to me was this guy who had dressed himself up as a hot dog!

While I was queueing up, I noticed quite a few people were trying to outdo each other by being very pretentious and over the top, which was sickening to see. Also, there were a lot of condescending and obnoxious people there as well, who I didn't get along with, which I guess is what *Big Brother* is all about, isn't it? Anyway, once I had registered, the *Big Brother* show assistants got us into groups of around twelve and gave us tasks and games to play to see how well we interacted with each other; you can't beat a bit of team building, can you? Then later on that day we all had one-on-one interviews with the production team. When it was my turn to be called in, I was led into a large conference room, where the producers of *Big Brother* were waiting for me, then I was asked to take a seat in front of a video camera which was set up in the room.

So, there I was sitting against a black backdrop with two massive photography spotlights shining down on me, along with a boom mic that was above my head, which didn't make me feel nervous at all! The producers then asked me a bunch of questions, which ranged from why I would make an excellent housemate to what I would have to offer the house and why they should choose me, etc. By this point, after I had stumbled and fumbled a few questions and came across as a nervous pervous, I was covered in sweat. After the interview was over the *Big Brother* producers thanked me for coming along and said if you hear from us you will know you have made it through to the next stage. I think the producers realised I wasn't made out of tough enough pirate material back then in 2009 because I never heard from them again. I'm pleased I auditioned, though, and I felt privileged they asked me to go along to the second stage. Auditioning for *Big Brother* was a fantastic and very nerve-racking experience.

Can you believe I originally uploaded my *Big Brother* audition video to YouTube in 2008, and in 2020 I saw on *The Sun* newspaper's *Big Brother* webpage that they had still been using my audition video from 2008 to show people how to apply to be a contestant on the show? I feel very honoured they have been featuring my audition video all these years even though they entitled that section of their webpage 'Wacky Big Brother auditions!' Anyway, here is a link to *The Sun*'s *Big Brother* website if you are interested in seeing my audition video featured on there, well, that is, if it's still there: bit.ly/TheSunsBBAuditionwebpage. And here is a link to my *Big Brother* audition video: bit.ly/MyBB10Audition. Because I didn't make it onto the show, I felt like I had let everybody down who was supporting me in my hometown. All I could think to myself, though, was that I gave it my best shot, but it just wasn't meant to be for me back then. I am sincerely grateful to all those who encouraged me in my campaign to make it onto the *Big Brother* TV show.

# THE PIRATE STEVE SHOW/THE POSITIVE PIRATE

I started the Pirate Steve Show in 2008 and it ran until 2019, when I rebranded and renamed it the Positive Pirate, with some inspiration and help from my good friend Matthew Squibbs.

What's helped me overcome my shyness and mental health issues has been putting myself in front of a camera and making vlogs and random green screen videos, which I am passionate about creating. Those videos have ranged from doing shout-outs for people – Pirate Steve Show Entertainment News – Helping to advertise people's businesses – Work vlogs – Singing: well, trying to – Random sketches – Making videos of my dad and me dancing in public, to creating promotional videos for Judge Jules and Amanda O'Riordan; Judge Jules is a world-famous DJ and Amanda O'Riordan has a well-known fashion blog called Amandazipsitup.

To give you an idea what the Pirate Steve Show was all about, here is a selection of videos I have compiled from my YouTube channel, well, that is, if you are interested in watching any them, of course. If you are, you will see how my Pirate Steve persona has developed over the years up until today. Also, you will see how I have now integrated Pirate Steve into my real life and become two personalities all rolled up into one. I'd better warn you, though, if you do decide to watch any of my videos, there are a lot of cringeworthy Pirate Steve moments, but, hey, I'm happy to embarrass myself for you; so on with the show.

The first video I uploaded to YouTube was titled 'My bb10 audition'. I uploaded this video on 20 December 2008, which is when I first created my Pirate Steve Show account on YouTube. You might have seen this video already; if you haven't, there's a link to it in the previous chapter. My *Big Brother* audition video received quite a few nasty comments from people, which hurt me a lot, if I'm honest, because they said some ruthless things about my family! I don't care what people have to say about me; there's no need to bring my family into it, though. So, onto my next video.

In January 2010, I created a feature called 'Happy News', which thinking about it I should have called 'Pirate Steve's Movie Reviews' instead because I talk more about movies than anything else! Also, in these videos you will be able to see how unprofessional I came across. So, let the embarrassment begin:

bit.ly/HappyNewsVideo1
bit.ly/HarryPotterAutographs

It's now 9 August 2010, and time for me to blow an apple up with the green screen effects I was teaching myself. It isn't as good as it sounds, believe me. Also, this is where I wear my Captain Jack Sparrow outfit for the first time on screen as well: bit.ly/PirateSteveAndTheApple

On 2 February 2011, I made my first ever episode of Pirate Steve News, where I talked about none other than *Pirates of the Caribbean*, along with other new movies which were coming out. You will also notice I changed my style a bit and turned into a punky pirate. For some reason, though, I started putting on an irritating voice, which you will hear me speaking in. I cringe when I hear how I used to talk in my videos; it's so embarrassing. I even remember my dad saying to me, 'Why are you putting that voice on for, Steven?'

'I thought it sounded good,' I would tell him; how wrong I was: bit. ly/PirateSteveNews

On 11 February 2011, I uploaded a video tutorial to try and help teach children the two times table and the alphabet. I wanted to do my best to take my channel into a new direction, you see. It didn't work, though, unfortunately, so I only ended up making two children's tutorial videos; I wasn't cut out to teach children about maths and how to learn the alphabet, that's for sure. Here, though, if you are interested, is a video link to my tutorial video: bit.ly/PirateSteveTheTeacher

Moving on, on 3 May 2011, I created the Pirate Steve Shopping Channel, where I transformed into a mad professor and set myself up in my dad's garage removing coffee, tea, red wine and permanent black marker pen stains from a carpet sample. So, to see me getting up to mischief in my dad's garage, here is a video link to my shopping channel video: bit.ly/ThePirateSteveShoppingChannel

It's been funny how my videos have been received over the years; people have either loved or hated them. Some people on YouTube love to criticise you when they see you having fun and enjoying yourself with the videos you create. Those individuals who scrutinise your videos sadly don't appreciate the hard work, time and effort you put into making them. People should encourage each other to be creative on social media, not go around being all negative and nasty for no reason! If you have got a YouTube channel and receive cruel comments from trolls, don't let them get to you. Show them you don't care what they say about your videos by ignoring them. Carry on with what you love doing because there are more people out there around the world who love what you do than those who don't.

Sometimes don't you wish you had a can of positive spray handy so you could spray some positivity on somebody who's being very negative towards you? Well, because of how people have treated me, I came up with my very own Positive Spray videos. The first Positive Spray video I uploaded, on 1 June 2011. And the second Positive Spray video I uploaded, on 26 June 2015. People loved the idea of having a can of Positive Spray handy to spray all over someone who needed it. I even had a few people messaging me saying they wanted to buy a few crateful of the stuff! So, without further ado, here are my Positive Spray videos for you to enjoy:

bit.ly/PirateStevesPositiveSprayTime
bit.ly/PositiveSpray

Around 2011, my dad and I used to go on camper van holidays around England, where I got to spend some quality time with my dad. As you will see from these videos, I did my best to turn them into documentary episodes of the places we visited. Hopefully, you will also be able to see how my videos started to improve a lot as well compared to when I first started making them in 2008:

bit.ly/PirateSteveGoestoDubDayzVWShow

bit.ly/CamperJam2012Part1
bit.ly/CamperJam2012Part2
bit.ly/WhitbyAdventuresEpisode1
bit.ly/WhitbySeason1

It's now 6 September 2011, and this was when I wanted to find out what it would be like to sing in front of a studio audience and face a panel of judges on *The X Factor* TV show. Because I can't sing to save my life, though, and to save me from humiliating myself on national television, I decided to upload my own spoof *X Factor* audition video on YouTube. In the spoof audition, you see me attempt to sing Nickelback's 'Saturday Night's Alright for Fighting'. My YouTube followers loved it. So, without further ado here is my spoof *X Factor* audition. I hope you enjoy it: bit.ly/PirateSteveSpoofXFactorAudition

Moving on now to 26 January 2012, which was when I made my first promotional video for a group of guys who were in a band called Toxin. I'm not sure if they're still around today; they were an excellent band, though. In this video, you can also see how my style was starting to change and the direction I wanted to take my YouTube channel in. So, sit back, relax and take a listen to some great music by the formidable band Toxin, in this unskilled promotional video I made for them: bit.ly/ToxinPirateSteveSpecial

It's now 11 April in the year 2012, and the year when I used to go to a bar in Leicester called Pirate's Bar, where they made these awe-inspiring cocktails in coconuts. I loved going to Pirate's Bar because I felt quite at home in there, as you can imagine. Unfortunately, Pirate's Bar has now closed down. In honour of Pirate's Bar, though, here is the promotional video I made for them: bit.ly/PiratesBar

I had never done a vlog before so on 4 May 2012 I uploaded my very first vlog, where I talk a bit about who I am. Although you're probably sick and tired of hearing about my life story by now: bit.ly/PirateStevesFirstVlog

So, as the years went by, I kept developing the videos I was creating to see which style would suit me best and also to observe if people liked what I was doing. Unfortunately, my YouTube channel never took off no matter what videos I produced. I never gave up, though, and I continued creating random videos with the ideas that kept popping into my head.

I'm also a huge fan of Disneyworld, so this gave me an idea for another new direction I could take my YouTube channel in. So, on 30 July 2013 I uploaded my first Disney Entertainment News video, which you can watch on the following video link: bit.ly/DisneyEntertainmentNewsEpisode1

Well, it's now 24 September 2013, and I have turned my hand to making educational history videos on parts of England my dad and I have visited in his camper van because my Disney Entertainment videos never took off. So, for your enjoyment and some mini history lessons on Whitby and Bradgate Park in Leicestershire, England, here are a few video links to those documentaries I made with the help of my dad while we were on our travels:

bit.ly/HistoryWithDadAndPirate
bit.ly/WhitbyAbbeyEngland
bit.ly/HistoryBramStokerDracula
bit.ly/HistoryBradgatePark1
bit.ly/HistoryBradgatePark2

Now here is a short special effect video I uploaded on 29 September 2013. I'll admit, it isn't very good, but I like it, and it tested my video editing skills to the max. This video all came about when my dad asked me if I wanted to join him and my mum on a camping holiday to Wales, and I thought, 'Yeah, that sounds like great fun.' So, before we went off on our trip, I wrote a rough script out and ran it by my dad because he was going to play a small role in it. I hope you enjoy this pirate themed video: bit.ly/BelieveDreamsDoComeTrue

On 1 December 2013, I uploaded my first Christmas special where I'm this crazy mad professor Pirate Doctor on board my pirate time machine with my little pirate robot dog. It's very amateurish but I hope you enjoy watching it: bit.ly/PiratesteveDoctorChristmasSpecial

On 27 January 2014, I started making work vlogs to show my followers on YouTube what my dad and I got up to during our workdays; my followers loved them. It was great fun making those work vlogs with my dad and if you would like to see what we used to get up to at work here are a few links for you to enjoy:

bit.ly/HavingFunAtWork
bit.ly/TheCarpetFitters

bit.ly/TheCarpetCleaners
bit.ly/PirateStevesWorkVlog
bit.ly/CarpetCleaningVlog
bit.ly/HowToWithTheCarpetFitters

On 2 February 2014, with the help of my dad, I made a six-second video clip where I'm combing my hair in front of a mirror and my reflection jumps out at me. My dad and I created this effect using an eight- by four-foot sheet of plywood, which we cut a hole into roughly the same size and shape as the mirror I was going to comb my hair in front of; we then covered the plywood with green-screen material. I then set the scene up and filmed myself standing behind the plywood and stuck my arms and head through the hole, which was acting as the fake mirror. And, finally, I then recorded myself while I was combing my hair in front of the real mirror on the wall in the dining room. It was then time for me to edit and green screen all the video clips I had made together. And here is the outcome of me scaring myself with my own reflection: bit.ly/PiratesteveAndTheMirrorEffect

As I was now getting a taste for adding special effects into my videos, I downloaded an app called FX Guru and came up with this next collection of videos I made from March 2014. It was great fun creating these videos and my favourite one is the UFO sighting that features my dad:

bit.ly/TreeFallsDown
bit.ly/CaughtInTheActVideo
bit.ly/AnimalStompede
bit.ly/CrazyUFOSighting

You are so funny, and I love that your videos always make me feel really happy and cosy somehow, and you are such a positive, vibrant, weird person! Team Steve, ha-ha.

Alice, Sweden/Germany, instagram.com/alt_lady_decay

Well, we are now moving up the years and on 3 June 2015 I made a video where I'm morphing in and out of various outfits where I shared an uplifting message to my friends online saying, 'It doesn't matter how you look or what you wear. You and I should accept each other for who we are,' so here are numerous versions of me changing outfits faster than a speeding bullet on its way to Mars: bit.ly/PirateSteveBelieveInYourself

In 2015, I upped my game and wanted to come across a lot more professional in my videos. So I revamped my Happy News videos I used to make in 2009, and created 'Facebook Entertainment News' instead, where I gave shout-outs to my friends on social media, helped to promote their businesses and any events they had planned, and also where I shared my tune of the week and final thought features:

bit.ly/FBENews1
bit.ly/FBENews2
bit.ly/FBENews3
bit.ly/FBENews4

Now here is a video I put together for the crowdfunding website Patreon. I should warn you, you will hear me singing a corny rhyme at the beginning of this video, so I do apologise in advance! Oh, and I uploaded this video on 6 August 2015: bit.ly/PirateStevePatreon

On 10 March 2015, my good friend Linda McCoy asked me to make her a promotional video for the first aid courses she held in Market Harborough, which I was excited to do. My dad was involved in this production as well because he had recently suffered having a cardiac arrest, so it felt very fitting to have him helping me demonstrate and explain to the audience how to help somebody who might need CPR, cardiopulmonary resuscitation. I also hope you pick a few tips on first aid up after you have watched this video and have a better understanding of what you should do if you see somebody unconscious when you are out in public: bit.ly/PirateSteveAndDadFirstAidTraining

When I first started my YouTube channel, I had a lot of positive and negative feedback from the community. Overall, though, my YouTube channel was going pretty well. Then, as the years went by, around 2015/2016, I slowed down posting on YouTube because I wasn't getting many people viewing my content, which I spent a lot of time and effort on creating. It was pretty disappointing, if I'm honest, especially after all the years of hard work I had put into the videos I loved making. So, instead, I started posting my videos on Instagram and Facebook, where straight away I received a lot of positive feedback and encouragement. And for the first time in years I was finally finding out what people genuinely thought about the videos I was producing. The Facebook and Instagram communities loved them, and still do to this day.

The videos I started making from 2015/2016 included shout-outs, promotional videos for DJs, random comedy sketches, vlogs on camping trips and work vlogs as well. I still post a few videos on YouTube, and I hope one day I can make my channel more popular again like it used to be. Now here in this collection you will see the style of videos I have made for my Instagram and Facebook friends to enjoy:

bit.ly/PirateSteveShowOnInstagram
bit.ly/StrangerPirates
bit.ly/PiratesOfDoritoIsland
bit.ly/JudgeJulesAndAmandaOriordan
bit.ly/PirateSteveShoutouts
bit.ly/JudgeJulesOnTour
bit.ly/PirateStevesPeople
bit.ly/PiratesteveAmandazipsitup
bit.ly/PirateSteveMusketeers

It has been my friends on social media who have given me the motivation to carry on doing what I love doing best, and that's making what I hope are fun and entertaining videos for them to enjoy watching.

Because of my love for trance, house and EDM, in 2015/2016 I made these following videos:

bit.ly/JudgeJulesPodcast
bit.ly/PaulOakenfoldPlanetPerfecto
bit.ly/TranceMusicIsStillAlive
bit.ly/JudgeJulesVsDavePearce

Here is a Christmassy video I made in 2017, well, it's me dressed up as Captain Jack Sparrow kayaking in the snow, just as any pirate would when it's snowing here in England: bit.ly/MerryChristmasFromCanoeJack.
And to end here are three videos of what my dad and I got up to during the pandemic lockdown of 2020 to lift people's spirits. I created the Pirate

Steve and Cowboy George Show which went live every week night on Facebook for ten weeks; we did fifty shows, made a collaboration video featuring over fifty of my online friends to the football anthem Vindaloo, by Fat Les, and I was kindly asked to hand over a special delivery of poems, birthday cards and gifts at my local post office to celebrate Colonel Tom Moore's 100th birthday.

bit.ly/BestBitsOfOurLockdownShow
bit.ly/VindalooTheCollaboration
bit.ly/JackSparrowColonelTomMoore

So, there you have it; that's what the Pirate Steve Show was all about. To summarise, the Pirate Steve Show, now known as the Positive Pirate, is about having fun – Positive vibes – Making a fool of yourself – Enjoying life – Being happy – Showing respect and thanks to everybody who watches and supports you – Never being afraid to express yourself – Showing the world your creative side – Inspiring people – Doing what you want to do in life no matter how ridiculous you will make yourself look to others, and it's also about helping other people who are alternative individuals to feel more comfortable with who they are and how they dress. So always be unique, be individual and be yourself.

You are very entertaining to watch. You should totally have your own Pirate reality TV show matey. You actually HAVE inspired me just recently, since I started getting on Instagram and posting again because I see the hard work and effort you put into your Instagram. I can see what a successful Pirate you are. That is VERY inspiring to me as a fellow Pirate. It inspires me to keep on going with my OWN 'Pirate's Life,' and hobby as well. Hopefully, one day, I could be almost as amazing and inspiring of a Pirate as you are! (just minus the beard though, for me) As for my opinion of you. You are probably one of the most hardworking, successful, interesting, fun Pirates that I know (and I know a TON of pirates) and you are even very nice to look at! Keep on living the Pirate's life, me matey! Cheers!

Rose Colbert, California, USA, instagram.com/rose_red_rum

Well, I hope this chapter has given you a bit of an insight into what the Pirate Steve Show/the Positive Pirate is all about, which you have often heard me mention throughout my book. The Pirate Steve Show was and still is an essential part of my life. It is a true reflection of the person I am on the inside. If I'm honest, I wasn't sure if to include this subchapter. For me, though, it was very significant because the videos I have made have been a massive part of my life. Thank you from the bottom of my heart if you did get a chance to watch any of them; it truly means the world to me. If you were wondering, I have never made any money from my videos on YouTube; that has never been my intention and isn't what I'm about. I have created the videos I've made because I have a huge passion for making them. I also hope I have been able to put smiles on people's faces who have watched them.

If you suffer from self-confidence issues, just like I have in my life, maybe you could start a YouTube channel where you help people by sharing advice on how you cope with your problems. Or you could talk about subjects that are close to your heart which you believe others will be interested in. If you do decide to create a YouTube channel, make sure you're full of passion and commitment on the topics you decide to talk about.

I believe my YouTube channel never did very well because it had no direction; I always focused too much on special effects, and also because I acted way over the top in my videos. What I should have been doing was showing people who I genuinely was as a person by focusing on meaningful subjects which were close to my heart.

Through my YouTube channel, I will continue to spread hope, happiness and positivity to everybody as much as I possibly can. So, all that leaves me left to say is: thank you for watching and see you again next time with me, the Positive Pirate. If you're interested in seeing more videos I have made, here is a link to my YouTube channel, The Positive Pirate: youtube.com/xxxpiratestevexxx.

# SCIENCE, TECHNOLOGY AND THE SINGULARITY

I am very passionate and love everything to do with science, technology and the Universe. We are so lucky to be alive today in this fast-paced technological society we're living in, where there are so many incredible opportunities opening up for us to learn, enjoy and discover the world around us.

# DO YOU WANT TO LIVE FOREVER?

Some people might laugh when I say this, but I have always from an early age wanted to live forever just like so many other people have dreamed of doing before me. I remember when I was around fifteen, I sent away for a brochure pack and a DVD to find out more about a company called Alcor, which is a life extension foundation program that cryogenically preserves your body. When I received it, I was fascinated with everything the company had to offer, well, that was until I looked at how much it cost to have your body cryogenically frozen and preserved! Some people regardless of whether they have an illness want to be frozen in this way by cryonics because they don't want to die and would like to see what the future holds for humanity if and when a way to safely unfreeze the human body and brain becomes available just like I do. To find out more about what Alcor do here is a link to their website, https://alcor.org.

I also follow the career of Aubrey de Grey, who is an English author, biomedical gerontologist and the chief science officer at the SENS Research Foundation. SENS stands for Strategies for Engineered Negligible Senescence. The work SENS are doing at their research centre is using regenerative medicine to repair the damage diseases of ageing do to our bodies. And I believe one day Aubrey de Grey and his team will find a cure for the conditions that contribute to you and me dying of old age. Aubrey de Grey's main aim is to end ageing.

De Grey's research focuses on whether regenerative medicine can prevent the ageing process. He works on the development of what he calls, 'Strategies for Engineered Negligible Senescence' (SENS), a collection of proposed techniques to rejuvenate the human body and stop ageing. To this end, he has identified seven types of molecular and cellular damage caused by essential metabolic processes. SENS is a proposed panel of therapies designed to repair this damage.

Taken from Wikipedia

When you look back over time, the average human used to live until they were only thirty years old in the 1900s and only up to around forty-eight years old in the 1950s. Nowadays, though, we are living into our mid-eighties, which is excellent, isn't it, and shows us how far medical advancements have come. Still, though, we want to live longer lives. The good news is our life expectancy is forever increasing. With modern-day technology and the scientific breakthroughs of tomorrow, I believe one day you and I will be living much healthier and longer lives even further on into the future than we can envision today. Just look at how long some people are living for already. There are far more centenarians living today than there ever have been. When I talk to my dad about living longer, he says, 'When you're gone, you're gone. I don't want bringing back and uploading into a computer. Don't go doing any of that to me.'

Some scientists believe you and I will be able to extend our lives gradually in around forty years' time with the advancements that are coming our way. So, with the medical advancements in science and technology we are told should soon be available to us, they will hopefully be able to keep us alive – that is, if you're young enough to be around in forty years' time, that little bit longer to survive for when the next medical breakthroughs arrive in the next forty or so years. And those medical breakthroughs will then help you and me carry on living even further on into the future. Just as long as when we are in our seventies and eighties – that is, if you're around the same age as me, forty-four as of 2020, that we are fit and able-bodied because we don't want to be living for years with illnesses and feeling poorly and bedbound, now, do we?

Would you want to be uploaded into a computer so you can live on and see what the future holds for humanity? I know I would. And if you have seen the movie *Transcendence*, which Johnny Depp starred in in 2014, you will know what I mean. Johnny Depp played Dr Will Caster, who got shot, and the only way he could survive was if his mind was uploaded into a computer! Another scenario where you might want to upload your mind into a machine would be if your natural body started to fail you. And then, once artificial intelligent robots have been created in the future, you could have your mind downloaded from the mainframe computer where you were uploaded to and transferred into an artificially intelligent body which would be free of diseases for you to continue on with your life. If that life isn't for you, though, you could always choose to die naturally of the disease your body has and your life as you know it would be over; the decision would be yours. I know what option I would pick; do you? It sounds pretty far-fetched, I know. One day, though, I believe it will be a possibility.

Q: If you had a time machine, would you go back and change something of your past or go to the future x.

**Dani Rust, Market Harborough, England**

A: That is an excellent question, Dani. I would go into the past and into the future. I have always wanted to see what the future holds for humanity, you see. I believe what has happened in the past cannot be undone because if it were then time would unravel itself and we might not exist in this very moment in time. Everything that has happened in the past has brought our civilisation to where it is today, although I would love to go back and stop the wars from happening so I could save the innocent lives that were so sadly lost during those times. I would also like to go to the beginning of time as well, when the Universe first came into being, and find out if another species has ever visited our planet because all those stone carvings and drawings in caves archaeologists find in various countries must mean something, especially when you see those symbols our ancient ancestors used to draw on the walls which resemble UFOs and extra-terrestrials.

And finally, Dani, I would love to go into the future to find out if we do make contact with another civilisation. I honestly believe there is intelligent life out there somewhere; it's only a matter of time until we make contact with them. And when we do, they are going to help humanity survive into the future, plus help us unlock the other ninety per cent of our brainpower. I know I must sound crazy, but this is what I believe; nobody knows what's up there in deep space waiting to be discovered. It's like if you travelled back in time and showed a mobile phone to somebody from the eighteenth century; they would think you're from another planet because that technology couldn't possibly exist to them. The advancements we have made as human beings so far have been incredible, especially when you look back over time and see how far we have come. What does the future hold for humankind? Only time will tell. And I, for one, can't wait to find out. Thank you for such a great question, Dani.

Steven M. Rippin

# THE SINGULARITY AND AI

The singularity is when computers will be able to teach themselves at an exponential rate. Artificial intelligence will one day surpass all you and I have come to understand, and in the near future it will take on a life of its own bringing unfathomable changes to the human civilisation as we know it today; this is what is known as the singularity. Technology is growing gradually year by year, our smartphones are becoming more intelligent, and we already have the capabilities to talk to virtual assistants. So, can you even begin to imagine what the next few decades are going to bring? I can see virtual assistants turning into artificially intelligent synths who will be able to walk, talk and become part of our everyday lives. As human beings, you and I strive for success and push ourselves as far as we can to the outer limits of our imaginations to see what we are capable of achieving. And we will never stop until we acknowledge all there is to know.

Technological breakthroughs that are happening today are increasing at what they call an exponential rate, which leads me onto quantum computers, which are in development right now. Once they have been created, they will be able to solve solutions to problems exceptionally quickly and with a lot less energy than a standard computer can do today. So, with the dawn of quantum computers on the horizon, they will be playing a big part in taking us nearer to the singularity.

At the minute, Google, IBM, NASA and the Universities Space Research Association are in the early development stages of learning to build quantum computers to help them move forward when it comes to creating even more advanced artificial intelligence and machine learning technologies. When quantum computers have been developed, it will be those companies I mentioned that will benefit from using them first so they can solve significant mathematical problems and generate even more powerful algorithms than we have today. So, unfortunately, quantum computers won't be available to the general public for the foreseeable future. If you would like to learn more about quantum computing, Professor Chris Bernhardt of Fairfield University in Connecticut, America, has a book out called *Quantum Computing for Everyone*. Furthermore, here is a link to Tom Simonite's guide to quantum computing, which was published on the Wired website on 24 August 2018: bit.ly/ TomSimonitesGuideToQuantumComputing.

I want to be around in the year 2045, because that's when futurist Ray Kurzweil predicts the singularity will occur. Ray Kurzweil is the author of the books *The Singularity Is Near: When Humans Transcend Biology* and *The Singularity Is Nearer*. Ray Kurzweil is also a computer scientist and inventor. Stephen Hawking, who I was a fan of and who was one of the greatest minds of our time, was very concerned, along with Elon Musk, that you and I as human beings should be taking more control over the development of artificial intelligence as we see it rise and become more of a reality in our everyday lives. Which makes me wonder: how long it will be until we start to merge with technology and become part synth? We'll just have to wait and see.

In the future, nanobots, I believe, will hopefully be able to help us fight off deadly diseases, such as cancer, heart attacks, strokes, motor neurone disease, dementia and Parkinson's by being injected into our bodies. Nanobots will also hopefully be able to roam around, clearing away all the build-up of plaque around our arteries, which can cause you and me to have either a cardiac arrest or a stroke. One day I hope nanobots can help repair and restore our eyesight and any other eye-related conditions we might be suffering from as well. Nanobots would unquestionably help to improve my vision a lot; I know that.

# LIFE BEYOND PLANET EARTH: WHAT DOES THE FUTURE HOLD?

In the future, you and I won't be bound to living out our lives here on planet Earth, because with entrepreneurs like Elon Musk, who wants to build a colonisation on Mars, we will be able to travel to the stars and then possibly out even further into the universe once we have colonised other planets and solar systems. And travelling to those distant planets once Earth has become depleted of its resources and overpopulated will be easy because in the future humankind will have learnt how to upload our subconscious minds into supercomputers. And travelling light-years across the Universe won't be a problem for us either because we will be uploaded onto advanced portable hard drive systems to be transported. Then upon arrival to our new destination – let's call it Earth 2.0 – we will be downloaded into an artificially intelligent living, walking and talking avatar body. OK, I'll come back down to reality now. Again, I got a bit carried away there, didn't I, but, hey, nobody knows what the future holds, do they?

We are such a primitive species, even though we have evolved from the dawn of man- and womankind around two hundred thousand years ago. And we still have a tremendous amount to learn. Most of us are on the right path, but there are a countless number of people on the planet who are holding our civilisation back from fulfilling our true potential and not letting us move forward as we should be doing. Racism, money, war, power and religion are all key factors holding our civilisation at a certain point in history right now. Once those issues are addressed and we can finally learn to get along with one other, then and only then will things start to improve for the human race. We're pretty much screwed, then, aren't we? Only joking; there's always hope, and I believe we will build a better world for everybody to live in one day.

The planet you and I live on is an incredible place, and we have accomplished so much as human beings. Now just envision for a moment, though, if extra-terrestrials existed and were observing us right now – which they might well be doing; who knows? – they would witness how we treat each other, all the wars that have been going on for decades, plus all the incomprehensible and appalling acts some human beings do to others. So, no wonder they have never made themselves known to us; then again, if they are ancient ancestors of ours, as some believe, they are probably too embarrassed to let other civilisations out there in the Universe know we are their offspring, so they're just leaving us to our own devices!

Q: How were the Pyramids built?

**Elijah Bennet, California, USA**

A: Hey, Elijah, well, there are a lot of theories on how the pyramids were built. One I like is that extra-terrestrials built them. Erich von Däniken believes the pyramids of Egypt were built using alien technology – Erich von Däniken is a Swiss author and has numerous books out claiming extra-terrestrials influenced human culture; you can find out more by visiting www.daniken.com/en. Now here is a brief description taken from the YouTube channel 'The Fifth Kind', followed by a video link on how Erich von Däniken believes the pyramids were built:

'It was written by the Arabian historian Al-Maqrizi that the great pyramid was built by a king who lived before the great flood named Saurid. King Saurid, was more commonly known in Hebrew as Enoch. With his advanced understanding of planetary events, Enoch was able to foresee the great flood. He then instructed the building of the pyramids to preserve treasures and written accounts of all valuable knowledge.'

bit.ly/MysteriesOfTheGreatPyramid2019.

For more fascinating and awe-inspiring videos, please check out The Fifth Kind's YouTube channel: bit.ly/The5thKind.

It is also believed the pyramids were built by Pharaoh Khufu, who reigned from around 2551 bc. Researchers have said the key to building the pyramids was down to using wet sand, which they used to make those enormous sand blocks with. Then those massive sand blocks, all 2.3 million of them, were moved using large ramps and pulley systems to put them in place, which over time formed the pyramids we see today.

Please remember, though, these are only theories; there are a lot of other explanations on how the pyramids were built. So, what I have said here may well be completely wrong. Thanks for your question, Elijah.

Steven M. Rippin

There are many exceptional minds and corporations all over the world, helping you and me move forward to become an enhanced civilisation of tomorrow. Some of those corporations include SpaceX, Google, Apple, Amazon, Facebook, Hanson Robotics, Human Longevity, Boston Dynamics and the SENS research foundation. People who think outside the box help keep our civilisation moving forward. They are the go-getters who reach for the stars and make the world a more exciting place to live because of their unique moonshot ideas.

Smart cities are being formed, robots are taking over our jobs and blockchain technology is said to disrupt the banking system. Times are changing so fast right now, so make sure you keep up with the developing world around you and don't get left behind. If you are interested in artificial intelligence, science and technology, here are a few website links I highly recommend visiting, where you can sign up for their newsletters and can keep up to date with everything that is going on: humanlongevity.com – kurzweilai.net – sens.org – bioviva-science.com – singularityhub.com – hansonrobotics.com – bostondynamics.com – opencog.org – lifenaut. com – brainpreservation.org – www.spacex.com – wired.co.uk – ai.google – deepmind.com – research.fb.com – aws.amazon.com/machine-learning

I have always wanted to see what the future will look like in one hundred years so I can witness how far technology and the human civilisation has advanced; I just hope I'm around to observe it. These are exciting times for the human race right now, and I can't wait to see what the future holds for us. So, remember, the future is here today and takes us both a step closer towards the singularity of tomorrow. The question is, though: will you be ready for it?

# PIRATE STEVE IS THE
# WEAKEST LINK. GOODBYE

I have spent a lot of money and done plenty of crazy things to promote the channel formerly known as the Pirate Steve Show on YouTube, now known as the Positive Pirate, from making a fool of myself on social media, thinking that by jumping out of a tree in my Jack Sparrow attire would get me on *Big Brother* to spending a small fortune on magnetic business cards and promotional T-shirts, which have all failed miserably. So, one day I thought, 'Wouldn't it be funny if I made a YouTube video where I'm walking off the set of a television game show saying, Yo-ho-ho and a bottle of rum.' Then I knew what I had to do; I had to get myself on a television game show and put myself in front of millions of people, where I could mention my YouTube channel! Why I hadn't thought of this idea before I will never know! So, I auditioned for *The Weakest Link*.

I knew it was going to be a tough challenge for somebody like myself to get on a BBC television game show, but it was a challenge I told myself I would succeed at accomplishing. I thought, 'What's the worst thing that can happen? Oh, I won't make it on the show.' So, I had absolutely nothing to lose and everything to gain. And I kept this mindset along with my positive attitude through the auditioning process, which helped me a lot. After I had filled in the application form online, a few weeks later I received a phone call from one of the production team, and I had only gone and landed myself an audition, hadn't I? I couldn't believe it: me, the eccentric pirate of Market Harborough! So, off my mum and I went to Leeds, where the auditions were taking place. I was so nervous on my way to Leeds. Once we had arrived, though, I felt a lot better, and I thought,

'They'll either love me or hate me.' While the auditions were under way, my mum waited for me in the hotel lobby.

During the audition, the first thing I was asked to do was fill in a questionnaire. Unfortunately, I filled in loads of wrong answers and didn't finish filling it in. I couldn't see the questions clearly, you see, due to my eyesight! I made a right pig's ear of my questionnaire. Luckily one of the girls who was running the auditions said, 'Ah, don't worry about it, it's all right.' After that, the other auditionees and I introduced ourselves to each other. We then got asked to stand in a circle answering a few questions in a mock-up version of *The Weakest Link*. It was good fun doing that and a little nerve-racking at the same time. At the end of the audition, we were told somebody would be in touch with us if they thought we had what it took to take on the Queen of Mean, Anne Robinson. I had a great time meeting the other auditionees that day and wished them the very best of luck. After the audition, I told my mum how it went, and she said, 'Well done. You've done your best; we'll just have to wait and see what happens next. It's exciting, isn't it?' I never thought I would hear from the production team again, so it came as a surprise a few weeks later when I received a phone call saying I was through and would be appearing on *The Weakest Link*! It was a daunting yet exciting feeling knowing I was going to be appearing on national television! My local newspaper, the *Harborough Mail*, heard I was going to be appearing on *The Weakest Link*, and here is the story they printed in their paper for me.

# PIRATE STEVE TAKES ON 'QUEEN OF MEAN' IN WEAKEST LINK BID

A PIRATE look-a-like from Harborough crossed mental swords with Anne Robinson on TV quiz The Weakest Link. Steve Rippin, known as Pirate Steve, appears in an episode of the show set to be aired on BBC One at 5.15 pm next Thursday. Steve got on the show after applying in January. He won over producers at an audition in May after telling them about his Pirate Steve channel on YouTube, to which he uploads humorous videos of himself getting up to a variety of capers. Though Steve must keep the show's outcome a secret until it has been aired, he told the Mail: 'It was awesome meeting Anne. I remember all the lights went off in the studio and all I saw was this dark figure walking towards me, it reminded me of Darth Vader. Then the lights go up, and Anne's there, and she stares right at me and says, welcome to The Weakest Link. I had a bit of banter with her, and I got her to smile. It was a fantastic experience, and I met some awesome people.'

*Harborough Mail*, **Wednesday, 6 October 2010**

The BBC certainly know how to look after you because when it came to filming the episode I was on they flew me up to Glasgow, where *The Weakest Link* was recorded, they paid for my evening meal and put me up in a hotel, all expenses paid! It was great, and I felt extremely privileged to have been given the opportunity to experience that kind of treatment.

You know when you're watching a game show on television, and you say, 'Oh that question's easy; they'll know that one,' then the contestant goes and gets it wrong, well, I did the same thing when Anne Robinson asked me a few simple questions! I couldn't think of the correct answers to save my life; it was so embarrassing! It was quite a surreal experience being there at *The Weakest Link* studio. I was well out of my comfort zone, but at the same time I felt so alive and privileged to be there.

When the filming of the show started, my heart was in my mouth, and I felt extremely nervous, especially when I heard those three magic words spoken: 'Quiet on set.' Then when the studio lights went down, the contestants and I were left standing in total darkness waiting for the Queen of Mean to arrive. After a minute, I then saw a figure slowly emerge from the dark and stop six feet in front of me on a raised platform which was in the centre of the studio. And BOOM! A BRIGHT spotlight was then shone down on Anne Robinson, who was standing there in front of me looking stony-faced and very dominating in her sexy leather outfit. After a few moments, Anne then said those famous seven words, 'Hello and welcome to... *The Weakest Link*.'

After Anne had introduced herself to the audience watching at home, a massive video camera came down from above and faced each of the contestants and myself one by one. When this monster of a camera faced me, I thought, 'Oh jeez, this is it.' Then this little red light came on, which was my cue to tell the audience watching at home my name, where I was from and what I did for a living. It was quite an experience, so I was relieved once Anne started asking her questions, which was just as nerve-racking as well, if I'm honest!

The show aired on Thursday, 14 October 2010 on BBC One at 5.15 pm. Soon after, I started receiving messages and phone calls from my friends telling me they had just seen me on TV and were laughing their heads off because I had got some straightforward questions wrong! Now here for your amusement are the questions Anne Robinson asked me when I made a fool of myself on national television.

# PIRATE STEVE MEETS THE QUEEN OF MEAN ON *THE WEAKEST LINK*

Anne: 'Steve, in old fashioned etiquette, when a gentleman met a lady out of doors, he would raise which article of clothing?'

'His coat?' I replied.

'His hat. Steve, in TV, which term suggests a rise in temperature as the job title of a comedian who entertains a studio audience before a recording?' Anne inquired very seriously.

'Pass,' I responded.

'Warmup. Steve, in film, the title of a 1990 comedy starring an eight-year-old child played by Macaulay Culkin is said to be left where alone?' Anne asked me.

'Home?' I said confidently.

'Correct. Steve, in children's literature, the German brothers who collected and published fairy tales, such as Snow White and Rapunzel, had what surname?' Anne then proceeded.

'Grimm?' I answered, knowing I was right.

'Correct,' Anne said sternly. Well, I survived round one. Unfortunately, after round two was over, though, I was sailing a sinking ship. Here is what one of the contestants, Emma, had to say about my performance when Anne asked her why she had voted for me, 'Because he got a question wrong in last round and one in this round.' And that was it; that was the end of my brief appearance on *The Weakest Link*, and it was man overboard for me – well, it was until Anne told me to walk the plank!

'Steve,' Anne said with a gleeful look in her eye.

'Hello, Anne, how are you?' I replied to Anne with a big cheeky grin on my face.

'It doesn't matter that you're not gonna win, does it?' Anne responded.

'No, not really, I just came here to have a laugh and all that, you know,' I said.

'Yeah, and as long as you can remember where you buried your treasure, really,' Anne joked.

'I thought you might say something about that,' I answered as I started feeling nervous of what her next question was going to be.

'Yes,' Anne returned.

'And I was gonna say, I think you need to do a collaboration with me on my Pirate Steve Show channel and call it the Pirate Steve and Anne Robinson Crusoe Show,' I suggested.

'OK, and what do you do on it?' Anne quizzed me.

'Something called Happy News, and I do a bit of entertaining,' I said as I was starting to get apprehensive.

'Well, do me some entertaining,' replied Anne as she looked intrigued as to what I was going to do next.

'Can I put my board down, please?' I politely asked.

'OK,' Anne answered with a look of concern on her face.

'Awesome, welcome to the Pirate Steve Show. This week we've gate-crashed *The Weakest Link*, and we've got Anne Robinson here; how cool is that? Now let's see if we can get Anne Robinson on our show this week, and, Anne, are you up for some crazy dancing?' I said, trying to get Anne up for doing a little jig with me on *The Weakest Link* studio floor.

'Have you started the entertaining bit yet?' Anne replied, looking disappointed.

'No, not yet no,' I said, feeling dejected.

'Ah OK, and when you're not doing that and looking like Johnny Depp, how do you earn a living?' Anne asked me in a condescending, jokey way.

'Carpet cleaning,' I responded, knowing my time was coming to an end.

'Do you?' Anne said in astonishment.

'Yeah,' I replied.

'In that outfit?' Anne questioned.

'Yeah,' I answered with a nervous smile on my face.

'How terrifying,' Anne said in bewilderment.

'I say, the old ladies love it, though,' I responded in my defence.

'Just put your board up. Steve; you are the weakest link. Goodbye,' replied Anne as she went back into character playing the Queen of Mean. And guess what: as I walked off the set, I said what I had planned on saying when I first thought about appearing on a television game show. Yeah, I said, 'Yo-ho-ho and a bottle of rum.' So, I accomplished one of my goals I had set out to achieve. When I was interviewed afterwards, here is what I had to say about meeting Anne Robinson on *The Weakest Link*:

> When Anne was chatting with me, I got the impression that she thought that I was a bit of an oddun. I'm not sure why because I think I'm quite normal, to be honest, compared to a lot of other people.

> Steven M. Rippin, 6 October 2010

Looking back, I cringe at how I acted on *The Weakest Link*. I have changed so much since then. I think I entertained quite a few of my family and friends who watched me on the show, though, plus I had an excellent conversation with Anne Robinson and even managed to make her smile. Oh yeah, I did try advertising my YouTube channel while I was chatting to Anne. Unfortunately, though, the production team edited out the word YouTube when I mentioned it, so nobody knew where to find my channel. Which I guess is a blessing to the people of Great Britain, although it was the foremost reason why I wanted to go on the show in the first place. Overall, I had a fantastic experience, and my parents were proud of me, well, I think they were, and I hope I didn't embarrass them too much. If you would like to watch my appearance on *The Weakest Link*, here is a link to the time when I embarrassed myself in front of the nation: bit.ly/ PirateSteveIsTheWeakestLink

A year after I appeared on *The Weakest Link*, I had a phone call from the production team, which surprised me, and they asked me if I would like to be a contestant on the show again! I thought, was this a joke? Had they not thought I'd humiliated myself enough already? Well, to cut a long story short, that's what they must have thought. You see they were putting together a collection of one-off specials of the show, and the special they wanted me to appear on was when contestants gave the silliest answers!

I felt honoured they had thought of me even though it was because of my lack of general knowledge and dim-wittedness. I was astonished they would even let me back on the set of *The Weakest Link* ever again!

Unfortunately, I was suffering severely with my arthritis, which had flared up in my knees, and my grandad, bless him, had recently passed away when they asked me. So, it was a tough decision whether or not I should appear on the show again. I discussed it with my parents, and they said I should go back on because it would have been something my grandad would have wanted me to have done, and something he would have been so proud of me for doing as well. So, on 6 December 2011 I was flown up to the BBC Glasgow studios.

While the episode was being filmed, the runners asked me if I wanted a chair to sit down on in between the questions being asked by Anne because they knew I was struggling considerably with my arthritis; luckily, I was all right and didn't need one. So, there I was for the second time on the set of *The Weakest Link*, and I thought, 'It won't be as bad as last time, when I was voted off in the second round. Surely I'll make it further this time and not embarrass myself again!' My second appearance on *The Weakest Link* aired on Wednesday, 28 March 2012, on BBC Two at 2.15 pm. And now here are the questions and the conversation I had with Anne Robinson this time around, all for your amusement of course.

# THE EMBARRASSING CONTESTANTS EDITION OF *THE WEAKEST LINK*

'Steve, in geography, which city is the capital of the United Kingdom?' Anne's first question was to me.

'England?' I replied with a look of confusion on my face at what I had just said.

'London. Steve, in chemistry, a thin cylindrical glass vessel opened at one end and often used in experiments, is called test what?' Anne proceeded, after looking shocked at my previous answer.

'Tube?' I said straight away, feeling relieved to have been asked another easy question to make up for my dim-wittedness from earlier on in the round.

'Correct. Steve, in cinema, the 1981 adventure *The Raiders of the Lost Ark* was the first film to feature which fictional hero played by Harrison Ford?' Anne asked.

'Indiana Jones?' I replied, thinking I was on a roll now.

'Correct,' responded Anne.

So, at the end of the first round, the votes were in, and I was voted the weakest link! Charlie and Betty, two of the contestants on the show, said, 'I think Steve was the only one to get a question wrong.' While Sarah, another one of the contestants, said, 'I think he jumped the gun a little bit and didn't listen to the question, so we had to vote him.' As soon as I heard what they had to say, I knew I was going to be walking the plank for a second time!

'So, Steve from Leicestershire,' Anne said.

'How you doing, Anne?' I replied.

'So, when you're in Leicestershire, and you're out and about, and you pass a woman who you know, what do you do?' asked Anne.

'I'll bow and curtesy in a pirate style and say, "Ahoy there, m'hearty."' I jokingly responded.

'That will explain why you couldn't answer the question last time,' replied Anne.

'Well, yeah, you know I was getting a bit confused there,' I said. Then after our conversation, Anne played the clip of my first appearance on *The Weakest Link*, then, when the clip ended, Anne and I started chatting again!

'I always get things a bit muggled up, you know,' I said.

'A bit muggled up,' Anne replied.

'Yeah,' I responded with a look of sympathy on my face.

'Steve, you arrr the weakest link. Goodbye,' Anne said and, just like that, my time on *The Weakest Link* was over. Unfortunately, as you have just learnt, I was voted off in the first round this time! How embarrassing! And what made it worse was that I was going to have to face my family and friends again just as everything was settling down from the first time I'd appeared on the show, when I got voted off in the second round! Here in my defence, though, is what I had to say after Anne gave me the old heave-ho off her show.

Well, the last time I was on The Weakest Link I was voted off in the second round, but I beat my record this year and got voted off in the first round, and I'm really proud of that.

Steven M. Rippin, 28 March 2012

Can you believe I still have people mention my brief appearances on *The Weakest Link*? I must have made quite an impression back then. If you're interested in watching me make a fool of myself for a second time, here is a link to my final appearance on the legendary television show which was *The Weakest Link*: bit.ly/PiratesteveIsTheWeakestLinkAgain

Q: Hi Steve, I wanted to ask you, I know you were on the Weakest

Link gameshow, may I ask, have you done any acting on stage, tv or film before? Does it interest you?

Jonathan R. Holeton, Edmonton, Alberta, Canada

A: Hey, Jonathan, great question. No, I've never done any acting, stage, TV or film work in my life. What I would love to have, though, is my own internet television show, which would feature special guests, comedy sketches, local bands, words of wisdom, facts on the Universe and extra-terrestrials, and a section dedicated to the music I love. Thank you so much for your question, Jonathan.

Steven M. Rippin

If you want to challenge yourself and step out of your comfort zone, I would highly recommend auditioning for a television game show. It will unquestionably help boost your confidence, self-esteem and any insecurities you might have about yourself. I had a fantastic time on *The Weakest Link*, and I will never forget meeting the Queen of Mean, Anne Robinson. Don't think about entering a television game show; just DO IT! What have you got to lose? Live your life outside the boundaries of your normal existence. And, finally, here is what my dad thought about me appearing on *The Weakest Link*.

I was surprised and proud because it was something I wouldn't do, and to go on twice was amazing. I knew you didn't go on there to win; you went on it to have some fun.

George W. Rippin, Market Harborough, England

# THE CNN DEBATE ON CLIMATE CHANGE TV SHOW

On 15 December 2009, I made a video for the CNN/YouTube Debate on Climate Change, which was being held live from Copenhagen. The video I made was for a competition so people from all over the planet could make their voices heard and tell the leaders of the world what they thought needed to be done to help save Earth from our carbon footprints. So, I thought I would get my message out there into the world and see if anybody noticed what I have to say. I doubted anybody would; you never know until you try, though, do you? So, I set to work on this new challenge I had set myself, and I made a poem expressing how I felt and do feel about climate change in my own unique way.

Once I had created my video entry, I submitted it to the CNN Debate on Climate Change channel on YouTube, then forgot all about it. That was until one day when a friend of mine on YouTube told me he had seen my video on TV! I thought, 'What's he going on about?' So, I continued reading his message, and I learnt he had seen my climate change video on the CNN news channel, where the Debate on Climate Change television program was taking place with Becky Anderson, who was the presenter of the show! I couldn't believe it!

So, I looked up how I could watch a repeat of the show, and – lo and behold! – it was on TV that evening; CNN repeated the Debate on Climate Change every night for a week at 7 pm, you see. Then I tuned into CNN and ran into the kitchen, where my parents were and told them I was on the television! They both looked at me and said, 'Are you serious? What have you been up to now?' So, they followed me into the lounge and there

I was talking about climate change on CNN news! It was surreal seeing my ugly mug on TV! There were thousands of video entries from people all around the globe who had entered the competition, so that made me realise how lucky I had been to have my climate change video chosen to be aired on their show. It felt in a small way that I was representing England on climate change as my video was the only one they featured from the United Kingdom. So, you can now call me, Pirate Steve, the Climate Change representative for England. Only joking. And here is how Becky Anderson introduced me on the CNN Debate on Climate Change television show. 'A question from Pirate Steve; now, you will not want to miss this, I promise you.' Then the show cut to a commercial break. When the show returned, Becky Anderson continued with, 'Our next video comes from Pirate Steve in the UK and brace yourselves for this.' Now for your entertainment, here is a video link to my appearance on the CNN Debate on Climate Change, followed by my message and poem: bit.ly/ PiratesteveCNNDebateOnClimateChange

# PIRATE STEVE'S CLIMATE CHANGE SPEECH AND POEM

Hi, I'm Steve from the UK and here's my video about climate change and how we can all help – and hopefully get a message across to the big government official world leader people and see what they have to say about it all. Because they're the ones flying around everywhere leaving their carbon footprints. What's all that about? Why don't they just use the internet? It'd be a lot safer and cheaper way to travel. And they wouldn't be spending all of our taxpayer's money flying around all over the place, would they? I hope you enjoy the video.

Does climate change affect you or me? Polar ice caps melting and the rising of the sea, I don't want the next generation to see the earth die, and to look up in the air and see no birds fly. Leaders of the world listen to what I have to say, you drive around in your fancy cars and go flying everywhere, leaving your carbon footprints high up in the air. It's one rule for you and one rule for us. You should practise what you preach and stop annoying all of us.

This is what it's all about, saving the environment and everything. Look at this awesome tree, the birds in the air, the fishes in the sea. All together, 1, 2, 3, I don't know I'm just trying to make it rhyme, but it didn't really work, but yeah, together we can beat climate change, peace, love, unity and respect.

As you can tell, after reading my poem, I am just as shocked as you are that CNN decided to choose my video to air on their major television network! Anyway, after my climate change video had finished, Becky Anderson said, 'Brilliantly done ha-ha, well, creative; some might say, a little odd. Of course, he has got a point though: the idea of the CNN YouTube debate was to give people a voice, and there are millions of people around the world who feel disenfranchised and, to borrow his line, how do we make this real?'

Then Becky Anderson spoke to the panel who discuss all the key points about making changes to the environment. Throughout the show, there were video messages from Desmond Tutu, who's one of South Africa's most well-known human rights activists and won the 1984 Nobel Peace Prize for his efforts in resolving and ending apartheid. He also became the first black Anglican archbishop of Cape Town and Johannesburg; Jet Lee, who's a Chinese film actor, film producer, martial artist and retired Wushu champion; and Kofi Annan, who served as the seventh secretary-general of the United Nations from January 1997 to December 2006. Kofi Annan and the U.N were also the co-recipients of the 2001 Nobel Peace Prize. Now here are who each of the climate change representatives were on the panel.

Representative number one was Yvo de Boer, who was the former executive secretary of the United Nations Framework Convention on Climate Change, which was a position he held from 2006 until 2010.

Representative number two was Daryl Hannah, who is an American film actress and famous for her roles in *The Fury*, *Blade Runner*, *Splash*, *Roxanne*, *Steel Magnolias* and *Kill Bill* volumes one and two, along with being an environmental activist as well.

Representative number three was Thomas Friedman, who is an American journalist, author and three-time Pulitzer Prize winner and who also wrote the book *Hot, Flat, and Crowded*. Thomas Friedman also has a foreign affairs column which is syndicated to one hundred newspapers worldwide.

And representative number four was Bjorn Lomborg, who is a Danish author, a visiting professor at the Copenhagen Business School and a director at the Copenhagen Consensus Centre.

So, I have no idea what those professional representatives for climate change must have thought to themselves after they had watched my climate change video, especially when they saw me dressed up as one of my eccentric YouTube characters, the Cyber Goth Kid! The best part about watching myself on the CNN Debate on Climate Change was observing the reactions of the panel of representatives and audience members after my video had finished playing because, when the cameraman panned onto them, I am happy to say they were laughing, clapping and smiling away. I wonder what they were genuinely thinking, though. I cringe at how corny I must have come across in my Debate on Climate Change video.

I can honestly say I never in my life thought I would be featured on the same television show as such renowned and famous influential people as Desmond Tutu, Jet Lee, Kofi Annan, Yvo de Boer, Daryl Hannah, Thomas Friedman and Bjorn Lomborg. I feel very honoured to have made it onto the CNN Debate on Climate Change TV show, where I was allowed to voice my opinions on how I feel about the environment.

Together we can help save the future of our existence here on planet Earth for the future generations of tomorrow.

# FAMILY, FRIENDSHIPS AND ADVENTURES IN PIGEON FORGE

Tennessee holds a special place inside my dad's and my hearts, so it's only right I dedicate this next subchapter to those fond memories we made together when we visited Pigeon Forge in Tennessee. I will also be mentioning a few of the outstanding people we had the privilege of meeting while we were over there who made a significant impact on our lives as well. So, where do I even begin to explain my adoration for Tennessee? Well, I guess the best place to start is the Great Smoky Mountains themselves. When I first witnessed the beauty of the Great Smoky Mountains, I was blown away by the phenomenal scenery and the blue mist you can see on top of them. It truly was a magical experience to behold. Then there was the southern hospitality my dad and I received from the local Tennesseans who we met, which was unbelievable! And, of course, not forgetting the legendary and awesome country music, which if I'm honest I never thought I would enjoy all that much, especially as I'm into Frenchcore, hardstyle, progressive house/trance, drum 'n' bass and happy hardcore!

> Pigeon Forge got its name by combining two popular characteristics of the area. The first is the passenger pigeons that once called the city home. Although they are now extinct; the pigeons were very predominant during the time of the early settlers. The second part of the city's name comes from the old iron forge that was located along the Little Pigeon River.

> Taken from bit.ly/visitmysmokies

Since my dad introduced me to country music, I am now, I'm proud to say, a huge fan of Dolly Parton, and one song I love listening to that takes me back to my time in Pigeon Forge with my dad, is 'Sha-Kon-A-Hey'. WOW, what a fantastic song that is! And I would highly recommend listening to the album *Sha-Kon-A-Hey* as well. All the songs on the *Sha-Kon-A-Hey* album pull on my heartstrings; if I'm honest, they bring a lump to my throat and a tear to my eye as well.

My dad's dad was a country music fan, and if you love your country music, then Tennessee is the place for you.

When I'm listening to certain songs at home, they will take me back to Pigeon Forge, and I will think of those unforgettable memories and experiences I shared with my dad while I was over there; they will be memories I will treasure forever. It was my dad's brother, my uncle Paul, who introduced my dad and me to Pigeon Forge many years ago. Uncle Paul, you see, suggested to my dad that we should take a trip over there because he knew we would love it. So, we took him up on his advice and travelled over to Pigeon Forge in 2009, and he was right: we loved it there.

When my dad and I arrived in Pigeon Forge for the first time, it felt like we were stepping back in time, and I say this because it gave us both a very nostalgic feeling. I will always remember when we drove down the Parkway because, off in the far distance, we could see the Great Smoky Mountains partially hidden away by the blue mist which was hanging over them. It was an incredible sight to behold and will always be my first ever true memory of Pigeon Forge.

Whenever my dad and I get a chance to travel to Pigeon Forge, we always visit the Great Smoky Mountain National Park along with the Great Smoky Mountain Wheel at the Island in Pigeon Forge, where there are loads of excellent places to eat and shops to explore; the wood carvings and rustic furniture you will come across in the shops there are spectacular. My dad and I love looking around those stores; they certainly aren't the kind of sculptures and home furnishings you would find in shops here in England. And one restaurant we fell in love with was Paula Deen's Family Kitchen; the food there was superb, and another reason why my dad and I want to go back to Pigeon Forge so badly.

Tennessee is a beautiful and homely state to visit where everybody makes you feel welcomed.

The shop assistants in Pigeon Forge are remarkably friendly, and, to give you an example, when my dad and I went into a store called Boot Junkies in 2016, we had the pleasure of being served by a guy named Kenny Forbes, who was a genuinely friendly guy. Furthermore, he made my dad and me feel very welcome. We got to know Kenny pretty well, and he told us he was getting married to his fiancée, Heather, who he's now married. We also got to meet Kenny's mum, who told my dad and me some great stories from her past while she was growing up in and around the Pigeon Forge area; it was lovely getting to meet Kenny's mum. So, there is just one example of the Southern hospitality you can expect to receive when you meet the locals of Pigeon Forge. People are so open and friendly over there.

A few theatre shows and attractions my dad and I love going to when we visit Pigeon Forge are the Country Music Tonight Show, the Tennessee Shindig, which unfortunately has now closed, the Smoky Mountain Opry, the Comedy Barn, Professor Hacker's Lost Treasure Golf, the Castle of Chaos, Outbreak Dread the Undead, the Hollywood Wax Museum, Dolly Parton's Lumberjack Adventure Dinner and Show, the Hatfield and McCoy Dinner and Show, and the Dixie Stampede Dinner and Show, which you will love if you adore horses. And one show I hope to watch one day is the Pirate's Revenge Dinner and Show.

Lastly, a show my dad and I thoroughly enjoyed watching on our first visit to Pigeon Forge was the Wonders of Magic. And after the show, we had the privilege of meeting Terry Evanswood, who is an incredibly talented and professional magician, along with his beautiful assistant Jessica Jane Peterson. Terry Evanswood was an amiable guy, and he very much appreciated my dad and me going to his show. So, if you ever get the chance, go and check the Wonders of Magic Show out in Pigeon Forge, Tennessee. You won't be disappointed: Terry Evanswood is one of the longest-running headliners in Pigeon Forge. And the International Magicians Society presented Terry with the Merlin Award one year, which is the equivalent of an Oscar.

The majority of young people in Pigeon Forge, Gatlinburg and Sevierville will call you sir/ma'am, open doors for you and even give up their seats when you're out on public transport, which was great to see and experience. Witnessing how the younger generation treated people in Pigeon Forge made me think, 'Wouldn't it be good if everybody in society acted this way? It would undoubtedly make people of all ages feel a lot safer when they are out in public.' What struck me the most about Tennessee and the people my dad I met was how friendly and courteous the younger generation was. And here is an example to show you what I mean.

One night my dad and I went to watch a group called the Drifters at the Memories theatre along the Parkway in Pigeon Forge. And, once we had sat down in the auditorium, my dad started fidgeting around in his seat. I thought, 'Does he need to go for a pee?' then he turned around and said, 'Steve, I've lost my wallet. I can't find it anywhere; it had all my money in it.' So, quickly, we started looking for my dad's wallet. We looked on the floor and underneath our seats, but we couldn't find it anywhere. Then my dad started panicking and said, 'I'm going to take a look in the lobby for it, Steve. It might have dropped out of my pocket.'

And when my dad stood up, he felt a tap on his shoulder from the guy sitting behind us, and this guy said to my dad, 'Excuse me, sir, is this your wallet?'

'Yes, it is thank you so much, where did you find it?' my dad asked.

'You dropped it in the lobby. I saw it picked it up and went to give it back to you, but you had already come to sit down in here,' the young guy said.

Then my dad replied, 'I can't thank you enough, here take this,' and my dad went to offer him $20, but the young guy wouldn't take it.

'No, I don't want anything, sir. Thank you anyway.'

My dad and I then got chatting with this young guy and his friends, who must have been in their early twenties, and my dad said, 'You guys could have kept my wallet, and I would have never known.' And one of the young guys said that wasn't how they had been raised. They had been brought up to show respect, honesty and courtesy to their elders. I have got so much reverence for people who go out of their way to help other people when they can. It is also refreshing to know there are young people like those my dad and I met, out there in the world today, isn't it, because not everybody would have returned my dad's wallet, would they?

I always felt so happy when I was travelling to Pigeon Forge sitting next to my dad on the aeroplane listening to my music; I was going back to the place I called home. Pigeon Forge, Gatlinburg, the Great Smoky Mountains, Sevierville, Cade's Cove, the Inn at Christmas Place and of course not forgetting Dollywood: I love you all. Well, without further ado, now follows some of the fun times my dad and I had while we were in Pigeon Forge, starting with the award-winning Family Comedy Variety Show, the Comedy Barn.

# THE COMEDY BARN

The Comedy Barn Show has been running for over twenty-five years, and it was in September 2009 when my dad and I went along to see what it was all about. I can truthfully tell you, we loved every second of it. Just as soon as the show started, my dad and I were mesmerised until the very end; we had never experienced a show quite like it in our lives!

Winner Funniest Show! Come see why year after year The Comedy Barn® Theatre is voted the most award-winning family comedy variety show in the Smoky Mountains. Featuring magicians, jugglers, ventriloquists, comedians, live country and gospel music! It's a night of a thousand laughs – guaranteed! Bring the kids and your granny for a night of entertainment EVERYONE will love! Showtimes are 5 pm and 8:15 pm nightly.

**Taken from the Comedy Barn website, www.comedybarn.com**

The Comedy Barn is a refreshing family show you can enjoy watching where you don't have to put up with those double entendre comedians you often see on TV today coming out with lewd jokes.

When my dad booked tickets for our first ever Comedy Barn experience, we were served by Tiffany Blackmon Schmedding, and my dad said to Tiffany, 'Hi, is this where we can book tickets for tonight's show?'

'Yes, it is, sir. How many tickets would you like and what name shall I put you under?' Tiffany said.

'We'd like two tickets please, and the name's Jack Sparrow,' my dad answered. Tiffany then looked at my dad and me and burst out laughing, as did the rest of the staff working there that day did as well. I have no idea what they were laughing about; anybody would think they had just seen a pirate! You should have seen the staff, though: they were belly aching with laughter, including my dad and me; we even had tears coming down our faces, so we knew we were going to be in for a treat that night.

During the show that evening which my dad and I attended, the host, Clyde Foley Cummins, announced to the audience, 'We have some special guests in tonight all the way from England. We have Captain Jack Sparrow and Crocodile Dundee.' Then the auditorium spotlights shone down on my dad and me and the audience erupted into applause and laughter, even more so when I stood up and started waving at them, while my dad sank lower and lower into his seat. After the commotion had calmed down, my dad said, 'Just wait until I see Tiffany later.'

I must have charmed Tiffany somehow with my magical piratey charm because we ended up exchanging contact details and met up for a meal and went to a show together in Gatlinburg. It wasn't a date, though. Come on: me going on a date? There's more chance of seeing a cow fly over the moon. And, of course, my dad was on this non-date with Tiffany and me. I wasn't going to abandon my poor dad, now, was I? On this non-date, we all went to an impressive Blues Brothers-themed diner which was next door to the Comedy Barn. And I have to say, when my dad's banana split came out it was quite simply beyond belief, a bit like Terry Evanswood's magic show! The servings of food you get in America are something you have to see to believe. I have no idea what Americans must think when they eat in our restaurants here in England because they wouldn't get half as much food as they would in their own country. After our meal, Tiffany, my dad and I headed over to Gatlinburg to the Sweet Fanny Adams Theatre, which has a very majestic feel about it; I felt like I was stepping into the 1920s. That night the Sweet Fanny Adams Theatre had a production on called *The King with the Terrible Temper*. We had no idea what to expect, and yet again we weren't disappointed. The show was fantastic and highly entertaining, well, that was until the performers on stage asked for three volunteers from the audience. And yeah, you guessed it, I was one of those unfortunate volunteers who got picked out, all because my dad and Tiffany were pointing at me continuously!

So off I went and joined the cast of the show on stage, wondering what kind of predicament I was going to end up getting myself into. After the leading actor explained to the other two guys who had also been picked out of the audience what they were going to be doing, he then came over to me. I thought, 'It's not going to be too bad. I'll probably get given a sword or something because I look like a pirate.' Well, I wasn't given a sword; I was given a pink dress to wear with a frilly pink hat! And let me tell you something else: the dress I had to wear had padded-out bosoms to go with it! I looked a right state!

So, there I was facing the audience feeling like a right plonker with my pink bosoms sticking out! And all I could think was, 'Why on earth have they dressed me up like this?' Then the two guys out of the audience and I were told by the leading actor that we were to play the parts of the king's daughters while he played the role of the king. The leading actor then told me I was the king's fat daughter, and when he would say, 'My fat daughter,' that was my cue to stand up and give an almighty growl to the audience! It was great fun; well, it was for the audience. I'm always up for a good laugh, though, and I can quite happily say I played my part terribly. Hey, after all, it was called *The King with the Terrible Temper*! Sorry, that was my feeble attempt at a joke there. I think my dad and Tiffany thoroughly enjoyed watching me make a spectacle of myself. And, if you fancy having a good laugh as well, here are the video links of my terrible performance on stage that night at the Sweet Fanny Adams Theatre in Gatlinburg.

bit.ly/TheKingsTerribleTemper1
bit.ly/TheKingsTerribleTemper2
bit.ly/TheKingsTerribleTemper3
bit.ly/TheKingsTerribleTemper4

Tiffany and I got on really well and have stayed good friends on social media since meeting all those years ago. Tiffany is now happily married and has a very lovely family.

It was a pleasure meeting you, Tiffany. All my best to you and your family.

Steven M. Rippin

The staff/cast members are all genuinely lovely people who work at the Comedy Barn. For example, when they get some free time they will visit the surrounding areas of Pigeon Forge, Gatlinburg and Sevierville, helping their regular customers out by either gardening or doing household chores for them, such as cutting lawns, weeding flower beds or doing a weekly shop. Now that's what you call Southern hospitality, isn't it? It truly touches my heart that the Comedy Barn cast members devote their spare time in helping others out in their local community in this way. What a beautiful place the world would be if more people loved their neighbours as those guys do.

In December 2016 my dad and I got to meet Stephen Knowles, Eric Lambert and Greg Franklin, who perform at the Comedy Barn. These three guys are absolute legends and amicable people. Every time my dad and I have been to the Comedy Barn, Stephen Knowles, who is an outstanding ventriloquist, always has time for a chat, and shares his captivating stories with us, which we love. Stephen makes my dad and me feel incredibly welcome when we visit the Comedy Barn.

Thank you, Stephen, for all the stories and laughs. You, sir, are a true legend. You rock, mate.

Steven M. Rippin

Eric Lambert, who I have also had the pleasure of meeting, got me on stage during one of his performances one night, which was quite an entertaining experience. And if you are interested in seeing me make a fool of myself while Eric had me doing a funny little dance, here is a video link to my mischievous shenanigans: bit.ly/PirateSteveAtTheComedyBarn

Also here is part of the conversation Eric and I had while I was on stage with him back in December 2016.

'Oh, man, good to have you here, brother. What's your name?' Eric asked me.

'Steve,' I said.

'Steve, where are you from?' asked Eric.

'The UK,' I replied.

'What?' responded Eric.

'The UK, England,' I answered.

'Oh, the UK, England, no kidding?' Eric stated in surprise.

'Yeah,' I confirmed.

'Is that how they're dressing there now?' Eric asked me as he looked me up and down.

'Yeah,' I said.

'No kidding? What part of England are you from, brother?' Eric asked me with intrigue.

'Leicester,' I told him.

'Leicester. Has anybody ever been there that didn't come here with him?' Eric asked the audience. And only one person answered and shouted, 'Yeah,' which was my dad, and I yelled out, 'Leicester.'

Then Eric asked me, 'What do you do for a living, my friend?'

'I'm a carpet cleaner,' I told him.

'You're a carpet cleaner?' Eric said in astonishment.

'I scrub the deck,' I answered.

'No kidding?' Eric replied, with his eyes nearly popping out of his head.

'Yeah, no, honestly,' I said.

'Yeah, you're kidding?' Eric asked me.

'Yeah,' I told him as I was getting confused!

'No?' Eric responded.

'Yeah,' I finally managed to get out.

'You're a carpet cleaner? Because you look at you right away and think, you know, carpet cleaner!' Eric said, still looking shocked.

'Yeah, I know,' I answered with a smile on my face.

Eric then started laughing. 'How long you been here in the country?' he asked me.

'About ten days,' I told him.

'About ten days, no kidding?' Eric replied yet again with a look of wonderment on his face.

'No, yeah honestly yeah,' I blurted out.

'We look a little different here, don't we?' Eric informed me.

'I need some of those dungarees,' I said as I pointed to Eric's country-style clothing he was wearing.

'Dungarees, dungarees, ha-ha we call them overalls,' Eric stated.

'Oh, sorry, boy,' I replied.

'We call this Captain Jack Sparrow. Whole different terms what we got here. Have you ever been on stage before, my friend?' Eric asked me.

'Err, no, well,' I answered as my brain was going into meltdown.

'That is a horrible waste, sir, you are going to be perfect for this. Thank you for coming. Stand right here; we'll get to you in just a second.' Then Eric started telling the audience the Comedy Barn story, which featured two other members of the public and me. It was a memorable experience meeting Eric Lambert and one I will never forget. And I am sure the audience was wondering who this strange English pirate was from jolly old England! The main thing, though, was that the audience was laughing away while Eric was interviewing me, so I took that as a good sign they liked me.

> Thank you so much for getting me on stage Eric; I loved that chat we had together. All my best to you and your family.

> Steven M. Rippin

And, lastly, Greg Franklin, who plays the highly entertaining Farmer Klemm, told me after the show had finished that I should look into working in Pigeon Forge because the locals would love my pirate get-up over there, which I appreciated him saying very much.

> Thank you for your encouragement and kind words, Greg. Keep on being the phenomenal Farmer Klemm everybody in Pigeon Forge loves and holds close to their hearts. All my best to you and your family.

> Steven M. Rippin

To keep up-to-date with the crazy shenanigans that go on at the Comedy Barn here is a link to their Instagram account: instagram.com/thecomedybarn

> Thank you to everyone who works and has worked at The Comedy Barn Theatre for making my dad and I feel so welcome over the years; until next time.

> Steven M. Rippin

# DOLLYWOOD

When my dad and I visited Pigeon Forge for the first time in 2009, we heard Dolly Parton had a theme park there called Dollywood, which we couldn't wait to visit; we fell in love with the place from the moment we got there.

> Dollywood has captured the essence of the Great Smoky Mountains magnificently within the park while also delivering an enchanting atmosphere and rustic feel to all who visit her.

Now, this might sound like a promotional advert for Dollywood, but it's the best way I can describe the theme park to you.

If you ever find yourself in and around the Pigeon Forge area and want to be entertained, then Dollywood is the theme park for you. With their heartwarming shows on throughout the day and family-friendly festivals, which are on all year round, you can't go wrong. And if you fancy doing a spot of shopping, then you can visit the local trade stalls, which sell impressive crafts in the workshop district, ranging from wooden rocking chairs to rustic beds. Also, while you're there, you can visit the breathtaking eagle sanctuary and get a bite to eat in one of the authentic restaurants. And if you're a thrillseeker, you won't be disappointed either, because there are plenty of rides and attractions to check out as well. Oh yeah, and get this: Dollywood has the world's fastest wooden rollercoaster ride, which reaches speeds of up to 73 mph. So, what are you waiting for? Get yourself to Dollywood.

One of the most memorable days my dad and I spent at Dollywood was with our good friend Brittney McMahan. My dad and I first met

Brittney in September 2009 while we were having a meal in the Pear and Partridge restaurant, where she used to work. Because we got on so well with Brittney while she was serving us, we decided to meet up and have a day out at Dollywood with her, where we all had an excellent time. My dad was cracking jokes every five minutes and making Brittney and me laugh so much that day. Then Brittney, bless her, got a wet patch on her jeans from one of the rides we went on. So while Brittney was trying to dry herself off with one of those large drying machines at Dollywood, I asked my dad to film me while I interviewed her for one of my video diary vlogs I was making on our trip to Pigeon Forge, which you can view on the following link: http://bit.ly/BrittneyDryingOffAtDollywood

Brittney, you were a fantastic sport that day. Thank you so much for putting up with our mischievous antics back then.

Steven M. Rippin

After leaving Dollywood, we finished the day off by meeting up with Brittney's mum, Deanna, who was lovely. We then went for pizza and ended our unforgettable day out by going to the Comedy Barn. Then it was time to say our goodbyes, which were very emotional, if I'm honest, because we didn't want the day to end. I have a lot of respect for Brittney McMahan and her family, and I will treasure those memories my dad and I shared that day with her and her mother forever. Brittney is now happily married, and I wish her and her husband all the joy in the world.

Thank you for the good times we shared Brittney and Deanna. Much love to you both and your families.

Steven M. Rippin

While my dad and I were walking around Dollywood in 2009, we were surprised to see members of Dolly Parton's family performing on one of the outdoor stages, which was a real treat and privilege. That day we saw Dolly Parton's Uncle Bill Owens performing, along with cousins Debi-Jo Hess and Dwight Puckett. And here for your musical pleasure is a video I took of them on stage: bit.ly/UncleBillPerformingAtDollywood

After the show, my dad and I had a brief chat with Debi-Jo and Dwight, and they genuinely appreciated that we had flown over from England to visit Dollywood. What got me, though, was how friendly they were. I could tell they meant every word they said to my dad and me that day.

After we had said our goodbyes to Debi-Jo Hess and Dwight Puckett, we saw a small tree that had recently been planted beside the side of the stage, which also had a small plaque next to it, so we went over to take a look, and as we were doing so we had the pleasure and honour of meeting Dolly Parton's uncle, Bill Owens, who appeared from behind the stage, so my dad and I asked him what the newly planted tree was all in aid of. And Bill Owens told us that a week earlier Dolly Parton had given a special presentation and ceremony regarding the excellent work he himself had done over the past thirty years to preserve the American chestnut tree. If only my dad and I had been at Dollywood a week earlier, we might have had the opportunity of meeting Dolly herself.

Bill Owens was an exceptionally down to earth and genuine guy; he explained to my dad and me that for over thirty years he has been part of the TACF – The American Chestnut Foundation – to help preserve the American chestnut tree, which also helps the community where he lives, especially the Appalachian Mountain families, who depend heavily on the American chestnut tree for food and shelter. Bill Owens and his wife Sandy also have an orchard of American chestnut trees, which they look after at the Dollywood theme park, where he has made it his mission in life to help continue research into the breeding of these trees.

When the American chestnut tree blight struck in the 1900s, it left nearly nine million acres of forest land empty. The pathogenic fungus – *cryphonectria parasitica* – was the main cause of the devastating American chestnut tree disease.

Did you know that Bill Owens discovered Dolly Parton's singing talent while she was washing the dishes in the kitchen at their family home? No, neither did I. And, when Dolly Parton was only ten years old, Bill Owens took her to Knoxville to perform on *The Cas Walker Show*. Then in 2013, at a special presentation at Dollywood, Dolly Parton said to the crowd, 'I know a lot of people get a lot of credit for my career, but if it hadn't have been for you, Uncle Bill, I never would have gotten out of these hills.'

How lovely it was that Dolly Parton said that to her uncle back then. I will treasure those memories when my dad and I met a few members of Dolly Parton's family forever.

Thank you, Bill Owens, Debi-Jo Hess and Dwight Puckett for taking the time to talk to my dad and me when we met you. Much love and respect to you all and your families.

Steven M. Rippin

An excellent place where my dad and I ate when we were visiting Dollywood was Red's Diner in the Jukebox Junction district of the theme park. Red's Diner was originally called Red's Cafe and in 1946 was first located in Sevierville, where Dolly Parton grew up. Dolly's dad used to take her into Red's Diner for hamburgers. So, it is a fitting tribute to Paul (Red) Clevenger, the owner of Red's Cafe, that Red's Diner has its very own place in Dollywood. Oh, and here's a small fact: Red's Diner is named Red's because Paul Clevenger had red hair.

The staff at Red's Diner are some of the friendliest workers you will ever meet. They always have time for a chat when they see you if they're free, just like they did when my dad and I visited Red's Diner in 2009. And can you believe, when my dad and I went back to Dollywood in 2011, the staff remembered us both from the first time we had visited! I always remember my dad saying to me, 'Steve, those ladies behind the counter over there are waving at us.' And when I saw them waving a huge smile appeared on my face, then my dad and I went over to those waitresses and said, 'We can't believe you remember us; it's so good to see you again.'

'Aw, we remember you guys,' one of the waitresses replied. The staff at Red's Diner made our visit to Dollywood that extra bit special that day. So, remember Red's Diner if you ever get the chance to visit Dollywood and mention you know Pirate Steve from England. You never know; they might still remember me.

While my dad and I were in Tennessee, we had the privilege of watching Dolly Parton perform live at the Grand Ole Opry in Nashville for their eighty-fifth birthday celebrations. Unfortunately, though, my dad and I were upstairs and a long way from the front of the stage, so we decided to go downstairs to try and get closer, essentially because I was struggling to see any of the performances due to my eyesight. So there we were crouched down in the aisle so the security guards wouldn't spot us, then the next minute we knew a security guard tapped us both on the shoulder and instead of telling us to go and sit back down in our seats, he said, 'Follow me; you guys will get a much better view up here.' My dad and I couldn't believe it! So, in the end, we ended up right at the front of the stage, where we must have been only a few feet away from where Dolly Parton was performing! It was such a surreal experience. Now, here is a video of Dolly Parton singing 'Jolene', which I filmed at the Grand Ole Opry while my dad and I were crouched down in the aisle: http://bit.ly/DollyPartonJoleneOpry

When we went back to Dollywood in December 2016, my dad and I had the pleasure of meeting Dolly's niece, Jada Star Anderson, along with Barry Jobe and her cousin Dwight Puckett. We met Jada, Barry and Dwight after watching them perform in the phenomenal show *My People, My Music*, which celebrates Dolly Parton's family, who inspired her to achieve her dreams. Regular family members of *My People, My Music* include Dolly's brother, Randy Parton, her sister Cassie Parton, her cousins Debi-Jo Hess and Dwight Puckett and her nieces, Jada Star Anderson and Heidi Lou Parton, who all perform songs of the family's faith, heartfelt love of the Great Smoky Mountains and resolute belief in Dolly. Dolly Parton's family are also joined on stage by a band of extremely talented and professional musicians, who help make *My People, My Music* the huge success it is today. Now, here is the lovely message Jada Star Anderson kindly sent me when she heard my dad had been diagnosed with cancer on his tongue.

> Hey, sweet man :) I'm sorry to hear you and your dad are going through such a hard thing. I'm sending him love and light and healing, and I have other's praying for him as well, and for you. Please give him my love, and know, we all love you in Tennessee.

> **Jada Star Anderson, Tennessee, USA**
> **instagram.com/jadastarandbarryj**

Thank you so much for the beautiful message, Jada.

**Steven M. Rippin**

Because Jada had taken the time to get in touch with me about my dad, I sent her a personal video message on YouTube. It is quite a private video I sent because at the time I asked Jada if she could ask her auntie, Dolly Parton, if she would be able to send my dad a short message wishing him all the best while he was in hospital recovering after his cancer operation. Unfortunately, though, Jada wasn't able to get in touch with her auntie in time, which I could totally understand and I realise it was a massive ask. And here is a link to the video I made for Jada if you are interested in watching it: bit.ly/AMessageToThePartonFamily

My dad and I also met and had a chat with Barry Jobe, who is an amiable guy. I chatted to Barry about the love I have for the music he plays and how friendly the people of Tennessee are. Barry asked me if I was a musician, and I told him, 'I wish I were. I did try learning to play the guitar once, but I never had the co-ordination in my fingers to pick the chords up properly; I found my passion in creating videos instead.' Barry Jobe and Jada Star write and perform songs together over in the Great Smoky Mountains, and the style of music they both love writing and performing has been described as Sugarland meets Fleetwood Mac with a hint of the Civil War mixed in as well. And if you would like to check out Jada Star and Barry Jobe's music and notable album *Long Way Home*, here is a link to their website: bit.ly/JadaStarAndBarryJ

All the best with your music careers, Barry and Jada.

Steven M. Rippin

And, finally, my dad and I had the pleasure of meeting Dwight Puckett for a second time. Dwight told us some compelling stories about his past and being on the road touring. He has unquestionably had a fascinating and exciting life; I could have stayed and listened to Dwight talk for ages. Unfortunately, though, my dad and I needed the restroom, so we had to say our goodbyes and run faster than greased lightning to the toilets! I will never forget the time Dwight took out of his busy schedule to talk to my dad and me that day. I feel very honoured having met members of Dolly Parton's family, and I can honestly say they are one of the most graceful families you could ever meet.

Thank you, Dwight Puckett, Jada Star and Barry Jobe; you made our visit to Dollywood very special and memories my dad and I will treasure forever.

Steven M. Rippin

Dollywood to me means love, family, being there for one another, and showing your family, friends and people who you don't know how much you genuinely love and care about them. One family I admire and respect are the Kidd family, who my dad and I were lucky enough to meet when we were at Dollywood in 2016. It was quite a humorous way that we introduced ourselves to the Kidd family from what I remember. So picture, if you can, my dad and me standing as still as we could in the entrance to Santa's Grotto at Dollywood so the first thing anybody entering would see would be the two of us standing there like statues; we were both playing the mannequin challenge, you see, which my dad started first many years ago, by the way! So, as you can imagine, we got quite a few curious looks, then the Kidd family walked by us, who all stared at what we were doing and burst out laughing as they queued up to have their photos taken with Santa.

My dad and I then joined the queue to have our photos taken with Father Christmas as well, where we met up with the Kidd family, who we got on remarkably well with. The Kidd family told us they had driven down from Knoxville to visit Dollywood, which is something they do once a year at Christmas time as a family together. It was great seeing the strong family bond the Kidd family had and how respectable and courteous they were. If I ever had a family, I would want to raise one just like Jill Kidd and her husband have done. Jill's sons and daughters were exceptionally cool. Brady, one of Jill's sons, and I took loads of selfies together and got on awesomely. It was the respect and traditional family values the Kidd family had that I admired.

Love and respect to you, Jill, your husband, Hannah, Brady, Kara and Dean Kidd. It was a pleasure meeting you all.

Steven M. Rippin

Dollywood is a magical place to visit, and it's more than just a theme park; it's a place where you can make memories with your family and friends which will last you a lifetime; after all, that's what life's about isn't it, creating those special memories with the ones you love. Dolly Parton has shown me, if you come from nothing at all, you and I can still achieve great things in our lives. We just have to believe in ourselves, no matter how big or how small our dreams may be. My dad and I have never felt more at home than when we have been in the presence of all the lovely people we have had the privilege of meeting while we have been at Dollywood. Family is and always will be the key to your happiness. Dollywood, we love you.

# THE TENNESSEE SHINDIG

Come on down for a rootin'-tootin' good time. Well, I would if the Tennessee Shindig was still open; unfortunately, though, it has now closed down. The Tennessee Shindig was packed full of fun, laughter and amazing performances which would have you clapping, cheering and stomping your feet on the ground throughout the show. It was a fantastic atmosphere, and the energy from the performers was amazing.

One evening when my dad and I attended the Tennessee Shindig, which I believe was around 2011, the Blues Brothers tribute act was performing, and they got me on stage as one of their backing dancers! The Blues Brothers even got me doing a bit of singing as well, can you believe? They soon pulled the microphone away from me, though, to save the audience from my dulcet tones! Now I will leave it up to you to decide if I was any good or not with this video when I appeared live on stage at the Tennessee Shindig: bit.ly/PirateSteveAndTheBluesBrothers

I still wonder to this day if it was because of my terrible singing and dancing skills that the Tennessee Shindig had to close! When the half time interval came, a lot of the audience members came up to my dad and me and said, 'You were great on stage; well done.' And somebody else said, 'Ah, that was staged, you're part of the show, aren't you?' I told them I wasn't, and I couldn't believe they thought I was even good enough to be classed as one of the professional performers. What a compliment, though. Oh, and they never did believe I wasn't part of the show, you know! The Tennessee Shindig is a show I really miss when I visit Pigeon Forge. Now I would like to dedicate the following pages to a beautiful soul who has been taken away from us far too soon.

# A SPECIAL DEDICATION TO AN EXCEPTIONAL LADY, ARTIST AND PROFESSIONAL PERFORMER WHO TOUCHED MANY LIVES

In memory of
Stacey Annette Morgan
24/07/1972–18/12/2018

It is with a very heavy heart I write this. Stacey Annette Morgan – Stacey Rivera – who to me was the essence of what made the Tennessee Shindig the show that it was and who I became good friends with, sadly passed away on 18 December 2018, which I still can't believe is real to this day. When I first heard Stacey had passed, I thought to myself, 'This can't be true!' So, I looked on Stacey's Facebook page, and sadly it was; my heart sank. I just couldn't believe it, and I was in shock and disbelief as was my dad when I told him as well.

Stacey was an angel sent down from above to bring joy into the life of everybody she touched.

One night my dad and I will never forget was when my dad was lucky enough to have the beautiful and talented singer Stacey Rivera pick him out of the audience while she sang to him. You should have seen the look on my dad's face, bless him. I don't usually see my dad get shy or embarrassed; on this occasion, though, he certainly did. If you would like to see my dad being sung to by Stacey Rivera, here is a video link to that unforgettable night back in 2009: bit.ly/StaceyRiveraSingingToMyDad

So, there I was thinking I had gotten away with not being picked out the audience, but oh no: I also got chosen by the lovely Stacey Rivera. There I was sitting comfortably enjoying the show, then the next thing I knew Stacey was pointing over and asking me to join her on stage along with two other members of the audience to be backing dancers! So if you would like to see me making a spectacle of myself as well, here is a link to my very first appearance on stage at the Tennessee Shindig in 2009: bit.ly/ PirateSteveDancingTennesseeShindig

I will always remember Stacey saying that I would be great on stage, which I appreciated her saying very much. Stacey unquestionably inspired me and gave me the confidence to be who I wanted to be in 2009, which helped to boost my self-esteem no end, especially after the previous year I'd had, when I had been assaulted, hospitalised and cyberbullied in my hometown. I also now believe in myself a lot more, thanks to Stacey.

One time when my dad and I had been to the Tennessee Shindig Stacey introduced us to the performers after the show, where we had some awesome photos taken together. One guy even took me backstage; hey, calm down: no, not like that; because he wanted to give me the shirt off his back, which he did! Stacey also told me one of her managers was interested in having me work over there in one of his theatres. I can never sincerely express how much Stacey Annette Morgan changed my life. I will miss Stacey dearly, as I know so many other people will whose hearts she touched as well.

My dad and I always felt welcomed by everybody at the Tennessee Shindig, and I believe if I lived over there in Pigeon Forge I would have even more self-confidence within myself than I do today. The Tennessee Shindig to me represented a place of happiness where everybody accepted you no matter how old or young you were.

To the performers of The Tennessee Shindig: I will always and forever remember those special memories you left my dad and me with. Thank you.

Steven M. Rippin

We were strangers in a city we had never been to before thousands and thousands of miles away from home, but it didn't feel like that one bit, especially when we went to the Tennessee Shindig and met Stacey Rivera because it always felt as if we had known her for years and that we had just popped by for a quick chat and a cup of tea with her on stage. Now here are a few lovely words Stacey wrote in a message to me on Facebook.

You and your dad so entertained us at my show. We were doing our job of putting on a show. Then you brought smiles to our faces when you were on stage with us. So fun! Your love and closeness with your dad and family is the most inspiring, at least to me. I grew up being passed around my family members. My grandmother pretty much raised me. Never have I even seen a photograph or picture of my dad. The family bond you have makes me smile. I know I have the DVD of you on stage somewhere in my collection of my show DVDs. And my cousin said for you to keep up the Pirate Steve, cause its HOT lol! Love you and your family.

**Stacey Annette Morgan, Knoxville, Tennessee, USA**

And when I messaged Stacey asking her if she would be happy for me to include her message in my book she said:

You sure can. I'm honoured. I love it! Thank you so much!

**Stacey Annette Morgan, Knoxville, Tennessee, USA**

It's so sad that Stacey never got to see a photograph or a picture of her dad. I can't begin to imagine what that must have felt like for her. Stacey never let her upbringing ever hold her back on chasing after her dreams throughout her life, though, and she grew into an incredibly talented and professional young woman who any father would be so proud of. I know I would be if I had a daughter like her.

Stacey found a family in everybody around her, from her friends she grew up with, her work colleagues she worked with and from people, such as my dad and me, who she met while she performed on stage throughout her career. I will always appreciate and never forget Stacey Rivera making my dad and me feel like part of her theatre family over the years in Pigeon Forge.

Stacey was one in a million; she had a heart of gold, and she was a very caring soul who always thought of those around her. I will never forget the love and support she showed my dad either when he was going through cancer, when she kindly donated to my fundraising campaign for Cancer Research UK. Here is what Stacey said in a message to me when my dad was going through cancer.

All of us in Pigeon Forge love you and your dad and want to help. My Aunt passed away from lung cancer a few months ago, and it hit hard, so whatever we can do.

**Stacey Annette Rivera, Knoxville, Tennessee, USA**

And now to finish my special dedication to a truly remarkable young woman, here is a personal message I have written out for Stacey.

Thank you, Stacey. I will never ever forget you. I loved coming over to Pigeon Forge with my dad to see you perform on stage at the Tennessee Shindig; you always made us both feel so welcomed. You were a phenomenal performer. I still can't believe you're no longer here with us; now, though, you're flying high among the angels. Until we meet again, keep on rocking and rolling up there and singing your heart out, making everybody happy. And thank you for what you said to me back in 2010 on Facebook, which was this,

'It was awesome to see you as well, and hey… I didn't take you to any pubs like I had wanted to do for a good ol' southern shot of Jack Daniels Whiskey… lol! Next time… for sure.'

And yes, Stacey, next time we meet we will have a shot or two of some of that good ol' Southern whiskey I never got a chance to sample with you. All my love always and forever, your friend Steve from England.

**Steven M. Rippin**

Again, that Southern hospitality and family bond my dad and I felt from the people of Tennessee keeps on shining through, doesn't it? It's such an incredible feeling and one I have never experienced before when I have been away from home. People in most places where you go on holiday are friendly and welcoming, but in Tennessee it's more than that though, because you create personal bonds and friendships with total strangers you know are going to last you a lifetime. For me, that is so special and means more than I can put into words here.

Thank you to everyone who worked and performed at the Tennessee Shindig and especially to you, Stacey Annette Morgan. With much love from my dad and myself, to you Stacey, to Tony, your loving husband, to Austin and Zac, your two awesome sons and to all of your family and friends. The love and joy you brought into this world will help keep us going on. You will forever be in our thoughts, prayers and hearts.

Steven M. Rippin

In memory of
Stacey Annette Morgan
24/07/1972–18/12/2018

# ENCOUNTERS WITH BLACK BEARS AT CADES COVE

Cades Cove is an eleven-mile loop you can either drive, cycle or walk around. There are also a lot of various trails you can go on, where you will stand a good chance of seeing tons of wildlife, such as white-tailed deer, bobcats, birds, cottontail rabbits, coyotes, beavers, bears, snakes and raccoons, to name a few. It truly is a beautiful place to visit, and you never know what variety of wildlife you're going to encounter. Take my dad and me, for example; we had our first showdown with a black bear while we were walking around Cades Cove in September 2009: an experience we will cherish forever.

Just before we came face to face with that black bear, the battery on my camera packed up, soon after my dad said, 'Quick Steve, get your camera back on; there's a bear over there.' So immediately I replaced the battery as fast as I could. Seconds later, this beautiful black bear emerged from out of the woods on the trail my dad and I were walking along. Then the black bear just stood in the centre of the path, looking directly at us! The first thing I thought of doing when I saw that black bear was to make a video clip for my *Big Brother* audition I was putting together at the time, obviously, not that the bear might be about to charge at my dad and me and eat us up for its dinner and feed our remains to its cubs!

Anyway, I gave my video camera to my dad and said to him, 'Do you wanna film me with the bear behind?' Please don't ever do this if you come across a black bear in the wild because you should never turn your back to a bear! So, there I was with my back to the wild bear as I slowly walked towards my dad and I said, 'Hi, as you can see we're in Cades Cove now and we've got some bears. Can you see them? How cool is this? I've been wanting to see these for years.' Why I said bears when there was only one of them, I have no idea; I clearly wasn't thinking straight, was I? My dad, bless him, said, 'Steve, don't go near it; just stay where you are!'

'Hi, I'd love to be on the *Big Brother* TV show; I love music and raving me,' I continued to say, then I turned around to make sure the bear wasn't running after me because, if I'm honest, I was pretty nervous!

By this point, my dad was starting to get concerned, and he said to me, 'Don't look at him; he's starting to come towards you. Come to me, Steven, don't run,' while I continued rambling on and said yet again, '*Big Brother.*' Then my dad said, 'STEVEN, STOP! You're all right; he's stopped. Just come this way; slowly come this way.' And, still, there I was talking away saying, 'I'd love to take part in the social experiment which is *Big Brother*; thanks for watching my video.' Then finally I finished waffling on, much to my dad's relief. The bear then sniffed at the air in my direction and wandered off onto the other side of the trail and into the woods. That was a moment in my life I will never forget.

Looking back, I'm sure that wild bear thought I was a bear, you know, with my long hair going halfway down my back, plus because of the black T-shirt I was wearing. From the black bear's perspective, I must have looked like a long Chinese black bean pepper profiterole from behind; then again, the bear might have sniffed at the air in my direction and thought to itself, 'Hmmm… I smell bad meat,' then just decided to wander off. If you are interested, here is a video link of our encounter with the black bear at Cades Cove when I waffled on about auditioning for *Big Brother*: bit.ly/ PirateSteveEncountersABear

So, after that encounter, my dad and I never thought we would be lucky enough to see another bear that close up ever again. In December 2016, though, when we returned to Cades Cove, sure enough, we were privileged to see another wild bear emerge from out of the woods and onto the trail we were driving along. And yeah, you guessed it, once we had pulled up into a lay-by along the trail, I asked my dad again to film me while the bear was behind me! I know, I know, I should have learnt my lesson after the last time that you should never turn your back to a bear; I did keep a clear distance between the bear and myself, though, which still isn't a good enough excuse, is it? So, while my dad was filming me, this time I said into the camera, 'How you doing everybody? As you can see, there's a bear behind me.'

'Steven, you'd better come towards me,' my dad said, sounding concerned. So, I started walking towards my dad slowly; this sounds like a re-run from our last encounter, doesn't it?

Then I continued chatting away and what better subject to talk about this time other than my favourite DJ, Judge Jules, and this is what I said, which doesn't all make sense because I was doing my best to stay safe and think about the situation I was in. 'Welcome to the Pirate Steve Show crew here on Instagram; as you can see there's a bear behind me at the moment, and for all you're the best podcast going around, it's Beartastic, the Judge Jules Global Warm Up podcast; check it out. Now I gotta be quiet now, though.' I certainly fumbled my words there, didn't I? Anyway, while my dad was filming me, a few American guys were watching the wild bear as well as it came closer and closer towards me. And the American guys who were facing me started backing away slowly, which made me feel nervous because I had no idea how close the black bear was to me or what it was doing behind my back. Then, as I was promoting the Judge Jules Global Warm Up Podcast, I could hear those American guys laughing away! I don't think they could quite believe what I was doing; they probably thought, 'Crazy Englishman!' And to be honest they did put me off a bit while I was trying to promote Judge Jules's podcast! Once my dad had finished filming the bear and me on his phone, the black bear then walked across the trail we were on and went up a grass verge for a snooze behind a fallen tree. And now here is the video of our second encounter with a black bear at Cades Cove for you to enjoy: bit.ly/ PirateSteveAndABearPromotingTheGlobalWarmUp

My dad and I feel very blessed to have had two meetings with wild bears at Cades Cove in the Great Smoky Mountains. They are memories we will treasure forever, and I am so happy I got to experience and share those special times with my dad.

# PIRATE STEVE'S BEAR ETIQUETTE TIPS

Now here are my six safety points when coming across wild bears.

- Stay calm and identify yourself to the bear by speaking quietly and calmly, so the bear knows you are human and that you are not the bear's next meal ticket. The bear might come closer towards you, more out of curiosity than anything else, but not in a threatening way.
- Keep very still, stand your ground and never make any sudden movements.
- Keep a reasonable distance between yourself and the bear.
- Make a detour and move yourself to higher ground, so you appear larger to any bears you come across when you are out hiking.
- Let the bears go about their daily business and don't bother them.
- And last but not least never face your back to a bear or any wild animals you encounter while you are out on your hikes in the wild because you never know if those animals will decide to come running up behind you and eat you up for their dinner.

There are a lot more rules to abide by so here is a link to a great website which has a lot of helpful advice on what to do if you ever find yourself in a sticky situation in the wild: bit.ly/SafetyTipsAroundBears

You only truly begin to realise how amazing the world is once you get yourself out there and start exploring and going on adventures.

My dad and I also got a chance to go horse riding in the Great Smoky Mountains in 2011, which was an incredible experience. Now, moving on, before I finish I have got one more encounter I would like to share with you which my dad and I had on our way back from Cades Cove to Pigeon Forge in December 2016. And, no, we didn't encounter any more wild bears but we did meet some of the good residents of Townsend when we pulled into a gas station to fill our hire car up. You see, when we entered the gas station to pay for our gas, my dad and I saw two guys sitting in chairs in the middle of the store who were having a chat with their friend who was working behind the counter. And my dad and I got chatting away with these guys, as you do when you walk into a gas station you have never been into before with complete strangers. So, my dad asked the store clerk what his name was, and he said, 'My names Jim O.M.S.T.E.A.D; Omstead, send me a Facebook, the Smoky Mountain Market, Townsend, Tennessee.' Jim was an amiable guy and straight away my dad and I felt welcomed by him into his store. Jim also gave us some excellent advice on places to visit around Townsend and the surrounding area as well. It was great meeting Jim Omstead.

Then my dad and I had a chat with the two guys who we saw when we first entered the Smoky Mountain Market who were sitting down on chairs in front of Jim's counter, and my dad said to me as I was filming him, 'Here's a couple of locals here; this is what they do most of the day, look,' then my dad asked them what their names were and they introduced themselves as George Carl Davies Jnr, who liked to be called Buddy, and Eddie Davies, who was Buddy's cousin. I then asked Buddy and Eddie what they did. Buddy was retired and used to park cars and his cousin Eddie was starting a new job later that month and was enjoying his time off. Meeting Jim, Eddie and Buddy in the Smoky Mountain Market was awesome. It was like Eddie and his cousin Buddy were watching the ball game on TV with Jim, and my dad and I had just gate-crashed their party. Jim, Buddy and Eddie showed the true essence of what it means to be a genuine Tennessean with the Southern hospitality they showed my dad and me that day.

Remember to take a time out in this fast-paced world you and I live in and don't let the pressures of everyday life get to you. So, relax whenever you can and hang out with your friends, just like Buddy and Eddie were doing. Now here is a video of the day my dad and I met Jim, Buddy and Eddie in the Smoky Mountain Market in Townsend, Tennessee: bit.ly/ JimBuddyAndEddie

It was truly a blessing meeting you and your dad here in Townsend at a very hard time (had just lost my dad) People are put in our lives for many reasons, and that day, I'm sure it was meant as an uplifting. My dad and I were so close, like you and yours. I suppose the message was, 'Gotta keep gettin up, and there is no hill for a climber,' dad would always say! It was also like we were friends for years.

**Eddie Davis, Townsend, Tennessee, USA**

What my dad and I didn't realise when we met Eddie Davies was that he had recently and regretfully lost his father. Just like Eddie said, though, it was like that day when we met was meant to be. I sincerely hope our meeting helped Eddie in some way. And it truly did feel as if we had been friends for years.

All my very best to you, Eddie; it was a real pleasure and a privilege meeting you along with your cousin Buddy and your good friend Jim Omstead back in December 2016. I was so saddened to learn about the loss of your father when you messaged me; he would be so proud of you. Love and light to you, my friend.

**Steven M. Rippin**

Most people, not all, are sadly always in a rush nowadays, aren't they, and I believe they need to learn to take a step back, relax and spend more time with their families and friends. If they took a leaf out of the Tennesseans' book of life and incorporated some of their ways into their own, I believe they would feel so much better within themselves and also learn to appreciate the world and the people around them a lot more as well.

# THE INN AT CHRISTMAS PLACE

My dad and I love the Inn at Christmas Place in Pigeon Forge because we always have a magical experience when we stay there; I have even become good friends with a few of the staff on social media. So, if you love Christmas, you will love the Inn at Christmas Place. And get this: there's even a daily newsletter in the lifts summarising the weather and events for the day. Most importantly, though, there's a countdown to Christmas Day. The Inn at Christmas Place feels like home to my dad and me; you can even go down for breakfast in your pyjamas, which a lot of the guests who stay there do because it feels so natural to walk around the hotel as you would at home. And the hotel beds are amazing; I have never slept on a more comfortable bed in all my life. If I could sneak one of those beds home with me in my suitcase I would! And what would the Inn at Christmas Place be without their very own Singing Santa? I write more about him later.

When my dad and I went back to Pigeon Forge in December 2016, Steve Myers and Lynne Lang Barbieri, members of staff at the hotel who my dad and I have known since we first started going there, came straight out of their offices to welcome us back with open arms, hugs and handshakes when they heard we had arrived! I have never experienced a welcome back to a hotel like that in all my life! And I don't mind admitting that it brought a lump to my throat. Steve and Lynne also both showed their love and support for my dad throughout his cancer scare back in 2017 with their prayers and well wishes. Steve even asked his family and friends on Facebook to join in and help pray for my dad as well, which is something I will never forget.

Thank you so much, Steve and Lynne; you guys are amazing, and you always make my dad and me feel right at home when we visit you.

Steven M. Rippin

Every prayer my dad received from our good friends in Tennessee meant so much to us. They unquestionably helped my dad on his road to recovery, and I say thank you once again from the bottom of my heart to all those people who prayed for him; Tennesseans have so much love to give to those around them, no matter how little they know them. Only once you have been blessed to have met the lovely people of Pigeon Forge, Gatlinburg and Sevierville will you genuinely understand what I mean. Now here are a couple of video vlogs my dad and I made while we were walking around the Inn at Christmas Place, which I hope gives you an idea what the hotel and surrounding area looks like in Pigeon Forge if you ever decide to visit:

bit.ly/ATourOfTheInnAtChristmasPlacePart1
bit.ly/ATourOfTheInnAtChristmasPlacePart2

One guy I will never forget is Scott Campbell. You see, Scott was one of the first members of staff my dad and I had the pleasure of meeting when we first arrived and booked into the hotel in 2009. Scott is just one of those guys you know you will get along with straight away and would feel comfortable having a few drinks with down your local pub.

Thank you so much for everything you did for my dad and I Scott and for all the laughs we had together. All my best to you and your family.

Steven M. Rippin

Also, on our first visit to the Inn at Christmas Place, while my dad and I were being booked into our room by Scott, I could feel a prominent figure approach the reception desk next to my dad, and when we turned round to see who was standing next to him my dad said in shock and awe, 'Father Christmas. It's so good to meet you; you look fantastic.' Then

Father Christmas turned around to my dad and said, 'Hello there, it's nice to meet you too.' That was a very magical moment for my dad and me when we met Father Christmas for the first time.

My dad and I then got chatting away to Father Christmas, who is the Inn at Christmas Place's very own Singing Santa, and, well, what an awesome guy Dean Townsend – the Singing Santa's real name – is. One year Dean kindly made our next-door neighbour's two sons a Christmas video message, which they both loved. And here is a link to that very video if you would like to take a look: bit.ly/AChristmasMessageForThomasAndWilliam

Dean has also had the time to do some video shout-outs for my YouTube channel as well, which I am very grateful to him for doing for me.

Thank you so much, Dean.

**Steven M. Rippin**

My dad and I used to love listening to Dean perform his Christmas songs on his guitar underneath the glockenspiel in the hotel during the evenings while we ate our milk and cookies. It felt so Christmassy and cosy; I loved it. It just doesn't get much better than that – well, it does, in fact, because, if you wanted to, you could help yourself to hot Christmas cider as well. You see, there is always free coffee, tea, milk chocolate or hot cider on continuously for the hotel guests, although I think the cider is only on throughout the Christmas period. And now if you would like to hear the Singing Santa live in action, here is a video I made in 2009. So, I hope you're feeling festive and have your Christmas jumper on: bit.ly/TheSingingSanta

Dean Townsend, the Singing Santa, has got quite a few CDs out with loads of awe-inspiring Christmas songs on them for you to sing along to and enjoy throughout the year, and, yeah, I purchased all of his CDs while I was in Pigeon Forge; I love listening to them. Two of my favourites are, *Let Them Be Little* and *Where the Eagle Fly*. Those two songs along with many others I think are outstanding. Dean Townsend makes an awesome Father Christmas and always makes you feel at ease when you first meet him, plus all the kids love him, well, who wouldn't? He is Father Christmas, after all. If you would like to discover more about the Singing Santa, here is a link to his web page on the Inn at Christmas Place's website: innatchristmasplace.com/singing-santa. Dean has been working at the Inn at Christmas Place as their incredible Father Christmas and very own Singing Santa since 2007, bringing joy and Christmas cheer to all the guests who have stayed there.

I used to love going for breakfast when my dad and I stayed at the Inn at Christmas Place because it always felt so cosy when we went downstairs and were greeted by Father Christmas or Mrs Claus, who would be sitting in their big comfy Christmas chairs. Blimey, I must sound like a big kid, mustn't I? Oh yeah, Dean used to say to my dad and I every time he saw us, 'You guys need to put some more meat on your bones.' That always made us laugh, and, hey, we both did put more meat on our bones after the two weeks we spent in Pigeon Forge because WOW the food over there is fantastic, especially the size of the portions! Now here is a Christmas message from Father Christmas and me: bit.ly/PirateSteveAndSantaClaus

> Dean Townsend, you, sir, are a true legend and a very talented guy who I am honoured to call my good friend from across the pond. Thank you for always making our stay feel that extra bit special. To me, you are the real Father Christmas. All my very best to you and your family and I hope to see you again soon.
>
> Steven M. Rippin

Never stop believing and never grow up. Some people, unfortunately, lose the enchantment of what life is all about, and they start criticising others for believing in things that are make-believe. What's wrong with make-believe, though? Make-believe makes the world a much more enjoyable place to live in, if you ask me. It also helps to give you and me hope when we are feeling down and at a loss, so, for me, make-believe makes life worth living.

One restaurant I always loved going to, was the Pear and Partridge, which was the Inn at Christmas Place's eatery. The food there was incredible. One memory which stands out the most from the Pear and Partridge was the conversation my parents and I had with a charming old lady who worked there; my mum joined my dad and me on one of our trips to Pigeon Forge in 2011. And the old lady sorrowfully told us that her husband had recently passed away. I have never known anybody in my life to open up about how they genuinely feel when they have lost a loved one to strangers in the way she did to my parents and me that day. It was heart-breaking. I realised more than ever from that moment that it's good to talk about how you feel when a traumatic event has occurred in your life. Soon after the old lady had told my parents and me about the loss of her husband, she started to cry, which then set my mum and me off crying as well. It was a very emotional moment we were all sharing. Then we all hugged and dried our tears away. Meeting the lovely old lady that day touched our hearts and made me realise how genuine, caring and loving the Tennessean people are towards one another. The connections you and I can make with strangers is unbelievable, isn't it?

Every time I am lucky enough to go back to Pigeon Forge, I feel like I'm arriving back home. And those feelings are what you and I should have no matter where we travel to around the world, aren't they? The world is our home and we should make it feel like that for one another. Love and respect your family, friends and strangers always.

All the hotel cleaning staff my dad and I met at the Inn at Christmas Place were the friendliest cleaners we have ever come across; they always had time to stop, talk and say hello to us in the mornings. And can you believe one young woman in particular who we met in 2009, Teri-Ann Cassman, remembered my dad and me when we went back to the Inn at Christmas Place in 2016! We always had a good laugh with Teri-Ann Cassman and her crew of house cleaners. Two more members of staff we became good friends with while we were there were Erin Arun Shell and Kathleen Gilbert. Erin and Kathleen always went out of their way to help my dad and me as best as they could when we needed anything, which we appreciated very much.

Thank you to all the hotel cleaning staff who looked after my dad and me and left chocolates for us on our beds.

Steven M. Rippin

My favourite books and movies were always about romantic pirates. In my teens, I fantasised about being a bawdy wench. I dressed like one for many Halloweens, lol. Every time I saw you in Pigeon Forge, I remembered all those swashbuckling memories, and I smiled. You are an inspiration for everyone to be themselves and to be happy. I'm also a hero with my Grandson because I know a real pirate.

Kathleen Gilbert, Ohio, USA

When my parents and I took a trip to the Inn at Christmas Place in December 2011, most mornings while we had our breakfast my mum told me she had spotted one of the female servers looking over and smiling at me, which I always missed this one particular server doing; I have always been rubbish at spotting when a woman is flirting with me, you see. Finally, though, I did notice the female server looking over in my direction one morning while I was eating my bowl of cornflakes, and she was the server I fancied, if I'm honest. I found out her name was Brittany, who also cleaned our room. And I don't mind admitting, every time I saw Brittany wheeling her cleaning trolley down the corridor as I was walking towards her in the mornings, my heart rate would rise; now, not many women have been able to do that! Jeez, I must sound like a right soppy pirate. Anyway, enough of this romantic talk. Brittany had long brown hair, beautiful big round eyes and a smile to die for— Hold on, hold on, wait a minute. I just said enough of the soppy talk, Steven! So, when Brittany came over to our table one morning to serve us, she and I got chatting away and arranged to meet up, where we spent a lovely day together at Gatlinburg.

On our day out we went to Ober Gatlinburg in a cable car and had a good laugh with Captain Cornelius, who I took out with me that day as well. Captain Cornelius, if you were wondering, is a pirate hand puppet I had with me for a bit of fun, although I think Brittany wondered what on earth I was going to whip out my jacket pocket when I produced Captain Cornelius. Luckily, though, Brittany loved my little pirate puppet friend. Then, after the adventures of Captain Cornelius, we carried on up to Mount Harrison in a chairlift that gives you a 360-degree view overlooking the Great Smoky Mountains, which was astounding!

As my parents and I were in Pigeon Forge over the New Year, Brittany came out with us to celebrate, and it was the best New Year's Eve I have ever had to date as of 2019. I felt so happy celebrating the New Year in with Brittany, and even though she wasn't my girlfriend it felt fantastic being out with her. The night was going really well until yet again I got picked out to go on stage at the show we were attending! I'm sure members of staff at those shows in Pigeon Forge communicated with each other and said, 'There's a pirate in town; make sure you get him on stage.' Anyway, this time I was on stage with half a dozen other people where we were given hula hoops, so you can imagine how ridiculous we must have looked hula-hooping away, especially me, who wasn't able to hula hoop to save his life!

Celebrating the New Year in with Brittany was very special for me, and a night I will never forget. It was also the last time I would get to see Brittany because my parents and I had a flight home two days later and Brittany had to work for the rest of the time while I was there. Brittany and I kept in touch for a short while until, one day, I never heard from her ever again. I have been told Brittany now has a couple of children and has settled down with her partner, and I wish them all the best. Brittany was adorable, and I'm so happy we got the chance to meet and hang out together back in 2011.

One morning my parents and I met the lovely Welborn family at the Inn at Christmas Place, and Poppi Welborn, who we met, has shown my dad and myself a lot of love and support through the messages she has sent to us through Facebook over the years. Poppi, who is a Christian teacher from North Carolina, also had her class at school pray for my dad while he was going through mouth cancer in 2017, which was so kind of them all to do.

> Hey! I wanted you to know that the boys and I are remembering you in our prayers. We have also put you on our church prayer lists. We talk about you guys often, and the children in my third-grade class pray for you at least once a week. (I teach in a Christian School) I do believe there is a higher power and that He loves us. Our faith in Him is a gift… It doesn't make all bad things go away, but life is certainly more bearable. I hope you guys have a terrific Christmas and a wonderful New Year!
>
> Poppi Welborn, North Carolina, USA

Poppi, thank you and your class so very, very much for praying for my dad back then, it truly meant the world to us how much you cared, and still do for my family.

**Steven M. Rippin**

When my parents and I met the Welborn family in 2011 I did a video interview with Poppi's sons, and, while I was interviewing them, her youngest, Bryson, made us all laugh when he said, 'I gotta lot of money, I got too much money.' Bryson was awesome. And now for your entertainment here I am interviewing Poppi's sons: bit.ly/ InterviewingTheWelborns

To say thank you for doing the video interview, Poppi's sons sent me a *She-Ra Princess of Power* DVD and some drawings they had done, which I never expected and appreciated very much.

Thank you so much Poppi and your family; it was an honour and a pleasure meeting you all. Thank you for the memories.

**Steven M. Rippin**

The doormen my dad and I met at the Inn at Christmas Place in 2016 were phenomenal and amiable guys, and I am not just saying that. David (I'm unsure of his last name), David Hinds and Alan Duhon are the three noble doormen my dad and I had the pleasure of meeting and having a good laugh with every day when we saw them on the doors. David, Alan and David were even happy enough to star in one of my Positive Pirate videos. Oh no, not more videos, I hear you say, so before you close my book and go and put the kettle on, here are two videos starring Alan Duhon, David Hinds and David working their magic on the doors at the Inn at Christmas Place:

bit.ly/TheDoormenofTheInnAtChristmasPlace
bit.ly/PirateSteveInAmerica

Thank you so much, David Hinds, David, and Alan Duhon. It was always a pleasure meeting you, and your friendly faces when we arrived back at the hotel after a long day out exploring. I hope I have the pleasure of meeting you all again one day.

Steven M. Rippin

In the two years I worked for the Hotel, I honestly, never met any two people more friendly than you and George. You were both very easy to talk to, had some interesting stories and, what I liked the most, was your sense of humour, Especially your dad. We had some good laughs together. His fangs came out when I called him an old fart.

David Hinds, Tennessee, USA

Now I couldn't miss out on mentioning the one and only Dallas E. Morrison, who my dad and I used to see at breakfast every morning back in 2016; Dallas worked in the kitchens as a server at the Inn at Christmas Place. I always used to look forward to hearing Dallas's impersonation of an English gentleman, which went a bit like this: 'Good day mate, would you like to go for a cup of tea?' I wish I had filmed him saying that. His pronunciation of the English language was spot on.

It was a pleasure meeting you, Dallas. Until the next time, mate, take care and I hope all is going well for you.

Steven M. Rippin

Eyes down for a full house, legs eleven and all the eights: eighty-eight, which can mean only one thing. Yeah, you guessed it, it's Christmas bingo time down at the Inn at Christmas Place. Have you ever played Christmas bingo before? Well, my dad and I hadn't until we found ourselves being led into the bingo room one cold December evening, where we had a surprisingly excellent time playing Christmas bingo. And guess what: we got two full houses and won some Christmas presents as well. How cool is that? Woohoo! And now here for your amusement is a video of our Christmas bingo game shenanigans: bit.ly/ChristmasBingoTime

To love and cherish the world, and everybody around you, is what I have taken away with me after meeting all of the awe-inspiring hotel staff and guests at the Inn at Christmas Place.

Because Steve Myers has always made sure my dad and I have had a pleasant stay at his hotel, we took him out for a meal on the last night of our holiday back in December 2016 as our way of saying thank you to him for making our vacation one of the best we have been on, which Steve appreciated very much. Unfortunately, though, my dad and I found Paula Deen's Family Kitchen the day we arranged to meet up with Steve! We had only planned on having a quick snack, but before we knew it we had stuffed ourselves silly, so when we met up with Steve that evening we weren't that hungry! Still, though, we all had a great night out.

If you ever get the chance to go to Pigeon Forge in Tennessee, I highly recommend staying at the Inn at Christmas Place because you will have the holiday of a lifetime and it will also be one of the most magical and festive experiences you and your family will have ever had. My dad and I miss everybody so much who we were lucky and privileged enough to have met at the Inn at Christmas Place.

> Thank you to all the management, staff, cleaners and maintenance workers at The Inn at Christmas Place for making our holidays magical experiences every time we have been lucky enough to visit you. Also, thank you for all the treasured memories my dad and I have made and taken away with us. Those memories will stay with us always and forever. The Inn at Christmas Place, we love you.
>
> Steven M. Rippin

I have made a lot of new life-long friends since staying at the Inn at Christmas Place, and they will always and forever hold a special place in my heart.

# THE GATLINBURG FIRES

The most devastating trip my dad and I took over to Pigeon Forge was when the Gatlinburg fires struck the state of Tennessee in 2016, which claimed many lives, injured 134 people and were one of the most significant natural disasters to hit the state in history. I was heartbroken when I saw on the news what was happening to the place I loved so much and called my second home. When I first heard about the Gatlinburg Fires, my thoughts and prayers went straight out to the people of Tennessee and to all their families and friends who had lost their homes and businesses. Thankfully, all my friends who live over there had survived, but so many others sadly weren't so lucky.

> In November 2016, two teen boys were videoed, on a cell phone, flicking burning matches out of their car into an extremely dry wooded area in the Great Smoky Mountain National Forest. These two boys started a fire that spread very quickly in unusually dry and windy conditions. Wind gusts reached 88 MPH that day, and the fire burned through the forest at an alarming rate. Fifteen people died, and more than 1500 structures were damaged or destroyed.
>
> **David Hinds, Kodak, Tennessee, USA**

My dad and I had planned to fly over to Pigeon Forge on 5 December 2016 but we weren't sure if we should go or not due to what was happening, so we called the Inn at Christmas Place where we were staying to see if they still wanted us to come over, which they did, because they wanted to show the world that they were still open for business. So, my dad and I flew over to Pigeon Forge not knowing what to expect, but we wanted to show our love and support to the communities of Gatlinburg, Pigeon Forge and Sevierville as best as we could.

Once my dad and I arrived in Pigeon Forge and were driving along the parkway we could see in the distance the smoke in the air coming off the Great Smoky Mountains, which was such a sorrowful sight to behold. My dad and I couldn't believe the amount of destruction those forest fires had caused. The forest fires started on 28 November 2016 and lasted until 9 December 2016. Once my dad and I had booked into the Inn at Christmas Place, we went across the road and had a meal at Denny's, and our server told us how distraught everybody in the community was. My dad and I then discussed with our server how upset we both were when we heard the news about the forest fires and that we were here to show our love and support. Our server genuinely appreciated us coming over from England and said, 'We need tourists to keep on coming over to help us survive right now, and we love it that you're here to support us.'

By the day of my birthday, 12 December, the forest fires had burned over 17,904 acres of land, which is nearly 28 square miles, around and inside the Great Smoky Mountains National Park, and roughly 14,000 residents and tourists had been told to leave and evacuate the area for their safety; also there were around 2,460 buildings which were either damaged or destroyed. Gatlinburg was closed for the first week while my dad and I were there and it reopened again on Friday, 9 December 2016. I remember walking through the shopping mall with my dad the day Gatlinburg reopened, when we witnessed first-hand the aftermath the forest fires had left behind for all the storeowners to clean up, which was so upsetting to see. There were industrial floor cleaning and drying machines everywhere, which I recognised because I use the same drying machines here in England for my carpet cleaning business. As we were walking around, I could feel the raw emotion and sadness in the air. At the same time, though, it was so good to see the community spirit of Gatlinburg had pulled together to rebuild all they had lost. And I will admit it brought a lump to my throat and many tears to my eyes to observe how much damage those forest fires had caused. Together the communities of Gatlinburg, Pigeon Forge and Sevierville are all Mountain Strong.

We are a very tight-knit community here in the mountains of East TN. The wildfires affected everyone. Fifteen people lost their lives, which our whole community mourned. Nothing can ever replace those lives. Many more people lost their homes and livelihoods. People from all over our country, gave of their hearts, time and resources to assist our community. Dolly Parton went above and beyond to assist her community as well. We have recovered and will continue to do so. My son, Patrick, was a zip line guide, at Zip Gatlinburg, until the wildfires destroyed those zip lines. The only good that came of his losing his job is the fact that I was able to spend so much time with him before he died Christmas Eve. So of course, every day I work at The Inn at Christmas Place, I am reminded of this.

### Lynne Lang Barbieri, Pigeon Forge, Tennessee, USA

One evening after my dad and I left Dolly Parton's Dixie Stampede Dinner and Show we came across a few soldiers from the National Guard in the car park, and one of the National Guard soldiers called over and said, 'Hey, do you mind if we get a photo with you?' which I didn't mind at all. In fact, I wanted to have my photo taken with them and tell them what a fantastic job they were doing in Gatlinburg. They were a great bunch of lads, and I felt very honoured to have met them.

My dad and I visited Gatlinburg once more before the end of our vacation, and on that visit, we went on the Ober Gatlinburg aerial tramway. And the young woman who was operating it that day told all the passengers that it was her first day back after the devastating forest fires and that she was finding it very hard and emotional being back at work. When she started crying, my dad gave her a hug, which she sincerely appreciated; I can't even begin to imagine what she must have been through. As we were travelling up to Ober Gatlinburg in the aerial tramway, we went over the top of the Great Smoky Mountains and saw the damage the forest fires had caused and left behind. Some buildings had been entirely destroyed and left blackened-out shells, while others you could see were still smouldering. I had never seen anything like it in my life. The rescue services did a remarkable job keeping those forest fires contained, and it is only when you're there to witness the size of the devastation for yourself that you can genuinely understand and appreciate the enormous amount of work and relief effort those rescue services had to contend with back then.

A massive THANK YOU to all the rescue services who helped to contain those forest fires in November/December 2016. The communities of Gatlinburg, Pigeon Forge and Sevierville, and I, can never thank you enough.

Steven M. Rippin

Once my dad and I got to Ober Gatlinburg we then travelled further up in a chairlift to Mount Harrison, which is 3590 ft, where we had a breathtaking 360-degree panoramic view above the clouds of the Great Smoky Mountains. There is usually a trio of bluegrass singers at the top of Mount Harrison. Unfortunately, it was out of season, though, so we didn't get to see them this time. Also, it can get pretty cold up there on Mount Harrison so my dad and I took our photos, went live on Facebook back home to our friends in England, then headed down to Ober Gatlinburg to warm ourselves up, where we ate at Seasons of Ober and had a very delicious meal.

While we were there, my dad got chatting away with the manager of Seasons of Ober, Rick Spragg. Rick was a great guy, and we must have spent a few hours in his restaurant while we warmed ourselves up with coffee, which his staff kept bringing out for us at no extra cost! England should start doing free coffee refills I think. How cool would that be? Then once we had warmed up, we said our goodbyes to Rick and his staff and headed down to Gatlinburg, where we saw the community was starting to get on its feet again. It was so good to see how busy Gatlinburg was that day when my dad and I visited for the second time. The spirit the people in the mountains of East Tennessee have is undoubtedly phenomenal; nothing will ever keep these exceptional individuals down for long, and they will always pull together and be there for one another because they are Gatlinburg Strong, Mountain Tough.

My deepest condolences go to all the families who tragically lost loved ones in the forest fires. We shall always remember, never forget and honour those who have fallen. And to the communities of Gatlinburg, Pigeon Forge and Sevierville, Stay Strong and Stay Tough. Remember that your loved ones who you have sorrowfully lost will be looking down on you from above showing you the way when times are hard and telling you never to give in and never to give up because you are Mountain Strong and Mountain Tough. Love thy neighbour, and thy neighbour will love you. Love and light to all.

**Steven M. Rippin**

In remembrance of the victims of
the Gatlinburg Fires
28/11/2016–9/12/2016

# MY FINAL THOUGHTS ON PIGEON FORGE

I love Pigeon Forge with all my heart, although I want to start my closing thoughts by saying how much I love my own country as well. Some people think the grass is always greener on the other side, don't they? I felt that way for years because of the enchanting and captivating people I have been lucky enough to meet. As they say, though, there's no place like home. For a start, I love the English heritage, the castles, the architecture and the history England has to offer, plus all my family and friends live here as well, which is the foremost reason why I could never move to another country.

> If you stop and look around the area where you live today, you might be pleasantly surprised how much you care and love the town, city or village where you live.

Now I have got that out my system it's time for my closing thoughts on Pigeon Forge. My dad and I have never experienced interactions in public like those we encountered in Pigeon Forge in all our lives. They started from the moment we woke up in the morning until we went to bed at night. We never knew who we were going to meet and become friends with, which made every day an unexpected series of wondrous adventures.

One thing I love about the Tennesseans is how they talk, especially when they say, 'How yawl doing, are you guys from Australia?'

What I admire about the shows in Pigeon Forge is that you always get a chance to meet the cast members in the reception area after their performance has ended, where you can have a chat and have your photo taken with them; I think that's awesome and a very memorable way to end your evening on.

What makes Pigeon Forge an exceptional place for me is how everybody treats you. There is so much respect for one another, and the Tennesseans genuinely care about how you are doing and how you are feeling, no matter if they know you or not. And if they can help you out in any way they will. After all, Tennessee is known for its Southern hospitality. What I especially miss are all the interactions my dad and I used to have with the people of Pigeon Forge, Gatlinburg and Sevierville. Those interactions were one of the primary reasons why we loved going back to the state of Tennessee time and time again. I believe if you and I learnt to be more loving, caring and respectful towards each other, just as the Tennesseans are, it would help make the world a better place to live. And it would be a planet where compassion and happiness rule instead of all the hurt, pain and misery we see today!

I love England to bits. I just wish as a country we could learn to have more time and respect for one another regardless of whether we know each other or not, whether that's when we are out shopping, walking around in public, down the pub with our mates or chilling out having a coffee somewhere. Love the community you live in and make it a safe, welcoming and respectable place for everybody to enjoy.

If you are ever lucky enough to visit America, I would strongly recommend visiting Pigeon Forge, Gatlinburg, Sevierville and, of course, the Great Smoky Mountains, the Inn at Christmas Place and Dollywood. Those places have changed my life.

I practise a lot of the Tennesseans' traditional family values they hold close to their hearts in my own everyday life, such as always showing respect and being kind, caring and courteous towards other people. Unfortunately, I don't always get treated like that in return here in England.

When my dad's wearing his cowboy hat in the UK, I find it very disheartening when some people say to him, 'Why on earth are you wearing that for? You're not in America now!' How disrespectful is that? Some people's attitudes stink, don't they? It just shows you though how small-minded those individuals are, doesn't it? Now here are two videos of my dad and me in the Great Smoky Mountains of Tennessee:

bit.ly/PigeonForgeRoadTrip2012
bit.ly/PigeonForgeLaurelFalls

I wanted to share those stories of our time in Tennessee with you because those people my dad and I have had the privilege of meeting hold a special place in our hearts. We have learnt a lot from being around them, and, most importantly, I have discovered how to become a better version of myself. The Tennesseans have shown me how to treat other people with the utmost respect. Above all else, though, the Tennesseans have taught me how to love my neighbour. Now here are a few final words on Tennessee from my dad.

> I think the friendliness of the people there is fantastic. They call it the southern hospitality; I love the laid-back attitude. I love the shows, such as the Dixie Stampede and all the theatres which are there. And also, you have the Smoky Mountains and the fantastic trails for walking.
>
> **George W. Rippin, Market Harborough, England**


> Tennessee, our hearts have grown with more love for the world since we have visited you. Thank you for the memories.
>
> **Steven M. Rippin**

Pigeon Forge has unmistakably had a significant influence on my life, and it has also helped to make me the man I am today.

# MY LOVE OF MUSIC, PLUS A FEW SHORT MUSICAL ADVENTURES

Music, well, what can I say? If it weren't for music I would probably be a broken mess by now; you see, music has motivated me in all aspects of my life, and it has also introduced me to many influential people over the years; where would you and I be without the music we love so much? The first song I remember listening to when I was a little boy was when my parents and family used to sing along to 'Shaddap You Face' by Joe Dolce, which was released in 1980/81. 'Shaddap You Face' always got the whole family singing along together; it was such a catchy little number. And, if you would like to listen to it, here is a link to 'Shaddap You Face' by Joe Dolce: bit.ly/ShaddapYouFaceJoeDolce

And the first record I ever bought was by Adam and the Ants, 'Prince Charming', which came out on a twelve-inch record. Thinking back, I reckon Adam Ant influenced me when I was younger and is the reason I turned out the way I have, especially when it comes to wearing eyeliner! You will understand what I mean if you check this video out: bit.ly/AdamAndTheAntsPrinceCharming

Music has helped me through a lot; it helped me when I was feeling depressed – When I was in hospital facing eye operations – When past relationships ended badly, and also when I was assaulted and bullied. And these three songs, in particular, I am going to share with you now assisted me tremendously throughout those times. The first song is by a band called Chumbawamba with their track 'Tubthumping'. This song supported me when I was first assaulted in my early twenties. Now here is a video link to 'Tubthumping' by Chumbawamba: bit.ly/

ChumbawambaTubthumping. This song was released on 11 August 1997.

The second song is by a band called Republica with their track 'Ready to Go'. This song helped me through a bad break-up in my early twenties. Now here is a video link to Republica's 'Ready to Go': bit.ly/RepublicaReadyToGo. This song was released on 15 April 1996.

I adored those two songs and still do. 'Tubthumping' by Chumbawamba helped me feel positive about myself again and also helped to clear my mind of all the negative and depressing thoughts I was having after being attacked. And Republica's 'Ready to Go' encouraged me to face the world again after my relationship ended.

Listening to music: Makes you feel happier – Motivates you when you're exercising – Helps to improve your health – Reduces depression – Makes you sleep better – Lowers stress – Helps you eat less – Improves your mood while you are driving – Helps to strengthen your memory – And helps you while you are learning new skills.

Certain songs we listen to can have powerful meanings for us, can't they, which leads me onto my final and third song, which unquestionably means the world to me. This song was written and performed by my all-time favourite musician, singer and songwriter, Avril Lavigne, and is called 'Anything but Ordinary'. The lyrics in this number are amazing, and I lose myself in it every time: bit.ly/AnythingbutordinaryAvrilLavigne. This song was released on 4 June 2002.

I went to see Avril Lavigne live in concert at the Birmingham NEC one year and I can honestly say she was astounding! I even managed to get myself to the front of the stage, which was so cool! Sorry, I'm fanboying now, aren't I? Ever since I changed my image the song 'Anything but Ordinary' has always been a constant reminder that I'm not alone when I'm made to feel like an outcast in society by small-minded people I meet in public. You might cringe at this, but I made a video where I'm dressed in my Captain Jack Sparrow costume singing away to 'Anything but Ordinary'. So, to warn you in case you do decide to watch this next video, I'm a terrible singer, and it's probably best if you don't watch it, to be honest: bit.ly/AnythingButOrdinaryJackSparrow

Whenever I feel low, anxious or depressed, I'll listen to hardstyle music because it's so uplifting and takes me on a euphoric journey away from all the nonsense I have to put up with from small-minded idiots in public every now and again. It's also a perfect style of music to work out to as well.

My love of dance music started when I was at secondary school, when a friend of mine, Richard Ashton, used to lend me his rave tapes in our photography classes. One of his rave tapes I enjoyed listening to was by a DJ called Jumping Jack Frost. And ever since then I have always loved happy hardcore, which then led onto my love of hardstyle, Frenchcore, trance, progressive house, dirty house and electro music. I will also admit I love a bit of country music as well, especially Dolly Parton. Furthermore, I believe listening to my friend's rave tapes in our photography classes helped me get the highest GCSE result out of all the subjects I took while I was at school, because I got graded a B, which was the best GCSE result I received, so listening to music while you study has its benefits.

Q: What's the best music event you have been to?

**Tinck Tincknell, Leicestershire, England**

A: Excellent question, thanks, Tinck, and it's the hardcore night you put on at the music cafe in Leicester called 'Critical Mass' back in 2014. What an incredible night that was; I had never danced so much in all my life. I even had one girl say to me, 'I see you were really into it there on the dance-floor and loving the music.' She couldn't have been more right. I also filmed that night on my iPhone, interviewed a few of the ravers, and turned it into a mini documentary, which you, Tinck, kindly shared with all your friends. Thanks, so much for doing that. Tinck, you're an awesome guy, and I've got a lot of respect for you because you put a lot of time and effort into the music events you organised and I say thank you. All the best mate and thanks for your question.

**Steven M. Rippin**

And here are two videos I made for Tinck's rave 'Critical Mass' at the music cafe in Leicester back in 2014:

bit.ly/CriticalMass2014
bit.ly/CriticalMassRawEnergy

The legendary DJ Paul Moore, who used to DJ at the Broadway nightclub, where my good friend Cameron Price and I used to go to in Market Harborough, used to play some outstanding European music his brother sent him over from Europe. And one of those tracks he played, which Cameron and I loved dancing to, was 'Forever Young' by a group called Interactive. WOW, what a tune that was, Cameron and I would dance like crazy to that song every Saturday night down at the Broadway. And now here is a link to Interactive's song 'Forever Young', which Cameron and I would party our socks off to: bit.ly/InteractiveForeverYoung

> Thank you so much, DJ Paul Moore; your musical influences all those years ago have helped me to become the raving loony I am today!

> **Steven M. Rippin**

When I was around eighteen I went on Market Harborough's local radio station, 102.3 Hfm, and played all my favourite electro, trance and happy hardcore tracks. Unfortunately, though, while I was on air the radio station had a number of complaints coming in from elderly people who were tuned in because they didn't appreciate listening to happy hardcore music while they were having their evening meals!! Luckily, though, my good friend Cameron Price was loving it while he was doing his homework.

> To one very special friend who found me lots of things, beer, dance music, clubs, and my wife many moons ago, love you, man.

> **Cameron Price, Market Harborough, England**

While I have been writing my book, I've been listening to cinematic, progressive house and hardstyle music, which have helped me enormously to pour my thoughts, feelings and emotions out.

Do you remember the song that went, 'Things can only get better'. Well, if you do, my claim to fame is that I was once lucky enough to meet the lead singer of that group. The band was called D:Ream and Peter Cunnah was their vocalist. I met Mr Cunnah when my parents took me to London one year when I was around thirteen, and as we were walking through Leicester Square we happened to walk by the Nickelodeon TV studio where you could look in through a window and see the presenters. And that's where we saw Peter Cunnah being interviewed. When his interview was over, Peter saw my parents and me standing outside looking in, and he said to us through the window, 'Come in and have a cuppa with me,' as he held his cup of tea up to us. So, my parents and I went and said hello to Mr Cunnah, and I remember feeling really nervous because here was this famous musician I had only ever seen on TV before and now he was standing right next to me while we had our photograph taken together by my parents! It was an excellent experience and a real pleasure meeting Peter Cunnah. And I can honestly say he was an amiable guy who had a lot of time for his fans.

I do find it funny because, when most people see me, they presume I'm going to love heavy metal music. I do like bands like Aerosmith, the Rolling Stones, Guns N' Roses, Slipknot, Kid Rock, Liam Gallagher, Oasis and most rock music, but believe it or not, instead of growing up and blasting out Iron Maiden and Metallica in my bedroom when I was younger, I was blasting out 'I Should Be So Lucky', because I was a huge Kylie Minogue fan when I was in my thirties. Only joking: I would have been around thirteen. I also had posters of her up all over my bedroom walls! I even went to one of Kylie Minogue's concerts with my good friend Neil Page, where we got pretty close to the front of the stage, and I could have sworn Kylie spotted me in the crowd; obviously she hadn't, or that would have made my night back then, well, it would have if I'd gotten to meet her after the show! I should be so lucky, lucky, lucky, lucky!

One type of music I never listen to is depressing music because it makes me feel sad. Saying that, though, my good friends Lillian Fox from Michigan in America and Pauly from Texas in America make valid points as you can see below.

Wavelengths are the best way to express it, if I ever have a huge headache, black metal seems to help me relax, and usually happy stuff is too much for me.

**Lillian M. Fox, The Queen of Foxes, Michigan, USA**

Music is a drug, a natural high, though, I do have a sad playlist if I feel wound up and need to cry it out. You cry and refresh! Sometimes get a good nap after too.

**Pauly, Texas, USA, instagram.com/the_other_paulyd2**

Thank you so much, Lillian and Pauly, for your musical inputs there on why people enjoy listening to music that some of us might find depressing.

**Steven M. Rippin**

And after hearing what Lillian and Pauly had to say about depressing music, I now understand why people choose to listen to it. I still believe uplifting music does our minds, bodies and souls no end of good, although you should always listen to what makes you feel happy on the inside. Various styles of music touch on our emotions in many diverse ways. Now, to give you an idea of the dance music I grew up listening to and still love today, here are a few tracks to check out.

bit.ly/RankOneAirwave – bit.ly/SolarstoneSevenCities – bit.ly/DuneICantStopRaving – bit.ly/CafeDelMarEnergy52 – bit.ly/ScooterMoveYourAss – bit.ly/TillmanUhrmacherOnTheRun – bit.ly/HerbieRightTypeOfMood – bit.ly/DuneHardcoreVibes

And here are some links to my favourite musical podcasts:

Judge Jules: The Global Warm Up - DJ Isaac: Isaacs Hardstyle Sessions - Brennan Heart: We R Hardstyle – Kutski: Keeping The Rave Alive - Paul Oakenfold: Perfecto Podcast

One song I find exceptionally inspiring is called 'Strength of a Thousand Men' by Two Steps from Hell. I love this piece of music, and here is a link if you would like to take a listen to it for yourself: bit.ly/StrengthOfAThousandMen. And here is another uplifting song by Two Steps from Hell I love called 'From Hell to Glory': bit.ly/2StepsFromHellToGlory

So, there you have it, that's just a small collection of the songs, artists and podcasts I have grown up listening to which have helped me to develop the positive mindset I have today.

I love dancing and letting the music take over my body. And when I feel at one with the music, I can feel the power it holds and possesses right through my bones to the beating of my heart.

Music can help relax you before and after surgery, because listening to the music you love can help take some of your pain away. And did you know music also helps Alzheimer's patients to remember things? Music improves recovery in stroke patients – Increases your verbal intelligence – Raises your IQ and academic performance, and music can also help to keep your brain healthy in old age. For a more in-depth look into the benefits of listening to music, please check out the following link from the lifehack.org website: bit.ly/15BenefitsOfMusic

# TWO MUSICAL ADVENTURES INVOLVING POLICE HELICOPTERS AND STOMPEDE CLUBNIGHTS

## RAVING INTO THE MILLENNIUM

When I was twenty-five, I thought it would be great to do something entirely different for the millennium, so when my friend Sam from California told me about an indoor rave taking place at the Staples Centre in Los Angeles, I knew that was where I wanted to go. All I had to do was get myself to Disneyland in California for 2 pm on New Year's Eve: no problem. So I told my parents what I was going to be doing and they said we should all go to California to celebrate Christmas and the New Year in together as we had never spent Christmas away from home before, so we planned our trip to California and off we went. It was so exciting knowing I was going to America to meet a bunch of Kandy Kid ravers who I had never met before.

So New Year's Eve came around, and my parents and I set off from the hotel to Disneyland. Then at 2 pm I left my mum and dad and headed over to the Haunted House ride, where I saw Sam and his Kandy Kid raver friends waiting for me. One thing I didn't realise until I met Sam was that he was gay, which is all cool with me because I have got a lot of gay and lesbian friends; the only problem was, when Sam introduced me to his boyfriend, he took an instant dislike to me straight away; he gave me some right evil looks. Anyway, after we had been on a few rides around Disney, we then headed to the Goofy car park, where one of the Kandy Kid ravers' cars was parked before we headed downtown into LA to queue up for the rave at the Staples Centre. When we arrived at the Staples Centre, I was blown away by the number of people queuing up for the rave; there were also police helicopters flying overhead with their spotlights shining down on us, and cop cars and police officers everywhere keeping law and order. Furthermore, going into the rave was like being at an airport because we had to go through security scanners, where we were given a good frisking, which if I'm honest did make me feel a lot safer that night. The Staples Centre rave was spectacular, then, after it ended, we all went to another club at 6 am, which was a bit dingy, but they had some awesome music playing, so it was all good.

Driving around the streets of Los Angeles in the early hours after the second rave ended with my new-found Kandy Kid Raver friends was awesome. Then, after our partying shenanigans were over, they dropped me off at my hotel around 9.30 am where I got about an hour's sleep until I met up with my parents for breakfast at 10.30 am. I was pretty tired on New Year's Day, as you can imagine. Well, that has to be one of the most random nights I have ever had out clubbing with people I have never met before in my life, and for me it was the perfect way to celebrate the millennium in, even though I didn't know anybody and anything could have happened to me, which thankfully it didn't. Celebrating the millennium in with Sam and his Kandy Kid raver friends was an unforgettable experience which I truly loved. And everybody I met welcomed me into their clubbing world with open arms, well, apart from Sam's boyfriend!

# BEING CHASED BY POLICE HELICOPTERS WITH BEN CRANE

One more musical escapade I will never forget – well, it was more like trying to get into an illegal rave I had no idea I was going to – happened to me back in the summer of 2018. You see, I had been out with a few friends of mine who I hadn't seen for a long time and after we had been around a few bars to finish the night off we headed to the King's Head pub in Market Harborough. Then, when it was time to head home around one-thirty in the morning, I said goodbye to my mates and went looking for a taxi to take me home. And as I was heading to the taxi rank that's when I bumped into my legendary friend Ben Crane and a few of his mates, who told me about a rave they were going to, so I thought, 'Oh, cool, I love clubbing; this will be a good laugh.' Little did I know, though, it was an illegal rave they were going to!

So, Ben bundled me into a taxi with his buddies and off we all went like Postman Pat and his black-and-white cat through the beautiful countryside of England in the pitch dark. When we got to where we were heading, one of the lads in the taxi said, 'Anywhere around here will do, mate; we can walk the rest of the way.' As I was sat there listening, I was thinking to myself, 'Where are we? We're in the middle of nowhere!' Anyway, we all got out the taxi and started walking along a country road, then one of the guys said, 'It's this way; we just gotta cut across these fields,' and I thought to myself, 'This is weird, where's the club I thought we were supposed to be going to with this rave on? And my white trainers: they're going to get all sh*t up walking through these fields! Oh, well, I'm here now; I might as well see where they're all heading.'

So, trekking across the fields we went at one-forty-five in the morning, and because it was pitch black I turned my torch on, on my phone, then everybody suddenly said, 'Turn your light out,' and I thought, 'Why do they all sound so worried? Surely the torch on my phone can help us see where we're going.' And, as soon as I turned the torch off on my phone, my good friend Ben Crane and I ended up losing everybody we were with because it was so dark!

So, there was Ben and me stumbling through muddy grass fields in total darkness trying to find everyone, and then I heard a helicopter hovering in the distance. I presumed it was a police helicopter looking for somebody on the run, which then made me think, 'This is great, here we are in the middle of a field at nearly two in the morning, and now there might be an escaped convict running around here somewhere! Can this night get any worse?'

A few minutes later I couldn't hear the helicopter anymore, so I thought nothing more of it, then my good friend Ben Crane told me the police helicopter had been hovering over where the rave was taking place! How slow was I? It had only just dawned on me that my friends were going to an illegal rave! It was too late, though, because here I was in the middle of a field at nearly two-fifteen in the morning not knowing where I was!

Then I came back to the situation at hand and heard Ben saying, 'It's this way, Steve; we just have to cut across this field, go over that fence and then over another fence into the next field.' So off Ben and I went once again, where we got covered in even more mud and stung by even more stinging nettles on our arms and legs as we traipsed our way through the field; we had shorts on, you see. Then finally, once we had arrived at the fence on the other side of the field, Ben climbed over it first, then I did, then we found ourselves on a country road which led us to the other fence and field we had to walk through! And that's when, as I was jumping over the other fence, the police helicopter Ben and I thought had gone came swooping across the midnight sky and lit us both up with its massive bright spotlight!

While the police helicopter was chasing after us, I went and tumbled over this fence I was clambering over, and I landed in a stream on my backside that had cow poop in it, which covered me from the waist down! My arms and legs got cut up, and my face got covered in scratches from the bramble bushes around me! I wasn't happy. Poor Ben, though, ended up losing one of his trainers in the stream we had landed in after jumping over that fence; he was also covered in cow poop, just like I was! Oh, yeah, you should have seen the state of my white trainers: it looked like I had a pair of attractive brown trainers on now; I was mortified! At least I had my trainers, though; poor old Ben, on the other hand, must have had a right soggy old poop-stained sock! The police officers in the helicopter above Ben and I must have been having a right laugh looking down on the pair of us running all over the place and falling into cow-pooped streams!

While I was doing my best to hide myself away from the police helicopter, I thought, 'Oh, bloody hell, they're bound to recognise me with this red bandana on my head!' So, I quickly tore my bandana off so the police officers in the helicopter wouldn't recognise me, but I guess they would have had special thermal imaging cameras onboard to get photographs of Ben and me if they had really wanted to, wouldn't they?

I never in my life thought I would end up being chased by a police helicopter in my forties! What an adrenaline rush it was, though, and an experience I will never forget! If I'm honest, I was pretty scared because it didn't matter where Ben and I ran; that police helicopter followed us everywhere! Anyway, while Ben and I were feeling like fugitives on the run from the police helicopter above our heads, we quickly hid away as best as we could in the trees around us, even though we knew we hadn't done anything wrong, plus I was innocently thinking I was going to an organised rave where you pay to get in! Then, luckily, while we were hiding away in the trees, the police helicopter disappeared a few minutes later, much to our relief! Apparently, the police helicopter had been called out because they wanted to keep the rave under control and contained as they didn't want any more people going to it.

So their Ben and I were around two-thirty in the morning, both covered and smelling of cow poop and we finally decided to call it a day and go home, then we realised we were going to have to do our best to get a taxi while looking like we had just gone for a swim in the local sewers! Luckily Ben knew where we were, and I managed to book a taxi for us home, then I thought, 'Hmmm, we both smell pretty bad,' and I remembered I had a can of hairspray in my pocket, which had miraculously survived the night; a pirate has got to look after his hair, hasn't he? So, I sprayed myself all over with my hair spray. Unfortunately, though, I forgot to spray

Ben because he was busy chatting away to a guy in a car who was asking directions to the rave! Then the taxi driver turned up a few minutes later, and I guess Ben and I didn't smell all that bad after all because the taxi driver didn't say a word about how we smelt or the state we looked when he picked us up that Sunday morning!

To summarise this very unexpected and crazy adventure we had been on, if I had known it was an illegal rave, I would never have attempted to have gone to it because the last thing I want to do is get myself arrested! All I know is that Ben and I made some special, memorable memories together that night, which will last us both a lifetime!

The foremost thing was that we were both safe and got ourselves home in one piece; minus one of Ben's trainers and a few scratches to my arms, legs and face, oh and a bump on my knee and the cow poop we were both covered in!

Please remember, your safety is the most important thing when you go on a night out clubbing. And make sure you stay safe and know exactly where you're going, not like Ben and me, who ended up covered in cow poop at two o'clock in the morning with a police helicopter's spotlight shining down on us! The most vital factor, though, after all the shenanigans we got up to that night, is that my trainers came up like new again. It's amazing what a bit of warm water, some Vanish whitening crystals and a lot of scrubbing can do, isn't it? Well, I hope you enjoyed this little adventure my legendary friend Ben Crane and I went on.

# DREW BIRKETT'S STOMPEDE CLUB NIGHTS

If it weren't for my good friends H. Henry. BK and Alice Cave, I would never have got to know Drew Birkett back in 2008 after I had been assaulted; he is now a good friend of mine. Drew's an excellent DJ, and he used to put on club nights in Leicester called 'Stompede' at the Rack'n'Roll venue, where I had a lot of memorable nights out with him and his DJ friends raving away all night long. Drew also has the same passion for music as I do and he loves his filthy electro, dirty house, hard house and hardstyle. So Drew and I clicked straight away when we met.

I first met Steve at the local rock/metal club around 2009. I'm not sure if it was called Retribution or Redeemer back then, I dunno, it was yonks ago. In fact, I first heard of him from a mate at work – 'I've got this cousin, Steve, he's a bit odd. He dresses like a pirate, like every day. He works as a carpet fitter and makes these funny YouTube videos. They call him Pirate Steve' – From that description, I recognised Steve straight away, out in the smoking area at the club. I was used to seeing people dressed up in all kinds of crazy outfits there, it was a metal club after all, but he stuck out like a sore thumb. He had his own unique style, kinda Steampunk, Pirate, Raver thing going on. He was there just posing away and chatting to anyone that would listen, very friendly he was. We hit it off right away. I loved his carefree, eccentric attitude. Literally 0 f###s given. We soon found we both shared a love of rave music too; chatting for hours of old classics past and exchanging new artists to explore. When I started running Stompede, a multi genre hard dance club night, he showed so much enthusiasm for it and encouraged me with my DJing. He made me these fan/promo vids that were so random, they're hilarious. I still watch them today, just to remind myself not to take life too seriously. As much as I used to see Steve out clubbing, I never saw him wasted. He was very sensible like that. He'd have a good time with a few drinks but never went too far, stay out too late or touch any naughty things, unlike most back then. One thing that has always touched me, is the relationship he has with his Dad, George. Through their posts and videos, I see such a close bond and joy of being around each other whatever they're doing, be it working together, on holiday or fund raising, their bants and antics always make me smile. We could all learn something good from them two. Overall, an all-round nice guy that has such a passion for life, I'm proud to call my mate, Pirate Steve.

**Drew Birkett, Leicester, England**

Many thanks for your lovely message there, Drew; it means a lot. Now here are a few promo videos I made for Drew's Stompede club nights, which he still watches to this day:

bit.ly/StompedePartOne
bit.ly/StompedePartTwo
bit.ly/StompedePartThree
bit.ly/StompedePartFour
bit.ly/StompedeClubnights
bit.ly/StompedeBirthdayBash

Drew founded Stompede back in January 2013 because he had always wanted to put a club night on for clubbers who loved hard house and hardstyle in the Leicestershire area. I thoroughly enjoyed going to Drew's Stompede club nights because nobody judged you on your appearance and everybody accepted you for who you were. Drew, though, has now sadly hung up his headphones and Stompede is no more. Everybody who loved going to Stompede dressed how they wanted to dress and acted how they wanted to act. And the crazier they looked and behaved the better, well, within reason, of course, which only added to the awesome party atmosphere that Stompede was all about. Becoming good friends with Drew Birkett helped me a lot after I had been assaulted because Drew and all his friends accepted me for who I was, and they never judged me on how I looked. I resembled a pirate, and that was the end of it. I always felt so happy, safe and comfortable at Drew's Stompede club nights, which is something I will always remember.

# CASEY ROBERTSON AND MY ATTEMPTS AT MC'ING

When I used to go out with my mates at the weekends – well, I still do occasionally – I would sometimes try to do a bit of MC'ing to impress them with, which I thought I was pretty good at; trust me, I wasn't! And, to give you a little taster of my lack of MC'ing skills, they would go something like this.

> Tommy Cooper, the Storm Trooper get your hands up in the air, wave 'em over here and wave 'em over there while you feel the bass in your face giving it some to the big kick drum. Let me hear you say YEAHHHH… You know the score keep it hardcore, Jump up and down on the dancefloor. Let's hear it for the DJ M. I. C. Shakin it over here and shakin it over there, get them hands up in the air. Hardcore you know the score oh YEAHHHH.

See, I told you I was terrible at MC'ing, didn't I? Anyway, one night when I was down the King's Head pub in Market Harborough doing my best to impress my mates with my MC'ing abilities, I saw my good friend Casey Robertson, who I hadn't seen for ages; he's one very cool dude who I have got a lot of time and respect for, and Casey said, 'Steve, it's good to see you, bro, I've got something for you to listen to. See what you think to this.' Then Casey played a song he had made on his phone to me, and I was blown away by his MC'ing talents. Casey put my feeble attempts at MC'ing to shame big time.

I couldn't believe how good or sik Casey sounded when I first heard him MC'ing; oh yeah, I am not sure either why the word 'sik' caught on with young people from around 2014 to 2018. Sik meant something somebody thought was really cool, like, 'Oh wow that's sik, man.' So, yeah, I thought Casey's MC'ing was 'sik'. Casey has unquestionably got a genuine talent with his MC'ing abilities and I would love to see him break into the MC'ing world and become the next big MC just like Biggy Smalls, Stormzy, Big Tobz, Mist, MC Whizz Kid, MC Storm and Skibba, to name just a few of the professional and talented MCs out there; I genuinely believe Casey's got what it takes. Now here are the song lyrics to 'My World', written by Casey Robertson, which are very compelling lyrics and are based on the world he lives in. Also, here is a video link to 'My World', which Casey uploaded to YouTube on 13 January 2013, where you can watch him MC'ing: bit.ly/MyWorldCaseyRobertson

# MY WORLD

I respect the world that I live in, but deep down, I just think it's a cruel place. I'm growing tired of the same news, same paper, just printed with a new face. I'm sick of all this fighting when deep down we're one huge race. When's it all gonna stop before it's too late, what's the world around violence, lies and huge hate. People fear in trust, and we choose who are your true mates. I'm trying to bring myself back up, but I'm finding it a struggle, kicked out of the circle, just left down in the rubble.

I've been doing this year after f*#king year; it's not the first time I've held back a tear. All I can say is thank you to the people who were here and to the ones who helped when no one would appear. All those hurtful years of painful suffering, for once in my life, I feel great, and now I'm starting to feel like something. I'm not where I wanna be, but deep down I have a whole lot of ambitions, I wanna be the role model who passed all his missions, I learned a lot about hard times, choose all the correct decisions. In the future, I wanna be with my kids, not just memories or visions. I learned a lot from school and a lot from watching television,

I seen a lot in person, and my brother told me a lot about prison. So, if you think you lived a hard life, come step in my shoes, I'll show you some hard times, you can come see my views. I've lost, hated, seen a lot of fury, and I've learnt so many lessons, and I've turned them into purity, and I've done a lot of bad stuff and gained a lot of notoriety. I hope Biggy Smalls is looking down, asking for more of me, I just wanna be the lad my family ought to be, I'm sick of being this figure of doubt, that's the past, but then I was growing up, so I see myself as an outcast, wanted to prove to the people what I was really about, but now I've been there, all I really want is f*#king out. Seen my friends stab friends, move from ends to ends, and now all I'm trying to do is make amends. I wanna show the world that deep down I'm trying, I'm done with all the fake sh*t and I'm done with all the lying.

**'My World', written and performed by Casey Robertson.**

What a phenomenal song 'My World' is. Some people with money and wealth have absolutely no idea what it's like when you have to watch where every penny you earn comes from. When you listen to Casey MC'ing in his video, you can genuinely feel the raw emotion that comes through in his voice along with how much every single word he MCs means to him, which shows you how much passion he has for the music he makes.

Thank you so much, Casey, for letting me share your song 'My World' with everybody in my book. I love you, bro, keep on doing what you love doing man and never change. Much respect to you and your family.

Steven M. Rippin

Music undoubtedly helps to express how we feel about our lives, and it can also be an outlet for so many people who are suffering in one way or another.

# MUSIC VIDEOS; SONGS PEOPLE HAVE MADE FOR ME AND ADVENTURES WITH DJ MANOS

On 18 August 2014, I uploaded my first attempt at making a music video. It gets worse. I sang on it as well, so you can imagine how cringeworthy and unprofessional this video is going to be. Still, I don't mind making a fool of myself for you, as you already know, so without further ado here is a video link to 'We are hardcore you know the score' and the lyrics you can MC along to: bit.ly/WeAreHardcoreYouKnowTheScore

# WE ARE HARDCORE YOU
# KNOW THE SCORE

Get your rhythm on the floor; you know you want to do it some more. Get your hands up in the air, shake them over here and shake them over there. You are the special one for me; when I saw you on the dancefloor, you take me to an ecstasy. All I can say is that I want it more.

Feeling the rhythm pulsating through your body, heart, mind and soul. You are the one for me, you wanna get down and party. We are hardcore; we are hardcore; we are hardcore; you know the score – repeat twice more. Feel the rhythm flowing over you; you want to get on down with the crew. Dancing here and dancing there, get those hands up in the air. I can see you standing over there with your hands up in the air. Come on now get down to this, stomp your feet and trance to this. We are hardcore; we are hardcore; we are hardcore; you know the score – repeat twice more. Feel the pulsating rhythm; it's pulsating through your body. Get on down you want to party, get those hands up in the air, Get on down.

'We are hardcore you know the score',
**Written by Steven M. Rippin**

Oh dear. If you managed to watch the whole of that music video, thank you so much for putting up with me crooning away there making no sense at all with my random lyrics! The music to 'We Are Hardcore You Know the Score' is by Tobu and called 'Higher'. All rights of the music belong to Tobu and you can find him by visiting tobu.io – youtube.com/ tobuofficial. Right, let's move on to what I believe is a much better music video I created, when there were four various versions of me dressed up on stage singing 'Hit the Road, Jack'. So if you would like to see what the other versions of myself – think of Captain Jack Sparrow when he bursts into a song by the Spice Girls – please follow the following link: bit.ly/ HitTheRoadJackSparrow

Have you heard of the German dance group Scooter? Well, I have been a fan of theirs since they first started back in 1993. They're not everybody's cup of tea or, as Hans Peter Geerdes, the lead singer of the band, says in one of his songs, 'Coffee isn't my cup of tea.' If you love your European dance music, though, then I'm sure you'll love Scooter. Scooter's music is full of energy and always gets me jumping up and down or, as one of their songs is titled, 'Jumping All over the World', so to speak, plus Scooter's music has a positive and uplifting vibe to it. Their music always puts a smile on my face. Some people though think Scooter's music is just cheesy pop music; to me it's so much more than that, because it brings people together from all over the world and for a dance group who have sold over thirty million records and earned over eighty gold and platinum awards they are doing something right, aren't they? Oh, and did I mention they have been around for over twenty-five years? How impressive is that?

Another reason why I wanted to mention Scooter was because I put together a music video with Scooter's song 'Jump that Rock – Whatever You Want', with my dad back in 2014, where I taught him a straightforward jump-style dance routine which we performed throughout the video while we were on holiday in the Lake District. And I have got to say my dad's a pretty good dancer, you know. He picked up the jump-style dance routine very quickly, although we did get a lot of funny looks from members of the public when we performed it! We filmed this music video in a number of various locations around the Lake District, which included dancing with statues of Laurel and Hardy in Ulverston – Dancing in a car park – Dancing in a forest – Dancing on a football pitch – Dancing with washing machines behind us in a laundry room, and we even did some jump-style dancing in a library where we had one family from the campsite we were staying on join in with us! So big thanks go to Andrew and Lisa Elliott from Suffolk for appearing in our music video and making it all the more fun and entertaining to watch, and especially to Lisa because she was struggling with her legs, bless her. Lisa did a fantastic job keeping up with all of us that day, and Andrew, her husband, really got into it as well and learnt the jump-style dance routine very quickly, which I was impressed with; he was a natural-born jump-styler.

When we filmed the library scene for this music video, while the library had always been empty, can you believe on this occasion there was a guy looking through the library books? Typical, eh? The show must go on, though, as they say, so I set my camera up and we started jump-styling in the library while this guy was stood right next to us browsing through the library books; he must have wondered what on earth was going on when he saw us jumping up and down all over the place. I'm sure he thought we were all just crazy campers! And, finally, here is a link to the Scooter vs Status Quo jump-style dance routine video we made while we were in the Lake District: bit.ly/ScooterVsStatusQuo

Because we had such a great time making that last music video in the Lake District, my dad and I wanted to make another one, so this time we asked a bunch of builders we knew if they would like to take part and do a bit of jump-styling with us in the back garden of the house where we were all working; they were well up for it. So, one by one I filmed the builders as they were working, then I set my phone up in the back garden, where the main dance would take place. The video turned out excellently and the song I picked for us all to dance to was by the Italiano Brothers – 'Stamp on the Ground'. And I have to say the builders picked up the jump-style dance routine straight away. So big thanks go to Steve Smith, Matthew Coe, Ash Woollatt and Steve Webb for helping my dad and me make such a memorable video and of course for making a lot of people laugh online as well. We all had a great time filming that video, and the builders' families and friends loved it when they saw it on Facebook. And now I would like a drum roll please because it's time for the builders of Market Harborough to show off their jump-style dancing skills, which they performed back in September 2014: bit.ly/DIYSOSHereComesTheFullMonty

The reason I wanted to include this video in my book with you was because, a few months after we had made it, my dad had a cardiac arrest and Ash Woollatt became seriously ill and went into a coma. I believe these severe medical health conditions occurred to my dad and Ash because they were both overworked and had a lot going on in their lives. My dad and Ash Woollatt survived, thankfully. So, as you can imagine, these two men appreciate every day when they wake up because they know they are blessed to be ALIVE today to enjoy the world around them.

Some people work too hard, get stressed, don't have time for their families, and can end up getting depressed with life when they let their work lives consume them. Please don't let this happen to you! Whatever you or I go through, we should always remember to look after ourselves – Make time for our families – Lesson our workloads and start living our lives for ourselves and having fun. So make crazy videos – Make a fool of yourself – Act daft – Don't give a crap about what other people think of you – Chase after your dreams – Fall in and out of love – Embrace the beauty of the world around you, and also, enjoy the feel of the sun on your face – The wind blowing through your hair and the ground beneath your feet.

Oh, and I hope you enjoyed those music videos I shared with you. Remember, life is for living and having an unforgettable time, so dance like crazy and let the music take you away on a never-ending journey of enchanting euphoric endeavours.

Music brings people together; it makes us feel happy; it invigorates us and always leaves us wanting more. So, embrace the power of music and let it lift you up when you're feeling down.

# GEORGIE GORMAN'S SONG, 'MY FRIEND PIRATE STEVE'

Now, you might remember me mentioning Georgie Gorman at the beginning of my book with the song he kindly wrote for me called 'My Friend Pirate Steve'. Well, here in this subchapter you will learn all about how Georgie Gorman has inspired and encouraged me over the years. Georgie and I first became friends on YouTube many years ago; he has always supported and believed in everything I do and helped me to understand that I can accomplish anything I put my mind to.

You never know whose life you're going to touch when you put yourself out there on social media, do you, and Georgie Gorman is one of those people whose lives I must have touched through the videos I have made online and the reason he reached out to me when he first saw me on YouTube. Georgie captured my personality bang on with the song he wrote about me, and he did all this without ever meeting me in real life.

So, without further ado, get ready for a good old-fashioned knees-up singalong song, a bit like how Chas and Dave used to sing on their pianos. If you don't know who Chas and Dave are, check them out on YouTube; they were famous for their rabbit song. And here finally is a video link to the song the very talented and professional musician Georgie Gorman from Sligo in Ireland wrote for me, which is titled 'My Friend Pirate Steve', along with the song lyrics you can sing along to. I hope you enjoy listening to it: bit.ly/MyFriendPirateSteve

# MY FRIEND PIRATE STEVE

I wanna tell you a story about my friend Steve. He's the kind of mate, he's really great, and would you believe, he always looks so happy, I can see him right now. His life's a bit of a bubble, he keeps out of trouble, and when Steve goes by all the people say, 'Wow.' Pirate Steve's got a trick up his sleeve, and I always knew he would. And if you're wearing a frown and you're feeling down, Pirate Steve is going to make you feel good.

So put away your troubles, you don't need them anymore, and say goodbye to the cloudy sky and leave your troubles behind your door. And if you're looking for a giggle, my friend you've come to the right place. My friend Steve is a mighty man; he'll put a smile upon your face. And when your sad and lonely and your heart is feeling blue, throw it in the bin and start off again, there's nothing much more that you can do, because my friend Steve's got a trick up his sleeve and I always knew he would. If you're feeling down and you're wearing a frown, Pirate Steve's gonna make you feel good.

Now if you're feeling lonely, sad and all alone, you've lost your one and only and your heart feels like a stone. All your friends have said goodbye, they don't see you anymore. Wipe those tears from your eyes, because Pirate Steve is knocking at your door. My friend Steve is a funny, funny man, he'll take all your troubles away. He's got a patch on his eye, and he won't pass you by; that's my friend Steve, what more can I say. So put away your troubles, you don't need them anymore. Say goodbye to the cloudy sky and leave your worries outside your door.

And if you're looking for a giggle, my friend you've come to the right place. If you believe in my friend Steve, then he'll put that smile back on your face. When your tears are lonely, and your heart is feeling blue, throw it in the bin and start off again, because there's not much more that you can do.

I've got a friend named Pirate Steve, you know he's a good friend of mine, He wears a patch on his eye, and every time I see him he says, 'Hi, Hello,' And I say, 'Hello Pirate Steve I see you on Facebook,' He says, 'Yeah that's me,' I said, 'What you up to next time Steve?' He says, 'Oh you never know where you'll find Pirate Steve, I'm on twitter, I'm on Facebook, I'm on YouTube, I think I'm gonna be on the BBC next ha-ha, ah, what do you think to that then eh? I'm only having a bubble.' Thank you very much; I have a dream.

> 'My Friend Pirate Steve', written by
> Georgie Gorman, Sligo, Ireland

Thank you so much, Georgie, from the bottom of my heart, for writing this amazing song and believing in me over the years. I will treasure your song 'My Friend Pirate Steve' always, and whenever I'm feeling down I will think of you and listen to it, which I know will always cheer me up and put a smile on my face.

> Steven M. Rippin

To think Georgie and I have never met each other and he came up with this remarkable song makes me feel incredibly humbled and honoured that he put so much of his time and effort into writing such an uplifting and inspiring number.

Now here in this next video is when I included Georgie Gorman in one of my Facebook Entertainment News episodes, which I uploaded on 22 September 2015, when I told my audience about the song he had written for me: bit.ly/GeorgeieGormanFacebookSpecial. Georgie Gorman has always given me a lot of encouragement over the years; he even said he would like me to record a song, which is something I would be interested in doing, although I have no idea if it will work because I am no singer, as you know; if Georgie Gorman believes I can do it, though, then I will listen to what he has to say.

> Hard work will pay off Steve, keep going, it's only a matter of time. I'm praying you get the break you deserve, your friend Georgie.

> **Georgie Gorman, Sligo, Ireland, instagram.com/georgiegorman**

> When you put out positivity into the universe and to those around you, you will always receive that positivity back into your life in one way or another.

Never give up on your goals in life; I never have and never will. And, just as long as there are people like Georgie Gorman around, then we will always have that determination and light shining brightly from within us to carry on doing what we so passionately believe in. When we help one another out in life, we can accomplish so much together and climb mountains we once thought were impossible to climb.

# THE SINGING GUITAR MAN OF DISNEYWORLD

Everybody says it hard to believe: is this Captain Jack Sparrow? No, it's Pirate Steve. Well, that's what the Singing Guitar Man burst into song with to my surprise back in 2012 when my dad and I went to Disneyworld; there we were, you see, queueing up to meet Minnie, Mickey and friends when all of a sudden this guy came out of nowhere playing songs on his guitar to members of the public. My dad said to me when we heard the Singing Guitar Man playing, 'Wow he's fantastic,' then to my surprise, my dad, without me knowing, went up to the guy playing the guitar and asked him if he could play a song for me! And if you would like to hear what the Singing Guitar Man of Disneyworld sang, here is a video link to that very rhyme, plus the song lyrics to sing along to: bit.ly/ TheSingingGuitarMan

> He's totally rad; he's right over there. He's got a bandana on his head; he's got the pirate hair. Everybody says it's hard to believe; is this Captain Jack Sparrow? No, it's Pirate Steve, Pirate Steve, Pirate Steve is the man, he's got the pirate face and huge mouse hands. All the way from England, here for you and me, everyone we know, including Jack Sparrow, wishes they could be Pirate Steve. Give it up for Pirate Steve.

**Made up by the Singing Guitar Man of Disneyworld,**
**September 2012**

I was gobsmacked the whole time while the Singing Guitar Man played this song! Then after he had finished his interpretation of me in his own unique way, I managed to quickly thank him before he disappeared into the crowds, where he left me in shock and awe while everybody around my dad and me were clapping and laughing away. I was blown away by the Singing Guitar Man's talent, and at how quickly he put his observations of me into a short song in the space of only a couple of minutes! The Singing Guitar Man was unquestionably a very skilled musician. So, if you ever find yourself at Disneyworld in Florida, be sure to be on the lookout for the Singing Guitar Man, and if you see him ask him to play you or your friend a song; I guarantee you won't be disappointed.

# DJ MANOS AND YIANNI KARRAS

Two fantastic nights out clubbing I had where all down to two excellent friends of mine, Manos and Yianni Karras. Manos used to invite me down to London, you see, where he would DJ from time to time in the Gallery Room at the legendary nightclub Ministry of Sound. Manos would hire a minibus and his son Yianni and his mates would all pile into it with a crate full of beer and whatever other alcohol they could get their hands on, then off we would all go down to London; those road trips were legendary. Yianni and his friends certainly knew how to party and would always start singing and shouting, 'London Bridge is falling down, falling down, falling down. London Bridge is falling down, my fair lady,' as we would drive by London Bridge, which we could see in the far-off distance. I still to this day have no idea how Manos put up with us in the back of that minibus; he certainly had a lot of patience, bless him.

One time when we took a trip down to Ministry of Sound Manos asked if I would be interested in making a promotional video for him while he DJ'd to help promote him in the DJ scene, which I was more than happy to do for him. So, once we got to London Yianni and his buddies went off to a bar for a few more drinks because they had drunk the minibus dry, while Manos and I continued onto the club. And can you believe I got to go behind the scenes where all the other world-famous DJs had been? Yeah, me: that lad who used to be called a geek and got bullied and beaten up all the time. So, it felt damn good to be welcomed into a world-famous nightclub and be treated with respect by the staff and security after all the crap I have had to endure from small-minded people in my hometown.

Once Manos and I were in the club, we were given VIP wristbands and led through to where Manos was going to be DJ'ing later on that night. After that Manos showed me around while I filmed him talking about the legendary night club before he started his DJ set. It was an incredible experience being in the DJ box with Manos while he was DJ'ing and watching the crowd go crazy every time he dropped a new track. After Manos's DJ set, people kept coming up to him in the club telling him how much they loved his set; Manos went down a storm! Then Manos and I went into the main room at Ministry of Sound, which is called 'The Box', and WOW the sound system in there was phenomenal; it must be one of the best sound systems in the world because once the bass kicked in it made us both bounce up and down where we stood. And that's not all: as we were bouncing around all over the place, smoke machines blasted cold air into the crowd, while lasers swooped down from above. It was an exceptional experience, and I loved it. To make that night even more memorable, Manos took me into the VIP area where the DJs were performing. So, from a club I had heard so much about while I was growing up, to now standing here on the sacred, hallowed ground where so many professional and talented world-famous DJs had stood before me; I felt humbled.

While Manos and I were in the DJ VIP area I didn't just stand around like everybody else was doing in there. I turned around, stood where the podium dancers usually performed, cleared the dancefloor and got told to leave! No, I didn't really: that was my poor excuse for a joke. What actually happened was that I faced the six hundred-plus crowd and started dancing and waving my hands in the air, giving it some, then a bunch of lads below me on the dancefloor looked up and started doing the same. So, there we all were, jumping up and down and waving our hands in the air, while smoke machines blasted out chilled air, and lasers swooped horizontally and vertically across us! What a euphoric atmosphere it was in the club; I didn't want it to end because everybody was so happy. That moment in time made me feel so privileged to be alive; my only wish was that it could last forever.

The power of music took me away that night; I could have stayed dancing all night long in the Box room. Unfortunately, we had to leave so we gathered up the troops – Yianni and his gang of mischievous ravers – and headed back home. What a memorable night it had been, though, and I have Manos Karras and Yianni Karras to thank for it. If that wasn't enough, Yianni invited me back to the Ministry of Sound for his birthday, which was another unforgettable night out we all had.

And here are the three videos I have made for DJ Manos and Yianni. The first video I uploaded to YouTube, on 27 October 2014 was to help promote DJ Manos's DJ career. The second video I uploaded, on 5 April 2014, was for Yianni Karras's birthday. And the third video I uploaded, on 12 January 2016, was for Yianni's YK Locksmith's business, which I hope helped to generate loads of work for his company:

bit.ly/DJManos
bit.ly/YiannisBirthday
bit.ly/YKLocksmiths

Thank you, Manos, for allowing me into the DJ booth with you in the Gallery Room while you were DJ'ing, and also for getting me a VIP wristband and taking me into the VIP DJ area in the Box. They truly are experiences and memories I will never forget. Much love and respect to you and your family, my friend.

Steven M. Rippin

And, finally, for all you budding DJs out there, here is an excellent piece of advice from DJ Manos.

Keep trying, don't give up, if you really want it, you will make it.

**DJ Manos Karras, Market Harborough, England**

My very good friend DJ Manos loves to play deep house music and you can find him on the following link: bit.ly/DJManosFacebook

# MEETING JUDGE JULES AND SON OF 8: MY IBIZA STORY

In the summer of 2016 – blimey, that sounds like a line from a Bryan Adams song, doesn't it? – I went to Ibiza with two friends, Chris 'Dingo' Simmons, who is an awesome hardstyle DJ, and his good friend, Dave 'Messy' Messenger, who also loves his hardstyle music. Chris, Dave and I had some amazing nights out in Ibiza and one of those nights was when we went to see Hardwell play at Ushuaia in Playa De Bossa. WOW, what an awesome night that was, well, apart from the price of the drinks. It cost around eighteen euros for a cocktail and eight euros for a bottle of water! Anyway, apart from the cost of the drinks, it was a fantastic night.

Because I knew I was going to Ibiza, I wanted to do my best to get a selfie with Judge Jules, which I tried to do when I was in my early twenties but failed at, so I thought to grab his attention I would make him some promo videos to advertise his Judgement Friday club nights. I also made a few promo videos for the DJ duo Son of 8, who were the resident DJs at Judgement Fridays that summer as well, and when both Judge Jules and Son of 8 saw those promo videos on social media they loved them and followed me on Twitter, plus Son of 8 invited me to Judgement Fridays as their VIP guest! I just couldn't believe it; I felt so honoured, as you can imagine, especially to get a follow on Twitter from one of my all-time favourite DJs. I thought to myself, 'Judge Jules following me? No way: this is awesome.'

I would just like to take this opportunity to say to all my haters who have assaulted, bullied and caused me a lot of hurt and misery throughout my life, 'Look who noticed little old me and the promo videos I made for him: yes, one of my all-time favourite DJs, Judge Jules!' Son of 8, if you were wondering, are Colin Airey and Paul Hampson from Liverpool, who DJ all over the world and create house music, which, as they say, is a fresh British frequency tailored for the crossover electronic scene. One of their songs I love is called 'With Every Heartbeat'. If you are interested, here is a video link to that outstanding track, bit.ly/SonOf8WithEveryHeartbeat. And here are some of the promo videos I made for Son of 8 which caught Colin Airey's attention on Twitter:

bit.ly/SonOf8Promo1
bit.ly/SonOf8Promo2
bit.ly/SonOf8Competition2016
bit.ly/TheJudgesonsHeadToIbiza

Love the videos you have done for Jules and Son of 8! They are amazing. Keep them coming; they are brilliant. Can't wait to meet you. I will reserve a VIP table for you and your guests that night as a thank you for all your support. We really appreciate the time and effort you put into your posts. I know it doesn't just take 5 minutes to put them together, so you deserve it. Thanks for all your support, mate.

**Colin Airey, Liverpool, England**

It meant so much when I received that message from Colin because he knew I had spent a lot of time making those videos. Colin and Paul of Son of 8, are the friendliest guys you could meet, and Colin was true to his word: he reserved a table for my friends and me in the VIP area at Judgement Fridays, which I was extremely grateful for. Son of 8 made my holiday to Ibiza one of the most memorable experiences to the White Isle I have ever had. I will never forget Colin and Paul's kind generosity back in 2016.

The night I loved the most in Ibiza was without a doubt when Chris, Dave and I went to Judgement Fridays, where we had a table reserved for us in the VIP area thanks to Son of 8. I was so excited, and I couldn't wait to meet those guys and hopefully Judge Jules as well. On the night we were at Judgement Fridays, my friends stayed in the VIP area with me for around half an hour, then they decided to go back into the main club to dance. I stayed, though, and got chatting with a really cool guy called Jules Marshall, who kindly bought me a drink and told me how much he loved the promotional videos I had made for Judge Jules, which I appreciated him saying. I have to admit, though, while I was in the VIP area on my own, I felt well out of my comfort zone, so as soon as Jules Marshall introduced himself to me I felt a lot more relaxed.

After Jules Marshall and I had a chat, I then heard a girl's voice shout, 'It's Pirate Steve,' which was the last thing I expected to hear! So I turned round to investigate who was shouting my name out, and I saw a bunch of people sitting around a table waving over at me, so I headed over to introduce myself, and it was Son of 8's family and friends, who all knew about the promo videos I had made. They were a great bunch of guys and girls, and one of them was Colin Airey's son Charlie, who's a fantastic musician.

After I chatted with Charlie and his friends, I stood by the balcony dancing away by myself, then I saw a bit of a commotion going on behind me, and I noticed the VIP area had all of a sudden got packed, and it was because Judge Jules had arrived after finishing his DJ set! As you can imagine, a lot of people were talking to him, so I thought I wouldn't bother him, well, to be honest, I was feeling really nervous and timid. So, I carried on dancing where I was, then a few minutes later I felt a tap on my shoulder, and it was only Judge Jules, who had come over to say hello to me and thank me for the promotional videos I had made for him, wasn't it? After Judge Jules had thanked me for making those videos, I got my phone out to take a selfie of the two of us, which I had wanted to get for years, and can you believe it the flash on my phone decided not to work. Typical, eh? That always happens when you don't want it to, doesn't it? Luckily, though, the Judge came to the rescue and whipped his phone out and took a selfie of the both of us; he then had to go because so many people were waiting to meet him.

Thank you so much, Julian, for taking the time to come over and thank me for the promotional videos I had made for you.

Steven M. Rippin

It just goes to show, doesn't it, when you genuinely want to achieve something in life, if you have got enough passion and devotion, you can make your thoughts become your reality, just how I had always wanted to go to Ibiza and meet one of my favourite DJs and have a selfie with him.

Oh, yeah, let me tell you about the last night I had out in Ibiza. Well, it all started one warm tropical summer's evening in the Bay of San Antonio, where I was staying. I decided, you see, to spend my last night partying back at Judgement Fridays to finish my holiday off in style, although I did have a bus to catch back to the airport in the morning, which was picking my friends and me up at 6.15 am. I thought, 'Ah it will be all right, I can go to the club, get back around 5 am, pack my case and have plenty of time to catch the bus back to the airport.'

So off I went at midnight, and before I headed to Judgement Fridays. I said goodbye to my good friends Steven 'Robbo' Robinson and his lovely girlfriend Karen, who both live and work on the White Isle. I also wished all the best to Robbo's crew, who I had got to know; Robbo and his crew work at the Slingshot, which is right next door to where Judgement Fridays used to be held. Before I left Robbo and Karen, two of the slingshot crew girls said they would join me at Judgement Fridays after they had finished work at 4 am, so I told them I would meet up with them outside the club just after four. Then finally I headed over to Judgement Fridays as a VIP guest for the second time, thanks again to Son of 8. I felt a bit of a Billy-no-mates this time, though, because I was on my own, I wasn't going to let that stop me from having an excellent night out, though.

Once I was in the VIP area of the club, I got myself a drink and took a look round to see if I knew anybody there, and I saw four people sitting down at the same table where I had seen Son of 8's family and friends on my last visit, so I headed over to see them. Unfortunately, though, it wasn't them! My eyesight is really bad, you see, especially in low light conditions. So, when I went up to those four people and asked them if they were mates of Colin Airey and Paul Hampson, they looked at me as if I was a piece of dirt they had just scraped off the bottom of their shoes. And one guy said in a very patronising way, 'What? No,' then turned away and carried on chatting with his friends!

Those people made me feel stupid and pathetic and like what was somebody like me doing in the VIP area talking to them for! I will never forget that feeling they gave me. I hate people who belittle you. Anyway, after that awkward situation, I then disappeared into the main club, where I thankfully met up with Paul Hampson and his lovely wife, Jessica. Paul and Jessica are an adorable couple, and I felt so much better after meeting up with them. After we had a chat, Paul and Jessica invited me into the VIP area with them, where we sat at the same table where the four condescending people had been sitting. And on the table there was now a large bucket of assorted drinks and champagne waiting for Paul and Jessica. And Paul said to me, 'Just help yourself, Steve, have anything you want.' I couldn't believe it; free alcohol in Ibiza: I nearly passed out! That whole experience left me feeling very overwhelmed because I have never encountered that kind of hospitality in my life when I have been in a nightclub. So, there I was helping myself to free bottles of alcohol with Jessica and Paul, who was the main-stage DJ that night at Judgement Fridays because, unfortunately, Colin Airey was ill. Then, after Paul had finished off his second bottle of vodka and downed six shots of Jägermeister, he went off and started his DJ set; sorry, only joking. I couldn't resist that one. Paul was teetotal that night and kept to his cup of peppermint tea. Then I told Jessica I had two friends to meet, and I would be back later on. So I went and met up with the girls from the Slingshot and headed straight back into the club with them, where we danced for a good hour before I told the girls I was heading into the VIP area to see Paul and Jessica, and they said, 'Yeah, that's cool; we'll be right here dancing.' Unfortunately, the girls didn't have VIP passes, and I couldn't get them in with me, which was a shame.

So, I met up with Jessica Hampson again, who said, 'Come on, Steve, let's go and watch Paul DJ.' Then the next minute I know, Jessica's grabbed me by the hand and led me straight into the DJ booth! And WOW just WOW, what a phenomenal experience that was! I never in a million years thought I would ever get the chance to experience what it would be like to stand behind the decks at a Judgement Fridays event!

And I can tell you it was an unbelievable feeling. There I was with Jessica, and Charlie Airey, who joined us later on in the DJ booth as we watched Paul Hampson of Son of 8 banging out some belting house music to the clubbers below us; as I was dancing away I saw my two friends from the Slingshot waving up at me. The atmosphere was electric and the bass in the DJ booth was incredible; I loved every second of it. Unknowingly to me, though, the time was flying by, and before I knew it I had a tap on my shoulder from one of the podium dancers, who said, 'Are you, Steve?'

'Yeah,' I replied

She said, 'Your friends over there dancing told me to remind you that you've got a bus to catch at 6.15 am and they didn't want you to miss it,'

'Oh, right yeah, I nearly forgot about that; thanks so much for letting me know,' I told her. Then, after the podium dancer had gone, I carried on dancing away for a further five minutes before checking what the time was on my phone, and it was 5.45 am! Which left me only thirty minutes to run back to my hotel, which was in the San Antonio Bay area, a good fifteen to twenty minutes' walk away, if not longer, plus I also had my suitcase to pack before catching the bus back to the airport! The question was: was I going to make it in time?

The funny thing is I didn't panic one bit because I was so happy where I was, and I thought, 'What's the worst that can happen? I'll end up missing my bus and have to stay in Ibiza. Oh no, what a shame.' I did leave the club in the end, though, but only after I had danced for an additional five minutes, of course. So, I said my goodbyes to Jessica, Paul, Charlie and the two Slingshot crew girls, then I headed back to my hotel pretty damn quickly; well, to be honest, I ran all the way back. I have no idea what the people must have thought who saw me running faster than the gold medallist Mo Farah as I went flying by them at a hundred miles an hour around 6 am that morning! Well, I arrived back at my hotel at 6.05 am, and by 6.11 am I was packed and downstairs where I saw my two friends. Then we went outside, and the bus pulled up within a few seconds. I just couldn't have timed it any better! WOW, what a night that was, or what my good friend Matt Squibbs loves hearing me say when we're on a night out: 'What a funny night that was, boy.' And to finish my Ibiza escapades off with here are a few links to my video diaries I made while I was on the White Isle back in July 2016:

bit.ly/Ibiza2016Part1
bit.ly/Ibiza2016Part2
bit.ly/Ibiza2016Part3
bit.ly/HardwellUshuaia2016

Ibiza, I love you and thank you for the memories, until the next time.

Steven M. Rippin

# FASHION BLOGGER AMANDA O'RIORDAN AND DJ JUDGE JULES

'It's our turn,' which can mean only one thing. Yeah, you guessed it, it's now time for me to write about a very inspiring and supportive couple I have followed on social media for many years, plus who I have made numerous promotional videos for. So, without further ado, I give to you the fashionista Amanda O'Riordan and her husband, Julian O'Riordan, who is better known as the world-famous DJ Judge Jules.

I was lucky enough to become online friends with Amanda through Facebook and Instagram around 2013. At the time, I was practising my video editing skills and enjoying making promo videos, so when I found out Amanda wrote a weekly fashion blog called amandazipsitup.com I thought, 'I know: I'll make her some promotional videos to help promote it for her.' So that's what I did, and I got to work and produced a whole load of videos for Amanda and her husband as well, which they loved; well, I think they did, anyway!

Did you know that Amanda O'Riordan was the voice behind the legendary group Angelic and sang the club anthem 'It's My Turn'? You see, back in 1999, Judge Jules and Darren Tate teamed up together, and between them they created Angelic, who Amanda O'Riordan was the lead vocalist for. And their single 'It's My Turn' reached number eleven in the UK charts when it was released in 2000. Now here is the official music video to Angelic's hit single 'It's My Turn': bit.ly/AngelicItsMyTurn

As Amanda O'Riordan is a fashion editor and blogger, I asked her what she thought of my style and she told me she loved it, which meant a lot to me and was a massive compliment coming from somebody such as

571

her. Knowing what Amanda thinks about how I choose to look makes me feel more accepted as an alternative individual in today's society, especially when I have had so many insults on my style from small-minded members of the public over the years. I feel very honoured having caught Amanda O'Riordan's attention online, and it truly means the world to me having her as a good friend in my life today.

I always remember the first time I met Amanda and Julian O'Riordan; I would have been around twenty-five at the time and on holiday in Ibiza at Judgement Sundays with my good friend Adam Epsly. And, while Adam and I were grooving away on the dancefloor to some funky house tracks, I saw Judge Jules DJ'ing, so I told Adam I would love to get my photo taken with Jules. Because I was so shy back then, though, I dared not go up and ask him, so Adam said, 'Come on Rippo, give us your camera,' then he went straight up to Judge Jules while he was DJ'ing and said, 'Hey up, Jules, can my mate have his photo with you?' which Judge Jules was more than happy to do.

So there I was waiting to have my photo taken with Judge Jules, which I had been waiting to get for years, well since I had been twenty-two, so around three years, and I was thinking to myself, 'Ah, this is fantastic, I'm so nervous right now; I can't believe I'm actually going to get the opportunity to meet Judge Jules and have my photo taken with him at long last!' Then, all of a sudden, this stunning young woman with long blonde hair appeared from out of nowhere and put her arm around Jules and posed with him for the photograph I was supposed to be in! And, just like that, the moment I had waited years for was over, and before I could ask Judge Jules for another photograph he disappeared back into the DJ booth. I was pretty gutted, I must admit. I found out years later the beautiful young woman in the photo was, in fact, Amanda O'Riordan!

So, Amanda, if you're reading this, you stole my photo opportunity all those years ago with your husband!

Steven M. Rippin

Luckily, years later, well, fifteen years later to be precise, when I was forty years old, I finally managed to get my photo taken with Judge Jules, as you know at Judgement Fridays in Ibiza in 2016, so everything turned out all right in the end. Then the second time when I met Amanda properly, was on 15 June 2018 on her birthday night out in Hampstead Heath for the Hacienda classical night at Kenwood House, which was one of the best nights out I'd had in ages. My good friend Troy Goodman came down to London with me that weekend, and we both had a fantastic night dancing, drinking and partying away with Amanda and her friends.

DJs Graeme Park and Mike Pickering, who used to DJ at the Hacienda nightclub in Manchester, created the Hacienda classical nights by picking a handful of classic dance tunes and teaming up with the Manchester Camerata orchestra to turn those tunes into classical compositions. My first experience of listening to the classics I used to love dancing to performed by the Manchester Camerata orchestra was amazing; I was blown away by this whole new experience of listening to dance music composed in this way. So, if you ever get the chance to go to a Hacienda classical night, you won't be disappointed, I can assure you.

Once Troy and I had arrived at the concert and spotted where Amanda and her friends were, we headed over to introduce ourselves. Unfortunately, though, as I was trying to get through the crowd to introduce myself to Amanda, I had several people asking me for photos. While I was having those photos taken, though, Troy went up to Amanda on his own, and I think she was quite surprised and puzzled when he introduced himself to her because she had no idea who he was! Troy, though, explained he was my friend and pointed me out to her in the crowd, where she saw me having photos taken with random strangers.

Then I saw Amanda coming over towards me with a huge smile on her face, looking outstanding as she always does, and she said to me, 'Steve, it's so good to see you, thanks for coming. How's your dad and his health? I love your style; you're a lot taller than I thought you were,' and my first impressions of Amanda were, 'She's so caring, and that was so thoughtful of her to ask about my dad.' I felt as if I had known Amanda for years, which I guess I had but only online. Amanda, her friends, Troy and I then took a few selfies together and afterwards Amanda said, 'How does it make you feel coming across as a celebrity to all those people who ask for your picture?'

I told Amanda, 'It's a great feeling, and I appreciate them coming up and asking for my photo; I always get really embarrassed and shy on the inside, though, when they do because I'm no celebrity.'

Amanda was even lovelier in person than I could have ever imagined, if I am honest, and I will admit, when I first met Amanda and her friends I was extremely nervous and felt as if I was intruding in on her party but straight away Troy and I were made to feel very welcomed.

I'm now good buddies with a few of Amanda's mates, who include Christina Armstrong, Hardeep Chahal and Harry Diver, who I am happy to say encouraged and supported me no end while I was writing my book. And, even though I don't get to see those guys very often, I know they will always be there for me as I will always be there for them.

Thank you for being such good friends, Christina, Hardeep and Harry. I love you guys to bits. All my best to you and your families.

Steven M. Rippin

Now here is a video link to the Hacienda classical night Troy and I attended for Amanda O'Riordan's birthday celebrations: bit.ly/AmandasBirthday2018

Thank you, Amanda, for inviting me down for your birthday festivities that June summer's evening in 2018 and thank you so much for your friendship over the years as well. All my very best to you and your family.

Steven M. Rippin

# PROMO VIDEOS: JUDGE JULES AND AMANDA O'RIORDAN

I unquestionably loved tuning into Judge Jules's *Weekend Warmup* on Radio One every Saturday night because it always got me pumped up and ready for a night of mischief and mayhem. Luckily after Judge Jules's Radio One show ended, he continued his show with a weekly podcast called *The Global Warm Up*, which I now love listening to every week. Judge Jules has undoubtedly gone from strength to strength with his musical DJ career. I first started making promo videos for Judge Jules when I was thirty-five, although I had no idea what he thought of them. I found out through his wife Amanda, though, that he found them very entertaining to watch, which I sincerely appreciated him saying. Now, how could I not include some of Judge Jules's classic one-liners he uses in his weekly *Global Warm-Up* podcasts? So, here to inspire and motivate your musical senses are a collection of the ones I love.

'Gems so special not even Jack Sparrow has them!' – 'Tunes so deep you'll need an archaeologist' – 'Hello and welcome to the *Global Warm-Up* as we plug you in and charge you up' – 'Chunky beats for your sound system, laying down the beats of the game' – 'Time to enter my musical vault, which has more hidden gems than the Federal Reserve' – 'Inviting you into our sonic apothecary, where you'll find the biggest and freshest in sonic antidotes' – 'Time to raise the sails, as we set off on another audio expedition' – 'Giving your audio appliances a battering, let's kick things off with my tried and tested song from last week'.

DJ Judge Jules, London, England, judgejules.net

And now here are a few of my own one-liners I made up for the promo videos I created for Judge Jules, well apart from when I say, 'Ice down your speakers': Judge Jules has credit for that.

'Bringing you more snap, crackle and pop than a bowl of muesli, it's the *Global Warm-Up*' – 'Bringing you more force and destruction than the Galactic Empire, it's the *Global Warm-Up*, which is packing that much heat you might want to ice down your speakers' – 'With more pulsating beats than Darth Vader can throw a light sabre at, it's the *Global Warm-Up* podcast'.

**Steven M. Rippin**

I know, I know, my one-liners are nowhere near as catchy as Judge Jules's are, so don't worry: I will stick to my day job and go back to cleaning carpets. Now, here is a collection of my favourite *Global Warm-Up* podcast promo videos I have made for the Judge:

bit.ly/GlobalWarmUp
bit.ly/GlobalWarmUpStarWarsSpecial
bit.ly/GlobalWarmUpJackSparrow
bit.ly/TheGlobalWarmUp

And here are a few Judgement Friday promo videos I made from 2015/2016, plus two promotional videos I made when Judge Jules played at Promise in Newcastle in 2016 and also when he DJ'd at the '90s Reloaded Weekender at Butlins in Minehead in 2017:

bit.ly/JudgementFridays
bit.ly/JudgementFridaysOpeningParty
bit.ly/JudgementFridaysReturnsToEden
bit.ly/PromiseNewcastle

bit.ly/MineheadButlinsReloaded

Now, here is a promotional video I made to advertise Judge Jules's *Trance Anthems* album, which was released in 2015 and is without a doubt worthy of any true clubber's musical collection: bit.ly/JudgeJulesTranceAnthems. Well, now the time has come for something slightly more embarrassing: when I dressed as Captain Jack Sparrow wearing a kilt to promote the *Global Warm-Up* while I sang a sea shanty. Oh yeah, and just in case you want to sing along, here are the lyrics I made up to go along with this next video: bit.ly/TheGlobalWarmUpSeaShanty

# THE *GLOBAL WARM-UP* SEA SHANTY

Tis the *Global Warm-Up* with the mighty Judge Jules with his download track and guest mix of the week. He'll get your feet a stompin', rompin' and pumpin'; while you've got your hands up in the air, wave them around like you just don't care.

He'll get your feet a rompin' and pumpin' some more while he slams on his main stage mix of the week. JudgeJules.net is the place to be for your full track listings, so get on down to your local iTunes store, Soundcloud or judgejules.net.

So, get in your cars and forget all your arrrs and crank it up some more and turn on your radio to the *Global Warm-Up*.

The '*Global Warm-Up* Sea Shanty',<br>
written and performed by Steven M. Rippin

And to end my promo videos for the Judge here is what I think is the craziest one I made when I had an encounter with a bear while my dad and I were on holiday in Tennessee at Cades Cove in 2016, which you might remember me writing about earlier on in my book: bit.ly/ GlobalWarmUpBeartastic

Well, I hope you enjoyed my collection of promotional videos I have made for Judge Jules.

The various genres of music Judge Jules has played over the years has helped to inspire me to become who I am today because if it hadn't been for the *Weekend WarmUp* I wouldn't have gone to Passion and

Gatecrasher and become a cyberkid, which then led me onto dressing more alternatively and progressing into the look I have presently. The type of music I enjoy listening to today might have changed slightly, but progressive house, trance, electro and the classics will always hold a special place in my heart.

When I first heard about Judgement Sundays in Ibiza, I knew I had to go and check those club nights out for myself, and I am so glad I did because I loved the euphoric atmosphere and friendliness of the clubbers who I have been lucky enough to meet at those nights over the years.

Thank you, Julian O'Riordan for all the music you have introduced into my life, and also for producing your *Global Warm-Up* podcasts, which I love listening to. All my very best to you and your family.

Steven M. Rippin

Now here are a collection of promotional videos I created for Amanda O'Riordan's weekly fashion blog, amandazipsitup.com:

bit.ly/AmandazipsitupPromo1
bit.ly/AmandazipsitupPromo2
bit.ly/AmandazipsitupPromo3
bit.ly/AmandazipsitupPromo4
bit.ly/AmandazipsitupPromo5

The reason I decided to create those promo videos for Amanda and her husband is because I have a lot of respect for all the hard work they have put into their careers. Amanda and Julian also do a lot of excellent work for Cancer Research UK, which is a charity close to their hearts, as well as mine, and why I made these final two videos:

bit.ly/AmandaOriordanRaceForLife2016
bit.ly/AmandaOriordanRaceForLife2017

# NOW IT'S TIME FOR QUESTIONS AND ANSWERS WITH AMANDA O'RIORDAN

## Question 1

Steve Rippin: Thank you so much for joining me today, Amanda, it's great to have you here, so the first question I would like to ask you is: what advice would you give to an individual who's being insulted on how they choose to dress in today's society? And what do you think of my fashion style and how I choose to look?

Amanda O'Riordan: I think you have a brilliant sense of style, and it's all about individuality. There's nothing worse than conforming or following sheep. I know I, 'Preach' about fashion, but ultimately you need to dress as you and nobody else. If you're being insulted – insult them straight back by telling them how boring they look and would blend into a boring crowd, no problem. Who will people talk about, discuss and remember long after you've gone?

## Question 2

Steve Rippin: Have you ever been bullied or been criticised by anybody through your life? If so, how have you dealt with that? And what advice would you give to other people going through some form of bullying right now?

Amanda O'Riordan: I haven't been bullied as such, but I do get a lot of bitterness and jealousy about my blog and how I look. Unbelievably from friends I thought knew me, rather than strangers. At the end of the day, they would sooner bitch about my life, to mask the fact they have huge holes in their own lives. I take it as a compliment and continue to post selfies! Ha!

## Question 3

Steve Rippin: What advice would you give somebody you now know which you wish you knew when you were younger?

Amanda O'Riordan: Biggest piece of advice I would give anyone is to look after yourself and your family because friends come and go.

## Question 4

Steve Rippin: What would your best piece of advice be to somebody who has lost a loved one?

Amanda O'Riordan: I have lost a few friends recently. The way to deal with death is to accept your grief, celebrate their lives, remember the good times and feel assured that everything gets better with time. We all have our time on earth.

## Question 5

Steve Rippin: Have you ever come across anybody who you find condescending, arrogant, obnoxious, or belittles you to impress their friends? If so, how do you deal with those kinds of people?

Amanda O'Riordan: As I said before, I hear through the grapevine that people bitch about me and my blog. They think because Jules is successful, we have our heads in the clouds and our noses in the air, but this behaviour makes me realise how fake people are. Trust no one! Keep everyone at arm's length and if you get hurt – block them and move on swiftly, time is a great healer.

## ~ And finally question 6 ~

Steve Rippin: What makes you happy?

Amanda O'Riordan: Being healthy and having clarity, not worrying and being with my family and friends make me the happiest I can be. I have to say, being a few pounds lighter on the scales puts a smile on my face too!

Well, thank you so much, Amanda, for answering all of my questions. See you again next time on Pirate Steve's Question Time with the Stars.

Steven M. Rippin

Oh, jeez, sorry about that. I'm getting a bit carried away, aren't I? Where was I? Oh, yeah, I think you will agree, there was some noteworthy advice there from Amanda. Isn't it a shame, though, how so-called friends can treat you just because they see you doing well for yourself in life? I have been treated this way by so-called friends as well, unfortunately. Just like Amanda says, though, it's best to keep those people at arm's length and well out of your life. Connecting with Amanda and her husband, Julian, through social media has been a massive privilege for me, and I sincerely appreciate their friendship and support in everything I do.

All my very best to you and your family, Amanda, and thank you for always asking about my dad and his health.

Steven M. Rippin

If you would like to check out Amanda's weekly fashion blog, please visit: AmandaZipsItUp.com

And to tune into Judge Jules's weekly podcast, the *Global Warm-Up*, please visit bit.ly/JudgeJulesGlobalWarmUp

# PIRATE STEVE'S GUIDE TO ALTERNATIVE FASHION

'What fashion sense do you have, Pirate Steve? You look a right state with the clothes you wear,' I hear you say. Well, my style might not be for everybody, but I have unquestionably developed my own unique look over the years, which believe it or not wasn't intentional; diversity is the spice of life, after all, so why not be eccentric and original?

As I grew up through my teenage years, I wore a lot of Ben Sherman shirts and fashionable jeans and trainers, just like everybody else was wearing, then when I hit my twenties I started dressing as a cyberkid and went clubbing with spikey fluorescent green and yellow hair! I also had short blonde hair for a while as well, and that was at the time when the iconic movie *Trainspotting* came out in 1996, so all my friends started calling me Sick Boy, who was one of the main characters in the film, because of his blonde hair.

A lot of people in small towns and villages around England are never too sure how to take me when they first see how I look, and I will often get insulted. If I'm in a city such as London, though, people will compliment me and ask for a photo instead.

Once I grew out of dressing as a cyberkid in my mid-twenties, I went back to wearing regular jeans and shirts and had a traditional hairstyle again. Then I decided I wanted to grow my hair out, so, as you can imagine, my image started to change quite drastically! Then in 2008, still into my streetwear fashion and now with long hair, I became friends with Alice

Cave, and it was hanging out with Alice and her friends which influenced me to change my style yet again. So the next time I visited the alternative district of Camden Town in London in 2009, instead of going to Cyberdog, which I always had done, I went to an alternative shop instead and bought what I have now learnt are 'GLP' – Goth, Lolita, Punk – clothes, which is a fashion style originating in Japan which I have grown to love and mix and match into my style today.

Q: My question is, as you are an awesome unique person with a look many love, even when not dressed as a pirate, would you bring out your own clothing range – like I'm trying to do – so others that idolise you can own pieces from your collection? xx

**Vicki Vaughan, Great Dunmow, England**

A: Hey, Vicki, oh WOW, thank you so much for your compliments. I honestly have no idea what the majority of people think of the clothes I wear; I just wear what I feel comfortable wearing. And I believe everybody is awesome and unique in their own way. Also, I doubt very much anybody would want to dress how I do, and I say that because of the negative comments and reactions I have received from members of the public. Bringing my own range of clothing out is something I have never thought of doing, Vicki. If I knew people were interested though, then, yes, I would consider it. Thank you so much for your question and all the best of luck with your clothing range; I hope it goes well for you.

**Steven M. Rippin**

The craziest style I have got which I still wear to this day is the industrial cybergoth look I created for myself when I was in my mid-thirties; will I ever grow up? I doubt it very much. My industrial cybergoth look involves me wearing my Cyberlox wig along with my cybergoth goggles and respirator, which both have LED lights and metal spikes on them. The cybergoth goggles and respirator I designed myself, and you will be able to see a photograph of this look later on in my book.

I wonder what people who have given me negative comments on how I appear would think of individuals who dress alternatively and come from places such as Camden Town in London, where you will find goths, punks and rockers, or from areas such as Harajuku in Tokyo, Japan, where people love to wear cosplay costumes every day in the district of Takeshita, where it is acceptable to look different and be who you want to be. I personally think those small-minded people would have a fit, wouldn't they? You and I should be allowed to wear whatever we want and not get judged on how we chose to look! I never judge people for conforming to society and wearing high street fashions which they feel comfortable wearing, so what gives small-minded people the right to criticise me?

I love Camden Town in London, and if you are an alternative individual like me or somebody who is open-minded and loves seeing people express themselves, then you will appreciate the diversity Camden Town has to offer. Whenever I have been to Camden, I have always been accepted for expressing myself the way I do by everybody I have met there. Camden Town also has a lot of unique shops. One of my favourites is Cyberdog, which I have been shopping at since I was sixteen years old.

The foremost thing I love about Cyberdog is the diverse style of clubwear they sell, plus the fact that it feels like you're in a nightclub as you walk around the store. So if you ever find yourself in Camden Town here in England, you will find Cyberdog in the Stables Market on Chalk Farm Road, where you will be greeted by two gigantic twenty-four-foot-tall cyborgs which stand either side of the store's entrance, then you will hear the thumping music. And if you love clubbing, you will want to start stomping away as soon as you step foot in there. Also, at the weekends, they have pole dancers to entertain you as well! So what are you waiting for? Get yourself down to Cyberdog! On 17 April 2015, to show my appreciation for the Cyberdog store, I made them a promotional video. I didn't get paid to make it; it was just something I wanted to do, and I found out they loved it. Now here is a link to that very video. Oh, yeah, and see if you can spot Chi-Chi the Cyberdog: bit. ly/CyberdogClothing

One of the best experiences I had in Camden was when wedding photographer David Griso from Barcelona came up to my friend Michelle Foster and me and asked us both if we wouldn't mind posing for a professional photograph. David Griso wanted to capture the essence of what Camden Town was all about through our unique styles.

> Every time I have been to Camden, I have often had people ask me if it's OK to have a photo, or I will hear them calling out Jack Sparrow as I walk by.

The world, like they say, would be a very dull place if you and I dressed the same, so I always love to mix and match my styles up as much as possible. I will find many clothes and accessories on market stalls, on online shops and around Camden Town. So please don't feel like you have to follow and copy your friends with what they are wearing; be adventurous instead and create your own unique looks.

My style today, you could say, is a mixture of casual rock, goth and rave wear, if that makes sense or even exists; well, it does now because I just made it up, and I like to call it 'the AltRaveRockStarLook' even though I'm no rock star; I'm just your average everyday pirate carpet-cleaning misfit! So, get out there and create your own individual look, just like I have. And to give you some ideas and inspiration I would start by going online and searching for alternative clubwear stores, such as cyberdog. net, attitudeclothing.co.uk, blackrose.co.uk, emp.co.uk or killstar.com, to name a few, that are packed with impressive alternative styles for you to look through if you're thinking about changing your image. So, remember: be unique, be individual and be yourself.

# THE EVOLUTION OF MY CAPTAIN JACK SPARROW COSTUME

As I have been writing about fashion, I thought I would write a brief explanation of why I started dressing as Captain Jack Sparrow and how my costume has developed. I never intended to resemble Captain Jack Sparrow; I just wanted to have long hair and a goatee beard, and it all stemmed from there, to be honest. Then as the years went by I got into YouTubing and found that by resembling a pirate was quite a unique thing, plus it made my videos more entertaining to watch as well, so I invested in a pirate outfit on eBay, and the first outfit to pop up happened to be a Captain Jack Sparrow one. So, when I wore that costume in my videos, it created quite a stir, and that's how the whole Captain Jack style I have today came about for me.

People have often said I should look into doing lookalike work; doing that isn't something I have ever been interested in though. I want to be known as somebody who helps inspires others and makes them happy.

Now here are two questions I get asked a lot along with my answers.

Q: How long did it take you to grow your hair?
A: It took me two years to grow my hair down to my chest.
Q: How long did it take you to grow your beard and who plaits it for you?
A: It took me six months to grow my beard to the length I like it, and my mum taught me how to plait it.

Oh, blimey, I just remembered: for a bit of fun back in 2014 I made a video demonstrating how I plait my beard. It's a very amateurish video, but if you would like to see me braiding my pirate plaits here is a link to that very video: bit.ly/HowToPlaitAPirateBeard

If you had said to me when I was in my twenties that I would be dressing as Captain Jack Sparrow in my thirties I would have laughed and thought you were mad; you never know what life has in store for you, though, do you?

I think it was 2007 when I first attempted to dress as Captain Jack Sparrow, and it wasn't until 2011 that I decided to buy an authentic Captain Jack Sparrow wig from a guy called Scott Blake of yordreem.com from Indiana, USA. The build and design quality of Scott's Jack Sparrow wig was excellent. I also purchased my boots, breeches and pirate shirt from Scott Blake, and that's when my whole Captain Jack Sparrow costume really started coming together. Oh, and I still use the same wig to this day. Then in 2017 I upgraded my outfit yet again and bought myself a waistcoat, which was handmade by Moniek de Koning, 'The Fairy Tailor', from the Netherlands; a tricorn hat, which was handmade by Paul Ventress from York in England; a frock coat from Halloween costumes in Minnesota; and a belt buckle from Martin Taylor of Martin Taylor Costumes of London. And doing all of that added a lot more BANG to my outfit when I went fundraising for Cancer Research UK in the summer of 2017.

I have never done a photoshoot before, well, that was until November 2017, when professional photographer John Robertson got in touch with me through Facebook and asked if I would like to take part in a personal project he was putting together of local characters of Market Harborough for an exhibition and possibly a publication in a national newspaper, which of course I was. The day of the photoshoot went great, and John and I had a good laugh. To thank me for my troubles, John gave me a cabbage! Who doesn't love a good cabbage, eh? So as you can imagine I was quite surprised; John had been taking photographs of cabbages for Waitrose the previous day, you see, and had a few spares in the back of his car. I'll tell you something; it was a delicious cabbage. I will certainly never forget my first photoshoot, that's for sure!

Thank you for the cabbage, John, and for including me in your photoshoot; those photographs you took of me are truly sensational. All my best to you and your family.

Steven M. Rippin

The second time I had my photo taken professionally was on 10 May 2019 by my good friend Philip Eldridge-Smith. This guy is a legend: he's cool, he's got style, and he would make a damn good pirate. I had an excellent time doing that photoshoot with Phil. Can you believe it, though: the day we did this shoot when I got dressed in my Captain Jack costume, my belt buckle broke and my breeches fell to bits! So, I had to get some double-sided tape to keep my breeches together so they wouldn't fall down because I didn't want to scare Phil while he was taking photos of me!

While Phil was photographing me, we spoke about how we have both been treated by members of the public because of how we look; Phil has been held up at knifepoint, you see, which he luckily came out of unharmed, and he has also had people insult him for no reason when he's been walking around our hometown of Market Harborough, which I can relate to all too well. And, just like myself, Phil lets those rude remarks go over his head because those types of people aren't worth his time of day. Hearing how Phil has been treated made me realise even more than I did before that it's not just me who gets abuse and insulted when I'm out in public. Phil's got a very positive attitude towards life and always takes people for who they are. If only people would do the same for Phil and me.

Thank you so much, Phil, for taking those spectacular photos and for all the great advice you gave me about marketing myself and my book. I really appreciated it mate; you're a great friend. You're a true inspiration to me, and I love the confidence and passion you have for the photography work you do. All my very best to you and your family, mate.

Steven M. Rippin

All in all, I love dressing up as Captain Jack because it makes me feel so liberated; it has also given me a lot more confidence within myself. Furthermore, it has taught me how people will treat you when you dress differently because, unfortunately, I have seen the good and the bad in people. Most importantly, though, I have had many positive experiences and made many new friends along the way who I wouldn't have met if it wasn't for Captain Jack Sparrow. So, thank you, Jack, you have certainly changed my life for the better and made it very entertaining.

Now it is time for you to go forth and let your own inner pirate out so you can experience how dressing as a buccaneer changes you as a person. And, finally, here is what my dad thought of my transformation into Captain Jack.

I was gobsmacked to be honest because when I first saw you, I thought you looked so much like him.

George W. Rippin, Market Harborough, England

# MY LOVE LIFE AND ADVICE
# ON RELATIONSHIPS

Oh dear, how embarrassing is this chapter going to be! I never thought I would be sitting here telling you about my love life! Here I am, though, about to spill the beans on my mad rampant sexual antics! Well, I am exaggerating quite a lot there; in fact, I am exaggerating one hundred per cent when I say that, because my love life is the total opposite of wild nights of passion and sexual encounters! The truth is I have only been in two relationships. Dating and chatting women up is something I have never been any good at; in fact, I'm rubbish at it! So please only take my advice I share with you throughout this chapter lightly. Well, here we go, let the embarrassment begin. I always get timid when I see a woman I fancy, and because I never go up to the ones I like somebody else will come along and whisk them away. I'll act as if it hasn't bothered me when secretly I am annoyed at myself for not having the guts to go up and talk to the woman I fancied in the first place.

When women approach me and ask me for a photo, which I still can't believe they do, that seriously helps me relax, and it also helps me feel less nervous when I am around them as well. The problem is I now no longer know if any of those women genuinely fancy me or if they are just curious about the way I look so they can show their friends that they had their picture taken with a guy who resembles a pirate. When I used to find myself in situations like that, I occasionally attempted to chat those women up; as soon as I did, though, they soon disappeared! So nowadays I no longer chat women up who I like when I'm out in public because the majority of them are never interested in who I am as a person on the inside; they are only ever interested in who they see me as on the outside. Furthermore, I feel like, if I did attempt to chat them up, they would only start laughing at me anyway.

If I'm meant to be with somebody, then it will work out if it's supposed to, and until that day I will carry on being happy, carefree and enjoying the benefits of not being under the thumb and being told what I can and cannot do. Oh, jeez, that sounds like a prison sentence, doesn't it? Only joking. When you meet the one for you, it isn't like that at all; well, I hope it isn't, anyway. Then again, what do I know? I've been single for the past twenty-four-plus years! Joking aside, I hope one day I do find a woman who wants to get to know me, Steven M. Rippin, and not the pirate they might see me as on the outside. I also believe how I have been treated through life has affected my confidence when it comes to approaching, being around and asking out women because in my mind I think women only see me as a joke. Thinking in this way has caused me to feel extremely nervous when I see a woman I like because I will imagine her thinking to herself, 'Oh no, it's that weird pirate guy. I hope he doesn't come over and talk to me. I'll ignore him, and he'll go away, hopefully; what a freak.' So much has contributed to making me feel this way. And I always seem to be more timid when I'm in Market Harborough, which I think is because a lot of people know who I am here. I know what my friend Matt Squibbs would say – and will say to me once he reads this: 'Dude, you're in your own head. Act on your impulses straight away; you miss out all the time by not going up to women; I've told you this so many times before, dude.'

Since I've changed my image, I have become more confident around women. At the same time, though, I think I must put a lot of them off me because of how I look and who I am, especially in my hometown. I guess you could say I've made a rod for my own back. I used to ask women out all the time when I was younger, and here is an example. When I would get my haircut in my twenties in Market Harborough, I used to like the girl who cut it, so one day I went into the salon and asked her out on a date. I felt well nervous, and when I asked her, 'Would you like to go for a drink sometime?' She said yes straight away, which I couldn't believe. Unfortunately, though, we only went on one date because she met somebody else, which I was gutted about. So, there's one example of how I used to be full of confidence and ask women out, which helped boost my confidence no end. It's like anything you do in life: the more you do it, the better you will get at it.

# PIRATE STEVE'S DATING TIPS AND ADVICE

So, are you ready for Pirate Steve's dating tips and advice? No, neither am I! Anyway, let's get straight on with it and start with how to overcome rejection when you are asking somebody to dance: not to be taken too seriously. Now imagine you are in a nightclub having a great night out with your mates and sitting across the dancefloor from you is a gorgeous man or woman who you want to ask to dance. Generally, in this situation, your heart starts beating fast, you feel nervous and your hands go clammy. Well, what you should do is go over to the guy or girl you like straight away without any hesitation at all because just as soon as you start overthinking asking somebody to dance or to go out on a date with you there's a good chance you will end up getting stuck inside your head and may say to yourself, 'What if they reject me?' So, don't do dally around, as I would, and walk up to that person you fancy right away. I always end up thinking too long when I want to ask a woman out, then, before I know it, I'll have talked myself out of going over to her.

> Remember always walk tall, show confidence, keep a friendly smile on your face and feel comfortable in the surroundings you're in when you're out in public, and even more so when you see someone you fancy.

So, as an example, which again isn't to be taken seriously, picture me walking across the dancefloor full of confidence to this beautiful woman I am about to ask to dance with me, then when I'm within four feet of her I say, 'Hi, I just wanted to come over and tell you how cool you look. I love your style; would you like to dance?' Yeah, yeah, yeah, I know, a very cheesy and corny chat-up line which no doubt if anybody I know is reading this right now will tell me when they see me! And, hey, if you have any better suggestions what I should be saying when I ask a woman to dance, please let me know because this might be where I have been going wrong all these years with my cheesy chat-up lines!

So back to what the woman who I have asked to dance is about to say, which is, 'Hi, no, thank you; you're not my type,' which has happened to me many times. And so what if she says no? Don't let it bother you. Politely smile, say goodbye, then turn around and head onto the dancefloor and start dancing like John Travolta from *Saturday Night Fever*, which is a film I have never seen, so I am not sure why I'm even mentioning it; I just thought it sounded good.

Anyway, don't worry about what song is playing in the club because you are there to have a great night out, plus when your friends see you dancing by yourself on the dancefloor, nine times out of ten they will come over and start dancing with you. If they don't, no worries; you will just end up looking like a right Billy-no-mates, but, still, you won't let it bother you, because you are having the time of your life and you're full of confidence. I have gone dancing on the dancefloor on my own before thinking my mates will come along and join me. Unfortunately, though, they didn't, and they just stood on the edge watching me make a fool of myself!

So there I am dancing away after being rejected and thinking to myself, 'Yeah, I might be here on my own dancing, but my friends will join me soon, well, I hope they do, and surely I must be impressing that woman over there with my groovy dance moves who I asked to dance earlier on.' Then, as I turn around, I see the woman I asked to dance coming onto the dancefloor with one of my mates! And, not only that, they start making out with each other in front of me! After seeing my friend and the woman I liked playing tonsil tennis together, I can't wait to make my escape off the dancefloor! I wonder if you have ever found yourself in a situation similar to this one, where one of your friends, has gone off with somebody you like. This scenario isn't too far from the truth for me, if I am honest. Also, it hasn't been the best example so far on how to overcome rejection when somebody turns you down, has it? Don't worry, though: the closing paragraph will rectify this. I hope it does, anyway, or you will have my guts for garters and make me walk the plank!

> Don't let rejection upset you, move on because there is somebody
> out there somewhere waiting for you.

So, if somebody you like says yes they would like to dance with you, then that's awesome. On the other hand, if they say no, they don't want to dance with you, you are going to be no worse off than you are right now because your life continues as it did before with the added bonus of knowing you had the confidence to ask somebody out who you fancied, which will then, in turn, have helped to boost your morale for the next time when you ask someone else out. When you look at it that way, you never lose, and you always come out a winner.

So now you can move on with your life, and not dwell on whether or not somebody you like will say yes or no to you when you ask them to dance, or out on a date.

Life's too short for 'Oh I would like to ask them out on a date; I wonder if they would go out with me? Oh, I'll leave it till next week when I'll have more confidence, and I'm feeling better about myself.' STOP wasting time and ASK WHO YOU FANCY OUT STRAIGHT AWAY, which I wish I had been doing years ago.

# QUESTIONS TO BUILD A STRONG HEALTHY RELATIONSHIP

Now let's move on to some excellent questions you and I can ask someone we like that can help build a healthy relationship.

If you woke up tomorrow morning having no fear of anything, what would you do? – Is there anything you would consider unforgivable? – When was the last time you cried? – What do you expect from a healthy relationship? – What has been the best thing to happen to you in your life? – What annoys you? – Does everything happen for a reason? – Do you usually follow your head or your heart when making decisions? – What makes you happy? – What is the one thing that makes you feel alive? – What advice would you give to your younger self which you now know? – Describe your perfect day – Where do you see yourself in five years?

Also, ask your new partner: What their interests and ambitions are in life – What places and countries they would like to visit or have visited – What their favourite music is – If they enjoy going to festivals – What the best concert is they have attended – What their favourite books and movies are – Who their favourite actors and actresses are – Whether they like camping or prefer staying in hotels – If they like travelling – If there are any countries, in particular, they would love to visit, and also ask your new partner what they would love to do in their lives which they haven't done yet.

Well, I hope you found those questions helpful if and when you ever need them. When you see somebody you like, always let the conversation happen naturally and never force it. And, if somebody is interested in you, you will know straight away because you will feel that special connection between the two of you, and, hey, you will undoubtedly feel that special bond if you're in bed together, won't you? Yeah, listen to me and you will go far because Pirate Steve the Love Doctor is in the house and always knows best, especially with his unsuccessful track record when it comes to women.

> When you're on a date, always show interest in your potential partner's life and don't talk about yourself all the time.

I have always found the women I like never feel the same way about me, while the ones who like me I never feel the same way about. It's all good fun, this dating business, isn't it? I wonder if you can relate to any of this. The best advice my dad gave to me about women was always be yourself and don't pretend to be somebody you're not. Which I think is excellent advice because in the past I have seen guys put an act on when they are in a relationship; why would you do that? When you don't portray your genuine personality, you will always end up showing your true colours because whoever you're in a relationship with will eventually get to know the authentic you, so be yourself and nobody else. Simples.

> I always find myself ending up in the dreaded friend zone when I try and chat a girl up, so make sure that never happens to you.

# ONLINE DATING

Well, I thought I had better mention online dating in Pirate Steve's Dating Tips and Advice chapter, especially when the majority of people I know have met each other through those sites. I'm not too sure about them myself. I will admit, though, that I have been able to connect with women I have spoken to online a lot easier than women I have met in real life. I think the foremost reason is that you get to know somebody for who they genuinely are online, other than when you're out on a Saturday night for a few hours; it doesn't help, either, when the majority of people you meet have had a few drinks, does it? Bars and nightclubs, I have found, are the worst places to meet someone. You always, like they say, stand a much better chance of meeting somebody when you least expect to.

Years ago when I was out with my mates in a bar in Leicester, we saw a bunch of girls we wanted to chat to but noticed they were busy on their mobile phones; still, though, we went up and got speaking to a couple of them while the rest continued to look at their digital devices. I said to one of the girls, 'Your mate loves her phone, doesn't she?'

And she said, 'Oh, she's just replying to one of my messages on Tinder to wind the men up who have messaged me on there.' I couldn't believe what she had said! This just shows you and me the sad world we are now living in, doesn't it? Where's it all leading, I wonder? Hearing what that girl's mate was doing on her friend's phone didn't give me any faith in online dating. Who's to say who's replying to us when we message people on those dating apps? We don't know anymore!

The dating apps I have been on are Plenty of Fish, Match, Tinder, Badoo and Bumble, which I have never had any luck on, and I can see why, if girls like the ones my mates and I met use them; saying that, friends of mine have met their partners on dating apps and are now happily married.

A friend of mine used to go on five to six dates in a week using sites such as Plenty of Fish, which shocked me, especially when I couldn't even get one date! I felt so sorry for the women he was playing off against each other; then again, I guess they might have been doing the same to him! By my friend going on those dates, though, he did find the woman of his dreams, and now he's happily in love. The only downside is that I no longer get to see my mate anymore. We used to go out most weekends, you see, and now I'm lucky if I get to see him once a year! Has that ever happened to you, I wonder, and your friend only reappears if their relationship ends, to only abandon you again when they find somebody new?

So, from my experiences with those dating apps, I don't believe they are pirate friendly at all! Although I thought Plenty of Fish would have been a fishtastic one for me, pardon the pun, being as people think I'm a pirate and love being out at sea. Surely, I should have been able to haul in netloads of fish on board my ship. Alas, I didn't haul in any at all, though.

Dating apps are really good to find new people, but I don't think it's really good when someone is searching for a relationship. To have a healthy and lovely relationship, it's very important to speak about everything, no matter what it is.

Julia Spaniol, Germany, instagram.com/thebluedarklight

I've had a baby with the person who I thought I'd be with forever! I thought the light shined from his eyes, and now we've gone our separate ways and don't even speak to each other. It's going to take a few heartbreaks to find the person who's right for you, and I've seen lots of people find their love from dating apps, so I wouldn't pass on it. But when you think about it, every heartbreak is one less on the journey to finding the one. No one is unlucky with love; you just have to be patient and find the person YOU want to be with without any input from anyone else, you only get one shot at life, so spend it with someone that loves you for you.

### Shannon L. Davies, Tonyrefail, Wales

Well, now it's time for my internet dating experience. The internet is a powerful tool, and you and I should always use it wisely when chatting to strangers we don't know, just as I found out when I got chatting with a woman from America, which was one of the biggest mistakes of my life! It all started when we met through Instagram in 2015, where we would message each other every few days, then as the months went by we started face-timing daily as we were getting on so well. After about four months of this, we decided we wanted to meet. It was pretty awkward, as you can imagine, as she lived in America. We didn't let the distance stop us, though, so we decided that I would go to the US and stay at her house. I always remember going online with this woman before I booked my flights, saying, 'Are you sure you want me to come over?' and she said, 'Yes, do it,' so BOOM! I booked my flights with the click of a button, and that was that I was going to America. I was so excited and nervous all at the same time.

I also got to know this woman's parents pretty well, and I felt like, 'Yes, I've finally found somebody who likes me for who I am, plus she's pretty quirky and similar to me.' So, as a friendly gesture, I went to London and purchased a few gifts for her mum and dad and her flatmate, who she had introduced me to online. I bought her parents some London teacups and a tablecloth, and I bought her flat mate a *Doctor Who* sonic screwdriver. Oh yeah, and I always remember buying this woman a lovely pink scarf from Cyberdog because she loved the colour pink, which I sent over to her for Christmas, and she loved it. It was so cool seeing how excited she was when she received my present while we were face-timing one day; she had also bought a gift for me, which she was going to send in December for my birthday, although I didn't expect anything in return from her.

So, I was getting really excited about going to America and had even packed my suitcase a month early. Then, a few weeks before my flight, this woman sent five videos to me where she's crying behind her sunglasses because she had been worrying about me coming over to visit her due to her finances. I felt so bad that she had been feeling this way and was struggling with money. She told me she had spoken to her parents about how she had been feeling and they advised her it was probably best I didn't travel over! And basically that's what she said in her recorded videos she sent me and not something kind and considerate like, 'Still, come over, Steve, but it's probably best if you book yourself a hotel then we can have some fun days out exploring my city together.' It would have been lovely if she'd said that because then I wouldn't have wasted my hard-earned money on a flight that cost me over £800! I was gutted and felt like a right fool after spending all that money on flights to go and see her! I never heard from her ever again after those five videos she sent me and her friends I had got to know couldn't believe how she had treated me. Furthermore, I had spent a few days out of my own time making a promotional video for her band she was in as well! Anyway, a few weeks later, she popped up on my Facebook newsfeed in the arms of another man where they were both embraced in a passionate kiss together! I thought, 'Wow, what a way to rub it in.' Then a couple of months after that I saw she was pregnant!

It's unbelievable how cruel some people can be, isn't it, when they play with your emotions in this way. I know I am not the only one this kind of thing has happened to because a lot of my online friends have messaged me in the past and explained how they have also been hurt by people fooling around with their emotions as well. People are despicable, aren't they? I should have deleted her off my Facebook a lot sooner, shouldn't I? Oh, yeah, and I never received the birthday present she had promised to send me. And the London teacups and tablecloth I bought for her parents went to my mum and dad, who sincerely appreciated them instead, and the *Doctor Who* sonic screwdriver I gave to my good friend Matt Squibbs. I will never forget that online dating experience, and I hope nobody else has to go through anything similar to what I went through. And, even though she upset me at the time, I wish her and her partner all the very best for the future. As you can imagine, that experience has made me very wary about online dating, so my advice is, if you do use dating apps or even sites such as Instagram, Facebook, Snapchat etc., then please always be careful who you are talking to! And if you are a parent reading my book always keep a close check on who your children are communicating with online.

Oh, yeah, if you were wondering, I didn't lose my £800 flight. I managed to change it, and I went to Pigeon Forge in Tennessee with my dad, which was one of the best holidays we ever had. So, out of a bad situation, my dad and I created a fantastic holiday experience which will last forever.

Never feel bitter or resentful against anybody who's done you wrong, because it will eat you up on the inside. It's best to move on with your life and be a better person. Remember, you only know a small percentage about the life of somebody on the other side of that screen you're typing away to, just as I have found out myself! How do you know if they have a boyfriend/girlfriend or not? Even worse, they could be married! Some people online will only tell you what they want you to know. Also, do you genuinely know what that person is like, who they are secretly chatting with apart from you and who they might be privately meeting up with behind your back? No, you don't, and you will never know! That's why it's so important to get to know somebody really well first. So please keep your guard up at all times when talking to people online who you fancy, and never give them any details about where you live! Also, never rush into anything with anybody, no matter how well you think you know them. And if you do decide to meet somebody from the internet, meet them in towns, city centres and coffee shops. Also, take a friend along with you for your own safety. Above all else, please be extremely careful and always get to know the person you like exceptionally well first!

> Hi Steve, I'm the same as you. I always meet the wrong people, the ones whom want control and want to change or hurt me. I have been through all of these. I have been on my own a long, long time now. I felt I had to do that as in these years I have been on my own, I've found me, I know how I like my eggs, I know what I like and dislike. I can do the things I love. But most of all, I can be me. I smile and giggle again; I don't look on the ground now when walking, I keep my head up high and smile, and I'm definitely a stronger me now and will never be put down or used again. I also have hope of finding love and companionship that works for us both. I think a lot of people do, to be honest. I have never been on dates or on the internet with anyone since being single. That's not what I'm about. If I'm meant to find someone, it will happen, and if not, well, I'm happy having my friends and family around me. All I can say is don't look for what you are longing for. Be happy

in what you do, and love will find you when you least expect it, but most of all, always be yourself.

**Maxine Sirs, Hartlepool, England**

Not all experiences of online dating are like the one I had. Take my good friends, Carl Andrews and Leigh Devin. They met on a dating app and have been together for well over ten years; they are also now happily married. I first met Carl and Leigh in Enigma, which was a nightclub in my hometown. And when Leigh introduced me to Carl I thought he was a bouncer because he looked like he could handle himself if any trouble broke out, then when the lights in the club came on at the end of the night I thought I was standing next to Bruce Willis! Honestly, I thought he was a dead ringer for him! Leigh and Carl are a lovely couple who I have had a lot of excellent nights out with over the years. Knowing how Carl and Leigh met has changed my attitude towards dating apps, even though I still don't have any luck on them!

# ADVICE ON LOVE AND RELATIONSHIPS

Now it's time to find out if my friends on social media can restore my faith in dating apps along with what advice they have to share on love and relationships from their own experiences, which I hope you find illuminating; I know I certainly have. And here is the question I asked.

What do you think of dating apps and do you have any advice on love and keeping a good healthy relationship?

Well, I had a great response and a lot of people I asked this question to said they had met their partners online, which did surprise me, but I guess because you and I lead hectic lives these days; we don't get time to meet a partner in the traditional ways anymore.

No one is unlucky. Life is giving you a chance to become your best before the right person enters your life. Dating can work for some, but it is, after all, only a place where vanity and so-called beauty prevails. Most are used as a way to meet someone for a fling. You cannot see a person's soul, personality or true beauty in them. For many, even myself, it is fuel for disappointment. I met someone who I thought was, 'the one' on an app, turned out to be a huge mistake, I'm just glad I had the strength to walk away before we were married. There are people out there for every one of us we just need to have our hearts and eyes open as they could be someone we would never expect. It is not a crime or sin to be single; it is a breath of fresh air, time to search yourself, to see the world around you. It is a strong person who can live a single life.

Maria L. Mills, Market Harborough, England

I myself have not had a girlfriend, but I would tell somebody not to be clingy, not to smother the person, give them space and listen to them when they're down.

Gavin Franz, Indiana, USA, instagram.com/__gavin_of_steel__

Tell your partner every day that you love them. Whenever they say it to you, say it back, because that is what they want to hear. NO SECRETS! Do not keep your feelings to yourself. If they hurt your feelings, LET THEM KNOW, so it doesn't happen again. Always be honest. Find someone you're compatible with. Do not attach yourself to someone you think you can change. People don't normally change; it will usually end badly. Good luck, my friend. Tell her you love her every day. When she tells you she loves you, tell her back, that is what she wants to hear. Be honest and open. If she hurts your feelings, TELL HER so it won't happen again. Spend a lot of time together before you commit.

David Hinds, Kodak, Tennessee, USA

Well, I met my husband on a dating site, we've been together for five years as of November 2017. I love him to bits. My advice would be, never take each other for granted, also for you ladies out there, remember that the man in your life likes to be complimented just as much as you do, it's not a one-way street you know. Yes, you'll have your arguments and ups and downs. If he/she is the one for you, though, you'll stay together no matter what life throws at you. I didn't meet my hubby until I was 47, so for you singles out there, don't give up hope as my friend always said to me, 'There's a lid for every pot,'.

Jenny Bennett, Melton Mowbray, England


My advice is to just forget about it, don't think about love. Let life take its course, and before you know it, you will be meeting your soul mate at the place and time you least expected it. Life has a way of working itself out.

Ray Mendez, USA


Tips on relationships: Trust each other, be there for each other, give each other space if needed, but never go to be angry. Communicate and sort out your problems before they become any bigger, go on date nights when you can and explore together.

Jessie-May Murray, Leicestershire, England


I find that most people tend to self-sabotage when something seems like it's going well. I believe this is done out of fear. It's a mechanism for guarding one's own heart from getting broken. Love requires taking chances. But in order to take that plunge, a person has to be 100% fulfilled and comfortable in their own skin. At that point, it doesn't matter how two people meet. It'll be the right two people together at the right time.

Nicole Morcos, California, USA


If you are well rounded, a good judge of character, streetwise, genuine, loving and kind, you will meet loads of scammers and some real genuine guys. I consider myself single, even though I live with someone. My ex-partner is my best friend – Wayne is my best friend too. Sex takes seconds or minutes. True friends are like gold they love and care for you but will tell you what they think of you genuinely passing on positive criticism. Straight people don't see us as a threat. Women love us, men, please don't think a gay man wants to get in your pants, as we don't. We feel just like you and want acceptance – I'm just me, nothing more or less, we all want to be liked. Be open, embrace, and I 100 per cent guarantee you will feel better. A good chat is so much better than a 10-minute bonk. Sex should be a part of a one on one relation which is loving; this is a system on the decline. A percentage have love with sex, or, sex for sex with no reason, or they just love the person. Me, I love the person, warts and all – sex is a no, no – friendship is king – we spend 24/7 together, except bed. What do you make of that lol x.

**Gordon Harrison, Leicestershire, England**

I can't tell you anything about dating apps, but here are my dating rules for a serious relationship… maybe these help you (I'm writing it as, 'he' and 'him', for you of course, 'she' or 'her') 1. The other one has to have separate hobbies, other than hanging on social media bugging me about not being on social media enough. Read, ride a bike, play games, build furniture, just something. Has to be able to have fun if we can't meet for a day or two – 2. I have to be included in the other one's future. If he talks about plans but doesn't mention where he could imagine me then yeah, that's a bad sign – 3. No passive-aggressiveness, that's a big red flag – 4. Has to be mature in the head. Having fun and being childish feels good, but when it comes to serious topics and decisions, let's be real. Respect is important. Chemistry is important no matter what people say and don't forget, there are literally millions of women out there, so don't get upset if one or two do not end up as a part of your life.

**Simon, Serbia**

Dating apps: like anything in life, just persevere. After meeting what seems like the entire world's population of head cases, I met my now-wife on an app. She's like my best friend too and perfect for me, and I couldn't be happier; we can just be ourselves around each other, there's no trying to change the person. It's pure acceptance of the person for who they are. It also helps if they put up with you farting in bed.

Andrew Burbage, Galicia, Spain

I don't know too much about dating apps, but as for relationships staying healthy, my best and most successful advice is to be 100% open and communicative with your partner, trust them, enjoy the little things with them, even through the tough times, talk, have fun, make jokes and do silly or cute things. Don't let people interfere with YOUR relationship! Being in a relationship is meant to be a shared emotional and physical journey through all of the good and the bad! If things go south a little bit, offer help and advice or a solution to the issue, don't post problems moaning on social media for attention, it'll cause a rift between the partnership! Smile, dance, laugh, talk and enjoy your adventures!

Samuel J.T. Conway, Leicester, England

You have to be able to love yourself to be able to love anyone else, it's important to be honest with yourself, so as to be able to be honest with others, as honesty is the best policy. We like people for their good points and we love them for their flaws apparently, as no one is perfect and this is what makes the world such an interesting and exciting place, variety is the spice of life and opposites attract, keep things fresh by shaking things up every now and again and doing something spontaneous and thrilling, as many relationships fall apart and people fall out of love with each other out of boredom and wondering if the grass is greener elsewhere – one love-one life-v2dheart 4 life!

Victor Vargus, Grenadines, Caribbean/Edinburgh

I would say, be very careful on these dating sites. In 2012, my friend set me up on one, well, I ended up dating a guy who turned out to be a psycho and attempted to have me killed, one that suddenly cheated on me out of the blue, and one stalker. My current boyfriend, Darren, was actually the 1st person I talked to on there, but he wanted to be friends, because of the distance (he lives in Bath) but we ended up being best friends. I made many great friends on there, including yourself. I gave up looking for love, but in 2014, me and Darren got together and have been together ever since. My advice would be, don't look for it, it will happen when you least expect with someone unexpected, love is like anything else, if you look for it, you won't find it. I personally wish, we could go back to meeting people normally, I hate how things are now, even in the pubs, things are so quiet, because nobody talks or interacts with each other anymore, they don't get to know each other before jumping into bed. Dating sites are so impersonal; you're essentially talking to a random photo you don't even know is real. As for a healthy relationship, you have to be honest about everything, always say sorry if it is you in the wrong, never go to sleep on an argument, and always support each other.

**Natasha Smith, Buckinghamshire, England**

WOW, a huge thank you to everybody who contributed their excellent advice on love, dating apps and how to have a successful relationship. I hope you found my online friends' knowledge as helpful as I have. And I am happy to say my faith in online dating has now been restored, slightly. The central points on love and dating apps are that you should always show your true feelings towards one another – To open up – To give each other space – To always talk about your problems – To treat your partner like your best friend. And furthermore, to share everything with them, and to let love happen when you least expect it; when you go looking for it, you never find it.

Another good way to meet new people and possibly a new partner, is always doing things you enjoy doing, such as by introducing new interests into your life, because, you never know, you might join an art class, book club, Zumba workout fitness class, or football, netball, tennis or running club, and find the love of your life waiting for you there.

People love being around happy, positive and uplifting souls.

You and I should give ourselves time to enjoy being single when the occasion arises, and doing so will help us learn what mistakes we might have made in any past relationships we were in, and it will also give us time to reflect and discover more about ourselves and what we want out of our lives. So please don't go jumping from one relationship straight into another. And, finally, when you are using dating apps and getting to know someone, please remember you are playing around with that person's emotions. So, it goes without saying that you should always be open, honest and respectful to that individual. Meeting your perfect partner online can take a lot of patience and perseverance, along with a lot of failed dates, before you find the ideal one for you. So good luck if you are on your quest in finding true love. From now on, I will take dating apps with a pinch of salt; I would rather meet someone in real life.

# WOMEN WHO HAVE COME
# IN AND OUT OF MY LIFE

Well, that's all my dating advice over with, you will be happy to hear. So, moving on, would you like to know about some of my past relationships I have been in? No? Oh, OK, then, no worries. Only joking. If you would, though, please read on, I will warn you, it isn't exciting, but it does get a bit soppy in places. So, let's start off when I went to Ibiza when I was seventeen years old.

While my friends and I were in Ibiza, I met the girl of my dreams, as corny as that sounds. And I met her in the romantic setting of a club called Play2 in the West End of San Antonio; her name was Tracey and she had gorgeous long blonde hair, beautiful hazel eyes and a smile to die for. I felt like the luckiest guy in the club and fell in love with her straight away – well, what I thought was love anyway; you have to remember I was only seventeen. Tracey and I danced all night long, staring into each other's eyes; I didn't want the night to end. When it came time to leave the club, though, I invited Tracey back to where I was staying. Unfortunately, I couldn't remember how to get back to my hotel. Typical, eh? So there we were standing in the street while I tried rattling my brains to recall my way home, then Tracey said she had better catch a bus back to the other side of the island, where she was staying, because it was getting late; well, it was around seven in the morning and we both needed some sleep, so we said our goodbyes and we never saw each other ever again! Shortest love story ever! Regrettably, back then technology was rubbish; neither of us had mobile phones, you see, and I didn't even think about writing Tracey's phone number down! I often think back to what could have been if only

I'd remembered my way back to the hotel that morning; there might have been some mini-mes running around today!

So, Tracey Murphy from Liverpool, wherever you are now, I hope you're having a wonderful life. It was a pleasure meeting you all those years ago in Ibiza.

Steven M. Rippin

I have had two serious relationships in my life, and the first one only lasted a few weeks when I was eighteen years old. The girl I was going out with back then wasn't sure what she wanted because she had just stopped seeing her ex-boyfriend and didn't know if she wanted him back or not. So, I was left feeling pretty confused, and my emotions were all over the place, plus I got the feeling she was happier staying friends. Then, while I was going out with Mary, which isn't her real name, another girl came into my life who I got on really well with, so I ended up going out with her instead and told Mary after she had done her first ever parachute jump that I had met somebody else! Looking back, I didn't time breaking up with Mary very well, did I? How stupid was I? I feel terrible looking back. Then, a few years after breaking up with Mary, I found out she had turned into a lesbian! I certainly didn't see that one coming. Mary and I had some great times together while we were going out, and I am happy to say we are still good friends to this day.

So, after Mary, I went out with Hannah, which isn't her real name either, for two years when I was eighteen, which I think for me was too young to be dating because I had a lot of growing up to do. I even proposed to Hannah and bought her an engagement ring! We never got engaged, though, and I ended up exchanging the engagement ring for an anniversary gift for my parents instead. A funny story which came out of the non-engagement was when my dad came home one day from work and said, 'Have you got something to tell me, Steven?'

'No, what's that then?' I replied, feeling nervous.

'Well, at the customer's house where I was working today, they said, "We hear congratulations are in order, George," and when I asked them, "Why's that then?" they told me because you were engaged!' my dad bellowed at me. That was a pretty awkward moment, as you can imagine, so I had a lot of explaining to do that day! Looking back, I now no longer recognise the person I was back then. How much you change as a person over the years is unbelievable, isn't it?

I am a loyal and honest person when it comes to relationships and to give you an example of this while I was going out with Hannah I went to Ibiza with my mates, and while I was over there I met a girl I got on really well with who wanted to sleep with me, but my heart and feelings were back home in England with Hannah, who I loved. And, for the record, I never did the naughty deed with the girl in Ibiza or even kissed her. My friends thought I was mad and couldn't understand why I didn't want to go off with her for a bit of hanky-panky! The truth is I felt very lucky being with Hannah, so the last thing on my mind was going off with someone else. I am just not that kind of guy who sleeps around. The funny thing is, when I got back home to England, Hannah and I soon ended our relationship because things weren't working out. We had some great times together, though, and we even got to meet Noel Edmonds once at his theme park as he drove by us in his beach buggy.

Unfortunately, some relationships are just not meant to be. Since my relationship ended with Hannah, I have grown and learnt a lot about myself over the years, and one life lesson I took away with me was to be more careful who I opened my heart and feelings up to. That relationship ended when I was twenty-one, and I have been single ever since.

I can't stand people who want to use you for one thing only. I want to be with somebody who wants me for who I am and not just for a bit of fun in-between the sheets! I have always had this mindset since I was a teenager, and this reminds me of a girl I took on a date once when I was around twenty-four because all she wanted was to get my sword and cannonballs out and put them where the sun doesn't shine after a night out we'd had together for all the wrong reasons. You see, she was going to university and didn't want to go as a virgin! Straight away, I thought, 'Oh great, she's just using me for one thing then!' So, I told her I wouldn't be firing off my cannonballs that night because I like to get to know somebody really well first before they go off! And after that night I never saw or heard from her ever again. You can't change who you are and how you feel about things, such as love and sex, though, can you? And I know I will get laughed at because I didn't sleep with that girl or the one in Ibiza. I have my morals, though, and you should never judge somebody on what they believe in, should you? I like to show respect and that it isn't all about getting your trombone and maracas out!

Here's a funny story. When my dad and I visited Las Vegas in 2012 while we were watching Blondie perform at the Luxor hotel, a girl who was with her friends in front of us turned around and went up to my dad and said, 'Would he' – looking at me – 'have sex with my friend?'

'Well, he's my son; you better ask him yourself,' was my dad's response as he stood there in shock!

Then it was my turn to feel as startled as my dad was when this girl asked me the same question! I just couldn't believe it! My reply was, 'Wow! I can't believe you asked my dad that! No, thank you. I don't even know who you guys are.' The girl's friend who wanted to sleep with me then came over and said, 'Hello,' looking all sheepish. It undoubtedly was one of the strangest situations my dad and I had ever been in! We soon made our excuses and left, I can tell you! Can you imagine being with your parents and a stranger comes up and asks your mum or dad if their friend can have sex with you! I couldn't; I can now, though! It truly is beyond the concept of my understanding how some human beings think it's acceptable to talk this way to strangers when they are out in public! It's unbelievable how forward some people can be, isn't it? Well, that concludes my love life, which wasn't all that exciting. I did warn you. Anyway, I hope you enjoyed my short stories and learnt a bit about my views on making love and commitment when being in a relationship.

It's a shame you've never had any luck finding someone. I hope the right person will come along soon! If I'm being totally honest, a guy with your background (the fact you haven't slept around etc.) would make me more interested in you and would make me want to date you more. A lot of people are against dating websites, etc., but I met my partner on POF (It's a bit embarrassing when we tell people how we met, as everyone is so against it), but we've been together for three and a half years, and we have a two-year-old together! I will say though, to anyone who goes on these dating websites, to always meet the person with a friend in a public place.

Francesca Alice, Wales, instagram.com/Francesca_alice90

# MY FINAL THOUGHTS ON LOVE AND RELATIONSHIPS

I have now reached a point in my life where I no longer worry if I will meet a woman. Too many people do worry, though, and need somebody in their lives, which I can understand because as humans we want to feel that special connection and close bond with another human being, don't we?

The majority of women I've fancied and got chatting with through my life I've realised have not been interested in me in a loving way; they just find me intriguing, then after a week or two they usually get bored and drift away. Some might stay in contact with me briefly, but only until they have found a more suitable guy to start a relationship with, then all ties with me are forgotten. And I swear I honestly don't mind anymore because I have gotten so used to being rejected and treated this way.

I used to feel under pressure from my mates to meet a woman. Now, though, that pressure has gone since I changed my mindset, well, to be honest, it's since my friends have all settled down, had kids and left me alone.

If you're single, don't worry about it; enjoy yourself and enjoy your life. Think yourself lucky, because you are free to do what you want to do, go where you want to go and spend your money on what you want to spend it on. Furthermore, you don't have to answer to anybody about what time you're getting home either. The world is at your fingertips and there is an endless number of journeys and adventures waiting for you when you're single, so get out there and party.

I could never sleep with a woman without knowing her genuinely well first because you don't know if somebody you have just met is carrying a disease. One of my friends thought he might have caught chlamydia from a woman he had slept with once. Luckily, he got himself checked out and he was all right. It just goes to show that you have to be extremely careful because you don't know who you might be jumping into bed with when you first meet them.

When I have found myself in situations I've not been comfortable in over the years, such as when a woman I have just met wants to take a trip to fantasyland with me, but I don't want to go to that magical place because I don't know her well enough, I've always made my excuses and run for it down the street with my bandana flapping in the wind!

Yeah, I can imagine, if you are a man reading my book, you might well be laughing your head off at me right now and thinking I'm a loser for not wanting to get my shrupney bits out and go full throttle into hyperspace! Which I don't mind at all if you are thinking that. And, as you can probably tell, I even get shy mentioning the word sex. So, I try my best to inject some humour into it as best I can; that way I find it a lot easier to write about.

I have never had any children, and I have never been married, whereas a lot of my friends have, which is fantastic, and I am happy for them. That lifestyle never presented itself to me, so now I have taken a different path in life.

Be yourself and do things you love doing, and don't go looking for love; love will find you.

It has always shocked me when men say, 'You must get loads of women'; the truth is I don't. I think when men see women coming up to me in bars and nightclubs, they presume I must get a lot of action! I'm sorry to disappoint, but that never happens. Some women like to get a photo with me, and that's all. There's certainly never been any mischievous pirate shenanigans going on out at sea for me and Mr Bojangles down below deck!

Q: Why are you still single, and how has being single shaped you? Do you aspire to be married one day with children?

Susan Barlow-Smith, North Carolina, USA

A: Hey, Susan, thank you for your questions. The reason I am still single is because I am very fussy with who I go out with and I'm always remarkably slow at making the first move, plus I haven't had much luck in finding a woman I can connect with. When a woman does like me, they either live in a different country or want to stay friends. It would be nice to meet somebody one day. Right now, though, it's just not the right time for me. And, if I met a compatible partner, I would consider marriage. Not too sure about children, though, because I find it hard enough looking after myself. All the best, Susan, and thank you again for your questions.

Steven M. Rippin

Q: My 5-year-old daughter wants to ask, 'Why do we love people?'

Vicky and Jess Day, South Devon, England

A: Hey, Vicky, please thank your daughter, Jess, for her great question. You and I love people, Jess, because they encourage, help and support us when we need them. Just how my mum and dad have always been there for me. I had a lot of eye operations done when I was younger, you see, Jess, and my parents were always there throughout those procedures, and that is something I will never forget. Also, as humans, we all – well, most of us – want that human connection and to be with somebody through our lives who will love us unconditionally. Unfortunately, though, I haven't met a woman who loves me. What I have got, though, is the love of my parents, family, friends and everybody else I know on social media who have always been there for me when times have been hard. So, as you can see, love comes to us in many various ways throughout our lives. Love is one of the most powerful emotions we have; love can also break our hearts. Above all else, though, love makes you and me who we are today. Thank you so much for such a great question, Jess.

Steven M. Rippin

My love life has been pretty dull, to be honest, due to my shyness and being reserved. Also, people who see me out in public at the weekends who think I'm some kind of Mr Pirate Lover, Lover man: I can assure you I am nothing like that at all, I'm the complete opposite, in fact, and I like to keep my pecker in my trousers!

So, what would my final piece of advice be on love and relationships? Well, it would be to ask out somebody you fancy the pants off straight away. And to always be open, honest and full of surprises to keep your partner on their toes. When you find that special someone, don't be all clingy and needy either; give them plenty of time and space so they can be with their family and friends.

When you do finally meet somebody you like, get to know them first before sleeping together, and that will show your potential new partner how much respect you have for them and that you are not just after one thing. Also, you will know when the time is right to show your love and affection in the bedroom department because it will happen naturally; for some people, though, that might be straight away. So please, if you can, hold off that urge you have in your nether regions wanting to rip each other's clothes off! And, until that night of jubilation, enjoy getting to know each other by going on spontaneous adventures together!

There is a lot of excellent advice online and in the countless self-help books that are available on relationships, so please only take my advice I have written here light-heartedly because I am no professional love doctor, that's for sure, as you now know! All I can say is I have written straight from my heart about my own personal experiences with women, love and relationships and by doing so I hope you have found some of my knowledge helpful.

When it comes to relationships always remember to be respectful, courteous, honest, kind, caring, spontaneous, upbeat, confident and happy. And stay safe out there because it is a crazy dating and relationship world you and I are living in today.

Don't take yourself too seriously when you're in a relationship; always have fun and give each other space.

# PART EIGHT

PART EIGHT

# HOW I LIVE MY LIFE

I live my life by looking through the eyes of my five-year-old self, where I am full of enthusiasm, confidence and happiness, where nothing scares me and where anything is possible. Sadly, though, as you and I get older, we can quickly lose our passion, determination and joy. We will get up and do the same job every day, come home from work, cook, shower, watch television, surf the internet, then sleep. And routines similar to this can get monotonous over the years if you're not happy with your life. That's why you and I need to keep our minds active and take up new interests that help motivate us to become the best versions of ourselves.

Learn something new every day and keep your mind motivated.

I believe because I have always lived at home with my parents, never had children, never been married and not had much experience when it comes to making love with a woman, I have in a way maintained my innocence, enthusiasm and happy mindset, like I had when I was a five-year-old boy; also, my health has had a significant impact on my life and slowed me down in some aspects of it, as anybody who suffers from a medical health condition will understand.

I haven't changed all that much since I was a child and I will be the first to admit I still act very childlike at heart. I can be sensible, but I love acting stupid and having a good laugh, especially when I'm out in public armed with my mobile phone making video vlogs for my social media sites. So, from living my life this way and coping with the medical health issues I have, it has given me more time to focus on my life goals. It has also helped me view the world from a different perspective. Don't get bogged down with your everyday life; it's easy to get caught up in the rat race and be a slave to the system.

If your life hasn't turned out how you thought it would and you're feeling unhappy, think of all the things that gave you joy when you were a child and all the activities you used to look forward to doing. By looking back on your childhood memories, it might help you reignite that happy magical spark into your life again.

I love all things to do with Disney, and I love listening to *Skulduggery Pleasant*, *The Dark Tower* and *Harry Potter* audiobooks before I fall asleep at night; they are my escapism from reality. I guess you could also say my head's up in the clouds because I am fascinated with the Universe, extra-terrestrials and time and space. These are all things I was passionate about as a child and which help keep that magical spark alive inside me.

You and I are both actors in life, and the planet we live on is our playground, which leaves it up to us the roles we want to play. Some people might want to play the extras in the background, while others will want to take to the stage and ride life like a rollercoaster, taking on every challenge and every risk that is thrown their way; it's those people who will live extraordinary lives. I wonder what role you're playing in your life right now and if you have ever thought of changing the part you play. Well, remember you can do anything you put your mind to, and you can choose to live any life you want. It comes down to you and me the direction we want our lives to take. So, remember, change the course your life might be taking you in if you're not entirely happy right now. I have changed the path my life has been taking me in by writing a book. Chase after those hopes and dreams you have; it's never too late.

Nobody's perfect, and whoever thinks they are there's something wrong with them. Take me, for example. I worry too much about my eyesight – I can be sensitive and get upset easily – I'm very clumsy; I'm always tripping up and bumping into things – I need to be more outspoken and confident – I can be untidy – I'm useless when it comes to chatting women up, and the thought of speaking in front of a crowd of people petrifies me. So, they are my faults; what flaws can you think of you have? If you can think of any, write them down and eliminate them from your life one by one, just as I'm doing with mine. The following affirmations have helped me a lot, and they still do to this day. And I believe they will help you as well if you incorporate them into your daily life.

'I will not let those who have held me back do so anymore.'
'I am in charge of my own thoughts and I feel fantastic.'
'I am conquering my illness, and I am getting better every day.'
'Although these times are hard, they are only a short phase of my life.'
'I have love and kindness to give to those around me.'
'I will not think negative thoughts ever again.'
'I will surround myself with happy, positive and confident people.'
'I will always keep negative people out of my life.'
'I am loving, kind and caring and have a heart of gold.'
'I always stand up for myself, and I never let others walk all over me.'
'I don't tolerate bullies; I will report them.'
'Today I am saying goodbye to my bad habits, and I am going to take up new hobbies and interests instead.'
'I am blessed to have loving family and friends around me.'
'I acknowledge my own self-worth and my confidence is soaring.'
'I can do anything I put my mind to.'
'My life is just beginning, and I will take every opportunity that comes my way.'

Do your best to read those affirmations to yourself first thing in the morning and just before you go to bed at night; also, copy and paste them into your phone, so you have got them with you all the time to remind you of how significant and fantastic you are, and even more so if some small-minded idiot tries to pull you down or insults you in any way during your day. I believe those affirmations will help you when you need your spirits lifting. If you are already feeling great, it's still a good idea to say those affirmations to yourself daily. And read Napoleon Hill's 'Self Confidence Formula', which can be found in his book *Think and Grow Rich*.

I also live my life by NEVER using the following words 'I can't – I blame – I'm useless – I'm pathetic – I'll only fail – What if I get rejected?' And what I say to myself instead and what you should too, is: I can – I will – If I don't try I will never know – I can achieve anything I set my mind to – There is no such word as fail – I can only learn from my past mistakes, and if I get rejected, it will be their loss and somebody else's gain.' By eliminating those negative words and replacing them with positive statements, you will see a dramatic change in your everyday life and attitude, just like I have. It all comes down to whether or not you want to live your life with a POSITIVE mindset, and, if you would rather be LOVED than HATED by people, don't live your life with a negative attitude. And remember Arnold Schwarzenegger's 'Six Rules of Success', which I believe you should also incorporate into your everyday life as well, which are: Trust yourself – Break some rules – Don't be afraid to fail – Ignore the naysayers – Work like hell – and give something back.

Well, I hope I have helped you understand how I live my life by keeping that magical spark alive which you and I have built into us from our childhoods. So, remember, always feel grateful, positive, confident and determined every day. And, if you're not feeling that way, you should change your life around and focus on what you genuinely want to achieve. I have now faced my fears and defeated ninety-five per cent of them. So, if I can do it, as I have said before, you can too. Believe in yourself; it's your life and how you live it is up to you.

# LIVING A HAPPY LIFE

It might seem odd at first that here I am writing about living a happy life, but I start by writing about what makes some people feel unhappy. As you read through this chapter and the subchapters to follow, though, you will learn what makes you and me happy and also the ways we can attract happiness and positiveness into our lives.

What does happiness mean to you, I wonder. For example, if you have just undergone a major life-saving operation, you might appreciate every day when you wake up in the morning, along with all the things you used to take for granted. Or you might find happiness in your work because it helps to give you a purpose in life, then again it could be you're in a long-term relationship, which allows you to feel contented.

Some people might think happiness comes from money – Being able to treat yourself to what you want – Going on holiday anytime you like – Committing to your partner and getting married, or when you go on a night out with your mates. Yes, all of those things can make you feel on cloud nine, but only for a short period. Blimey, I know a few people who are wealthy and are right grouch bags.

Our moods change all the time, and just how doing regular exercise and eating right can make you and me feel good; if we stopped doing those things, we would feel entirely different, which would undoubtedly reflect on how happy we are.

Joyfulness comes from having consistency in our lives, doing the things we love, and spending time with those who we hold close to our hearts.

Life is about being full of enthusiasm and having a healthy, happy, positive mindset. Unfortunately, that isn't always possible, though, especially with the problems you and I face throughout our lives. So, we have to cope as best as we can don't we because, if we didn't, we could end up letting everything get on top of us and become depressed.

I have unquestionably noticed an increase in mental health issues since the internet has been around. Before we were living in a connected world, though, mental health was hidden away from us, wasn't it? So now the internet is here, it has exposed all of us for who we genuinely are. And only now can we fully start to understand how many unhappy people there are in the world due to mental health problems.

# SOME REASONS THAT CONTRIBUTE TO FEELING UNHAPPY

Before social media was around, you and I had no idea how others lived their lives and now all of a sudden we get to see daily how impressive some people's lives are compared to our own. All you have to do is open Instagram, and straight away you will be bombarded with models with flawless features. I will admit I would love to have a six-pack and go out with a model. Unfortunately, though, I don't have a six-pack, and I have never wooed a model with my looks. The point is, I'm not going to let my social media apps make me feel unhappy about myself or my life, and neither should you.

Social media is a fantastic way for you and me to connect but, if you are the kind of person who has low self-esteem, is always looking up to other people and wanting to be just like them, for example when you see on your feed everyone jetting off on holiday, splashing out on clothes every other day and pictures of people you follow in passionate embraces with their loved ones, it might start to make you feel a bit depressed. If that's the case, then you need to take a break from social media, so you stop filling your head with other people's lifestyles which you envy. What you need to be doing instead is concentrating on your own life. Then think about what you want to achieve and the places where you would like to go in the world. And, if you're not happy with how specific parts of your life are going right now, write down the areas of it which you want to improve on.

You should always concentrate on your own life. Don't worry about what other people have in theirs; they have worked hard to achieve that lifestyle. Be grateful for who and what you already have. And remember you are just as good as anybody else.

> Absolutely this! Social media tends to only be a highlight reel to people's successes. What you don't see is all the blood, sweat, tears and failures that it took to get to where the person is today. Also, being a woman and seeing the expectations that social media's society has put on us. Our bodies, our careers, the way we mother our children, etc., it's hard. I totally get it. Sometimes, even with my own successes, I find myself comparing to other people and feeling down that I don't have what they have. But that's when you really have to dig to find your own ground to stand on and snap out of it and realise that you're doing amazing too.

> **Kase, Tennessee/Alabama, USA**

One thing social media has helped me with is feeling accepted. If I'm lonely or upset, then I will post a status online because I know my friends will be there to help me as best as they can through any hardships I'm facing. I am concerned though about the implications social media is having on the younger generation, who have grown up with apps such as Facebook, Instagram, YouTube, Snapchat and the 'like' society we are all living in today because some young people might start getting depressed because they want to look and live a particular lifestyle, just like the models they might be following on their social media apps are doing.

> Mobile phones are like slot machines; you can't get enough of them once you're on them.

Social media can be a scary, intimidating and upsetting place. I have lost friendships because of it and found out when mates have gone on nights out together and not invited me along, which has annoyed me, but I'll think, 'Yeah whatever, I don't need friends like you in my life,' and I will just move on from them. For a young person to find out by social media that their friends have all gone and done something together without inviting them along, though, must be very upsetting. In a way, the social media apps on our phones, which are supposed to connect us, can just as easily divide us and end friendships. They can also make you feel more stressed, worried, anxious and depressed if you are not careful as well, especially if you're experiencing cyberbullying, which can go on 24/7 these days. It also worries me when I hear the big tech giants of today making sure that their children aren't on their digital devices for long periods of time because they know only too well how addictive they can be and the problems they can cause our mental well-being.

So please make sure you limit your time as best as you can when you're checking your social media apps and don't try competing with anybody who you idolise online either. Remember, you are your own person, and you will only get out of life what you put into it. Create your own life, not somebody else's.

Speaking to each other in real life is extremely important; it can help our social skills, self-esteem, confidence and how happy we feel on the inside. So, to feel happier, you and I should make more of an effort to get out there into the real world and go on adventures with our family and friends instead of being on our phones and tablets all day long.

When I was younger, I used to play football – well, tried to – with my friends down the park, and if it hadn't been for one of my mates asking me to go along and join in, I would have stayed in my bedroom playing on my computer. Nowadays most youngsters are glued to their phones, tablets and gaming consoles, so you won't see many of them playing down the park like I used to anymore. Instead, they close their bedroom doors and isolate themselves away from everybody. And rather than having physical interactions and meeting up with their mates they will chat with them either through the game they are playing online or an augmented reality chat room on one of their social media apps, which I can totally understand them doing if their friends live in another country or miles away. I just hope those young people who are stuck to their digital devices for hours on end are getting out with their buddies and not cooped up inside the house all the time.

I definitely agree! And it's getting worse with the younger people. When I was a child, we were outside as much as possible, climbing trees, playing kickball and using our imaginations. Now the kids want to stay inside and play video games. I recently witnessed a table full of teen boys who weren't even talking to each other because they were all looking down at their phones. It's like a virtual life.

LeeAnne Murrell, Virginia, USA

I hate iiiiiit. I loved living a quiet life without the need for the internet, or an online following. Such a strange age we live in when my childhood was spent running around castles and medieval camps. Children now have ridiculous phones and all sorts of things. It is mind-blowing. And now there's video gaming addictions that are recognised as mental health disabilities, blows my mind.

Xenia Von Carstein, Northern Ireland,
instagram.com/luna_nymph

What is the society you and I live in coming to, I wonder. Well, here is a great video to explain in more detail; this video was made by Gary Turk titled 'We Need to Start Switching Off Our Phones and iPads and Look Up': bit.ly/SwitchOffOurPhonesGaryTurk

Don't let social media consume you. Always make sure you strike a healthy balance with your online presence and with your real life.

So finally, on that note, that is why social media is one of the foremost reasons I believe there are more unhappy people in the world today. Now here are all the other reasons why I think you and I are more troubled in today's society, which include: Money – Health – Hopelessness – Lack of self-confidence – Mental well-being – Having to compete with other people in life or at work – Feeling mentally fatigued by doing the same thing day in and day out – Envy of others – Worrying about what other people's opinions are of you – Thinking people aren't giving you as much credit, respect or appreciation as you deserve, and finally, having feelings of guilt and shame, such as thinking to yourself, 'I've overindulged yet again, I need to lose weight, I'm working too many hours, and I'm not paying enough attention to my family and friends.'

The planet you and I live on is massive, and we should remember that we both play tiny parts on it. The roles we do represent, though, are appreciated by our families and friends and the people we meet and attract into them. They are the ones who help you, and me feel happy from within. I might not earn much money, but I still consider myself rich and happy because I have a job I enjoy doing, I get to travel all over the beautiful English countryside for work, and also because I have a loving family and fantastic friends who love and support me. What more could I ask for?

Think of the people you have in your life today who admire and encourage you in everything you do because that is where true happiness comes from. Now here is a piece of advice on living a fun and fulfilled life from my dad.

I would say not to take life too serious and don't be in a hurry to grow up too quick. And don't be envious of others. Be happy with what you've got.

George W. Rippin, Market Harborough, England

# WHAT DO YOU BELIEVE MAKES PEOPLE UNHAPPY IN SOCIETY?

Now, here is another one of the questions I asked my friends on social media to get their views and opinions on what they believe makes people unhappier in today's society.

Social media, looking at screens for hours on end, the types of jobs we have, money, mental health and having to compete against other people are some of the reasons why I believe people are more unhappy in today's society. Would you agree? If not, what do you think makes people unhappier?

Potholes and speed bumps make me unhappy.

Gary Randall, Rothwell, Northamptonshire, England, instagram.com/buffmaster71

Comparison: Looking at Facebook and comparing your life with what you see other people doing (even though you only see one side of the story on FB). Nevertheless, comparison steals your joy.

Anna Larke, Hertfordshire, England

Being brought up without the internet and social media but being one that embraces modern technology and thinking of my own experiences, I am of the opinion social media is good and bad. Good points is a shy person like me, means others can know more about me thru my posts. Bad thing is that a shy person can use this medium as a way to communicate, rather than real-time interactions. For me, as an untrained user of the internet when it was in its infancy, and I was young and inexperienced, I would say it's been VERY damaging and caused me many problems. But it's here, and we have to embrace it. The internet should have tighter controls and kids need education on the damage it can do. To see couples split up and cyberbullying, young people committing suicide and terrorists using it on horrendous crimes, means action is needed, but as it is big bucks for many including the government, a blind eye approach is taken.

Gordon Harrison, Leicestershire, England


That money rules everything. We work to die. And to die, we need to work to afford to die. It's an unfair circle of misery.

Susan Dilks, Leicestershire, England, instagram.com/suzy0826


We are in a shift. I tell you an amazing thing that happened when I was alone in a magical place talking to nature and asked if there was a message for me. A fish dropped out of the water, and when I walked the path, this guy shouted, 'Aquarius!' And after this, I met a guy, and his name was Ariel. It is the Aquarius time we are in. The awaking of a new wave in consciousness. (YouTube) Together we can raise our consciousness by meditation and becoming more aware. I, therefore, also don't watch news fear based. So true what you mention. People would be much kinder if they are happy. I try to meditate as much as I can to raise our vibration.

Bella Beleza, Amsterdam, Netherlands,
instagram.com/_bella_beleza_

I agree! I don't even want to start; I'll just say, it's not fair on today's youth because they don't have a choice, it's imposed on them, this is life today in the modern world, and it's getting worse. Question everything! Ditch the TV! Be a part of nature, not above it. Mother nature slowly but surely balances things out by taking matter into its own hands. Its gut and heart-wrenching. We have to simplify our lives, know and believe within us that we can do things that they like to make us believe we can't, that we, 'Need' this and that, they'll do everything for us but at a cost. Start doing things and fixing things yourself; knowledge, research and power on. It's a brutal life, just bury me in my garden, but can't even do that. Everything is so systematic and controlled, even, 'fun,' is controlled, it all starts with our birth certificate and goes on from there.

**Andjelka Bikić, Western Australia**


What makes me unhappy is the section of society that thinks the world owes them. They've done nothing, given nothing, take everything and make the lives of others unbearable.

**Su Ablitt, Leicester, England**

Thank you to my friends on social media who shared what makes them feel unhappy in today's society. There are a lot of diverse opinions on this as you can see, from money problems to social media, which has highlighted mental health a lot more, and not forgetting Gary Randall, who is unhappy with the state of Britain's roads!

# WHAT YOU THINK ABOUT, YOU ATTRACT INTO YOUR LIFE

A few years ago, I listened to an audiobook called *The Secret* by Rhonda Byrne. After listening to that audiobook, I couldn't believe how much I related to it. My attitude used to be very negative towards life, you see, because of what I have been through in my past, *The Secret*, though, helped me get my life back on track again. It also made me realise the mistakes I was making. So, if you find you're always having negative feelings and things never seem to go your way, I would highly recommend reading what the Law of Attraction is all about. When you practise the Law of Attraction, what you think about won't just come to you; you have to have a positive attitude, be full of confidence and have plenty of commitment and determination. These are all key factors to attracting what you want into your life.

Unfortunately, not everybody believes in the Law of Attraction, although I have read a lot of stories about how it has helped many people. If I didn't believe in it, I honestly wouldn't write about it.

100%! I fell across it by chance years ago. I started writing down my goals and visualising me achieving them. Low and behold, I started to achieve them, and everything I desired came to me. I've put a lot of study time into it, and I talk about it a lot in my training sessions I give to businesses. The law of attraction is everything; those that believe in it, respect it and practice it, will achieve great things.

Robert Spence, Leicestershire, England,
instagram.com/robjohnspence

Since I have been practising the Law of Attraction, I can tell you it does work. I have always been realistic, though, because when you do want to draw something into your life it is best to start small then gradually work your way up to the more essential things you would like to attract. So, for example, if you think about that long weekend break you have wanted to get away on or that festival you have wanted to go to but have been unable to afford, then those are things you can attract into your life. You just have to set out a plan of action and save up each week so you can afford to do those activities. And when it comes to the more significant things you would like to attract into your life, such as that big six-bedroomed house you have always dreamt of owning or that brand-new sports car you have had your eyes on, then you have to set out more extensive plans of action on ways you are going to be able to afford to buy them over a certain period by saving up. If you want something bad enough, you can get it if you put your mind to it and have enough determination.

I think trying to have a positive outlook on life helps a lot. If you try to think positively, I think it helps to attract positive things back to you. Also, the more you put into life, the more you can get out of it. It's hard to stay positive all the time as life has its ups and downs, but it's helpful to be that way as much as you can. I really admire people who try to do that in their lives.

Debbie Barnard, Booneville, Arkansas, USA

Have you ever had a negative experience when you have been somewhere and said to yourself, 'I'm not going there again'? I know I have. For example, I used to love going to Enigma, which was a nightclub in my hometown. Once I had been assaulted in there though, I stopped going for around a year. I was associating Enigma with all those sad memories of when I had been head-butted twice in the face, you see. When I finally went back to the club, though, I had a great time, and all my fears melted away. So, just because you have had a bad experience somewhere, it doesn't mean it is always going to be like that when you go there again. Although, if you do keep thinking in a negative mindset that something terrible will happen to you, then there is a good chance that something unfortunate will happen. Remember, you are the one who is subconsciously attracting those negative thoughts into your mind.

By keeping a negative attitude, you will be portraying to those around you how you are feeling through your body language, which might attract the wrong kind of attention your way. So, the best thing to do is to surround yourself with your good friends; also think positively and remember the great times you had in that place where the negative experience happened.

If you surround yourself with negative people, you will have negative experiences. So always encircle yourself with positive individuals, and then you will have fantastic adventures.

I do indeed believe in the law of attraction and the fact that your thoughts have the power to manifest themselves into reality, as I always say, you have to perceive it, to believe it, to achieve it, mind over matter.

### Victor Vargus, St Vincent, Caribbean/Edinburgh

When I think negatively, I will listen to my music, exercise and talk to my family and friends, who help make me think more positively again.

If you say to yourself, 'I'm never going to win the lottery,' then there is a good chance you will never win it. If you believe you will win the lottery, though, then there is going to be a much higher chance that you will win it, even if it is only a small amount. It's a bit like when you say to yourself, 'I think I'm coming down with a cold because somebody sneezed on me,' then there is going to be a good chance you come down with one! So always remember to attract positive, healthy and happy thoughts into your mind, thus changing your whole attitude.

Yes, when I put my focus on dreaming of what I wanted to be each day, I soon found it easier to rid my life of the things that got in the way of that dream. I discovered what it took to achieve my goals. Once upon a time, I was a homeless needle junkie, using a t-shirt as a blanket and a flattened box as a barrier between my sleeping body and the rough ground behind a mechanic shop, not even a pair of shoes to my name, and clutching my book bag so nobody would steal it from me while I slept; true story. So, I stopped being so focused on the misery of my situation and started doing what I had to do to get out of it. Now here I am, three years later, a two-bedroom apartment, in love, and I have a beautiful baby boy; completely sober. A lot more than Law of Attraction got me here, but that sure did help.

Rhiannon Hennessey, USA

When you put positive energy out into the Universe, you will always receive that positive energy back. So, by looking at life on the bright side, having a positive outlook and a smile on your face, being grateful for your health, the house you live in, all the possessions you own and your family and friends, you will attract good life experiences to you. On the other hand, if all you do is moan and groan about everything and everybody in your life, then you are going to draw negative energy and encounters your way.

Also, be grateful for the money you have in your bank account, no matter how small or large the amount is. And when those bills come through your letterbox, don't get all stressed and think, 'Oh great, here's another statement I have to pay.' Instead, say to yourself, 'Thank you for charging me. If it weren't for this payment I have to make, I wouldn't have fresh, clean running water every day. And thank you for this electricity bill because without it I wouldn't be able to enjoy my favourite TV shows and surf the internet.'

Always be grateful for the public services people provide us, so massive respect to all the Delivery drivers – Power station companies – NHS staff – Post office workers – Car mechanics – Farmers – Government; even though we don't always agree with the decisions they make, they do keep law and order – Police force – Fire Brigade and ambulance workers out there, along with key workers who help keep the planet running smoothly today.

My dad and I are forever grateful to the NHS because they have saved my eyesight on several occasions and my dad's life twice! So, to show our thanks to the NHS and my opticians, my dad and I will take them in a box of chocolates or a thank-you card every so often, which they always appreciate.

I find that when I write, the Universe opens up to me. Some of my characters even come to life, in the most uncanny way. This just proves to me that I'm on the right track, and I should continue to pursue my dreams. Thank you for being a constant inspiration, Steve.

Nicole Morcos, California, USA

Have you ever thought to yourself, 'Oh, it's all right for them isn't it? They have everything.' Well, you should never think that way. I used to, and by doing so I would put myself into a negative mindset and say to myself, 'Nothing good ever happens to me. Why can't I have a house like they have and why can't I go on holiday more often?' So never use the words 'I can't'. Say instead, 'I can,' and then you will see the difference it makes to your life.

You and I come into this world with nothing, and we both leave with nothing. It's the mark we leave behind on other people's lives which we will be remembered for.

# GRATITUDE ROCKS AND CRYSTALS

You know when you have had one of those days you can't wait to be over and find it difficult to sleep at night because your head is full of negative thoughts? Well, why not get yourself a gratitude rock and hold it in your hand before you go to sleep at night and be thankful for all the positive things that have happened to you during your day? Some people do this by writing down their thoughts into a diary each evening. If you're not into gratitude rocks and writing your feelings down, then you could find something else to hold in your hand which you find comforting, such as your favourite teddy bear or, if you have got a stress ball, that would work as well.

Holding a gratitude rock, teddy bear or stress ball while you think of all the positive outcomes of your day and the people you care about the most can help relax your mind before you go to sleep at night, so when you wake up the following morning you will have a clear head free of any negative thoughts from the day before. All this might sound a bit strange, I guess, but it's a therapeutic technique which does help a lot of people. I first heard about gratitude rocks when I read *The Secret* by Rhonda Byrne, if you were wondering. My dad thinks I'm nuts, but, hey, it would be a boring world if we were all the same. If you do try using a gratitude rock, I hope it helps you as much as it has helped me. I found my gratitude rock in my garden, by the way.

Another alternative is crystals, although when I mention crystals to some people they laugh at me, which is fine because they are not everybody's cup of tea. I do believe in the power they possess and put out there into the Universe, though. So, if you are somebody who is learning what the Law of Attraction is and are interested in crystals, I would highly recommend buying yourself a few that are linked to the Law of Attraction. I have been into crystals for a short while and only know the basics of what each one does. All I can say is that they make me feel fantastic when I am around them; whether that's in my mind, though, I honestly don't know. Now here are the crystals I would recommend to help you with the Law of Attraction, plus a brief description of what each one does. Amazonite: communication and truth – Citrine: abundance, positivity, personal power and energy – Clear quartz: amplify energy, inner power and clarity – Carnelian: passion, confidence and strength – Amethyst: clarity, wisdom, higher vibration – Goldstone: growth, goals and luck – Smoky quartz: creativity and manifesting success and power. All of these crystals can also help with spiritual healing.

I hold the crystals I have at home close to my heart and say, 'Thank you, Universe for all you have given me throughout my life. I am grateful for my eyesight, my family and friends, and I am grateful for my health.' Or if a family member or friend is poorly I will say, 'I would like to send positive, healthy healing vibrations to my family and friends. I believe in you, Universe; thank you for listening to me'; you could also say this or something similar. And communicating with the Universe while I am holding my crystals helps clear my mind and comforts me. I became intrigued in crystals when my good friend Kelly Charlton told me some of the health benefits they possess. So, open your mind to the power of crystals because who knows what they could do for you. Now here are a few words of wisdom on crystals from my good friend Kelly Charlton.

Crystals help to focus the mind but not in a negative way, in a healing, positive way. When I did the crystal courses which all in all was about 18 months, one of the best things was the fact it drew like-minded people together. It's also amazing to watch people who do not believe in it at all choose a crystal, and when the properties of that crystal are explained, the surprise on their face is great. I always carry grounding stones in my jacket and even though I haven't recently – meditating with crystals is great for clearing and making your mind quieten down. They can also bring clarity. Crystal healings are excellent and can help with lots and lots of things. It also helps to understand that a lot of illnesses are caused by emotional problems. Basically, it can open a lot of doors to learn more knowledge and expand your mind and soul. Amethyst is one of my favourites and is a great all-round stone. If you have trouble sleeping stick some smoky quartz under your pillow as well.

**Kelly Charlton, Lutterworth, England**

Here is a story how the Law of Attraction has worked in my life because of my dad's caring attitude. It all started around 2014, when a guy got in touch with my dad to have some carpets fitted in his flat. Unfortunately, this guy was unable to pay for his carpets straight away so my dad said he could pay his bill off weekly to help him out, which the guy genuinely appreciated, and he thanked my dad for being so understanding. Then in 2017, when I was raising money for Cancer Research UK, towards the end of my fundraising campaign, I had a very generous donation from the guy who was struggling to pay for his carpets. I just couldn't believe how much money he had donated! It blew my mind! So, I messaged the guy, and he explained why and how he was able to donate such a large amount. Basically, he had come into some money and said he always remembered how kind my dad had been to him, plus he thought what my dad and I were doing for Cancer Research UK was excellent. Again, this is just another example of how the Law of Attraction works. When you are kind and help other people out in life, those acts of kindness will always come back around to you. So be happy, kind and caring towards others, and you will receive kindness back into your life in one way or another in the future.

I know the Law of Attraction works. Unfortunately, though, you do have to be careful because there are a lot of scam artists out there who will take you for every penny you have got, so you should always keep your wits about you and use your common sense. And, if something does sound too good to be true, then it usually is. Always do your homework first and read up on what you are looking into before parting with any money.

Now follows a great piece of advice from my good friend Carol Atkinson, which you and I should remember while practising the Law of Attraction in our everyday lives.

I don't believe that positive thoughts alone can transform anyone's life, and I know many people have been disappointed by the Law of Attraction. Positive thought, combined with positive action and determination is a different story, so it's all about interpretation. Also, there are a lot of charlatans around, and I was reading about a woman who invested £80K in some venture to do with 'The Secret' and was left bankrupt by a con merchant. The Law of Attraction has become a lucrative business for some. I like the exert from the Desiderata – Exercise Caution in your business affairs; for the world is full of trickery. But let that not blind you to what virtue there is; many persons strive for high ideals, and everywhere life is full of heroism – In fact, anyone who hasn't read, The Desiderata, should look it up. Sorry to have gone off-topic a bit.

### Carol Atkinson, Liverpool, England

In our lives, we can never choose what positive or negative experiences we are going to be faced with, so it comes down to how you and I respond to those events the direction the rest of our lives will take. Take me, for example; I have faced a lot of negative encounters which I have not wanted to attract into my life. Unfortunately, though, things do happen to us which are out of our control. Always remember, you are in command of your thoughts, feelings and the responses you make to any life decisions.

If teachers taught schoolchildren the principles of the Law of Attraction, and gave them books to read such as *The Secret* by Rhonda Byrne, Napoleon Hill's *Think and Grow Rich* and Dale Carnegie's *How to Win Friends and Influence People*, they could teach them so much.

So, you must, in whatever negative circumstance you have no control over, respond to it correctly, which will then help improve your life just as bullying helped to transform mine. Say you have been bullied and now you have learnt how to overcome it; you could assist others who face bullying daily and do your best to teach those people how to ignore, rise above, deal with and stop the bullying from happening to them. From any negative experiences you have gone through, create positive outcomes from them.

# STARVATION AND POVERTY VS THE LAW OF ATTRACTION

When you look at the terrible atrocities happening in the world, let's say famine and the death of 100,000s of innocent children every year. Those children aren't attracting starvation into their lives, because they are already surrounded by deprivation from the day they were born, and sadly they don't know any other way of life.

The fundamental thing those Third World children are attracting into their lives, though, are the thousands and thousands of people from all over the planet who are trying their best to stop poverty and hunger around the globe with the excellent charity work they are doing by sending out clothes, food and water to those countries who need it the most.

Also, there are thousands of aid workers who go to those Third World countries to construct homes, put water systems in so they can have fresh, clean running water, and plant crops so they can harvest their own food every year, which can serve in building a stable community for them to live in.

In some Third World countries, there is a lack of education in the schooling system that seriously needs to be addressed.

Those children living in those deprived regions are having reinforced into their mindsets every day that it is normal to live their lives how they are right now, plus they don't know what the outside world is truly like. They should be getting the same opportunities you and I have.

Enough isn't being done to help those children, although the Law of Attraction is at work even though some people might not think it is; it's operating through you and me who donate money to the charity organisations which help provide food, water, shelter and clothing.

I sincerely hope, one day, famine and poverty are eradicated forever. Until that day, though, you and I can only do our best to help those in need and pray to the Universe no more innocent lives are lost.

# DOMESTIC VIOLENCE VS THE LAW OF ATTRACTION

Very sadly, I know a few women who have suffered from domestic violence. I am happy to say though, they have overcome their horrific ordeals and have turned their lives around for the better. These women are an inspiration and show you and me, no matter how bad things can get in our lives, that we can still climb back up to the top of that mountain and gain back control of our lives and be happy once again.

If you are suffering from domestic violence, you need to have the courage, strength and determination to speak up and come forward and let your family, friends and the authorities know what is happening to you, so it's put a stop to once and for all, and the person harming you gets the punishment they so rightly deserve.

One of my friends, Susan from America, asked me if I would like to share her story in my book with you because she would like other women who have or are going through domestic violence to know that you can survive and overcome a terrifying ordeal like this, just as Susan has done herself. Susan used to live with an alcoholic who put her through a horrendous ordeal and nearly beat her to death, which left Susan needing two spinal cord surgeries to save her from being paralysed! Luckily, Susan survived the beating, and she is now living a happy life, which is all down to her positive attitude. Now here are Susan's views on the Law of Attraction.

> I think if we all never had problems, were always nice to each other, never got sick, had perfect bodies, hair, relationships, jobs, etc., then no one would ever appreciate what they had because it would always

be perfect. We live in a world where evil (my belief from the bible – The Devil) runs the world; if you've ever read the bible and read the parables in it that give us examples through stories (parables) like the prodigal son or the rich man or Job whose faith in God was tested. Job had open sores all over his body, his children and wife were killed, he lost all his cattle and sheep, lost his livelihood and lost all of his riches – BUT he still praised God through it all! He then came through it all and was blessed with a new wife, children, great wealth, cattle and sheep (even more than before)! And had a great home. Job stayed faithful and humble through it all. And God blessed him for his faith and loyalty. My reason for being faithful and (try) to stay humble is because I know I could have it so much worse! I could be blind, deaf, paralysed (I was so close after the beating), or a multitude of horrible things. It's what you DO with the situation given to you that makes you the person you are.

I was beaten for fifty minutes straight because I was living with an alcoholic who was jealous of me working two jobs and always being gone. I thought I could change him, but that NEVER worked. THEY have to WANT to change. I ended up having two separate spinal cord surgeries to save me from being paralysed. I have only eighty per cent balance and walk with a walker to be independent. I had to teach myself to walk again, drive my car, and go places on my own. NOW, the positive thing that came from this situation is that I put a violent person behind bars (prison) for 4 yrs. (not enough) And I use my brutal beating story as a testimony to my BAD choice. It's been 11 yrs. now, and I still walk with the walker outdoors and a cane indoors, but I'm free from a man that could have shot me (he owned A LOT of guns and used to point them at me and laugh) he tried to suffocate me during the beating, and he could have taken my life! But I'm stronger than I think I am, and I persevered and struggled, but I'm still here, and now I know I have a new purpose in life. I make better choices in my life due to the bad choices I used to make. That situation taught me so much about myself, and I am much wiser and careful when I make ANY decisions now. I'm not perfect, but I'm striving to be MY best!

Going through something like that makes you more resilient, stronger, wiser and mature. It's not to say that you or I don't get into a funk once in a while, because we are imperfect people. How you handle situations that happen to you negatively, depend on how you were raised, the parents you had, the support you had from teachers, friends and parents; life choices, such as to do drugs or not, to smoke cigarettes or not, etc. Where you go in life after you make a yes, or no choice, determines whether or not BAD things happen to you, OR GOOD things happen to you. You CAN, to some extent, plan out your life for yourself, in turn, resulting in a happy fulfilled life or a disastrous worry-filled life never knowing what real happiness is. You're the ONLY one that makes you happy or unhappy. We ourselves control the bad or good that happens as far as just decision making goes. Such as – 'Should I drink then drive my car or give my car keys to a friend that doesn't drink.' Either decision will lead you to a comfortable outcome (good) or (bad). Only YOU control whether you FEEL good or bad. It just takes self-control to control your anger if someone makes you mad by what they say to you just as it makes you elated inside if someone gives you a compliment or some other nice gesture. I think if you are inherently a positive, contented person, then you're able to handle situations a little better than a negative, angry person. A person who is positive has a better outlook on all different situations, while the negative person sees nothing but bad – in the world, in those around him and life in general.

Susan, USA

Thank you so much, Susan, for your thoughts and views on the Law of Attraction, I sincerely appreciate you opening up about your past experiences and sharing them with me for my book. You truly are an inspiration to so many people around the world with how you have overcome everything you have been through in your life. All of my very best to you for the future and may your life be filled with love and happiness forevermore.

Steven M. Rippin

I hope you found Susan's story enlightening and inspirational; I certainly did. So, as you can see from what I have written about starvation and poverty vs the Law of Attraction and domestic violence vs the Law of Attraction, these circumstances are out of our control and can change the course our lives can be taken in forever. It's the Law of Attraction, though, that can help give us purpose again so we can focus on the path we want our lives to take.

Be courageous and strong-minded and move forward with your life when you have faced a disastrous or frightening ordeal. Turn those experiences into positive outcomes and become the best version of yourself starting TODAY!

# VISUALISING WHAT YOU
# WANT OUT OF YOUR LIFE

When you want to attract something, visualise it into your mind. Say, for example, there's an expensive car you want to treat yourself to, then you should envision yourself sitting behind the steering wheel in those lovely soft plush seats while you take in that beautiful new car smell, then imagine yourself turning the ignition on for the first time and hearing that baby roar to life. This is what's called a visualisation technique, which brings your dreams to life. If you work hard enough at envisioning what you want, you will eventually manifest it into your reality. It won't come easily; it takes a lot of patience, commitment, determination and hard work. And if you have all four of those personality traits, then you will stand a good chance of attracting what you want.

Another great way to visualise is to create a visualisation board where you cut out images from magazines of what you would like to attract into your life. On my visualisation board, I have got a collection of photos of people who are very important to me and of the places and possessions I would like to draw into my life. My visualisation board includes a photograph of my dad and me, along with pictures of my good friends, an apartment looking over London, a villa in Ibiza, images of Disneyworld and Harry Potter World and a photograph of my dad and me in Tennessee, where I would love to go back to one day. So, every day, take a few minutes out of your daily life and find somewhere quiet where you can close your eyes and think of the people and things you love. Open your mind and let your thoughts take you away to where you want to be.

If you have visualised about something you want but are unable to afford it, then open a bank account and put a specific amount of money into it each week, then you can gradually watch your money grow. And every time you make a deposit you will be another step closer to your dream holiday or whatever it is you are saving up for. Now here are a couple of examples of how you can attract various interests into your life. If you visualise yourself becoming a DJ, then you are going to want to connect with DJs and musicians by joining sites such as Soundcloud, Mixcloud, Twitter and Instagram. There are also DJ courses you can go on to help you become the next superstar DJ. Or, if you have always wanted to become an author, a bit like myself, then you are going to want to attract people who have written books into your life; those novelists will be able to help you out with ideas while you're writing and ways you can get your book published. Always start by setting out plans on how you are going to achieve your goals, then get to know people who can help you in those fields you are interested in; social media is ideal for this. Whatever you are envisioning into your life, there will always be somebody out there who is willing to help make your visualisation come true.

To visualise a healthier lifestyle for yourself, use affirmations. For example, if you want to give up smoking, you could say, 'I will feel healthier every day once I have packed up smoking, plus I will have more money to put towards my dream holiday.' Or, if you want to lose weight, you could say, 'I am going to feel so good once I start losing weight; I will eat more healthily and exercise more, then I will be able to buy those smaller sized clothes I have always wanted to fit into.' Say your affirmations out loud to yourself and believe in what you're saying with all your heart. Most importantly, take action to make those changes in your life become a reality because, as they say, actions speak louder than words.

When you say statements to yourself daily, you will start changing your mindset from how you used to think, plus you will also be on the right road to achieving your objectives because you will be embedding into your subconsciousness the person you want to become and what you want to accomplish. Doing this can seem strange at first; it's like anything new you try, though: it can be daunting at the beginning, a bit like when you are learning to ride a bike; the more you practise, though, the easier it will become.

Let go of any fears you might have and step out your comfort zone and let your visualisations become your reality, then picture the life you are going to have through your mind. The world is your oyster and the stage is set for you to come forward and shine.

Maintain the following rules while visualising. What you think about you attract into your life – Surround yourself with people who can help you achieve your ambitions – Set out a plan of action to accomplish those goals you have visualised about – Stay devoted – Envision what you want – Repeat your affirmations to yourself every day, preferably in the morning, at midday and just before you go to sleep at night – Never think negatively; always think positively, and remember you are awesome, and you can achieve anything you set your mind to, and, most importantly, believe in yourself.

It is also a good idea to set yourself lifetime plans so you can see where you will be in five, ten and fifteen years' time. So please don't get disappointed after a year or two and think nothing has changed in your life and that you must be doing something wrong; you're not. All the big companies in the world today had to start somewhere, and it took them years to get off the ground. Just look at Apple. Steve Jobs and Steve Wozniak first met in 1971, when Wozniak was twenty-one years old and Steve Jobs was only sixteen, then in 1975 Jobs and Wozniak began working on the prototype for the Apple 1 in Steve Jobs's parents' garage and look at how far Apple has come today. And the same goes for Jeff Bezos, who is the founder, chairman and chief executive officer of Amazon, which he first started back on 5 July 1994, again in his garage as an online bookstore. And it's incredible how far Amazon has come today as well, isn't it? So, don't give up and, even if you fail over and over again, look at those mistakes as lessons learnt which you won't make next time.

When you put all your time, energy, dedication and soul into something you believe in, you can accomplish great things. Please remember, though, always look after your health. I have been working towards the life I have wanted for years, and I will never stop until I have achieved all I have set out to obtain. Visualisation is a powerful tool that can help transform your life; first, though, be realistic, start small and have an open mind about what you what to conceive, then you can chase after your dreams, so they become your reality.

# DAD AND HIS PIRATE SON: ROAD TRIP USA

Part of a road trip my dad and I went on in 2012 will show you how we attracted specific outcomes into our lives because of our positive attitudes, which were all down to the Law of Attraction. I hope you find these short stories and interactions fun and entertaining to read and recognise the powerful message I am trying to get across.

Disneyworld, in my eyes, is, as they say, one of the most magical places on earth. So, when my dad and I decided to go to Disneyworld along with a few other locations on our road trip, I felt like a big kid and couldn't wait to meet Mickey Mouse, well, Minnie, if I am honest. So, let's begin. Our enchanting journey started in the year of 2012 when my dad and I stayed at the Pop Century Resort at Disneyworld. We had a right laugh when we were checking in. You should have seen the pair of us; we were like a couple of little kids because we had made it to Disneyworld! Then, me being me, I decided to interview some of the cast members who were playing Disney songs and dancing around in the lobby, where of course I joined in and had a dance with them. Now for your entertainment here is the interview and random piece of dancing I did while my dad queued up to check us in. Unfortunately, the audio decided to stop working while I was dancing, so you don't get to hear the Disney songs! You could, if you like, though, think of one of your favourite Disney numbers: bit.ly/ PirateStevePopCentury

After my random acts of dancing, the holidaymakers in the queue asked if it was all right to have their photos taken with me, which I didn't mind at all; my dad and I made a lot of people happy that day, and we also had a good laugh with the cast members when we checked in as well. I felt quite at home walking around the Disney parks as a lot of people thought I was Captain Jack Sparrow, funnily enough, plus my dad and I had countless parents ask us if it was all right for their children to have their pictures taken with me; they genuinely thought I was Captain Jack Sparrow, bless them. I also signed a lot of the kids' autograph books while I was at Disneyworld, which I felt very honoured doing because they were magical memories those boys and girls would remember forever. Oh, yeah, I nearly got married to Minnie Mouse as well, when it was my turn to have my photograph taken with her at Epcot because soon as she saw me she waved one of her big mouse hands up and down, asking me to go down on one knee so I would propose to her, then the next thing I knew, once I had done that, Minnie has grabbed hold of my arm and run off with me down the corridor, all to the dismay of the children queuing up to have their photos taken with her!

Then, as Minnie and I were skipping along the hallway, Goofy saw us both arm in arm and gave me a bunch of fives! So, Minnie and I went back to where she was having her photographs taken so I didn't get a good hiding, and then Mickey Mouse saw the two of us together! And he gave me such a look as he stood there with his arms crossed over his chest, then he started waving one of his big mouse fingers at me in disgust for running away with his girlfriend, which I don't blame him for! It was such a surreal experience!

Everything turned out well in the end, though, and you will be happy to know I proposed once again to Minnie Mouse a week later while my dad and I were having breakfast on the day we were leaving Disneyworld to continue with our road trip to Cookeville, Chattanooga and the Kennedy Space Centre. Unfortunately, Minnie and I never got married because I called the whole thing off in the end. I told her she would be better off with Mickey Mouse, who she would have a much better life with at Disneyworld than she would with me in England. If you would like to see me proposing to Minnie, here is a video link to our non-marriage shenanigans: bit.ly/PirateSteveProposesToMinnieMouse

And here are a collection of Disneyworld Diary videos I made for my Pirate Steve Show, now known as the Positive Pirate, on YouTube:

bit.ly/DisneyWorldDiaries1
bit.ly/DisneyWorldDiaries2

bit.ly/DisneyWorldDiaries3
bit.ly/DisneyWorldDiaries4
bit.ly/DisneyWorldDiaries5
bit.ly/DisneyWorldFacts

After our mischievous endeavours at Disneyworld, it was then time for my dad and me to travel to Chattanooga, but before we arrived there we were feeling a bit peckish, so we pulled off the highway and headed for the next town we came across, which was called Cookeville. And as we were driving through Cookeville my dad spotted a barbershop and said, 'I wouldn't mind getting my haircut,' so we pulled into the parking lot of this authentic-looking American barbers, and when we walked into the barbershop one of the barbers said, 'We thought Johnny Depp had just pulled up!' So, we had a good laugh about my appearance. Then, once Brian Neeley, one of the barbers, had cut my dad's hair he said, 'Do you guys wanna game of corn hole?' My dad and I just looked at each other with confused looks on our faces because we didn't have a clue what Brian was talking about!

Now, I have probably seen too many American movies because I thought Brian and his barber friend were going to tie my dad and I up, take us out the back of their barbershop and put us in some holes they had already dug out for tourists who come a-wandering into their hometown, then force us to get into those holes and bury us in corn, where we would spend the rest of our days! A bit far-fetched, I know, but, hey, haven't you seen 'The Little Barber Shop of Horrors', which was in an episode of *The Simpsons* featuring Itchy and Scratchy?

Luckily the barbers didn't bury my dad and me in corn, although they did take us outside into the parking lot to teach us how to play corn hole, which was great fun. If you are wondering what corn hole is, corn hole is a game where you have bags of corn and throw them onto a raised platform which has a hole at the far end of it. And if you get a bag of corn into the hole that will win you three points, and one bag of corn on the platform will earn you one point. And this continues until whoever you are playing against reaches a final score of twenty-one. It was a great afternoon, and my dad and I had an excellent experience learning all about corn hole in Cookeville. I am happy to say I'm still good friends with Brian Neeley on Facebook today. Oh, yeah, and here is a video of my dad and me in action at the Corn Hole Olympics in Cookeville: bit.ly/CornholeInCookeville

Thank you, Brian and your friend, for teaching my dad and me how to play corn hole that day. All my best to you and your family, matey.

Steven M. Rippin

We then continued on our road trip to Chattanooga, where we stayed at the Chattanooga Choo-Choo hotel, which is a historic former railway station. While we were visiting Chattanooga, my dad and I went to Rock City, where you can walk through the beautiful gardens and see the astonishing rock formations. One guy I will never forget while we were walking around the Rock City gardens was a preacher who kindly said a prayer for me to relieve the pain my arthritis in my knees was causing me that day, and to top it off the preacher also did a shout-out for my YouTube channel! Which by the way was the best shout-out anybody has ever done for me! And here, if you are interested, is the preacher giving my YouTube channel a shout-out and praying for me, which, come on, somebody needs to: bit.ly/ThePreacherAndPirateSteve

Now, here is a brief piece of history about Ruby Falls, which my dad and I also visited while we were in Chattanooga. In 1928, Leo Lambert, a chemist and cave enthusiast, started drilling through the limestone on the side of Lookout Mountain, where he discovered a small passageway which was only around eighteen inches high and four feet wide. Eventually, Leo Lambert found a large cavernous opening and in that vast space Leo found hiding away an incredible 145-foot-high waterfall, and when he took his wife down into the caves to show her what he had discovered that's when he told her he would name the falls after her; ever since that day, the falls have been known to the world as Ruby Falls.

Lookout Mountain is a mountain ridge located at the Northwest corner of the U.S, state of Georgia, the Northeast corner of Alabama and along the Tennessee State line in Chattanooga.

Information taken from Wikipedia

Ruby Falls was a phenomenal sight to behold, and it is more than 1,120 feet underground, which caused a problem for my dad and me when we went to visit because we both suffer from claustrophobia. We had to travel down in a lift, you see, where there, straight in front of us, was a solid sheet of rock as we plummeted underground. We faced our fears and made it to Ruby Falls, though, I'm happy to say. I would highly recommend visiting Ruby Falls if you ever get the chance. To learn more about it, here is an amateurish video I made back in 2010. If I were you, though, I would Google Ruby Falls instead of watching my video: bit.ly/RubyFallsWithPirateSteve

After visiting Chattanooga, my dad and I then continued on our road trip towards the Florida Keys and visited the Kennedy Space Centre, where we had a great time and had lots of lovely interactions. Well, that was until we went on the tour bus! You see, while I was filming, I also recorded the tour guide, who was explaining about the history of NASA. Then, all of a sudden, the tour guide's hand shot up right in front of my camera, and he said in a very stern and severe voice to me, 'There'll be no video taking of me, I don't have rights to YouTube at all!' He then carried on speaking, and the tour continued. I was expecting the tour guide to apologise to me after the tour and say, 'Sorry about that. I hope you can understand why I couldn't let you film me,' but he never did. Instead, he just stood at the entrance to the bus as we disembarked, waiting for a tip! And yeah, I should have given him one as well shouldn't I, which would have been to be more courteous to the patrons on his bus tours! My confidence just evaporated when that incident happened. That tour guide was not a happy man and could have done with learning about the Law of Attraction. Unfortunately, I hadn't heard of it back then, so I was a bit down after that experience. When I arrived back home, though, I sent the Kennedy Space Centre an email explaining what had occurred; they never replied back. So, as you can see, because of that tour guide's discourteous attitude towards me that day, he drew negativity into his life from me. And here is the video I took where you can see the tour guide's hand shooting up in front of my camera: bit.ly/RudeTourGuideAtNasa

Towards the end of our road trip, my dad and I had a few days left, so we decided to head back to Disneyworld to finish what had been a fantastic holiday at the Pop Century Resort. Now, this is the foremost reason I wanted to include this road trip straight after I had written about the Law of Attraction. You see, when my dad and I booked ourselves back into the Pop Century Resort, we thought we would be able to use our Disney passes again to go to all the theme parks. Unfortunately, though, the cast member who was booking us in on the reception desk told us our Disney passes had run out and that we would have to purchase new ones, which was pretty annoying, because they cost a few hundred pounds. Then a lady came out of one of the offices and asked us what the problem was, so we told her, and she took our passes away, then disappeared back into her office. A few minutes later, she returned with our passes and said, 'Here you go, guys. You now have full access to all the parks at no extra cost.' We couldn't believe it! When my dad asked her why she had done that for us, she said, 'I remember you guys from a couple of weeks ago when you first checked in and made the cast members and holidaymakers so happy, especially when your son took the time to have his photo taken with the other guests, so this is our way of saying thank you.'

Now, if my dad and I had been standing in the queue at Disney's Pop Century Resort looking all serious, not smiling or having pictures taken with the other guests, do you think we would have had the same outcome of being given those free passes, which were worth over £300? I don't think so, do you? Our attitudes can have influential impacts on the people around us, so always live your life with a positive mindset and a smile on your face. When you are positive, happy and friendly and have time for those around you, you will attract incredible consequences back into your life; positive mindsets attract positive outcomes. That experience my dad and I had checking into Disney's Pop Century Resort for the first time in 2012 has always stuck with me, and I now practise how we both acted that day every day of my life. Life is about making people happy, putting smiles on their faces and joining in with others who are having fun, just as I did with those two Disney cast members I started dancing in the lobby with that day. People will always notice if you are happy or unhappy, and if they see you smiling it will make them feel comfortable being around you. For me, all I truly want to attract into my life is happiness, good health, fun, laughter, respect and good times.

Thank you, Dad, for an unforgettable road trip, which I have been able to look back on and realise that we have already been living our lives just as the Law of Attraction teaches us to.

Steven M. Rippin

# THE SECRET TO LIVING A HAPPY LIFE

Happiness is the best feeling in the world. When you live a happy life you look forward to every day, you love the job you do, you are thankful for your family and friends, you grab hold of opportunities that come your way, and you get on with whatever life throws at you. If only we could feel like this all the time, though. Some people do, I guess, but let's not forget it doesn't matter how happy we are, because there is always something that comes along at some point and throws a spanner in the works, isn't there? And it's at those times when we have to be at our most positive.

People who are happy don't get upset, stressed or offended as easily as someone who lives an unhappy life.

# HAPPINESS, MONEY AND WHERE YOU LIVE

When my parents were growing up, they used to live in Nissen huts as children, and their parents didn't make much money, so they had it tough, not like how we have it today, where we are able to flick a switch and have central heating and electricity. These days the majority of us are able to treat ourselves to the latest must-have gadgets and clothes, go out for meals and nights out partying with our friends, and take short weekend breaks abroad, which wouldn't have been possible years ago for the average family, and something only the rich and wealthy families could have afforded to do.

Life hasn't always been easy for my mum and dad, and I have seen the struggles my parents have been through when it comes to paying bills and having to work all hours of the day just to put food on our table. Thankfully, though, things have got better for us, which is down to my parents working extremely hard over the years.

Unfortunately, not everybody in society is quite as lucky as the majority of us are today, and they still face difficult times as they are growing up, especially when it comes to where they live and being able to afford to put food on the table for their families.

So, for example, say you live somewhere where there is a lot more crime on the streets. It isn't always safe to walk around at night, and there are no job opportunities for you. Growing up in an environment like that is going to have a significant impact on how your life is going to turn out and how thankful you feel to the world around you, isn't it, which is caused because of the lack of money you have. Money isn't everything, though, but it does help give you more comfort and security.

What upsets me is when you hear about families on the news having to watch where every penny comes from that they earn to pay for their weekly shopping, and that's only if they can afford to do a weekly shop. Then you will hear about how much money bosses of banks pay themselves with their yearly bonuses, along with the ludicrous amounts of money politicians and people in the entertainment and sporting industries get paid as well! And a prime example of this was when one famous sportsman was paid one hundred million pounds over ten years to wear a particular brand of clothing back in 2018! Like, what is that all about? It's disgusting, if you ask me! What a screwed-up world we are living in!

Surely one hundred million pounds could be divided up a lot more equally between the less fortunate in our society and distributed to the areas that need it the most in our deprived towns, cities and communities. Also, that amount of money could help create youth centres with community projects and schemes for the younger generation to get involved in, which would help make the neighbourhoods they live in feel a lot safer and more like home. It would also give those youngsters a sense of purpose and direction in their lives. Paying celebrities, bankers, politicians and sportsmen and women a regular wage packet just like the rest of us receive each week would undoubtedly help to bring the divide in our society closer together. And the money those well-known individuals would usually receive could go into the development of helping to move our nation forward in becoming a much more civilised and fairer place to live in where everybody would get paid equal amounts.

One thing I will add, though, is that a lot of well-known people do fantastic work for charities, which helps to make a big difference in the world to people's lives. And a few of those famous individuals include Sir Elton John, J.K. Rowling, David Beckham, Martin Lewis, Coldplay, Ringo Starr, Jamie Oliver, Rory McIlroy, Colin Montgomerie, One Direction, Brian May, Roger Taylor and Taylor Swift. And I say, 'Thank you so much to all of those celebrities.'

Can you believe I have worked at some people's houses who are well-off, but they are still unhappy? What's that all about? Plus they have their health and families around them as well! Then I have worked at other people's houses who don't have two pennies to rub together, and they love life, always have their families around them and are so happy.

Happiness isn't to do with the amount of money you have. Happiness is to do with feeling contented and having your family and friends around you.

People with a minimal income know the true value of wealth and happiness. They will put all they earn towards either a new appliance for their home or a family holiday, which they will save up for for a couple of years. Families on a limited wage appreciate everything and everybody around them, from their family and friends to the roof over their heads and the food on their table. I have also noticed people with just enough money to get by have more time to spend with their families because they are not striving for that big house with a swimming pool or want to become the next multi-billionaire and work every hour of the day; they are already happy with everything they have in their lives. And I have seen this for myself when I have been working around customers' houses over the years, because parents who don't have much have time to play with their children and take them away on holidays, which helps to create those special parent/child bonds, which is something I don't see happening as much with some of the families who are very well off doing; their parents are too busy out at work and need to rely on a nanny to look after their children, which is so sad, isn't it?

What a happier planet you and I would live on if money were given out more fairly, or, hey, what if money didn't even exist and we had to work for rewards instead? Hmmm I'm getting sidetracked now. I am probably completely wrong with what I have written about; these are just my personal opinions. You and I need to do something, though, to create a more balanced society if we want to bring about more happiness between one another here on earth.

# MY THOUGHTS AND FEELINGS ON HAPPINESS

Happiness for me comes from making other people smile and laugh, from my love of music, from my family and friends and from the beauty of the world around me.

Feeling sadness, anger, anxiety, grief, fear, surprise, disgust, envy, love, pity, shyness, rejection and joy are all normal emotions you and I go through in our everyday lives, aren't they? I would say ninety-nine per cent of the time I feel happy these days because I have a lot of positive thoughts going on inside my head, and if I ever start having any negative thoughts, for example if I think back to the times when I was bullied and assaulted, I will stop reminiscing about those moments and bring myself back to the present and remember all the great things that are going on in my life today; when I think that way, I truthfully start feeling positive again. Now, here is a video that always makes me laugh and features my dad when he got up to his usual mischievous antics on one of my Pirate Steve Facebook Entertainment News episodes: bit.ly/ FacebookEntertainmentNewsWithGeorgeRippin

The following message is from a charming guy I met while I was in a tearoom in Market Harborough when I was fundraising in June 2017 for Cancer Research UK dressed as Captain Jack Sparrow. So, without further ado, here are Tim Wykes's wise words of wisdom.

I got held up in a Tea Room, but life is an open book of ideas and endeavours, sometimes adversity brings up situations to question our own path and response. I saw a genuine warmth and belief in being who you are as a person and what you want to achieve. And in that, whatever life brings, you will always carry a Silver lining, because negativity will never win with an honest heart and endeavour.

**Tim Wykes, Brixworth, England**

Learning to forgive those people who have caused me hurt and misery in my life has been difficult, because I am always reminded of what they did to me every day mentally on the inside and outside when I look at myself in the mirror and see the scars around my eyes, which cause me a lot of discomfort daily. Instead of thinking of those scars I have as bad memories, I now see them as milestones in my life which have helped me become who I am. And those people who have made me suffer will never take my happiness away. If anything, I am grateful for my scars and the torment those individuals have caused me to live with because my injuries and the agony I go through make me feel ALIVE like I have never felt before in my LIFE! My wounds and pain have also given me a purpose, which has led me on the path I am on today, which is to bring HOPE, HAPPINESS and POSITIVITY into as many people's lives as I can. Forgiving others is essential, especially if you want to move forward with your life and get your true inner happiness back. So don't let those who have upset you ruin your life and take your happiness away; stay strong and positive and think of the person you want to become.

My dad started his carpet career after leaving school, and he has been fitting carpets now for over fifty years! I believe the key to my dad's happiness and positive outlook on life is that he found a job he loved doing and is very passionate about. A lot of my dad's customers have said to him, 'You really love your job, don't you, George?' and another said, 'Let me shake your hand, George; it was a real pleasure having you in my house. You're such a nice guy. I could tell the first time I spoke to you on the phone.' How lovely of those customers to say. I know he's my dad, but he is unquestionably one in a million.

Finding a job you love doing will help you discover true happiness.

Happiness is the simplest things in life, it's not money, or going down to your local, it's about family, your loved ones and to be able to smile whatever the occasion, my son, my daughter and my granddaughter makes me happy and keeps me going, and not forgetting Debs, who has been by my side for 31 years.

### Andy 'Chappers' Chapman, Market Harborough, England

If you are feeling unhappy with your life, maybe it's down to the lifestyle you're leading. So, ask yourself, 'Am I exercising enough and eating the right foods, and do I need to cut out any bad habits?' Breaking your normal behaviours can have a significant effect on how you feel about yourself; it can also help to increase your happiness. My dad made a couple of lifestyle changes after he had his cardiac arrest in 2014, and he did that by altering his diet and going to a weekly fitness class for people who suffer from heart problems, which has undoubtedly helped to prolong his life. I have seen for myself the benefits my dad's gained. He is now a lot fitter, less stressed, more relaxed, healthier and happier within himself, plus he has a lot more energy and loves to keep as active as he can on a daily basis.

Is being successful in life the key to happiness? I guess it all depends on how you view what being successful is. To me, it shouldn't be about how large your bank balance is – How huge your house is – How well liked you are on social media – What possessions you own, or if you have the latest gadgets and wear all the top designer labels. It should be about how good a father or mother you are – How well you bring your children up, and the love and devotion you give to those around you, I believe.

It doesn't matter how old you are, it is never too late to bring genuine joy into your life.

# WHERE DOES TRUE HAPPINESS COME FROM?

Here follows where I believe true happiness comes from.

Feeling comfortable with who you are as a person – Your family and friends – The unconditional love of your pets – Not getting stressed – Thinking positively – Being honest and trustworthy – Keeping negative people out of your life – Learning who you are as a person – Eating healthily and exercising a minimum of thirty minutes every day – Raising money for charity – Not worrying about what other people think of you – Healing yourself from tragic experiences and moving forward – Smiling as much as possible; when you smile more, it helps lighten your mood and relieves stress – Showing your true feelings – Stepping out of your comfort zone – Being thankful – Getting at least eight hours of sleep a night – Not overworking – Listening to your favourite music – Dancing with your mates – Walking in the countryside or along the beach – Giving compliments – Visualising – Being ALIVE – Doing activities you enjoy – Not worrying; worrying makes you ill so stay optimistic and positive – The influential impact you have on people's lives – Being authentic and living your life as your true self – Having a purpose in life – Giving to those less fortunate – Never expecting anything in return – Showing others respect – Accepting people for who they are – Helping and supporting one another – Remembering to love yourself. And, lastly, true happiness comes from living your life in the present.

Most people worry about the future or reminisce about the past. What they don't do is consider living for today in this moment right now. When you live in the present you focus on the people in your life and the things that matter the most to you, such as creating a piece of art – Watching a beautiful sunset – Writing a book – Dancing – Having deep and meaningful conversations with your family and friends – Walking in the countryside – Being in the arms of your loved one, or feeling the ocean waves brush up against your feet; these, along with many other examples you can think of, are what we should be focusing on.

So, live your life in the now, and by doing so you will feel a lot happier and invigorated. And every day will feel more meaningful and brighter for you to shine like the star you are. Live for today. Well, I hope that has helped give you a greater understanding of where real happiness comes from. Find what makes you feel joyful on the inside so you can benefit from that feeling every day for the rest of your life.

Pure happiness is enjoying this moment in time. It is being in the present and not worrying about what the future holds. So LIVE, LOVE, LAUGH and ENJOY every second of your LIFE, starting NOW. The foremost thing I believe to perfect happiness is not forgetting who your authentic self is, along with the activities you used to love doing when you were younger. So, remember, make time for yourself or one day you might wake up and think, 'What's happened to the young boy/girl I used to be? Who have I become? I'm just not as happy in my life as I used to be any more.' So, get out there and start enjoying your life again before it's too late!

To help you get a better understanding of how you are feeling today, write down a list of the things that mean the most to you and also what makes you who you are, such as: What makes you feel happy? – What are your strengths and weaknesses? – What are your goals in life? – What sports and hobbies did you used to love doing but have stopped doing now? – What activities would you like to take up? And also, where do you see yourself in five years? Then, once you have given those questions plenty of thought and written your answers down, read them back to yourself every day and focus on what you want to achieve and the areas of your life you want to improve on.

I live my life by always thinking positive thoughts – Never judging people – Being thankful for everything and everybody I have in my life – Showing my family and friends I am there for them when they need me – Listening to music which lifts my spirits when I am feeling down – Feeling blessed when I wake up to the magnificent world around me every day – Appreciating my eyesight and health, and thinking back to how happy I was as a child growing up before I started school. I will also look back on old photographs at the innocent little boy I was and who I still am, then I will think of how far I have come and what I have achieved. And I also live my life by appreciating the life I have been given by my parents who brought me into this world. It's all down to you how contented you feel, and only you can make those changes you need to make if you believe you should be living a happier life today.

Q: How do you feel making people happy every day by just being who you are, and how do you feel about sharing your life with us?

Keith Larkin, Northern Ireland, instagram.com/hatguy96

A: Hey, Keith, that's a great question; thank you so much for asking it. I didn't realise when I first started posting on social media the impact I would have on people's lives. I have always been myself and been open and honest with everybody I have met. Knowing I can make a difference in my online friends' lives is an incredible feeling; I am honoured they see me this way. Also, my online friends, including you, Keith, have always helped me to believe in myself. And I could never imagine living my life without sharing it with everybody on social media. Again, thank you so much for your question.

Steven M. Rippin

Now, to finish, I would like to share a short story with you about how seeing somebody smiling can have a significant impact on how you are feeling. Isn't it amazing how just one person can alter the way you feel if you are having one of those days when you're feeling really miserable? Just like how I was when I was working at a customer's house one dull drizzly day, then just as soon as I met the customer who had a friendly smile on his face my mood changed just like that, and I felt much happier. And that showed me that day that smiling is a very influential superpower we possess. So, if people smiled a lot more in today's society, it would make the world a much brighter and happier place to live in, wouldn't it? You are the one in control of your thoughts. So, if you're feeling down, remember that it is you who is making yourself feel that way.

# WHAT MAKES YOU HAPPY?

Happiness can mean many different things, so to find out what makes other people happy I asked my friends on social media the following question.

## What makes you feel happiest in your life?

Happiest moments are the family times, the times when you have a gathering, but not intentionally, when last-minute you all come together, change plans and make sure you do everything you can to arrive at this one place, or time with your family. The laughing lines appearing at the jokes that are shared, the heartfelt concern when you share how difficult you're working day, week or month has been, and the love and strength that is shown from hugs that are so strong, you know if you fall or ever need anyone, your family are there.

**Ann-Marie Studd, Leicestershire, England**

Making other people smile, whether it's when I'm paying for petrol or walking down the street, I love to see people smiling and think it's great to spread happiness, even if it's just a brief encounter. A moment of light, in a sometimes dark day.

**Kelly Charlton, Lutterworth, England**

I am at peace and truly happy, when I know my family are at true peace with themselves. It's a great feeling to be together and have that feeling inside, that all is well, believe me, a parent can feel that.

Dean Townsend, Tennessee, USA

Dancing, seeing my children happy and genuine honest people to spend time with, oh, and animals! I'm more likely to say hello to a cat in the street before a human.

Sam Bingham, Waikiki, Western Australia

When I watch Pirates of the Caribbean ha-ha! No, well that does make me really happy! But taking care of animals makes me happy. I love what I do. Horseback riding relaxes me. Pretty much anything with animals.

Crissy Rose, Pennsylvania, USA

On an Island, with no hustle and bustle, taking in the steady breeze, sound of the waves crashing to meet the sandy beach and enjoying a frozen Margarita with no salt. BUT what WOULD really make me happy, is knowing that EVERY ANIMAL in the world is free from harm/abuse/slaughter.

Julia Thornhill, North Carolina, USA

My job being a support worker and knowing that my clients know I'm there to care, support and talk, no matter what.

Sam Thurston, Market Harborough, England

672

What makes me happy has changed a lot over the years. In the mid-to-late 1990s, what made me happy was dressing in black velvet, putting on makeup, and going to goth clubs to dance. From 2007 to 2015, working at a university and helping young people to learn, made me very happy. Now though, I am no longer able to work, because of my health problems, so only two things make me happy: My wife makes me happy and getting dressed in costumes to show off my art, and having people appreciate my art makes me happy.

Caelyn Nagle, Richmond, Virginia, USA

Being with someone and feeling comfortable with no conversation at all, looking at the moonlight sat on a park bench and saying nothing at all, and enjoying the moment of peace and happiness, that's when you know it's right.

Ian T. Walden, Leicestershire, England

Seeing friends for a meet up after not seeing them for ages, going on adventures, forgetting my troubles of dull everyday life of responsibility, plus, Disney films and creating art xx.

Monica Sanders, Northampton, England

Walking, or running in the rain, really soothes my soul and quiets the noise, so I can think.

Sophie Webster, Oadby, England

Being at the seaside, walking along the beach watching the tide coming in and out, you can't beat it.

Susan Wilson, Derbyshire, England

I love work. I am at my happiest when we have lovely customers in the shop and have friendly banter with them xx.

**Ruth Gamble, Market Harborough, England**

Rain and cloudy days. I know it makes a lot of people feel gloomy, but I love it, it's peaceful.

**Nyx St-Cyr, Canada**

It's the little things in life that make me happy, happy songs, all things nature, coming home after a long day's work to my cats and a hot dinner, the smells of summer, bright colours, smiling people, sitting by the fire on a cold wintery evening, dancing uncontrollably to music, waking up every morning with the love of my life, my friends and family, and of course pizza.

**Samuel J.T. Conway, Leicestershire, England**

A big thank you to my friends on social media who contributed to my question on what makes them feel the happiest. Happiness comes down to the simple things in life. I wonder what makes you happy.

# QUESTIONS AND ANSWERS TIME
# WITH STEVE RIPPIN

Well, if you have reached it this far through my book, you deserve a Positive Pirate sticker. Anyway, enough of my random ramblings, the reason I decided to do a questions and answers section is that I often have people asking me questions when I am out in public about my appearance and why I choose to live my life the way I do. So, I put myself out there on social media and let my friends ask me anything they would like. And what better way to start than to share with you a video I uploaded to YouTube on 26 July 2014, when I interviewed myself! Strange and weird, I know, but I have never been conventional in my way of thinking when I do things: bit.ly/PirateSteveQAndA

Now here are the impressive and thought-provoking questions I was asked. And, hey, why not have a go at answering them too? Well, the questions you think are relevant to you.

> What would you talk about if you had sat at the table with John Lennon, Jesus, Hitler and the Dalai Lama? The other question is a bit more personal. What do you think about when you are alone?
>
> **Maria L. Mills, Market Harborough, England**

A: Hey, Maria. Oh, wow, fantastic questions there. Thank you. Well, if I had the privilege of sitting at the table with John Lennon, Jesus, Hitler and the Dalai Lama, I would ask John Lennon,

'Where did you get your inspiration from for the songs you wrote and which Beatles song is your favourite?' I would ask Jesus, 'Are you the Sumerian God Anu's son, Enki of the Anunnaki who is said to be an ancient God of Mesopotamia, or are you an extra-terrestrial visitor from a planet called Nibiru?'

I would ask Hitler, 'Is it true you fled to Antarctica after the Second World War ended, developed a UFO and discovered an underground civilisation where extra-terrestrials lived?' I would also ask Hitler, 'Why are you so evil? Why kill so many innocent people who did nothing wrong to you? Are you the devil in disguise? What is the biggest regret of your life? And if you could have one wish, what would it be?

And to the Dalai Lama, I would ask him, 'What do you think of all the terrible atrocities that are happening in the world today? Do you ever get angry and swear? Do you listen to music? If so, what is your favourite song? Do you believe in extra-terrestrials? And what is the best piece of advice on life you could give me, please?'

When I am alone, I often think of how I could help change the mindset of small-minded people who see alternative individuals negatively in today's society. I also think about the future because I want to live as long as possible and see where technology and science will take us. Ideally, I would love to be cryogenically frozen or have my mind uploaded when the technology becomes available so I could be downloaded into an artificially intelligent body and see how far human civilisation will have evolved. And, lastly, I think about what life would be like if I didn't have any eye problems; I would love to be able to see out of my eyes correctly and have no pain or redness in them for once in my life. One last thing I think about when I am alone is life without my parents, Maria, which is very hard for me to imagine. You just don't know how those events will alter the course of your life, do you? And on that note, Maria, I will say thank you so much for those profound and meaningful questions.

Steven M. Rippin

Q: What were the most difficult/hardest challenges you have had to face growing up?

**Maggie S. Cox, Kettering, Northamptonshire**

A: Hey, Maggie. They would be all the eye operations I have been through so far in my life, along with the bullying, cyberbullying, being beaten up a few times and seeing my dad in hospital. Thank you for your question.

**Steven M. Rippin**

Q: If you could get a message across to a large number of people, what would your message be? xx.

**Danielle Tredgett, Leicestershire, England**

A: Excellent question, Danielle, thank you. I would say in a message to a large number of people: Treat others how you wish to be treated in return – Don't judge others – Don't follow the herd – Think outside the box – Believe in your ambitions – Never let anybody walk all over you – Stand up and be proud of who you are – Ask questions – Step out of your comfort zone – Always be willing to take challenges – Face your fears and be the change you want to see in the world today! Thank you so much for your question, Danielle.

**Steven M. Rippin**

Q: If you could change anything in your life, what would it be? I know some say they would change some things x.

**Sheryl Fernley, Market Harborough, England**

A: Hey, Sheryl, the truth is I wouldn't want to change anything; I am happy with who I am even though I have gone through my fair share of pain and suffering at the hands of others. Thank you so much for your question, Sheryl.

Steven M. Rippin

Q: What do you think has been your greatest achievement in your life? You, George and Sheila, are really wonderful people xxx.

Pam Campion, Market Harborough, England

A: Hey, Pam, lovely to hear from you, my greatest achievement would be how I fought my way back out of depression after I was assaulted. That experience showed me how strong I am as a person on the inside, and it made me want to show those around me that whatever knocks you down in life, you can overcome it and become an even stronger individual than you were before! I also feel privileged that my friends on social media are inspired by my posts to the point that I have helped to save lives. Thank you so much, Pam; that is lovely of you to say about my parents and me. All my best to you and your family and thank you for your question.

Steven M. Rippin

Q: What in your opinion, is the most important part of being a public figure? Or, do you feel a responsibility to the people who look up to you as a public figure, and if so, how do you deal with this?

Kimberly, Montreal, Quebec, Canada

A: Hey, Kimberly. Good question, thank you. I have never viewed or seen myself as a public figure, although I do have a lot of friends and followers on my social media sites who say I inspire them. So, I feel I have got a responsibility when I share any content online. When you know you are going to be influencing people, you should always give out a positive and uplifting message. I think the most vital part for me when posting online, is to show others that we should love and respect one another and always be honest, courteous and caring. Thank you so much for your question, Kimberly.

Steven M. Rippin

Q: Where in the world would you like to take Pirate Steve that you haven't already?

Elly Wilson, Nuneaton, Warwickshire, England

A: Hey, Elly. I would love to visit Italy, Japan and Europe. Thank you so much for your question.

Steven M. Rippin

Q: In the past, people were buried with the items they would need in the afterlife, what would you want buried with you, so you could use it in the afterlife?

Danielle Tredgett, Leicestershire, England

A: Intriguing question, Danielle. Thinking along the lines that once you are in the afterlife your body becomes whole and healthy again, which would mean I wouldn't need my glasses, contact lenses or medication, I would want to be buried with clothes, food, a survival kit in case I need to fend for myself, a mode of transport so I can get around to see who else is about and what's around me, a compass, and also a how-to book on surviving in the afterlife. And the foremost thing I would love to have is my mind and sanity intact. Great question, Danielle.

Steven M. Rippin

Q: If you could be any hero or villain, who would you be and why?

Bam B. Crowley, Leicester, England

A: Good question, Bam. My favourite superheroes are my mum and dad, because they have been the most influential people in my life, and for a fictional superhero it would have to be Superman because I have always wanted to be able to fly and know what it feels like to have perfect vision. Thank you for your questions.

Steven M. Rippin

Q: My question is if you could choose only one person/pet to come back from the dead for a day, who would it be? (The person doesn't have to be a relative, it can be absolutely anyone) xxx.

Natasha Smith, Buckinghamshire, England

A: I would love to bring back my grandparents, my cousin, my uncle and all of my friends who have sadly passed away so I can tell them how much I love them. I couldn't pick only one relative I'm afraid, Natasha. Thank you ever so much for your question.

Steven M. Rippin

Q: What are your long-term career goals? Do you plan on meeting Johnny Depp one day? How about taking your pirate act on the road in America?

Susan Barlow-Smith, North Carolina, USA

A: Hey, Susan. My career goals would be to help and inspire as many people as I can through the power of social media. I want people of all ages to know that it is acceptable to be unconventional. And I would love to have my own Positive Pirate Show where I would invite professional counsellors and doctors on who would give their best advice on subjects to help improve various aspects of our lives. There would also be comedy sketches, bands and of course alternative, unique and quirky individuals who would share their stories of how society treats them. As you can see, I have my head in the clouds and a very long journey ahead of me; that is only just beginning. And Susan, I have never planned on meeting Johnny Depp, although that would be pretty awesome, and unfortunately I haven't got a pirate act. I would travel over to America, though, because I love it over there, especially Tennessee. Thank you so much for your questions, Susan.

Steven M. Rippin

Q: My question is. What do you think about how transgender people should have a say in this world? What are your thoughts about our country and how we are handling life?

Jodie L. Chapman, Nevada, USA

A: Hey, Jodie, thank you for your questions. I believe as human beings you and I have as much right as one another to be who we choose to be in society no matter what sexual orientation we desire to become; we are both made out of skin and bone, and transgender people are no different from anybody else. I don't see what the problem is, personally. Look at Martine Rothblatt, who is one of the highest-paid CEOs in America, who is transgender herself. Martine Rothblatt is a highly respected lawyer, author, founder of SiriusXM satellite radio and also a futurist, so to me she is an astounding woman who has accomplished so much in her life. Martine Rothblatt is an inspiration to so many transgender people all over the world. I love America, and every time I have been there I have been treated with the utmost respect from everybody I have had the pleasure of meeting; I can't wait to go back and revisit one day. And I think from what I can see you're handling life really well, although I know not everywhere in America is doing all that great, sadly, and that improvements are needed, especially with gun crime. I sincerely hope things improve for the sake of the new generations of young people growing up over there today, for tomorrow. I wish I could answer your question in more detail about America, Jodie, but I don't know your country well enough to do so, I'm afraid. I do love visiting, though, and I always miss the US when I come back home to England. Thank you for your great questions.

Steven M. Rippin

Q: What is life without imagination?

Gavin Franz, USA, instagram.com/__gavin_of_steel__

A: Hey, Gavin. Life without imagination to me would be incredibly dull. You and I would be like sheep following the herd being told what to do all the time. Also, without our imaginations we wouldn't have invented all the outstanding products that make our lives more comfortable today. And breakthroughs in medicine and science wouldn't have advanced, we wouldn't have ventured into space, and all the TV shows and movies we love watching wouldn't exist either. Without imagination, the internet wouldn't exist; companies such as Apple, Google, Facebook and Amazon wouldn't be around either. My imagination has given me the courage to live my life as an alternative individual where I get to express myself how I want. Our minds are the most powerful tools we own, and, hey, who knows what we are truly capable of achieving? Thank you for your interesting question, Gavin.

Steven M. Rippin

Q: What influenced you the most to become the person you are today?

Heather Witt, Pennsylvania, USA, instagram.com/hthrwtt

A: Hi, Heather, my parents and my eyesight conditions have influenced who I have become today. If it weren't for my mum and dad, I would never have grown up to have a positive attitude. And if it weren't for my eyesight issues, I would never have grown my hair long, which then led me onto becoming known as Pirate Steve. Thank you for your question, Heather.

Steven M. Rippin

Q: Who is your favourite Pirate and would you move to Ibiza with us and form a band?

Linda Owens and Molly Byrne, Liverpool, England

A: I love the questions, Linda and Molly, and I thought you might have known who my favourite pirate was: Captain Jack Sparrow, of course, who is the ultimate rock star pirate of our generation. And that sounds like an excellent idea to me. Unfortunately, I don't play any musical instruments; I could pretend to be a world-famous pirate DJ for the audience's amusement, though, I guess.

So, pack your bags, because Ibiza here we come. Thank you for your questions.

Steven M. Rippin

Q: Is there one defining moment that changed your life? If so, what was it, and how did it change you? What goals and purpose do you now have, versus before?

Ryan Edwards, Florida, USA

A: Hey, Ryan, the defining moment that changed my life was when I was attacked in 2008. That incident made me want to inspire people and show them that you can look however you want in life. I also love spreading happiness and positivity into everyone's lives as well because of that occurrence. Thank you so much for your questions, Ryan.

Steven M. Rippin

Q: If you could be anyone else other than Pirate Steve, who would it be? Keep doing what you do. Love you lots.

Claire B. Hughes, Leicestershire, England

A: If I weren't Pirate Steve Claire, I would want to be just like my dad, who's my hero and inspiration in life. Thank you so much for your question.

Steven M. Rippin

Well, there you have it: questions and answers are finally over. If you have been answering any of those questions yourself, I hope they helped you learn a bit more about the type of person you are. And a big thank you to everybody who kindly posted their questions to me. I thoroughly enjoyed answering all of them. And now I have some questions for you, so are you sitting comfortably? Excellent; let's begin.

What makes you special, unique and talented? – What advice would you give your ten-year-old self? – What promises have you never carried through? – Who do you need to get in touch with because you haven't spoken to them for a while? – How are things going in your life right now? – If you could invite six guests round for dinner, who would they be and why? They can be family, friends or celebrities who are alive or have sadly passed on – What answers are you searching for? – What negative experiences keep happening time and time again to you, and when are you going to learn from them? – What are you always attracting into your life that is no good for you? – Whose permission are you waiting for to achieve your goals in life and will they come true? – Do people show you the respect you deserve? – Do you learn something of value from the mistakes you make? – When you're nervous about something, do you resort to alcohol or cigarettes to calm you down? If you do, why not try willpower instead? – Do you let people walk all over you? Why? And when will you put a stop to it and learn to stand up for yourself? And, finally, do you have a goal and purpose in life? If so, what is it, and what plan have you set out to achieve it?

Well, I hope those questions got you thinking. Now, here is a game I love trying out on my family and friends, which is called 'The Four Questions Game.' And it's all about NLP: neuro-linguistic programming, which is to do with your brain and mind. So, here are the four questions I would like you to ask yourself or your family and friends.

1: Imagine yourself in a white room, and everything is white, including the walls, ceiling and floor. Now do your best to describe how you're feeling and the experience being in that white room gives you.
2: What is your favourite colour? Describe it, and what feeling does it give you?
3: What is your favourite animal? Why? And please describe it.
4: Imagine yourself near a large body of water and describe the first thing you do when you see it and how it makes you feel.

Now here are the meanings to those questions you have just asked or answered.

Question number 1: Is your perception of death and dying.

2: Is how you see yourself with those qualities you described.

3: Is how people see you with those qualities.

4: Is how you feel when you make love; this one always gets people embarrassed.

Only ask these questions if you know your family and friends are going to feel comfortable responding to them, especially when it comes to revealing what their true meanings are because you might not want to know how a large body of water makes any members of your family feel! And there you have it, a few questions I hope you enjoyed answering to help you learn more about the person you are.

# ENVISION YOUR PAST, PRESENT AND FUTURE SELF

This technique I have come up with might get a bit confusing, so please stick with me while I do my best to explain it to you. You see, this technique, depending on how old you are, can help you visualise how a past, present, or future version of yourself, can see the person you are today and what changes you should be making in your life right now.

So, back to the present day and on with this visualisation technique. What I would like you to do is look at yourself in a mirror and imagine you can see a reflection of your younger self from either five, ten, twenty or thirty years ago.

Now think and write down what you would like to say to that younger version of yourself that will help improve your life, along with what you wish you knew when you were that age. For example, would you tell yourself: To carry on the way you are and to never change anything – To be proud of who you are because you have already been through so much in your life – To make better life decisions – To stop drinking alcohol and eating junk food – To exercise daily and watch what you eat – To always follow your heart – To stop hanging around with negative people who are holding you back from reaching your full potential in life – To be ready to face life's challenges, because there's a bumpy road ahead for you – To be more supportive to those around you – To believe in who you are, no matter what people think or say – To live your life with a positive attitude – To stop thinking negatively – To treat other people how you wish to be treated – To chase after your dreams – To never let people intimidate you, take away your happiness, confidence or self-esteem – To always love who you are – To never worry if you make mistakes – To spend more time with your family and friends who love you, unconditionally – Or to face your fears, because you're stronger than you think you are? Whatever you decide to tell your younger self, make sure it hits home and comes straight from your heart.

Now take a few moments to reflect on what you have written down and would tell a younger version of yourself. Then when you are ready look into the mirror again and see the YOU of TODAY who is staring back at you.

Now, what would you like to say to yourself? And, again, write down your answers so you can see what you would like to improve most about yourself right now so when you look back in the future, you can see if you have made any of those changes in your life. Are you still with me? No, don't worry: I'm confused as well, so let's carry on.

So would you tell the YOU of TODAY: To remember who you once used to be because you have now lost your way and need to regain that confident and happy, positive persona of the person you once were again – To change your habits and live a healthier lifestyle – To listen to other people more – To be more understanding – To be less stressed and overworked – To spend more time with your family and friends – That you still have a lot to learn – To take up new interests – That you are proud of who you have become and what you have accomplished in life, or will you tell the YOU of TODAY, that you are contented with your life and grateful for your health, happiness and family and friends?

So, if you feel you need to make any critical changes in your life, make those necessary improvements starting today. And now it's time to take the final step of my visualisation technique, which I am sure you will be happy to hear.

When you're ready look into the mirror again and now envision you're staring at your future self, which can either be in five, ten, twenty or thirty years' time, and think to yourself, 'What type of person have I become today and did I listen to the advice I gave myself when I was younger?' And write down any thoughts you might have while you are doing this, such as: Have I learnt from any of my past mistakes? – Am I proud of the person I have become? – Am I surrounded by happy, positive people in my life? – Have I lived my life the way I wanted to live it? – Have I stopped worrying about what other people think of me? – Have I stepped out of my comfort zone and learnt new skills, taken up new challenges and hobbies? – Have I got fantastic stories and adventures to tell my grandchildren, family and friends? – Have I become somebody who other people look up to and admire? – Have I had incredible life experiences? – Do I have wise words of wisdom to share with other people? – Has my life been full of fun, love and laughter? – Did I chase after my goals I had when I were younger? And, finally, have I become the best version of myself today?

Then, after you have had time to reflect on the type of person you have become in the future, take one final look in the mirror and with a big smile on your face say out loud:

> I am beautiful. I am full of confidence. I have my whole life ahead of me. I can change and live my life the way I want to live it. I have been at my worst and now it's time for everybody to see me at my best. I have been through my fair share of heartache and turmoil, and now I choose to love myself because, if I don't love who I am, I won't be able to believe in myself and accomplish my dreams. I love my family and friends, who I am so lucky to have in my life, and I will always let them know how significant they are to me. And I embrace my past because it has made me who I am today. At this moment, right now, is where I can make any improvements I need to make for my brighter future self of tomorrow, and then I can be proud of the person I am going to become. The future is what I make it, and I am going to make my future self proud of the person I am today.

> **Your name here**

Well, I hope you have found my visualisation technique helpful and not too confusing. And I genuinely hope it helps to guide you on the right path you would like your life to take you on. Always love who you are and remember your future is what YOU make it.

# ADVICE YOU WISH YOU KNEW WHEN YOU WERE YOUNGER

Here are a few pieces of advice I would tell my younger self, which I wish I knew when I were younger: Always be there for your family and friends – Visit your grandparents as often as you can – Always stay true to yourself – Don't let anybody change you – Stand up for yourself – Don't smoke – Don't take drugs – Don't drink alcohol – Eat healthily – Exercise regularly – Never be afraid of taking challenges – Listen to your family and friends when they give you advice – Don't let people disrespect you – Chase after your dreams – Travel as much as you can – Encourage others – Learn about the world around you so you have a better understanding of people and life in general – Learn what the Law of Attraction is – Always accept people for who they are – Never judge on appearances – Keep negative people out of your life – Be happy – Don't be small-minded – Live your life outside the confines of modern-day society – Have moonshot ideas – Stay positive – Learn what mental health problems are, and make your dreams become reality.

And a few questions I would tell my younger self would be: How are you going to make the world a better place? – What do you want to be remembered for? And what will your legacy be you leave behind? Above all else, though, I would tell myself to be confident in everything I do. And, if I fail, to look at those failures as mistakes I can learn from the next time around.

Well, that is the advice I would give my younger self, which I would like to think would help me. Now have you ever thought, 'Oh, I wish I had known what I know now when I was younger?'

If we knew what we know now though when we were younger, then we wouldn't be who we are today would we? Hmmm, anyway, this got me wondering what piece of advice you would tell yourself or somebody else which you wish you knew when you were younger. And here is what my friends on social media had to say when I asked them this question.

What advice do you wish you knew when you were younger, which you know now?

I would say, learn from your mistakes you made in life. I would also say, do what you need to do for you. Do not be someone you are not to please others. You do what you do because it pleases you. If people love you, they need to love you, for who you are, not what you are not.

Kimberly Barnard, Arkansas, USA


The advice I would give is never judge anyone. Every person has a struggle in their personal life that no one knows they are facing, so never judge and be your own person. We are all unique, so let your individuality shine, it's what makes us who we are. I would also say kindness doesn't cost anything, so be kind xx.

Wendy Rudge, Essex, England


Don't start smoking, Don't start gambling, you never win in the long run, Don't let bullies get to you, and feel your own self-worth, and stick to the close friends you have, as, at school, you don't need everyone to like you. There will always be people that don't like you, and that's ok, it's part of life. Be kind and understanding to people, as you don't ever really know what they are going through, take risks and be brave, as it's better to make a mistake and learn from it than to live with the regret.

Claire Colasurdo, Peterborough, England

That's a good question Hun, I think most children are told to be happy, and live life as much as possible. Personally, I think be told to, accept people for who they are, do not judge them by what they look like. Accept them for what they believe but keep your morals and beliefs true to yourself; believe in yourself. If you want something, fight for it, but do not hurt others along the way. Maybe a little more appropriate considering the world today.

Maria L. Mills, Market Harborough, England

Listen to your gut, and don't let others tell you how to feel and what to think. The truth is, what you see with your own eyes, not what others say.

Bethany, USA

That being yourself is more important than doing what everyone around you is doing. You will be a more interesting person as you get older and you will make better friends. Hang on in there, because great things are what you make of them. Also, peer pressure is the lamest thing, never surrender x.

Roseanna Kat, London, England

I would say in matters of the heart, put your own feelings first, because you need to feel happy while you are trying to make everyone else happy.

Tarah Price, Whitby, England
instagram.com/tarahmerle

I think I would tell anyone who is young, that there are always things to be grateful for. Try to be happy and appreciate what you do have in life. Enjoy everything as much as you can.

Debbie Barnard, Arkansas, USA

Great question! I'd say, don't sweat the small stuff and enjoy the moment you are in. Life is anything you want it to be, so if you want something, go for it!

Nicole Morcos, California, USA

REALLY listen to your parents, because what they say is true and with love!

Jonii Hagene, Florida, USA

I would say to not be jealous – don't be jealous of a boyfriend leaving you for someone else, he probably wasn't worth it. Don't be jealous of your friend with the new phone, clothes, etc., she may be happy on the outside, but crying on the inside. Don't be jealous of the kid whose parents let them do anything they want while you have rules. That kid may not have his/her parents love, and attention like your parents give you. Just some examples, I wasted so much time being jealous when I was younger that I didn't appreciate what I had. Looking back, I had a LOT, and it had nothing to do with money, status, etc.

Carla Nelson, Ohio, USA

You cannot change the life you have lived. You can change the life you are living. Always go with your gut x.

Paula Greenfield, Coventry, England

Always believe in yourself. Walk away from negativity. I was brought up to treat people like you would want to be treated yourself and if you don't have anything nice to say, don't say it. In other words, respect everyone. These have stood me in good stead. Please don't think I am a saint, because if anyone does try to put one over me, I can stand up for myself. Time has taught me that there are many sad people out there. Some just need a smile.

Alison Twomlow, England

I would say, to be grateful! Grateful for the family you have, the love they give you, the friends you have made, the choices life has given you, the good decisions you've made and the bad, the little everyday wins and mostly, be grateful that you have the freedom to live life however you choose. I am grateful for, love, family and friends and for the choices I made in regard to those things xx.

Rebecca Frances, Leicestershire, England

Well, fantastic advice there. I hope you found what my friends had to say helpful with their words of wisdom. I only wish I had known half of their knowledge when I was younger.

# PART NINE

PART NINE

# FINAL THOUGHTS

And now the end is near, so you and I face the final curtain. Writing my alternative self-help autobiography has been one incredible eye-opening journey; I have certainly learnt a lot about myself. Would I change any part of my life if I had the chance to, though? Yes and no; you see, the foremost thing I would change is the pain and hurt my parents went through after seeing me have numerous eye operations done, and the times when my mum and dad saw me in hospital after I had been attacked, which are moments in my life I would never wish on anybody. Unfortunately, they will be with my parents and me forever. All the discomfort I now suffer with in my eyes has empowered me to become a more determined human being in everything I do, and I will always be who I truly want to be.

I am sure certain people would rather see me shy away and become a depressed person with no self-esteem or confidence! Sorry to disappoint those individuals but I have been there and done that; never again, thank you very much. I am here to stay because I want to help inspire as many people as I can! I feel like the timid and low self-esteemed child I once was has come a long way to become the man I am today. I hope now you are coming towards the end of my book that, whatever somebody might have said or done to you in your life, you now feel more in control and have a better understanding of how to deal with those past damaging experiences. I also hope you believe in yourself more and know that you can overcome your fears.

You inspire me to be outgoing and made me realise everyone goes through hard times. That I shouldn't dwell on the past and I

697

should focus on my amazing future! Everyone goes through hard times; it's how you get through it that matters! You've overcome so much, and I'm really glad to call you a friend xx.

Danielle Tredgett, Leicestershire, England

I look at where I am today, a carpet cleaner from a lovely market town in Leicestershire, and I visualise where I see myself in five years. I might still be where I am right now, which I will be happy about, because I love my life, but I am going to do my damned hardest to get to where I want to be. It doesn't matter what kind of life you have led, or background you have come from; you and I can achieve great success in our lives. Enthusiasm and a positive attitude are all you need.

If you want to transform your life and see yourself somewhere else in years to come, then write down your aspirations and goals; it's never too late to chase after your dreams. You might have some people say to you, 'Get back to the real world; stop dreaming.' Never listen to those individuals; they will only hold you back. So, get out there and do what you have always dreamt of doing.

Writing my alternative self-help autobiography has helped me deal with specific events that have taken place in my life which have always festered in the back of my mind and often made me feel depressed. Now, though, I feel free, confident and not afraid to walk around with my head held high for the whole world to see me for who I genuinely am.

Thank you to my family, mates and online friends and followers for all your support throughout my journey while I have been writing my alternative self-help autobiography; it has been an unbelievable experience sharing my life with you. Furthermore, thank you to everyone who contributed and answered the questions I posed to them through social media; I am so grateful to you all. I hope I have done you proud and you have enjoyed reading my book. I don't mind admitting that I'm feeling very nervous as to what reaction I'll receive. All I can say is that I wrote from my heart and let my emotions flood out.

Steven M. Rippin

You are such an outstanding and inspiration to me and so many people!

The other Sanderson sister, USA,<br>instagram.com/Spiders_and_cider

I wish you all the best with your book and your journey forward; you're a great person inside and out. Your courage in life has helped others to also move on because you have shown us no matter what we have gone through and the pain we have felt, that we can move on from that. We all have a purpose in life; we just have to find it as you have found yours.

Maxine Sirs, Hartlepool, England

We went to the Smokey Mountains (2011) one Christmas to get away from family drama and had the most magical time. We were at a Christmas show at the Opry, and my son turned around and said, 'Mom there is a pirate in here' a few rows back, so he was only eight at the time, and I had to introduce him to you, and we got his picture with you. He was more thrilled with seeing the pirate than the show. That moment added to our magical vacation, and that's how we met you for a brief moment in time. I then followed you on social media because I thought, 'I wonder what his story is, a handsome fellow, no wife that I have seen and with mom and dad.' I thought wow what kind of blessed people are these to have such a relationship and family love. I then learnt you travel around blogging/vlogging with your dad at work and on vacation in all kinds of places and even eating at fun restaurants you recommend. I thought how cool is this, I can watch your adventures, and I never have to leave my little town of Geneva, Ohio. Not really but I certainly have never gone where you have and don't think I will do, it's fun to see Pirate Steve here there and everywhere. I love your accent and even when or if you swear you sound so amazing and kind. And my favourite video was you and George playing Christmas bingo this past Christmas at the Christmas hotel in Tennessee. You inspired me to have a Christmas themed birthday party for myself. Only I couldn't find the bingo game. We decorated ugly sweater Christmas cookies. You're always in my prayers, and I still don't know your story so I would love you to write a book because I would read that book and truly be able to say I knew a real pirate who was kind and loving and wild and crazy. I never knew the love you have with your parents, so I love that too. Jesus last commandment to us was to love, and you are such a fun example of that. God Bless you and your adventure. P.S. You don't have to mention me, but I thought you would enjoy this little memory I had of you. I don't think you're self-indulgent at all. I think you're a motivator and an inspiration to all who meet you.

Lee n Stacey, Talmo/Unsinger, Ohio, USA

Steve Rippin, I think your bleeding radio rental, but we all love you for who you are, and you're a genuine person xxx.

Pauline Jones, Market Harborough, England

Q: Do you think that sharing what you've gone through in your life has helped you get through it all? You've stayed positive throughout it all, and I personally think that helps you get through these things xx.

Paula Jarvis, Market Harborough, England

A: Hey, Paula, yes I do; knowing people are out there who love and support me has helped me enormously. And on another subject, even though I have never found love, I have found admiration through Facebook and Instagram from my online friends, such as yourself, Paula, so I now no longer feel alone.

Steven M. Rippin

Awww Steve, you have found love in us all. You're an amazing guy with great family values, and we've all loved being part of your journey in life. You're an inspiration to all who know you, and you'll never be alone because too many people care xx.

### Paula Jarvis, Market Harborough, England

I now have more of a purpose in life, and for the first time when I am out in public I have a lot more self-esteem and confidence as well, especially when people ask me, 'Why are you dressed that way?' in a condescending manner; it's water off a duck's back to me now.

It's a big world out there and remember 7.8 billion+ people live on the planet today, with the average human living for around 27,375 days, so what are you waiting for? Make every day count and get yourself out there and live a beautiful life! Don't worry about the past or the future. Think about that moment you are living in right now. So, delve deep and take a journey of self-discovery in becoming the best version of YOU; peace, love, unity and respect. Now, before I leave you, it's time for one final act and a singalong song, where I sing in my own karaoke style, Frank Sinatra's classic, 'I did it my way' on this following video link: bit. ly/PirateSteveIDidItMyWay

Thank you so much once again for reading my book, and I hope you enjoyed the singalong song. Never be afraid to be who you want to be in life and live for today, the Pirate Steve way.

### Steven M. Rippin

# DEDICATIONS TO FAMILY AND FRIENDS

You never know who you are going to connect with and the impact they will have on your life. Our friends can inspire and help us through the tough times we face, and genuinely understand who we are on the inside. When you are a kind and honest person, you will attract loving and trustworthy mates into your life.

I would now like to say an enormous thank you to the following people for being the best friends anybody could ask for.

Thank you, Simon Wellard, Tom Cooper, John Burnham, James Boulton, Phil Wellard, Matthew Green, Nick Freer and Owen Wright, Mark Tolhurst, Faye Moore, Adrian Holliday, Cameron Price, Kris Taft, Adam Epsly, Steven Robinson, Chris Palmer, Jack Jacovou, Aaron P. Trigg, Matthew Squibbs, Lee Brace, Joe Elliott, Chris Twiselton, Jono Holder, Harry Brown, Gary Randall, Mark Russell, Warren Lee, Troy Goodman, Chris and Mel Owens, Jonathan Almond, David and Melanie Bones, Andy and Debbie Chapman, Mark Stephenson and Steve Smith. I will treasure the good times we have shared forever. Thank you for accepting me and for never judging me as many have done. Much love to you all and your families.

Steven M. Rippin

I would now like to say thank you to my family for always being there for me. Without the following people, I honestly don't know how I would have coped after leaving school. So, to begin with, the two most influential people in my life have been my parents.

> Thank you, Mum and Dad, for all your encouragement and guidance you have given me, and for putting up with the unconventional person I have transformed into today. You sincerely are the best parents any child could wish for. Thank you so much for bringing me into this topsy-turvy upside-down world of chaos, love and unpredictable series of unfathomable outcomes which I have loved being a part of. You both mean more to me than you will ever know. Mum and Dad, I love you both very, very much, always and forever.
>
> Steven M. Rippin

My mum's sisters and brother, Auntie Janet, Auntie Lella and Uncle Nino, have always shown a lot of love to my parents and me. When I was a child in hospital having my eye operations, my mum's family always came to visit me, which meant so much; I always looked forward to their visits. My mum's sisters and brother have supported me in everything I do as well, which means so much to me. When I think of my aunties and uncle, the first thing I think of is their happy smiling faces, because they are always so contented, no matter what they go through in life.

> Thank you, Auntie Lella, Auntie Janet and Uncle Nino. I will never forget you being there for my mum and me when my dad was in hospital. Much love to you all.
>
> Steven M. Rippin

My dad's brothers and sister, Uncle Andrew, Uncle Paul and Auntie Julia, are very caring and confident people. Uncle David sadly passed away. I miss him very much, because he was such a friendly and down-to-earth guy who always made me feel comfortable when I went around to visit him with my dad.

I still think about you, Uncle David, and miss you very much. I hope you're behaving yourself up there and not having too many whiskeys.

Steven M. Rippin

Uncle Andrew, Uncle Paul, Auntie Stephanie, Auntie Julia and her husband, my Uncle John, have always been there for me when I have needed them. Also, they helped my mum and me out a lot when my dad was in hospital, which is something I will never forget. I would also like to say I have a lot of love and respect for my Auntie Stephanie, who has always shown interest in everything I do. Auntie Stephanie was very supportive while I was writing my book, which meant so much to me.

Thank you, Auntie Stephanie, for what you said about my book when we met up at the family get-together in February 2019. All my love to you, Uncle Paul and Kerry and Tara.

Steven M. Rippin

And thank you to my cousin Sandie Hart. I will never forget Sandie keeping me informed how my dad was doing after his mouth cancer operation in 2017.

Thank you, Sandie, for inviting me to your school in 2008 when I dressed as Captain Jack Sparrow, and then again in 2017 when you gave an assembly and invited my dad and me on stage with you where you spoke about my dad's cancer journey. We are very grateful to you for helping us raise awareness of cancer and with our fundraising campaign back then. Much love to you and your family, Sandie.

Steven M. Rippin

# MY DAD, MY BIGGEST INSPIRATION

A moment in my life I will never forget is when I heard my dad say to me, 'I'm going,' while he was lying there on the hospital stretcher at Kettering General Hospital. Then, moments later, I saw my dad's eyes roll up into the back of his head, and he died right there in front of me. It wasn't until around ten hours later when I heard him say, 'I'm back,' to only be told two years later he had cancer! Which he also survived! This is the story of the most inspirational man I know and the journey he has been on. This is the story of George W. Rippin, my dad.

My dad didn't have it easy growing up. He lived in a Nissen hut, woke up freezing every morning because there was no central heating, walked four miles to school and back every day, had his dentist drill straight into his teeth when he needed fillings without giving him an anaesthetic to numb the pain, shared bathwater with his brothers and sister, and also had learning difficulties when he was at school and was given no help or encouragement by the teachers; he found that was the toughest part about growing up when he was younger. Money wasn't easy to come by for my dad's parents back then, either, but my dad and his family got on with it and were grateful for all they had.

My dad, George William Rippin, grew up in Melton Mowbray with his parents, Katherine Zeta Nash and Gordon William Rippin, along with his brothers, Paul, Andrew and David, and sister Julia.

Not many people can work with their parents. Luckily, though, my dad and I get on really well and we have built up a strong bond over the years; we're the best of friends and know each other inside out. I sometimes think, though, my dad wishes I wouldn't tell him everything that's on my mind, especially when I go on about living forever and being uploaded into a computer! We do have the odd argument now and then, but who doesn't? I think an argument here and there helps to keep relationships with our parents, family and friends healthy, doesn't it?

> My dad has worked extremely hard all his life and earned every penny he's made through the hard graft and long hours he's put into the fitting and supplying of carpets over the past fifty years.

I have laboured for my dad since I was sixteen; I used to go around picking up the carpet offcuts for him. With my dad employing me, it has helped me out immensely. I don't think any company would have put up with the amount of time I have had to take off work over the years due to my health problems, you see, so I have a lot to thank my dad for.

> Thank you, Dad. I'm so grateful for everything you have done for me throughout my life.

Steven M. Rippin

I always remember as a child my dad working very long hours through the day fitting carpets, then when he would get home around 6 pm he would have his dinner and go straight back out again on his night calls and not get back home until around 10 or 10.30 pm! Which I used to think was normal! I would never be able to put that number of hours in at work myself, I know that. Would you? So I have a lot of respect for the work hours my dad did over the years. It really winds me up, though, when I hear people calling my dad saying things like, 'It's all right for him; he's done well for himself,' in a very negative way. Yes, he has done well for himself, which is because of the hard work and hours he has put into his career.

I'm extremely proud to call George William Rippin my dad. He has taught me so much in life, and he has always been there for me through the ups and downs it has thrown my way.

When my dad was a teenager, he used to take the stair carpet up and refit it for no reason. And when I asked my dad why he did that he said it was something he enjoyed doing. So, as you can see, from an early age my dad has always known what he wanted to do with his life. Now here is a brief history of the carpet shops my dad has worked for over the years. My dad first began his career in carpets when he was fifteen years old, and the first job he had was at Portess's in Melton Mowbray, which is a home furnishing and flooring shop, then when my dad was eighteen years old he moved to Market Harborough, where he continued his carpet career and landed himself a job working for Cyril and Nelly Smith, who owned a home furnishing and flooring shop as well; my dad worked for Mr and Mrs Smith until he was twenty-one years old. Then he moved on yet again to work for a business called Glenfield Carpets for a short while. After his stint at Glenfield Carpets, he then worked for a company called Robinsons until he was twenty-four. After that job, he moved to DCS until he was twenty-seven years old.

And, finally, the last carpet company my dad worked for was Potters Carpets in Anstey, and he left Potters when he was thirty-one because he wanted to become self-employed. So, he set his own business up, called George Rippin Carpet and Flooring, which he ran for over thirty-five years. When he came to retirement age, he joined forces with Brookside Carpets and Curtains of Market Harborough, who he delegated a lot of his carpet orders to, to help lessen his workload, which worked out really well. Now, here is a short story from when my dad worked for Portess's in Melton Mowbray.

When my dad was working for Portess's, he noticed the other workers were making £27 a week, which was big money back in the 1960s, compared to the £7 a week Portess's were paying him. So, my dad went and had a chat with the owner of Portess's, and the owner told my dad that he would never make that much money. So, my dad handed his notice in and went and worked for Holwell Works, where he made £33 a week placing drains on a conveyor belt.

Then, one day, while my dad was working at Holwell Works, the manager said, 'Who wants to make an extra £5 by working nights?' My dad shot his hand straight up, much to the annoyance of the employees he was working with. Those employees told my dad not to work the night shift because the union wouldn't be happy about it. My dad didn't listen to them, though, and worked nights as well.

Then one night, when my dad was working, he fell asleep on the job, and when he woke up he was surrounded by fire! The dissatisfied workers had only gone and placed oil rags around him in a circle and set fire to them! When my dad woke up, he was dripping with sweat, and he said to the unhappy employees while he rubbed his hands together, 'Ooh this will keep me lovely and warm, thanks, lads.' I couldn't believe they did that to my dad! The things that go on in the workplace! Oh yeah, and my dad took his first paycheque from Holwell Works into Portess's to show his ex-employer that he was now making £33 a week, compared to the measly £7 a week he was making with them. So that shot Portess's up the ####!

Can you believe, if my dad hadn't become a carpet fitter, he would have liked to have been a vet instead. I can just imagine my dad as a vet, if I'm honest, because he has always been very fond of animals.

When my dad moved to Market Harborough when he was eighteen, he lived in a flat up Northampton Road, where he had his own room and shared the bathroom and kitchen with two other residents. Now, my dad doesn't tolerate drugs and hates everything to do with them, so when he found out one of the residents he was living with was into drugs, he wasn't very impressed! Then, one day, one of my dad's flatmates told him the other guy living there had stashed some drugs in his room in a tin of paint! He went mad when he found this out.

So when my dad got home from work one evening, he saw this guy who had stashed the drugs in his room high on pills and crashed out on the living room settee, and my dad thought to himself, 'Right, I'll wait until he's come round and then I'll sort him out.' So, while this guy was coming down off his high, my dad went and had a shower. Then, as my dad was drying himself off, he heard this guy and his girlfriend trying to creep out the flat, so my dad quickly wrapped a towel around himself and confronted the guy on the landing about the drugs he had stashed in his room, which the guy denied putting there. My dad was fuming by this point and then started beating the crap out of him. Unfortunately, while my dad was punching this guy, his towel fell off, leaving him stark naked, then the bloke's girlfriend started screaming as my dad carried on beating her boyfriend up on the landing! That guy never stashed any drugs in my dad's room ever again after that.

My dad first spotted my mum when he was driving through the town of Market Harborough in his work van while she was walking down the street with her friends. And from that moment he knew he wanted to ask her out on a date; I guess you could say it was love at first sight for my dad. So, my dad asked my mum out, and they started dating and going to dances together at the village hall in Foxton, where my dad's friend Andy Mathias held the Frolicking Kneecap Northern Soul nights. Then a few years later they decided to get married and have a baby.

When I was around three and my dad was twenty-seven, my parents and I moved to the town of Syston in Leicestershire so my dad would be closer to where he worked at Potters Carpets in Anstey. That's when I first started struggling with my arthritis in my knees, so we moved back to Market Harborough, into a bungalow, because I was struggling to walk. Then, a few years later, my dad handed his notice in to Potters Carpets and became self-employed, which was the best thing he ever did. My dad was worried at first about working for himself, but he had an excellent reputation and customers were always asking him to fit their carpets, so it worked out really well for him, plus he rarely had to advertise for business either. And, just like my dad has always told me, 'Word of mouth is much better than any kind of advertising, and if you do a good job and go that extra mile for your customers, they will always come back to you.'

> My dad is a perfectionist and does a fantastic job fitting carpets, and I'm not just saying that because he's my dad; he truly is one of the most professional and skilled carpet fitters I know.

When I look back on my childhood, I always remember my dad being there for me and taking me on holidays to the beach, where we would build sandcastles and have water fights in the pool together. Oh, yeah, and when my dad used to come home from work he would often say to me, 'I've got a surprise for you, Steven,' then he would produce from inside his coat pocket the latest *Star Wars* action figure, which he had picked up on his way home from work for me that evening. I'll never forget my dad doing that for me.

A childhood memory I will cherish forever is when my dad took me to a village fete one day, where I got to meet my childhood hero, Worzel Gummidge, just after I'd had my cataract removed from my right eye.

I can honestly say I have never met anybody more thoughtful, considerate and loving than my dad; he is the kind of guy who will help you out as much as he possibly can.

Dad, you are the strongest and bravest man I know. I love you with all my heart.

Steven M. Rippin

# MY DAD'S KIND NATURE AND LOVE OF ANIMALS

Over the years my dad has helped to get money back for people, shovelled snow from neighbours' driveways and gone to customers' houses doing odd jobs for them, such as hanging paintings and putting light fittings up; this is why I admire my dad so much.

If my dad sees an animal in need of rescuing, he will do his very best to save its life.

One time while my dad was driving around in his work van he spotted a dog running down a main road weaving in and out between traffic, so he pulled his van over to the side of the road, got out and started slowing the oncoming traffic down who hadn't seen the dog, just like a police officer would when an accident had occurred. Luckily, my dad managed to rescue the dog that day, although the poor dog's paws were all cut up and bleeding badly. So, my dad took the dog to a vet, who cleaned and patched him or her up. My dad found out that the dog had escaped from boarding kennels where the owners had taken their dog to stay while they went on holiday.

Thankfully there was an address tag around the dog's neck, and my dad was able to reunite the dog with their owners. The dog's owners were ever so grateful and bought my dad a bunch of flowers and a card and gave him £100 as a way of saying thank you; what a lovely gesture and my dad spent the money on bird feed to help the wildlife.

Now one final animal story I would like to tell you about is the time our cat went missing, and the incredible amount of passion, determination and commitment my dad put into finding her. So, I hope you are sitting comfortably because now it's time to tell you the tale about Bootsy's five-day adventure away. One cold Thursday morning in April 2019, Bootsy the cat was roaming around, as she usually did outside, but more so this day because there was a lot of building work going on at our house and many workmen's vans to explore.

Unfortunately, my dad and I weren't around to keep an eye on Bootsy that day, so when we arrived home that evening and couldn't find her anywhere we were a bit concerned as it wasn't like her to disappear like that. So, the following morning I designed a poster of our missing cat and Rogers and Co Estate Agents and Brookside Carpets and Curtains of Market Harborough kindly printed off two hundred copies of it which my dad posted around our neighbourhood. Sadly, though, nobody had seen Bootsy anywhere.

After a couple of days, we thought we would never see her again. We didn't give up, though, and I lost count of how many times my dad walked around our neighbourhood calling her name out and shaking her treats box, all to no avail. I also shared two posts on Facebook about Bootsy going missing, which got over 165 shares between them both! I couldn't believe it; the amount of love from my online friends was amazing. Then, on the third morning, I thought, 'We've not checked the CCTV footage yet!' So I told my dad, and we got on the case of tracking Bootsy down with this new lead of investigation we could pursue. As we went through the CCTV footage, we saw Bootsy jumping into the back of a worker's van! Then a few minutes later we saw the tradesperson close the doors of his vehicle and drive off with our cat, unknowingly to him!

So, my dad called the tradesperson to find out where his next job was after he had worked at our house that Thursday, and it was in the village of Ashley, which is about five miles away from Market Harborough. So, this gave us a glimmer of hope that we might be able to find Bootsy. My dad spent over three hours posting flyers in every house in the village of Ashley, and a few hours later his time and effort paid off because he started receiving phone calls from people saying they had spotted a cat who looked like Bootsy in the villages of Stoke Albany and Wilbarston. So, my dad shot over to Stoke Albany, called Bootsy's name out but couldn't find her there, then he had another phone call from a lady who was walking her dog, who said she had spotted Bootsy in the Maltings in Ashley. So, my dad drove over to Ashley again, met the lady walking her dog, got Bootsy's treats out and started calling for her. And that's when he heard a meowing coming from somewhere behind a wall, and, as he looked over this wall, he could just see Bootsy walking by the side of it underneath some brush. Then Bootsy spotted him, looked up and started crying and meowing. My dad quickly got around this wall to Bootsy to pick her up, where she continued to cry and meow while he held her in his arms.

I felt so much relief when I first saw her; I felt joy and happiness, it's a funny feeling in your stomach, a good feeling, like yes, I've got her. And I picked her up and gave her a big cuddle, and I told her how much I loved her; obviously, she understood every word I said.

George W. Rippin, Market Harborough, England

That day in Ashley, my dad walked over 30,000 steps and did around fifteen miles, and that's not counting the previous days he had spent walking around looking for her. My dad has a heart of gold and so much love to give animals, especially Bootsy, who he loves very, very much.

When my dad called me up to let me know he had found Bootsy, I can't begin to explain how I felt. I was so relieved, and I will admit I shed a few tears. For five nights, our cat went missing, but with our love, determination and detective work we found her in the end. She had lost a bit of weight, bless her, and looked really tired; other than that, though, she was in good health. After I had posted an update on Facebook letting everybody know that we had found Bootsy, our local radio station, Hfm, got in touch with us and did a news feature about her going missing, as did the *Leicester Mercury*:

bit.ly/DetectiveWorkFindsMissingCat
bit.ly/MissingBootsyTheCatReturns

Thank you so much, Nick Shaw, for featuring our cat on your news segment, and also, thank you to my friends on Facebook and the lovely people of Ashley as well; it meant so much.

Steven M. Rippin

And finally, to thank Rogers and Co Estate Agents and Brookside Carpets and Curtains for their help, my dad and I made them a couple of promotional videos as our way of saying thank you, which you can watch on the following links:

bit.ly/RogersAndCoEstateAgents
bit.ly/BrooksideCarpets

# WALKING IN THE COUNTRYSIDE WITH MY DAD

I was never much into walking in the countryside until I was in my mid-thirties and started walking with my dad in the Lake District and Yorkshire, which are stunning parts of England. I used to love going out every weekend partying, you see, which I still do, but not as much anymore. Oh, and here is a video when my dad went hiking in the Lake District with his friend Chris, who he nicknamed Chutney after Chris nearly gave him some mouldy old pickle in a sandwich he was making while my dad fitted his carpet. It was quite windy the day Chris and my dad went hiking as you will see. And please excuse how I used to present my videos because I used to act over the top in them, I'm afraid: bit.ly/WindyDays

A walk my dad and I love doing takes us along the Grand Union Canal, through numerous fields, over a railway bridge and then into the beautiful village of Great Bowden, where we will have a cup of coffee at Bowden Stores, which I highly recommend visiting if you are ever in the Leicestershire area here in England, especially if you love your coffee. I even made Bowden Stores a promotional video in 2017, which you can watch here: bit.ly/BowdenStoresPromoVideo

My dad will talk to anybody; he's a real people person and always knows what to say to somebody even if they give him any backchat, and his quick one-liners always help open conversations with strangers we meet while we are on our walks. I only wish I had some of my dad's magic when it comes to speaking to people so easily.

One time, when we were in Cumbria, we visited a town called Ulverston, where you will find the impressive Laurel and Hardy museum;

Stan Laurel was born in Ulverston on 16 June 1890. And here is a video I put together from that day, which you may find interesting if you are a fan: bit.ly/TheLaurelAndHardyMuseum

Also, while my dad and I were in Ulverston, we came across a charming cobbled street which was full of cute little independent shops, and, as my dad and I were strolling along taking in the sights, all of a sudden three young women came running up to us all excited. They told us they were intrigued, obviously by my dad's appearance and I think mine as well. One of the women, Rachael Weaver, owned one of the adorable independent clothes shops we had walked by called Two by Two. It was a real pleasure meeting Rachael and her friends, Sara Charlesworth and Ceri Hutton, that day.

But the story doesn't end there because a year later my dad and I revisited Ulverston and went and said hi to Rachael Weaver in her shop. Rachael was so happy to see us both again; in fact, she was so happy she said, 'We should all sing a pirate song. Come on, set your camera up,' so I set my camera up and as I was doing so Rachael's friend Ceri Hutton appeared to say hi; it was so good to see Ceri again. Then the next minute there we all were singing 'What Do You Do with a Drunken Sailor?' in the middle of the street in Ulverston! It was awesome. What the passers-by thought I will never know. Thank you to Rachael Weaver of the clothes store Two by Two in Ulverston, and to her good friend Ceri Hutton, for such a good laugh that day.

Now here is the video of us singing 'What Do You Do with a Drunken Sailor?': bit.ly/WhatDoYouDoWithADrunkenSailor

After our encounter with the lovely women of Ulverston, my dad and I headed back to the car; before we left the car park, though, we filmed our final scene for the jump-style dance video I was putting together. So, there my dad and I were dancing away – well, trying to – then my dad spotted an elderly man who was going back to his car, so my dad went up and had a chat with him. The old man asked my dad what we were doing, which I could totally understand because it's not every day you see a grown-up adult and a pirate dancing around in a car park, is it?

Now, here is the conversation the elderly man and my dad had together, which I would like to share with you because it gives you a clear picture of the kind of guy my dad is with how he can strike up a conversation with somebody he has never met before and act as if he has known them for years. Also, I was able to capture this conversation on video because I forgot to turn the camera off on my phone while I was filming my dad and me dancing, so as a bonus here is the actual conversation to watch as well: bit.ly/ALovelyInteractionMyDadHadInUlverston

'You can join in, if you want?' my dad said to the elderly man.

'No, I've come to see where your hat and coat is,' he replied.

Then my dad and I laugh politely because we think the elderly man is referring to what Frank Sinatra and Fred Astaire used to wear when they were on stage dancing together. 'That's called the scooter dance,' my dad told the elderly man.

'Is it?' he said, looking confused.

'They're a group who've been going around for 20 years; he will do a dance and put it on YouTube' my dad responded referring to me.

'Oh, I watch YouTube,' the old man replied.

'Steve, give him a card. Have you just bought yourself a watch?' my dad asked the elderly man.

'Oh, I can't get it out of there,' he said, referring to the packaging it was in.

'Have you got some grandchildren?' my dad then inquired. My dad's quite nosey, isn't he?

'Oh, hundreds of them,' replied the elderly man.

'Well—'

But before my dad could reply, the elderly man said, 'How old do you think I am?'

'Seventy-eight?' returned my dad,

'Eighty-two!' the elderly man responded.

'Seventy-two?' my dad remarked.

'Eighty!' said the elderly man.

'Ninety?' my dad replied, having a laugh.

'Eighty-two!' said the elderly man again.

'I'm only winding you up; congratulations. So, you came up to some stranger, and you let me take your watch? You might have thought I'd hit you on the head and run,' responded my dad.

'Ahhh I would have tackled ya,' the elderly man countered.

Then my dad laughed politely and said, 'Aw, God bless.' Then the elderly man, my dad and I all started laughing together and said our goodbyes. That was a lovely interaction the three of us had that day, and also a great example of the kind of interactions my dad has with strangers he meets.

You come across some people in life who have a very negative attitude, and you will want to avoid them like the plague, then you come across people such as Rachael Weaver, Sara Charlesworth, Ceri Hutton and the lovely elderly man, and you know straight away they have hearts of gold and positive attitudes towards life and are the kind of people you love being around. So always surround yourself in life with positive, happy loving people.

# CUSTOMERS: THE GOOD, THE BAD AND THE LOVELY

Before I tell you about specific customers my dad and I have encountered, a question I get asked a lot is how customers react when they see me turn up on their doorsteps looking how I do. Well, one old lady thought I was a Native American Indian, another couldn't weigh me up, and one woman took an instant dislike to me as soon as she saw me. The majority of customers, though, are fantastic and never say a word about my appearance. Some clients have even said they love how I look and can't wait to tell their kids that a pirate is going to clean their carpets.

Can you believe my dad has been fitting carpets for over fifty years! He has got a fantastic reputation as well, and I believe that has helped a lot when I go around customers' houses with him and why people feel more comfortable accepting me into their homes.

When we used to work on building sites fitting carpets, they were experiences I will never forget. I can get pretty shy, you see, so when I used to hear builders shouting, 'Hey, it's Jack Sparrow,' I would get embarrassed and worry about whether I would have the mickey taken out of me all day long. Luckily I wasn't, and after a few minutes things would calm down. Now let me tell you about a lovely lady my dad and I cleaned carpets for one year who took a fancy to me.

One day while I was cleaning a bedroom carpet, I felt something brush through the back of my hair, which made me jump, so I turned around and there standing behind me was the lady of the house stroking my long locks! She said, 'Ooh, haven't you got lovely hair, if only I were younger. Do you drink? I'll get you a bottle to take home with you?' Which was very kind of her, but I was quite nervous at this point because I didn't know what the customer was going to do to me next! Luckily, though, when I declined her offer of a bottle to take home with me, she left me alone to carry on working. Then, when my dad and I had finished cleaning and were stood chatting in the kitchen to the customer, she started running her hands up and down my chest! I tensed right up and didn't have a clue what to do! What would you do if you were in my position being touched up by a lady while your dad's standing there laughing his head off!

The lady then said, 'Ooh, isn't he lovely, George? I need a new lodger; would you like to move in, Steve?'

'I'm all right thank you; I don't normally get in until two or three in the morning at weekends,' I told her.

'Oh, that's no good, is it, George?' she said to my dad. Then the lady went up to my dad and put her hand up his T-shirt and started stroking his chest hair and said, 'Ooh, George, do you think Steve will mind if I kiss him?'

'You'll have to ask him,' my dad said. And before I knew it, I was being kissed by the customer! I should mention, the lady was in her eighties, and her husband was in the kitchen laughing away at his wife's mischievous behaviour while all these shenanigans were going on. That lovely elderly lady was quite a character. Oh, and she only kissed me on the cheek, if you were wondering.

What an experience that was; you just never know who you are going to meet when you're a tradesman! Luckily, there are more good customers than bad ones though, and this lovely elderly lady was one of the pleasant ones. Which leads me nicely onto this next little encounter my dad found himself in when he was twenty-seven and working for Potters Carpets. You see, when my dad arrived at this customer's house to measure up for a new bedroom carpet, a woman in her forties answered the door to him wearing a tiny little nightgown which left not much to the imagination! And this lady said to my dad, 'Ooh aren't you a big boy? Come in, I won't bite. The room I'd like you to measure up is upstairs on the right; I'll be up there in a minute.' So, off my dad went upstairs to measure up, and I think while my dad was measuring her bedroom carpet that woman was busy measuring my dad up!

Then just as soon as my dad had finished working out the sizes, the woman entered her bedroom, sat on her bed and said to my dad, 'Come over here and sit next to me.'

My dad replied with, 'No, I'm all right thank you. It's all measured up; I'm going to get going now,' then he quickly said goodbye, and off he went feeling rather uncomfortable in the situation he had just found himself in.

A few weeks later when my dad was in the showroom at Potters Carpets, one of the other estimators called my dad over and said, 'You remember that woman you priced a new bedroom carpet up for?'

'Oh yeah,' my dad said.

'Well, she asked when she placed the order with us if you were gay!' Then my dad remembered the awkward situation he had found himself in a few weeks earlier! She was what you would call 'the flirtatious customer'.

My dad and I are very respectable and honest hard-working tradespeople, and if those scenarios occur we always finish the job we are doing and flee out of that customer's house as quickly as possible. Well, now it's time to hear about the annoying customer who said my dad gave him a load of old waffle, who has pretty much gone down in history as the most irritating customer we have ever encountered!

One day, when I was working with my dad, the lady next door asked if I could price her carpets up to be cleaned. So, I went around and priced them up for her, and she said she would have a chat with her husband and be in touch.

I didn't hear anything from her for a few days, then the weekend came round and I went out with my friends on a Saturday night, so on Sunday morning I had a lie-in, then around 7 am the phone rang, which my dad answered and it was the husband of the lady who I had priced carpet cleaning up for, and he said, 'Hello, is that Steven Rippin?'

'No, this is George Rippin. I'm his dad; what can I help you with?' responded my dad.

'Well, I want to talk to Steven Rippin about my carpets; have I got the wrong number?' the lady's husband demanded.

'Well, obviously you have else you wouldn't be talking to me. Anyway, you'll have a job talking to Steve: he's in bed; he went out last night,' my dad told the customer.

'Well, I don't really need to know that do I,' returned the lady's husband in a patronising tone. By this point, my dad had weighed this customer up and knew he was going to be hard work, but my dad kept his patience and said, 'Will I be able to help? I clean the carpets with him.' So, then the customer started asking my dad a list of questions about how we clean carpets, including pH scales, carpet fibres and how we remove stains.

This client was one of those know-it-alls who had been online reading everything he could about carpet cleaning, which is fair enough; I bet he knew more about carpet cleaning than the whole of the National Carpet Cleaning Association! Anyway, my dad answered all the customer's questions, but still he continued asking for me, and my dad told him he would have to call back on Monday. So when the customer called back on Monday I answered the phone and he said in a very condescending voice, 'Ah Steven Rippin, yes, your dad gave me a load of old waffle the other day about carpet cleaning, and now I want to ask you about how you clean carpets,' which left me shocked on the other end of the phone after what I had just heard this customer say about my dad; I had to do my best to keep my cool and be as professional as I could! Looking back, I wish I'd said something to him.

What I did say to that disrespectful customer, though, was that my dad wouldn't have given him a load of old waffle, and also that he knows just as much if not more about carpet cleaning than I do. Still, he just brushed what I said aside and continued with the list of questions he had already asked my dad. This bloke was really starting to get on my nerves.

Later that day, I told my dad what the client had said about him and how annoyed I was. My dad said, 'Calm down, Steven; I'll call him back later and sort this out.' So that evening, my dad called this discourteous customer back, and his wife answered the phone, and my dad said, 'Can I speak to your husband, please?'

'Oh, he's in the garden. I'll go and get him for you,' she replied.

Then about a minute later, the impolite customer eventually came to the phone out of breath and said, 'Oh, I'm a bit out of breath... I was just at the bottom of the garden,'

'Well, I didn't really need to know that did I? And my son told me you said I gave you a load of old waffle the other day,' my dad said, feeling offended.

'Oh, no, no, no, no, no he has it all wrong I didn't say anything of the sort,' the ill-mannered customer said.

'So, you're calling my son a liar, now, are you? And let me tell you something else: I would never step foot over your threshold, and I don't like being woken up at seven o'clock on a Sunday morning either! Don't you ever call here again!' bellowed my dad, then he put the phone down while the rude client carried on talking at the other end! And guess what: we never heard back from him ever again! Now here is the episode of the bothersome painter we had to contend with on another job!

When my dad and I were working at a customer's house one year while they were away on holiday, we had the misfortune of having to put up with an unpleasant painter who was working there as well. I thought when I first met this painter that he was a pleasant enough guy; how wrong I was, though! So, my dad and I prepped the rooms we were fitting, and everything seemed to be going fine. That was until the painter said to my dad, 'Your son smells bad, doesn't he?' My dad thought he was joking around, but he was deadly serious, the cheeky s#d!

So my dad said to him, 'What did you just say? I think you're mistaken; the underlay we use gives a funny smell off,'

'Ah, right. Can you believe he hasn't made me a cup of tea yet?' replied the arrogant painter.

'He's not your tea boy, is he? He's my son. You know where the kettle is; go and make yourself one!' my dad told him, getting annoyed. So that painter caused a right atmosphere. I couldn't believe I thought this guy was all right when I first met him!

As you can see, this painter had a very negative attitude and obviously something against me! I thought tradespeople all stuck together and respected each other! That rule didn't apply to this guy, apparently. Also, while we were working at that house, the painter had his dog running around all over the place! I don't know about you, but I wouldn't like a tradesman's dog running around my house while I was away on holiday, would you?

Then my dad and I put the carpet rubbish from the job we had accumulated into the next-door neighbour's skip, which the next-door neighbour was happy for us to do. That was until we arrived back at the house the following morning and saw the next-door neighbour must have changed their minds because they had gone and dumped the carpet waste onto the pavement! My dad and I couldn't believe it! So, we put the carpet debris into our work van and thought nothing more of it. This job seemed to be turning into a nightmare!

Anyway, so my dad and I carried on working away and got the job done over the next couple of days. Then, once the customer had returned home from there holidays, my dad phoned them up to make sure they were happy with the job we had done and to also ask for his money. My dad must have rung the customer four or five times, but nobody would ever answer or reply to his calls, which was very strange. So, one Sunday morning my dad went around the client's house and asked, 'Is everything all right? I've tried calling you, but you haven't been replying to any of my messages.'

'You better come with me,' the customer said in a solemn voice. Then the client showed my dad into their house and what they weren't happy with about the job we had done, which was very strange because my dad and I thought the job looked fantastic.

My dad found out that the painter had been stirring it and had told the customer we had come into her house rushing around like a couple of rhinoceroses in a china shop, banging around here, there and everywhere, which we never do, and also that we had put the carpet waste into her next-door neighbour's skip, which we shouldn't have done, and that we had left her furniture outside in the garden, which we had to because there wasn't enough room to fit the flooring down with all the furniture in at the same time; we placed the old carpet we had taken up to throw away on the patio so we could set the furniture on it, which helped to protect it and keep it clean. Furthermore, it was a lovely hot, sunny day, and we put the furniture straight back into the room once the flooring had been fitted. Oh, and there was a bit of dust on the skirtings from where we had cut the door so the flooring would clear properly, which my dad did for the customer at no extra cost; we must have accidentally missed the dust while hoovering up, which is easily done. As you can see, it wasn't the customer's fault; the client had just been misinformed and wound up by the painter who had painted – pardon the pun – a black picture of my dad and me! That painter had clearly not heard about the Law of Attraction.

My dad explained to the customer that the painter had been acting very negatively towards us and that their neighbour had been all right at first about us placing the carpet waste into the skip. Whether they believed him, though, I don't know. As my dad is an honest and hard-working, civilised man, he had a chat with the customer and sorted everything out they weren't happy with, then all was well. So, as you can see, that job started fine and would have been straight forward if it hadn't had been for the unpleasant painter talking to the customer behind our backs. The story doesn't end there, though, because around a year later, when my dad and I were on another job, who did we come across? Yeah, you guessed it, none other than that negative-minded painter!

Oh, it was brilliant. My dad and I walked into this room where this bloke was standing with the repulsive painter, and he said, 'Oh it's you, have you finished stirring the sh*t for my son and me?'

'Uh, what do you mean?' replied the defensive painter as he carried on painting and acting as if nothing was wrong.

My dad then said to him, 'You made it really awkward for us on that job, didn't you? What have you got to say for yourself?' Then the horrid painter went as red as a strawberry milkshake and didn't say a word. 'Huh. I didn't think you would have anything to say,' my dad snapped back at him. After that, my dad and I walked off and left the foul painter standing there, feeling embarrassed with the other guy he was working with. As they say, what goes around comes around.

So, after putting up with those annoying people, my dad and I came up with 'The Most Annoying Customer of the Year Award', where we would keep a mental list in our heads of the clients who had annoyed us the most. And, once we had agreed who the most irritating customer had been, we wanted to award Mr or Mrs X with their very own Annoying Customer of the Year Award trophy and present it to them. And, as a bonus prize, we wanted to give them a book on how to be more courteous, so it would teach them how to treat tradespeople with the respect they deserve.

Ninety-nine per cent of our clients are great. It's just once in a while we will come across one or two who will wind us up. And, unfortunately, we have never handed out any annoying customer of the year awards. Yet!

# SPECIAL MEMORIES:
# ALASKA AND THE CARIBBEAN

Years ago, my dad and I used to watch a TV show called *Buffy the Vampire Slayer*, and because we loved the show so much we ended up going on two different *Buffy the Vampire Slayer* cruises with fans of the show! The first cruise we went on was around the Caribbean in June 2005, and the second one was around Alaska in June 2007. I never in a million years thought my dad would be interested in going on either of those two cruises, but he surprised me and thought it was an excellent idea. On those cruises, my dad and I met Joe Motes and his daughter Ashley. Joe Motes was the organiser of the cruise conventions we went on, and he founded his company, Vulkon Entertainment, back in 1986.

While my dad and I were on the cruise around Alaska, we went panning for gold in the Alaskan mines, where we managed to find a few tiny shards, which we got to keep in little souvenir jars. The street value of our gold would only have been one to two pounds. Unfortunately, I lost mine; some pirate I make! Another memorable expedition we went on in Alaska took us on a helicopter ride onto a glacier, which felt like being on another planet. Oh, and as usual I made a fool of myself when I attempted to dance on it! I have no idea what the pilot must have thought when he saw me dancing around shouting, 'Hardcore, you know the score, come on, let's have it.' Luckily, I didn't break the ice with my stomping around and fall through! Although I'm sure a lot of people would have loved to have seen that! Now here are a few mini romance stories I had while I was on those cruises with my dad, which you might or might not be interested in reading.

When we were on the cruise around Alaska, there was one young woman who had a crush on me. I liked her but not in that way, and me being me I made a right mess of things because I desired another woman, named Dana Ridenour, so, unfortunately, I ended up upsetting the woman who fancied me because I told her I only wanted to be friends, then I went on a date with Dana, who I genuinely favoured. I will never forget meeting up with Dana. There we both were on board the vessel's posh cocktail bar sitting down with our arms around each other sipping on cocktails while we chatted and sailed by the icecaps of Alaska on the Pacific Ocean. Dana was an undercover FBI agent, and I felt like I was James Bond conversing with the lovely Miss Moneypenny in the phenomenal setting of Alaska, where we were both about to uncover the evil crime lord's secret lair and expose his illegal activities to the world. Back to reality, though, we had a fantastic evening and got on really well. Dana is now happily married to her husband, and to date, she has two books out, called *Behind the Mask* and *Behind the Cabin*.

Thank you, Dana; it was lovely getting to know you while we were cruising around Alaska in 2007. All the best with your career as an author. And all my very best to you, your husband and your families.

Steven M. Rippin

My next romance, well, it's more like a fanboy crush I had on a woman called Iyari Limon. Iyari played Kennedy in *Buffy the Vampire Slayer*. I first met Iyari when I queued up to get her autograph at the Showmasters Collectormania convention in Milton Keynes in 2003, where I also gave her a bunch of CDs I had made, which she loved. Then I met her again in 2005, when my dad and I were on the Slayer cruise around the Caribbean. I was so timid when I saw her because of how much I still fancied her! And then one night when Iyari walked by me as I was going to the nightclub on board the ship, she stopped and said she remembered me giving her a collection of CDs from a couple of years ago, which she still had on her shelf at home. I couldn't believe she had kept my CDs! I just wish I'd struck up a conversation with her back then; again, though, I was too shy!

And, finally, one last encounter I will always remember from the

Caribbean cruise was getting a kiss from Danielle Benson, whose sister, Amber Benson, played Tara in *Buffy the Vampire Slayer*. It was only a kiss on the cheek, though, so nothing serious, but, truth be told, I did like Danielle; again, though, I didn't have the confidence to chat her up! Danielle and her sister Amber were awesome. I even got to hang out with them in the restaurant one evening. Those guys were such a good laugh and were always messing about.

Now, moving on, while my dad and I were on the Caribbean cruise we docked up on the beautiful island of Nassau, and after we had done some exploring of the island we went to find somewhere quiet to relax on the beach. Then, once we had settled ourselves down underneath a palm tree, the *Buffy* stars saw my dad and me and said, 'Do you guys mind if we sit next to you?' Which we didn't mind at all, and before we knew it most of the stars of the Slayer cruise were all around us; it was fantastic! While we were onboard the Caribbean cruise my dad became good friends with Andy Hallett, who played Lorne in the TV show *Angel*; Andy even invited my dad over to his dining table in the restaurant one evening to have photos taken, which showed me how much Andy genuinely admired my dad. I thought that was really lovely of him to do. Sadly, Andy Hallett passed away from heart failure at the age of only thirty-three years old in 2009. Andy was a lovely kind soul with a heart of gold.

> Love and light to you, Andy. Every time I think of you, I think of
> that beautiful smile of yours. And still, to this day, I can't believe
> you are gone, I love you, man.

Steven M. Rippin

Some fans can get starstruck when they see their idols in real life. Not my dad, that's for sure. You see, one day when my dad was walking around the cruise ship he said hello to a woman he was walking by, then all of a sudden this woman turned around to my dad and said, 'Do you know who I am?'

'No, sorry. I have no idea who you are. Should I?' replied my dad.

Then she said, 'Wait a minute; let me do my hair,' so she buffed her hair up and posed for him! How funny is that? Like, who actually does that?

Anyway, after she had sorted her hair out and done a bit of pouting for my dad, he still had no idea who she was, and he said to her, 'I'm sorry, I still have no idea who you are.' She then made her excuses and walked off in a huff and a puff. It turned out she was one of the actresses from a *Star Trek* TV show my dad had never watched; there were a few *Star Trek* actors on the Slayer cruise with us as well, you see. Then, get this, another *Star Trek* actor thought my dad was an actor on a TV show! As you can imagine, my dad was loving that cruise with the *Buffy* and *Star Trek* actors complimenting him.

A lot of the male guest stars of the *Buffy* TV show loved my dad because he was down to earth and didn't act all starstruck when he saw them. They also held him in high regard because he treated them just how he would treat anybody else he would meet in his everyday life. I would now like to give my thanks to Joe Motes, who organised those conventions, because, if it hadn't been for Joe, my dad and I would never have had all those incredible experiences of going around Alaska and the Caribbean!

> Thank you, Joe, for the great times we had on those conventions you organised. My dad and I made many special memories. All our best to you and your family.
>
> **Steven M. Rippin and George W. Rippn**

I feel fortunate to have had the opportunity to go on those two cruises with my dad. And, if you ever get the chance to go on a cruise, I would definitely recommend it; they are great fun.

> Thank you for the wonderful memories we made together on those cruises dad. I will cherish them forever.
>
> **Steven M. Rippin**

# NUISANCE PHONE CALLERS

One thing I love about my dad is his fantastic sense of humour and how he's always up for a laugh and not afraid of making a fool of himself. My dad's one-liners are exceptional, and, if somebody tries to get one up on him, he will always have a witty remark to reply back to them with. To give you an idea of his sense of humour, here are some funny nuisance phone call conversations my dad's had. The first one is when an insurance company told my dad he was owed money because of an accident he had apparently been in the year before, which obviously had never happened.

Insurance guy: 'I heard you had an accident last year.'

'Oh, yes? When was that then?' asked my dad.

'Last year,' the insurance guy said.

'What month?' insisted my dad.

'June,' responded the insurance caller.

'What date?' my dad requested.

'The 20th,' said the insurance caller, getting agitated.

'What time?' inquired my dad. And they went back and forth like this for a couple of minutes, then the person on the other end of the phone rang off after getting frustrated with my dad's sense of humour.

Another funny nuisance phone call my dad had was when an insurance company asked him to take a loan out. And here is how that phone call played out.

Insurance guy: 'Hi, Mr Rippin. Can I interest you in taking a loan out with us?'

'Oh, you just wouldn't believe the day I've had,' replied my dad.

'Oh, why? What's happened?' asked the insurance guy.

'Well, I was driving on the motorway, and I got a flat tyre, then it started raining, and I got wet through, then my phone rang, and it was the hospital saying that my wife's in hospital, and now you're asking me about taking a loan out. Can it get much worse?' my dad said, winding the insurance caller up.

'Oh, I'm sorry to hear that. Err...' Then the nuisance phone caller rang off!

And here is one more conversation my dad had on the phone to a nuisance phone caller.

Insurance guy: 'Is that Mr Rippin? This is accident and claims. I understand you were in an accident last year.'

'Yeah, my wife died,' my dad responded, sounding depressed.

'I'm so sorry,' replied the insurance guy.

'And then my son lost his arms and legs in a car accident, so now I have to lift him onto the toilet seat!' my dad said next, trying to keep a straight face. Then he had to put the phone down because he was laughing so much! It's terrible what my dad comes out with, I know, but those are the kind of things he says when he receives nuisance phone calls because they wind him up so much!

So, hey, the next time you receive a nuisance phone call, you will hopefully be more prepared with how to deal with them now; don't let those nuisance phone calls wind you up; have fun with them instead. You could even turn those phone calls into a game you could play with members of your family to see who can keep the nuisance phone caller on the phone the longest. Or, as my dad's done in the past, you could answer the phone then leave it on the side somewhere while you carry on with whatever you're doing. Trust me, the nuisance phone caller will soon get the message and ring off.

Thank you, Dad, for being such an incredible father to me and for always making me laugh.

Steven M. Rippin

# THANK YOU, DAD, FOR BEING AN ETERNAL INSPIRATION TO ME

Well, I hope that has given you a brief insight into the kind of dad George William Rippin has been to me over the years. We have certainly had a lot of exciting times together and made memories that will last us both a lifetime, which I am sincerely grateful for. What I admire about my dad is that he's down to earth and what you see is what you get with him; he puts no airs or graces on, and he's always courteous, respectable and honest with everybody he meets. My dad has taught me through life never to judge anybody, never to put anybody on a pedestal, to always believe in yourself, to live life with a positive attitude, to never let people walk all over you and to show affection, courage, compassion, reverence and devotion towards one another.

Having spent a lot of time with my dad, I have got to know him remarkably well, and I feel extremely lucky to have had the chance to have bonded with him how I have.

One thing my dad has said to me many times over the years is that he would love to come back as an eagle and soar through the sky. So, if I ever see an eagle soaring overhead once my dad has passed on, I will know that eagle might well be my dad watching over me. And I can imagine the message he would send me through the supernatural airwaves; it would go something like: 'Stop getting upset, Steven, and get yourself out there and do what you want to do, because, as long as you're happy, then I'm happy. Enjoy yourself and enjoy your life. You're only here once, so make the most of it and look after your mum.'

Thank you, Dad; you have been an exceptional part of my life, and I have so much to thank you for. I hope we have many more years to create magical memories together. I will always look up to you, now and forever. And with those final words, I will say, Dad, I love you with all my heart, and I hope one day I will be half the man you are.

Steven M. Rippin

When you have a positive attitude towards life, it transforms how you view the world and the people around you. All of my family and friends have helped me to believe in myself since I was assaulted. They have also given me the confidence to get myself back out into the world again to be who I want to be. And still to this day they continue to help and support me when I get insulted by small-minded individuals. And I say thank you to everybody who has been there for me, just like I will always be there for them when they need me.

Writing my book has been a significant outlet for me. I have been able to gather my thoughts and emotions in my head and get them out into the open. I also feel the life experiences I have been put through by a small minority of individuals in Market Harborough who have ridiculed and threatened me because of how I look have all contributed in me creating this alternative self-help autobiography. The bottom line is: always be there for your family and friends and wear a smile on your face. So, saying that, I am now going to end my book with one final video of my dad and me singing 'When You're Smiling' by the late, great Seger Ellis, which he wrote in 1929: bit.ly/WhenYoureSmiling

The song 'When You're Smiling' in my video was made and produced by Vic Gilmore of VJAG Entertainments. And here is a link to Vic's website, where you can find loads more excellent songs he has created for you to listen to: bit.ly/VicGilmoreYouTube

My parents have been phenomenal. I am forever grateful to them for everything they have done for me in life.

I'm very proud to see how Steven's coped with his health, especially his eyes, and I find him a very positive person, very sensitive and very loving. His hearts in the right place and I'm proud that he's my son.

George W. Rippin, Market Harborough, England

Thank you so much, Dad, for inspiring me to write this book. I love you more than words can say.

Steven M. Rippin

View life as an adventure, so every day when you wake up you will look forward to a brand-new journey of self-discovery of becoming who you were born to be. Be unique, be individual, face your fears and become the best version of you. Your life is what you make it, so stay positive, always believe in yourself and make your dreams come true.

 Matador